ON ESSENCE

XAVIER ZUBIRI

ON ESSENCE

TRANSLATION AND INTRODUCTION
BY
A. ROBERT CAPONIGRI

THE CATHOLIC UNIVERSITY OF AMERICA PRESS
WASHINGTON, D. C.

Library of Congress Cataloging in Publication Data.

Zubiri, Xavier.
    On essence.

Translation of Sobre la esencia.
1. Essence (Philosophy).   I. Caponigri, Aloysius.
Robert, 1915.   II. Title.

B105.E65Z813   111.1   78-68067.
ISBN 0-8132-0546-8.

Depósito Legal: M. 43595-1980

Impreso en España. Printed in Spain

Gráficas Cóndor, S. A., Sánchez Pacheco, 81, Madrid, 1980. — 5213

To

Sister Theresa Sandok, O. S. M.
gratefully for her tireless collaboration
in this work

ACKNOWLEDGEMENT

This publication has been assisted by a grant from the
United States-Spanish Joint Committee for Educational
and Cultural Affairs of the 1976 Treaty of Friendship
and Cooperation between the United States and Spain.
A most grateful acknowledgement of judicions counsel
to Edmund D. Pellegrino, M. D., President, The Catholic
University of America.

INTRODUCTION

BY

A. ROBERT CAPONIGRI

ABREVIATIONS OF WORKS CITED

Symbol   *Title*

NHD   Zubiri, Xavier: *Naturaleza, Historia, Dios,* Editora Nacional, Madrid, 1942, 1963[5].

SE   Zubiri, Xavier: *Sobre la esencia,* Sociedad de Estudios y Publicaciones, Madrid, 1963.

HOM.   Varii: *Homenaje a Xavier Zubiri,* Editorial Moneda y Crédito, Madrid, 1970, 2 volúmenes.

REAL.   *Realitas: Seminario Xavier Zubiri,* I: *Trabajos* 1972-1973, *Sociedad Estudios y Publicaciones,* Madrid, 1974.

Zubiri, it has been claimed, has achieved not only a new philosophy, but a new *idea* of philosophy as well.[1] Like all such claims this, too, savors of a certain extravagance and must be greeted with a certain reserve, a reserve, however, which is sensitive to the element of truth which this claim undoubtedly contains. Zubiri's claim to attentive audience does not derive primarily from the novelty of his philosophical doctrine or of his idea of philosophy, although both exhibit this quality. Novelty, of itself, generates no obligation and ministers only to curiosity. Zubiri's claim has a far more solid and compelling basis, namely, the manner in which he addresses the most fundamental problem of western philosophy and the powerful personal insights he brings to its illumination. It is this continuity with and enrichment of the old and the abiding which gives significance to what is new in his thought.

This most ancient and fundamental problem of western thought is simplicity itself; indeed, overwhelming in its simplicity but far more so in the profundity which this simplicity conceals. This problem is, in Zubiri's own words «el esfuerzo por entender el último de las cosas,»[2] the effort to comprehend the first principle of things. This principle, whatever its character, is what is really real in itself and what, in turn, through the communication of itself, its «dar de sí,»[3] is the source of all else that is *real* and that really *is*. The quest for this principle is philosophy. Its presence is the most distinguishing mark of western culture. The form which this quest has taken, the methods by which it has been approached and the resolutions which have been offered for it impart to that culture its distinctive quality

---

1 Ellacuria, Ignacio: «En Zubiri ... no sólo se ha logrado una filosofía nueva ... sino ... una idea nueva de lo que debe ser la filosofía,» *HOM.* I, 486.

2 *NHD*, 221; cf. *HOM.* I, 463.

3 «dar de sí»; cf. *HOM.* I, 522.

and character. This is the problem which Zubiri addresses. In this address he has exhibited great perspicacity and inventiveness and has given evidence of powerful personal insight. He has elaborated the classical formulations of the problem in significant fashion and has drawn from the ancient and classical resolutions of it dimensions hitherto latent. His claim to audience, consequently, stems neither from antiquity nor from novelty taken in abstraction but from that penetration of the two of which the fabric of history is woven.

Particular force and interest accrues to Zubiri's claim from the fact that in all that is novel in his idea of philosophy and in his philosophical doctrine the most ancient resolution of that fundamental problem receives fresh vindication. To this most ancient view of «el último de las cosas» the venerable term «realism» has consistently been assigned.[4] Behind this historical term lies a complex insight. This is the insight that whatever «el último» — the principle of all that is real and which itself is most real, because real «de suyo» and as «suyo»[5] — may prove to be, it is a principle independent of man and of man's knowledge of it and must indeed be recognized as the principle of the reality of man — of the reality *that* he is and of the reality of *what* he is. At the same time, and through the agency of what man is in his reality, the reality of that principle is reciprocally realized. This is the insight, expressed in roughest outline, which historically first signalizes the presence of philosophy in western thought and first establishes western culture as philosophical in its most profound dimension. This is also the position to the defense and deepening of which Zubiri, drawing upon, and in no wise rejecting or opposing, the powerful insights and formidable resources of modern and contemporary thought, returns. Under this aspect his thought constitutes, not metaphorically, but quite literally, a *ricorso*

---

[4] Ellacuria, Ignacio: «la metafísica, por tanto, tiene que ser una forma de realismo,» *HOM*. I, 477.

Zubiri, Xavier: «ni tan siquiera en la propia inteligencia hay una primicia del inteligir en cuanto tal sobre la realidad. En el exordio mismo de la metafísica hay, pues, una radical primicia fundante de la realidad sobre el inteligir. ... La metafísica jamás podrá ser una lógica. Es insostenible el supuesto primordial de la metafísica hegeliana.» *SE*, 47.

[5] Ellacuria, Ignacio: «El 'de suyo' es lo que se hace presente en la actualización primaria de lo real, como algo anterior a la presentación misma.» *HOM*. I, 483; cf. also *op. cit.*; 488; *SE*, 417.

in the Vichian sense: [6] the great circle in which the human spirit returns to its source, not however, there to be lost in a featureless identity, but to re-emerge enriched and illuminated.

This fresh and deeper penetration of the classical realism of the west, through the most sophisticated agencies of modern and contemporary thought, is a position at which Zubiri arrived by no easy route. On the contrary, his has been a long and arduous journey, to the term of which he has not even yet finally arrived. As in every significant pilgrimage of the human spirit, this journey's end, as the poet says, [7] is in its beginning. The work of Zubiri here presented for the first time in English translation *Sobre la esencia, On Essence* is recognized as the culmination, though not the termination, of that long and arduous pilgrimage which has been his life. By this same principle, consequently, the appreciation of this work, too, must lie in its beginning.

It has become a commonplace, after the numerous reiterations of Croce and other critics, that the extra-philosophical life of the philosopher, like the extra-poetic life of the poet, is of little interest. Yet it does help in the comprehension of a philosopher's thought to know something of his life and particular circumstances, especially as, in Zubiri's own view (we hear an echo of Ortega), philosophy is always projected from a «situation.» [8] A few indications of Zubiri's life and career will not, therefore, be amiss.

Xavier Zubiri was born in San Sebastián in eighteen hundred and ninety-eight. After preparatory studies he enrolled in the University of Madrid where his intellectual interests quickly found their focus in philosophy and theology. To a great extent, no doubt, this was due to the influence of the masters it was his good fortune to encounter, above all Don Ángel Amor Ruibal, Don García Morente, Don Juan Zaragüeta and Don José Ortega y Gasset. [9] Each of these men pre-

---

[6] Caponigri, A. Robert: *Time and Idea*, Routledge and Kegan Paul, Ltd., London, 1953, Chap. VII: 'Ricorsi'.

[7] Eliot, T. S.: «In my beginning is my end,» *East Coker*, Faber and Faber, London, 1950.

[8] *NHD*, 28.

[9] Angel Amor Ruibal, 1869-1930. Longtime professor of theology and canon law at Santiago de Compostela; canon of the Cathedral there. Cf. López Quintas, A.: *Filosofía española contemporánea*, La Editorial Católica, S. A. Madrid, 1970, pp. 38-92.

sented him with a model of the intellectual life marked by its own special virtues but all characterized by a common trait, absolute integrity. If, however, the specific accents of the influence of each on Zubiri's thought may be noted, it may be said that the example of the weighty Zaragüeta more than all others placed his feet firmly in the paths of classical western thought while that of the adventurous Ortega, always open to the new and unexplored, urged him into the wider fields of modern speculation.

His studies at Madrid were varied by periods of residence at the University of Louvain and the Gregorian University at Rome. The former was the center of the new scholastic and Thomistic movement which had been inspired by Pope Leo XIII. This center was under the aegis of the magnetic and enlightened figure of Cardinal Mercier and was attracting the best Catholic intellectual talent from many parts of Europe and abroad. The Gregorian, of course — the lineal descendent and continuator of the Collegio Romano of Counterreformation fame from which much of the creative energy of that movement had flowed — was a bastion of solid traditional philosophical and theological learning, while at the same time programmatically sensitive

García Morente, Manuel, 1886-1942. Influential theologian and philosopher; held a number of professorial posts 1912-1936. Chair of Ethics, Madrid; Dean, Filosofía y Letras 1931-1936; Tucumán (Argentina), 1937-1938; ordained priest 1940; resumed Madrid chair 1940. López Quintas, *op. cit.*, 136-148.

Ortega y Gasset, José, 1883-1955. After Miguel de Unamuno, the most articulate and versatile intellectual in Spain during the first half of the twentieth century. After wide-ranging studies in Europe held the Chair of Metaphysics in the University of Madrid, 1910-1936; founded influential *Revista de Occidente* 1926; foreign residence 1936-1945; cofounder, with Julián Marias, of the Instituto de Humanidades in Madrid. López Quintas, *op. cit.*, pp. 113-137.

Zaragüeta, Juan, 1883-1973. Long time dean of Spanish philosophers: doctor of Louvain University 1908; professor Madrid Seminary 1908-1917; Escuela Superior de Magisterio 1917-1931; chairs of pedagogy, rational psychology and metaphysics, Madrid, 1947. Influential posts in numerous philosophical institutes and societies.

Husserl, Edmund, 1859-1938. Student of Franz Brentano from 1884-1886; founder of the phenomenological movement; professor of philosophy at Halle, Göttingen, Freiburg; established Jahrbuch für Philosophie und Phänomenologische Forschung: wide influence: Adolf Reinach, Max Scheler, Eugen Fink, Martin Heidegger, Xavier Zubiri, cf. Caponigri, A. Robert: *History of Western Philosophy*, Volume V, pp. 152-181.

Heidegger, Martin, 1889-1938. Student of Richert and Husserl; founder of «Existenz philosophie»; wide and enduring influence; chief work *Sein und zeit* (Jahrbuch, 1927); cf. Caponigri, A. Robert, *op. cit., vol. cit.*, pp. 263-276.

and responsive to the currents of modern thought. At the Gregorian, in nineteen hundred and twenty, Zubiri received the doctorate in theology. Thence he returned to Madrid to receive the equivalent degree in philosophy the following year. His thesis, published in 1923 and entitled *Ensayo de una teoría fenomenológica del juicio* [10] already projects the range and quality of his mind.

Zubiri entered upon a university career and the year nineteen hundred and twenty-six finds him occupying the chair of the history of philosophy at the University of Madrid. His more urgent interest, however, lay in the enrichment of his own culture and in extending contacts between philosophical thought in Spain and the dominant movements in other countries of Europe; he was also much concerned to extend and strengthen his own bases in the physical, biological and humane disciplines. The years nineteen hundred and twenty-eight to thirty-one, consequently, found him resuming the role of student and traveling to various centers of learning in Europe, seeking out masters of thought in various areas of study. His interests were and remain encyclopedic. These years find him studying classical philology with Werner Jaeger, philosophy with Husserl and Heidegger, theoretical physics with de Broglie and Schrödinger, biology with von Geluchten, Spemann and Goldschmidt, mathematics with Rey-Pastor, La Vallée-Poussin and Zermelo. [11] Despite this diversity of interests, Zubiri's real talent is not encyclopedic. On the contrary, it is highly concentrative and all of these interests served only to minister to his sustained central concern — philosophy and philosophical theology. The years nineteen hundred and thirty-six to nineteen hundred and thirty-nine find Zubiri in Paris, exercising the dual role which defines his life: teacher and scholar. While offering courses at the Catholic Institute in Paris, he is engaged in the study of oriental languages

---

[10] Zubiri, Xavier: *Ensayo de una teoría fenomenológica de juicio*, 1923.

[11] De La Vallée-Poussin, Charles, Jean, 1886- . Mathematician, professor, Louvain, Sorbonne, Collège de France, prime numbers lower than 4.

Zermolo, Ernst, 1871-1953. Mathematician; professor, Zürich, Freiburg.

Schrödinger, Erwin, 1887-1961. Mathematician; Schrödinger equation (1926), professor Zürich and Berlin; Nobel Prize, 1933.

De Broglie, Louis-César, 1875-1960. Physicist, «ions» of de Broglie.

Rey-Pastor, Julio, 1888- . Professor Oviedo and Madrid; Buenos Aires; projective geometry.

with Deimel, Benveniste, Labat, Dhorme and others at the Sorbonne. [12]
In the subsequent years 1940-1942 he occupied the chair of the history
of philosophy at the University of Barcelona.

The year nineteen hundred and forty-three must be accounted
crucial in Zubiri's career. Never an academic man in the narrower
sense of the term, in this year he left the university to strike out on
an original program of research and teaching on a model all his own.
This led to the creation of his own particular organ: the *cursos*, which
he has presented and continues to present since that date. The
cursos, even more than the treatise or essay, must be recognized
as Zubiri's personal and original mode of expression and communication. In them, even more than in his books and publications
in learned journals, is to be found the living movement, the vital
rhythm as well as the weighty insights of his thought. To have
assisted at them, even occasionally, as the present writer has, proves
a memorable experience. Their texture is dense, but lucid. Above all
it is the sense of direct participation in the quest of truth, in the
immediate communication with the deep personal quest of a powerful
intellect informing a personality of unshakable devotion and integrity
that most impresses one; this and the particular didactic style, in
which the auditor is not passive, but rather drawn directly into the
active intellectual emprise in which the lecturer is so manifestly
absorbed. The full force and quality of Zubiri's thought, as has been
suggested, is to be found in these *cursos*, even more perhaps than
in his formal publications.

Ignacio Ellacuria has suggested that Zubiri's activity falls into
three major phases. The first phase runs from the appearance of his
first published writings to the establishment of his program of private
cursos, embracing the twenty years, that is to say, from about nineteen
hundred and twenty-three until nineteen hundred and forty-two. The
second phase covers the period from the establishment of the *cursos*
until the appearance in 1962 of *Sobre la esencia* when the third and
present on-going phase was initiated. Prior to this last event, Zubiri's
major, though not, of course, exclusive, preocupation had been with

---

[12] Benveniste, Emile, 1903-   . Professor at the Collège de France since 1937;
comparative grammar.
   Deimel, S. J., Anton, 1865-1954. Professor Biblical Institute, Rome; Assyriology.
   Labat, René, 1904-   . Professor at the Collège de France, Assyriology.

the «idea» of philosophy; more precisely, both the idea as represented by the actuality of its history and the idea as an «ought,» an ideal. His concern had been to determine what philosophy has been in its historical actuality, as a basic dimension (indeed, in a phrase he will come to use more and more, as the constituting principle), of western culture. Even more, he had been concerned to identify philosophy in its «idea»: that is, the kind of knowledge in which it ought to reside, the kind of attitudes and operations it demanded of the «philosopher» and above all the way in which this kind of knowledge and these operations affect the philosopher in his existence and especially in the state of being and the relation to reality in which philosophy establishes him. For it seems clear that if philosophy is not effective in this way — that is, if it does not establish its subject, the philosopher, in a particular, and is a particularly real, relation to reality, and to reality, not in its mere factuality but «principially» (the term is his own), in its effective principle — all that can be said of philosophy is what St. Paul said of faith without charity — it is sounding brass and tinkling cymbals. The second phase is marked by the program of the *cursos*. In these *cursos* as we have noted much of the most valuable material for an understanding of Zubiri's thought is to be found; indeed, they possess a unique value, because here are to be seen not merely the results of his thought but its *process*. Were the present essay concerned with his total system and not intended to serve principally as an introduction to the English translation of *Sobre la esencia* the *cursos* would unquestionably serve as a principal source.

The appearance of *Sobre la esencia*, nevertheless, must be considered the major event in Zubiri's work; this treatise (and its similarity to the «tractatus» of the second scholasticism has been noted) does two things: it brings to focus certain basic strains in the *cursos* of the preceding years and it opens a new constructive phase of his activity. In this work and henceforward his chief concern will not be with the idea of philosophy, historical or normative; his purpose will now be effectively to *do* philosophy (as a current English phrase has it); that is, to construct his own philosophy («cada filó-

---

13 *Hom.* I, 461.

sofo ha construido su propia filosofía» [14] as that «sistema de pensamiento unitario y deliberadamente organizado» [15] which philosophy must always be. Our concern at this point will be to identify the salient points of the earlier phases during which the concern was principally with the «idea» of philosophy for it is this «idea» which he will seek to realize in his construction of philosophy in *Sobre la esencia.*

In these earlier studies Zubiri approaches the «idea» of philosophy along three paths: first, by way of the analysis of what it is to «philosophize» [16] as an attitude and an activity peculiar to man; second, by way of a contrast between philosophy as a form of knowledge and science in the modern understanding of that term; finally, by way of the identification and characterization of philosophy by the «object» of philosophy.

Zubiri introduces his reflections on the idea of philosophy with the observation, noted earlier by Hegel, [17] that the history of philosophy is the history of the idea of philosophy. [18] What this history teaches, in the first place, is that the «content» of philosophy, the «doxai» of Diogenes Laertius and even their systemization have but a secondary and conditioned importance. [19] These remain but an inert mass, without significance or life, providing merely matter for scholastic erudition, unless grasped in their creative and generative principle; it is the latter which truly concerns the quest for the idea of philosophy: «el principio que la mueve.» [20] The characteristics which Zubiri attributes to this generative activity of philosophy are striking; here we can but touch on a few salient features. In this activity the philosopher seeks «recibir original e indeformada, ante su mente, la

---

[14] *HOM.* I, 461.

[15] *NHD*, 135.

[16] The way, it may be noted, taken by Heidegger and Jaspers in their extensive studies of Nietzsche.

[17] Hegel, G. W. F.: *Vorlesüngen über die Geschichte der Philosophie*, heraus. Hermann Glockner I, 33.
Caponigri, A. Robert: «The Pilgrimage of Truth through Time: Hegel's Concept of the History of Philosophy» in *Miscellanea di studi Filosofici*, Palermo Presso l'Accademia, 1974, pp. 94 ff.

[18] *NHD*, 121.

[19] «Los contenidos filosóficos y su sistematización tienen una importancia derivada y condicionada.» *HOM.* I, 462; *NHD*, 28.

[20] *NHD*, 221; *HOM.* I, 462.

realidad del mundo y de la vida humana»;[21] it is not an «occupation» of man, that is an activity which does not affect him as a subject, in his radical relation to being, to reality. Instead «es un modo fundamental de su existencia intelectual.»[22] All philosophy is executed or carried on from a «situation»: «como todo hacer verdadero, es (la filosofía) una operación concreta, ejecutada desde una situación.»[23] This «situationism» does not, however, give license to subjective philosophical lyricisms. The process of philosophy is governed not by such subjective movements but by the dynamism of reality itself which is actualized in the mind of the philosopher. Reality holds primacy over philosophy, and philosophy holds primacy over the philosopher: «no es la filosofía obra del filósofo, sino el filósofo obra de la filosofía.»[24] The process by which this subjectivity of the man in situation is transcended is the inner movement of philosophy. This movement cannot, however, be characterized or formalized *a priori*. Philosophy can never be turned into a technic by being formulated into rules which can be applied universally by all manners of men. It always remains the work of the individual and the philosophy to which he gives expression is *his* philosophy. «La idea de la filosofía es distinta en cada filósofo porque cada filósofo ha construido su propia filosofía.»[25] Finally, the philosopher in his individuality cannot construct his philosophy *a priori*, by any plan or rule; it can only be the result of an inner movement of his own soul of which his philosophy is the expression. The philosopher is a philosopher only in view of the philosophy which he has constructed and he is a philosopher of a certain character because of the character of the philosophy which has issued from the inner movement of his own soul. «Ante una filosofía ya madura, y precisamente ante ella, es cuando resulta no sólo posible, sino forzoso preguntarnos hasta qué punto y en qué forma responde a su propio concepto.»[26] Nevertheless, despite all of these highly personalistic dimensions of philosophy and the process of philosophizing, philosophy in its ultimate character is

---

[21] *NHD*, 136; *HOM.* I, 463.
[22] *HOM.* I, 463.
[23] *NHD*, 28.
[24] *HOM.* I, 463.
[25] *HOM.* I, 461.
[26] *NHD*, 121-122.

one; the reason lies in the fact that in all philosophers and in all philosophies the ruling principle is reality which is not many but *one;* the one which all seek in a diversity of ways from a diversity of situations but with a unity of ultimate orientation.

The principle of philosophy, consequently, that on which its idea depends, cannot be an «objective,» i.e., impersonal and quasi-mechanical principle, like the «method» of certain figures in the history of philosophy, involving no personal commitment or transformation of the philosophizing subject. The result of the operation or application of such a method would be a «fact,» «hecho,» a product and would always be an «other» to the philosopher himself, something alien and alienated. Philosophy is never a fact, «hecho,» but rather «es cosa que ha de fabricarse por un esfuerzo personal.» [27] Even under the aspect of system — and philosophy must eventually be system — the aspect under which it might seem most «impersonal» and «objective,» philosophy is unauthentic unless the systematization itself is the result of an authentically philosophical effort. This insistence on the personal dimension of the philosophical activity raises immediately the question of its intrinsic character and, less directly, the question of the transformation which the activity of philosophy and the achievement of its end effects in the philosophizing subject. Both questions receive an initial but determining response in Zubiri's formula already noted: «recibir original e indeformada ante su mente la realidad del mundo y de la vida humana.» [28] The presence of reality «original and undeformed» to the personal consciousness of the philosophizing subject clearly cannot leave that subject unaffected in its status in existence and in being. Indeed, the ultimate impact of philosophy under this most important aspect is upon this personal transformation of the quality of the act of existence of the philosophizing subject. And since it is reality «original and undeformed» which works this transformation, the transformation itself cannot be other than in the direction of the revelation of the reality of the subject and its establishment in that reality.

These observations must not, as suggested, lead one to conclude overhastily that philosophy is an entirely «subjective» operation. Such

[27] *NHD,* 27.
[28] *NHD,* 136.

a view would be in obvious contrast to the view that philosophy places «realidad original e indeformada» before the subject; that reality can by no stretch of the imagination be constricted to the limits of subjectivity. Quite the contrary, it is not the limits of subjectivity which define reality, but philosophy, reality, which defines and establishes the philosopher as subject. He is established in his character of philosopher by philosophy and not conversely: «no es la filosofía obra del filósofo, sino el filósofo obra de la filosofía en el sentido ... de que no somos nosotros los que poseemos la verdad sino de que nosotros somos los poseídos por la verdad.» [29]

Thus at the heart of the «idea» of philosophy innests this reciprocity: philosophy is the result only of a personal effort of the philosopher not, however, in the sense that philosophy is the work of the philosopher but rather in the sense that the philosopher is the creation of philosophy, of reality and of truth as these take possession of him. Paradoxical as this may seem, it is essential, for Zubiri, to the understanding of philosophy and it is this reciprocity which supplies the inner dynamic of the process. Finally, this view of the «idea» of philosophy has a direct reference to the interpretation of Zubiri's own thought, for it provides a most important entry into the structure of his own system.

Philosophy establishes the philosopher in a particular state of being and existence, his «estar siendo.» The condition of actual existence, «estar siendo,» in which philosophy establishes the subject is essentially a condition of knowing, of knowledge. The quality of this knowledge obviously demands clarification and the path by which this clarification is best achieved is by a contrast between it and the concept of science especially as the latter takes form in modern thought.

This is the path which Zubiri takes and he concretizes this process in a contrast between the Greek notion of *epistemé* and the modern conception of *science*. His position is complex. It is no part of his concern (as happens in the case of certain other philosophers concerned to vindicate the specific, even privileged, station of philosophy as knowledge) to denigrate the modern conception of science. On the contrary, it is his view, as will be seen more clearly, that science is

---

[29] *HOM.* I, 463.

essential to culture and — even more importantly, in this conjunction — to the project of philosophy; he makes every effort in the constructive phases of his thought to incorporate modern science, materially and methodologically, into its systematization. At the same time, he is concerned to keep these kinds of knowledge — philosophy (epistemé), and science carefully apart; the distinction between them, however, must be dialectical and not abstract. If released into abstract autonomy, these kinds of knowledge will lead to distinct concepts of reality, the one contradictory to and nugatory of the other. The real task is to identify the character of each as authentic knowledge, while locating them within the one reality, since the real can only be, transcendentally, one. The character of this difference — and at the same time the authenticity of each — may be exemplified and illuminated by a comparison of the manner in which science and *epistemé* respectively address common points of issue.

The first of these points of issue is movement and phenomenon. For science, in Zubiri's view, movement is the passage from one place to another, the course of which must be plotted by the correlation of a number of factors. For *epistemé*, what is important in movement is the *mobile*, in its condition as a changeable thing, internally unstable, and *movement* as a mode of being (ser) in relation to the non-being (no-ser) which it implies. For science, according to Zubiri, the phenomenon is a real event (acontecimiento) whose temporal and spatial area must be circumscribed by precise measurements and which further involves an observer, a measurer: e.g., the equations of modern physics as anticipations of observables. [30] For *epistemé*, by contrast, what is important about the phenomenon in its manifestation is not the observer to whom it appears but that which appears, the «ens phenomenale» the thing itself which appears in the appearance. [31]

Finally the respective address of *epistemé* and modern science to nature may define these differences even more clearly. Both seek the *nature* of things, but the idea of nature in the case of each differs. For science, nature is the system of laws, the norm of variations, the mathematical determination of phenomena that vary as, for example,

---

[30] *NHD*, 281.
[31] *NHD*, 74.

in Galileo, or the distribution of observables, as in the new physics. For *epistemé*, nature means movement, actual or virtual, emerging from the very depths of the being which moves — the principle of movement, a movement viewed from being (ser) and from causes.

It must be concluded then that science and *epistemé*, philosophy, are two different kinds of knowing. Both seek a «because,» thanks to which we may know the inexorable necessity which penetrates reality. The «because» of science, however, is a «how»; that of *episte-mé* is a «why.» Zubiri sums up the difference by saying «La ciencia trata de averiguar dónde, cuándo y cómo se presentan los fenómenos. La epistemé trata de averiguar que han de ser las cosas que así se manifiestan en el mundo.» [32]

This difference as knowledge, however, finds its full impact in the fact that it is the *idea of reality* proper to each which inevitably differs as well as their ideas of what things are and of what the universe is, reality in the sense of what makes things *what* they are and what makes them *that* they are. For *epistemé*, things are not many notes united together, but a unity which is diversified in its notes. According as we place ourselves on the side of unity or on that of diversity we see what the thing is in itself and what it is for the observer. Science tends to believe that things are clusters of notes more or less united in their appearances and does not focus on the unity from which the notes are diversified.

While these different modes of knowing may be considered two valid approaches to things, equally *authentic*, they cannot, by this mere consideration, be thought to be of equal force. The point of view of science which seeks «la unidad ... en la totalidad de los fenómenos es su conexión objetiva ... la ley» [33] which totality is in turn interpreted as the totality of objective experience, is a great gain. It is not, however, at the same level, in the order of knowledge, as philosophy for which «el problema de la realidad de las cosas es esencialmente el problema de lo que ellas son y no simplemente de las condiciones intramundanas o transcendentalmente mundanas de su acontecer.» [34] It is to the former problem that philosophy, differently from science,

---

[32] *NHD*, 78.
[33] *NHD*, 86-87.
[34] *NHD*, 88.

addresses itself and it is this difference which establishes its higher status as knowledge.

It would be easiest, in dealing with the «object» of philosophy, if philosophy might simply be said to have an «other» or different object than that of science; the different objects might then be characterized by different notes but in an identical idiom. But this is not the case because the relations of the one, science, to its object and that of the other, philosophy to its object, are completely inverse. Science has its object given *before* it and proceeds to illuminate and explore it. Philosophy, by contrast «... no se sabe cuál es su objeto. Determinar el objeto de la filosofía es la primera de sus tareas y el esclarecerlo debidamente es su coronación.» [35] In Zubiri's own words: «La filosofía tiene que ser, ante todo, una perenne reivindicación de su *objeto* (llamémoslo así) ... Mientras la ciencia versa sobre un objeto que ya se tiene con claridad, la filosofía es el esfuerzo por la progresiva constitución intelectual de su propio objeto, la violencia por sacarlo de su constitutiva latencia a una efectiva patencia.» [36]

This observation does not imply for Zubiri, as an analogous observation did for the idealists, that philosophy must *create* its object. The intellectual anguish (angostura) which oppresses the philosopher and from which he tries to escape by seeking the proper object of philosophy does not lead him to the fantastic evocation of new objects; rather, it leads him to the discovery and possession of something which is not a concrete object, but which, nevertheless, has its own consistency. Some might conclude from this that philosophy is a useless quest, doomed to failure. Zubiri does not see it so. Philosophy cannot be thought useless because even its failure, if failure it prove to be, would tell us more of reality than the ostensible successes of the sciences.

What can be said with certainty is that man, in all his stances, is orientated toward reality. His first orientation toward reality is toward reality as realized in real things and over these he deploys his sciences. There is always the danger of conceiving philosophy as another of these sciences — a confusion the consequences of which must prove disastrous. Philosophy — the philosophic quest — is born when

---

[35]   *HOM.* I, 471.
[36]   *NHD*, 120.

man perceives that while reality itself can be approached only by way of things that are real, it cannot be equated without residue with those things so that the character of reality, even as it is the principle of the reality of those things as *real*, does not make itself patent to us in the same form or manner as do the real things which we encounter. [37] In Zubiri's own words: «Es menester que después de haber aprehendido los objetos bajo quienes late, un nuevo acto mental reobre sobre el anterior para colocar el objeto en una nueva dimensión que haga, no transparente, sino visible, esa otra dimensión suya. El acto con que se hace patente el objeto de la filosofía no es una aprehensión, ni una intuición, sino una *reflexión.*» [38]

The object of philosophy, consequently, is transcendental. The sciences consider things *such* as they are; philosophy, by contrast, considers things as they *are*. Suchness and transcendentality — these are the dynamic polarities of philosophy in Zubiri's system; the structure which emerges from their interplay — essence — will be explored in *Sobre la esencia.* Philosophy is not alien to things in their *suchness, such* as they are; this seems to Zubiri to have been the error of the idealists (on the Platonic, and not the Hegelian, model, it is needless to say). Neither does it raise the qualitative properties of things to a transcendental status; this was the complimentary error of the empiricists. The task of philosophy is more difficult than these two positions assumed: it must isolate and characterize the transcendental function of things such as they are. This will become the theme of *Sobre la esencia:* essence: the structure of things as they are, such as they are, which establishes them as *real.* The pretension to do this may be a scandal to the scientists; but it defines the problem of philosophy in its central focus. [39] The object of philosophy is not formally our mode of knowing; even less is it a kind of macro-object (the Idea) which emerges from the dialectical play of things. Neither is the object of philosophy the «Being» (ser) of things, in the sense given this concept either by Heidegger or by Hegel. Being — ser — does not (although Zubiri was inclined to think so in his Heideggerian period) fulfill the condition of ultimacy — the condition of transcendentality. As Zubiri wrote in an early (1931)

[37] *HOM.* I, 473.
[38] *NHD,* 116.
[39] *NHD,* 110.

conference on Hegel: «el primer problema de filosofía, el último ...
de sus problemas no es la pregunta griega *¿qué es el ser?* sino algo ...
que está más allá del ser.» [40]

The comparison with Heidegger throws considerable light on
Zubiri's position because the thought of Heidegger is a constant point
of reference of his own. The effort has been made to establish a
positive relationship between what Heidegger means by *Being* (ser)
and what Zubiri means by «realidad.» But this relationship proves
under careful analysis to be untenable. Not that no relationship exists
for, in fact, Zubiri develops the notion of «realidad» with a certain
reference precisely to Heidegger's *Being*. Eventually, however, he
decides that what Heidegger understands by Being is not sufficiently
radical and ultimate to constitute an adequate response to the question
of metaphysics. On the contrary, Being and reality appear to Zubiri
to constitute two different formalities at the metaphysical level-for-
malities which must be carefully distinguished. Zubiri does not mean
that his idea of «realidad» is to dislodge or substitute for Heidegger's
notion of Being, but rather that the latter must be purified and
transcended, but *not* negated, in the idea of «realidad.» [41].

The Doctrine of Sobre la esencia

Between the earlier works of Zubiri such as *Naturaleza Historia
Dios* and *Cinco Lecciones* and *Sobre la esencia* there is, as Ellacuria
has remarked, not rupture but evolution. The path of this evolution
is from concern with the *idea* of philosophy, seen principally from
the point of view of the philosopher, to the construction of philosophy
itself as the quest for «el último de las cosas» — from idea or
paradigm of philosophy, that is, to actualization. Obviously the
achievement of *Sobre la esencia* rests heavily on these earlier reflections for in them Zubiri had formed in dialogue with other philosophers, contemporary and past — according to his own dictum: «la
historia de la filosofía no es cultura ni erudición filosófica. Es encon-
trarse con las demás filósofos en las cosas sobre que se filosofa» [42]

---

[40] *NHD*, 240.
[41] *HOM*. I, 475.
[42] *NHD*, 222.

— his own idea of philosophy of which the doctrine of *Sobre la esencia* is the actualization. As Ellacuria notes: «en su última etapa Zubiri ha dejado de lado el tema de que es la filosofía para ponerse de lleno a hacerla.» [43]

Περὶ τῆς οὐσίας ἡ θεωρία

It is this phrase from the *Metaphysics* of Aristotle that Zubiri chooses as the motto of *Sobre la esencia* and the choice is portentous: for his quest and that of Aristotle are identical though pursued in ways diverse and to significantly diverse terms. What Aristotle meant by οὐσία — not what he ultimately offered as οὐσία, that is, what in *fact*, in his view, fulfilled the condition of οὐσία, but what οὐσία is — what Aristotle meant by οὐσία, is that which is *really real;* that which is real in *fact*, to be sure (but this would be merely the object of *science* as Zubiri has already indicated) but the *principle*, that by which that which is really real is *real*. And this is clearly indicated by Zubiri as the end of all philosophic quest which he accepts as his own: «el último de las cosas»; [44] not «las cosas,» (though these make the only possible starting point and the eventual point of reference of all θεωρία), but «el último de las cosas.» Ultimate from the point of view of philosophy as man's quest but *principle*, that is *beginning*, in an absolute sense from the point of view of what is really real: beginning and necessary ground of necessity and actuality.

At the very beginning a point of confusion threatens which Aristotle and Zubiri are equally concerned to avoid — the latter more concerned, perhaps, because he has seen this confusion posited and compounded by some of the greatest philosophers of the west: Plato, Hegel, in a word all those to whom the epithet «idealist,» with whatever justice, is assigned. This confusion involves the notion of *principle* itself and resides in the substitution of the *idea* as principle for the real principle, or the principle of the real as itself supremely real — and the attempt to derive the latter from the former: the really real from the *idea* — and to demand that the latter conform to the former, compounding the problem by confusing the *sollen* and

---

43 *HOM.* I, 485.
44 *NHD*, 221.

the *sein*. But this, from the point of view of Zubiri, is an inversion of both the order of truth and that of reality. For clearly, he holds, the truth is determined by what *is*. Truth is in the order of *physis* when *physis* is understood, as Aristotle understood it, as the actually real principle of what is actually real. For Zubiri, as Ellacuria writes, «una metafísica que no fuera suficientemente 'física' dejará de ser lo que es para convertirse en lógica, fenomenología, etc. ...», [45] echoing the even more emphatic statement of Zubiri himself «La metafísica jamás podrá ser una lógica. Es insostenible el supuesto primordial de la metafísica hegeliana.» [46] What then is the «physical»?

Here Aristotle contributes on his part to the confusion from which this concept of the «physical» must be delivered. He makes the distinction fall heavily on the difference between natural and technical or artificial. Zubiri points out, however, that modern experience has shown that it is technically possible to *make* something that is perfectly *real*, real in the same sense that the real things are real. «Physical» must be taken as meaning, not that which has a «nature»; it must be recognized as the synonym of «real.» Others have equated the «real» with the existent, the existential, the vital, the ontic, the ontological, the logical, the experimentable, etc. For Zubiri, none of these proves sufficiently «ultimate» to meet the conditions of the end of the metaphysical quest. The formula real-physical may be a pleonasm; if so, Zubiri replies «un puro pleonasmo pero muy útil.» [47]

No empiricism is implied, Zubiri contends, in a false opposition, also traceable, at least in part, to Aristotle, between «physical» and «metaphysical.» The physical has two aspects: one positive, the other «meta» physical (talidad-transcendental). That is to say, the «physical» must be understood as that which *is* real (i.e., as a matter of «fact»); this is the positive dimension of the physical. The «physical» must also be considered as the formal and ultimate principle of the real as such. These two aspects of the physical are not identical, but are related in a special manner which Zubiri will investigate extensively when he takes up the question of «transcendental function» in general and of the «transcendental function» of «essence» in particular. «Realidad física es realidad *qua* realidad, por tanto su carácter es *eo ipso*

45 *HOM.* I, 478.
46 *SE*, 47.
47 *SE*, 13.

un carácter metafísico.» [48] Metaphysical does not mean escaping from the physical into the conceptive order by way of predicative logic or any other mental construct, but means fixing the transcendental bond between what is actually real and the principle of its reality, not as *such* reality merely, but as real *qua* real. «Positive» knowledge focuses on what *is* real, i.e., what exercises reality, exemplifies, etc.; metaphysics addresses in what is real that which is its reality, that which establishes it as *real*, and not merely as actual or as *this* (such). This second enquiry goes beyond — «más allá» — the range of positive knowledge but the real in this second sense is entirely actualized in what is real in the first and hence can be sought successfully only when that which is real, in the sense of *actual* and *such* is taken as point of departure. The «más allá» does not imply a latent «other»; it is a *depth* dimension of what is actually real. Physical knowledge may, therefore, be schematized as «physical-positive» and «physical-metaphysical»; the former addresses what the thing is, its «talidad,» in its «talidad,» in its real concretion; the latter addresses the *same* thing insofar as it is *real*, not *this* or *that* real, but its reality *qua* real. Thus Zubiri transcends the dualisms: empirical-rational, ontic-ontological, etc., which have bedeviled western metaphysics. He addresses the reality in its dual aspects as suchness (talidad) and as transcendental function and in the transcendental linkage between these. His philosophy is neither a «conceptive» or a «materialistic» nor yet a «physicalistic» metaphysics; neither is it a theory of objects (Meinong) nor an «ontology.» It is a «realistic» metaphysics in the full sense of the word — for it goes directly to reality, to the reality which surrounds us, under its dual aspect. In his philosophy there is no opposition between scientific and metaphysical but a strict transcendental interfunctionalism.

These considerations lead ineluctably to the conclusion that metaphysics must be an *intramundane* inquiry. It takes its point of departure in the things that are real about us (mundo) to determine their dual aspect: *what* they are as real things (talitativamente) and in what their reality as real, and not merely as «talitative,» resides. He writes: «Puedo proponerme ... describir la estructura y la condición metafísica de las realidades en cuanto tal.» In his system, it is

---

[48] *SE*, 292.

true, this inquiry will not prove metaphysically ultimate; he will discover that the reality of the real things of the world is not itself ultimate: «se radicalizará últimamente, por intrínseca y rigurosa necesidad, la estructura metafísica de lo real en tanto creado.» [49] This is a further step, however, to which he is moved precisely by the initial inquiry as to the character of the real things of the real world as *real*. Such further inquiry «caería en el vacío si no se apoyara en una filosofía primera intramundana.» [50]

As a consequence, Zubiri rejects two of the pillars of classical metaphysics: analogy and the concept of general metaphysics. The latter would prescind from intramundane reality to address itself only to transmundane reality and its science would constitute «first philosophy,» its object «ens ut sic.» That «general metaphysics» in Zubiri's view must prove a phantasmagoria, a product of the speculative imagination. The question of what reality is can be met only from the ground of real things as they are in the world and as they are there present to the intelligence of man: *sentient intelligence.* [51] Since reality presents itself to us only in real things and since the real things which are present to us as real are present to us as sentient intelligences and the things so present as real are the things of this world, there is no other point of departure for first philosophy, no other form first philosophy can take save that of an *intramundane* metaphysics. For this reason, the method of analogy, on which that general metaphysics rests, appears to him to be inadequate, for it supposes that the ways of *being real* may be many, when they cannot (although the ways of being [ser, estar siendo] may be, or that the ways of knowing the real may be many when they cannot). This intramundane metaphysics must therefore be accounted *first philosophy*, for only by way of this intramundane metaphysics can reality as principle be reached, even when this principle stands revealed as «más allá» the real things of the world, and of the world itself as «creado.» For that «más allá» is not a phantasm beyond real things, but an inner depth of their reality. [52]

---

49 *SE*, 292.
50 *SE*, 210.
51 An excellent exposition of this fundamental Zubirian notion is to be found in López Quintas, A.: *op. cit.*, pp. 196-271.
52 *SE*, 290.

Intelligence and reality

One of the first questions to which Zubiri addresses himself is that of man's primary and fundamental access to reality. He replies to this question by his theory of «sentient intelligence.» The theory of «sentient intelligence» as a theory of man's primary access to reality must be distinguished from the «epistemological question» or the theory of knowledge. The theory of the intelligence is logically antecedent to the epistemological question and every epistemological theory eventually reveals that it presupposes a theory of the intelligence in its account of what and how man can know.

For Zubiri the nexus between intelligence and reality is strict. What is understood by reality inevitably depends on the manner in which things present themselves to us, the way in which we encounter them. [53] *The determination of the fundamental way in which things present themselves to intelligence constitutes in itself a determination of reality.* Zubiri avoids two extremes, which in the past have perplexed this issue: first, that of considering human reality, the reality of the intelligence itself, as *closed*, in such wise that it must go «outside» itself in quest of things and second that of considering it as pure *openness* so that reality becomes nothing but its precipitate. Rather, there is a mutual implication between them, but not necessarily one which implies a perfect equivalence of status in this reciprocity.

The salient feature of this mutual, but not equivalent, implication between intelligence and reality for Zubiri is the status of reality as principle with reference to the intelligence: «la principialidad de la realidad sobre la inteligencia.» [54] This status as principle means priority; the priority of the real means that the real is present to us as something the presence of which is consequent and subsequent to the real, as already real in its own character. [55] This priority is not merely that of reality before the Ego, nor before reason, the predicative *logos*, the concept, intentionality or «unveiling.» It is these and more. The character of this priority is based on the primary and

---

[53] *SE*, 389.
[54] *SE*, 417.
[55] *SE*, l. c.

formal activity of the intelligence: *actualization.* This actualization, which must be called the very essence of intelligence, means that reality which is actualized of itself antecedently to its presence to the intelligence *of itself* compels the intelligence to *actualize* itself conformably to that antecedent reality. The intellective actualization takes place *in* the intellect and is *of* the intellect but the act which actualizes itself in the intellect is the act and actualization of the thing. Therefore what reality *is* (as distinct from merely what is real) appears formally only in the pure actualization of the intelligence, while what intelligence *is* appears formally only in the pure formality of reality as *prius* to intelligence. Together these moments yield, — in due hierarchical relation, — the real truth *(verdad real)*. [56]

In the case of the human intelligence, the force with which reality presents itself exhibits special characteristics. Human intelligence is not *pure* intelligence. Human sensibility renders it a *sentient intelligence.* Human sensibility renders reality present in impression; nevertheless it presents reality in its specific character as *real*. Man is «animal de realidades.» [57] His impressions are not mere «affections» of his own state but of reality itself. In this he differs from all other animals. Nevertheless, he has access to reality only by way of sensible reality given in impression; but that of which he has the impression is reality itself as it is «de suyo.» [58] This radical realism of the human intelligent condition is the basic principle of Zubiri's intramundane metaphysics.

Reality as principle

The principle, then, which permits us to explain the ultimacy and the totality of the real is, for Zubiri, reality itself in its character as «de suyo»: its absolute priority in itself to the intelligence. The character of reality as *principle* is here anterior to and more fundamental than the principle proposed in other metaphysical systems. These others are, rather, derived from it — from the presence of the thing in its character «de suyo.» This is true with respect to nature, to existence and the existent, to aptitude for existence, to essence as

---

[56] *HOM.* I, 488-490.
[57] The contrast is with the Aristotelian characterization.
[58] *HOM.* I, 494-496.

classically understood and to Being (ser) in any and all of the three meanings assigned to it classically: copulative, substantive, transcendental. It is reality as «de suyo,» the irreducible and non-deducible *prius* of all presence which is the principle by which all is totally and ultimately explicated.

Essence as the Structural Principle of Reality

Zubiri has insisted throughout his investigation that reality is to be reached only in and through real things, things that are real — that reality cannot be reached or attained by any logical process or dialectical ploy. In this sense it can therefore be said that reality itself has its principle in real things — «realidad está principiada en las cosas reales.» [59] What then is the reality of things that are real? His answer is — essence. Essence is the principle of the reality of real things, of things which are real. The real thing *is* its essence. And the essence itself, in its turn, must be understood both as quidditative and transcendental: as endowing the real thing with its quidditative or talitative status as a real thing of this or that kind and as real *simpliciter*. [60]

Zubiri's concept of essence differs from all other concepts of essence heretofore advanced in the history of philosophy. For him, essence is identified and characterized through the function which it performs in the real thing, the thing that is real — «según la función que desempeña en la cosa real.» [61] When we answer the question: what function does the essence perform in the real thing, we indicate what the essence is as *principle*. Now the essence, in Zubiri's view, functions in three ways, does three things. It establishes the real thing in its quidditative and qualitative status as a thing of this or that kind: the status we indicate in replying to the questions what is it, what kind is it? Secondly, the essence establishes the thing, in its quidditative status, as *real*, real in the same sense in which all things, though quidditatively distinct among themselves or from one another, are real *in the same sense*. Finally it establishes the rela-

---

[59] *SE*, 59 and *passim*.
[60] *HOM.* I, 496.
[61] *HOM.* I, 496-498.

tionship between these two orders: a relationship which Zubiri calls functional identity. The consequence of this functional identity is that in discourse of one order, the talitative, we speak of the reality of that order (and not of mere appearance, etc.) and in discourse of the order of reality we speak of all things that are real. But the ability to speak in this way is not constitutive; it is derivative; it reflects the complex structure of the real in its immanent quidditative and transcendental dimensions. The emphasis on the mutual imma- nence is crucial. For the transcendental is not then itself the tran- scendent (though the transcendent is by no means excluded from reality, may, indeed, on the contrary, be rigorously implied in it) but that which establishes the transcendental reality of all, each and every thing that is real. Neither is the talitative order something which accrues «accidentally» to a constant, self-identical substratum: the real in its transcendental character is realized and actualized only in the things that are real in their total talitative character.

This complex structure is what constitutes the world. The *world* is constituted by the fact that the order of suchness and the order of transcendentality are intrinsic to each other. The link between them consists in the fact that the «talitative» order performs a transcen- dental function. It establishes the real as «de suyo.» Reciprocally, when the essence is considered transcendentally it is seen to establish the entire real thing as «de suyo» as «res» or «thing»: the transcen- dental-talitative complex in its «de suyo» character.

Open and Closed Essence: the Person

There are two fundamental types of essence, Zubiri holds, the closed and the open. The distinction between them is highly refined but important since it is the basis for the concept of *person*. The closed essence is closed because, due to its «suchness,» its «talitative» status, its entire transcendental reality is exhausted in being «de suyo» in itself. The open essence, by contrast, is open because it is not merely *such* as it is, but in addition, because of *what* it is (ser talitativo), it belongs to itself. It is formally and reduplicatively «suyo»; it possesses itself in its formal character as reality. The manner of being «suyo» is what constitutes a person.

The structure of the closed essence is the reason why something is a fact: «hecho»; a closed essence, as structural principle, is a merely «natural» thing. The structure of the open essence is the reason why something is an event: «suceso.» The open essence, as structural principle, is not merely a «natural» thing, though it is that too, but, even more, is an event-reality.

The «essential» then as principle is a structural principle. [62] The essence is not only principle of the substantivity, but is the structural principle of all that the real thing is and of all its ways of being real. The essence, in its turn, is so real of itself — de por sé — that everything that is real is real only in function of it.

---

[62] *SE*, 100; *HOM*. I, 496.

PART ONE

THE PROBLEM OF ESSENCE

Περὶ τῆς οὐσίας ἡ θεωρία.
This is a speculation on substance.

(Aristotle, *Meta.* 1069 a 18.)

INTRODUCTION *

Essence is the name of one of the central themes of every meta-physics. The Latin word *essentia* is a sophisticated term; it is the abstract form of a presumptive present participle *essens* (being) of the verb *esse* (to be = *ser*). Morphologically, therefore, it is the exact homologue of the Greek term οὐσία, which is, in its turn (or at least was so perceived by the Greeks), the abstract form of the present participle feminine οὖσα of the verb εἶναι (to be = *ser*). This homo-logous relationship might lead one to think that οὐσία meant es-sence. Nevertheless, such is not the case. The Greek word, in ordinary linguistic usage, is very rich in meanings and relationships; and Aristotle employed the term in all of them. When, however, the philosopher employed it as a technical term, it meant not essence but *substantia*, substance. By contrast, what this Latin term translates exactly is the Greek term ὑποκείμενον, that which «lies underneath,» or that which «is the support of» accidents (συμβεβηκότα). This is no mere complication of linguistic accidents; the fact is that, for Aristotle himself, the οὐσία, the substance, is above all and in its first meaning (μάλιστα) the ὑποκείμενον, the subject, the *sub-stante*. Essence, on the contrary, corresponds more to what Aristotle called τὸ τί ἦν εἶναί and what the Latins called *quidditas*, that which, or what, the οὐσία, the substance, is. For Aristotle, what is real is radically substance, and the essence is a moment of substance. The essence is, therefore, always and only, essence of the substance.

This implication or mutual reference between essence and sub-stance, within their undeniable distinction, has run, as cannot be 4 denied, through the whole course of the history of philosophy, though

---

* Marginal numbers refer to pages in Spanish texted. 1963.

taking on a different character (at different times). During the Middle Ages, the ideas of Aristotle on this point were repeated without fundamental alteration. From the end of the fourteenth century, however, and culminating in Descartes' idea of it, essence begins to be dissociated from substance and remains referred to substance in what might be called a loose manner. Actually, Descartes did not doubt that immediate evidence, of itself, guaranteed that the essence of the ego is to be a *res cogitans*, a thinking something, while the essence of the world is to be a *res extensa*, something extended. In this context, however, *res* does not mean thing, that is, substance, but only what scholasticism understood by *res*, that is to say, essence in its widest meaning, the «what;» for this reason I have translated *res* by the term «something.» This *res* or essence is so different from «thing,» or substance, that, in order to apprehend the former (i.e., essence), evident cogitation would be sufficient. In order to be sure, however, that the essence is found as realized in «things or substances,» not only was evidence insufficient for Descartes, but he held it necessary to take the problematical, roundabout way of invoking the divine veridiciousness. Essence and substance remain implicated with each other, consequently, but only in the loosest conceivable way: only by the mere *potentia Dei ordinata*, that is, by the «reasonable» power of God.

From this moment, this link breaks down from its own weight and substance remains something beyond essence; it could not have happened otherwise. Still, essence continued to be referred to a special substance, namely, thinking substance, which, insofar as it was thinking, would be a substantial subject. Essence would be, consequently, a formal act of conception of this thinking, or at least its merely objective term; it is idealism of the essence in its different forms and contexts.

In contemporary philosophy, it is true that even this implication seems to be disappearing. Thus Husserl, faithful to the spirit, it not 5 to the letter, of Cartesianism, and following a scholastic thinker, Brentano, will affirm that essences have nothing to do with substances, because consciousness itself is not substance but pure essence. As a consequence, the entire world of essences rests solely on itself. Substances are nothing but the uncertain and contingent realizations of these essences. This is the most Cartesian deformation of Cartesianism. One step more and consciousness, having been de-substantialized, remains reduced to being «my consciousness,» and this «my» takes on the character of being simply «my own existence.» The result is that, what before was called thinking «subject,» con-sciousness, etc., is nothing but a kind of existential *impetus* (impulse) whose possibilities of being realized within the situation in which it finds itself are exactly the essence, something like an essential pre-cipitate of the pure *to exist*. This is the thesis of all forms of existentialism. What is real has become desubstantialized and essence realized only in a purely situational and historical form.

It might be thought, then, that the intellectual transformations have fallen more heavily on substance than on essence, as though the identical concept of the latter had been preserved imperturbably identical in philosophy. Nothing could be more mistaken. Still, it is an error which can be explained, because these terms, consecrated by a centuries-long tradition, can produce, by the mere fact of this consecration, the deceptive impression that, when they employ them, everyone understands them in the same sense; whereas the truth is that, many times, they involve different concepts. This is what does in fact occur in the present case. In the wake of the transform-ation of the concept of the «what» this reality is, namely, the essence. By a singular paradox, consequently, we find ourselves con-fronting the same problem which, from the beginning, Aristotle himself had to debate: the implication between the radical structure of reality and the character of its essence.

This is the reason why I have set up as the motto of the present 6 work the phrase with which Aristotle opens the twelfth book of his *Metaphysics:* «This is a speculation about substance.» In this passage Aristotle reaffirms his idea of reality as substance, and undertakes in a formal manner to find its causes. Nevertheless, nothing prevents us — quite the contrary — from applying that phrase to an investi-gation about the essence of substance such as is carried out in the seventh book. In invoking this phrase I do not take it as an indication of my intention to repeat Aristotle's ideas but as a reminder that Aristotle was the very first to broach the problem and as an invitation to posit it anew. There is no question here, consequently, of taking two concepts which are already complete and fully formed, that of substance and that of essence, and of trying to couple them in one way or another, but rather to lay out the problem which underlies these two terms, the problem of the radical structure of the real and of its essential moment.

CHAPTER ONE

THE PROBLEM OF ESSENCE

Before all else, let us indicate the form in which, in a first attempt 7
to focus it, we shall confront the problem of essence. Let us call
essence — later we shall enter upon the matter of its more precise
determinations — as «that which» or «what» a real thing is. And
this «what» can constitute a problem under three clear-cut aspects.

Along a first line of inquiry we can put the question of the «what»
with respect to the fact that it has existence. Every real thing, as a
matter of fact, can be stated or conceived from two points of view:
either by saying of it «what» it is or by saying that that which it is,
is an existing reality. These are two perfectly distinct points of view.
I can, as a matter of fact, understand what a thing is while completely abstracting from whether or not it has existence; and I can
understand the fact of its existence without intellection, or at least
without any precise intellection, of what it is. Hence it results that,
conceptively, the essence (the «what») and the existence are two
moments of our exposition or conception; even more, they are two
moments of the real thing as it is the term or subject of the conception
in question. Of these two moments, each refers to the other: in every
thing, the existence is the existence of «something» and the «something» is something «existing,» for if this were not the case, it would
not be anything, but rather a pure nothing. As a consequence, when
once the real thing has been considered as the term of a λόγος, of
a conception, it is undeniable that essence and existence are two 8

distinct moments of the thing *qua* λεγόμενον, that is, of the thing
insofar as it is expressed in a predication. It is possible, therefore,
to ask why every thing possesses this «conceptive» duality. Here,
then, we have the first form in which the problem of the essence
with respect to the existence can be stated. Classical philosophy will
tell us that the foundation of this conceptual duality is found at least
in the fact of «causation»: because it is caused, everything justifies
our asking this question concerning the very fact of its existence
(since it has acquired it through causation) and concerning the character of that which exists. And this is the precise point at which, along
this line of inquiry, a serious problem arises: the problem of whether
the two suppositions from which the point of departure has been
taken are correct. First: is this duality primarily and formally «conceptual» in character, that is to say, does it consist in the manner of
stating a thing by way of the λόγος? Second: is «causality» the radical
foundation of this duality? This is a question of transcendent importance. Nevertheless, it is evidently not a question which has
reference to things in themselves but rather to our manner of confronting them intellectually.

Once this question has been solved another arises, a graver one,
though still in this same line of inquiry, concerning essence under the
aspect of the manner in which it differs from existence. Does the
fact that there may be two conceptually distinct and grounded moments in the same thing mean that the real thing, precisely as it is
real, that is to say, in its own «physical»[1] structure, possesses two
characters both physically and actually distinct, independently of all
possible intellectual considerations? For the structure of a thing,
insofar as it is the term of the predicative λόγος and the internal
«physical» structure of the thing taken in and for itself, are not the
same — and I will insist upon this point at great length in the course
of this work. Every reality can be made the term of a predicative
λόγος; this does not mean, however, that it is physically «composed» 9
of an attribute and a subject. Is the essence something physically
distinct or different from the existence? Here we have the second
aspect under which the problem of essence may be stated. It may
be supposed that essence and existence are only two moments or

---

[1] On this term consult the general note at the end of this chapter.

aspects which an identical and single thing offers to conception or
to the predicative λόγος. Independently of all intellection there would
be purely and simply the thing, and nothing but the thing. Only a
false conceptism would have led one to transform these two conceptual aspects of the reality into two physically distinct moments
of it. Basically, it would be a question of the fact that all things are
caused; nothing more. And, as a matter of fact, historically only the
idea of creation *ex nihilo* has led to the contra-position of *essentia*
and *existentia*. By contrast, in other philosophies, the essence-existence
duality is a physically real duality. The essence, therefore, would have
a physical relationship toward existence and the question of what this
respect might be would arise. The essence would be the internal
potentiality of the thing for existence, at the same time that the
existence would be the actuality of that potentiality.

It is evident, consequently, that no matter what solution may be
given to this problem, that is to say, whether or not it be true that
the essence involves a real respect to existence, the essence is something in itself; quite otherwise, it could not even be asked whether
or not it is really respective to the existence. Consequently, prior to
the problem of essence with regard to existence, there is a problem
of the essence under another aspect, namely, the essence considered
in and for itself. This is the third aspect under which the problem
of essence can be brought to a focus. Let us take any real thing
whatever. We say of it that it is this or that other. It may be that
not all that it is, is essential to it. Our immediate problem, then,
consists in ascertaining what, within all that a thing is, is essential
to it. This is a problem internal to the «what» itself, the problem of
the essence as the moment of the «what.» What is it that is essential
to a «what?» This essential moment is a real moment in the thing
itself, is a real moment of its «physical» structure. What we are
trying to ascertain is, then, in what the real character of this physical 10
structural moment of the thing, which we call «essence,» may
consist.

Precisely we are asking, in the first place, for the essence considered, not as the term of our way of confronting real things, but
rather as a moment of those things themselves. In the second place,
we are asking to get inside this moment considered in itself and not
in its eventual relationship to existence. In the third place, we are,

finally, inquiring about this moment as structural and physical moment of the real thing. Such is the line of inquiry along which we are going to confront the problem of essence. At first glance, it might appear that this is a reduction of the metaphysical problem of the essence of the thing to the «merely essential» element of it; that is to say, solely to the most important element of what the thing is. We will see in the course of this study, however, that not this, but the exact contrary, is the actual situation.

Let this, then, be the first step on the path of our investigation. Anticipating some ideas, I will begin by a provisional determination of the concept of essence, which will, at the same time, be a more precise formulation of our problem. Thereafter, I will examine some of the most important concepts of essence that have been given in philosophy, and this not so much through a desire for information, legitimate though that be in itself, but rather as a means, in a certain sense dialectical, of bringing the vision of essence into focus. We shall then be in a position to undertake a direct and positive confrontation of the problem of essence.

11   GENERAL NOTE

Throughout this work the term «physical» will appear continuously. A reader who is not familiar with the history of philosophy may find himself disoriented, because this word does not have, in ancient philosophy, the same meaning that it has in modern philosophy and science. «Physical» has designated, for some centuries now, the character proper to a clearly determined class of real things: namely, inanimate bodies. In itself, however, this meaning is nothing else than a restriction or specialization of a much wider and more radical meaning, linked to the etymology of the term and to the concept originally signified by it. This latter is the meaning which the term possessed in ancient philosophy. As this meaning is enormously expressive I believe that it is necessary to recover it and to introduce it into contemporary philosophy. More than through definitions or theoretical considerations, what I am trying to say will be understood by appealing to concrete examples.

«Physical» does not designate a circle or class of things, but rather a mode of to be. The word comes from the verb φύειν, to be born, to increase, and to germinate. As a mode of to be, then, it means to proceed from a principle intrinsic to the thing which is born or grows. In this meaning it stands in opposition to «artificial.» The «artificial» has an entirely different mode of to be; its principle is not intrinsic, but extrinsic to the thing, since it is found in the intellect of the artificer. Hence the word took on the form of a substantive and the intrinsic principle itself from which the thing proceeds «physically,» that is, «naturally,» came to be called φύσις; the same term was applied to the intrinsic principle of a thing from which all its properties, whether active or passive, proceed. Everything that belongs to the thing in this form is physical. The physical, consequently, is not limited to what we today call «physical,» but embraces the biological and the psychic as well. The emotions, all modes of understanding, the passions, the acts of the will, habits, perceptions, etc., are something «physical» in this strict sense. Such is not necessarily the case with what is understood or what is desired, for these may be merely intentional terms. A centaur, non-Archimedean space, are not physical things but, as we tend to say, intentional things (I will be excused from entering at this point into the rigorous distinctions which would be absolutely necessary if we were treating this theme explicitly). That which is understood, taken in this precise character, is not a physical part of the intelligence; by contrast 12 however, the act of understanding, itself, is something physical. Here, consequently, the «physical» is being set over against the «intentional.» And hence «physical» becomes the synonym of «real» in the strict sense of this latter term.

What has been said may become clearer if we pay attention to the notes or properties of things. The weight and the color of an apple tree are physically distinct; they are, in effect, two real notes each in its own right, (and) which contribute to the «integration» of the reality of the apple tree. They are at the same time an act of memory and one of passion. By contrast, two notes such as the «life» and the «vegetation» of an apple tree are not notes which are distinguished physically, because in the apple tree we do not have «life,» on the one hand, and «the vegetative functions,» on the other. Life and being a vegetable do not make the apple tree one whole thing. Rather than

notes possessed by it, these are aspects which the apple tree, taken as
a totality, offers to us according to our mode of looking at it, that is,
according as we consider it as a thing which possesses a mode of
being different from a stone or as a thing endowed with the constitutive functions proper to this mode of being and different from those
of a dog. They are not distinguished in the apple tree independently
of my mode of considering it; by contrast, in the apple tree, its
weight and its color are, each one, what it is, even though there may
be no intelligence considering them. For this reason it is customary
to say that these last properties are physically distinct, while the
aspects mentioned above are distinguished only «logically» (I would
prefer to say «conceptively»). In order to have a real distinction and
physical composition it is not sufficient that two concepts be independently of each other; it is also necessary, further, that what is conceived
be notes actually and formally independent in a «physical» thing.
Evidently «integration» is not the only type of physical composition.
It is enough to consider, for example, two constitutive principles
of a thing such as prime matter and substantial form in the Aristotelian system.

Physical and real, *in the strict sense*, are synonyms. The word
«reality,» however, also has many different usages in our languages,
usages which do not contribute in any precise manner to the clarification of the ideas involved, above all, in the post-Cartesian centuries,
which are so little demanding in matters of precision. Sometimes
those things we earlier have called «intentional» are also called real;
13 for example, when one speaks of real numbers, etc. It is clear that
numbers and figures, etc., are not realities as are a piece of iron, an
apple tree, a dog, or a man. For this reason, in order to underline that
one is treating of realities of this last type, I am accustomed to call
them sometimes «physical realities» or «physically real» things. This
is a pure pleonasm, which is, nevertheless, very useful.

In order to be exact, it would be necessary to go on to make
more precise distinctions at every level. These few lines, however,
may prove sufficient at least to orientate the reader who finds
himself unprepared.

CHAPTER TWO

A PROVISIONAL DETERMINATION OF THE CONCEPT
OF ESSENCE

Let us begin by delimiting the concept of essence in a provisional manner. Unless we hold before our eyes the essence itself, all our considerations would run the risk of falling into the void, and above all we would lack a point of reference to give a basis for those considerations and enable us to discuss them. Naturally, this demands that we have recourse to ideas which will acquire adequate clarity and justification only at the end of our discussion, precisely because they will be the proper result of that work. Nevertheless, nothing impedes our anticipating, in a summary manner, though rather vaguely, some of the characteristics which, as I view the matter, what we call the essence of something, must possess.

Taken in its most originative meaning, the word «essence» means that which responds to the name or to the question «what» something is, its *quid*, its τί. In a wide sense, the «what» of anything comprises all its notes, properties, or characteristics (it matters little which term we employ). These notes are not free-floating or detached, but constitute a unity, not by external addition, but an internal unity, the unity in virtue of which we say that all of these notes belong to «the» thing and, reciprocally, that «the» thing possesses such and such notes. The notes, therefore, possess unity, a unity which is internal. If they lacked this unity and if each one stood by itself, we would not have «one» thing but a number of things. If the

unity were merely additive or external, we would have a conglomerate
or mosaic of things, but not, in any strict sense, «one thing.» In this
very wide sense, the «what» means all those things which the thing
in question, as a matter of fact, is, with the totality of notes which
it possesses *hic et nunc*, including this very *hic* and this very *nunc*.
Thus, it is as though each thing were present to us in our first apprehension of it and is, in this apprehension, the term of a deictic
function, that is, of mere nominal indication: it is «this.»

The «what,» however, may have a more restricted meaning. In
apprehension itself, if not in first apprehension, in the strict sense
of the terms, at least then in the simple apprehension (we must not
confuse the «mere apprehension» of something with the «simple
apprehension» [1] of it; *apprehension simple* / simple apprehension),
that is, in that which includes the apprehension of a real thing among
other real things, this thing presents notes which rapidly take on a
function which is characteristic or distinctive of it, differently from
other notes which it possesses, so to say, indistinctly in a real, though
indifferent, manner. It is an apprehension of the thing as being «the
same,» despite the fact that these indifferent notes may vary; even
more, to apprehend them as a mere «variation» of the «same» thing
is something congenerous with the apprehension of those notes as
characteristics «of it.» The respect under which this sameness exists,
however, matters little: it may be the sameness of a class (man, dog,
apple, etc.) or a sameness proper to an individual (it is the same
person with different garments, hairdo, etc.). However, in this case
we do not possess a mere δεῖξις; this has rather been transformed
into a true «denomination» or naming, whether proper or specific. The
«what,» understood in this manner, does not respond to the question
of a deictic *quid*, but rather to the demand for a demonstrative *quid:*
it is now no longer «this thing» but rather Peter, a man, a dog, etc.
This *quid* does not embrace the totality of the notes that the thing 17
comprehends *hic et nunc*, but rather only the conjunction of those
notes which it possesses as its distinctive properties; not those which
are indifferent, but only those which constitute its characteristic
sameness. We are not accustomed to calling this «what» essence, but

---

[1] «simple apprehension» = a fairly technical term in the analysis of knowledge
in the classical tradition of scholasticism.

it should be called essence, because it is absolutely necessary to refer to that «what» in order to understand how, from the first meaning of essence, its widest meaning, the problem of the essence in a third sense, essence in a strict sense, arises.

To take a step further, also in the «what,» understood in the second sense, the thinking intellection has to carry out a difficult task in order rigorously to conceive the essential «what» of anything, because the strict line of distinction between those notes which characterize the sameness of a real thing and those others which are indifferent or accessory to it under this aspect is very vague and fluctuating. We have to understand whence those characteristics of the notes begin and end; that is to say, which may be the notes which, taken in and for themselves, not only characterize a thing more or less so that it may not be confused with other things, but rather, that they can in no sense fail or that they can in no sense be absent from a real thing without this latter, in a strict sense, ceasing to be what it is. It is these last notes which, in a strict sense, ought to be called the essential notes. The essential *(esencial)* of anything is precisely the minimum of that which it must possess in order to be what it is in the second sense. The unitary conjunction of all of these essential notes is what in the strict sense I shall call essence. In order to be exact, let us add that the essence, understood in this sense, is not only the unitary conjunction of the notes that the thing necessarily possesses, but rather that, in this unitary conjunction, its unity exhibits an extremely precise character. This unity, as a matter of fact, is not only internal, but, even more, is primary and radical, that is to say, it is a unity such that, with respect to it, the notes are nothing but moments in which, so to phrase it, the unity in question exhaustively 18 deploys itself. In the classical example of man as rational animal, we would say that he is an animal and rational because he is man, and he is not man because he is rational and animal. Animality and rationality are the moments in which what we call being a man is exhaustively deployed. Therefore, the unity of animality and rationality is not only intrinsic but is also «primary.» The essence, therefore, is a primary necessitating unity. It is clear that the essence is, then, the principle of some other necessary notes of the thing even though the latter are not strictly essentials *(esenciales)*. Under this aspect, the essence is, further, the primary unity, the principiating unity of the

non-essential. For the nonce, let us be content with this provisional
determination of the concept of essence. We will soon add some
additional characters.

In this third, and strictest, sense, the conceptualization of essence
presupposes the apprehension of the «what» of something in the
second sense. Precisely because we already know what the thing is
(Peter, dog, man) we find ourselves compelled, by the thing itself, to
seek out the concept of its strict essence. That is to say, we know
what the thing is, but we do not understand, in conceptual terms,
what its essence consists in. However, since we already know (in the
second sense) what the thing is, we also know whither we must
direct our mental gaze, in order to assure the correctness of each one
of the further steps in our investigations. The «what,» in the second
sense, is that, then, which forcibly confronts us with the problem
of essence in the strict sense and, further, that which makes its
treatment possible.

To sum up, the question concerning the essence in itself is nothing else but the quest for the principiating unity of the real thing.
19 Of what kind is this unity? What is its character? What is that which
is inessential to something? That is our question.

Responses to this question have been forthcoming in distinctive
ways according to the interpretation given of the principiating, necessitating unity. Before undertaking to treat the problem of essence
directly, it is necessary briefly to review the most important of these
answers, and to examine them with some rigor.

PART TWO

SOME CLASSICAL IDEAS CONCERNING ESSENCE

CHAPTER THREE

ESSENCE AS MEANING

The classical ideas concerning essence which we are going to submit to rapid examination may be reduced to three groups. In the first place, there is the idea that essence is a «meaning.» In the second place, there is the group in which we find the different ideas according to which the essence is, in one form or another, the «concept» of the thing. Finally, there is the idea of the essence as the correlative of the real «definition.»

We will begin with the first group. We ask, then, in what does the primary necessitating unity of the real thing consist? A first attempt at an answer to this question — first only in order of this exposition — depends precisely on the conceptualization of the kind of necessity to which the essence refers. This is the conception of essence which Husserl held. It is not enough that something be necessary to insure that it be strictly essential, because there are different types of necessity. All natural laws involve some kind of necessity (whether it be statistical or causal is unimportant at this point); nevertheless, we do not say without further consideration that they are essential laws. Essential necessity is more than natural necessity. For Husserl, natural necessity is merely the necessity characteristic of a fact. Natural necessity, in a word, refers to individual realities, that is, internally determined realities situated in a certain place and at a certain moment of time. Every individual reality, we are told, is, in 24 itself, contingent; it is «thus» but it could be otherwise. It might be

found in some other place and encountered at some other moment
of time. In its characteristics, this individual reality is what and as
it is, but only as a matter of fact. Reality is, then, for Husserl, individuality, and for this reason contingency, and for the same reason,
fact. Hence it is that natural laws are mere laws of matters of fact,
factitious regulations of the factitious; as such, they share, in the last
analysis, the contingent character of all matters of fact: things are
as a matter of fact, subject to determined necessities. However, in
their particular character *(de suyo)* they could be subject to other,
different necessities. This factitive necessity is what the law of nature
expresses; it is a hypothetical necessity because it rests on the supposition that things are regulated as they are, as a matter of fact,
regulated. Hence, in its intrinsic character, no matter how necessary
it may be, knowledge of natural laws is an empirical knowledge.

An essential law is something very different. It expresses an
absolute necessity. Absolute here means not only that it admits of
no exceptions, but also that it cannot have any exceptions because it
does not depend upon any hypothesis concerning matter of fact: the
essential not only is as it is, but also has to be as it is; it is impossible
on the basis of its intrinsic character *(de suyo)* that it should be
otherwise. For this reason, the essential law does not rest on reality
as such but rather on something independent of all factitive reality.
This object on which the essential law rests is what Husserl calls
essence. While apprehension of matters of fact constitutes empirical
knowledge, the apprehension of essences is the term of an absolute
knowledge. It is clear that essences and realities are not totally
independent of each other: an essence is independent of all reality,
i.e., matters of fact; a reciprocal independence of matter of fact
relative to essence is not certain. That is, every reality is founded on
an essence. It has a to be, being, relative to an essence, and all
empirical knowledge is based on an absolute knowledge. Essence, by
contrast, has an absolute to be and is also the term of an absolute
knowledge.

25   On this basis, what, for Husserl, is this essence in itself, what
is its absolute «to be» *(ser)*? Granted that the essence is the terminus
of absolute knowledge, it will be enough for us to arrive at this
knowledge: its object, the essence, will, by this very fact, be characterized. Empirical knowledge attains to the real thing insofar as it

is real and is the terminus of an act of apprehension by my consciousness, an act which in itself is also a real act, possessing psychic
and psycho-physiological mechanisms of execution. Empirical knowledge, consequently, exhibits all of the relativity inherent in the
character of reality of its object as well as of its act of apprehension.
Without, however, abandoning this act, I can effect a change of
attitude which would consist in taking the term which is apprehended
solely in its character of being apprehended, and the act of apprehension solely in its character as a taking account of, that is, setting
aside the mechanism of its execution. We thus place the character of
reality «within parentheses.» And, in virtue of this simple operation,
we have opened an unsuspected world before our eyes. In these
conditions, effectively, the object apprehended, insofar as it is apprehended, and the apprehending consciousness, insofar as it is a
consciousness of this character, cannot be posited the one without
the other; they are in strict, rigorous, and indissoluble correspondence, the traits of which can be precisely determined. That which
is apprehended, strictly as apprenhended, does not form a part or
moment of consciousness even though it is given evidently only in
that consciousness. Reciprocally, consciousness, in this case, is not
a real act, psychic in character, but is only «consciousness of» that
which is apprehended, and cannot be posited without it. This is
precisely what the «of» *(de)* expresses. This «of» belongs, then, to the
structure of «pure» consciousness and is what Husserl calls intentionality. In its turn, that which is apprehended in this precise
character is nothing else than what is intended *(intentum)*, the intentional correlative of that «*de*», the intentional term «toward» which
consciousness directs itself, that is, the «sense» *(Sinn)* of this intention.
As object, this *intentum* is a new object, so new that it is irreducible
to any matter of fact and remains unaffected by all the vicissitudes
of reality; this is the case whether that which is apprehended, in its
precise character as apprehended, be, in addition, a reality or not 26
(illusion or hallucination). This new object, which is the «meaning,»
is not, consequently, a real object, but pure «*eidos*.» For this reason,
that which is apprehended as apprehended, that is to say, not as
the factitive term of a fact of consciousness but as the objective
meaning of its intention, is now not a reality but *eidos*. For this
reason, that knowledge in which that which is apprehended is not

relative to empirical conditions but is independent of them, is absolute knowledge. Its object is precisely the essence. The essence, consequently, is nothing other than the eidetic unity of a meaning or sense. And consciousness itself, on having been reduced to an «intending» meaning, exhibits to us, in this intentionality, its own proper essence; consciousness would be, in a certain way, the essence of essences, because it is the essential *(esencial)* support of all of the essences. Consciousness is, then, effectively, an act of «giving» meaning *(sinngebender Akt)*. Simply by the process of reducing reality to meaning, empirical knowledge has been turned into absolute knowledge, and fact into essence. The laws of the realm of essence, we may say, are absolute. For Husserl, this means that any attempt to violate them not only is false as a matter of fact, not only is, further, impossible because contradictory, but is something much more simple: it is «counter-sense» *(contra-sentido) (Widersinn)*.

The essence, then, is the eidetic unity of meaning. As such, it is, in the first place, as we have said, «an object of a new character» and separated, that is, independent, of any reality of fact; it has indeed nothing at all to do with realities. Essence and reality are two distinct and separate worlds. In the second place, essence is that which establishes or grounds reality. Every reality is «thus and so;» it might, however, be in «some other manner;» this «thus and so» and this «other manner» refer back to the essence; every individual and contingent, by its very meaning, sends us back to an essence of which it is the realization in fact and to which it must accommodate itself; the supreme condition of every reality is that what is realized in it must have meaning. Essence, as I was saying, is separated from fact, because it is independent of the latter. The fact, however, is not separated from the essence, but, quite the contrary, refers back to it and is founded in it; it is in itself inseparable from the essence. The essence is, then, the foundation of the possibility of the real. In the third place, essence as meaning is not only independent of reality and that which establishes the latter; it is also sufficient to itself. It is the unique entity *(ente)* which has no need of another in order to be what it is: pure meaning. Its to be, therefore, is absolute.

To sum up then, the essence, for Husserl, is an eidetic unity of meaning and as such rests upon itself in a world of absolute to be,

distinct, independent, and separated from the world of reality of
fact.

Despite all the richness of the phenomenological analysis, this
conception of essence is radically unsustainable, both in its presuppositions as well as in its content.

It is untenable before all else in its very suppositions. In the first
place, by reason of the very form in which it focuses the question.
Husserl, as a matter of fact, takes his point of departure from the
absolute laws or necessities of things. Stated in this way, the obvious
course would be to concentrate on things in order to arrive with
much effort at their absolute moment, without ever being secure of
having reached it. Nothing could be farther from Husserl's mind.
Husserl does not go directly to things because what he wanted, in
the first place, was apodictic evidences, absolute evidences, that is, a
knowledge which, by reason of its proper character as a form of
knowledge, will guarantee these evidences and would, therefore, be
an absolute knowledge in and for itself, quite different from every
form of empirical knowledge. The radical differentiation, from which
Husserl takes his point of departure in all his philosophy, is the contraposition between absolute knowledge and empirical knowledge;
it is not the difference between two modes of to be — «the» absolute
and «the» relative — but between two modes of knowing. He subsumes 28
the concept of essence under the concept of absolute and makes the
absolute in its turn a form of knowing. With this, in place of seeking
the absolute of things, what he does is delimit among them that zone
to which this kind of knowledge, absolute by itself, attains. Husserl
has projected the problem of essence by way of knowledge, by way
of the act of consciousness, in which I apprehend it. However, in this
way, the essence of things remains irretrievably lost beforehand and
can never be recovered. The philosophy of Husserl, phenomenology,
never tells us what anything is but only the mode of consciousness
in which it is given. With his celebrated essences Husserl will never
tell us what the essence is, but only what it is which is given to us
in the absolute mode of consciousness; and this «what» is that which
he will call, without qualification, essence. This is to twist that which
is apprehended to make it take on the character of a mode of apprehension; it is to call absolute that of which we have absolute consciousness. This, however, is inadmissible. By departing from things

and directing himself to consciousness for the sake of an absolute knowledge, Husserl has lost, in the very focusing of the question, the essential element of reality. He will attain, at most, a kind of «essential thinking» but never the essence of things.

However, even if we should accept this focusing of the question, the very idea of consciousness, with which Husserl operates, is inadmissible, namely, his supposition that the formal character of consciousness is «intentionality.» Let us pass over the grave problem which (the manner of) speaking about that which Husserl, following philosophy since Descartes, calls «the» consciousness, constituted. It is not possible to speak of «the» consciousness for the simple reason that consciousness lacks all substantivity, all substantive *to be*. Consciousness is nothing but a character or property which some, but not all, the acts which man carries out, possess; there are conscious acts, but there is no «consciousness». For this reason, the radical problem does not lie in the moment of consciousness, but rather in the «physical» character of those acts. Therefore, I repeat, let us not linger over this important question on which I have insisted extensively in my courses, and let us acknowledge that one speaks of consciousness as an entity in itself. Husserl tells us that this entity is «intentional.» That means that the inner character of this act is to be «consciousness of» and that the character of the object is to be its intentional term, to be «correlative to» the intention in consciousness. What is true as a mere establishment of properties which the act and its object effectively possess is completely false as an affirmation concerning what they formally are. Consciousness does not consist formally in «being intention of» but in being «actualization» of its object. The intention itself is a mode of actualization and nothing more. Conversely, the to be of an object does not consist in «to be correlative to.» To be sure, the object is correlative to the act; however, since the latter is an act of actualization, it follows that the formal character of the object, insofar as it is the term of the act, is merely to be actualized. To be the intentional object of consciousness not only does not exclude being reality — this should be obvious — but rather that it futher «consists» in referring formally to that which the object is independently of consciousness and its meaning, and this in virtue of the formal character of consciousness: to actualize. It is a question, then, of a remission not of a «meaning,» but a «physical» remission just as the actualization is also physical. Hence it follows that the essence is not formally «meaning.» To be a meaning is, in the essence, a character which it possesses only for the intentional moment of consciousness, but not the character in which the essence formally consists. As we shall see later on, consciousness by reason of its proper character, which is not intentional but physical, sends us back to this other character proper to the essence and, there- 30 fore, does not exhibit it to us as mere meaning.

Consequently, in its very suppositions — both those which regard the focusing of the question as well as those which refer to the idea of the act of consciousness — the Husserlian conception of essence is inadmissible. However, what is still more serious, the very idea which Husserl forms of essence is radically erroneous in its content. The essence, he tells us, is an eidetic unity of meaning. We have just said that the essence is not the «meaning» of the intentional dimensions of consciousness; now we may add that, taken in itself, neither is it a meaning with respect to things. Things do not «send us back to» the essence as to a meaning which is regulative *a priori* of their reality. Things actually have a more intimate relation with the essence: they do not send us back to the essence but rather they «possess» the essence intrinsically; essences are realized «in» things; they are an intrinsic and formal moment of them. It is this moment that may be called *eidos*. The essence, however, is not an eidetic unity of meaning, but rather, it would be at most the structural *eidos* of the reality. To the degree that the matter stands in this way, the reality is not a pure contingent fact, but encloses within itself, as an intrinsic moment, essential necessity (the necessity proper to the essence). Hence it follows that to violate essential laws would be an absolutely impossible effort, not only through logical impossibility (contradiction) and less by way of counter-meaning *(contra-sentido)*, but, ultimately, for a much more profound reason: by the «real» impossibility of the thing, should those laws be violated, continuing to be physically the same thing that it was. It is not a counter-sense, but a «counter-to be,» a «counter-reality,» that is, a radical and primordial destruction of the thing.

Hence, it follows that the reality of fact and the essence are not opposed to each other in the form which Husserl suggests. To the degree to which the essence is realized «in» the thing, it is «of» the thing. Every essence is, by reason of its proper «to be,» the essence 31 «of» the thing, a moment of it. The «of» belongs to the formal structure of the essence itself. The essence is necessarily «the essence of.» There is no essence apart, as Husserl would have it. By its intrinsic character, in the first place, the essence is not something independent of the reality of fact. It is true that the color that I perceive, insofar as it is perceived, or a geometrical circle, are what they are in their pure suchness so long as my perceptions do not prove to be hallucinatory; the naturalist would be upset, but the painter and the geometer would continue unperturbed. This, however, does not mean what Husserl would have it mean. For the color which has been perceived, insofar as it is perceived, and the geometrical circle, are not essences, but objects *sui generis;* proof of this resides in the fact that I am necessarily compelled to inquire into the essence of this color and of this circle. These presumptive «objects,» like all objects, have their proper essences. And of this essence we have to repeat that it is not independent of the object itself as though the essence were «an ideal thing,» but is, rather, an intrinsic and formal moment of the object itself. That of which the essence is independent is the accidental contingency, but not the real thing, for this real thing has in itself and formally something more than its contingent moment, namely, the moment of essential necessity. The color which has been perceived insofar as it is perceived, and the geometrical circle, owe their indifference to existence not to the fact that they are essences but to the fact that they constitute another class of objects different from real things. The reduction in character of reality does not turn the fact into an essence, but the real thing into a phenomenal object. The essence, as such, issues untouched from this operation.

In the second place, the essence is not that which grounds the reality as the regulative meaning of the reality itself. We have already said: it is the *eidos* of the reality, a structural moment of it, but not its physical «meaning.» The essence is not like an ideal pole toward which the thing would be directed in its contingent mobility and individuality.

Finally, in the third place, the essence has no absolute to be 32 whatsoever; it is not the being *(ente)* which is sufficient to itself in order to be what it is. And this for a simple reason, because, as «separated» from the thing, the essence «is» not an entity; as to be *(ser)* only the thing «is.» The essence is not an entity, but only a moment of the unique entity which the real thing is. Therefore, the essence does not repose on itself; it reposes on the real thing according to that mode of reposing on it which is «to be it.» Consequently, it follows that the essence is in itself something completely made factitive *(fáctico)*. There are no essences which are really and physically immutable and absolute.

In a word, then, the essence is always and only the essence «of» the real thing and nothing more: it is an intrinsic moment of the latter. Essentiality and facticity are not two regions of entities, two classes of «things,» but only two moments of every reality. The essentiality pertains to the structural moment of the real and not to the objective meaning of my absolute knowledge. By separating these two moments — essentiality and facticity — and by substantivizing them to the benefit of two types of knowing — absolute knowledge and empirical knowledge — Husserl has disjointed the real, and the reality has escaped forever from his hands.

CHAPTER FOUR

ESSENCE AS CONCEPT

Essence is, then, an intrinsic moment of the thing. In order to bring the question into focus in this second line of inquiry, let us anticipate some ideas again, that is, let us make some addition to the provisional determination of essence.

Since essence is an intrinsic moment of the real thing, the contraposition, or I might better say, the difference between the «simple» real thing and its essence remains carried back to a difference within the real thing itself between what is essential and what is not essential in it. Among the notes which the thing effectively possesses, there are some notes of a more profound character than that of their mere effective possession, because they are those notes upon which rests all that the thing is. This is what is essential; everything else is real in the thing, but non-essential to it. This difference between what is essential and what is non-essential is expressed, before all else, in the idea of truth: what is essential is what is truly real in the thing, the essence is its true *(verdadera)* reality. This is what we must add to our earlier provisional determination of the essence. Let us say then that the essence is primary unity and at least an intrinsic principle which necessitates the other notes of the real thing; we add, then, that it is the true reality of this thing.

The conception of essence as «meaning» does indeed indicate the character of the primary unity and of the necessitating principle of the real thing, but states it as extrinsic to the thing. Having seen, 34 however, that it is intrinsic, we have turned our gaze toward the interior, so to say, of the real thing itself, and we try to verify in just what its truth may consist. Only in this way will we encounter the essence. What, then, is the true reality of anything?

It is not a question, in the first place, of truth, in the sense of true knowledge, but in the sense of the real character of things; as when, for example, we speak of a true wine in contrast to a wine that has been adulterated. It is customary to speak, in this sense, of an ontological truth. We may set aside, for the moment (though recognizing clearly its importance), the question whether this truth is, properly speaking, ontological; for reasons which I shall explain later, we will see that it is not an ontological truth, but another kind of truth, real truth. For the purposes of a simple exposition of philosophical positions other than our own, however, let us employ the idea of an ontological truth. By this term, what is usually meant is that it is not a question of a truth of the λόγος, but of a truth of the thing. What is this truth, truth in this sense? In this truth of the thing, the thing is not what we might call its reality without qualification, that is, the immediately apprehended reality, but rather it is the reality of that which we apprehend insofar as it corresponds to the concept of the thing. The truth of something would be its concept, or, if one prefers, conformity with its concept. When the thing corresponds to the concept of it, we are accustomed to say that it possesses ontological truth. Thus, authentic and true wine, that is, a liquid which is truly wine, is one which possesses all the properties which are included in the concept of wine.

On this supposition, this true reality would be, properly, the essence of the thing. As a consequence, we can say that the essence is the reality of the concept «of» the thing. Naturally this expression proves ambiguous; and it is deliberately so because it leaves in the shadow the meaning of this «of.» The only thing that we have wanted to say is that reality and concept are two dimensions in the correspondence between which essence is truly found. This correspondence is what is expressed in the «of.» And the different interpretations of this «of» offer a corresponding number of distinct notions of the essence as the concept of the thing.

THE ESSENCE AS FORMAL CONCEPT

The essence, we are told, is the reality of the concept. This phrase, however, as I have just said, is enormously equivocal, because the concept itself can be understood in two ways. The concept is, on the one hand, that which is conceived and, on the other hand, the conception itself, that is to say, the act of conceiving that which is conceived and the thought in and with which I conceive it: this is the classical distinction between the objective and the formal concept.

In a first sense, to speak of the reality of the concept can mean that one is considering the reality of the formal concept itself. The formal concept would not be a form empty of content, but rather that in which the very activity of reason would formally consist: to engender, to conceive, to create something in and by thought. What, however, is this conception, and what is that which is conceived in it? This is the question.

That which is conceived, in the first place, is an objective concept; as such, it contains no more being than that which its formal conception confers upon it; that is, its being consists solely in being thought. Hegel will tell us that this is not enough; that which is conceived is not merely an objective concept, but is identical with the real thing itself, as real. If there should be a separation or distinction between the objective concept and the real thing, possession of the truth would not be possible. Therefore, the *to be* which the formal conception confers on that which is conceived is more than objectivity; it is the «physical» reality itself. All the *to be* of the real thing as real would be conferred upon it by the formal conception of reason. To be consists in being conceived. «To be is to think» *(Phänom. Vorrede,* 3); «the concept as such is the being in and for itself» *(Logik, Einleit.).* In this manner the concept would be «the living spirit of what is real» *(Encyk.,* Section 162) and only that «is true in reality which is true in and by the forms of the concept» *(ibid.).* Conception, therefore, has the strong meaning which it has in biology;

the formal conception, the act of reason, would be the generation or realization of things. Reciprocally, the whole of reality would be nothing else than the realization of reason. «Logical reason itself is the substantial element of the real» *(Logik, Einleitung)*. Because it is the root and foundation of the whole of reality, this logical reason is in itself the divine reason. Nevertheless, it is, at the same time and as unity, human reason, because the latter is, in its proper concept, identical with the divine reason. To be sure, human reason is finite in itself; its finitude, however, in the same manner as the finitude of all other things, consists simply «in not as yet having within itself completely the reality of its concept» *(Logik,* III; *Abs.* 3, p. 40). The divine reason, by contrast, is reason in its full concept, is «the» absolute reason. By what it contains on the basis of reason, human reason is, then, identical with the divine reason; on the basis of what it has of the human, it is nothing but the realization, as yet fragmentary and deficient, of that divine reason. There is, between these two, only a difference of degree; human reason is only a moment of the divine reason, of «the» reason. From this it follows that the content of human reason, insofar as it is actually reason, namely, the *Science of Logic,* «is nothing else in its content but the exposition of God as He is in His eternal essence before the creation of nature and finite spirit» *(ibid.).* Metaphysics and theology, consequently, are nothing but logic. That is to say, the structure of reality is identical with the formal structure of «the» reason and is founded on it. Such is Hegel's interpretation. What then is essence?

E v i d e n t l y , it will be a moment of conception, that is, of the realization of reason. In a first moment, that is, immediately when we conceive something, we conceive it provisionally as «actually being» *(siendo). To be* is pure immediacy, because it is nothing but the setting in motion of conception. Therefore, reason cannot conceive pure *to be* and nothing more, because «to be and nothing more» is «not to be,» determinately nothing: pure to be is the same as pure nothing, Hegel will tell us. That is to say, *to be* contains within itself intrinsically its own negativity; this «no» can rest in itself. Therefore, *to be* is seen as forced to emerge from itself; it is not rest but process, becoming *(Werden).* Reason is seen as forced to continue the process of conception; it has to conceive *to be* as «something;» this is to say, in its process of becoming, *to be* acquires its specific notes, or quantitative and qualitative determinations. The oak is not only the tree; it is also the fruit and the seed; and it is these three things at one and the same time, as moments of a single process.

But let us not be deceived. To speak of *to be* has been, since the time of Parmenides, to speak of something supreme and ultimate. In Hegel's view it is exactly the contrary: *to be* is the most impoverished (of concepts). Not, to be sure, in the sense that it possesses the least comprehension; because this, in addition to being the oldest (point of view) would be false for Hegel, since for him *to be*, by reason of its processive character, is endowed, as we have just said, with specific determinations. The poverty of *to be* is for Hegel much more profound: it consists precisely in its pure immediacy, its being nothing more than setting the process of conception in motion. For Hegel, «to be» is «to be and nothing more.» And to say of anything «only» that «it is,» is to level off everything: all things «are» and are «equally;» when we look only to the fact of *to be*, all things have the same rank. Immediacy, therefore, is pure indifference *(Gleichgültigkeit)*, and for the same reason, dispersion. This is what the poverty of *to be* consists in. Reason conceives that this «no» can be in this way. Therefore, it folds the notes back upon themselves *(Reflexion)*, it interiorizes them, in a certain way, that is, it conceives them as the manifestation of a kind of internal nucleus of the thing. This is the essence: the second stage of conception as 39 realization. After the first, which was the immediacy of becoming, that is, the mere «setting in motion» of conception, we now have, so to say, «the concrete motion itself» of conception, a movement of the folding of becoming back upon itself, a quiescence of becoming which is the constitution of its internal supposition: the essence. What does Hegel understand by essence?

First of all, the manner in which Hegel arrives at the essence already foretells its proper formal character. For Hegel does not discover the essence by distinguishing, within real things, the essential and the non-essential notes. Not that it is the case that Hegel is entirely ignorant of this difference, but rather that he eliminates it as «superficial» and external *(etwas äusserliches)*. For Hegel, the difference between the essence and that which is not essence is not a difference of notes but a difference of condition. It is not a question of what is essential in a thing, but of the essentiality *(esencialidad)*

of *to be*. All the notes of a thing, considered as notes which merely
«are,» constitute what is non-essential; non-essentiality *(inesencialidad)*
is precisely the pure indifference of *to be*. However, *all* these same
notes conceived as «growing out of» the interiority of the thing which
«is» are what is essential in it, what is essential in *to be*. For this
reason, that which Hegel calls non-essential *(un-wesentlich)* would
have to be properly translated as «a-essential.» That which is constitutively a-essential is for Hegel pure *to be*, because it is pure indifference. The essence, therefore, in a certain way stands beyond *to be*.
Hence follows the formal proper character of the essence. The essence,
in effect, because it stands beyond *to be* as such, is, *eo ipso*, the
negation of the constitutive immediacy of pure *to be;* it consists in
the «no» of simple *to be (Nichtigkeit)*. Therefore, essence is formally
40 «pure negativity»: here we have its specific formal character. On this
supposition, the problem of essence is nothing else for Hegel except
the problem of the structure of this pure negativity.

Hence, negativity is not a pure «nothing,» because, for Hegel, the
essence arises in a movement of refolding, in a «reflection» of becoming back on itself. It is the first structural moment of the essence
as negativity: the reflexivity of *to be*. Reflection is not a movement
of knowing, but of *to be*. As a character of *to be* it is not a transitive,
but an intransitive movement, a «remaining» in itself, something, as
it were, like a stationary movement, a «relation» rather than a
process. In this reflection, and established upon the *to be*, what
movement does is to open the vacuum in it, the ambit of its interiority.

Reflexivity is, under this aspect, a negation of the simple immediacy
of *to be;* it is not, however, an annihilation of *to be*. *To be* is con-
served, but as something negated. In opening the ambit of the interiority of *to be*, reflection lodges in it precisely the *to be* itself,
though «negatively,» so to say. Rather than an annihilation, it is an
annulment of being. I should say that, for Hegel, essence is not
«nothingness» *(nada)* but rather «nullity» (this would be my translation of *Nichtigkeit)* in the order of *to be*, something which «is not
actually being.» And this is, concretely, «appearance» *(Schein)*. Appearance, in fact, does not mean here a thing which appears other,
that is, an apparent thing, an «apparent *to be*,» but rather «an appearance of *to be*,» pure and constitutive «appearanceness» *(aparien-*

cialidad). Appearance is not a nothing; nevertheless, it is not *to be;* *to be* is preserved in the appearance, though negated in its *to be,* that is to say, affirmed only as appearance; it is precisely the nullity of *to be.* Neither does appearance mean here that, for example, what I have before me appears to be an oak but is not such. Appearance is not «only appearance.» Appearance means that the reflective refolding of all the notes of that which I have before me makes of them that which we call an oak precisely when I take these notes, subtracting *(restando)* from them their character of *to be.* As nega- 41 tivity of *to be,* then, the essence is positively appearanceness. For this reason I would call the Hegelian essence a «positive negativity.» It is *to be* which, in the process of negating itself to itself, remains as pure appearance. Here we have the second structural moment of essence as negativity: appearanceness. This is the terminal moment of the reflexive movement. As such, essence has a peculiar character. Because it stands beyond *to be,* essence is «in itself»; pure appearance lacks otherness, it does not send us back to an other thing. Even more, it has within itself that which is apparent; it consists, therefore, in its appearanceness; it is something «by and for itself.» These two characters taken together constitute what Hegel understands by identity. The essence is constitutive identity with itself: it consists in what appears.

Examined carefully, however, reason cannot pause at this point. By way of the negation of *to be,* essence arises; things, however, are (or are not) what they appear. That is to say, it is precisely the character of essence as appearance which forces us to return to the thing, to that *to be* which we began by negating. Essence lies beyond *to be;* nevertheless it belongs to *to be.* This movement from the essence to the thing is the contrary of doubling; it is the unfolding of the essence into the *to be (ser).* Just as unfolding is also a negation, the negation of doubling; however a negation of a negation, s i n c e doubling (reflection) already was a negation. And every negation of a negation is a «positing.» In the essence *to be* is not annihilated, but is preserved as «appearance;» in the explication the essence is not annihilated, but rather returned to *to be.* As returned to *to be,* it still possesses a *to be;* and this new *to be* is what. Hegel calls «ground» *(Grund).* Here we have the third structural moment of essence as negativity: groundedness *(fundamentalidad).* That which ap-

42 pears as an oak is what «makes» the thing an oak. To be, itself, insofar as it is the «grounded» in the essence, is what Hegel understands by existence. Hence it is that for Hegel things already «are» even before they exist: existence is an exit from the essence. Therefore, what the real thing is, is something which «already was» *(gewesen)*. For this reason, that which already was is essence *(Wesen)*.

To sum up then, things are, but they «not» merely «are.» This not is the essence in its pure negativity. Therefore, things are «not» simply, «but are» internally grounded. This «but are» is the structure of the essence as pure negativity: it is the reflexivity of *to be*, the appearentiality and groundedness of to be. The intrinsic and structural unity of these three moments is what Hegel understands thematically as essence: it is an intransitive movement, a movement of interiorization and exteriorization. Because it is intransitive, it does not separate us from the thing itself: it is a self-motion. The essence is not something that moves, but is the very movement of interiorization. This movement is the conceiving movement. In conceiving a thing, I conceive it as «being» *(siendo);* however, in making it I conceive it already as an interiority. That is to say, my conceiving movement conceives the reality by preconceiving it as interiorized. The essence of the oak is none of the three moments (seed, tree, fruit) taken in themselves, neither is it their unity as moments of a process. To invert the statement, the essence is something preprocessive; becoming and its moments are what they are precisely because they are the becoming of something which «already was» an oak. Let us call this «to be an oak.» What, according to Hegel, would this prior «to be an oak» be? It is not to possess the formal characteristics of the seed, nor those of the tree, nor those of the fruit; that is to say, it is not to be in the sense in which the seed or the tree or the fruit are. Neither, however, is it «pure» process or becoming which leads from
43 one of the terms to the other; because, in being «pure,» process is always a «going» from one to the other, whereas in the cycle of the oak (as well as in any other thing whatsoever), we are confronted with a «going» which «already» is internally «qualified» (this very un-Hegelian expression will be forgiven me on the grounds of clarity), a qualification in virtue of which the process is intrinsically an «oaking» (the word may be tolerated) process, and not, for example, a «dogging» process. This internal character of process as such is

what Hegel intends by «to be an oak,» this is the «essence» of the oak. For Hegel, it is not something which qualifies becoming as a consequence of «coming from» or of «going toward» a term; on the contrary, it is the character which predetermines the internal quality of each of the three terms. The process ends in an acorn or begins from it or expands into a certain tree because the process is already in itself «oaking.» The «first» oak is seed, «then» the oak is a tree, «finally» the oak is fruit, however it «always» is actually the same: an oak. To be-an-oak, therefore, predetermines its three moments. It is an internal motion, a self-motion, the internal and intransitive dynamism of reality. The essence is thus the internal determination of *to be*, that which, when we conceive *to be*, we are also forced to conceive: its intrinsic presupposition. In this its truth consists; essence is radical truth. Reciprocally, *to be*, that is to say, the thing in its becoming and with all its notes, is nothing but «manifestion» *(Erscheinung)* of the essence, of its interiority. And in this resides its truth: real to be is grounded truth.

Essence, then, is, for Hegel, the formal concept as the grounding truth of the *to be*. Therefore, for Hegel to discover the essence of anything is to construct conceptually, speculatively, the presuppositions of its reality; it is to re-engender the thing. Correlatively, reality itself is something «posited;» it is the «positing» of the *to be* as essentiated formal conception: the reality as «position,» as essence. 44 Such is the second stage of the reality as «positing», as essence.

However, this is a singular «positing.» Because, in «positing» the essence as the presupposition of the becoming, reason adds nothing to the essence; rather, it merely conceives expressly something which, without knowing it, it had already conceived when it conceived becoming. Interiorization is, in a certain sense, recall. At this point account is necessarily given of that fact. Reason «knows» that the essence is something pre-conceived, that is, reason conceives how the essence is conforming in and by a conceiving act of reason. This kind of conception Hegel calls *Idea:* it is the explicit and formal concept of the concept itself as the general conception of the real thing. It is the third and definitive stage of the realization of reason. In it, reason conceives itself as pure formal conception; it is the conception of the conception and, for this reason, of the whole of reality as «concept» of reason. In this entrance of reason into itself,

in this *self-conception*, we have the final term of the process of conception: as Idea, reason, in conceiving things, realizes itself conceptively to itself as absolute reality, unique and radical. «The Idea
shows itself as a thinking which is pure and simple identity with
itself, but which, in order to be sufficient to itself, is, at the same
time, an activity in which it situates itself to itself before itself (as
some other thing) in order that, in being with this other, it is only
in itself.» *(Encyclopedia*, Section 18.) Thinking, reason, is the Idea
in itself and for itself; Nature is the Idea itself in its being other
than itself; and Spirit is the Idea which from this condition of
being other to itself turns back upon itself in order to be itself. As
such, this reality of the Idea is justly God; νόησις νοήσεως, thought
of itself, Aristotle called it, *(Meta.* A, 1072b 18-30;) and as a synthesis
of his own philosophy Hegel, in paragraph 577 of the *Encyclopedia*,
45 reproduces literally in the original language the entire Aristotelian
passage.

The whole of reality, then, would be nothing else but the process
of the self-realization of God himself, of logical reason as formal
conception: *to be*, essence, Idea, that is, becoming, positing, self-conception, are the three moments of the unique process of formal conception. And each of them is the truth of the preceding: the essence
is the truth of *to be*, and the Idea is the truth of essence.

In the introduction I said that in a good part of modern philosophy essence has reference to a unique substance, the I. And where
this process actually culminates is in Hegel. For him the unique
substance is the thinking subject; its essence is its function of conceiving, that is, of engendering, of producing things; and the essence
of these things is nothing else than to be mere positings, mere «concepts» of thinking, that is to say, of the thinking subject. This would
be the meaning of the «of» in the phrase «the essence is the reality
of the concept 'of' the thing»: it is the generating genitive.

Despite this mighty Hegelian effort, however, the essence cannot
be understood as a moment of formal conception. This is absolutely
untenable for various reasons.

In the first place, (it is untenable) by reason of its unitary and
univocal concept of reason which leads it to assert the primacy of
the logical over the real. What Hegel calls «the» reason does not
exist. Reason is not a singular principle of which the divine reason

and the human reason would be two moments differing only in degree.
On the contrary, the difference between them is essential; a difference between reasons precisely in their quality as reasons. In a
word, to know the whole of reality, both actual and possible, in all
its aspects and characteristics, solely by means of a formal concept,
is something of which only an infinite intelligence, the divine intelligence, is capable; consequently it is chimerical to attribute it to
human intelligences, intrinsically finite as they are. Human consciousness demands, not only different formal concepts, but objective 46
concepts which are dependent on things as well; and one of the
essential moments of its intrinsic finiteness consists precisely in this
dependence. This finiteness is not a mere «defect» or a deficiency of
human reason; quite the reverse is the case: it is its positive and
constitutive structure. Human intelligence and the divine intelligence
are not different from each other only in degree, through their range
of influence, so to say, as though the human were only less than the
divine; a divine intelligence, as it were, which is cut back or diminished, a diminished divine reason; rather, they are essentially distinct
in themselves by reason of the very structure of intelligence as intelligence. What we call intelligence is not the same when we are
treating God as ti is when we speak of men. Human reason is not
identical with the divine reason, not even in that specific character
of reason. They are not two levels of one same intelligence, but two
distinct intelligences in their very character as intelligences; they
are, so to say, two irreducible species of intelligence and intellection.
Let me repeat in more general terms: the finiteness of things does
not consist, as Hegel would have it, merely in the failure of the
realization of the plenitude of their concept. There is another kind
of finiteness, more profound and radical: the intrinsic limitation of
the concept itself, that in virtue of which the plenitude which is conceived in one concept is not identical with the plenitude conceived
in another; it is a question of a diversity within a generic unity;
it is a question, above all, of a total diversity of a transcendental
order. Correlatively, infinity is not only plenitude in the line of that
which is conceived, but rather entitative plenitude in the line of
reality as reality; the former would be a merely extensive infinity,
whereas the second is an intensive infinity, so to say, an infinity in
the transcendental order. Consequently, the difference between the

divine and the human intelligence belongs to this last order; it is
47 a transcendental difference. Therefore, what Hegel calls «the» reason
does not exist; there exist only reasons which are intrinsically
distinct.

Even less, consequently, can that grounding primacy of reason
over reality exist. Because the difference between two modes of intellection, that is, the difference between intelligences as intellective,
depends on the character of the physical reality of those intelligences,
that is, the intelligences insofar as they are real; and in its turn,
the difference between the intelligences as realities depends upon
the difference of the character of the realities which possess the
intelligences in question. The divine intelligence and the human intelligence are distinct precisely in their character as intelligences, because
they are distinct in their physical reality; and they are distinct in
their physical reality because the reality of God and that of man
are essentially different. It follows that not even in the intelligence
itself is there a primacy of understanding as such over its reality.
In the very first appearance of metaphysics we have a root instance
of the grounding primacy of reality over intelligence.

Therefore, neither does «the» reason exist nor does there exist a
metaphysical primacy of reason over the real. Metaphysics can never
be a logic. The fundamental supposition of the Hegelian metaphysics
is untenable.

In the second place, the identification of the real thing with its
objective concept as the product of formal conception is untenable.
Hegel makes this identification rest on the argument that, if such
an identity did not exist, truth would be impossible. However, this,
in turn, is untenable, both because of what it implies concerning
human reason and what it implies concerning the divine reason. To
consider, first, the way in which it touches human reason, if that
identity did exist, error would be impossible. Were *to be* and to
think identical, what we call error could consist only in the failure
48 to realize fully the concept of truth, that is, in the fact that *to be*
and *to think*, although identical, would not constitute, through their
identity, the whole of the thing; error, then, would be, and Hegel
himself recognizes this fact, a finite truth, therefore, a fragmentary
and partial truth, a provisional stage on the road of absolute truth,
of full and complete identity. Now, although it may many times be

the fact that, materially, error may be a partial truth, nevertheless, formally, error is never partialness but rather disconformity, resulting from a bad direction of thought with respect to the thing, a deviation; at most, the partialness would be the cause of a further deviation and nothing more. This means that thinking consists only in thinking «toward» *(hacia)* the thing and, therefore, in holding the thing at a «distance,» not in «identity.» It this were not the case, error would not be possible. Error is disconformity based on deviation. Correlatively, the truth of reason is conformity based on standing «in the way» *(en vía)*. Therefore, human reason has, in its radical structure, antecedently to its judgments, true and erroneous, the double intrinsic possibility of being either on the right path or deviated. This essential co-possibility of truth and error in human reason proves, then, that in it there is no identity but rather distance and distinction between to be and to think. This fact does not mean, as Hegel claimed, that the truth of human reason would not be possible, but signifies, rather, something entirely different, namely, that the truth of human reason does not rest, in the first instance, on reason itself.

However, even in the case of the divine intelligence itself, it is completely false, because impossible, that the *to be* of that which is conceived would consist merely in a kind of intellectual gestation. Even in the case of God, the mere objectivity — science of simple intelligence — rests at least upon a «previous,» «physical» fecundity of the divine reality. However, even setting aside this problem of the science of simple intelligence, that which proves to be undeniable on this basis and what is most important for us here is that if that which is known possesses «physical» reality, the intellection of it — the science of vision as the theologian would call it — is not a question of pure intelligence, either with respect to the reality of that which is known or with respect to the medium of intellection. For that, there is necessary a creative *fiat*, that is to say, an act of volition which would confer on the merely objective character of simple intellection a physical reality; without that volition that thing would lack any reality at all. Physical reality is not, even in the case of God, a movement or projection of mere intelligence; real things are something more than mere «divine concepts» (taking this last expression, which is in any case, an improper one, in a broad sense).

Hence it follows, in the third place, that the real thing is not, even in the case of God, a merely immanent and formal moment of intelligence. To be sure, it is the terminus of His intellection; however, a terminus which is terminally transcendent to it and even to His creative volition. The infinite character of the divine intellection does not in any way consist in a monism of the intelligent spirit of God. The divine intellective act, formally immanent to the reality of God, is, from the point of view of the reality of that which is conceived, terminally transcendent. The real thing is not, formally, a formal moment of the divine intellection itself. Hegelian idealism has nothing to do with the idea that the metaphysical essence of God might be His subsistent intelligence. Even if this thesis, clearly problematical for that matter, were true, it would never mean that there is no more reality than the divine intelligence, and that all that is understood might be formally and terminally an immanent moment of the divine act of intellection. Idealism does not consist only, as has been asserted so many times, in the affirmation that absolute and radical being is an intelligence; it consists rather in the further affirmation that all that is understood in and by that intelligence is only a formally immanent and identical moment of that intelligence itself, a content of it which is merely thought, having no more formal and terminal 50 reality than pure intellection. That is, idealism consists in affirming that the infinite intelligence is not only the absolute and radical reality but also that it is «physically» the unique reality. But this is impossible as the reasons adduced make clear.

Hence follows the radical falseness of the Hegelian idea of essence and of the path by which it is to be apprehended. For Hegel, essence has two characteristics: it is the presupposition of being (let us call this «suppositionality») and it is the truth of being. I agree without more or greater demands for rigor that these two characteristics do undeniably belong to essence; however, they are in no sense specifically Hegelian. What is specifically Hegelian resides in the interpretation of these two characteristics as structural moments of negativity, and, therefore, as moments of the formal conception. And this interpretation is untenable because, as we have just seen, the primary suppositions of the Hegelian philosophy are untenable. Nevertheless, let us permit our attention to dwell for a bit on each one of these three characteristics: negativity, truth, and suppositionality.

In the first place (let us consider) the formal character proper to essence according to Hegel: its formal and constitutive negativity. It is a central concept in the whole Hegelian philosophy, because negativity constitutes the *primum movens* of the entire dialectical process of thought: it is that which causes the antithesis to emerge and that which advances to the synthesis. In the case of essence, negativity is that which compels reflection, doubling (antithesis) and the unfolding in the ground (synthesis).

As, for Hegel, the dialectic is the formal conception as generating physical reality, it becomes necessary to introduce negativity into *to be* itself as one of its constitutive moments. And this is the 51 question; can it be said that to be, that reality itself, is constitutively affected by negativity? This is impossible. Reality is that which is, and, in that which is, there is distilled all its reality, no matter how limited, fragmentary and insufficient it might be. The negative, as such, has no physical reality whatsoever (we are here using *to be* and reality as synonyms). Of two real things we say, and we see with truth, that the one «is not» the other. This «is not» does not, however, affect the physical reality of each of the two things, but it affects this physical reality only insofar as it is present to an intelligence, which, when it compares those things, sees that the one «is not» the other. Negativity, therefore, is a constitutive moment of the objective concept of reality, but not of physical reality itself. In the case of essence this observation is decisive. Hegel considers the essence as a pure «appearing;» it is the concrete form of the negativity of simple being. This, however, is impossible. In reality there is no pure apparition of being. Every appearance rests on a previous reality. And this resting with which appearance is constituted is negativity only in the objective concept and not in the thing itself. Hence, it results that Hegel calls essence, not a physical moment of reality, but its objective concept. And it is the fact that Hegel begins by identifying physical reality with the objective concept; and since the latter has no more *to be* than that which is conferred upon it by formal intellection, it follows that reality remains submerged in the intelligence from the very beginning. And this is impossible for the reasons adduced above. To anchor the problem of essence in negativity is to make of the suppositionality and of the truth of essence moments in formal conception. But this cannot be maintained. Let us examine this, independently of those general reasons.

In the first place, (let us consider) essence as the «truth» of *to be*. What does Hegel understand here by «truth?» Naturally, there is no question here of logical truth, but of ontological truth, of truth as a constitutive moment of *to be*. This truth is, for Hegel, the «manifestation» *(Erscheinung)* of the essence in the reality of the thing. Is this maintainable? The identification between reality and its objective concept tends to return. In this oak which I have before me it is certain — later I shall have to insist upon this point at great length — that its notes manifest the essence, the *to be an oak;* the fact is, however, that here «essence» is a physical, structural moment of the thing itself, of the oak. However, if by essence one understands something that lies beyond being, this *to be* is not the manifestation of the essence. Quite the contrary. As we shall see in the following paragraph, it is things which manifest themselves in objective concepts and therefore it is they which send the intelligence on to something which stands beyond *to be*. Only in a secondary sense may we call the thing the manifestation of that which is conceived. It is the problem of ontological truth, as conformity of the thing with its objective concept. Hegel, however, has greater pretentions; for him ontological truth would consist, in the last analysis, in the fact that the formal act of intellection was physically and formally the very configuration of the thing; stated in the Aristotelian terms which Hegel favored so much, in which the formal conception would be the very «form» of the thing. And this, independently of the fact that the essence would be beyond being, is impossible. For then you would not have «conformity» between the thing and its concept, but rather «conformation» of the former by the latter. Well then, this is false, both as it touches on God and as it refers to things. It is false, with regard to God, since the divine Idea, considered objectively, is not really the informing form of things, but only their formal paradigm. And if one takes the Idea as the act of ideation, that is to say, as the formal act of intellection, then the impossibility is even more manifest. Because, as the formal act — I will say it in general terms without entering into the problem — the Idea is nothing else but the intellection of God's own reality insofar as it is the «fountain» of reality, not insofar as it is a reality which in and by the intellection of that which is not identical with it will, in giving form to things, give form to himself. And this is also false with respect to things. Things are not the Ideas but merely transcendent projections of ideas. And in their character of reality, things are infinitely more rich than the Ideas, because in the Ideas there is to be found, objectively and determinately, «that which» things are or are going to be; but not, however, their physical reality itself for which there is necessary, as we have said, an act of infinite divine volition. Ontological truth is not the identity of thought and thing; rather it presupposes, in some form or other, a kind of distance between the intellective moment and the physical moment of reality. Without the former there would be nothing but brute reality without Idea, or Idea without reality. There is ontological truth only when there is conformity, not when there is conformation. This means that the essence is not the Idea as the formal act of intellection. At the very most it would be the Idea as objective concept. We shall see immediately, however, that neither can it be this latter. For the present moment, however, it is enough that we see that the essence is not the formal act of intellection and that, as a consequence, the essence does not show that the truth of to be is thought itself.

It would only show us that, if it made us see that essence is the presupposition of to be and that to be «the presupposition» is something formal and exclusive to thinking. And this is the last character of essence that we must examine: the essence as the presupposition of to be. What is the internal characteristic of this presupposition? And in what does «to be a presupposition,» that is «suppositionality,» consist?

In the first place (let us consider) the internal character of the essence as the presupposition of to be. Hegel tells us that essence as the presupposition of to be is the intrinsic principle of its becoming, in such wise that the essentialness of things would be self-motion.

Hegel, then, leaves unclarified, first of all, the character of presup- 54 position which essence would possess. He has told us that essence is interiorized, folded back upon itself, that is, as the principle whence there flow or flower the notes which it possesses by the mere fact of being what it is. That is to say, that to be a presupposition — let us repeat it — would be simply «to be a principle» through which all the difference between the essential and the non-essential would prove to be a simple difference between that which is principiated as such and the merely happening and indifferent, a difference which, for greater clarity, I have called the difference of condition. Well then, this surely is not enough, because if this were true, all the notes which the thing possesses here and now, on being folded back into their principle, would, by that fact, be essential to it. And this is impossible. The non-essential is not simple indifference, but rather a real moment of each thing, a moment within it physically distinct from that which is essential to it. The real thing encloses as a reality not only the essential notes, but «in addition» many other notes by no means less real than those. The difference between the essential and that which is not essential is not a difference of conditions of some of its notes, but a difference among the notes themselves. In his effort to arrive at the problem of the essence by way of the concept, Hegel, like Plato (although for radically different reasons), glides over this distinction between essential notes and non-essential notes within a thing itself; he does not tell us in what this difference would consist; he is satisfied to call it superficial. And it is here that we may see the complete obscurity in which he left the formal character of «to be a presupposition,» that is, the principle character of essence. The fact is that all of the notes, both the essential and the non-essential, have a single principle in the «interior» of the thing. This principle, however, does not have the same character in the case of the essential notes and in the case of the non-essential. For 55 the essential notes, the interior principle is the primary unity which determines their formal character as notes. The non-essential notes, however, even though they rest on, or are grounded on, this primary interior unity, nevertheless are not necessarily determined by that same unity. This makes it clear that, although Hegel says correctly that the essence is the presupposition of *to be* as its principle, he has, nevertheless, left in complete obscurity the unitary and formal character of this supposition or principle as such; that is, he does not tell us what «to be a supposition» is or in what the proper and formal «suppositionality» of the essence with regard to the notes which unify «what» a thing is, consists.

Even when the essence is taken without this necessary clarification, however, is it true that the internal character of this supposition consists in being self-motion? Hegel underlines the character, in a

certain sense dynamic, of the essence, that is, the intrinsically determined character of the process of becoming as such; the essence
is not ascribed by Hegel to one alone of the three moments, for
example, to the «oak-tree,» but rather to the *to become, «oaking»* as
such. This conception of Hegel's is, at best, problematical. It is difficult, as a matter of fact, to conceive what *to become* might be if it
is not «reality in process of becoming,» that is to say, reality becoming; and in that case it will be a matter of discussion, if one wishes,
what this reality might be, whether it is the seed, the tree, or the
fruit, or something distinct from all three; it will always be the case,
however, that the essence resides in the moment of reality and not in
the moment of becoming. Nothing is gained by underlining the
moment of the αὐτός; quite the contrary. For what is to be understood by the αὐτός? A real thing is αὐτός, the «self-same,» when
it possesses a character of physical «sameness» in virtue of which
«it moves itself.» Here the αὐτός, the reality which is itself or «the
same,» is a *prius* with respect to its «self-motion,» is its principle.
As such, it is beyond movement. It might be that this principle is
not a mere support or a subject of movement, but something intrinsically and formally enveloped in it; a metaphysics of becoming   56
will have to make clear in what form the principle of movement
stands beyond the movement which is principiated. It always will
be a principle, however, a *prius*, with respect to its own self-motion.
This is not the αὐτός about which Hegel speaks. In Hegel there is
no question of a *prius*, but rather of a *posterius* (at least in the
order of dialectical development) with regard to self-motion. For
Hegel, self-motion does not consist in the fact that something which
already is an αὐτός «moves,» but rather only in the fact that this
movement is intransitive; in that case the αὐτός is not a principle
but is, quite the contrary, the intrinsic result of the movement itself.
Sameness or selfness would be the compass constituted by an intransitive movement. In other terms, for Hegel, the essence «is» not
already something at hand, but rather something which is in «process
of» making itself in and by an intransitive movement; even better, the
essence is that intransitive movement itself. But this position is radically untenable. The decisive question remains unanswered: on what
is the intransitive, that is, reflexive character of the movement
grounded? For Hegel it is based on the negativity of simple to be,

But we have already seen that negativity is not a moment of physical reality but only its objective concept. Only because the notes are what they are can they constitute this intransitive dynamism in intellection. The essence is already a physically constituted principle and, as such, is not the intransitive movement, but rather its principle. In a word, this dynamism (we may call it such in order to simplify «becoming»), is not, for Hegel, a physical and temporal becoming; that is to say, he does not undertake to elaborate an ontogenetic theory of the real, a natural history of the universe. The becoming to which Hegel refers is quite other: it is an a-temporal becoming in which its different moments do not succeed each other but are grounded in one another κατὰ λόγον, for its own «reason.» What Hegel understands by becoming is this «logical» deployment of the
57 process of fundamentation of the formal conception, not its possible temporal process. And the «reason» of this whole deployment is precisely what Hegel calls essence. The essence of the oak is the «reason» through which this process «seed-tree-fruit» is a process intrinsically «oaking.» And this character of process which is the essence, Hegel will tell us, is something which we see ourselves forced to conceive in order that there may be becoming; and «forced to conceive» is precisely a character of thinking. And this is the reason why the Hegelian becoming is not a causal «ontogenetic» process but, in a certain way, a «logogenetic» process. And just as it is «necessary» to conceive this in order that there may be «to be» it follows that, for Hegel, the conceptive character of the essence will show that, fundamentally, *to be* itself is conceptive in character; essence, as the supposition of *to be*, will be the «positing» in and by thought. But this is impossible. In what effectively does the necessity, according to which essence must be conceived, consist? In thinking, that is to say, «in» the thinking, is where we see ourselves forced to conceive it; however, we are not forced «by» thought but by the force of things, that is to say, by the force of the «to be» previously intellected. What thinking «posits» is not the essence in the «to be,» but the essential character of *to be* in the intelligence. As a formal act, thinking does not generate *to be* but, at most, the actualization of «to be» in the intelligence. Hence, this necessity, this logical dynamic character of essential thinking, is not what constitutes the proper character of the essence as the presupposition of *to be*, but the proper character

of the essence as the reason for the intelligibility of *to be*. The essence as the presupposition of *to be* is not intransitive dynamism, but physical structure. It is not «the presupposition» of «to be» but the «to be a supposition.» The necessity is the *ratio cognoscendi* of the essence, not its *ratio essendi*. The essence is not a necessity of *to be;* things are, as a matter of fact, what they are, and nothing more. The essence is necessity only for the intellection of things. 58 And precisely in this rests the whole reason why the essence is intellective: it is what forcibly plunges us in the things themselves.

This is a matter of the utmost seriousness. In submerging itself in pure intellection by itself, reason, for Hegel, occupies itself only with itself, and it occupies itself with itself not insofar as it is reality, but insofar as it is intelligent; its very mode of being so occupied is also purely intellective. Hence it is that, despite its presumed becoming, reason in Hegel does no more than conceive itself; in reality, in this Hegelian becoming, nothing happens, everything is preserved. And this conception of itself is purely «logical.» It is a conceiving becoming in which there is no true innovation, no true creation, neither in things nor in the human spirit itself. It is a gigantic conservation of itself in pure conception. If one wishes to go on speaking of becoming in Hegel, that is, of a «real movement,» he would have to say that it is a singular movement, a transformation like that which the mathematicians call «automorphism.» In our case, it is a logico-dynamic automorphism. But this is impossible. By intelligence, man is in things (including himself among them) as realities; he is necessitated by them and, therefore, in a real, rather than logical, becoming. As a matter of fact, we see ourselves compelled by the reality of things to bow before them modestly and problematically. Modestly, that is, with an effort to submit ourselves to them, no matter how irrational they may appear to us; it is not possible to apprehend the essence of anything by pure conceptual dialectic. Problematically, because we can never be sure of being able to apprehend, either in fact or in principle, the essence of anything, and even less to apprehend it wholly and adequately. Before the conceptualism of Hegel it is necessary to underline forcefully the givenness of the real, whether or not we can conceive it adequately. Formal concepts are one thing, then, reality another.

SECTION TWO

THE ESSENCE AS OBJECTIVE CONCEPT

I have said that the phrase «the essence is the reality of the concept» is equivocal because one cannot tell whether the concept in question is the formal concept or the objective concept. For Hegel, as we have seen, it is a matter of the formal concept. However, that phrase can be understood by referring it to the objective concept. Such is the point of view of all forms of rationalism which have their origin in the philosophy of the fourteenth and fifteenth centuries, become incarnated in Descartes, and culminate in Leibniz and in Kant himself. The objective concept of a thing is not, consequently, the thing itself. However, we are told, the objective concept is the locus where, formally, we are presented with «what» the thing really is; this is the reason why this presentation is, in a certain sense, a «second» presentation of the thing itself, that is to say, its «representation.» Whether this is enough to enable us to know the real thing, as Leibniz held, or whether it is not enough, as Kant believed, it will always be the fact that, in these philosophies, the objective concept is the representation of what the thing is. And since «what» a thing is, is precisely its essence, it follows that the essence, for these philosophies, is nothing else than the content of the objective concept. Naturally, the concepts to which reference is made are, in the first case, the divine Ideas; the essence would be the objective content of these Ideas. However, essence may also be applied to human concepts, when they exist, because in their objective dimension these have the same content as those Ideas. Consequently, in order to ascertain what the essence is, it will be enough to ascertain what the objective concept is.

Every real thing, we are told, is the factitive realization of an objective concept; to realize anything is, in a word, to realize 60 «something,» that is, «to make» what is conceived. Dogs, men, oaks, are realizations of what it is to be dog, man, or oak. The first characteristic of an essence would, therefore, be its «anteriority» with respect to reality. And this is clear precisely when it is a question of the radical origin of things, that is to say, of the divine creative act: God creates the world on the pattern of His Ideas. Human concepts do nothing more than reproduce this anteriority of the divine objective concept.

Hence flows a second characteristic of the essence as objective concept. Since it is anterior to the real thing itself, it will be «the ground» of that thing; it is not a question of temporal anteriority but of an anteriority of ground. What is this character of the objective concept of anything which makes it the foundation or founding principle of the essence? The objective concept would be the ground of the reality in at least three respects.

In the first place, since, in the concept, there is represented what the real thing is anteriorly to its reality, it follows that the thing, in being realized, is referred to, is measured by, that which is represented in that concept. The concept is, then, the ground of the thing, before all else, as the measure of its reality. And since this concept is the essence of the thing, it follows that the essence is the measure of the reality of things. Or, making use of the medieval idea of ontological truth — the conformity of the thing with its objective concept — rationalism will say that the essence, as objective concept, is the ground of the ontological truth of things. And this truth will be the primary and radical truth of those things.

However, in the second place, what is the objective concept in as far as it is the measure of the reality? That is to say, in what does its grounding character consist? To be sure, the essence is the ground of the real thing, but it is not its causal ground, because the objective concept, by itself, does not produce the existent reality. Nevertheless, it contains objectively «what» the thing is going to be if there is anyone who might produce it. What is objectively conceived «is not» reality by the mere fact of being conceived, but is 61 something which «can be» real. The world of concepts and, therefore, of essences, will be the world of the possibles. In this context, possible does not mean that there is anyone or anything capable of producing the thing, but that the thing is, in itself, producible. This internal possibility is what is proper to the objective concept. Anterior to things, the objective concept will be their ground as their proper internal possibility. In what, then, does this internal possi-

bility consist? Objective concepts are composed of notes which
possess two characteristics: they are notes independent among
themselves, and are, moreover, compatibles, that is, non-contradictory.
Therefore, it follows, the objective concept of a synthesis of independent and non-contradictory notes will correctly be the essence in
its strict sense. And that non-contradictoriness will be formally the
internal possibility: and everything which is not contradictory is
possible in itself, and everything which is contradictory is impossible
in itself. Therefore, the essence, as objective concept, is irreducible
internal possibility of the real.

In the third place, what is the objective concept, what is the essence in itself, not as measure and as possibility but in its proper
and positive *to be?* What is objective in itself is certainly not a real
thing; nevertheless, it has a positive *to be*, it is «something» in
itself; if the contrary were the case, it would not be able to be the
ground of the real, either. This *to be* is not the *to be* which the
intelligence as a «faculty» possesses; for while it is true that what
is objective possesses no other existence save that in the intelligence,
it is no less true that it «is» not, formally, the intelligence itself.
Hence, neither is this *to be* that which the real thing possesses, since
what is objective lacks all physical existence, to state it in this way.
Different from the intelligence, as well as from physical reality, what
62 is objective, nevertheless, as Descartes said, is not pure nothing, but
rather is «something.» That is, it is «thing;» but a thing *sui generis*,
an «ideal thing.» It is a thing which, despite the fact that it has no
real existence, still does have an ideal existence. With respect to it,
the real thing will be the factitive realization of an ideal thing. And
since it is capable of being converted into the real thing, the ideal
thing can also be called «possible thing.» Existence will be something
which is «added to» this anterior thing, which is the essence as ideal
thing; to realize will be to confer existence on an ideal thing. The
fundamental *to be* will be the essence, and existence will have,
inexorably, to rest on it. And, since this essence is an objective concept of reason, it follows that the fundamental and absolute *to be*
is rational objectivity: this is rationalism.

In a word, the essence is what is objectively represented in the
concept. As such, it is anterior to the real and the ground of its

reality in a triple dimension: as measure or ontological truth of the real, as internal possibility of the real, as the ideal thing in itself.

However, this is inadmissible. In this conception of the essence, there interweave, without criticism, the most disparate themes, while, fundamentally, the problem of essence remains untouched.

On the one hand, let us consider the theme of the objective concept as such. If I prescind from the existence of a real thing and form in my mind the concept of «what» that thing is, the objective content of this concept contains — let us establish this without further question — the pure «what,» that is to say, the essence of the thing. This is true; however, it does not even remotely follow from this that the essence consists formally in being the objective dimension of a conception, because the objective concept of the essence is, as we have said, posterior to the real thing and to «what» that thing is. We have, then, on the one hand, the objective concept of the essence and, on the other, something very distinct from this, namely, the essence itself. Rationalism, however, by a singular paradox, inverts the terms and converts the objective concept into the essence 63 itself. How could this have been possible, and what grave reason could have moved rationalism to do this?

It is that, together with the theme of the abstractive conceptuation of the real thing, there appears the theme of the radical origination of things, as Leibniz pointed out: the theme of divine causation. The causal origin of things leads rationalism to establish an identification between the essence and the objective concept, which is fundamentally a quasi-identification of logic and metaphysics. And the reason is evident: it is that God, the first cause, is an intelligence as well. As such, in order to produce things, God knows «what» He is going to produce. Therefore, He orders His causality according to His ideas. And in this respect the ideas are anterior to the things; and since, in those ideas, there is represented objectively «what» the things are going to be really, it follows that the objective term of these ideas is not only anterior to things but also constitutes the pure essence of what is real; «pure» essence, because it lacks real existence; it is an *esse essentiae*.

To locate the problem of essence on this line of thought is to dislocate it *ab initio;* and to dislocate it in two ways.

(a) The way of intelligent causality leads us to the discovery of the ideas as anterior to things, and as the sole and exhaustive canon of their individual reality. However, this is to set the question on a wrong path, because the divine Idea is the paradigm of every thing, but only the paradigm or, as we are accustomed to say, exemplary cause; in no manner whatsoever is it the essence of the thing, because only when the thing realizes the idea in its breast, does it possess an essence as its intrinsic moment. When the essence is confounded with the intellectual paradigm, the problem of essence is sent off on a false path, because, taking refuge in the ideas, it
64 avoids saying what the essence is in itself as a real moment of the thing. To trace the origin of this thing contributes nothing to the solution of our problem: the anteriority of the Idea leaves the problem of essence untouched.

(b) In the second place, the way of causality leads one to distinguish «in a certain manner» what the thing is from the fact of its really existing. Hence, by an easy illation this distinction in made to coincide with the merely abstractive formation of the concept of what the thing is, to «prescinding» from its real existence. In this way, the problem of essence is launched on the path of its contraposition to existence. Once more it avoids telling us what the essence is in itself.

At the very focal point of the question, consequently, rationalism evades the problem of essence, that is to say, the question of ascertaining what the essence is, considered in itself (and not in as far as it is opposed to existence) and as an intrinsic moment of the real thing (and not insofar as it is the ideal paradigm of that thing).

Hence it follows that the «fundamental» character of the essence as rationalism understands it is formally inadmissible.

1. We are told, in the first place, that the radical truth of the thing is its measure or conformity with the objective concept of that thing: the ontological truth. To be sure, it is not possible to deny that this conformity is really to be found in things. Is this truth, however, their radical truth? This is a question which affects equally both rationalism and medieval metaphysical systems. It is undeniable, in a word, that reality is «true» solely by reason of its respect to an intelligence. However, is this respectiveness, which formally constitutes the truth of things, basically and primarily a respectiveness to

the intelligence, insofar as it is a «conceiving» intelligence? The reply to this question depends on what may be the primary and radical function that is assigned to intelligence, and, therefore, what intelligible or that which is intellected as such may be. If the formal function of the intelligence were to form concepts, to conceive or to form ideas, then all respect to intelligence would repose on the respect- 65 iveness to concepts, and the radical truth of things would be their ontological truth. However — to anticipate some ideas to which later on I shall, in a certain way, return — the formal function of intelligence is not to conceive, but to apprehend real things as real. The formation of concepts is an ulterior function which rests upon this other primary function and derives from it. And this is the case whether we are speaking of human intelligence or of the divine intelligence. God does not, in the first place, know real things *qua* real in objective concepts *qua* concepts, but rather in a «vision» of them as real or as realizable. The intelligible, and intellected, is formally the real as real. In fact, therefore, the primary and radical respectiveness of things to intelligence is not a respectiveness to concepts, but to their being apprehended as real in the intelligence. Consequently, prior to an ontological truth (which might well be called a conceptive truth), there is what I shall call «real truth» which is the basis of that other, ontological, truth. The real truth does not separate us from things in order to carry us towards something else, toward their concept, but, on the contrary, consists in holding us and holding us firmly, formally submerged in the real thing as such, without ever sallying forth from it. We shall see this later on. The essence, then, of the thing is found enveloped in this real truth and is, as a consequence, an intrinsic moment of the thing, and not its extrinsic measure, whether in the form of a paradigm or in the form of an objective concept. Consequently, the essence is not a ground anterior to the thing, and ontological truth is not the radical truth of real things.

2. We are told, in the second place, that the essence as objective concept is the internal possibility of the real thing, understanding by this possibility merely the state of non-contradiction between the notes of its concept. This position is, however, for various reasons, untenable. Because, before all else, we must ask what is the force or reach of this non-contradiction? If two notes are contradictory they 66

will never be realized joined formally in one same thing. However, if we know nothing more than that they are not contradictory, nothing follows from this fact, because here we are not asking about the thing insofar as it may possess a multiplicity of notes, but insofar as it may possess an internal structural unity; the essence, in a word, is not an addition of compatible notes, but a *positive* unity of which those notes are o n l y moments. Non-contradiction signifies nothing relative to the positive constitution of this essential unity. Non-contradiction is merely a negative limit, and not a source of positive *to be* as an entity. In the divine intelligence itself, the possible is not merely the non-contradictory, but that which is positively the terminus of the divine essence insofar as it is imitable.

However, the difficulty of identifying the possible with the non-contradictory increases immediately if we turn our attention to the objective concepts of the human mind. I may be permitted to repeat what many years ago I expounded in one of my courses. It is true that the contradictory never will be able to be realized. When, however, is something contradictory or non-contradictory? This is the question; let us examine it in each of its two terms.

In the first place, let us examine that which concerns non-contradiction. The truth is that the non-contradiction of a true system of notes or objective concepts can never be positively demonstrated, not even in the realm of mathematics (Gödel's theorem). It will be said that the fact that a thing is real is already a manifest proof of the non-contradiction of its notes. This is true. However, in making appeal to this consideration, we have already abandoned the anteriority of the objective concept respective to the real thing. And then, already installed within the latter, we repeat what we said before, but now with greater reason, namely that the internal possibility of a real thing is not a merely negative possibility, but has to be a real positive possibility, that is to say, something which is actual in that real thing as its intrinsic principle. That is to say, as
67 the internal possibility of the thing, the essence is not an un-contradictory concept, but a real principle of the real thing in its reality.

In the second place, let us consider what concerns contradiction. The truth is that we are in no better situation on this matter. The principle of contradiction is true; two notes which are formally contradictory can never be realized in one same thing simultaneously and under the same formal aspect. This is supremely evident. However, this does not prove to be applicable with security, save in the order of that which is formally conceived, insofar as it is formally conceived. If we transpose it from the order of objectivity to the order of reality, that is to say, to the things in which the objective concepts are realized according to their formal, proper character, the question presents a different aspect; because the condition under which the principle of contradiction is applied is that the thing being considered is nothing more than that which the notes, objectively conceived, formally contain. And here the difficulties begin. For, we may ask, is this condition itself possible? I do not believe so. Not only treating of real things, but of objects as well, the mere fact that various notes which are objectively conceived are realized in those things, or that we ourselves realize the objects, carries with it, inexorably attached to it, the fact that through this very condition these things or objects possess more properties than those which we have conceived objectively. And this is not only true in the sense of implication, which is obvious: in a word, if a thing possesses N properties, it must also inexorably contain all those others which may be deduced from those notes, that is to say, it contains more properties by implication. I am not referring to this, but to other properties which are not implied, but which are even more intimately involved («com-plicadas») with the initial properties simultaneously posited («co-puestas») by the fact that these others have been «posited» and by the mere fact that they have been posited or realized. Realization, whether in the physical order or in the order of objects, is, as such, the root of other properties. In this case, it is not that the principle of contradiction 68 is not true with respect to these things, but rather that its application proves problematical and fragile, given that the subject to which it is applied is complex and the formal purity of the concept can undergo important limitations.

However, even if we pass over this difficulty we encounter others which are still more serious. In order to apply the principle of contradiction it is necessary to isolate a reality and to consider it in itself; only in this way can it become the subject of the attribution of a predicative *logos*. The principle of contradiction forbids me to state that this reality, substantivated in this way, is something

contradictory. However, this is only half the question; the other half
is to be found in the very supposition of the presumed subject of
attribution. For *in re* this subject is not isolated from others, but is
intrinsically connected with them. Hence it is that many things which
have persistently appeared to be contradictory are not in fact so,
and the contrary is true as well; this is the case, not because the
principle of contradiction is not true, but because reality does not
validate the supposition of the «diction,» that is to say, it is not
made up of unconnected subjects. In order that the principle of
«contra-diction» might have, in the human mind, the exhaustive and
definitive application to real things which Aristotle claimed for it,
it would be necessary that man should have before his eyes, as the
subject of the attribution of its *logos*, the totality of the real in its
integrity. The fact is, this *logos* does not exist in man. I may put
it in other terms: the principle of contradiction rests on the unity
(ἕν) and the sameness (ταυτόν) of the being (ὄν). However, this is
equivocal, because a being may be, on the one hand, that to which
the *logos* is referred formally and intentionally, that which is signified
by the vocables (ὀνόματα), that is, the being as declared (*qua*
λεγόμενον*); it may, on the other hand, be the thing itself about
69 which I think and speak with my *logos*. Are these two «beings» identical? This is the question. If they were identical, not only would the
reality not be contradictory, but we would positively and firmly know
the conditions and limits of its non-contradictoriness, because the
presupposition on the basis of which we would be able to speak of
contradiction *in re* would then have been realized. The fact is, however,
that this identity between the being as signified intention and as
thing (πρᾶγμα), is highly problematical. Proof of this lies in the fact
that Aristotle himself, in book Γ of his *Metaphysics*, is aware that the
being as signified intention is not enough, and that the being as thing
is also necessary (οὔ ... τὸ ὄνομα ἀλλὰ τὸ πρᾶγμα, *Meta.* Γ 1006 b
22).   Nevertheless, despite the fact that he had divined the difficulty,
Aristotle does not formulate the problem, and goes on to admit that
identity without further ado. The only thing he does is to justify the
principle of contradiction, in each of the two meanings o f b e i n g ,
a s t e p which breaks the unity of the exposition and makes, it for
the moment, disconcerting. In a word, after he had defended the
principle in its reference to the being as signified intention — resting

his case on the «meaning» of the terms — insofar as he wants also to justify it with reference to things, Aristotle finds himself forced to enter into a discussion with the physicists and physiologists, that is, to ascertain if all be permanence or change in reality, without raising the question whether the «being,» with which the physicists and the physiologists concern themselves, were the same as that with which he himself had been concerned when he was speaking of the *logos* as such. As it appears to me, in this stage of his exposition more than the truth of the principle — which he takes as established — what Aristotle is trying to see is whether the presuppositions for its application are given in reality. He is then constrained to examine the three hypotheses (which are exactly the three ways of the *Hymn of Parmenides*, and this observation is of enormous importance): whether everything is at rest, or whether everything is in motion, or whether everything is sometime at rest and sometime in motion. Here, instead of appealing to «being» or to the «meaning of being,» what he does appeal to is nothing less than the *Theós*, to the unmoved 70 mover, something immensely remote from the principle of contradiction in itself. The real application of the principle of contradiction is, then, exceedingly difficult and every precaution which we may take in this order will be too little. Aristotle himself, more than anyone else, sensed the difficulty in trying to conceptualize change, that subtle unity of being and non-being in movement.

It will be said that these are merely difficulties of application which do not invalidate the principle as such. This is true. These difficulties of application, however, are not mere difficulties in the «management» of the objective concepts, but difficulties in application of the principle, touching its applicability, difficulties which touch the very supposition on which this management as well as the principle which regulates it, rest. And this is reason enough and more not to identify, without qualification, the possibility of something with the mere fact that its concept involves no contradiction.

3. If, in the third and final place, someone should say to us what the objective concept represents is an ideal or possible «thing» in itself, we should say the following: this presupposition is equally inadmissible for a serious reason which is to be directed both against rationalism as well as against a number of the great medieval metaphysical systems at least insofar as these touch on human intel-

lection. They confuse the «objectivity» in what is conceived, in its character as conceived, with what I would call the «objectuality,» that is to say, the fact that something may be an object. Taking their point of departure in the fact that the *objective* has no entitative character, many medieval metaphysical systems go on to deny all entitative status to objects. Taking their point of departure in the fact that objects have a certain entitative status, a number of other medieval metaphysical systems, and rationalism joins them in this, attribute positive entitative status to the *objective*. The fact is that neither of the two theses is true, because objectivity and objectuality are not the same thing. Without treating this problem thematically, we may content ourselves here with indicating the unequivocal differences between them. Any geometrical figure whatsoever, and *a fortiori* entities such as non-Archimedean space, are examples of «objects.» It is undeniable that they have some positive entity, that they are «something» whether they be called ideal things or by some other term; solid proof of this is the fact that laborious investigations are conducted upon them. Nevertheless, these objects are *toto caelo* distinct from the objectivity of a concept. The proof resides in the fact that I find it necessary to elaborate only with difficulties, sometimes enormous ones, the objective concepts which represent those objects, sometimes exactly, many times inexactly, and at all times in a fragmentary way. Objectivity is the terminal moment of the concept, but a purely intentional dimension of it. For this reason, while the object has «a certain» entitative status proper to itself, the *objective* has no entitative status whatsoever in its own right; it is only that which I conceive about things, whether these be real things or merely «objectual.» That which is objectively conceived about a thing is distinct from the thing itself, not only when it is a question of real things, but when it is a question of objectual things as well. The *objective* is so devoid of entitative status that I can form objective concepts of privation, of not to be, etc.; that is to say, the *objective* not only is not an object, but is not even necessarily positive.

On this supposition, the essence is a moment of the thing (whether real or objectual) while the objective concept of its essence, as objective concept, lacks all to be, that is to say, is not a possible object. If the essence is «an object» or ideal «thing,» it is not «objective» possibility, and if it is objective possibility it is not a thing or an

ideal object. As a matter of fact, the possibility of an object belongs
to the domain of objectivity, but not to that of objectuality. That is
to say, even were the possibility of a thing to consist in the objectivity of its concept, it would never be possible to transpose the
«possibility of a thing» into «a possible thing.» There is no «anything»
in itself except insofar as that «anything» would, in addition, be
possible, because this presumed anything is not «anything» but only
the «possibility» of something. If this were not the case, we would
have further to admit an impossible «thing,» given the fact that objective impossibilities are conceived; but this is absurd, because, if 72
it is impossible, it manifestly is not anything. There is not «anything,»
consequently, which would have two statuses, that of possibility and
that of reality; there is only a pure objective possibility on the one
hand, and, on the other, a thing (whether real or objectual, in this
context, matters little). Hence, it follows that to realize something
is not «to add» an existence to the essence considered as an ideal
object, but rather to produce, at one and the same time, the existent
essence or, what comes to the same thing, the essentiated reality.
Prior to this production there is nothing but the causes capable of
producing the real thing. The objective possibility is nothing else
than the intentionally conceived terminus of that real capacity.
Reality, therefore, does not rest on ideal objects. The essence as
objective concept is not the ground of the reality, in the sense of an
ideal thing, because the objective concept is not a thing, either objectual or real.

To sum up, then, the essence of which rationalism speaks could
at most be the objective concept of the essence, but not the essence
itself of the thing. Therefore, that concept is not the ground of the
thing, either as its radical truth or as its internal possibility, or,
finally, as an ideal thing. Clearly, rationalism cannot be unaware, nor
is it unaware, that the essence understood in this way is realized in
the thing and is, consequently, an intrinsic moment of the thing. In
this it would be differentiated from any conception of the essence as
pure «meaning» or any other conceptions possessing affinities to this
one. This, however, is to be thought of merely as a concession in
rationalism, a concession rather obvious in itself. Installed thus in
the line of intelligent causality, rationalism does not believe that to
be an intrinsic moment of the thing is the primary and radical note

of the essence; nor does it tell us anything about this real moment in itself, but only by counterposing it to existence. The only thing which could distinguish the essence as an intrinsic moment of the thing from the essence as mere concept would then be the mere
73 contingent «fact» of its existence. Only by abstraction from this latter would we lay hold on the pure essence, and this pure essence would *eo ipso* remain reduced to the pure objective concept. This, however, is merely to avoid the problem of essence, because the primary and radical character of it is that of being an intrinsic and real moment of the thing itself, independentally, not only of all intellective conception, but also of all eventual relationship to existence. In a word, the problem lies in the physical essence in and for itself. To have confused, or at least to have involved the «physical» essence with that which recent scholastics call the «metaphysical» or abstract (I would say conceptive) essence, that is to say, to have confused that without which the thing cannot have formal reality with that without which the thing cannot be conceived: this has been the serious error of rationalism in dealing with our problem.

CHAPTER FIVE

ESSENCE AS THE REAL CORRELATE OF THE DEFINITION

Neither the formal concept nor the objective concept, then, yields 75 us a satisfactory idea of essence. Nevertheless, the phrase «the essence is the reality of the concept of the thing» can point in a third direction: the reality intended need not be the conceptual reality (whether formal or objective) but rather the thing itself as the correlate of its concept; that is to say, the reality of that of which the concept is the concept, the reality which is conceived, but not as *conceived* but as *real*. In that case, the determination of the essence would rest, not on the truth of the concept, but on that reality. The concept would be no more than the organ with which we apprehend that, in the thing, which constitutes its essence; and the essence itself would be that which, in the thing and, as a real moment of the thing, corresponds to the concept. This is the point of view of Aristotle. However, what we here have called «concept,» Aristotle, more properly, calls «definition.» And the reason for this preference is clear: the essence is the «what,» the τί of anything; and the response to the question what something is, is, for Aristotle, exactly the definition.

Having brought the question of essence to a focus in this manner, Aristotle begins to approach the real thing by way of the definition, in order then to tell us what the essence, as a real moment of the thing (τὸ τί ἦν εἶναι) is.

76   In the first place (we must consider) the route of the definition.
It is not a question of logic, but of ascertaining what the real thing
must be in order that a definition of it may be formed. Aristotle
characterizes this process as «proceeding λογικῶς.» The *logos*, called
the definition, is composed of a number of predicates to which a like
number of notes of the thing correspond. Of these notes, there are
some which the *logos* predicates of its subject in virtue of that which
it is in itself (καθ' αὐτό) while there are others which are, indeed,
predicated of the thing, but which are accidental to it (κατὰ συμβε-
βηκός). Thus). «animal» belongs to Socrates in virtue of what Socrates
is in himself that is to say, because he is a man, while «musical»
does not belong to him in the same way, because being «musical» is
something accidental to him. All the predicates of every definition
belong to the first type. Not all of the predicates of a definition,
however, are parts of the definition of a thing. Only those definitions
state the essence of a thing in which the predicate is not a «property» of the subject, and in which, therefore, the subject does not enter
formally into the predicate of the definition. If I want to define a
white surface, the «whiteness» is a note which the subject, the surface,
demands in virtue of «what it is in itself;» but it demands it merely
as a property in such wise that this subject is formally different
and distinct from the whiteness. Actually, in the definition of a white
surface, the term and the concept «surface» must, in one way or
another, enter in the predicate. Only those definitions, then, express
the essence of a thing in which the predicate belongs to the subject
in virtue of what the latter is «in itself,» without this subject entering
formally into the predicate itself, that is to say, without that which
is defined forming part of the definition.

On this basis, we may ask which are the beings in which this
actually happens? That is to say, which are the beings of which there
are definitions in the strict sense we have just expounded? To be sure,
nothing that we today would call an «ideal thing» is for Aristotle a
being in the proper sense of that term (leaving aside the obscure
problem of what «mathematical entities» were for him). However,
77 even among real things, beings have very diverse entitative character.
Indeed, only «natural» things have the character of beings in the
strict sense. Here, then, Aristotle takes another route, that of nature,
of φύσις, that of generation and corruption. Only natural entities

(φύσει ὄντα) deserve to be called beings and only they, therefore, have essence. It is clear, of course, that, for Aristotle, there are entities which are separate from nature: the stars and the θεός, indeed, are not subject to generation and corruption. So far as our problem is concerned, however, the latter are not distinct or different from natural entities, since, equally with the latter, they are counterposed or contrasted to «artificial» things, and this is the only point which is of interest to us here. Without diminishing the general character of the problem, consequently, we can limit ourselves to speaking of everything non-artificial as though it were natural. For Aristotle, artificial beings (τέχνῃ ὄντα) are not beings in the strict sense and, strictly speaking, do not have an essence. A bed of chestnut wood is not, in a strict sense, a being. The proof is to be found in the fact that if it were planted in the earth and if it would be able to germinate, not beds, but rather chestnut trees, would grow from it. The chestnut tree, not the bed, is the being. For the Greeks, τέχνη, that which we, in a clumsy expression, call *technic*, is something inferior to nature. In any case, the technic of the Greeks does not do what nature does, but rather that which nature does not do; at most, it helps nature in its processes and actions. What really and truly possesses the character of being is nature. Therefore there is essence only of natural beings.

These natural beings, in their turn, are of very different kinds. There are some which are, not so much beings, as beings of beings, affections or dispositions of other beings. They are, as a matter of fact, predicated of other beings and have no being separated from the latter, but only with reference to them and, by analogy, with them: these are the accidents. In contrast to the accident, substance (οὐσία) is the ultimate subject of all predication: it is not predicated of any thing else nor does it exist in any thing else. Substances alone, consequently, possess a true «what,» a τί. They exist in themselves, 78 separately (χωριστόν) from every other being. Therefore, in a strict sense, only of them can there be a definition; accidents can be defined only analogically. Because substance is the ultimate subject of predication, consequently, it is only of it that notes can be predicated in virtue of what it (the substance) is in itself, without that which is defined entering into the definition. Therefore, every definition is a λόγος οὐσίας, the *logos* of a substance. Propositions in this form or definitions can be formulated about anything one may wish, but there can be a definition only of substance. Only substances, therefore, have essences.

What, then, is the essence as a real moment of substance? Before all else, the essence is not identical with the substance; on the contrary, it is properly recognized as something «of» substance, and, therefore, may be predicated of it: Socrates is a man, etc. The distinction between Socrates and man is not merely logical, but real. Socrates, in fact, in addition to the human notes which are essential to him, has many other notes which are not essential. As a consequence, Socrates is the complete and total being, while the essence is only a part of him. Strictly speaking, when we say Socrates is a man, the predicate is distinguished really from the subject, as the part is from the whole. In order to verify the essence in a positive sense, it is enough for Aristotle to point out to us which notes are not essential, that is, the other «part» of the total entity Socrates. These non-essential notes, he will tell us, are of two classes. Some are the notes to which we alluded earlier: the accidental notes, those which are superadded to Socrates, that is to say, the accidents of the substance. There are others, however, which do not supervene to Socrates but only to his essence. Of what kind are these? That is the question.

At this point Aristotle finds it necessary to recur to the structure of the natural substance. At first glance, it might be thought that the essence is the substantial form, that is to say, that which conforms to indeterminate matter in order to make of it a determined sub-
79 stance, in such wise that the essence would be distinguished from the thing only as the formal part of the substance is distinguished from the whole, from the complete hylomorphic compound (τὸ σύνολον) in which the substance under consideration consists. It is of this substantial compound that the substantial form would be predicated as its essence, its formal part. This, however, is not true when we are considering natural substances, because it is «naturally» essential to all of them (with the exception of the θεός) to have matter. The difference between substance and essence does not lie between the substantial principles as such, but rather at another point, for the discovery of which it is enough to observe the natural generation of substances. When Socrates begets a son, this son, no

matter how different he may be, as an individual, from his father, will always be, just as his father is, a «human» being. This character of being «human,» consequently, is a «specific» character. As such, it is not something «logical» but something real and «physical,» since really and physically fathers beget sons of the «same kinds» as themselves. This moment of specific sameness is precisely the essence of the man. Into it, matter enters as much as does form, though in a supremely special way: not «this» matter, but «matter.» It is, of course, clear that just as there is an immaterial substance, the θεός, which is pure form, and just as, even among material substances, the form is the substantial act, it follows that it may be said that, in a certain sense, the essence is the form. For this reason, the difference between essence and substance is not a difference between form and substantial compound but between specific substantial compound and individuated substantial compound. The characters, consequently, which supervene on the essence are these individuating moments.

This interpretation of the essence as something which includes «the» matter itself, is not the only possible one, for on this point, as on so many others, Aristotle's expressions are not easy to reconcile or put into clear relation to each other. In some passages Aristotle 80 seems to say that the essence of every substance is solely the substantial form. However, even in this latter interpretation, the essence consists in nothing other than the moment of specificity of the form. And, in the last analysis, this is the only thing of importance to us.

The essence as a real moment of substance is, then, its physical moment of specificity. And all non-specific characters — whether they be accidents or individuating moments — are, for Aristotle, non-essential.

And here the concept of essence as the real correlate of the definition and the concept of essence as the real moment of substance converge. Let us remember, in fact, that, to designate the essence understood in this manner, Aristotle made use of a word which, though already philosophically consecrated, was, nevertheless, colloquial among the Greeks: the term *eidos* (εἶδος) which the Latins then translated as *species*. This word, in Aristotle, has two meanings. The first is simply the one customary among the Greeks, and which is the decisive use in reference to our problem. *Eidos* designates the unitary conjunction of features or characters in which «one sees» (and this precisely is the reason why they are called «*eidos*») the class of thing to which the reality in question belongs, the mode of being of this reality: dog, parrot, man, oak, olive, etc. It is the typical form «which manifests» the mode of being of the thing. For Aristotle, the substantial principle of these characters is the substantial form (μορφή), that is, the «conforming» form of the being of the thing in the «*materia prima.*» For this reason, Aristotle calls the substantial form itself *eidos*. However, on the other hand, I can make of this *eidos* the term of my predicative *logos*, comparing it with other *eidos* (εἴδη). I then discover that there are some, more or less vague, characters which may be attributed to all those *eidos* equally and which announce their lineage, their common descent, their unique trunk, their γένος, on the basis of which there can be traced something like a geneology, clearly not physical, but according to the *logos* by way of the more «general» affinities. In that case, *eidos* does not signify that which physically manifests the mode of being of the thing, but rather that which identifies the «genus» to which it belongs in a determinate manner. The *eidos*, then, is only one of the many configurations which the genus can determinately present, and includes not only the form but «the» matter as well. Though originally it signified the same as *eidos*, the Latin word *species* persisted almost solely in this second sense, that is, as signifying the species as the determination of the genus.

In the first sense, *eidos* is the essence as a real and physical moment of the thing. Each one of its parts (form and matter) are precisely this: «parts» of the thing. By contrast, in the second sense, *eidos* is that in the thing which is the real correlate of the definition. The species, as defined, is compounded or composed of two «notes» (genus and difference); however, each one of these is not a «part» of the thing, but an aspect of «all» the entire thing: the genus is the whole thing as determinable, and the species is the genus as determined by a difference. Here the essence is not formally a physical moment of the thing, but a «defined» metaphysical unity. We have said that the notes which are predicated of the substance in the definition and which constitute its essence are those which belong to it in itself or by reason of itself in such wise that that which is defined does not enter into the definition. These notes, then, are those which belong to the substance by reason of its own specificity.

These two notions of essence, however, have a point of convergence, because the characters which manifest the mode of being
of the thing are the same as denote its *genus*. And this point is easy 82
to see. In effect, the essence as real *eidos* is a physical moment of
the thing, though it is its physical moment of specificity; the *eidos*
is always typical. And precisely this real *eidos*, insofar as it is specific,
is what the *logos* defines by way of genus and difference; one does
not define Socrates, but the «man» that Socrates is. It follows, then,
that the species as defined is «materially» identical with the species
as a real moment of the thing. This is the reason why the species
as defined is not a mere «objective concept» but is rather, if not
formally, then «materially,» the real correlate of the definition. It is
in the specificity, then, that there is found the unity of the concept
of essence, because the essence as *eidos* has two slopes, the physical
and the definitory, which coincide in the specificity.

To sum up, the essence is the specific, both as the physical
moment, and as the defined unity.

This concept of essence, unfortunately, suffers from a murky
ambivalence. The ambivalence consists in this, that, as in all the
problems of his first philosophy, Aristotle addresses the problem
along two paths: that of predication (λόγος) and that of nature
(φύσις). It is true that, in some cases, it appears that he follows only
one path; however, this is not the case, for it is only a matter of the
predominance of one way over the other. As a matter of fact, the two
ways are always present. And since they are radically different and
independent of each other, it is very difficult for them to lead to a
single and identical concept of that which is sought. In our problem
there exists, fundamentally, a clear preponderance of the λόγος over
the φύσις, of predication over nature. Even more, the very appeal
to φύσις was used to attack the position of Plato who was, correctly,
looked upon as the great theoretician of the «λόγος of ὄν,» the one
who delineated the problem of the «*eidos*» and delineated it properly
in terms of the λόγος. For this reason Aristotle tells us, somewhat
hesitantly, that he is going to begin «according to the λόγος»
(λογικῶς). As a matter of fact, while it is very true that he is seeking
the essence of anything by way of the φύσις, nevertheless, insofar
as he is seeking to apprehend positively that which is the essence of 83
a natural thing, what he does is simply to emphasize in the natural

thing, as «natural,» those characteristics which belong to it only
insofar as it is λεγόμενον, that is, as a term of predication, as
object of λόγος. This confuses the concept of essence.

In order to facilitate our discussion and to orientate it toward
the object of our quest, let us propose that the problem of essence
be deployed in three successive steps:

1. Define the ambit of those things which I propose to call «es-
sentiables.»

2. To indicate, within this ambit, those things which have an
essence: «essentiated» things.

3. To determine in what the essence of this latter class of things
formally consists.

When the question is brought to focus in this manner it is clear
that, for Aristotle, the ambit of the «essentiable» is «nature;» the
«essentiated» entity is the natural «substance;» the essence itself is
its «specificity.» On none of these three points, it must be protested,
does the Aristotelian conception prove satisfactory.

In the first place, let us consider the point which concerns the
ambit of the «essentiable,» that is, nature. Aristotle defines this area
by contrasting it to τέχνη. In this contraposition one encounters a
serious confusion which invalidates the entire Aristotelian intention
on this point. Nature and τέχνη are indeed, from one point of view,
two principles of things and, in this sense, they are counter-opposed
to and exclude each other in the manner that Aristotle indicates to
us. Each being emerges from a principle and realizes, so to say, the
«design» *(sit venia verbo)* of that principle. In τέχνη this principle
is extrinsic to the things in question: it is to be found in the imagination or in the intelligence of man. In nature, by contrast, the
principle is intrinsic to the things in question. For this reason we
speak, in the first case, of «production» of things while, in the second
84 case, we speak of the «birth» of those same things (and this is what
φύειν fundamentally signified). This is true, but does this complete
duality of principles also involve a complete duality in the entity of
the beings generated according to those principles? This is the single
question which is decisive for our problem. And when serious thought
is given to it we must respond, without the slightest hesitation,
negatively.

Perhaps Greek technology and, in general, all ancient technology was able only to produce «artifacts,» that is, things which nature does not produce and which, once they have been produced, have no «natural activity.» In this case, the duality of principles leads to a duality of entities; the example of the wooden bed is decisive on this point. In our world, however, this is not true. Our technology produces not only artifacts, that is, things which nature does not produce, but also the same things which nature produces and which are endowed with an identical natural activity. And it is in this sameness that the decisive factor is to be found. An abyss separates our technology from ancient technology; nor is it only a difference of degree, but a fundamental difference of incalculable philosophical impact. The whole of our chemistry is clear proof of this fact. In this dimension our technology has achieved undreamed of proportions and finds itself on the brink of achieving results which were before considered impossible. It produces not only those things which are called compound bodies, but also elements and even elementary particles, identical with the compound bodies, the elements and the particles which emerge from nature. It produces synthetically molecules which are essential to the structures of living beings. It intervenes prodigiously in ever more extensive zones of living being and it is possible to believe that the day is not far distant in which there will be produced the synthesis of any type of living matter. In these conditions the difference between artifacts and natural beings disappears: 85 *our technology produces natural entities artificially.* (It is not important that the capacity of producing natural entities artificially is very limited.) This is the idea of the new technology. For a Greek this phrase would constitute an inadmissible paradox. The duality of φύσις (nature) and τέχνη, valid in the order of principles, fails to prove so in the order of the beings generated by those principles. Nature and τέχνη are, at times, only two possible ways for producing the same beings. The serious Aristotelian error on this point has been to have confused both things. When this confusion is eliminated, the intention of delineating the area of «essentiable» realities by way of the contra-position of nature and τέχνη also proves invalid.

Within this area, poorly defined as we have seen, Aristotle tells us that only substances possess an essence properly so called, because only the substance is a true being. However, we may ask, in what

does this priority of substance in the entitative order consist? This
is the question; and it is a question which, to be sure, is not as
simple as it may appear. Aristotle establishes this range by appealing
to that which he calls the figure of the categories, in which substance
is counterposed to the accident of which it is the subject. Only from
this point of view is it justified to speak of substance, ὑποκείμενον,
sub-stans. That which is proper to substance, its formal *ratio*, and
its metaphysical prerogative, would consist, according to Aristotle, in
its irreducible status as subject. Aristotle comes to this conception
by the double way of predication and of nature: substance is the
ultimate subject of predication, while the accidents are nothing
more than affects of substance. To be sure, he tells us that substance
is the only «separable» reality. For Aristotle, however, separability is
merely a consequence of subjectuality: the reason why the substance
is separated is that it is the ultimate subject and the subject deter-
86 mined by a τί. The Platonic ideas are not separated realities since
they are predicated of individual subjects, and prime matter, despite
being subject, is not separable because it is indeterminate in itself
(de suyo), it lacks all τί. The true being possesses its character as
such by reason of the radical and determined subjectuality in which
it consists. To be sure, there is a special substance, the θεός, which
is pure form. However, apart from the fact that it performs no
function in the Aristotelian theory of substance, Aristotle himself
conceives his θεός somewhat after the manner of a subject of itself;
his *autonoesis* fundamentally means only this, something very different from what, for example, reflectivity in medieval and modern
philosophy will be. Scholasticism will continue to consider substance
as being *par excellence;* in general, however, it affirmed that the
formal *ratio* of substantiality is not subjectuality but *perseitas.* Later
on we shall see what must be thought of this idea of *perseitas;* for
the moment our attention must be limited to Aristotle. And substance, that is, true being, whatever may be its formal *ratio* (did
Aristotle even ask this question?) has for Aristotle a formal subjectual character. This concept, we must conclude, is justified neither
by the way of the λόγος nor by way of the φύσις.

It is not justified by way of a λόγος because every reality, no
matter what its character may be, can be converted into a subject
of predication. And precisely because this can be done with every

reality, the fact of being λεγόμενον, of being the subject of predication, leaves untouched the question of the physical character of the
reality to which we are referring, that is to say, its subjectual or non-
subjectual character. It would be a serious error to invert the formal
structure of the λόγος and the thing itself. Under this aspect Aristotle
leads to Leibniz and even to Hegel. To be a subject in the sense of
the terminus of a λόγος is not to be physically a subjectual reality
as a reality. To be the subject of attribution is not the same as to
possess the attribute as a physical property of the subject. The
λόγος is nothing more than one way, always the same, the way of
predication, to enunciate truths about realities of the most diverse 87
structure, of structures which are, perhaps, irreducible: the identity
of the way does not involve the identity of the real structure of that
to which this way leads; that is to say, not all realities which are the
subject of predication are, for this reason, *sub-jectum* in their character as realities.

Neither does the way of φύσις impose this subjectual conception
of reality. It is one thing that, «within» a transformation, there
should be persistent structural *moments:* another that the persistent
element should be a *subject-thing* which persists «beneath» the
transformation. In the first instance, the transformation — or at least
the movement — affects the entire reality of the thing; in the second,
it takes place on the surface, no matter how substantial one seeks
to make it.

There is no reason to think, therefore, that every reality, as such,
would have to be necessarily subjectual in character. It is true that
all the realities which we know through experience are, in one way
or another, subjects; this does not mean, however, that subjectuality
is their radical structural characteristic. Precisely to elaborate a
theory of reality which does not unqualifiedly identify reality and
subjectuality have I introduced a terminological distinction: I have
called the radical structure of all reality, even though it involves a
moment of subjectuality, substantivity, differentiating it from substantiality, which latter would be the specific characteristic of reality
only insofar as it is subjectual. Substantivity expresses the plenitude
of entitative autonomy. The hierarchical priority in the order of
reality, as such, resides not in substantiality but in substantivity.
Substantivity and subjectuality are two irreducible moments of

reality, while of these two the moment of substantivity is anterior to that of subjectuality. The failure to discriminate between these two moments causes the Aristotelian notion of «essentiated» being to lack
88 sufficient precision or at least sufficient exactitude. For, as we shall see, the essence is a moment proper, not to subjectuality, but to substantivity.

However, when we have passed, even lightly, over these important questions concerning the «essentiable» and the «essentiated,» the third point remains: namely, what is the essence in itself? For Aristotle, the essence is the specificity of the substance. He arrives at this opinion, once again, by way of «the convergence» of the two ways, that of the λόγος and that of φύσις. On the one hand, the essence is the real correlate of the definition; on the other, it is a moment of the physical structure of the substance. And the presumptive point of «convergence» would be precisely the moment of specificity. However, despite the appearances, this last moment is determined, in its turn, in function of the definition itself, in such wise that, in the problem of essence, there is revealed a decisive preponderance of the λόγος over φύσις. Responding to the pressure of the Platonic tradition, Aristotle goes to the thing, in our problem, with the organon of the notion which it is possible to have of the thing in the form of a definition. And since only the universal is definable, the result is that the essence, for Aristotle, involves, before everything else, a formal moment of specific universality. It is the predominance of the λόγος which has launched the problem of essence on the line of specificity.

It is true that Aristotle appeals to the process of generation in order to come to the specificity of the essence by a way that is truly «physical.» However, he does not state with formal rigor what this physical species might be. On the contrary, he takes from the process of generation only the fact of the multiplicity of «equal» individuals and their inclusion in the «identity» of a single concept (ἕν καὶ ταὐτόν). Aristotle energetically rejected the Platonic conception according to which species have «separated» reality (χωριστόν) and repeats to the point of satiety that species are separate only in the
89 order of νοῦς and λόγος. According to this position, the species possesses physical reality in the individual; however, that which, in the individual, is species is the unity of the concept insofar as it is

realized in many individuals. This, however, is more than questionable. Does the mere identity of the concept univocally realized in many individuals suffice to constitute these individuals as a «species?» In its proper time, we will see that this is not the case. That identity is indeed necessary for the species but in no sense is it sufficient. In every case it is manifest that, even in this presumed physical characterization of the essence, there is to be observed an undeniable primacy of the conceptual unity over the individual physical unity to the point that the latter remains formally unclarified and, as a matter of fact, is not even formulated properly as a problem. That is to say, there is an undeniable predominance of the essence as something defined over the essence as physical moment. This predominance leads to an inadequate idea of the essence for, no matter how important the structure of definition (a logical problem) may be, it is something entirely secondary with respect to the structure of things (a metaphysical problem). Let us examine, then, these two concepts of essence separately.

1. When the essence is taken as the real correlate of the definition, the least that must be said is that it is a question of a very indirect way of arriving at things. For, as we have already said, instead of going directly to the reality and asking what in it may be its essence, one takes the roundabout way of passing through the definition. This might be admissible if it was a matter of no more than a roundabout way. It is, however, something more; it is a roundabout journey which rests on an enormously problematic presupposition, namely, that the essential element of every thing is necessarily definable; and this is more than problematical. It is one thing that by means of our concepts we approximate more or less closely to realities and that we even succeed in characterizing some of them in such wise that they may be distinguished more or less unequivocally among themselves, but another, very different thing, to say that the whole of reality can be explicated in concepts and, even less, its essence defined. It were better to say that we could give definitions 90 of some essences. Even in this case, however, the question remains, what is it in reality that these definitions define? We have already said, they define the essence as species. However, the essence «man» is one thing; the essential characteristics of a determinate individual are something else. Aristotle will permit «matter,» but not «this mat-

ter,» to enter into essence; not «these» bones, «this» blood, etc., of
Socrates. This would, indeed, be true of the essence as abstract
specificity, but not as a physical moment of Socrates for whom what
is essential is precisely «these» bones, «this» blood, etc. With his
pertinacious orientation toward the definition, Aristotle leaves us
without what is most important for us in the essence, namely, the
physical essence. Aristotle will say, naturally, that the individual
cannot be defined, that only the specific can be defined. This is true.
It does not follow from this, however, that the non-specific is not
essential; rather, quite the contrary, that the essence, as such, does
not consist in that which can be defined. An individual can possess
many characters which are essential for it, and which are not specific.
Despite the fact that they recognize this, some scholastic philosophers nevertheless continue to be faithful disciples of Aristotle,
limiting the essential to the specific, and precisely for logical reasons.
The investigation of essence, however, is not the elaboration of a
definition. It is one thing to ascertain what the essential of something is, another that that which has been ascertained should be
formally a definition. Instead of making the essence the measure of
the definition and recognizing that the definition corresponds to only
one aspect or other of the essence, Aristotle makes the definition the
measure of the essence. And this, even from a logical point of view,
is unacceptable, unless by another path it will justify the view that
the strict and formal function of the essence is to be the principle of
specification. This latter, however, is not the case: and this fact
leads us to the second concept of essence.

91   2. Let us take the essence as a real and physical moment of
substance. Aristotle brings to focus the structure of the individual
substance by considering it as a subject endowed with certain notes
which are the same as those possessed by other individuals, and it is
these identical notes which he calls essential notes. In this way the
essence appears to him as a physical moment of specification. Instead
of confronting the question of the essence in itself and trying to see
in what, *within a determined individual,* its essential physical moment
may consist in respect to the totality of the notes which it might
possess *hic et nunc,* Aristotle is looking for something else, namely:
how *this individual* articulates itself *within the species;* the structure
of this articulation would be the essence. Thus the essence would

consist in that which collocates a thing within a class of things. What is this? It is a «man,» a «dog,» an «apple.» This and this alone is what the Greeks called τί, *quid*, what. The rest would not belong to the what, but rather to the τίς, *quis*, the who or what kind of. Indeed, that the specific essence should be a moment of the individual, because the species does not exist separately from the individual, as Plato pretended, will be a question as important as one may wish with respect to the species, but will, nevertheless, leave untouched the prior question of knowing what within this determined individual may be that which we call its essence, independently of the fact that it may further serve to constitute the possible unity of a species. These are two entirely distinct questions, because specificity supposes the plurality of individuals, so that the essence, in its own character *(de suyo)* makes no formal reference to other individuals. So much so, that, if this were not the case, it would not be possible to speak of essence in those realities which, for any reason whatsoever, do not admit of numerical multiplication. But this is absurd, because in that case what would happen is precisely that the τί and the τίς «would change into each other» *(se convertirían)* by reason of their content: the entire content of the τίς would enter into the τί, and vice 92 versa. The multiplicity of individuals is certainly an inevitable means for arriving at the knowledge of the essence, but nothing more. Specificity is formally alien to essentiality. Within the individual, those characters which we call essential, fulfill a function proper to themselves, independently of whether or not there may be other individuals with possible identical characteristics. This function, therefore, is not a specifying function, but a structuring function. There is a moment, to be sure, when Aristotle seems as though he is going to treat of this aspect of the question, namely, when he refers to the substantial form, because the form is a physical moment of substance. Nevertheless, for him, the form is in itself specifying; between its specifying function and its structuring function there exists nothing more than an abstractive difference; independently of the act of constituting the substance, the form, in itself, is only a principle of specification. And this is not enough. The essence, as a physical moment of the substance, exercises a structuring, and not a specifying, function; and it exercises this function in the order of the properties of the thing themselves, and not solely in the order of the actuation of matter by form.

3. The insufficiency of this conception becomes more sharply apparent if we consider what happens, in Aristotle's case, when he considers these two concepts of essence together. For Aristotle, the essence seems always to be supported by a substantial subject: it is the subject of «attribution» of some predicates, it is the subject of «inherence» of certain real notes. It is a theory of essence established on a theory of reality as subjectuality. Hence, the failure to distinguish the abstract essence and the essence as a physical moment of the reality. Since, for Aristotle, the essence is specific, instead of arriving at a unitary idea of the essence and of the «essentiated» substance, 93 he becomes trapped in an irreducible duality. If the essence is something specific, it follows that it, the essence, is the species insofar as it exists in the individual and, therefore, this species is the true subject of attribution of the essential notes. Hence, it follows that even though the ultimate subject would seem to be Socrates, nevertheless, the true and proper subject of his human notes is not Socrates, but rather the humanity which is in him. Consequently, this humanity is something like a subject within the subject Socrates, a second substance, as Aristotle himself says, within the primary substance. What might be the nature of the strict articulation of these two surprising substances is something that forever remains obscure, and not by accident, but rather as a result of the very way by which, primarily and preponderantly, approach is made to things, the way of the λόγος. Hence arose, as is well known, the medieval problem of universals.

To sum up, when we are told, with Aristotle, that the essence comprises those notes which are predicated of a thing in itself (καθ' αὐτό), it appears very clearly that the essence possesses what I would call a function, very precisely determined, which certain notes fulfill in the real thing. What might this function be? For Aristotle, it is the function of specification: the essence proves to be the principle of the specificity of the substance. We have already seen that this is difficult to admit. The function of the essence, as we have said, is something else: it is a structuring function independent of all specification. Neither is this function what Aristotle would call an actuation of prime matter by substantial form. This is not the question here. The question concerns a structuring function, but *in the order of the very properties* of the thing. The Aristotelian idea of essence is woven of the thread of the λόγος and, for this reason, ends necessarily with the specificity of the subject of this predication. It is a conception of essence based on a theory of reality as subjectuality. And in this consist its intrinsic limitations.

In medieval philosophy, a return is made to this theme for the 94 first time in that celebrated *opusculum* of St. Thomas, *De Ente et Essentia.* Following this, there is an uninterrupted series of texts and commentaries concerning this problem. As a matter of fact, however, medieval philosophy does nothing more on this matter than rethink the Aristotelian ideas, making use of the elaboration of those same ideas by Avicenna and Averroës. Its originality is encountered in two points: it raised and considered the problem of the distinction between essence and existence and it penetrated more profoundly the problem of universals, which is so intimately connected with the essentiality of substance; I shall refer to these points as they arise in the course of our exposition.

* * *

Let us sum up. Rationalism and Hegel represent two ideas of essence which rest upon the concept we have of the thing: the essence would be the reality of the concept of the thing. This equivocal phrase may be understood as referring either to the formal concept (Hegel) or to the objective concept (rationalism). In Aristotle, by contrast, the essence is a moment of reality; of reality, however, taken as the physical correlate of its definition. After the extreme Hegelian idealism, by way of rationalism, we fall back with Aristotle to the reality itself. This return, however, comes about in a very special way, namely, by considering reality as λεγόμενον, admitting that its essential character is always and necessarily expressible in a definition. Having made clear the insufficiencies and the vacillations of this special contact with reality — special in the sense of being indirect — we are now free to take a step forward: to go directly to reality and to try to ascertain in it and by way of it what the reality of essence may be.

PART THREE

ESSENCE. STRUCTURAL MOMENT OF THE REAL

which

Chapter Six

INTRODUCTORY RECAPITULATION

Our purpose is to ascertain what essence is. With the purpose of approaching the problem more closely, I have lingered over the discussion of some classical concepts concerning essence. The most tangible result of this discussion has been to show us that if we wish to know what essence is in a fundamental and formal sense, we must turn back to the reality itself and inquire what in it may be this structural moment proper to it which we call essence, taking it in itself, independently of every further function which it might be able to exercise, whether in the order of existence, in the order of specification, or in any other order whatsoever.

To achieve this purpose, let us turn back to the original point of departure of our investigation. I began with a provisional determination of the concept of essence. At that point I had no other purpose than to link up this discussion with the customary ideas concerning essence. Now, however, as we take up the direct treatment of essence as a structural moment of the real, it is necessary rapidly and systematically, to recapitulate what was said in that provisional determination in order to direct our own steps.

In its most innocuous acceptance, essence is purely and simply the «what» of anything, that is, the totality of the notes which it may possess, taken in their internal unity. This «what» however, immediately exhibits itself to us in our experience as something more or less variable, while, despite this variability, the thing remains the 98 same. Essence, then, is the internal unity of those notes which presumably constitute the sameness of a thing, and prevent its confusion with other things. This conclusion forces us to seek, among these notes which pertain to the sameness of the thing, those which strictly cannot be absent from that thing, and which that thing necessarily must possess if it is not to cease to be that which it was in the earlier acceptance. The unitary conjunction of these notes, which the real thing necessarily possesses, is what, in the formal and proper sense, we call essence. This unity of the essence possesses two fundamental characteristics. In the first place, it is a primary unity, because in it the different notes are nothing more than abstract moments in which that original unity deploys itself. In the second place, since not all the notes which a real thing may possess *hic et nunc* are essential to it, it follows that the essence, in contrast to everything else the thing has or may have or may not have, constitutes, in its unity, the true reality of the thing in question, the principle of its other notes. Primary unity and true reality in the order of principles: here, then, are the two characteristics which the essence possesses as the internal unity of that which the thing cannot fail to have, which necessarily belongs to it.

In a word, in our provisional determination, essence comprises five points at least, which it will help to clearly set over against each other:

1. The essence is a moment of a *real* thing.
2. This moment is the primary unity of its (the real thing's) notes.
3. This unity is *intrinsic* to the thing itself.
4. This unity is a principle on which the other notes (whether necessary or not) of the thing are based.
5. The essence, understood in this way, within the thing, is its *truth*, the truth of the reality.

Our summary analysis of the most customary ideas concerning 99 essence has not been conducted out of mere historical curiosity nor has it been a simple dialectical discussion, but it has been the road which has brought us near, in a positive way, to the precise formation of what is problematic about essence. Further, our analysis has done this in two ways. In the first place, it has made clear to us that those conceptions are not totally false, but so radically insufficient that the discussion has made us see what the essence cannot be, and, at the same time, what it formally has to be; that is to say, it has led us to a thematic distinction of those five points. The primary unity, in fact, cannot be extrinsic to the thing, but must be intrinsic, in such wise that it is inadmissible to interpret the essence as a «meaning» which would sustain itself, independently of the reality of fact. On the other hand, as the true reality, it is the essence which has to be the foundation of any formal and objective concept, and not the reverse; the essence does not belong to the concept, but the concept is concept of the essence. Finally, the essence is not formally the principle of specification which is expressed in a definition, but is rather the physical structural moment of the thing taken in and by itself. Correlatively, the non-essential is not the purely factitive; it is neither «a mere being,» nor the extra-conceptual, nor the individuating.

However, our discussion had a still further objective. Not only has it differentiated those five points, but it has also shown us in what way they are radically problematic. In this sense, the discussion has not been a «refutation,» but, quite the contrary, a kind of first approximation, by way of so many aporiatic efforts, to the correct conception of those points. To make this clear, we need only let our reflection dwell for a moment on every one of these points. For example, after what we have said concerning the insufficiency of the differentiation between natural and artificial in Aristotle, what is to be understood by «real thing?» We know, since Aristotle, that the essential notes constitute a *per se* unity, and Descartes and Leibniz repeat it. But, we must ask, of what kind of unity are we speaking? 100 It is not a conceptive unity as Leibniz would say. Our discussion with Husserl has shown us that this unity must be intrinsic to the thing; however, we do not know, with scientific certainty, to what the essence in the thing itself is formally intrinsic. It is clear that the essence must be a principle; however, we must ask what is the principle here and of what is it the principle. It is not, certainly, a generating principle, as Hegel would seem to wish; neither is the essence the principle only of the necessary notes. Finally, it has been made clear that the essence is the true reality of the thing; and this is always true because by this truth there is not understood, in the first instance, correspondence to the concept, as Leibniz and Hegel, following, in part at least, medieval philosophy, held. That this correspondence exists is undeniable; but it is formally alien to the essence and the primary truth of the thing. What, then, is this truth of the thing?

By our discussion we have discovered that the provisional formula of essence proves to be no more than a vague indication whose possible errors earlier ideas have made clear to us. It is necessary, consequently, to impose a rigorous precision on that formula. Addressing ourselves directly to the reality itself, therefore, we must seek in it what its essence may be and what may be the true character of those five points; that is to say, what is that which I have called «special function,» which, what we designated by the name essence, exercises within the real thing itself and by reason of which that thing is in itself. This function is what constitutes the essence as a structural «physical» moment of the thing. Here we have what we are looking for.

In order to establish its character precisely, let us proceed by successive steps. In analyzing the Aristotelian idea of essence, and anticipating my own arguments, I have suggested the examination of three questions which I then designated in a purely nominal fashion: the «essentiable,» the «essentiated,» and the «essence» itself. By «essentiable» we understand the compass within which alone things
101 which possess essence may exist, even though not all of the things within that compass possess it. I call «essentiated» that thing which, within this compass, possesses essence in a strict and proper sense. Finally, the «essence» itself must be encountered as the formal and structural moment of the thing so designated. These three concepts are the rubrics of the three porblems to which the idea of essence points:

1. The essence, we say, is the conjunction of what cannot be lacking in the real thing, what is necessary to it. We must ask, however, of what necessity are we speaking, and what is understood here by reality. This is precisely the strict delimitation of the area of the «essentiable.»

2. The essence is the true reality. That is to say, within the «essentiable» there are some realities, but not all, which are «true» in

contrast to others which are not. Which are these that we call «true realities?» These will be the «essentiated» realities.

3. The essence is a primary unity of the notes of the thing and the necessitating principle of at least some of the other notes of the thing. Which are these notes? In what does the special and proper function of that system of notes consist? In what does the intrinsic character of the essence as principle consist? Only by ascertaining the answers to these questions will we have apprehended the «essence» in itself as a physical and structural moment of the reality, and that which constitutes, within the reality, the difference between the essential and the non-essential.

The essentiable, the essentiated, the essence itself: here then we have the three circles of the problem that we must confront.

CHAPTER SEVEN

THE COMPASS OF THE «ESSENTIABLE»

In order to delimit this compass, let us try to see, before all else, what necessity is in question when we speak of essential necessity. In general terms — without entering into more precise determinations at this point — we may say that a note is essential to a thing when that thing cannot be without that note, when it «must possess» that note, under penalty of not being the kind of thing it is. In this sense, it is essential for a knife to have a blade, just as it is essential for an animal to possess sensibility, etc. What we say is true, though of course absolutely inadequate. When we speak of a thing «having to have» a certain note in order to be a thing of a certain kind, if the moment of necessity is centered in this moment of «having to have,» we are given a merely negative concept of necessity: «have to have» is the same as «not to be able to lack.» The positive element of the moment of necessity lies, rather, in the other half of this phrase, in the subtle «in order that the thing may be such and such.» Hence it follows that the first thing we have to do is to determine precisely what is to be understood by «such and such a thing,» this thing to which the «have to have» must refer if one wishes to speak of a rigorously essential necessity. This thing is not just any of those items which we call things, but is a formally real thing: essential necessity is a formally real necessity. It will be necessary to say, then, what is to be understood in this context by reality. It is precisely the determination of the compass of the «essentiable»: the compass of the «essentiable» is the compass of reality.

104   A reality is everything and only that which acts upon other things or upon itself formally, in virtue of the notes which it possesses. Let us explain ourselves.

In order not to evoke false ideas which might cause the problem to enter upon a line of development different from that which we are going to follow, let us say, once and for all, that when speaking of «notes» I take this term in its absolutely greatest generality.

Ordinarily, it is taken as a synonym of property, while giving to this latter term a restricted meaning: something which the thing «possesses» as previously constituted as a thing of a certain kind. For example, to be a biped is a property of man. It is, in the last analysis, that which the ἴδιον, the *proprium*, means in Aristotle, to be differentiated, for example, from generic, specific, and individuating characters which are not properties «of» the man but are the man himself. Here, by contrast, when speaking of «notes,» I am referring not only to these «properties» of the thing, but rather to all of the moments which it possesses, including among these even that which is ordinarily called «part» of the thing, that is to say, matter, its structure, its chemical composition, its psychic «faculties,» etc. Sometimes, for reasons of convenience of expression, I shall employ the word property as a synonym for note, that is to say, giving it, not the restricted sense which it possesses in Aristotle, but rather the very extended meaning it possesses etymologically: everything which belongs to the thing or which forms part of it «as a property,» as something «its own.» The cells of an organism, or the soul itself, are, in this sense, properties of that organism or of the man, etc.

Having said this, let us turn to the concept of reality. In it, actuation is a mere *ratio cognoscendi*, since precisely what one seeks to say is that, when it is given, this type of actuation is real and constitutes, therefore, a moment of the reality of the thing. This rigorously circumscribes the area of reality. Minerals, mountains, the 105 galaxies, living beings, men, societies, etc., are real things. To these things are counter-posed other things, such as a table, a farm, etc. These latter things are certainly real, but they are such only by reason of the properties or notes of weight, color, density, solidity, humidity, chemical composition, etc. In virtue of all these notes, as a matter of fact, they act upon other things, on the air, on the light, on other bodies, etc. By contrast, however, they do not act upon other things in virtue of their formal characters as table or as farm. This character, consequently, is not a real property of them, is not a moment of their reality. Hence, these things in their formal and proper character as table and as farm, are not, formally, real things. They are precisely «another thing,» another type of «thing»: they are possibilities of life. It is clear that, if they did not have their real notes, they would not be such possibilities. However, the converse is not certain: things can have real properties, including known properties, and nevertheless not be all of the possibilities which might be constituted by them. Until the beginning of this century the air, despite the fact that its resistance was known, was not a means of travel; only land and water were such. In every case, possibility and real note are two completely different dimensions of the thing. And not only are they different, but the second is anterior to the first, with an anteriority, moreover, which is κατὰ φύσιν, as is obvious, with an anteriority καθ᾽ αἴσθησιν, that is, contrary to the opinion of Husserl and Heidegger, an anteriority by the first and primary way in which the thing is perceived. The properties spring from the reality and are based on it; possibilities spring from the meaning which real things possess in life and are based on that meaning; we will, therefore, call them «meaning-things.»

This contra-position has nothing whatever to do with the Aristotelian opposition between τέχνη and φύσις. We have already seen that this latter is a difference between beings solely with respect to their status as «principiated.» By contrast, the contraposition between «real thing» and «meaning-thing» is a difference which refers to the formal character of the thing itself. If one wishes to continue to speak of «nature» to designate real things, he will have to say that the concept of nature here expressed differs *toto caelo* from the Greek concept of φύσις; it also differs from the modern concept of nature which has been employed since Galileo.

Nature, as a matter of fact, does not here signify φύσις: the intrinsic principle whence things are born or grow, that is to say, an originative principle, but rather their mode of existing and acting once they have been produced. The elementary particles may be natural or artificial in the Greek sense, that is, by reason of their

106

principle: insulin, nuclear acids, etc.; these, once produced, act formally in virtue of the properties which they possess. As such, they are natural realities in the concept of nature here expressed. Conversely, the «meaning-things» are not necessarily artificial: a field as a farm, or a cave as shelter, are not artificial, yet they are nevertheless only «meaning-things.»

Neither does this concept of nature coincide with that suggested by Galileo and which reaches its full expression in Kant: the system of natural laws. Laws, as a matter of fact, are mere functional relations, while what is important in our concept is not the relations but the things themselves; and a thing is not natural because it is subject to natural laws but rather it is subject to natural laws because it is natural. And it is natural because it actuates formally in virtue of the properties which it possesses. This is true independently of the fact that the complex of natural laws would never be able to explain everything present in the thing, because there always exists in a thing a margin of individuality and contingency which those laws would never succeed in exhausting.

107 In opposition to the modern concept of nature as law, we must here vindicate the concept of nature as thing. With respect to the Greek concept of natural thing, as a thing which comes into being by reason of a principle intrinsic to it, there must be defended the concept of thing which acts formally in virtue of the properties which it possesses, whatever may be its origin.

At the same time that we propound the concept of nature, it is necessary to delineate the problem of τέχνη. Although there is little accord as to the precise point of change or as to its ultimate meaning, as we have seen, it has been recognized, nevertheless, that the concept of nature has changed from Greek times to our own. Nothing similar, however, has taken place with respect to τέχνη. Our technic seems to differ from that of the Greeks only in amount and perfection. As a matter of fact, the difference is much more profound, because, just as in the case of φύσις, the difference lies in the very concept of τέχνη. The present, however, is obviously not the moment to take up this problem.

Only real things, real in the sense defined above, can have and do have essence. There is a concept of «meaning-things;» however, they do not possess essence. We have already seen, when we were speaking of rationalism, that essence and concept cannot be confused. That which is conceived can be the essence when it is a real thing that is conceived; not everything, however, which is conceived is reality and, much less, essence. The compass of the «essentiable» is, therefore, the compass of reality conceived as the set of things which, endowed with certain properties, act formally in virtue of these properties. Despite what, at the beginning of our investigation, seemed obvious to us, the knife, as such, has no essence. That moment of «having to have» must concern only the reality, if it is to constitute an essential necessity. All essential necessity, consequently, is, always and only, a real necessity, conformable to the concept of reality which we have just expounded. Obviously, this does not prevent us speaking in current language of the essential with respect to all kinds of things, whether or not they are real; what happens is that we 108 consider them as though they were real things. And we do so for a very profound reason: it is that, apprehended by man, these things, though unreal in themselves, produce real effects on man. Man, in a word, is the only being which, in order to be fully real, must give the «essential» twist to the unreal. This is a point which we have no reason to develop here, and with which I have concerned myself extensively in my courses.

Chapter Eight

«ESSENTIATED» REALITY

Having thus outlined the compass of the real as the compass of that which is formally «essentiable,» we now ask which are the things, within this compass, that possess essence, that it to say, which are «essentiated» realities.

In order to establish this point, let us begin by observing that the necessity expressed in the phrase «to have to have» is always eminently relative. It is already such in the order of the «meaning-things.» On my table there is an ash tray which holds down some papers. In order for this object to be (an) ash tray, it is essential that it have a cavity or a plane surface in which the ashes may be deposited; in order to be (a) paper weight this note is non-essential to it, because it could fulfill this function perfectly even were it spherical or solid. However, the only point that is important for us is the necessity of the real order. In this order, the «have to have» is also relative. In order to reflect light in a determined manner, a piece of silver «has to have» a very smooth and polished surface; in this sense this note is essential to it. However, for this same piece of silver to float in water, that note is non-essential to it, whereas it would be essential to it to have a certain volume which might displace the water, conformably to the principle of Archimedes. As a floating object and as a light-reflector, this piece of silver «has to have» very different notes; we may call them essential, in a relative sense, however. Essence is, then, not only essence «of» something, but also essence «for» something. In the cases we have cited, these two moments, of the «of» and the «for,» are really distinct. To the moment of the «for» we might apply the name ἀγαθόν, of which Plato said that it was the basis of the essence of everything, a thesis which, as we are going to say, cannot be accepted without qualification. The relativity of the «have to have» resides in the difference between the «of» and the «for,» since one same «of» may have different «for's;» whence it follows that what is essential in one respect is not in another. Even more, for this same reason, one same thing may have and does have various different essences in this relative sense; the same piece of silver may at the same time be a floating object and a reflector. This, however, is not a true essence.

In order that there may be an essential necessity, it is not enough, then, that there should be real necessity. It is necessary, in addition, to indicate of which «for» one is speaking. When a system of notes is necessary, not in order to act in a determined manner (as a floating object or as a reflector in our example) but rather in order simply to be real (in order to be silver) only then will we have essential necessity in a strict sense. In that case, the «for» becomes identical with the «of» in the «what;» the real distinction between the «of» and the «for» disappears. The «what» is the very reality of the «of,» in such wise that now one can not even speak strictly of an «of.» The essence «of» the silver is the characteristic structure of silver itself, its nuclear and cortical system. I can, logically, say that this is the structure «of» the silver; *in re*, however, this structure is not «of» the silver but, rather, is the silver itself, the reality silver *simpliciter* in distinction to the reality of the silver *secundum quid* or under a certain aspect, namely, «to» float or reflect light. And for this reason, the reality *simpliciter* of the silver is what this thing truly is, is its true reality. The truth here is — we will see why — the reality *simpliciter*. Hence, essential necessity is not relative; one same thing cannot have different essences. I may say in other terms: essential necessity is absolute. Here «absolute» means only that the structure of the reality proper to the thing does not depend on a «for,» on an ἀγαθόν, distinct from itself. It, the reality, is its own ἀγαθόν. Only in this way is the Platonic idea admissible; what happens then is that it is no longer Platonic.

With these considerations we have circumscribed the compass of the «essentiated»: only and all real things have essence in that and by that by which they are real. That is to say, the «essentiated» is the reality *simpliciter*, the true reality.

Having reached this point it would seem that we have exhausted the question of the «essentiated.» Such, however, is not the case, because reality *simpliciter* and true reality remain up to this point, as it were, mere denominations. They serve to designate the proper reality «of» something, or better, the something real itself, differentiating it from that reality which is such «for» something. These denominations, however, tell us nothing concrete about reality in itself. We have the thing in our hands, but we have done nothing more, as it were, than touch it and give it its proper name without yet knowing clearly what is actually at stake. Therefore, it is necessary that we say with greater precision what this reality *simpliciter* may be. We may embark on this question by the analysis of the truth element in the real. That will permit us to conceptualize more rigorously and with fullness of content what the reality *simpliciter* of anything is.

SECTION ONE   112

REALITY AND TRUTH

We speak of true reality. The truth under consideration here is not logical truth, the conformity of thought with things. Here truth is not conformity but something much more profound: the ground of such conformity. Of what ground are we speaking? Obviously without intelligence there would exist no truth. From this point of view, consequently, the ground in question would be the intelligence itself, and what we would be looking for concerning this ground would be a theory of the intelligence. Here, however, we are not proposing a theory of truth in this sense, but in another. In this other meaning, the ground of the truth means that which brings it about that there is truth in the intelligence. Without intelligence, what this ground «makes» *would not be (no sería)* truth; however, without this ground there *would not be (habría)* in the intelligence what we call truth. It is this ground, as such, that is to say, as ground of the truth of intellection, that we call «the true» *(lo verdadero)*. Here «the true» means, then, that which gives truth; if the expression may be permitted me, that which «truths» (as a verb) in the intellection. This is the sense in which we are asking for the ground of truth. What is this ground? What is it that «truths» the intellection?

In order to reach the answer to this question, let us identify some constitutive moments of the truth.

1. In the truth there is a moment of intellection; without it what we call truth would not be truth. As I have just said, however, this is not the sense in which I am now referring to intellection. I am not referring to intellection as the act of the intelligence, but to intellection insofar as it involves or implies a ground which gives truth. Therefore, even though there is no truth without intellection, it is not the intelligence in and for itself which «gives» truth to intellection, it is not the intelligence which «truths» in it. For we may ask, what is, with respect to the effects upon that which is intellected, the formal character of the act of intellection? It is not to be «position» of things, because, as we have seen, these are not formal concepts, as Hegel opined. Neither is it to be «ideation,» that is, the elaboration of objective concepts, because these latter are, in any case, posterior to the things themselves, which must be antecedently present to the intelligence. Neither is it to be «intention» as though the *to be* of that which is intellected might be formally and exhaustively «to be correlative to» the intellective intention; thàt is to say, although, in effect, that which is intellected is the correlate of the intellection, nevertheless, its *to be* does not consist formally in being the intentional correlate. The proper and formal act of intellection with respect to that which is intellected is to be mere «actualization» of the thing in the intelligence and therefore that which is intellected, as intellected, is only «actualized.» There is no necessity, at this point, to enter upon a precise determination of what this actualization, as an act of the intelligence, might be in itself, since, as I have said, the elaboration of a theory of the intelligence is not at this point our theme. I take actualization to be a simple, easily ascertainable fact; the only thing

which a thing acquires through intellection is its mere actuality in the intelligence. Intellection is a mere actualization of the thing. Every other conception is unacceptable, before all else, by reason of the absence of ultimate radicality. Position, ideation, intentional correlation, could not be even what they pretend to be (and what they at times effectively are) if they were not simple modalizations — certain modalizations among various others — of what it is to actualize. Further, we must not confuse this character with that other which has so much prestige in contemporary philosophy, thanks to Heidegger, namely, with «unveiling.» Unveiling is not formally an act of intellection, but is rather, in its turn, a special character of actualization. 114 If the thing is unveiled, this is because it is already actualized. The moment of unveiling is based on the moment of actualization. The proper and formal condition of that which is intellected is to be «only» actualized in the intelligence. In this case, «in» does not have the sense of «container and contained» but rather the harmless meaning of to be the terminus of the act. Even less necessary is it for us here to explain this terminal character, because we have no reason to enter into a theory of the intelligence as such. All the so-called intellective acts are either modulations, consequences, or ways of actualization. The intelligence may, for example, «create» objects, but this is because it is «already» moving in the «element» of that which has been anteriorly actualized, etc. And as intellective actualization, because it is «mere» actualization, involves that which has been actualized as something which «already» was something proper in itself (this is what «mere» actualization precisely consists in) it follows that that which «truths» in the intellection is the thing itself, in its own proper character. It is the thing itself which, in actualizing itself, grounds the truth of intellection. The first moment of truth, then, is to be the actualization of the thing in the intelligence.

2. However, this is still not enough, because it is not enough to say that the thing itself is actualized in the intellection. If something more were not the case, there would be no truth. For actually, of what are we treating here? This question refers, naturally, not to what the things may be of which we, as a matter of fact, have intellection but to the formal character of what is intellected, as such. This formal character is «reality.» Here reality does not mean what the thing is in itself, its nature, etc., but, as I have just indicated,

it means only the formal character of that which is apprehended, even though what is apprehended may be a most ephemeral, fugitive, and insignificant quality. This is the sense in which I say that, in
115 truth, one is always concerned with something that «really» is. (And-though I cannot here enter into this question, — the reader should not confuse what I have just called here «reality» with what is ordinarily called *esse reale,* «to be real,» because this *esse reale* is for me, as we will see in its proper place, something impossible *in adjecto.)* That which is intellected is reality not only as a matter of fact, but in its formal mode of being apprehended: to intellect, as such, is to apprehend something as reality or, as I have said so many times in my courses, to come face to face with things as realities. There can, indeed, be other modes of apprehending them; in such cases, however, these apprehensions would not be acts of intelligence. For example, in pure sensation, the things which are apprehended are apprehended, not as real, but as «stimuli.» That things may be *stimuli* which the animal senses, that is to say, that stimulation may be something sensed, is so obvious that there is no need even to mention it. What, however, must be underlined, because sufficient attention has not been paid to it, is that «stimulus» is the proper and constitutive formality of sensing as such: what is sensed *qua* sensed is always and only stimulus. The theory of sensibility is nothing else than the theory of «stimulation.» «Reality,» by contrast, is the proper and constitutive character of the act of intellection as such. What is intellected *qua* intellected is formally «reality.» Stimulus and reality are, before all else, as I am in the habit of saying, the two formal characters, the two formalities of that which is apprehended in its condition as apprehended. This is not the place to work out the precise articulation of stimulus and reality. Let us content ourselves with saying that the stimulus itself can be apprehended in the stimulation itself as really stimulating, that is, as a real stimulus. What happens, in such a case, is that it is no longer pure stimulus and the act of apprehending it is no longer pure sensation. Therefore, that which «truths» in the intellection and is its ground, that is to say, that which is actualized in the intellection, is the real thing itself, as
116 real. This is «one» of the reasons why truth cannot be defined as «unveiling.» In pure sensation the animal possesses the thing as «unveiled;» he lacks truth in a formal sense, however, because the

thing is unveiled only as stimulus and not as reality. Without a real thing «there would not be» truth; without intelligence, however, that is, without an apprehension of the real thing in question as real, what there is with this thing «would not be» truth.

It is clear, as I said before, this actualization is «mere» actualization, that is, the real thing is actualized as something which, on being intellected, does nothing more than become actualized in that which it already was in and by itself, namely, its own proper reality. Reality, although it is the ground of the truth, does not exhaust itself necessarily in this grounding function, because the reality is the ground of truth, but does not, however, *consist* in being the ground of truth. We have already seen this to be true in the particular case of the definition when we discussed Aristotle: the radical structure of reality is not necessarily definable in a *logos*. And we must say the same of all the dimensions of intelligence, including those which do not constitute a formal part of the *logos* itself: reality is not exhausted in nor does it consist in being intellected. In its actualization as reality, therefore, the real thing grounds the truth: however, it is actualized to itself as something which indeed is ground, and is such precisely because it already was reality in a proper sense independently of being intellected, in such wise that in the intellective actuality of the reality, the moment of reality presents itself to us as a *prius* with respect to the moment of its intellective actuality. This is the reason why we can and must say that in the intellective actualization of the real thing, the truth is a truth which belongs to the thing itself, and is a truth of the thing. This is what we express when we say, on the one hand, that the reality as intellected is a «true reality» and, on the other hand, that the truth which it contains is a «real truth.» Let us 117 explain both these ideas, beginning with the second.

(a) Before all else, the real thing as intellected has a «real truth.» This «real truth» is not, however, a «logical» truth, since logical truth is a truth of knowledge, while the real truth is a truth of the thing. Neither is it to be identified with that which is ordinarily called «ontological truth,» that is, with the «conformity» or «measure» of a thing with its concept or objective idea, because in real truth there is no conformity of any kind. All conformity, as a matter of fact, demands two terms, and, therefore, the «exit» from one of them (the real thing) «toward» the other (the concept). In real truth, however, there are not two terms but only one, the real thing itself, since intellection is nothing other than «mere» actualization. What is present in real truth are not two terms, but rather something like two «conditions» of one single term, of the real thing, namely, the condition of «proper» reality and the condition of «actualized» reality. It is a kind of duality intrinsic to the real thing itself on being intellected. These two conditions do not function *ex aequo;* rather the second, as we have already said, (precisely because it is «mere» actualization) not only involves the first formally, but also consists formally and constitutively in immersing us in the former. That is to say, in the act of being intellected, the real thing is not actualized in any indeterminate way but rather in an exceedingly precise form, that is, as an actualization in which the real thing not only is real, but also, in a certain way, itself «refers» back formally from the intellective actuality to its proper reality; that is to say, it is found actualized in and for itself as formally and reduplicatively real. Because, in a word, this sending back and, therefore, this reduplication is an act which is given «in» the intelligence, and solely in it; 118 nevertheless, it is not an act «of» the intelligence, but of the thing, an act in which the latter not only is real, but is in the act of realizing itself as real. And this «act» of being in the act of realizing itself *(estar realizando)* as real is precisely the «actualization» itself; therefore, it is a reduplicating actualization. The reality resides in it two times, as I said before; once, as a moment of the thing («real»), a second, as a moment of its actualization («realizing itself»). The reference back or reduplication is, therefore, a moment or property of the thing itself insofar as it is actualized. This is what I meant by saying that in being intellected the real thing refers formally in and for itself to its proper reality as to a *prius* with respect to intellection. In intellection there is not only the reality, but even more, a ratification, as it were, of the reality on the part of the thing itself. And it is the thing itself which, by the «physical» necessity of this actualization which refers to the reality, «holds us back» in it. The thing holds us back *velis nolis* because its intellective actualization is «physically» a sending back. And, therefore, in the act of intellection, not only is there no «exit» from the real thing to something different from it (concept, idea, etc.) but also, on the contrary, there is a positive and necessary act of «not-exiting,» the act of «standing fast» in what the thing really is, in its proper reality. In the act of intellection, the intelligence «is» *(está)* in the thing (precisely because the latter «resides» *[está]* in the former), though it is a mode of being *(estar)* internally qualified: it is a «to be remaining» in that which the thing is. In the act of intellection, consequently, the real thing is, as I say, ratified in and by itself in its own reality. What I call real truth resides precisely in this: the real truth consists in being in and by itself formally and reduplicatively what it already is. The real truth is not cut-off reality, but «true,» because in the thing, as actualized, there is a duality; nevertheless, it is «real» truth because this duality is not a duality of things but only of conditions; that is, the reality as intellected is a reality such that in the act of being intellected it does not leave the real thing itself but rather that the latter formally 119 ratifies, in and by itself, its reality as such. If one wishes to continue speaking of *measure*, he will have to say that, in real truth, the thing is not measured by the concept, but that the thing is its own measure. For this reason real truth is not identified with ontological truth, but is rather the first and primary supposition of the latter.

This is also, and *a fortiori*, the supposition of all logical truth. Even more, it is the supposition of error itself. Just as there are many modes of actualization, and the intelligence can excercise functions of creation, etc., so also, «already» installed in what is actualized, the intelligence can «err.» Error is possible only in this further act of intellection, and only because the formal act of the intelligence is to actualize. In the primary actualization there is not, nor can there be, anything but real truth. The real thing, in as far as it is intellected, possesses, consequently, a real truth.

(b) For the same reason, however, it can and should be said that the real thing as intellected is a «true reality;» it is that thing itself, in effect, which generates truth in the act of the intellect. The expression «true reality,» however, lends itself to an unavoidable equivocation. For it means, on the one hand, what I have just indicated: reality insofar as it generates truth. On the other hand, however, it signifies only a structural moment of this reality which generates truth; that moment to which we allude when we speak of the «true reality» of anything, of silver, of a ruby, of a dog, of man, of angel, etc. It is clear that «real as opposed to unreal» *(«realidad verdadera»)* is not the same thing as «real as opposed to something else

that is real of a different kind» *(«verdadera realidad»)*. However, since both expressions are so cognate, I will employ them, save when I specifically indicate the contrary, as synonyms; that is to say, when I speak of the *«realidad verdadera,»* I will speak only of the *«ver-*
120 *dadera realidad»* of something, and not of its entire reality. Let us avoid, consequently, for the time being, speaking of «true reality» *(«realidad verdadera»)* and let us say simply that truth is an «attribute» of reality itself.

As a matter of fact, we can use the real truth as a guideline to enable us to enter into the structure of reality. This does not, however, lead us to a third moment of truth.

3. The real truth of any thing, I have said, consists in being in and for itself reduplicatively and formally that which it already is; or, what amounts to the same thing, it consists in a kind of formal ratification of the reality as such, intellective actualization. Although in the intellective act, however, it is always a question of a «mere» actualization, nevertheless, this reduplication or ratification has a structure proper to itself: it is a pluri-dimensional actualization. The real thing formally and reduplicatively ratifies its own proper reality under different aspects. That is to say, real truth has different dimensions, and as in relation to it, it is a question of a ratification of its «own» reality, it follows that real truth discloses to us the different dimensions of reality itself. In each one of these dimensions, however, the entire real thing is projected according to its different dimensions or facets.

Although this pluri-dimensionality is a structure of every real truth as such, and, therefore, although these dimensions are dimensions of every reality, nevertheless, in order to perceive them with greater clarity we can, without diminishing the generality, give our attention more especially to a determinate type of intellective actualization.

There is, to begin with, a «simple» actualization; that in which the real thing is actualized in such a form that, although its notes and qualities are distinguished, nevertheless, these latter are not apprehended, each one by itself, as actually and formally counterdistinguished from the rest and from the thing, that is, as though they were component moments «of» the latter. Not that the real
121 thing does not have different notes, nor that these are not actualized

in their variety in the intellective apprehension, but rather that this variety is, as it were, absorbed into the primary unity of the thing. This happens when there is a question, for example, of an elementary color or elementary sound, as long as we do not make an effort to perceive what intensity or tonality they may have within the optical or acoustical range. The same thing happens when it is a question of realities which are complex to the highest degree, when the active intellection apprehends them in a certain way *en bloque,* and as absorbed in them in, so to say, a compact form. Insofar, however, as we perceive those elemental realities by actualizing, in their mutual distinction, these qualitative characteristics, such as intensity, etc., we no longer have a simple actualization of «reality,» of «a real thing,» but rather, a different actualization: the actualization of reality which «possesses» or has those characteristics. In such a case, something happens which might be characterized as an unfolding between «real thing» and «note possessed.» And this, which is true when it is a question of such elementary realities as a color or a sound, is much more true, one can see, when it is a question of almost all the other realities which we intellect, because practically all of the rest are intellected as things which have such or such notes, as their real moments. Every act of intellection, therefore, in which the thing is actualized as possessing certain notes as its real moments, is clearly a «mere» actualization, but is, nevertheless, a complex actualization. For example, the actualization of «hardness» would be a simple actualization and nothing more; by contrast, the actualization of a «thing which is hard» would be complex; we will call it, for reasons of simplicity «a hard thing.» We shall consider this last type of actualization in order to discover with greater clarity the pluridimensionality of real truth as such.

In a word, we may ask, in what does the «complexity» of this actualization consist? In the «hard thing,» the «hardness» is a physical 122 moment of the reality (which is also physical) of the «thing.» Let us not prejudge the character of this «moment,» that is to say, the character of the presumed «relation» between the thing and its hardness; we are not, at this point, examining the meaning of «to have.» For example, we will not wish to say that the thing is the «cause» of the hardness, and even less, that it is the subject «of» that hardness, the subject which «has» that hardness, etc. For

precisely this reason, we will say, in a manner which is neutral, but
still radical and formal, that the thing is actually hard, that is to say,
that it is actualized «in» hardness, and that the hardness is actual
«in» it, etc. This actuality has nothing to do with intellection, but is,
rather, a structure which is, in a physical sense, proper to the thing:
hardness is, in itself, something real; the thing is real and so too is
the actualization of hardness in the thing. From this it follows that
when the hardness is intellectively actualized, the «thing» is also
actualized intellectively, not by itself nor before itself, but neither
by something that would be a «representative» of it *(«representa-
ción»)*, but rather «in» the hardness itself, that is to say, insofar as it
is physically actualized in this hardness. There is, consequently, the
physical actualization of the thing in its hardness, the intellective
actualization of the hardness, and in its turn, the intellective actualization of the thing in its hardness, that is to say, the intellective
actualization «hard thing.» There is no question of an illative apprehension, since, as we have said, it is not necessary that, between a
thing and its notes, there exist a distinction such that there is «first»
an apprehension of the note and «afterward» an apprehension of the
thing, but rather that, because the thing is physically actual «in»
the hardness, when the hardness is intellectually actualized, the thing
itself is *eo ipso* intellectually actualized. It is, then, a primary but
special form of «mere» actualization because it is the actualization
of a reality physically actual in its notes. It is not a complex of
actualizations, but a complex actualization.

　　This complex «hard thing» is that to which, as to a reality in the
123 proper sense, the intellectual actualization formally and reduplicatively refers, that which makes the act of the intellect true, veridicous.
The ratification of the reality in its proper character, that is, real
truth, has a complex character. What it is now important for us to
determine about this complexity is its proper structure.

　　A. In the first place, it is a ratification of the reality of the «thing,»
as hard, to be sure, but nevertheless of the «thing» itself. Insofar as
this is a thing which is physically actual in its notes or real moments,
we call it reality *simpliciter*. And since it is actualized in the act of
the intellection, in virtue of these same notes, it follows that this
reality is that which ultimately and radically makes the intellective
act veridicous. This is the reason why it is true reality *(realidad ver-*

dadera). And it is this in two senses: because it makes the intellective act veridicous and because it is what is physically actualized in the notes, it is, preeminently, the true reality *(verdadera realidad).* True reality, reality *simpliciter,* is not, then, the whole of the reality of the thing, but rather the ultimate and radical grounding reality of all that is real «in» anything.

The sending back to this reality is, as I have said, primary; there is no question of a process of reasoning. To be sure, it is something more than problematical to grasp intellectively what in each thing may be its reality *simpliciter,* its true reality; this is one of the most difficult tasks of human knowledge, more liable to error than any other, and which, even in the greater number of the most favorable instances, can achieve only modest approximations. Nevertheless, that which is immediate and in which no error can befall, but what is primary real truth, is the mere sending back to this reality *simpliciter,* to something which, as «thing,» in the most unconstricted and free acceptance of the word and, no matter what kind of thing it might be, is actualized in its notes as in real moments of itself.

B. The real truth, because it is a ratification of the proper reality of the thing, is the rigorous way of access to the structure of reality. Therefore, since the physical actuality of the reality *simpliciter* 124 in its real notes, and, consequently, in its intellective actualization, is complex, it follows that in the process of sending back to that reality, an entire compass of different and possible dimensions of ratification, that is to say, of real truth, remains open. These different dimensions of the real truth are nothing more than ratifications of the different structural dimensions of the reality *simpliciter* itself and therefore the pluri-dimensionality of the real truth constitutes not only a plurality of ways of access to the reality, but also the intellective actualization of the different dimensions proper to the real, taken as real. In order to discover these, then, we must necessarily have recourse to the real truth.

Before doing so, we lay stress for the last time on an observation which earlier insinuated itself into our considerations, namely, that, although we speak now only of «complex» actualization, nevertheless, what that form of actualization teaches us is valid for all actualization, even simple actualization. For what it teaches is not specific to complex actualization, as complex, but precisely as actualization.

10

The different dimensions of real truth are to be found exactly equal
in simple actualization. What happens is that in simple actualization,
differently than in complex, the different dimensions correspond
exactly to each other so that it is difficult to distinguish them at first
glance. By contrast, in complex actualization, the very complexity
serves as a physical analyzer which, in a certain way, separates the
different dimensions of the truth. However, there is nothing more; as
dimensions they are dimensions of every real truth and every intellection, whether simple or complex, and of every reality whether or
not it be elemental. It is clear, of course, that there are other types
of actualization, different both from the complex and from the simple.
We need not enter upon a description of them here, because we are
not engaged in the elaboration of a theory of the intelligence. We may
be content to say only that these other actualizations formally presup-
125 pose complex actualization. As a consequence, what we have said or
may say of the latter is, *eo ipso*, valid for all intellective actualization as such.

Having established this much we may ask, what, concretely, is this
pluri-dimensionality and what, effectively, are these different dimensions of reality?

We grasp a real thing intellectively in its notes. However, this
actualization, expressed in the «in» can be seen in different ways.
One way consists in going from without inward. The point of departure is taken in the notes and these are viewed as something which
affects (as accidents) the real thing, their subject (substance). In this
case, it is seen that the entire reality of the notes is based in this
their inhesion in the thing-subject. This inhesion may take different
forms such as: qualification, quantification, localization, etc. Each
of these modes of inhesion is a «mode of to be» of the accident. As
this inhesion is expressed in a judgment, the copula «is» not only
states the inherent note, but also «recognizes» the very mode of
inhesion. What is expressed by «recognizes» is expressed in Greek as
κατηγορεῖν. The different modes of to be of accidents, that is, the
different modes of inhesion, are, for this reason, «categories» of the
being. Such is Aristotle's point of view.

However, it is possible to see in the real thing, not the subject
which «has» the notes, but something which is «actualized» in them.

In that case, we follow a path the inverse of the former: we proceed from within outward. One takes his point of departure in the thing and we see in the notes, not something which a subject has, but rather that in which the thing is actual. In this actualization, we find the entire thing actualized in each of its notes; or better, in their totality; a kind of projection of the thing in the entire body of its notes. Then there is no longer any question of a mode of inhesion, but rather of a structure of actualization or projection. The difference from the earlier point of view is clear. Considering them from the point of view of the substance in which they inhere, Aristotle sees the notes only as a mere «flowering» from the substance (under- 126 standing the term flowering in the widest sense, as active as well as passive, etc.). This flowering is undifferentiated; differences exist only in the mode of inhesion. Each mode excludes the others; for example, quality has nothing in common with quantity, etc. (We may prescind, for the moment, from the question whether «all» the categories which Aristotle enumerates are, as a matter of fact, really distinct). By contrast, in this other way of viewing the matter, of which we have spoken, there is no question of a «flowering,» but of an «actualization» or «projection,» of the real thing in the totality of its notes, not only in each of them in itself, as happens in the flowering of Aristotle. Further, it is an actualization which can take place in different ways, under different formal aspects. Each of these latter, then, is precisely what I call «dimension» because in each of them the entire thing is measured or determined. Since the real thing is totally present in each dimension, it follows that in its projection in one dimension, all of the other dimensions are found implicated in one way or another; therefore, instead of excluding each other, as happens in the case of the modes of inhesion, these dimensions imply each other, mutually. This, clearly, limits the concept of dimension. Physical or geometrical dimensions have to be independent of each other. This is not the case in what we call «dimensions» of the reality, because, as we have just said, and as we shall see again and again, these dimensions mutually imply each other; their independence of each other is only very limited and relative. In this sense, they cannot be compared to physical or geometrical dimensions. Strictly speaking, it is a question of the «formal respects» of the actuality of a thing in its notes; and as respects they are distinct. If I call them dimensions, it is because, in each of them, the reality of a thing is determined or measured and because, as respects, they are first or basic. Thus clarified, the term dimension can and ought to be used.

127   The view from without inward is a way of viewing as inhesion and leads to a theory of the categories of being. The view from within outward is a view of actualization or projection and leads to a theory of the dimensions of reality. These two manners of viewing are not incompatible; rather, both are necessary for an adequate theory of reality. Our concern at the moment, however, is only the discovery of the dimensions of reality.

Which are these dimensions? To ascertain this point, let us remember that the real truth is a ratification of the reality itself. Since reality is pluri-dimensional, the projection of the reality in each dimension will give rise to a precise or special mode of ratification, that is to say, a specific mode of real truth. Therefore, the real truth will also have different modes or dimensions of truth which are mutually implicative, although in some cases one dimension may dominate the others. The structure of projectivity consists precisely in this. This is a matter of fact. The real truth is the necessary guideline, not only for arriving at the reality *simpliciter*, but also for discovering its dimensions. These dimensions of the real truth are, fundamentally, three.

(a) In intellection, the real thing is actualized when the multitude of the notes in which it is physically actual, is realized. There notes, however, actualize the thing in determined formal respects. In a first respect, they actualize it as notes which, in being intellected, place the thing (wholly or in part) in the open. Then, the ratification of the reality in its proper character as merely revealed in and by its notes, is what we call «patentization» *(patentización)*. This is the first dimension of real truth. The «patentization» to which I here allude is not the «unveiling» *(Unverborgenheit)* of Heidegger, but only the

128 mode in which the thing is actualized, that is, by way of its notes which place it in the open. The thing, then, is something «unsound-able» *(«insondable»)*, which the notes tend to disclose. The thing, as a matter of fact, is physically actualized in its notes. Insofar as they are revealers of all that it unfathomably is or can give of itself, the thing itself remains actualized in the notes under a very determined

respect: as a thing endowed with internal «richness». The notes are richness, not as taken in themselves, but insofar as they actually reveal the thing. Richness, therefore, as a physical aspect of the actualization of the thing in its notes is, for this reason, a «physical» dimension of that thing; its first dimension. Viewed from its own viewpoint from within, the thing «is rich» in notes. In this dimension, the revelatory character of the notes, that is to say, the projection of the entire reality of the thing in the dimension of richness, is what we call «manifestation» («*manifestación*»). This denomination is not sufficently exact, because there is no manifestation save before someone (in this case, before an intelligence), and the manifestation to which we are alluding has nothing to do with whether the thing is or is not intellected. In its own proper character, what we call manifestation is nothing other than a physical actuality in the dimension of richness. But since this same actuality is that which, on becoming intellective, manifests the thing, makes it patent, we may call it, *a potiori*, manifestation. Hence, we will say that patentization is nothing other than one type of manifestation which the richness of the thing possesses among a thousand others: intellective manifestation. In a word, the real truth has a primary or basic dimension, «patentization.» In it, the proper reality of the thing is ratified in its internal dimension of «richness.» And the actuality of the thing, as a whole, formally in this dimension of it, is «manifestation.»

(b) The notes actualize the real thing intellectively in another dimension: as something which merits the confidence which the notes arouse. The ratification of the reality in itself as something actualized in notes which make it an object of confidence is what we call 129 «securidad.» Joined to the dimension of patentization, real truth possesses the dimension of security: that is true of which it is possible to be secure, in which and about which one can rest confident. All reality, to be reality, must have a minimum of this quality. In their character as credentials of the security of the thing, the notes actualize this thing in another, perfectly determined, formal respect: «solidity.» In this context, the term does not have a geometrical or physical meaning. Quite the contrary, physical and geometrical bodies possess only a certain kind of solidity, «material» solidity. Etymologically, solid means firm, resistent. In this strict sense, solidity leaves open the possibility of different types: static solidity, dynamic solidity, or some other type different from, and superior to, both. In the actuality of its notes, then, everything is endowed, in addition to richness, with internal solidity. Here we have the other real dimension of the thing as seen from within: solidity. In a word, real truth possesses a dimension of «security» in which the proper reality of the thing is ratified in the internal dimension of its «solidity.» The actuality of the thing as a whole in its notes, in this formal dimension of solidity, is what we call «firmness.» This, too, is a denomination *a potiori.* In itself, firmness is nothing else than a formal respect of the physical actualization of the thing in its notes, and has nothing to do with intellection. However, since this same formal respect is that which is actualized in the intellect in the form of security, we may call it, *par excellence,* firmness.

(c) Finally, the notes actualize the real thing in the intellect in a third dimension: as notes which «proclaim» (make public) the «real» character of the thing, or, if one wishes, the character of reality of its actualization in determined notes. The ratification of the proper reality of the thing as actualized in notes which promulgate it simply as real, is what we call «constatation» *(constatación).* Together with the dimensions of patentization and of security, real truth possesses a dimension of constatation. As constatation of the real character (character as real) of the thing, the notes actualize the thing under a formal and precisely determined respect, a respect which we may call «being in actual being» *(estar siendo)* (actually exercising the act of being), placing the emphasis on the «*estar.*» We may recall that, in classical Latin, *stare, estar,* sometimes has the meaning of *esse, ser,* to be, but in a «strong» sense. The word then passed, in this way, into some other romanic languages to express being, not in any manner whatsoever, but «physical» reality precisely as «physical.» With this development, *esse, ser,* to be, remained ascribed almost exclusively to its sense in grammatical usage, as the copula. Only rarely does the «to be» express the profound and permanent, in contrast to the circumstantial, which is then expressed in the «*estar;*» as when one says of anyone that he *is* a sick man (constitutively), something very different from «not being well» (circumstantial). Exceptions do, of course, occur to what we have just said, but the basic shade of meaning is perfectly perceptible. For the circumstantial, precisely because it is circumstantial, involves the «physical» moment of its realization, while the profound and permanent «to be» denotes much rather the «mode of to be» and not its «physical» character. For this reason the phrase *estar siendo*, «actually to exercise (circumstantially) the profound act of (constitutive) being» is, perhaps, the phrase which best expresses the character of «physical» reality with which every real thing is endowed, and which is intellectively ratified in the constatation. In the actuality of its notes, every thing, in addition to richness and solidity, is also endowed with that which we call its «*estar siendo*,» actual, though circumstantial, exercise of the act of to be *(ser)*. The thing then, is actualized in its notes under the general aspect of «actually exercising the act of being» *(estar siendo)*. This is the third dimension of the real thing viewed as real from within. This character of «physical» reality is not «mere» reality, as though it left outside itself the «what» that is real, to wit: these determined notes of the thing. Quite the contrary, it is 131 just these notes which are under consideration, in their most determinate «suchness» and in which, precisely as these notes, the thing possesses its «this» physical reality. Just as the notes are not richness taken in themselves, but rather taken as revealing actuality, neither are they in themselves an «actual exercise of the act of being» *(estar siendo);* they have this latter status only as actuality which proclaims the thing. This is why the «actual exercise of the act of being» *(estar siendo)* is a physical dimension of the thing. Therefore, the actuality of the thing as a whole in its notes, in this physical and formal dimension of «exercising the act of being» is what we call «effectivity» *(efectividad)*. It is a real moment of the thing which has nothing to do with intellection. However, the effectivity of the thing in the act of intellection, that is to say, the intellective effectivity of actually exercising the act of being *(estar siendo)*, is constatation.

Real truth, that is to say, the ratification of the reality in itself in the act of intellection, has then three dimensions: patentization, security, constatation. Every truth possesses then indefectably and indissolubly. None of the three has a preferential status, nor any kind of prerogative over the other two. The three are generated together as structural moments of the primary intellective actualization of a real thing. Nevertheless, they are formally different, so much so that their deployment in *further intellection* modifies fundamentally the tone of man's attitude before the problem of reality.

Man, in a word, can move about intellectually according to his preference amid the «unfathomable» richness of the thing. He sees in its notes something like its richness in eruption. He is in a state of insecurity with respect to every and all things. He does not know whether he will reach any part, nor does the paucity of clarity and of security which he may encounter on his path disturb him overmuch. What interests him is to stir up reality, to make manifest and to unearth its riches; to conceive them and to classify them with precision. It is a perfectly defined kind of intellection: intel-
132 lection as adventure. Other times, moving cautiously *(a tientas)* and, as it were, in the twilight, as he must in order not to stumble or to become disoriented in his movements, man seeks in things securities on which to base himself intellectually with firmness. It is possible, that, proceeding in this fashion, he may let fall by the way great riches in things; but this, however, is the price of reaching what is secure in them. He pursues the firm as «the true;» the rest, no matter how rich it may be, is no more than the shade of reality and truth, the «verisimilar.» It is intellection as achievement of the reasonable. On other occasions, finally, he precisely restricts the range and the figure or pattern of his intellectual movements amid reality. He seeks the clear constatation of his own reality, the aristate profile of what he effectively is. In principle, nothing remains excluded from this pretension; however, even when it is necessary to carry out painful amputations, he accepts them; he prefers that everything in which he does not achieve the ideal of clarity should remain outside the range of intellection. It is intellection as science, in the widest sense of that term. All true intellection has an element of hazard in it, some element of reasonableness and some element of science; because patentization, security, and constatation are three constitutive dimensions of real truth and as such cannot be renounced. However, the predominance of some of these qualities over the others in the development of the intellection qualifies the intellectual attitude.

These three dimensions of real truth (patentization, security, constatation) are three dimensions in which the thing is ratified in its proper reality and they correspond, therefore, to three structural moments of the thing, whether or not it is intellected: manifestation, firmness, and effectivity. And each of these three moments is the projection or actualization of what the thing «really» is: in manifestation there is actualized the reality of its richness, in firmness the reality of its solidity, in effectivity the thing is actualized in its 133 exercise of the act of being *(estar siendo)*. Richness, solidity, existence, are, then, the three formal respects of the actuality of a thing in its notes. In these dimensions, the reality of the thing is determined and measured; these dimensions, as we shall see in another place, are what determine and measure its «degree of reality.» Degree of reality thus receives its univocal and precise definition. This is the reason why those three formal respects of physical actualization are, strictly speaking, called «dimensions» of the real thing as seen from within as real. They are not respects extrinsic to the reality of the thing, as though we «first» had the real thing actualized in its notes independently of every dimension, and «afterward» this reality is modulated «by adding to it» these three dimensions. On the contrary, these aspects belong intrinsically, as its constitutive dimensions, to the reality of the thing as such, and cannot be dissociated from it. The contrary would be, as it were, to pretend that a cube or a sphere were geometrical realities independently of all dimensions, and that the dimensions were three aspects under which I contemplate them extrinsically. This is simply absurd; as realities, the sphere and the cube are intrinsically «dimensioned,» are intrinsically «dimensional;» without dimensions they would be nothing. Reality is intrinsically and formally dimensional, insofar as it is real. Correspondingly, what is actualized in them is precisely reality *simpliciter*.

The analysis of truth, which we have just sketched, has not been, then, a vain speculation on the fringe of our problem, but quite the contrary: it has laid bare for us, within the truly real, the reality *simpliciter*, not as an empty logical or conceptual determination, but in its intrinsic dimensional texture, in the entire plenitude of what the thing is: richness, solidity, actual exercise of existence *(estar siendo)*. The dimensions are not merely formalistic aspects, but express the internal fullness of what the thing is in its reality. 134

These three dimensions are mutually implicated in the structure of the reality *simpliciter*. Only a determined richness of notes can possess the solidity necessary for its actual existence, the actual exercise of the act of being *(estar siendo)*; only that which has solidity in its actual exercise of existence *(estar siendo)* can possess a true

richness of notes; only that which truly actually exists has a minimum
of richness and solidity, precisely because it exists, etc. As a consequence, the character of essentiated reality is found in the primary
unity of these structural dimensions of reality. What is this unity?
What is its formal character? These are the questions to which we
must address ourselves. Let us begin with the first.

SECTION TWO

STRUCTURAL UNITY OF REALITY *SIMPLICITER*

The road we must take in order to encounter the structural unity
of reality *simpliciter* has already been traced out in what we have just
finished saying. That implication of the three dimensions in the structure of reality already clearly indicates that the three terms, richness,
solidity, and the actual exercise of existence *(estar siendo)*, do not
have the vague, even metaphorical, meaning which they usually
possess but, rather, designate three structures, or, I might say with
greater rigor, three eminently precise structural dimensions. In
speaking of richness, for example, one runs the risk of thinking that
it is a matter of a simple abundance of notes. This is not the case,
however; it is the richness of the thing «with reference to» its solid,
actual exercise of existence. The same is true of solidity and of the
act of existence. Consequently, in trying to learn the unity of those
three structural dimensions as the reality *simpliciter* of any thing,
we suspect that, perhaps, not all of the notes which a thing may
possess *hic et nunc* may help us in the solution of our problem,
because not all of these notes are moments of the rich and solid
exercise of existence *(estar siendo)* of that thing. To begin, consequently, we must discern the type of notes which belong to reality
simpliciter.

In the first place, in every real thing there are notes which refer
to its connection, whether active or passive, necessary or contingent,
with other realities. A living thing, for example, has need of nourishment. However, in this meaning these notes belong to that thing

in what might be called an oblique manner. In notes of this type, richness is a kind of profusion very similar to mere abundance; solidity is more nearly consolidation; and the exercise of existence *(estar siendo)* is a kind of self-maintenance, a self-conservation in 136 reality. However, this profusion, consolidation, and maintenance presuppose the more radical richness, solidity, and actual existence of the real thing. For this reason, the notes with which our problem is concerned are those which the real thing would possess when considered in itself, independently of the notes which it might possess by reason of its connection with other realities or by reason of the absence of such connection. A man, a dog, are gaunt or fat, in part by reason of the nourishment they take; however, what is important to us at this moment is the obesity which, as a matter of fact, they possess independently of its connection with the food they consume. And this is true *a fortiori* if it is a question of notes which are not derived from any connection of a thing with other things; for example (if we prescind from genetic considerations), the heart, the brain of a dog, his weight, his visual sensibility, etc. These notes, not derivative from any connection of a thing with other things, or even things so derived as long as we consider them in themselves independently of any such derivation, are what we call, without especially belaboring the denomination, notes of a formal type; these refer to the thing considered in itself. By contrast, we will call those notes which constitute the connections among things notes of a causal type. Only the notes of a formal type are relevant to the richness, the solidity, and the actual act of existing of which we are speaking.

In the second place, not all the notes of a formal type belong to the reality *simpliciter* of a thing. There are notes which, as we have said, the thing may possess only by reason of its connection with other things, even though that which is acquired through this connection may be in itself a formal note. There are, by contrast, other formal notes which are not due to any such connection, but rather to the very character of the thing or at least to the synergy of both factors (character and connection). As examples, we may take obesity itself, if a special metabolic disposition contributes to it; the specific heat and the valency of a chemical element; the normal color of the skin of a given race; the phenotypical peculiarities, whether belong- 137 ing to a type or to individuals, more or less indelible, perhaps controlled by the genes, whether of a morphological or a functional order; etc. All these notes which form part of what is commonly called the nature of a thing, we will call notes of a constitutional type, in contrast to the others which are notes of an adventitious type.

The primary structure of a thing, then, is the «constitution.» This is exactly the reason why I have decided to give philosophical status to this concept. The constitution understood in this way is «physical» and not logical in character; it is also strictly individual.

It is above all something «physical.» In biology, especially in human physiological pathology, it is customary to call constitution that conjunction of individual morphological and functional peculiarities which are «innate»(?). However, it is necessary to broaden the concept and introduce into it physical characteristics of a specific type (the genotype). The constitution then is, in effect, the *compago*, the basic physical complexity or structure of the real thing which determines, even physically, all its other characteristic notes as well as its characteristic actions and passions. In saying that it is «physical,» I am averting to the fact that it is, in the first instance, neither formally conceptual nor something merely objective. That is to say, we are not speaking of a «species» which is articulated by genus and difference. For the rest, the question of what, in each particular case, constitutes the «physical» complexion, remains open: its physico-chemical, psychological, social, moral, historical, etc. properties.

Integrated through all these notes, the constitution is also something strictly «individual.» Individual, before all else, «in itself;» that is, because there is nothing real which is not individual. Individual also «for itself» and not something merely individualized. Individuation, in a word, is not a special «principle» within the reality 138 of the thing, but rather a simple «moment» of it, that moment which establishes the thing as this irreducible physical unity, by reason of which, for example, we say that this individual is formally «this.» To be «this» is to be formally an irreducible physical unity. This character, however, must be correctly understood. The term «individuality,» with which it is customary to designate that character, has the double inconvenience of being purely formalistic and merely negative. Formalistic, because it moves exclusively in the line of the multiplicity of the «one» and of the «other» without paying any attention to the inner character of this unity. Negative, because it centers itself in the idea of «*in*-division,» which ends by «formalizing» the pure «one.» Nevertheless, since no other term is available, we will use this word «individuality» to designate that character of every reality by reason of which this reality is not physically the other.

Adverting, then, not to this formalistic character of the individual unity itself, we discover two radically different types, not only of individuals, but even more importantly, of individuality. One is the reality, the individuality of which consists in being merely a numerical unity; the individual in question is not other and in this not-being-other all its individuality is exhausted. Every individual, no matter what its character, is not other; however, in the individuals to which we are now referring, their individuality consists «only» in not being other. By reason of their content, consequently, these individuals are exactly and exhaustively equal; they differ only through forming a mere numerical mulitplicity. I will call this type of individual a *singulum*, or also an individual or a *singular individuality*. There is, however, another type of individuality whose unity and internal content are eminently positive and are expressed by the term and the concept «constitution.» Individuality, *sensu stricto*, is not a simple numerical unity. This numerical unity, so fundamental for many aspects of the problem (we will return to this point and, in general, 139 to the problem of individuality in the following paragraph), is, nevertheless, radically insufficient in these individualities. Individuality, properly so-called, possesses, in addition to this numerical unity, an internal determination. The individuality of this type of individuals I shall call *strict* individuality, in order to distinguish it from singular individuality, a distinction which, many years ago, I stated in my courses in opposition to the interpretation of these terms as synonyms as is usual in scholasticism which always speaks of *singulare sive individuum*. It is necessary, however, to understand this unity of internal determination correctly.

In the first place, strict individuality does not indicate what distinguishes one thing from another within the same species. We do not know, as a matter of fact, whether or not other individuals of the same species do exist or can exist for the simple reason that we do not as yet know anything about the «physical species» as such.

Strict individuality means the real integral constitution of the thing with all its notes, whether these be different from those of other individuals or whether, on the contrary, they are totally or partially common to other individuals or even to all individuals. The internal differentiation does not, in the first place, fulfill a differential function, but a constituting function proper to the thing.

In the second place, the determination belongs formally to the individual as such. Let us make ourselves clear. In the perspective of the «species» — which we shall later discuss in greater detail — it is customary to say that the moment of individuality affects primarily and formally the mere numerical multiplicity of the specific moment, and that the rest are nothing but modifications which supervene upon this numerical multiplicity. Let us take, for example, an albino man. In the interpretation to which I am making reference, its structure would be the following: «this man» + albino. Albino would be a
140 modification of this numerical human individual. This, however, cannot be admitted. Physically, strict individuality, the «this,» affects primarily and formally the entire constitutional complexion of the man in question, and not the human «species» of which «this man» would be nothing but a «singular» example or instance. Albinism is a constitutional character. In this way, the structure would be: this «man + albino.» Thus, the moment of irreducible unity would be merely numerical in the first interpretation, while in the second, by reason of the physical complexion of the thing, the unity itself, in each one of the things, possesses its own proper and peculiar way of being one. The unities do not differ by reason only of their contents, but also by reason of the very way in which they are one, or unities. This is to say, in every strict individual reality, there is a unity of content of its notes and a merely numerical unity, according to which that reality is irreducibly «this one.» There is no question, however, of two unities, but only of two aspects of one sole and intrinsically unique unity. This modification is what we call internal determination. The numerical unity thus modified or determined is what I understand by constitution: it is the peculiar or proper way which «each» thing has of being «this,» or being numerically one; if one wishes, the nature of its «being-unity.» The unity proves to be numerical thanks precisely to the constitution, and not the reverse. In the first interpretation, to which I referred earlier, «this man» would be a *singulum* to which

a modification «albino» would be added; in the second, which we are proposing here, «this albino man» is a true individual, intrinsically individual. Thus, then, the intrinsic and proper «mode» of being physically and irreducibly one, is precisely that which we call, from the philosophical point of view, «constitution.» When this has been stated, it becomes possible to call this structure, pleonastically, «individual constitution.»

In order to treat the point completely, it should be said that 141 reality offers the two types of unities: there are merely singular individual realities and there are others, like human individuals, which always are, and alone can be, individuals in the strict sense. I will return to this point. Strictly speaking, the concept of constitution can be applied to these singular individuals also; however, it is useless to do so here, because, even if it be admitted that they might be substantive realities, their constitution would be reduced to the possession of minimal characteristics, exactly and exhaustively repeated in all these *singuli*. Since these singulars are rare and, furthermore, have a special character, I shall refer in what follows only to individuals. When I have occasion to refer to all individuals, both singular and in the strict sense, I shall either do so expressly or the context will not lend itself to confusion.

On this supposition, it is clear that suchness, solidity, and the actual exercise of the act of existence *(estar siendo)* must be sought for in those notes which are constitutional in character. The real thing projects itself in these three dimensions, and it is in them that the differences of reality among things are, in the first instance, measured. Things, then, in fact, have a different constitution, before all else, in the dimension of richness; there are realities which are either more or less rich than others and which manifest this richness in different notes as much by reason of their wealth *(caudal)* as by that of their specific quality. Realities may, however, differ not only in richness, but in some other dimension as well. There are realities which by their constitution are more or less solid than others and which evidence this solidity in notes which are more or less firmly constituted. A material body is, with respect to constitution, less solid than a spirit; and this not in the sense of the «forces» which hold these realities together (in the case of spirit these would be no 142 more than metaphorical) but by reason of the very character of the thing which is actualized in its notes, of which some are in themselves more inadmissible than others. Finally, real things are variable and differ in the very manner of exercising the act of existence *(estar siendo);* there are some which in their notes have greater or less individual effectuality than others. Once the constitution has been determined in its three dimensions (what I have already said about this conception of dimension is not to be forgotten) what we call their «degree» of reality is actualized in them. I said before that these three dimensions mutually imply each other in the reality of the thing and that for this reason richness, solidity, and act of existing *(estar siendo)* must be taken «as one.» But this «as one» is nothing other than the structural unity of the reality *simpliciter* of any thing: its individual physical constitution. What this tri-dimensionality affects, in the first place, is the constitution. The structural unity of the real, then, is, taken concretely, «constitution.»

143   SECTION THREE

FORMAL CHARACTER OF THE UNITY OF THE REAL

Having arrived at this point, it is necessary to take a further step and ask ourselves what type of unity is proper to the constitution. Only when we know this shall we have arrived at an understanding of the reality *simpliciter* of anything and, therefore, of the essential reality. Of course, constitutional unity is not an additive unity. Addition presupposes the unities, or units, as such, and what one does with them is a mere unification or union, an operation following upon the previously given unities; the unity which results is one in which every element formally retains its own unity; it is a unity, therefore, which is also consequent on the process of addition. A heap or crowd, a wall of bricks, a rock, a colony, etc., are additive unities, unifications, unions.

Such is not the case with constitutional unity. An atom of silver is not a simple addition of elementary particles, nor is water a mere addition of atoms; a dog is not a conglomerate of chemical elements, nor of cells additively coupled; it is not a mosaic either in the order of its constitution or in that of its functioning. Were such the case, we would not have one thing, but many. Anticipating ideas which I shall explicate in detail at a later point, I will say that constitutional unity is not a union or unification, but a primary unity. Primary means that, whatever be the mechanism of its production, in that unity, once it exists, each note is a function of the others, in such wise that only in and by reason of its unity with the others is each note what it is within the real thing. In this sense, the unity dominates, is a *prius*, with regard to the possession of each note considered in isolation. The unity is not the «source» of the notes, though each 144 note is present in the thing in and by reason of its «pre-existing» function with respect to the rest. For this reason, once this primary unity has been established, the elements which constitute it no longer retain their individual unity within that constitution. In a multicelled organism, each cell is something different from what a unicellular living thing might be. Hence, the constitutional notes, as moments of a primary unity, constitute that which we call a «system.» It is this system which is formally tri-dimensional. Individuals constituted in this way are systems of notes.

In what does a system consist concretely? A system possesses a variety of fundamental characteristics. Before all else, there is the internal concatenation and interdependence of all its notes. Internal: as the result of its primary unity. Interdependence, because they are mere moments of this unity. In virtue of this unity, these notes are relatively indissociable. Not in the sense that the notes can never be separated, but in the sense that, if they are separated (as happens in some systems), the system disappears by disintegration. In what does this concatenation of interdependent notes precisely consist? It is not the question whether some notes derive from others; this can occur and necessarily must occur with some notes though not with all (we will see this later). Neither is it the question whether each note has a repercussion on the rest. It is true that each note acts or reacts in one way or another and in one measure or another on all the other notes. This process of action and reaction does not, however, constitute the system but is, rather, a consequence of it: every note has a repercussion on the others precisely because it forms a system with them. The concatenation of interdependent notes consists formally in

a «position» of each note with respect to all the others. The position
is something which is expressed in the function which a note fulfills
145 with respect to the others. Let us take an example from an order
which is very clearly functional. Every animal organism has a weight.
It has this weight, without the least doubt, by reason of the substances
of which it is composed. However, independently of this «origin» the
weight possesses a very determined biological «signification.» This
signification is nothing else than the functional expression of the
«position» which the weight has in the system of the constitutional
notes of the organism in question. Only this position *enters* formally
into the constitutional system as such. However, we must not confuse
this idea of «position» with another, very different, Aristotelian idea.
Aristotle «ordered» the notes of a substance according to *genera,
differences*, and *species;* one might be led to think that this is an
effort similar to that of fixing the position of a note in the system.
However, this is not the case. In the first place because, as we are
about to see immediately, there is no question here of substances, but
of systems. In the second place, because this ordering of Aristotle's
is an ordering by inclusion of some «aspects» in others, while here it
is a question of a connection or concatenation of some «notes» with
others; Aristotle's ordering, therefore, is «conceptive» and «objective,»
while that of a system is «physical.» If one should wish to call
genera and *differentia* notes, it would be necessary to say that they
are incomplete «notes» in the order of notes. Life, taken in itself,
without further qualification, is not a note, properly speaking; only
«vegetative life» or «sensitive life» can properly be called notes.
Moreover, in the strictest sense, not even these notes are complete
notes, because a complete note would only be something like «the
sensitive life of this individually determined living thing.» And these
notes, «physically» complete in the order of notes, are those of which
we say that they form a system, in that each of them has its perfectly
determined position with respect to all the others; for example,
nervous stimulation with respect to the metabolic functions, etc.
146 «Position,» then, is a physical, and not a conceptive or objective
character; it is at once, in itself, the systematic connection of notes
while each one of these latter is a note endowed with complete physical
reality in the order of notes. As a consequence, we say that a system

is a concatenated or connected conjunction of positionally interdependent notes.

However, in every constitutional system there is something more.
The conjunction of notes which constitutes it is, as it were, closed
in upon itself. This closure is not an incommunication with other
realities, that is to say, it is not a question of a closedness within
the order of the connection of realities, but rather in the order of the
connection of the notes of a reality within itself; meaning that these
notes form something complete or concluded in the order of formal
characteristics. If it were permitted us to suggest a figurative idea of
this conclusion, we would say that a constitutional system is a cyclical
system of notes; in the figure of the circle, what we are trying to say
is figuratively expressed. We do not, however, place excessive emphasis
or reliance on this figure or think it over-successful. Not all systems
are circular, though all possess what the circular systems have in
their circularity: conclusion, closedness.

Constitutional unity is, then, a primary unity whose distinct notes
are nothing other than concatenated moments positionally interdependent in closed form; it is the unity of a system. This constitutional
character is precisely what we call «substantivity.» What the constitution constitutes is a substantivity, and the reality constituted in
this manner is a substantive reality. When I explained the idea of
complete *intellective* actualization, I made a point of the fact that I
did not insist on the presumed «relation» between a thing and its
notes, and that I was limiting myself to saying in a neutral, though
nevertheless basic, way that the thing is actual «in» its notes. Now
we can go a step further. The thing to which I was then referring was
the thing insofar as it was substantive. This thing, in its substantive
character, is the system itself; it is not «another thing» hidden behind 147
it. The notes are no more than real «moments» of it and what is
physically actualized in the notes is the system itself insofar as it is
their primary unity, that is to say, the substantivity. The dimensions
of the real thing are nothing other than dimensions or formal aspects
of the actuality of the substantivity of its notes; in the richness, in
the solidity, and in the act of existing *(estar siendo)*, what is actualized is the reality *simpliciter* of something, that is, the substantive reality. The essentiated reality is, then, the substantive reality.
The question which remains to be answered, then, is the question

of stating more precisely what substantivity is. To this end we may proceed step by step.

(a) *The notes of substantivity*. In order to treat the problem of substantivity, let us begin by analyzing, a bit more extensively, the constitutional notes of the substantive system.

Through experience we know only compound substantivities, that is, those realities whose substantivity is found to be constituted formally by other realities which, when they are separated from the substantivity which they constitute, can possess their own independent substantivity. These we will call components or elements of the system. It is evident that not every substantivity has to be, in its own character, a system compounded of elements; however, only in taking our point of departure from compound substantivities are we able to conceptualize simple substantivities and to disengage «epago-gically» («*epagogicamente*») the formal reason of the substantivity as such. Let us analyze, then, the notes of a compound system.

To this end let us recall, first of all, what we have been saying in the preceeding pages, namely, that I call notes or properties not only what, in a restricted sense, is a *proprium*, but also everything which forms a proper «part» of the thing, whether as *proprium*, or as matter, structure, chemical structure, psychism, etc. Therefore, in this very
148 wide sense, the notes or properties of a substantive reality are of two kinds or classes. Some are of a merely additive character and, as such, they can be adequately distributed or deployed among the elements which compose the system. For example, if we prescind from the lack of mass, the mass of any body whatsoever is the sum of the masses of its component elements. However, there are other properties which belong *pro indiviso* to the system as such and cannot, therefore, be distributed among its component elements. Thus, in mechanics itself, the potential energy of a system of masses cannot be distributed among the diverse masses, but belongs solely to the total system; the chemical properties of hydrochloric acid cannot all be distributed between hydrogen and chloride, but rather constitute a new and irreducible system. Between the systematic properties and the properties which the elements of the system can contain in themselves, there is a strict relation; this relation may be stated in the following precise way: although distinct in each type of system, the properties of each element become complicated in the systematic

property. If this were not the case, the system would float on top of itself, independently of its elements. However, I repeat, the form of this complication is very different in different cases; it depends, in the instance, on the inner character of the elements of the system.

If a compound reality possessed no other than additive properties, this would indicate to us that it was not a unitary system, a unity, but rather a union, a unification. However, if various elements enter into the composition of a true systematic unity, then each one of them contributes to this in two ways: as conveying some of its properties which can be added to those of the other elements, and as constituting with them the basis of new systematic properties. For this reason, by being integrated *a radice* in a closed system, the elements, despite having lost their individuality, can, nevertheless, contribute, through the primary unity which all together compose, to the additive properties of the system. 149

On this supposition, the systematic properties of a substantive system can be of very different character. And this is a point of decisive importance. There are systematic properties which have the same character that their components possessed, so that the system is, in such a case, like a compound element. Thus, hydrochloric acid has as systematic properties a certain specific heat, a certain electric character, etc., different from those of hydrogen and chloride, each of which, in its own right, possesses a specific heat and an electric character. Strictly speaking, hydrochloric acid, differently from hydrogen and chloride, is, like them, one more body. It is not, however, necessary that this should prevail in every case. It can happen that the unity of the elements determines systematic properties in the system which are merely functional, and not new properties like those of the component elements. Such is the case in an organism. The organism is not a system endowed with physical and chemical properties distinct from those which its structures possess; nevertheless, it functions in a manner radically different from that in which the elements which compose it function; it is a substantive system with a new substantivity which is irreducible to the substantivity of its components, but only in the functional order. If I may be permitted to hark back to the old distinction between mixture and combination, in order to designate by the latter the constitution of a specifically new system, we would be able to say that in the organism and in

similar cases we are in the presence of a kind of «functional combination.» The mixture is not a combination; rather it is something
merely additive; for this reason its properties are, in a certain way, of
150 a «medial» character with regard to the mixed elements. The combination, by contrast, produces something specifically new. Chemical
combinations are combinations of a corporeal type because their
results are bodies with a specifically new unity and formal character.
The functional combination, by contrast, is certainly a combination,
since in it, too, something specifically new is produced, but the
novelty does not affect the formal character of the elements of the
system, that is, the functional system as functional. There are systems
whose manner of functioning is not of the «combinatory» type but
is a mere «complication,» something like a functional mixture; such
is the case in any of those things which we call machines; however,
there are systems whose manner of functioning is truly an «innovation,» that is, a functional combination. Such is the case of organisms.
An organism is not simply a machine but neither is it a body in the
sense that hydrochloric acid is. Its corporeal unity, insofar as it is a
substance, is enormously lax; it is not «one» corporeal substance in
the rigorous and specific sense of the term. Its functional unity,
however, is strict and rigorous. It has not been said therefore, in any
sense, that a substantive system is endowed with systematic properties
which are necessarily of the same type as those which its components
possess; that is to say, it has not been held anywhere that a system
is necessarily a kind of composite element.

This analysis of compound substantivities allows us to conceptualize what a simple substantivity might be, although we have no
experience of such a substantivity. The simple substantivity is also
a closed system of notes or properties. It is clear that it does not
possess additive properties precisely because it is simple. A simple
substantivity, we must energetically insist, possesses no properties
151 save systematic ones, not in the sense that it includes all the elements,
since it has none; but in a higher sense, namely, in the sense that
each new note involves, in one form or another, all the others, not
because it «implicates them» formally (in that case, they would not
be distinct) but because it presupposes them physically in the undivided and indivisible unity of the substantivity. The interdependence
of the notes of a system here acquires its maximum purity. And this

is of decisive philosophical importance. Compound substantivities, in effect, place very clearly before our eyes the fact that, in them, substantivity is not necessarily homogeneous with the type of reality which its elements possess. It suggests that simple substantivities are not, properly speaking, anything like isolated or dissociated elements, but that their substantivity is of a completely different order; they are much more substantive, so much so that they cannot enter into composition.

Simple and compound substantive realities, taken together, deploy before our mind something which, anticipating what we shall immediately explain, may be formulated in the following terms: a substantive reality is not necessarily a new substance, that is to say, substantivity is not to be identified formally with substantiality. This is precisely the problem of the formal reason of substantivity.

(b) *The formal reason of substantivity.* In reality, in what we have already expounded we have also already stated in what the formal ground of substantivity consists. It will be enough, at this point, to turn to it once more in greater detail and with closer attention. Substantivity, from every point of view, involves a character of sufficiency. As a consequence, what is lacking is a precise determination of what this sufficiency consists in.

To this end, let us remember that substantivity is nothing other than what we have called «system,» but rather consists in the system as such; it is nothing hidden behind it. We said, at the same time, that a system is a primary and intrinsic unity in which the different notes are nothing other than partial moments, positionally interdependent, in which the system, as unity, is actualized. The notes to 152 which we refer are the constitutional notes: that is to say, notes which are formal and not adventitious, in the sense of being due to the connection of one thing with another. When that unity forms a closed conjunction we have a system. Under these circumstances, we have substantivity in the strict sense. This «closedness» confers on the unity of a system a character proper to it, the character of «totality.» The stricter and stronger the constitutional unity, the greater is this character of a «whole» possessed by the reality constituted in this way, and the more it is and acts as a whole. In the limit case we would have absolutely simple action. This character of wholeness, or totality, is a character of the unity itself and not of the notes

considered in their «extension.» And this is to be seen in the operative order, as well as in the constitutional order. Operatively, the
thing acts as a «whole,» that is, the «entire» thing is involved in the
action, with all its notes, precisely because this thing possesses a
primary «integrity» which is what is involved in the action; total
integration in the order of action, for example, in the responses of the
nervous system is nothing other than the operative actualization of
the primary integrity in the constitutional order; here we are dealing
with a thing which is intrinsically «complete.» In its turn, this integrity is nothing other than the actualization of the primary unity:
the thing is «entire,» it is «complete,» because it is primarily «one.»
From this point of view, the unity of the system is not only closedness,
by reason of what it does to the «extension» of its positionally interdependent notes, but is also «totalizing» of its multiplicity (i.e.,
confers on its multiplicity the unity proper to a totality). The actualization of the unity of its notes is what confers on the system the
character of totality, and is in itself a totalized unity in them. We say
of this primary unity, insofar as it is actualized in constitutional notes
153 which *ab intrinseco* form a totality, that is, insofar as it is a totalizing
and totalized unity, that it is a unity which possesses constitutional
sufficiency. The substantive reality constituted in this *manner*, then,
exists «sufficiently.» Therefore that intrinsic and closed unity of
constitutional notes, makes of the thing something plenary and
autonomous, that is, sufficient, within a very precise line: in the
order of constitution; constitutional sufficiency, consequently, is the
formal ground or reason of substantivity.

In order to understand what this means, it is enough to reflect
that not every grouping of notes is capable of having substantivity
in the sense in which we have just defined it, because it is possible
that a grouping may not possess constitutional sufficiency, either
because the notes are lacking to it, or because the notes which it does
possess do not support a sufficiency in the order of constitution.
Thus it would not be possible to have a thing which would consist
in nothing more than the possession of a certain spatial figure and,
at the same time, be conscious. It would have no substantivity at
all, because, in order for the notes to have sufficient constitutional
unity, it would be necessary to have another group of notes among
them, for example, a certain mass, a certain intelligence, etc. Shape

and consciousness do not constitute a sufficient unity. It would not be possible to have an atom whose nucleus would be constituted only by five neutrons. Reciprocally, it is not enough to separate a determined note from a substantive reality to insure that the rest should possess constitutional sufficiency. If, for example, we take intelligence from a man, what would remain would not be simply an animal organism. The animal is irrational; but this note is negative only in a logical sense, because physically the difference is positive and constitutional, and belongs to the structure of the animal itself. For this reason, when intelligence is withdrawn, if we should desire that what remains should have constitutional sufficiency, it would be necessary to modify, among other things, the cerebral structures, and, even more, to modify them in a very precise way, according to the type of animal we wished to obtain because we would not be able to remain merely with «animal» but with a dog, a horse, a monkey, etc. An animal is not a *homunculus*, not even in an organic sense. For the same reason, a man is not obtained «by adding» the note of intelligence to the structures of some animal or other in a determined *phylum*, but rather by adding it to the structures of an animal whose cerebral structures must have undergone a precise or certain structural evolution. Were this not the case, the grouping of animality and intelligence would lack constitutional sufficiency and, therefore, substantive reality. Within the series «animal» itself, a certain animal which might have certain deformities of a genetic character, that is, constitutional deformities, would not have sufficiency in the order of constitution. Its decomposition would give rise to other different substantivities, not of just any kind indifferently, but determinatively to those which would have been formed of notes capable, in their turn, of forming constitutionally sufficient unities.

On this basis, let us fix more explicitly this formal reason or ground of substantivity. Substantivity, we say, is a sufficiency; however, it is necessary not to confuse constitutional sufficiency with other types of the same. We have seen that, for Aristotle, the proper reason of reality *simpliciter* is substantiality, while he understands substance as the subject of those notes which are the accidents. Sufficiency (for him) would be substantiality, subjectuality. The medievals noted that, strictly speaking, the sufficiency of substance resided formally in the order of existence and not in that of subjectuality; that sufficiency would be the capacity for existence. What I have called substantivity is a sufficiency in an order which is to be identified neither with subjectuality nor with the capacity to exist.

In the first place, it is not to be identified with the capacity to exist. The scholastics understood by this capacity the aptitude which a substance possessed in itself to have its own proper existence. It is *perseitas*, something very different from *aseitas*, because it is not the same thing to have through oneself the capacity for existence *(perseitas)* and to have existence from oneself *(aseitas)*. The confusion of these two was, as is well known, the profound error of Spinoza on this point. Although the scholastics never distinguished between substantiality and substantivity, they nevertheless affirmed that the formal ground of substantiality is its *perseitas;* the result might be the tendency to think that what we have called substantivity would be precisely identical with this scholastic *perseitas*, that is to say, that substantivity might be the sufficiency which a thing possessed for having its own proper existence. However, even prescinding from the fact that the scholastics, as I have said, never distinguished between substantivity and substantiality, it would be completely mistaken to believe that substantivity might formally be sufficiency in the order of existence, whether in the sense of *aseitas* or in that of *perseitas*. This sufficiency in the order of existence would more properly be, as a matter of fact, existential aptitude: a completely different problem from that of substantivity. The terms apart, the attributes which the scholastics assigned to substance in the order of its capacity for existence were one thing, while what we have in mind here, that is, the attributes to be assigned to substantivity in its own right as counter-distinguished both from substance and from the capacity to exist, are something very different. Sufficiency in the order of aptitude for existence is, in fact, consecutive on substantive sufficiency in the order of constitution; in no sense whatever is it its formal reason (or ground). If substantive reality is capable of itself of having its own proper existence, it is precisely because it is substantive, and not the reverse. To say that the substantive is that which has *perseitas* is not to state in what substantivity formally and intrinsically consists. To center substantivity in the capacity for existence, in *perseitas*, is to evade the problem of substantivity. As a consequence, substantivity in not only not identical with the capacity to have one's proper existence, but this capacity presupposes sufficiency in the order of constitution, that is, substantivity. Therefore, substantivity is not *perseitas* and much less *aseitas*.

In the second place, the sufficiency of substantivity is not formally identified with substantiality, that is, with subjectuality. All the realities which ve know by experience do certainly have a moment of subjectuality, but they also have a moment of substantivity. And these two moments are perfectly distinct, even though they may be articulated from within.

In a word, we have seen that, in compound realities, there is a certain dissociation between substantivity and subjectuality. And this for various reasons.

(a) The elements which compose the system are many, while the substantivity, which they constitute, is one.

(b) These elements have a peculiar condition. They can certainly be given independently of the composition; in that case they are substantive realities in their own right. However, on entering into the composition they take on or gain a special character. They do not lose any of their properties, but they cease to constitute a closed and total system. What they lose on entering the composition is precisely their substantivity, and they remain reduced to mere nonsubstantive substance. As a substance, sugar is identical in a flask in the laboratory and in an organism. However, when it is integrated into the latter, it loses its substantivity; the substantivity has passed from each element to the system.

(c) Not only is this the case, but the compound substance may also possess certain properties as a system of a totally different kind from the systematic properties of its elements, and may be of the type which we have called functional combinations. There are composi- 157 tions in which the compound, because it possesses substantivity, is, equally with its components taken in isolation, a substance; this is the case with any chemical substance. However, there are other compounds, such as living beings, in which the characteristic and differential moment of their substantivity is of a purely functional type, so that the total compound is not, properly speaking, «one» substance. The organism, as substance, is not «one» substance, but «many.»

Substantivity and substantiality, or subjectuality, are, then, two distinct moments of every reality *simpliciter*. Substantiality is that character according to which there spring forth or emerge from this reality determined notes or properties, active or passive, which, in one form or another, are inherent in it; for this precise reason they are *subjects*. I say active or passive, because the inner character of the substance also determines the type of passivities to which it is susceptible. Substantivity is, by contrast, sufficiency in the order of constitution. Both moments are so clearly distinct that it is perfectly possible for an insubstantive substance to occur: all the elements of a compound, while they form part of that compound, are instances of this case.

It is also the case that, as we have said, the «origin» of the notes cannot be confused with their «position» in the system. The notes may have their origin in the substances; this, though possible, is not always the case, as we will see later on. However, what is formally decisive in substantivity is not the origination but the positional interdependency within the system, the position in it. Only the systematic and positional unity of these notes is formally substantivity. Reciprocally, the notes are nothing else than the physical actualization of the constitutional sufficiency, of the substantivity. And the different formal respects of this sufficiency are precisely what is meant by dimensions. Richness, solidity, actual existence *(estar siendo)*
158 are dimensions of constitutional sufficiency. While the categories are categories of the substantiality, the dimensions are dimensions of the substantivity, that is, of the constitutional sufficiency as such.

Both moments, however, substantiality and substantivity, are nothing other than this: moments. It is not the case that there are two classes of things, the class of substantives and the class of substantials. In fact, since all the substantive realities which we know through experience are composed of substantial elements, it follows that those realities, as substantive, take the substances up into themselves; as a result, the compound reality, although it is substantive, inevitably possesses a moment of subjectuality. Substantivity and subjectuality, then, are only two moments of one same and unique reality *simpliciter*. However, the reason why this reality is substantive is not the same as the reason why it is subjectual.

Further, there exists a precise articulation between these two moments. Substantivity is, as a matter of fact, superior to subjectuality, precisely because it is the reality as substantive which, on absorbing the substances, receives from them its character as subject. However, by reason of this absorption, the moment of substantivity can be defined only in a way very different from the moment of subjectuality. Let us take the two extreme cases.

At times, what the substantial elements together compose is, in its turn, a new substance. When this is the case, the compound reality has a substantivity superior in rank to the mere substantial character. However, superior only in «rank,» because the area of substantivity covers exactly the area of substantiality and does not exceed it. In that case, the compound reality is substantive as a closed and total system of constitutional properties; however, it is, further, a principle of their emergence in the manner of nature (φύσις). Insofar as it is the natural principle of its properties, this reality is, then, «underneath» them, is a true ὑπο-κείμενον, *subjectum, sub-stans*, substance.   159

In the extreme opposite situation or instance, that of substantivities characterized by functional combination, there is a substantive reality, the human, in which the substantivity is articulated with the subjectuality in a partially very different manner, because the human substantivity has an area which enormously exceeds the area of the component substances as substances. In a word, in addition to the formal properties which emerge «naturally» from the substances which compose it, the human substantivity possesses others whose root is not an «emergence» but rather an «appropriation»: the appropriation of possibilities. In that case, the subjectual moment of the human reality acquires a singular character. On the one hand, this reality is, like any substance whatsoever, the subject of properties which it possesses by reason of the substances which compose it. On the other hand, however, it does not stand «beneath» its properties, but, quite the reverse, it «stands above them» since it appropriates them by acceptance. For this reason, I would say that under this aspect it is not ὑπο-κείμενον, but rather ὑπερ-κείμενον, something not only *sub-sistent* but also *super-sistent*. That is to say, it is a subject, but not in the sense that these properties spring from its nature and are inherent in it as the «subject of» them. Virtue or

science, for example, are not notes which man has by nature, as he might have talent or stature or the natural color of his eyes. In man, antecedently to his free decision, there is talent, but he has no virtue or science; he is the «subject-of» talent and color, but he is not the «subject-of» virtue or science. Virtue and science are only two possibilities of life and of human reality different from others, vice and skill, for example. In order to «have» them, man must choose among
160 these possibilities and appropriate them to himself. Therefore, with regard to them he does not stand in the condition of «subject-of» them, but of the subject which determines them; he is *superstans*, above them. As standing above them, the human substantivity is such that, by reason of its intrinsic constitution, it finds itself exceeding the area of its substances, and that, not just in any manner whatsoever, but in a very precise manner, that is to say, by finding itself «naturally» immersed in «situations» which it must necessarily resolve by its own decision, in view of the different possibilities. Insofar as it is immersed in situations, the human reality is «subject-to» the necessity of appropriating possibilities to itself. To be sure, other realities, for example, animals, are in situations and, therefore, are also in a certain wide sense «subject-to» illnesses, etc. However, in the case of man, the situation is such that he has to resolve it by decision. This is why he exceeds the area of his substances and why we say that he is «subject-to» *par excellance*. He is «subject-of» only after he has appropriated his possibilities; for example, he is the subject of virtue and of science only when he has made himself scientifically informed and virtuous. *In this aspect*, then, substantivity is not only different from subjectuality, but is the ground of it; substantivity is the ground of being «subject-to,» and «being subject-to» is the ground of being «subject-of.» The Greeks spoke only of properties, distinguishing among them only on the basis of their contents; they did not observe that, before being differentiated on the basis of content, properties are to be distinguished on the basis of their very mode of being «proper;» some are properties by reason of «nature,» others by reason of «appropriation.» The first is the case in merely substantial substantivities, the second in superior substantivities. The substantive reality whose «physical character» is to have, necessarily, properties by appropriation, is precisely what we understand by moral reality.
161 Morality in the usual sense of goods, values, and duties, is possible

only in a reality which is constitutionally moral in the sense which
has been explained. Morality is in its own way something «physical.»
This, however, is not the place in which to develop these ideas.

In human substantivities we are in the presence, then, not only
of a dissociation between substantivity and subjectuality, but also a
dissociation between «substantial» subjectuality and a higher «moral»
subjectivity; something which is «subject-to» is not a subject only
in the sense of «natural» ὑποκείμενον. It is certainly a «subject of
attribution,» like every reality, by reason of the fact that we speak
of it; however, in reality, it is not a «subjectual reality» in the sense
of substance. It is, to be sure, something «physical,» but it is not
substantial. The «physical» is not to be identified with the substantial.
It is «logically» subjectual, but «physically» may not be identified
with the substantial. Its physical reality is not formally substantial,
but rather substantive, and its possible subjectuality is not of the *sub-
sistent*, but of the *super-sistent type*. The precise differentiation
between the two dimensions of human subjectivity, obviously, falls
beyond the limits of the present work.

Even in those realities in which the substantivity covers the area
of the substantial exactly, it is possible to apprehend such realities
in terms of pure substantivity. Let us take purely material things
— those which are usually called physical by *antonomasia*. Evidently,
in expressing them in language, I always make them subjects of
attribution. However, the belief that they are necessarily nothing
more than substances, that is, real subjects of the physical inherence
of accidents, is a mirrorism produced by predicative description. The
predicative *logos* always has, as a matter of fact, a subject and a
predicate perfectly determined in their function as predicates and
subjects. Thus we say that a body — let us call it improperly mass — 162
produces a force upon another body or undergoes the action of a
force. This description tends to implant in our minds the idea that
the «body-mass» is merely a thing, a substance, whose physical
character is to be the subject of a force, that is, be the subject of
inherence of the accident «force.» This, I say, proves to be no more
than a mirrorism. Not that it is not true that this thing is a substantial subject, but rather that it is not true that this is its only real
dimension. If we were able, in fact, to express this same dynamic
phenomenon in terms of pure substantivity, we would never arrive

at that indiscriminated identification of the subject of attribution
with the subject of inherence or substance, but rather we would
express the phenomenon in purely structural terms, that is, considering
this phenomenon as the variation of a structure of substantivity and
not as an action or passion of a substantial subject. This is no chimera
or fiction. The description of that phenomenon in physico-mathematical
terms is precisely a non-predicative description. Newton will tell us
that force is equal to mass multiplied by acceleration. In this predicative expression of Newton's law, there is clearly a subject and a
predicate. However, we observe that — as I have contended at length
in my courses — these three «realities» (mass, force, acceleration)
are three realities irreducible in themselves and that, therefore, «to
multiply them» has no meaning. What Newton's law states is that the
numbers which measure these realities are what are multiplied and
what stand in the indicated relation. This means that, even as realities,
they are structurally linked by a purely functional relation. And this
does not imply in any sense a subject of attribution. It is enough for

me to describe the phenomenon by «writing» $f = m \cdot \dfrac{dv}{dt}$ and it

will be seen immediately that none of the three terms has any
163 prerogative over either of the other two. *In re*, it is a mere functional
structure, that is to say, the expression of a linkage of substantivity
and not of substantiality. The same thing happens with all physical
laws. At the beginning and the end, all the functions which physics,
at least classical physics (and this is enough for what I am proposing)
introduces, are analytical functions. And even if they were infinite
forms they could always be uniform in principle (theorem of Poincaré,
Klein and Kobe), which we discover to be the same as in the simple
case of Newton's law. I do not mean, by saying this, to say either
that mathematics is capable of describing the whole of the reality of
bodies and their laws, or that the mathematical description of reality
is the only possible functional description. The only thing which I
have suggested is to propose an example (within the strictest limits
of the realities of bodies and those, perhaps, only under one aspect)
of a non-predicative description of reality, which would be merely
structural and functional.

And the truth is that, when one reflects upon it, it will prove to be the case that this happens constantly in ordinary language. The form of expression is almost always a predicative «phrase,» but the thought is not always necessarily predicative. Many times all I do is express predicatively a reality in its pure structure of substantivity.

Hence, it follows that substantivity is different from subjectuality and superior to it.

Let us draw these observations to a conclusion. Substantivity is nothing distinct from the system of constitutional notes itself insofar as that system is total and closed. The formal reason of substantivity is nothing other than this sufficiency in the order of constitution. It is not, therefore, either *perseitas* or capacity of having its own existence, or subjectuality. It is more than subjectuality, but is anterior to *perseitas* because only that which is sufficient in the constitutional order has *perseitas*. 164

(c) *The Non-substantive (The Insubstantive).* To complete our outline of this reason *(razón)* of substantivity, we shall permit ourselves a few words concerning its opposite: the non-substantive or insubstantive. Just as substantivity is not identical with substantiality, so the insubstantive is not identical with the accidental. For Aristotle, an accident is that which can have no other reality save as inherent in a subject, a substance. It is clear that every accident is non-substantive; the converse, however, is not necessarily the case: not all that is insubstantive is accidental. There are insubstantive realities which are still strictly substantial in character, insubstantive substances: all of the substances which compose an organism. When they become integrated in that organism, they loose their substantivity; as substances they continue to be just as they were before they became part of the organism. The formal reason of the insubstantive is not inherence, as little as the formal reason *(razón)* of substantivity is the subjectuality. The formal reason *(razón)* of insubstantivity is insufficiency in the order of constitution, that is, the condition of being merely a «moment-of» a closed and total system. Every accident finds itself in this condition, but so, too, at times, do the substances which are component elements of a system. What happens is that the accident is doubly insufficient: in the first place, as insubstantial, because it can exist only as inhering in a subject and, in the second place, as insubstantive, because it can only exist as a moment of a substantive system. The formal reason *(razón)* of its insubstantivity is not, then, identical with the formal reason *(razón)* of its insubstantiality.

(d) *Substantivity and individuality.* Substantivity understood in this way, we have been saying, is the formal structure of the constitutional unity. I have already noted that, in a strict sense, the
165 concept of constitution can also be applied to a merely singular reality. Let us apply it for a moment, so as not to remain general, to some concrete affirmations. Since every constitution is radically individual, it follows that substantivity is formally individual in the wide sense, that is, whether singular or strictly individual. In order, then, to bring to an end our treatment of the theme of substantivity we must determine more precisely the nature of this radically and formally individual character.

To this end, even at the risk of boring repetitions, it is necessary to review what we have already said about the individuality of the constitution. Individuality does not, in the first instance, perform a differentiating function; that is to say, we are not referring to those characteristics which, «added» to the specific character of a reality, make it different from others of the same species. The substantive reality is not found to be composed of specifying characters plus characters of individuation. By contrast, individuality is not one more «character,» but a moment which is primarily constitutional: that moment by reason of which every substantivity is radically, determinatively, and irreducibly «this» substantivity. And this means two things. In the first place, it means that we do not know whether or not what is called «species» exists. Here there is only the question of «this» substantive reality which I hold before me. In the second place, not only do I not know whether or not the «species» exists, but I am also ignorant of whether or not its existence is possible in all cases. Individualization is a moment which refers to the substantive reality considered in itself, in such wise that it is *within* this reality, and not outside it or anteriorly to it, that one must ascertain, beyond the moment of individuality, whether there may be in the thing any moment which, precisely considered, might be susceptible of multiplication in other individuals. That is to say, the problem does not lie in the individual within the species, but rather
166 in the species itself as something outside, or at least as something

above, the individual in question. There is no individuation of the species but specification of the individual.

Individuality, therefore, is a moment of substantivity as such. Properly speaking, there does not exist any «physical» principle of individuation, but rather, every substantivity is individual not only in itself, but also through or by itself; that is, by reason of its whole substantive reality: the whole of substantive reality is formally «this.» To be «this» means that the autonomy and total fullness of the substantivity is a sufficient and irreducible unity.

«This,» however, is a unity which possesses or contains different relational aspects. In the first instance, in the perspective of the species, this unity possesses, before all else, a numerical character: it is «one» individual among «many.» But, as I have said, this does not constitute a strict individuality, but only a singularity. There are substantive realities which have no other type of sufficient unity. The elementary particles of contemporary quantum physics, all atoms and molecules, possess only this character. Two atoms of silver are distinguished only in being two, and not by any internal characteristics. However, not all substantive realities fall into this class. A living being possesses, at least inchoatively, that which, in the case of man, is strict individuality. «This» reality has not only a numerical unity, but an internally determined unity as well. To designate this second unity is the reason why I have introduced the concept of individual constitution: the constitution is something eminently positive and full of content. Each substantivity has its own peculiar way of being one and total, a whole, of being «this.» And this mode is precisely the formally and strictly individual constitutionality. As I have already noted, the concept is also applicable to the singular individuality; however, for greater clarity, we will again prescind from the *singuli.*

Between the two moments of singularity and individuality there is a precise articulation. There is no individuality without singularity, 167 though, as we have just seen, there are s i n g u l a r s which are not individuals. Further, every individuality, by reason of being an internally determined unity, is determinatively non-repeatable, while singularities are numerically multipliable. It is clear that, *de potentia absoluta,* God could create two true individuals exactly alike without their ceasing to be two. We would then have two internally determined individuals, which were only numerically distinct. Differently from the singularities of the physical world, which do not succeed in becoming individuals, that is to say, which are infra-individual singularities, we would now find ourselves confronted with super-individuals: even though they might be «indiscernibles» — we may say it with deference to Leibnitz — they would not cease to be two «this's.» However, this proves to be no more than a speculative possibility; as a matter of fact, it does not happen that way. As a matter of fact, the strict individual, as such, is substantively «one» and, even more, «unique.»

To sum up, then, individuality is a moment which belongs to the substantive thing by reason of its whole proper reality. Primary unity and total enclosure of the system are the two positive and real characters which form a substantivity, which is, *eo ipso*, constitutionally and by itself, an individual. It will never cease to be such and to be individually identical to itself so long as that constitutional system perdures. This is the reason why the term «this» suffers from serious ambiguities, which one must dissipate because it points to, or identifies, different characters of substantive reality.

As I said at the beginning of this exposition, metaphysics, placed in the perspective of the species, has generally projected the problem of individuation by way of the differences; a way which, for reasons which I will immediately expound, I call the way of «concretion.» Just as the difference «specifies the genus,» so too, it is thought, do the individual differences «contract» the species into the individuals. But such contraction does not exist, no matter how one may choose to interpret these presumed individual differences.

If they are interpreted as mere individuating «moments,» then, as we have already seen, there is no contraction of the species, because the species is not something primary which is individualized, but just the opposite, the species is a possible (no more than a possible) specification of certain constitutional notes of the individual. There is no «contraction» of the species, but «expansion» of the individual.

If the individual differences are interpreted as true characters added to the species, then such individuation is still more impossible. And for this assertion we can give two reasons.

In the first place, the formal reason (*razón*) of the individual is perfect constitutional determination; perfect, that is to say, in the sense of being an irreducible character. This is not individual «con-cretion» save in the conceptive and logical order, that is to say, in the sense that I can predicate of an individual substantivity the notes which constitute this, its individual reality; and under this aspect it would appear that it is these predicates which individualize the sub-ject. However, *in re* this is not the case: the elements and the notes which compose a substantive system are individuals *per se;* they are «this» color, «this» face or feature, etc. The individual is not constitu-ted by concretizing it each time with more notes, but rather by the total constitutional sufficiency in irreducible form. The predication of notes is a mere «logical» and objective apprehension of the individual reality; and, therefore, it is possible only if the «subject» of the predication is already individual independently of the predication.

In the second place, in order that concretion succeed in constituting an individual, it would be at least necessary that it should be a final and exhaustive concretion. Concretion, then, can always be variable 169 and, furthermore, can fail ever to exhaust itself in the reality, and this is the way in which it comes about that the individual already exists and is always the same. And it is because the substantive reality is something already individually determined in the order of consti-tution, that it is a subject (either in the sense of «subject-of» or of «subject-to») further determinable in the order of non-constitutional notes; and this is the reason why I say that this determination is not yet constitution, but merely concretion. A piece of silver, a star, must necessarily occupy some portion of space, a place; but not necessarily a determined place; they change place and in each moment the new location of each is a new note of concretion. The same must be said of all other changes. «Things» can change color. An oak, a dog, changes size, or height. In addition, a dog links together the various moments of his actions. A man changes occupation, his way of looking at things, his situation in life, his intellectual formation, his physical condition, his moral attitudes, etc. None of these new determinations are what constitute him an individual; they are only the moments of a variable concretion. Even more, they are, at times, also the moments of a progressive concretion. It is a matter of indifference to the con-cretion of a star to have occupied determined points on its orbit, but to no living thing is its life-course or development a matter of indifference, because this becomes inscribed progressively (in the

form of «engramas» or in some other manner, no matter which) in the notes which, at each instant, constitute its concrete *present;* in such a case, the concretion, in addition to being variable, is also progressive, and by reason of its very character is interminable; it comes to an end only with death. Not so the individuality. Hence, it
170 is, that the real is always «the» *(el)* same (identical) but never «the» *(lo)* (qualitatively) s a m e . It is «the» *(el)* same, in the first sense, as an individual perfectly individuated *ab initio;* it is never «the» *(lo)* same in the line of concretion.

From whatever point the question is approached, then, such a contraction, that of the species to the individual, is seen not to exist; the substantivity, rather, is something individual in itself (both in the case of mere singularity and in that of individuality in the strict sense) in a primary and radical way. Individuality implies an internal determination, but this determination is not concretion; it is something anterior to and more radical than concretion, the presupposition and ground of all concretion. The individual is not reached by a constant accumulation of more concrete notes. This is chimerical. It has reached this state by the mere fact of having been constituted as a closed and total system, a substantive system of constitutional notes.

With this analysis we have discovered the primary ambiguity which is always latent in the demonstrative «this.» This term can signify either the individual or the concrete. Both are real, but perfectly distinct, aspects of the thing; the second, moreover, is based on the first. Let us add, finally, that individuality is incommunicable.

To sum up, «this» has four moments proper to itself:

(a) the moment of «numerical» unity;
(b) the moment of intrinsic individual determination or «constitution» individuation properly so-called;
(c) the moment of «concretion; »
(d) the moment of «incommunicable» reality.

These four moments are distinct and different. Only the first three touch on the question with which we are concerned. Much later we will treat of the fourth, namely, incommunicability.

By these considerations we have delimited, with a certain rigor, the formal character of the structural unity of the reality *simpliciter;* that is to say, of its constitution: *substantivity*. Its formal reason *(razón)* is sufficiency in this order of constitution, that of being a closed and total system of constitutional notes, whether these be elementary, additive, or systematic. In contrast to the substantive, 171 everything is insubstantive or non-substantive, which — whether substantial or accidental — is only a moment of this system: it is insufficiency in the order of constitution. This substantivity is intrinsically and formally individual (singular or individual in the strict sense) by itself. However, by reason of its component elements, or by reason of any other dimension of its intrinsic finitude, every substantive reality has in itself, in addition to the moment of substantivity, a moment of subjectuality, in virtue of which it finds itself subject to further determinations in the line of concretion.

It is necessary, then, to concede that, in the world, what we possess is, rather than a connexity of strictly individual substantive realies, a gradation, or better, a progressive and evolutive movement from the merely singular reality to the strict individual substantive reality. In the order of simple matter, substantivity, strictly speaking, does not belong to any of the so-called material «things;» rather, it belongs to the material world, taken in its total integrity, because each one of those material things, properly speaking, is only a fragment of the total substantivity. This substantivity is not singular, nor, for that matter, individual, in the strict sense, because, even though it is undivided in itself, it is not, nevertheless, something divided from all the rest: the «entire» material reality, in a word, has nothing outside itself from which it might be divided. However, if, by a concession, natural in a certain way, we consider the elementary particles, atoms and molecules (and sometimes, perhaps, crystals) as realities in and by themselves, we find that they are nothing but mere singular substantivities; for this reason, in principle, they constitute an indefinite, purely numerical, multitude; even more, they are capable of conserving their number unchanged in processes, 172 of exchange, of certain types of collision, etc. However, in matter immediately constituted of atoms and molecules a step forward has been taken, intermediate between mere singularity and the first indication of individual substantivity; it is the *stabilization of matter*.

In it, there appear no new «unities» but merely simple «conformations,» that is, mere aggregates of singular unities endowed with «unicity;» there are no two pieces of microscopic matter which are identical. These conformations can be stable only in their global «configuration;» the stability of dynamic configuration is what characterizes the stars in the widest sense of the term. Among them, there are some, like the planets of our solar system, which have, in addition to the stability of dynamic configuration, a stability which, in a certain way, is static in their «internal» parts, due to dominantly molecular grouping; this is the case, for example, with the earth we inhabit. Living things constitute a further advance. They are functional combinations endowed with a certain independence of medium *(medio)* and with a certain specific control over it: *this is the vitalization of stable matter.* Here we have, not a simple unicity of conformation by mere aggregation of singularities, but rather a strict unicity based on a true intrinsic unity of functional character. It is the first sketch or *primordium* of individual substantivity. We will call it quasi-individuality. It is more than mere singularity, but less than strict individuality. And this is true for two reasons. In the first place, because the living thing is, after all, purely material and therefore continues to be a mere fragment of the total material reality. In the second place, because even if life is taken as an autonomous domain, each biological species and, therefore, *a fortiori* each living thing, is, perhaps, nothing else than a mere modulation of this basic structure which is *life.* In that case it is to the latter and not to each living
173 thing that substantivity belongs. However, this «life» possesses a relative unity of independence and control proper to itself. Hence it follows that each living thing, in having these same characteristics, possesses an individual peculiarity much greater than the mere singular individuality. Each living thing is much more than a simple «number» of «the» life and of the species. For this reason it is quasi-substantive and quasi-individual. Among living things, the vegetables do nothing more than nourish themselves from their medium in dynamic and reversible equilibrium with it. However, animals are more substantive, since in addition, they sense their medium or environment and their own reality in the form of «stimulus.» Only in man — and this by reason of his intelligence — do we find ourselves in the presence of a plenary and formal constitution of strict indi-

vidual substantivity: this is the *intelligization of animality.* By his intelligence man confronts his environment and himself as «realities» — this is what intelligence formally consists in — and in virtue of it he is in possession of himself as a reality which is formally «its own.»

Stability, independence of the environment with specific control over it, facing things as realities; here are the three *schemata* of the substantivization of reality. Each of these presupposes the previous and, further, carries it as formally implied in itself.

This is «essentiated» reality. The essence, I said at the beginning of this exposition, is the primary unity and, at least, the intrinsic and necessitating principle of the rest of the notes which belong to the thing. These notes are those the conjunction of which (now we would say more properly «system») is what is necessary, not in order to be this or the other (for example to be something which floats or which reflects) but in order to be reality *simpliciter* (silver); this system of notes is not «of» the reality («of» the silver) but is the reality itself (the silver). This identity of the «for» and the «of» in the «that» is reality *simpliciter*. This reality simpliciter is the true reality, that 174 is to say, that which is primarily and dimensionally realized in its richness and solidity in its act of existing *(estar siendo)*. And this true reality is reality insofar as it possesses a strict «constitution,» that is, insofar as it is a primary and intrinsic unity, insofar as it is a closed and total system of constitutional notes. In sufficiency in this constitutional order consists the formal character of the structural unity of reality *simpliciter,* the «individual substantivity.» Here we have the essentiated reality.

On this basis we may then go on to ask: what is the «essence» itself of this «essentiated» reality?

CHAPTER NINE

THE «ESSENCE» ITSELF OF THE REAL

In order to direct our inquiry as it should be ordered, let us keep before our eyes what we have been saying up to this point.

In what has been said we have progressively encircled the precise point at which the essence is to be found: it is to be found within the compass of the «essentiable,» in the «essentiated» reality, that is, in substantive reality. But this progressive definition of limits has not been a merely external circumscription; that is to say, it has not been a process of setting aside all that does not touch the essence. Quite the contrary. What has been said indicates that the essence is to be found in a reality which, because it is substantive, possesses, in its turn, the characteristics of what we have called the «essentiable,» in such wise that the characteristics of the «essentiable» and of the «essentiated» are formally and intrinsically characteristics of the essence itself. We must now, therefore, fix precisely what may be the proper character of essence. This effort will make it possible, thereafter, to achieve a rigorous internal analysis of essence itself.

THE SPECIFIC CHARACTER OF ESSENCE

Let us review the path which has been traversed. The essence, I have been saying, is a moment of the real thing, as reality *simpliciter*, that is, of the substantive reality as substantive. Therefore, the essence will be found in the system of characters or notes which physically form this substantivity, as its grounding principle; that is to say, of that by reason of which a real thing is real and acts as real, and is, therefore, «natural» reality, in the concept of nature which I expounded at the beginning; that is to say, things as they act upon other things by reason of the properties which they possess in and by themselves, whatever their origin might be.

Let us begin by fixing with greater precision the character and the function which essence must possess; this is what will enable us to carry through its internal analysis.

A.   The essence is something «physical;» or, if one prefers, what we are looking for is the «physical essence» of real things, that which, in the thing, makes it «one» thing, clearly circumscribed and determined. This circumscription, however, as we have seen, may be understood in at least two ways. It can be understood in the sense of a *species*, of an εἶδος; that is to say of that conjunction of features which permits us to locate a thing in the line, in a certain sense geneological, of the *genera* of things and which, within its *genus*, represents a determined figure proper to itself; thus the species states the ancestry of the thing. In such a case, the «what» signifies the kind of thing the thing in q u e s t i o n is. And the essence would then be what has usually been called the «metaphysical essence.» The reply 177 to the question «what» is it? in this sense, is the definition. However, this circumscription can be understood in a second sense, namely, as that which constitutes the profile of formal sufficiency of a thing as a reality in itself, independently of its specific or generic connections with other things; that is to say, that which gives it proper sufficiency in the order of constitution. Then the «what» is the sufficient constitution for the substantivity. The essence, then, is not *species* but substantive constitution. Formally, it is not that which corresponds to the definition; therefore, the essence is not to be sought in the metaphysical analysis of the predicates which are attributed to the thing, but rather, on the contrary, in the analysis of its real structures, of its notes, and of the function which these fulfill in the constitutional system of its individual substantivity, both strictly as individual and as singular. It is the essence as «physical» moment of the real thing. Aristotle, as I have said, made the question clear in speaking of the substantial form. But he only pointed it out, because the notion of form in Aristotle is a notion of the substantial order, while essence belongs to the order of substantivity; and in the second place, because Aristotle, as I have said, turned the problem from its proper path by seeking in the form only its moment of specificity. We have seen that, for this reason, the way of definition is not enough. It is not a question, then, of the species, but rather of the individual physical moment as such, that is, of the nuclear moment so to say, of the root of the substantive reality taken in itself, where one finds the secret, the basis, the key, or the source — the terms are not important at this point — of all the properties or actuations of the thing in its primitive, or first order, individuality. And the difference between both concepts (because of their inevitable points of contact) is so profound that, in this «physical» sense, the essence of a thing might be constituted, not by the cadre of formal features of its physiognomy, but only by the properties capable of producing or engendering that physiognomy.

The essence we seek, then, is the «physical» essence and not the so-called «metaphysical» essence. Personally, I call the latter the «conceptive essence» because what we have to say of the physical essence is also, in a strict sense, metaphysical. It is not a question of preferences. The fact is that by reason of its formal ground the essence as species is something grounded in the physical essence. The fact that the first, but not the second, can be defined is what has, in the past, in metaphysics, given a preferential position to the first. And this is not as it should be. 178

B.   The essence, then, is physical. However, it is only a physical «moment» of the thing. This fact requires further clarification because there are different possible ways of conceiving the physical essence of anything.

In fact, by essence there might be understood an «element,» that is, a «part,» of the thing, precisely its «essential part.» The essential part of anything is not any part whatsoever, but a part of exceptional and preferential rank or range, because it is that part in which, in the manner of a nucleus, the very roots, which determine the characteristic properties of the thing in question, are concentrated. The physical essence would then be the element or nuclear part of the thing. Because it is a part, it can, on occasions, be extracted from it,

and it is this «extract» which is sometimes also called essence. It is
the conception, diametrically opposed to that of the species, which
is merely a specific «abstract.» An essence is, in common parlance, an
article of perfume or of pharmacy; thus one speaks of rose essence,
of belladonna, of a sleeping potion, etc. What interests us here is why
these articles should be called, precisely, *essence*. They are called thus
179 because they are an extract in which, presumably, there are embraced
all the «virtues,» all the active «power,» all that gives these realities
the properties which they possess. The essence of the sleeping potion,
for example, opium, embraces that which «makes» anything a sleep
inducer, that is to say, its pure saporific being. And, in its turn, as the
isolated extract of the sleeping potion, it carries with it the virtues
of the latter and is its «essential extract.» It is not a question of an
essence defined by way of genus and specific differences, nor of a
specific concept of things, but rather of something, in a certain sense,
«active,» of the «active principle» of things, as we are accustomed
to say.

This is not a mere liberty of language; quite the contrary. In this
«physical» sense, the concept is already found in the strictly
philosophical strain of the India tradition. Already in the *Rig-Veda*
and, above all, in the most ancient *Upanishads* (one should see the
beginning of the *Chāndogy-Upanishad)* and later across the full breadth
of the philosophy of India, what we call essence is called *rasa-*. In the
basic and usual sense it means vital juice, sap, elixir of life, etc.;
that is to say, that which contains the greatest qualities and the most
radical properties of anything, that which, for this reason, has the
power to communicate them and to maintain or sustain the reality
of the thing; it is the active principle of this thing and can at times be
isolated as the dynamic extract of it. The commentators, in fact,
explain *rasa-* by *sara-*: vigor, marrow, nucleus, the most effective, the
most important and decisive part of anything. And this is what Indian
philosophy strictly understands by essence. *Rasa-* possesses a dynamic
value, not in the sense of movement as opposed to the static, but
dynamic in the sense of strong, vigorous, that which imparts its
power to the thing *(bhūta-,* τὸ φυτόν, τὰ φόντα) so that it may be
what it is *(svabhāva-),* manifest itself as such *(svarūpa-)* and can be
distinguished from others. The essence as *rasa-* is not then, physiognomy, *species;* sap possesses none of the formal characteristics of the

species, but is, however, the active principle which produces them
intrinsically. Here may be seen the entire difference between the 180
essence as *species* and the essence as «physical» moment. The species
(svarūpa-) is the physiognomic manifestation of the proper constitutive character *(svabhāva-)* of the thing *(bhūta-);* a character which is
the product of the *rasa-,* which, nevertheless, does not have that
physiognomy. For this same reason, that which, in the final instance,
differentiates one thing from another is the essence as *rasa-* and not
as *species.* Differently from the distinction by *species,* which is a
«visual» type of distinction, the distinction by *rasa-* is, for this
philosophy, «gustatory;» it is taste which makes it possible to
distinguish one thing from another. The word *rasa-* also has, as a
matter of fact, the sense of taste and of savor; hence it goes on to
mean some of the movements, dispositions of soul, or its fundamental
humours (ten of them especially). It is a question, consequently, not
of a visual but of a gustatory intellection.

The ordinary language and the philosophy of India possess, then,
a physical conception of the essence as «essential part» of the thing.
However, this is not admissible simply in this sense. The essence is
not, as it were, a second thing within the thing which possesses the
essence. The essence is not an «essential thing,» but «that which is
essential to a thing.» Sap, vital juice, etc., that is to say, the dynamic
extract, are one thing within another, a more subtle thing than that
which possesses them, but, still, a thing like it. But this is impossible because the essence is something which touches the substantivity,
and the substantivity is, in its turn, only a «moment» of the real thing.
Therefore, the essence cannot be a true «thing,» whether nuclear or
seminal, cannot be an extract, but can be only a mere «moment» of
the real thing, at most, its «nuclear moment.»

C.   In the third place, this moment does not concern the operative,
but the entitative order. When one says «the essence or the nature»
(essentia sive natura), essence is considered at most «materially» but
not formally. Formally, it is not a question of a moment which 181
concerns the activities or the passivities of a thing in contrast to the
rest, but of a moment which concerns the notes which we have called
formal and constitutional. And this, no matter what may be the type
of activity or passivity being considered. Activity, in the most favored
of beings — such is the case in all living beings, including man in all

the aspects of his life — is always and only a second act. The essence, by contrast, is a primary act in them. And in all beings in general, the essence concerns what is formally entitative and constitutional as such. To be sure, every reality is, from a certain point of view, «respective,» as I have been accustomed to say in my courses. Reality is «*syntactical.*» This does not mean, however, that this relatedness or syntax is the «resultant order» of actions and passions. Entirely the contrary. The actions and passions are consequent on the respectivity in which real things find themselves by reason of their entitative constitution. Precisely because reality is respective, each real thing has its «proper» constitution in order to this respectivity. For this reason, the syntax or respectivity is a structure which touches the proper constitution of every thing. And it is this last which touches the formal and proper moment of essence. What this respectivity may be in itself is a problem into which we do not have to enter at this moment. We shall be concerned with it later in this discussion. At this time, it is enough to note that it is not «specification.» All things may have to be specifically and generically distinct; but this would be no reason why reality would necessarily cease to be respective or syntactical. Essence, as a physical moment, is, then, constitutional and not merely operational in character.

D. However, as I added at the very beginning, the essence understood in this way fulfills a precise «function» in the real thing. It is the fourth feature which completes the determination of the proper character of essence. What does this mean?

182   We have referred to this feature on different occasions, especially when treating of the Aristotelian concept of substance. And I added that scholasticism, in rethinking these ideas, brought important clarifications and precisions of detail which were absent in Aristotle. One of these clarifications has its origin in the problem of universals. The second substance, that is, the Aristotelian essence, is found in all individual substances; therefore, it has, with respect to these substances, the first substances, a character of universality; it is species. In reality, however, nothing is formally universal; rather, everything is individual. It is, therefore, to be asked, what kind of reality does the essence have? It can be universal not *in re*, but only in predication. However, if it is not universal, then it is individual and, as such, incommunicable, incapable of being predicated of all

individuals. In resolving this difficulty some of the scholastics, including Saint Thomas himself, offer us a concept of what the essence is in itself. The essence of a real determined thing, we are told, is always individual as is the thing itself, with, however, merely numerical unity. In order to obtain the essence as such, it is enough to abstract from the thing what is numerically individual. Then I have the essence «according to its proper principle, that is, considering it absolutely» («*secundum rationem propriam et haec est absoluta consideratio ipsius.*» *De ente et essentia*, Chapter IV, ed. Baur). The essence, as such, prescinds from whether it is realized in many or in one only; it is neither universal nor singular. Let us set aside the problem of universals, which provided the motive for this concept, and give our attention only to the concept itself. It is clear that what is given us in this concept is the essential content, the essential notes of any thing: man, dog, apple. What Saint Thomas is telling us is that the essence of man, for example, «according to its proper principle» is rational animal. This does not at all, however, allude to the 183 other aspect of the question, namely, what it is «to be essence.» Essence, whatever it might be in any and every concrete case, that is, no matter what the essential notes might be, is always «essence of» the thing and only that. The concept of essence «according to its proper principle» responds to the first question, for example, humanity in itself. This consideration, however, leaves intact the second question. What is called the «proper principle» of the essence is, then, an ambiguous expression. It can mean, on the one hand, what kind of thing the essence is, that is, of what kind the essential notes according to its proper principle, may be, considered in themselves; however, it can mean, on the other hand, what may be the proper principle of essentiality (of any and every essence) as such, what it is to be essence. The essence is not essence by reason of the notes considered absolutely, but rather according to the function which these notes fulfill in the real thing. And this second question is precisely the one with which we are concerned: not what may be the essential notes, as notes, but rather in what their «essential» function consists as such within the real thing. To meet this question the «absolute» consideration is of indifferent importance to us; even more, because it is «abstract,» this consideration can make us glide over the function. The essence then, as physical moment of the real thing, fulfills «according to its proper principle» a very precise physical function within the thing possessing essence. It is precisely this function by reason of which the essence is essence. Let us circumscribe a bit more exactly the character of this function.

(a) It is, in the first place, an «individual» function. What does this mean? We saw, when speaking of Aristotle, the difficulties over which his idea of essence as species stumbled, in the interpretation of the individual reality. Nevertheless, scholasticism accentuated much more sharply, in confrontation with all Platonism, the rigorously individual character of all reality. It would appear then, that it should have developed the idea of the individual function of the essence. This however, was not the case. Scholasticism took up its position at the Aristotelian point of view of the essence as species in order to elevate itself thence to the essence «in itself.» However, as Saint Thomas tells us, the essence «considered» thus «absolutely» prescinds from being realized in the individual. Hence it was that the only problem which the essence occasioned in the individual was that of its relation to, or distinction from, what was individual in the substance. Saint Thomas' answer to this question — it was not the only one and we refer to it only because it was the dominant one — is clear: between the essence and the real individual there is no real difference whatsoever, but only a distinction between mere concepts based on the reality (distinction of reason *cum fundamento in re*). If, then, it is asked what t h e function of the essence is, the answer which would be given us would be clear. If it is taken in itself, as distinct from the individual, essence is a «being of reason.» If it be taken physically, it is identical with the individual, it is the individual itself. However, with this answer the individual function of the essence still remains unclarified. That physically the essence should be identified with the individual reality, does not mean that within, it, the essence does not formally have an individual function proper to itself. This function is not primarily or formally a function of specification; we have said as much repeatedly. For the essence has no formal reference to other individuals. Even more, because individuality does not mean individualization. Every reality is individual; however, it is not such necessarily by individualization, that is to say, by «contraction» of the species, but rather may be individual in its own right. Actually, the only thing which the physical identity of the essence with the individual means is that the essence is not a second thing within the individual thing, but rather is only a moment of it. However, for precisely the same reason, it fulfills in that thing a particular function, not in the order of specification, but in the order 185 of the structure itself of the individual reality. The essence is essence by reason of a function which it fulfills physically in the individual reality.

Some scholastics (Suarez, for example), recognize that, in addition to its specific notes, there are, in every individual, notes — almost infinite in number — which are essential to it. Our science, he tells us, nevertheless, must limit itself to the specific; to know the individual exhaustively in all its essential notes would be proper only to an angelic intelligence or to the divine. In this conception we are not told why these innumerable notes within the individual are formally necessary or required. In our own reflections, we have seen that these notes are formally necessary for the «constitution». It was necessary to have tried to delineate a theory of the individual physical essence and not merely to have recognized its existence.

(b) Finally — let us take note of it once more — this individual constitutional function does not concern the substantiality but the substantivity. It is not a matter, in a word, of the root whence the properties «emerge.» This root might be a substance, though it is not necessarily such; the systematic properties of a substantivity are not always of the type of accidents emerging from a substance. What is decisive for the essence is only that these notes or properties constitute among them, so to say, the substantivity. The essence can be «materially» something substantial, though «formally» it is something proper only to the substantivity. The substantivity is then, actually, the essentiated reality as such. The substantivity is, as we have seen, sufficiency in the constitutional order: that is, the closed and total system of constitutional notes. As a consequence, the individual, physical, and constitutional function of the essence is a function in the order of «sufficiency,» that is, in the order of the closedness and totality of the constitutional system as such. If we should want to 186 express the same ideas in classical terms, we would say that it is a question of a theory of the physical essence which would not be formally a theory of substance and even less necessarily a hylomorphic theory of it.

By these considerations we have sharpened, somewhat rigorously, the proper character of essence. The essence, I have said, is a principle, a necessitating principle, at least, of the reality *simpliciter* of anything. The essence understood in this way has, as we have just come to see, a precise character. It is, in the first place, something «physical» and not merely conceptive. In the second place, it is a «moment» and not a thing or force. In the third place, it is an entitative moment. It is, finally, the conjunction of notes of a thing insofar as this conjunction possesses an individual «particular function» in the constitutional order, and which formally concerns the substantivity, that is, the constitutional sufficiency of a thing. With these conclusions established, we may enter upon the internal analysis of the essence.

187   SECTION TWO

INTERNAL ANALYSIS OF ESSENCE

Substantivity, I have said, is the closed and total system of constitutional notes. The constitution is the manner in which the notes determine the unity of the substantive reality, a unity whose formal reason *(razón)* is precisely the constitutional sufficiency. As a consequence, the essence must ground, within the substantive reality, both the determinants of its mode of unity and the unity itself. Only by understanding it in this way will we understand the essence in itself and in its function and will we be in a position to conceptualize the kind of principle the essence is within the substantive reality. If we are then to ascertain what the essence is of this substantive reality, we will have to examine the question in four successive steps:

(a) What is the internal ground of the substantive reality in the order of its constitution and of its mode of being one by reason of the notes which it possesses; this is the problem of the *essential notes.*

(b) What is the ground of the systematic unity itself in its character as unity; this is the problem of *essential unity.*

(c) In the light of the results obtained in the two earlier stages, we will then be able positively and formally to conceptualize what the essence is as a moment of the reality; this is the problem of *essence and reality.*

(d) Finally, in what does the *character of essence as principle (carácter principial)* as such consist?

ARTICLE I

THE ESSENTIAL NOTES

188

The essence, I, say, is a moment of the substantive reality as such. Since the substantive reality is a system of constitutional notes, the first thing we must do is to ascertain which among these notes are essential and in what their essential character *(esencialidad)* consists.

Let us recall that the essential notes are those notes of a formal type which are not due to the connection of the reality in question with other realities; that is to say, they are non-adventitious notes; this constitution is the primary structure of the thing. Those constitutional notes which compose the primary structure of the thing in question are of a different character because not all of them are absolutely independent among themselves.

There are some notes, in a word, which form part of the constitution of the thing because they are necessarily determined by others. It matters little, for the rest, what the character of this necessity might be. In some cases it may wear the vestige of strictly «logical» necessity, so to say. This happens in the case of the specific heat and the valency of a chemical element, which derive with mathematical rigor (whether statistical or otherwise is not important at this point) from its atomic structure. At other times, it is more a matter of a necessity which is, in a certain way, merely «natural» or normal. Nor is it that, rigorously speaking, the presence of these notes may not be impeded. It may be impeded by some special cause, though what this cause does is determine the presence of other notes which, even though abnormal or unusual, do not, for that reason, cease to be constitutional. When this does not happen, the natural foundation of 189 these notes in others is what is called «normalcy.» Such is the case of the phenotypical pecularities, whether individual or typical, of primary and secondary sexual characteristics, or racial characteristics, and of certain hereditary characters (in a restricted sense), etc.

Joined to these notes or properties, which are necessarily founded on others, there exist others which are strictly and rigorously ungrounded. I do not mean to say, naturally, that they are not produced by causes which are their reason for being. All the substantive realities which we know by experience are caused and, in this sense, have a foundation or ground. However, in speaking here of ungrounded notes, I do not refer to origin, but to the formal structure of the substantive reality; that is, I take my position in the order of constitutional sufficiency. And in this line, or order, there are notes which do not derive from other constitutional notes but, rather, rest on themselves. And this is the precise sense in which I say that they are ungrounded. Evidently they are those which determine the entire structure of the constitutional system. As such, they are more than «constitutional,» they are constitutive. The constitutional, therefore, is not to be confused with the *constitutive*. Both the grounded and ungrounded notes are constitutional, but only the ungrounded are constitutive. These constitutive notes are those which I call formally essential notes.

The expression is not infrequent; what is decisive is what I want to express by it. In the first place, «constitutive» is a concept which is found here, not as it is usually found, in the line of formal «metaphysical» reason (which I prefer to call «conceptive») of the real (genus, difference, species), but rather in the line of the «physical» character of substantivity as such. It is a question, then, not of a metaphysical or conceptive, but of a physical constitutive principle
190 which is, in its own way, also metaphysical. I will return later to this character of the «constitutive.»

In the second place, «constitutive» is not distinguished here from all the «other» notes or predicates which do not enter into the metaphysical reason, but rather is distinguished only from the grounded constitutional notes; the insubstantive remains on the periphery of the delineation of the concept «constitutive.» Let us recall, in fact, that «constitution» has a strict philosophical meaning; it is the system of notes which determine the intrinsic and proper mode of being, something physically and irreducibly «one,» that is, substantive. «Constitutive,» then, means that which precisely and formally within this constitutional unity (which is substantivity) forms primarily and *simpliciter* that aforesaid physical unity. And this is no question of mere objective concepts, nor of concepts with a foundation *in re*. Much more enters into the constitutive, as much more entered into the constitutional, than enters into the real correlative of the definition. In explaining the character of the constitutional unity, I took as example «this albino man.» Naturally, albinism, as such, is not constitutive, but merely constitutional, because, as is known, it is a genetically controlled characteristic. The constitutive would be that or those genetic notes which establish this character. It is not enough, however, to have «arrived» at the gene which controls it, because, in its turn, this character of the gene may perhaps be nothing else than something based on biochemical or biophysical structures which are more elemental; these latter would be the constitutive notes of the albino. Hence, to arrive at a truly constitutive note must always be an open problem; what today appears ultimate may not appear such tomorrow. The goal, however, is philosophically clear. Only with these notes would we have the primary unity of the real; that is to say, the primary mode of being instrinsically and irreducibly «one.» To this and only to this do I apply the term «constitutive.» It is a concept, then, which falls in a different order than that in which the term is usually employed: in the order of constitution. 191

By these reflections we have made the concept of «constitutive» more precise. These constitutive, or essential, notes are, then, moments of substantivity, which, as I have repeatedly said, is in its turn a «sufficient system» of constitutional notes. Therefore, if the essential or constitutive notes are ungrounded, the result will be that, as I have just said, it is they which primarily form the system, that is, the formal unity of substantivity. It is not the case that there are two systems of notes, one of merely constitutional notes, the other of constitutive notes. As system, there is but one: the constitutional substantive system. What happens is that, in this system, the merely constitutional notes are moments of the unity of substantivity by reason of their being supported in the system or unity of constitutive notes; however, neither with the one nor the others do we pass out of the unique unity of substantivity. Let us recall, then, that when

speaking of substantivity, I insisted that this substantivity is nothing hidden, or still less, something situated «behind» the system of constitutional notes or «beneath» it; rather it is the system itself as such. Neither, for this same reason, is essence something which is found beneath the substantivity; it is, rather, an internal and formal moment of the system itself as such. In order to understand this it is enough to note that, among the notes of a substantivity, there may be formed groups which have a certain character of unity and of system; for example, an «organ» of a living being or an «apparatus» with the respective moments of its functional cycle (digestion, breathing, etc.). In these examples there is, to be sure, no question of systems in any strict sense, that is, of different substantive unities, because if such were the case, we would not have «one» substantive reality but, rather, the articulation of different substantive realities supported or posited in mere juxtaposition. Nevertheless, even though they do not possess strict constitutional autonomy, these
192 groups possess certain systematic traits within the total system. For this reason, we may call them «subsystems.» The expression clearly indicates that a subsystem of notes is not something which necessarily forces us to leave the total unity; because «sub» here does not mean «underneath» but rather «within;» or, if one prefers, a system or partial quasi-system. Subsystem is the exact philosophical concept which indicates that what is signified by the term is nothing hidden behind the system or situated beneath it, but rather a formal moment of the system itself. The essential notes, then, form a sub-system. As such, it is not a system which is found beneath the constitutional substantivity. In that case it would be a ὑποκείμενον and the essence would be a moment of the substantiality. No, the essential notes form a subsystem within the constitutional system of the substantivity itself. As such, the constitutive notes are a mere moment of the substantivity. However, this subsystem is distinguished radically from all the subsystems to which we have alluded. Those subsystems were partial systems of mere constitu-tional notes; for this reason they lacked complete sufficiency. When we turn attention to the constitutive notes, however, the situation changes. The subsystem, in this case, has two peculiar features. It is, in the first place, a subsystem endowed with full sufficiency; only because they are supported by it, do the merely constitutional

notes take on systematic character. In the second place, it is a «primary» subsystem in the sense that it rests in itself; its unity derives from no other source; it is rather «one» thing in and through itself. In this sense, it is a partial system but in a way different from that in which all the other subsystems are partial systems: it is the «formal» nucleus of the substantivity; it is, if one prefers, the fundamental subsystem. By reason of these two peculiar characteristics I will almost always call this subsystem of constitutive notes *a posteriori*, simply «system.»   193

On this basis, we can now say, in the strictest sense, what the physical essence of anything is *from the point of view of its notes:* it is the system of the constitutive physical notes necessary and sufficient to insure that a substantive reality may possess all its other notes. The essence is not then either subject or substance (ὑποκείμενον) nor is it a moment of the substance, but an internal moment of the substantivity. In other terms, it is not essence of the substance, as Aristotle thought, but essence of the substantivity. We said earlier that constitutional sufficiency is the formal character of substantivity. What confers this sufficiency and, therefore, this formal character, on the substantivity, is precisely the system of its constitutive notes, the essence. The essence is, then, what constitutes the substantivity as such; that is the reality *simpliciter* of anything. Reality *simpliciter* is nothing other than the essence as the system of constitutive notes. Here we confront the essence, and its proper functions, from the point of view of the notes. It is something physical because it is found physically formed of notes which are, in their turn, physical; however, because it is a subsystem, it is only a moment of the substantivity. And, within the substantivity, its proper function is that of being «constitutive,» in the sense which has been explained, and not in any sense of specification. Later we shall see what the essence is from another point of view: from the point of view of the *unity* of its notes.

However, all this makes further clarification necessary. We have, as a matter of fact, characterized the constitutive notes by calling them «ungrounded.» Left without further clarification, this proves to be something predominantly negative; it is necessary, therefore, now to point up, with greater rigor, in what this character may positively consist. And this will become apparent when we consider

¹⁹⁴ the notes both in themselves and in their relation to the others. Considered in themselves, the essential notes are the «ultimate moment» of the substantivity; considered with regard to the other constitutional notes, the essential notes are the «grounding moment» of them. These two traits — that of being the ultimate moment and that of being the grounding moment — express in rigorous fashion and in a positive manner what it is to be constitutive. Let us analyze these two characteristics separately.

¹⁹⁵

SECTION ONE

THE ESSENCE, ULTIMATE MOMENT OF THE SUBSTANTIVITY

Let us consider then, in the first place, the essential notes taken in themselves. Ungrounded as they are, I have said, the essential or constitutive notes are ultimate and constitute the ultimate reality of the substantive reality, that which this is in the last instance. The constitutive is, before all else, the ultimate. Essentiality is, then, constitutional ultimateness. This ultimateness manifests itself, in its turn, in the triple order of what I will call its «metaphysical condition,» its «entitative character,» and its «constitutive content.» By reason of its metaphysical condition, the essence is absolute or, as I shall say, *factual.* By reason of its entitative character, the essence is individual ultimateness. By reason of its constitutive content, the essence in unalterable.

I. *Essence: Its Factual Metaphysical Condition*

Before all else, the essential or constitutive notes, since they are ungrounded and, therefore, ultimate in the constitutional order, do not depend formally on the other constitutional and adventitious notes. As a consequence, since they do not depend on any others, the only thing which can be or ought to be said of them is that they «simply are.»

However, it is necessary to understand this condition of the es- 194
sential notes correctly, because something can «simply be» in many
different ways. One such way may be called the way of precision, so
to say: something is taken in and by itself, prescinding from whether
or not it has any ground. This precision may be the fruit of a deliberate
logical act, or it may well be an immediate lived *experience* in which
the reality is apprehended only as something which is; that is, a kind
of reality in brute form. Thanks to this logical or living precision,
the reality is the term of mere constatation. In ordinary language,
reality apprehended in this manner is to be called «fact.» The notion
of fact understood in this way, since it is purely the result of precision,
does not imply that the reality of fact is nothing more than mere fact;
all the realities in the universe — even the most necessary — can be
considered, by way of precision, as mere fact. In this sense, «fact»
is only a way of considering reality *(modus rem considerandi)* and
does not imply the least qualification concerning the condition of the
reality in itself. The essential notes do not constitute any exception
to this rule. Even more, according to this manner of considering
reality, there is no place for speaking of essential or non-essential
notes; all the notes equally «are.» This is the only point on which
Hegel is right when he tells us that pure *to be* is total indifference.
What happens is that this notion of being, which is reached merely
by precision, is nothing primary. I have extensively developed this
matter in my courses over many years and, as we shall see later,
to be is never primary, either formally or objectively; reality is
primary. As a consequence, what remains precisely qualified from
this point of view is not the indifference of *to be* but the character
of the reality. And this qualification is «mere fact;» it is not «indif- 197
ferent being» but reality considered as real in the perspective of
precision.

However, this is not the condition of the things to which I refer
when I speak of the essential notes, nor is it, for this reason, the
primary and radical meaning of «only to be.» As a matter of fact, if I
take reality, not in a perspective of precision, but in a reverse manner,
in its real condition itself (whether through an act of reflection, or
through one's own *direct experience* [*vivencia*]), that is, if I consider
reality in what looks to its fundamental character, then is precisely
when I discover what is peculiar to the essential notes, that which I

have called «*only to be*.» Intellected * «fundamentally,» of things and their notes, some are, as a matter of fact, contingent; they *are* in this way, but they might be or might have been in quite another manner. In this sense, i.e., a sense not consequent on precision, but on a real condition, we can call these things and their notes «realities of fact» or «matters of fact.» Others, however, are necessary because their reality is determined necessarily by reason of the character of the connection among things. Finally, there are others, the systems of essential notes, for example, whose real condition is neither contingent nor necessary, but is that of «*only being reality*.» Then the adverb «only» does not indicate my manner of considering things, but rather, under its negative appearances, expresses the positive metaphysical condition of the reality of essence. If we want to go on talking about «to be» we will say that it is not the indifference but, quite the reverse, the «sufficiency» of to be in the order of constitution.

In order to understand what this means, and in what this sufficiency consists, a brief digression is necessary concerning what I have called «metaphysical condition.» Here condition does not mean what is ordinarily expressed by the «if» of a conditional proposition, but rather what is ordinarily meant when we say, for example, that various persons are of different condition. In this sense the condition is certainly not a property or note of the real thing, but is, nevertheless, a real character of it. This condition may be of two classes. One is, in a certain way, subsequent (logically, not temporally) to the formal structure itself of the thing: it is something like the simple modulation of the previous reality of the thing. This is the sense it has when we speak of the conditions of the character of a person. The conditions of character belong to the real structure of the person, but they presuppose this structure and limit themselves to modifying it in its properties and notes, for example, giving some notes preference over others or giving them greater stability, etc. This is the formation of the personality. The condition in this sense «conditions» something which is already real. The metaphysical range of condition in this sense is incalculable; this is not the place, however, to enter into this problem; we shall do so later on. However,

---

* In Zubiri intellection is the first act of mind prior to conceiving and concept.

there is another kind of condition: a condition which is not subsequent to the properties and notes of the thing, but is rather, in a
certain sense, anterior to them, or at least concomitant to them,
congeneric with them, because its roots stand in relation to the
groundedness on which the thing in question rests. In a word, if we
refer a thing which is given to us intellectively to that which we call
«ground,» we find, before all else, that it is the thing itself which
reveals to us a real *characteristic* intrinsic to itself, namely, its respectivity to that ground. This *respectivity*, in the first place, is an
intrinsic character of the thing, something which touches on its inner
quality itself and is not merely an extrinsic point of view taken with
regard to it; this is why we say it is a «condition» of it. Further,
however, in the second place, it is not a condition which rests on the 199
previous reality of the thing, but precisely the reverse: it is a fundamental condition, an intrinsic condition on which the thing's possibility of having reality depends. It is something «in» the thing;
not something *a posteriori* with respect to itself, but rather *a priori*
with respect to it. It is not, then, any effective causal «connection,»
whether positive or negative, with any other thing, with the presumptive cause, but rather the proper inner character of the real
thing itself, that which either demands or excludes any connection of
the kind indicated. The effective causal connection is the consequence
of this proper inner character. When we intellect the thing, then, in
its fundamentality, it is the thing itself which «sends us back» or
does not send us back in one manner and not in another to the
ground in question. It is then a real moment «in» the thing, «antecedent» to its reality itself or at least of congeneric origin with it.
What, in this process of reference, the thing shows us, is its intrinsic
a priori respectivity. It is, then, a moment of the real; in the first
place, «real,» and, in the second place, «antecedent» to its reality
itself, or at least *congeneric* with it. This is what we call a «metaphysical condition» of any reality. It is not something which belongs
to the thing as one of its «material» or «formal» properties. Neither,
however, is it a mere extrinsic denomination or a mere objective concept of it, but rather, is a respective moment, but one intrinsic to
the real thing, and the ground, also real, of its concept. It is the
intrinsic character which the thing possesses in its way of being real

with respect to a «ground.» In addition to their properties, both material and formal, things have «condition.»

This is one of the most weighty themes of the whole of metaphysics. From the time of the Greeks, philosophy has called the totality of real things the «world» or «cosmos.» In my courses I have offered another concept of world. World is the unity of all real things «in and by» their mere character of reality, in contradistinction to the 200 determined content of those things; by contrast, the unity of real things by reason of their content, that is, by reason of *what* they are, would constitute a «cosmos.» Both concepts are different *in re;* the «world» is always one, the same, but it may have many «*cosmoi.*» Our present concern does not require us to enter into this problem; I shall refer to it more extensively at a further point; it is enough for us now to refer to «world» as the system of real things.

Christendom has a different concept of world than the Greeks had. The idea of world was one of the most important points of encounter between Christianity and philosophy, and that which forced Christian thinkers to work out a system of philosophical thought of their own. It is possible to hold that, originally, the entire radical innovation which Christianity introduced into philosophy consisted in a new idea of «world.» While the Christian metaphysicians, save on some concrete points, absorbed, purified, and elevated Greek metaphysics, on the point of the concept «world,» by contrast, they broke with it. And before all else, on the question of its origin: the world is «created.» This is the ultimate character, and for many thinkers a formal and intrinsic character of world as such. World, then, is the totality of created being *as created*. With this idea, metaphysics was transformed into the «theory of creation.»

Therefore, with respect to this its ultimate ground, its first cause, created reality possesses before all else, a characteristic metaphysical condition: *contingency*. The world freely created by God is an intrinsically contingent reality. It was created, but it might not have been created. Hence it is that reality, as already created, involves in its intrinsic contingency a second metaphysical condition with respect to God: *possibility*. Contingency and possibility are thus the two unique metaphysical conditions of created reality with respect to the first cause. They are not two states of one same thing which, of itself, would be neither real nor possible. Neither do they indicate here two classes of entities, one of which is the class of possibles, the other of real things. Rather they are two conditional marks formally inscribed in actual created reality. All created reality is 201 already, insofar as it is real, a possible reality in the sense of the actuality of a possibility. The moment of possibility is precisely that which confers on actual reality its character as contingent. As a consequence, from the point of view of their *respectivity* to their ultimate ground, the contingent possibility and reality of all created entities, that is, the possibility and contingent reality of the world, are homogeneous. All created beings are equally possible and equally contingent with relation to God.

For mediaeval philosophy itself, there was nothing to impede, without in any way diminishing the first cause, our taking the world in and by itself and looking at things as realities, which reside in the world, as intramundane realities. Even more so, because, despite the fact that they are «second» beings, the reality and the causality of the world are, nevertheless, truly and strictly, reality and causality. Then it is possible to develop a metaphysics, which would be proper to those intramundane realities, from this other point of view: I may propose to myself, before all else, the task of discovering the structure and metaphysical condition of the realities of the world as such. This would be a metaphysics of «worldly» reality as such. This is not an easy task, and even less is it a task which has been brought to any conclusive state; quite the contrary. Only after it has been established, will it be possible to rise to the first cause of the world, and the metaphysical structure of the real, as created, be «ultimized» in the strictest sense of the word, that is, finally radicated in intrinsic and rigorous necessity.

The realities of the world, then, which enjoy a homogeneous metaphysical condition with respect to God, do not enjoy a similar condition with respect to each other. Possibility and reality, from an intramundane point of view, take on a different character from that 202 which they possess with respect to God. Even more, intramundane metaphysical conditions not only are not homogeneous, but are not reducible to two. Let us make this point clear at once so that we may be able to consider with precision the problem of the metaphysical condition of essence.

In the first place, that which concerns possibility and reality: as intramundane conditions, that is, as characteristics of the mode or manner of *to be* of the real thing with respect to its intramundane grounds, these are different than they are as metaphysical conditions of created reality *as created*. Referred to God, there are infinite things which are in the condition of being able to be created; that is to say, which, in this sense, are also possibles and which, nevertheless, are not possibles or even actually impossibles with respect to the intramundane grounds. Reciprocally, to be possible in the real world, means not only to be creatable by the first cause, but also to be realizable by intramundane causes. As a result of this consideration, «to be in the condition of a possible» takes on a new, very precise character. The mammifers were thus possible in the Precambrian stage; that is to say they were in the condition of possibles with respect to the world. Hence it follows that these possibles are in a certain sense doubly possibles; possibles for God, as able to be created; and possibles, further for the intramundane realities of that geological age. When traditional metaphysics has set itself the problem of «possible being» it has almost always considered the possibles from the point of view of the first cause. By contrast, when Aristotle and the Greeks in general spoke of δυνάμει ὄν they were referring to physical intramundane capacities.

In the second place, intramundane metaphysical conditions are not reducible to two. When the real thing is referred to its intramundane ground, we discover that its condition of possibility, for example, is of a very different type; that is to say, that there are 203 different ways of being possible. There are possibles by nature, natural possibles (realities in potency, realities which are virtually real), possibles by chance, possibles by «possibilization» (*posibilización*), possibles by freedom, etc. And even among those types, there are still profound differences. Thus, for example, not all natural possibles are equally possible; rather, some are «more» or «less» possible than others. This is the case with the state of the elementary particles and with the atom in contemporary quantum physics. And the quantitative measure of this «grade» of possibility constitutes precisely what we call real probability (at least this is the concept of *probability* which I have been accustomed to propose in my courses); a proper conditional character. Probability, chance, etc., are

internal conditions of real things in their relation to an intramundane
ground. Correlatively, the conditions of actual reality are no less
varied. With regard to God, everything is contingent; with respect
to things in the world, however, not all are contingent; rather some
of them are in another condition, are necessary. Necessity and contingency (I repeat monotonously) are not formal structural moments
of reality, but rather intrinsic characters of it in its manner of being
real with respect to intramundane grounds; that is, they are metaphysical conditions. Even more, contingency itself has different
types. For God, not only is everything contingent, but, even more,
everything is *equally* contingent, because everything created is an
equally free realization of something creatable. However, with regard
to intramundane realities, contingency is merely exemption from
intramundane necessity. There comes into view, at this point, a vast
variety of ways of being contingent, from mere coincidence to free
determination. With liberty, moreover, we come to a new metaphysical condition. What is free is certainly contingent; this, however,
indicates only the negative character of liberty: that of not being
necessary. Positively, what is free is beyond or above the necessary
and the contingent: it is the manner of *to be* of *the domain of the* 204
act, «domination» as a mode of *to be*, the mode of *to be* of an act
of «absolute position,» *of the act of love* source of *the real as such.*
Necessity, contingency (in its different modes), and freedom are
three metaphysical conditions of the real.

From another point of view, there is among human realities a
radical difference of metaphysical conditions. The human reality,
as a matter of fact, executes acts which, as such, are the realization
of something possible. As is the type of the possible, then, so too
will be the metaphysical condition of its realization. There are two
types of possibles. One is the possible in the sense of the potential
(including chance). Reality, as the realization of what is potential,
is «fact.» It is the third concept, and the strictest, of what is called
a fact. However, there is another type of possible: what are called
the possibilities (whether offered to him or of his own creation)
which a man has in his life. Here «possible» means «making possible»
(*posibilitante*). The realization of these possibilities confers a precise
and special condition on the real: this is «event.» With regard to
its intramundane ground, reality has a different character according

as that ground is a potentiality or a possibility. Fact and event are the two great differences of metaphysical condition in the realm of the real. They are not necessarily distinguished by reason of their content. The proof of this is that sometimes one same thing may be, from one point of view, fact, and, from another point of view, event. Nevertheless, the reason why it is fact is different from the reason why it is event: these are two different metaphysical conditions.

In order not to induce confusion, let us bring together the three concepts which, as I see it, must be given of what is called «fact.» In the first place, «fact» is what exists simply as existing. In the second place, «fact» is what exists contingently. In the third place, fact is what (necessarily or contingently) exists as the act of natural 205 potencies. The first is a concept reached by precision and is extrinsic to the thing which, as a mater of fact, exists; the other two, though in different form (we cannot engage this question at this point) are metaphysical conditions of the real as realized. In these pages, unless the contrary is indicated, I will mean «fact» only in the second sense.

I do not, in these remaks, pretend to have enumerated all the metaphysical conditions of intramundane reality and, even less, to have sketched (however lightly) their metaphysical treatment. I have tried only to give a certain idea of what I understand by metaphysical condition of the real: the character which the reality of anything possesses intrinsically in its manner of being real with respect to what we call «ground.»

On the basis of these considerations, let us turn to our problem, to the metaphysical condition of what is the essential element (*lo esencial*) of the real. I have said that the systems of essential notes lack ground, they «only are.» Now we are in a position to understand what this means. This «only being» is not a concept reached by precision, but the expression of a metaphysical condition of essential reality. In a word, what I am doing is apprehending a substantive system of constitutional notes and referring it to a presumed ground. This reference, and the ground in question, can be given in different orders. It can be, in the first place, in the order of origination; in that case, the system of notes, like any reality in the world whatsoever, sends us back to another, different reality of the same system; for example, to its efficient cause. My reference to the ground, however, may be carried out in the order of the constitutional sufficiency of the substantivity. In that case, some notes refer me to others, while others do not. That is to say, the notes themselves disclose to us, in our apprehension of them, their respectivity to the ground, to the intrinsic character of their reality. Grounded and not grounded are, then, metaphysical conditions of the notes. What are these conditions? This is the question.

Grounded notes, if they are constitutional, are necessarily grounded 206 in the constitutive notes; they are the realization of what is possible or necessary on the basis of these latter. Their intramundane condition is, then, *necessity*. If the notes are not constitutional, but, rather, are either causal or adventitious, their metaphysical condition is contingency with all its varieties. What is the metaphysical condition of the constitutive notes? That is to say, in what does the metaphysical condition of the ungrounded positively consist, of that which we have called «only being?»

If my effort is to refer the essential notes to their presumed ground in the order of formal structure, the result is that these notes do not refer us to anything different from themselves, but rather, quite the contrary, «fold us back» upon themselves. This positive «folding back» is not, as Hegel would claim, a movement of reality itself, but only a movement which the real thing imposes on our intelligence. Since it is the real thing which imposes it on us, it is also the real thing which, on being *intellected* in this movement, shows us its internal condition or respectivity: its lack of ground. In effect, «to lack» does not mean here merely «a not having,» because, differently from what happens in the case of objective concepts, physical reality does not have negative determinations. «To lack» is the simple objective expression of something positive *in re*, which becomes transparent in that process of folding back: it is a positive resting, really and effectively, on themselves.

What is it that we call «to rest?» From a merely objective point of view, to rest is «to be sufficient (*bastarse*) to oneself.» However, *in re*, things neither are sufficient to themselves nor cease to be sufficient to themselves; they are what they are and as they are, and nothing more. «To be sufficient» expresses, objectively, the positive element of a precise real character. The constitutive notes, as

a matter of fact, because they are ungrounded, are not found formally
207 linked, tied, or attached to others, but are rather «loosed from» all
the others, that is, «absolute.» Here we have, positively, the precise
metaphysical condition which expresses the «only to be» (*solamente
ser*). That which simply is, is, *eo ipso*, ab-solute (without bonds);
reciprocally, absolute means real «*simply* to be.» The essential notes
are neither contingent nor necessary; they are simply absolute. Our
problem then is to state more concretely what we understand here
by «absolute.»

Absolute, as metaphysical condition of the real, points here only
to the order of constitutional sufficiency and not to the order of
origination. It is not a matter of a reality which, from the point of
view of its origin, has no need of any other reality to exist, but
rather means that the essential notes, in and by themselves, are
formally sufficient to constitute a substantive system. Absolute, then,
here means «autosufficiency» in the order of the constitution of a
substantive system. We said, a few pages earlier, that the formal
reason (*razón*) of substantivity is sufficiency in the constitutional
order. The formal reason (*razón*) of essence, however, is not to be
identified with the formal *ratio* of substantivity, because not all sufficient notes whose systematic unity is constitutional, are capable
of constituting this substantivity «by themselves.» Some of them, as
we have already seen, are structural moments of a sufficient system
only resting on or grounded in others, in the constitutive or essential
notes. These last not only form part of the sufficiency, but also are
sufficient, «by themselves,» to constitute a substantivity. The formal
reason (*razón*) of essence, then, of the absolute, is not sufficiency
in the order of constitution (substantivity), but the sufficiency «*by
itself*» (essence) in that same order. The absolute is the self-sufficient
in the sense of sufficiency «by itself» to constitute a system. It is in
this that not only its constitutional, but also its constitutive, character
consists; it is to essence that the character of closed and total system
208 belongs formally and in the first place. Aristotle spoke of the character
of the «through itself» (καθ' αὐτό). However, with him, this referred
to the predication of the notes to their subject of attribution, or to
the unity of the «metaphysical» moments of a substantial form.
Here it is a question neither of the one nor of the other, because
we are not referring to the subject of attribution as such but rather

to its physical reality, and because in it we are treating of the «physical» notes in themselves, according to their capacity to constitute physically sufficient unities. The essential notes are those which have this capacity; and this, their autosufficiency, is precisely the metaphysical condition which we call «absolute.»

Absolute, then, is self-sufficiency. Let us take a step further in this conception of the absolute. Understood as we have just proposed to understand it, the absolute seems to approach the status of a pure fact. However, this is not the case. The absolute is not, first of all, the character, based on precision, of «simple fact,» but is rather a metaphysical condition of the real. Neither, however, is the absolute *fact*, in the sense of something which is «as a matter of fact,» and which might have not been. Although the absolute is certainly not necessary, neither, however, is it formally contingent. If we call facts, both in the sense of based on precision and in the sense of the metaphysical condition of contingency, the «factive» (*fáctico*), then it will be necessary for us to forge another word to designate the metaphysical condition, the manner of *to be* (*ser*) real, of the essential, of the absolute. We may then speak of the «factual.» The factual is one with the factive (*fáctico*) in «not» being grounded in any necessity; however, it differs profoundly from the factive (*fáctico*) in that the latter, no matter how contingent it may be, is found to be grounded, precisely contingently, in reality, while the factual is grounded in nothing intramundane, either necessarily or contingently. The absolute is that which *is* and nothing more: it is *simpliciter* 209 reality and nothing more. If one wishes to proceed further in analyzing the term «fact» one would have to say, paradoxically, that it might seem to appear that the essential is «absolute fact;» not simple fact, but *pure fact*. We cannot fail to note in passing that for these effects the distinction between fact and event, that is to say, the third sense of «fact,» is inoperative, at least if we take the essence, as it must be taken in first philosophy, in all its generality. If, in its place, we limit ourselves to an essence which is highly determined, namely, the human essence, then we would have to face up to the presumed possibility that everything that man «is» might be only «*event*;» what we call the human essence would be simply the realization of possibilities and, therefore, his metaphysical essence would be pure «*event*.» This is the thesis of a number of philosophies, among them all the existentialisms. This is impossible, even in the case of man. However, since this concerns the essence of only one type of reality, the human, we shall reserve reference to this problem to another place in this work.

Essence, then, has as its metaphysical condition, to be absolute in the sense of autosufficient; therefore, the absolute is, as we have said, purely «factual.» Essences are, in the order of constitution, the last elements on which the entire world is based, its physical principles (ἀρχαί). The structural ultimacy of the world is pure essential «factuality.» The world, in every instant — (later we shall see the reason or justification for this temporal nuance) — is based on certain ultimate systems of constitutive notes. These systems, the essences, are the web and woof of this ultimate fabric or ensemble. Everything that occurs in the world must be either necessary or contingent; however, there is something at the base of this ultimate structure which is neither necessary or contingent, but simply «is.» In this order of worldliness, the world is nothing factive (fáctico), 210 but something factual, it is pure factum.

To be clear, let us recall what we said at the beginning of our exposition of this problem; it is a matter of an intramundane metaphysics or a first philosophy. All these characters, and before all else, factuality, are intramundane. A transmundane investigation yet remains to be undertaken; this latter would, however, fall into the void if it did not rest on an intramundane primary philosophy.

To sum up, to say that the essential notes are constitutive means that, taken as moments of substantivity, they are ultimate in their metaphysical condition; they are absolute in the sense of autosufficient, they are factual. Precisely for this reason, they can constitute a physically substantive system, that is, a system with full sufficiency in the constitutional order.

211   II. *The Essence: Its Individual Entitative Character*

Factual ultimacy is, in another respect, an ultimacy which is entitatively individual in character. For this reason, it is a matter of indifference whether one speaks of a singular individuality or of an individuality in the strict sense. We have seen, as a matter of fact, that the essence, in addition to a content, has a function proper to itself, and that this function is not a «specifying» but a «structuring» function. Even though the real be merely singular, its essence has, *in re*, a structuring function proper to itself: that of conferring on the real thing its numerical unity. As a result, the specific content of the essence also has, in this case, an individual character proper to itself: and that character is precisely *singularity*. For the moment, however, the really serious problem is the one which arises with respect to individuality in the strict sense. For this reason, in all that follows, although mention is made only of individuality and essence, it should be understood that I am referring, unless specific indication to the contrary is given, only to individuality in the strict sense. In this latter, the structuring function of the essence does not consist in giving the reality mere «numerical unity,» but in giving it «constitution»: it is a constituting, structuring function. Hence, the 212 very content of the essence has something more than mere singularity; it has constitutive notes which are proper in each individual. And here re-appear, from a new point of view, the difficulties with which we had to struggle earlier in regard to substantivity. Let us repeat them in order to fix our ideas, even at the risk of monotonous repetition.

I said, at that time, that every substantive reality is, of itself, individual, is «this» substantive reality; hence, the «this» affects, formally and primarily, the entire constitutional complexion of the thing in question. The substantive reality, I then said, is not a merely singular unity, but an intrinsically determined unity in its very way of being «one;» and this way is what I have called «constitution» in the philosophical sense. From the point of view at which we here find ourselves placed, the constitution is the formal reason (*razón*) of the strict individual, as distinct from the merely singular individual. However, having now distinguished, within the constitutional system itself, the properly constitutive characters from the rest of the constitutional characters, grave difficulties arise, both with regard to the «materially» individual character of the essence and with respect to that which concerns the «formal» character of its individuality. As a consequence, it is necessary to encircle rigorously that which we call the individual «character» of the essence, and not only of the substantivity. (This last we have already done.)

In the first place, I say, there are difficulties with regard to the materially individual character of essence. I call individual, in the «material» sense, that which has independent, physical unity. It might, therefore, be thought that only the entire constitutional complex is individual and that, therefore, the mere system of constitutive notes is not such. We say, on the contrary, that the constitutive structure, within the constitutional system, is by itself something individual. It is true that only the complete constitutional system is the individual; its individuality, however, accrues to it radically from its system of constitutive notes. This system is not a nuclear individual within the great individual which would be the constitutional system, because we have already said that the essence is not an essential «thing» but only an essential or nuclear «moment» of the thing, a subsystem, the fundamental subsystem. The «individual» is, to be sure, the substantive system, and it alone is such; its «individuality,» however, accrues to it from its «constitutive» moment. We must not confuse the individual with its individuality itself. 213 The latter is only a moment of the former. The constitutive cannot be separated from the rest of the constitutional order, nor is the converse possible. They are nothing but two moments of the one single thing; moments, of which the first is the root of the individuality and, thanks to which, the second takes on individual character. Only the unity of the two moments is the individual. In that individual, the true and radical individuality is precisely the constitutive; the other notes, since they are grounded, would not be individuals if the constitutive notes were not already individuals. In this sense of «moment» and *only* in this sense, do we say that the essence is not only factual, but individual as well. The essence is not only «absolute fact» but also «absolutely individual fact.»

In the second place, (there arise) difficulties concerning the formal character of the individual in the strict sense. There are, as we have already said, substantivities which are only singular. Singularity, however, is not the formal reason (*razón*) of strict individuality; rather, the latter involves an internal determination in the very manner in which the thing is «irreducibly one.» We now affirm, therefore, that the essence is formally individual in the strict sense. This appears difficult to admit, because if, from the constitutional system, we remove all the other notes which are not constitutive,

it appears that all the individuals, no matter how internally determined they may be, are of the same constitutive character, and that,
therefore, the character of the essential would consist in being merely singular. Nevertheless, this is not the case. To suppose that
the constitutive (element) is necessarily identical in all constitutive
systems, is to believe that the constitutive is necessarily only the
specific. This is false. «Constitutive» means purely and simply ultimate
constitutional sufficiency, self-sufficiency. Therefore, there is no reason
why the essence should have nothing but the specific moments of the
thing. On the contrary, I recognize s h a d i n g s *(matices)*, moments 214
(call them whatever you will), all that I have encapsulated in the
idea of internal determination and which is proper and peculiar to
each constitutive system. For this reason, despite the fact that all
the other grounded constitutional notes may have been separated
from the substantivity, the remainder will continue to be formally,
not a mere singular, but a true individual moment. The substantivity
is individualized, because its constitutive notes already form by themselves and of themselves *(de suyo)* a formally individualized subsystem, or, to put it better, the formally individual moment of the
substantive individual.

The difficulty, however, then re-appears in another, still much
more serious form, the form which goes to the heart of the matter.
It is clear, as a matter of fact, that individuals are different in their
irreducible condition: each one is itself and is, in addition, something
whose notes belong to it as non-transferable properties and make
it, therefore, incommensurable with all other individuals; without
those notes it would not be what or the kind it determinatively is.
This, however, is not the problem to which we are referring, because
many of these notes belong to what we call the order of concretion
or, at most, the constitutional order. In this character, they are not
what makes the thing «determinatively» irreducible but, on the contrary, determine something which is already determinatively irreducible; that is to say, something which possesses an intrinsically
and formally distinct unity in its own constitutive system. Stated
in other terms: the differences to which we are referring here are
intrinsic entitative differences, distinct in each individual. And these
distinct differences must affect nothing less than the constitutive
moment of each thing, its essence; this is what must be individual.

That they should be individuals by themselves is not something obvi-
215 ous; however, we have established that fact earlier. But that they
should be individually, in the strict sense, and not only singularly,
different in their proper essences: this is the greatest difficulty. For
then, some one will say to us, individuals would differ essentially; that
is, they would all be essentially different — an assertion which seems
absurd, because all men, for example, are essentially equal: their essence is precisely that in which they do not differ. Every difference
between them, apart from their incommunicable singularity, must
necessarily be non-essential or, — as is said in the terminology of the
schools, — accidental.

Mediaeval philosophy, in its last period, discussed a question
which has a certain homological similarity with the problem which
now preoccupies us: the question whether there can be, within the
human species, souls which are substantially distinct. Our problem,
however, is really much more serious, because both those who resolved that (mediaeval) problem affirmatively and those who resolved it negatively agreed that, speaking precisely, no essential differences exist between animate substances. We, however, have taken
up our position, not on the level of substantiality, but on that of
substantivity, and we say that individuality touches the essence, that
is, that substantivities must be essentially different in an intrinsic
and entitative way. Individuals differ essentially. Is this possible?

In order to answer this question, let us ask ourselves, first of
all, something which touches the problem at its most external aspect
namely, what is to be understood by essential difference? Only thereafter will we engage the matter more in depth.

Through the weight of the Platonic and Aristotelean tradition, a
primary metaphysical status is assigned to individuals, not insofar
as they are individuals, but only insofar as they realize and insofar
as there are attributable to them intrinsic predicates in which all
share among themselves. Let us try to place in clear relief the struc-
216 ture of essence and of essential difference in this conception. Although
this analysis has never been fully carried out, capital importance
must be assigned to this question.

What this conception looks for in the reality of individuals, provisionally, is a minimal intrinsic predicate in which all coincide. It
is a question, then, in the first instance, of finding a «minimal quan-

tity» of coincidence. But, it must be asked, «what minimal quantity?»
It is not a question of just any minimal predicate whatsoever, but
of a minimal predicate such that, between it and the rest of the
predicates which are individually attributable, no intermediary whatsoever falls. The minimum predicate in question is then, in a certain
sense, a maximal predicate. It is minimal because it does not involve
individuating notes and moments; it is maximal, however, in the
order of pre-individual coincidence. That is to say, it is a minimum
such that, in this order, it is an ultimate predicate. The minimalness
in question would be, then, concretely «ultimateness;» it would be
that in which all the individuals ultimately coincide in all their pre-
individual notes. And the minimal and ultimate intrinsic predicate
is the «eidos» (εἶδος), the species; it is that which would constitute
the *quid* (the «what») of the thing; in that case, essence would be
simply *quidditas*, «whatness.» This is precisely what is expressed, as
we have seen, in the second part of the present work, in the definition.
It is necessary, however, to take a further step in order to tighten
traditional thought. Minimalness, I have said, is concretely ultimateness. However, what is this ultimateness of this minimal predicate?
It is not, in the first place, an ultimacy which can be reached by
trying constantly «to add» more and more predicates to that predicate in which individuals agree or which they share. Plato was the
first to state this problem and he saw clearly that the predicates
which count in our problem are not those which are added to the
subject in just any manner, but those which express the natural
articulations of the «whatness;» that is, those predicates which reveal
its natural and intrinsic divisions. «Division» (διαίρεσις) and not 217
addition is what is decisive here. Division, however, of what? Precisely of the notes of the «eidos.» The philosopher who wants to
know what the «eidos» is, Plato tells us, is like the good cook who
cuts a bird along its natural jointures and not like the bad cook who
hacks it apart any old way and therefore what he does is break and
shatter it (*Phaedrus*, 265 E). What are these natural lines of jointure
of the eidos? Let us take a minimal note in which, perhaps, there
may coincide not only the individuals of the species we are looking
for, but also other individuals of other species (γένος, *género*). The
genus lacks ultimacy; it is none of the various species, but necessarily
belongs to one or another of them, as I have been accustomed to

explain in my courses. The jointure is that point at which a new note divides or separates both possibilities of the reality and reduces the genus to a single species. If we succeed in carrying this process of articulation to its extreme point, exhaustively, we will then have the «eidos;» that is, something in which no further division is possible; the «eidos» is predicatively an «ἄτομον εἶδος,» an indivisible «eidos.» And this would be what formally constitutes the «quiddity,» the «whatness,» the essence, as minimal and ultimate intrinsic predicate, in which all the individuals coincide. Ultimacy would then be concretely the natural «indivisibility» of the «eidos.» In this conception every note is a «divider» which separates the two parts of that which is to be divided, leading us to the one and separating us from the other; it is a δια-φορά, a difference. Every essential difference, in this conception, possesses a concrete character: that of being a «divider.» Therefore, every essential difference is a «quidditative» difference, a specific difference. The last of these differences is what, strictly speaking, constitutes the ultimacy of the species; it is what brings it about that one essence is not quidditively another. Whence it follows necessarily that an essential difference would be simply a difference «of» species.

On the basis of this supposition, to say that two real individuals are essentially equal or different is the same as saying that they are 218 specifically the same or different. In this sense, to say that two individuals of the same species can differ essentially is simply absurd... precisely by definition. This was Aristotle's thesis.

However, as soon as one reflects on the matter a little, one notes that all this depends on a precise point of view, namely, a predicative point of view. The essence would be the minimal quantity of coincidence and the ultimate possibility of division: the essential difference would be a «divider» and, therefore, would mean difference «of» essence. But this is unsatisfactory for two reasons.

In the first place: because predication rests on something prepredicative. Predicatively, the essence — ἄτομον εἶδος — is not univocally determined. As moment of coincidence, the ἄτομον εἶδος would be nothing more than that in which the individuals, as a matter of fact, coincide, and then different possibilities of ultimacy and indivision would be opened to the intelligence. In the case of human individuals, we might have come to a stop, not at rationality, but at the condition of being bipeds. What happens is that the ἄτομὸν εἶδος, is not that in which all the individuals coincide but that in which they must necessarily coincide if they are to be quidditatively equal. This means that antecedently to all predication, point of departure is *already* taken in an ἄτομὸν εἶδος, which I have before my mental vision (νοῦς) and its «natural» lines of juncture are looked for afterward in order to make so many other predicates of them. Point of departure is already taken in the fact that we «see» that man is animal and rational, and afterwards, only afterwards, is rationality made the ultimate specific difference. Now this is expressly to abandon the predicative way (*via predicativa*) and to assign primary status to physical reality. The ἄτομὸν εἶδος, as a matter of fact, because it is pre-predicative, is something physical and its very lines of jointure are precisely «natural;» that is, physical. To the very degree to which they are natural, they are pre-predicative. Therefore, we find ourselves referred back from the *quiddity*, as predicate, to the physical reality. It is not a question, as some scholastics already thought, of amplifying the compass of quidditative predication with indivi- 219 dualizing predicates, but of abandoning all predication in order to go to the thing in its physical reality and to ascertain what in it confers on it its minimal and ultimate character. Only then will we be able to see whether all essential difference is difference «of» essence and whether the quiddity is the whole of the essence. The insufficiency of the predicative point of view rests then, for the first reason, in being a point of view which is not sufficient to itself, not even in its own order or line, because it depends on something antecedent, namely, on the physical point of view. And then (the second reason for the insufficiency), the physical reality of the essence, without ceasing to be quiddity, but, even more, precisely in order to be quiddity, is something more primary and fundamental within which the essential difference possesses a different character from that which it possesses in the quiddity. This is what we must now try to make clear.

As physical essence, we have seen, the essence is the system of notes necessary and sufficient to insure that a substantive reality possesses the rest of its characteristics; and its formal basis (*razón*), we have been saying, is the auto-sufficiency of those notes, that is, their capacity to form, by themselves, substantive systems. And in this sense, the physical essence is a factual absolute. As a consequence, in its character as a physical and real moment of substantivity, the essence is not, in the first instance, that in which all the individuals which possess it coincide, that is, it is not *quiddity* but rather intra-individual *constitutivity*. Hence, it is, that an adequate conception of the characteristics of the essense, different from the usual conception, becomes necessary.

The analysis of the traditional concept of essence has revealed to us three fundamental characteristics of it: minimalness *(quantity)*, ultimacy, and essential difference. These three characteristics are not, primarily, proper to essence as «quiddity;» but proper rather 220 to the essence as constitutive essence. For this reason, the fact that we have discovered them in the process of analysis of the traditional concept of essence as quiddity opens to us the possibility of dissociating those characteristics from the interpretation of them which traditional metaphysics gives us. Minimal character, ultimacy, and essential difference, in and for themselves, are one thing, while the quidditive manner of conceptualizing them is quite another. It was fundamental that this dissociation be carried through to its ultimate point. Traditional metaphysics has given an extremely precise interpretation of those characteristics: the minimal means the minimal point of coincidence, ultimacy is undividedness, essential difference is difference «of» essence, i. e., specific difference. In the conception of the physical essence these three characteristics are not quidditative, but constitutive moments; as a consequence, the manner of conceiving it proves to be very different from the traditional one; *minimalness*, in a word, proves to be, not that moment of inter-individual coincidence, abstracted in the form of a minimal predicate, but rather a moment of the physical constitutional intra-individual notes, the minimum in the sense of «necessity and sufficiency» in order to have the rest of the notes, whether constitutional or other; precisely what we have called the constitutive. It is not a minimum of coincidence but a minimum of constitution. Neither is ultimacy that quidditive moment which is indivision. Ultimacy is not quidditative «indivision,» but systematic «closure,» auto-sufficiency in the constituting order. It is not a question of a predicate such that it admits no «intermediate» between itself and that which individuates; but of a constitutionally independent subsystem, factually absolute, that is to say, auto-sufficient in the order of the individual substantivity itself.

Naturally, it is not the case that this physical essence is something in which a certain inter-individual coincidence does not fall; that is, it is not the case that the physical essence is not, in any form whatsoever, quiddity or species. It can be these — no more than «can 221 be» — and we shall immediately concern ourselves with this problem; however, let us suppose for the moment the case in which there is species. In order to fix these ideas, we will call the physical essence of each individual «constitutive essence» and the specific (element) of it, we will call «quidditive essence.» We might have called it simply specific essence, because in reality «quiddity» is nothing but the abstract form of *quid*, and in this sense the term is fully applicable to the constitutive essence as well. However, since the tradition, when it treats of intramundane realities, always calls «quiddity» that which situates an individual within its species, I have decided to treat species and quiddity as synonyms and to call the specific essence quidditive essence. The constitutive essence is much wider than the quidditive essence; for example, the constitutive determinant note of albinism belong to the constitutive essence of the albino man; it does not belong to his quidditive essence. Nevertheless, the quidditive essence is not a «part» of the constitutive essence, but rather only a physical «moment» of it, that moment by reason of which the constitutive essence of this determined individual coincides with the constitutive essence of all the others. This determined man, in a word, does not have «the» (*el*) animal organism and «the» (*la*) reason as its constitutive notes, but only «this» (*este*) animal organism and «this» (*esta*) reason; its quidditive essence, however, is not «this» (*este*) animal organism and «this» (*esta*) reason, but what «this» (*este*) animal organism and «this» (*esta*) reason possess of animal organism and reason respectively. It is this physical moment as numerical realization of «the» (*el*) animal organism and of «the» (*la*) reason; that is, this physical moment as the numerical realization of the human species that, in the first place, I will call the quidditive essence. In a derivative sense, I will designate by this same name the quidditive essence insofar as it is «common» to all the numerically distinct individuals of the same quidditive species; that is, the quidditive essence as «conceptual unity.» With the distinction 222 between constitutive essence and specific essence I am not referring then, in the first instance, to the difference between common or abstract unity and its numerical realization in an example of the former (this would be the classical problem of universals) but to the difference, within the numerical example itself, between its constitutive essence and this its physical moment of quiddity which I call quidditive essence. To be an example of the human species is not, simply by that fact, to be constitutively such a particular individual man. I leave undecided until a later moment the problem of the character and range or compass of this difference. In any event, the meaning is not that they are two adequately distinct and complete essences, each in its own order; in this sense, there is but one essence, the constitutive essence. This is what I have already implied by saying that the quidditive essence is only a «moment» of the constitutive essence. I call them essences only in order to simplify the exposition of our problem, and above all because usually there has always been understood by essence the quidditive essence of each individual of the species. In reality, it is a question of a physical moment of the constitutive essence. However, as a moment, at least, it is something which is not identical with this last. This is to say that there is in every physical essence, which is individual precisely as essence, a difference between the quidditive individual and the constitutive individual, a difference which is an essential difference and which, nevertheless, leaves intact the specific, quidditive identity when that exists. It is precisely the other meaning of essential difference which has to be clarified.

To do this, let us take our point of departure, provisionally, in the quidditive essence. In the essence we must distinguish its content and its individual structuring function. The essence, considered quidditively, concerns only the content of that in which the individuals conceptually coincide. However, if we consider the quiddity in its 223 structuring function, that is to say, if we consider the quidditive essence insofar as it is physically and numerically realized in each individual, then it is perfectly possible to think that there are different ways of individually realizing one same specific content; that is, different manners of being *in* the same or *of* the same species, according to the way in which the quidditive essence performs, so to say, its structuring function. And this is not a mere possibility but, as we have seen, a necessity which is at least «natural.» From the point of view of the structuring function there would be, for example, different ways of having the human quiddity, different ways of being man. These different ways are based, or at least manifest themselves, in so many other physical notes which, therefore, are already notes of the content of the individual physical essence. They are precisely notes of the constitutive essence. As we have seen, some pages earlier, thanks to them, the strict substantivity is not merely a singular but also something intrinsically determined. And the way in which each strict substantivity has of being «one» is precisely the constitution. As a consequence, by reason of its structuring function, the quiddity is something constitutionally differentiated. The functional considera-tion thus uncovers possible essential differences in its own proper physical content. It is not enough, then, to say that individuals have almost infinite different predicates of the merely quidditive order; but it has been necessary, abandoning the predicative point of view, to find a conception of essence which would involve, of itself, the moment of «constitution.» With that conception, there appear dif-ferences which touch the essence itself. This is what must be shown metaphysically. We ask, then, what is the character of these differ-ences, according to which the quiddity exercises its structuring function in different ways?

Above all, they are not merely accidental differences. It might be thought, in fact, that the different ways of realizing one same 224 specific quiddity, for example, the different functional or structuring ways of being man, precisely because they are «ways,» are something accidental to that which we call being man *simpliciter,* to the human quiddity. However, here again the predicative point of view tends to assert itself surreptitiously. The different ways of realizing one same quiddity are predicated of the subject in an accidental form; evidently, however, *accidens* is being taken in the sense of the «pre-dicables,» according to which the *accidens* is opposed to the generic, to the specific difference, to the species, and even to the *proprium.* In our problem, however, it is not a question of the predicative rela-tion as such, but rather of a physical-real structure. Hence, the least which must be said is that the different ways in which a quiddity may be realized are accidents in the «categorial» predicamental sense. But this is also impossible because, apart from the fact that substantivity cannot be confused with the category of substance, the different ways in which a quiddity may be realized are not properties or notes of a subject (which would be the quiddity); they are in no way similar to a color, an action, a similarity, etc., which are «inherent» to a colored subject, an active subject, or a subject which resembles another. And the reason is clear; the differences in question affect the entire reality of the thing. No quidditive moment is, in the strict meaning of the term, «affected» by individual differences; rather, only in primary unity with them does it «constitute» itself a reality. These differences, then, are not accidental, either in the sense of predicables or in the categorial sense.

Nothing remains save differences. And this is the most serious point of the question. These differences are not non-essential because strict individuality is not mere singularity but is, rather, something intrinsically and formally determined. Although it is «indifferent» to the abstract quiddity as such, whether it be realized in one form or another, nevertheless, considered physically, it is essential to it to have to be realized in some form or other, because the physical essence is not exhausted in its mere quidditive content, for its structuring function is also essential to the essence. That is, physically, even though not conceptively, the quiddity is from itself and by itself (if this pleonism be permitted) something essentially «to be differentiated.» The essence is not, primarily, something «defining,» but something formally «structuring.» As a consequence, the «different» in its reality is an intrinsic and formal moment of the essence itself as realized. And the structuring unity of the purely quidditive in its intrinsic essential difference is precisely the constitutive essence. *From the quidditive point of view*, the constitutive essences are the different modes of the realization of the quidditive essence; this is the reason why, *from the point of view of the physical essence*, quidditive essence is only a «moment» of the constitutive essence. This line of thought leaves us the unresolved question of a more complete formal characterization of the constitutive essence and the quidditive essence. We shall take up this question in what is to follow. To sum up, then, the different ways in which a quiddity may be realized are not formally quidditive differences but are, rather, formally essential differences.

The fact is that in the predicative conception of the essence as quiddity, the difference exercises a clearly marked function, which is extremely specified: the function of dividing. The difference is a «divider» as such, and every quidditive difference is *eo ipso* a difference «of» specific essence; in this sense, two essentially different men would be two realities of different species. This dividing function is, however, only one of the many functions which the difference may have, but nothing more. It is necessary to dissociate the dif- 226 ferential function from the divisive function; the latter is only a specialization, a specialized form, of the former. From the physical point of view, to differentiate is not the same as to divide because not every difference is «something added;» determinations may be and are added to the individual, but only in the order of concretion; the individuality itself is not something added but is rather the character of the reality as such of the individual thing. To differentiate is not to divide, neither is it necessarily «to add;» it is also «to constitute» something in reality. Such is the case in the differences we are discussing. In their true character, they are not differences «of» quidditive essence, but rather differences «in» the quidditive essence, within the quiddity itself. Not every essential difference, consequently, is a difference «of» quiddity, for it may also be a difference «in» the quiddity. Two men inexorably have differences «in» the quiddity and, nevertheless, are not «of» different quiddity, are not of different species. Within each strictly individual substantivity, there is, then, a difference between its quidditive-individual moment and its constitutive-individual reality. The articulation of these two moments resides in the necessity with which the quiddity, in itself, is physically to be differentiated. Hence, the constitutive difference is essential without being quidditive. The essential individual differences leave intact the possible specific quidditive identity.

To sum up, minimalness, ultimacy, difference, are structural moments of every essence from the point of view of its notes; they are not, however, necessarily quidditive moments, but rather something *toto caelo* different: physical moments, moments of that which constitutes as such. Mimimalness is not coincidence, but minimal constitution; ultimacy is not indivision, but the self-sufficiency of that which constitutes (*lo constitutivo*); essential difference is not difference «of» but difference «in.»

227   We asked, at the beginning of the exposition of this problem of
the individual essence, how the articulation «essence-species-individual» is possible. And I said that, in order to answer this question,
we were going to begin with the most external aspect of the problem,
namely, by ascertaining what the essential difference might be. We
have just seen what it is: the constitutive difference «in,» within, one
same quiddity. This, however, is only the most external aspect of
the problem. We took our point of departure from the quiddity
itself, in order to see how to differentiate it. That is, we supposed,
provisionally, that the problem consists in seeing how it is possible
to differentiate a quiddity. The truth is, however, that the fundamental problem lies in seeing the possibility of «specifying» or «quiddifying» individuals. The problem concerns, not the different ways
of realizing one same quiddity, but of elevating individual substances
to specific unity. Then the radical problem becomes: what is understood by species? That is to say, is every individual substantivity
specifiable? Only the reply to these questions will enable us to touch
the question «essence-species-individual» at its most profound level.

    For this purpose it is necessary to indicate precisely what is
understood by quiddity. The quiddity is always the answer to the
question concerning the «what» of anything. This «what,» however,
is not necessarily quiddity; every quiddity univocally characterizes
a thing, but not everything which univocally characterizes a thing
is *eo ipso* quiddity. For example, if I ask myself «what» a man is, it
might be said that he is an animal characterized, among other things,
by being two-legged and by speech. This answer does tell us univocally
what man is; this is, however, neither *quid* nor quiddity. In order
to be *quid* the answer must, first of all, express that which cannot
be absent in a thing, if it is to be what it is; namely, that it must
228 express or state not only those notes which univocally characterize
a thing, but those which are its «constitutive» notes as well. For
example, if I ask what an electron is, I might reply that it is an
elementary particle with a negative charge (-1), of gross mass (in
electronic units), and of spin $\frac{1}{2}$. These are constitutive notes of the
electron and furthermore are its *quid*, its essence, in the strict and
formal sense. Nevertheless, this does not mean even remotely that
this is the quiddity of the electron. To be this it would also be necessary that the constitutive notes be further articulated in themselves

and in a highly precise manner; for example, in the form of proximate genus and ultimate difference. (Further on we shall see a more «physical» concept of quiddity.) A mere enumeration of the constitutive notes is not enough. In the «what?» of the electron, as we have indicated it, no one of the notes expressed is related to the others in the form of genus and difference. On the contrary, if I say, adducing the traditional example, that man is an animal (proximate genus) which is rational (ultimate difference) then not only have we expressed the strict and formal essence of man, but his *quiddity* as well. When one says, then, that the essence, in the strict sense, is that which cannot be absent if it is to be all and only what it is, this essence, this *quid*, has two perfectly distinct aspects. The *quid*, the strict essence, means, in the first place, the conjunction of the constitutive notes of a thing. It also means, in the second place, within these notes, those of its moments which are articulatable in the form, for example, of genus and difference. Only this ultimate *quid*, only this essence, is quiddity, that is to say, species.

At the beginning of this work, in tracing the provisional outline of the concept of essence, I said that the «what» has three meanings. One is the conjunction of all the notes which a thing possesses *hic et nunc*. In another sense, the «what» is to be taken as all the notes which univocally characterize the «sameness» of a thing in contrast to the rest of things or in contrast to its own variations. However, I went on to add that there is a third sense: the least number of minimal notes which a thing must have in order to be all and only what it is. The second meaning yields the essence, but only in a «wide» sense. Only in the third sense do we encounter the essence in a «strict» and formal sense. We may now add that, in this third sense, the essence divides itself into two other meanings. One is the essence as the conjunction of the «constitutive» notes of the thing; it is the essence *qua* «constitutive.» Another, as the complex of the articulated notes, articulated, for example, into genus and difference, the essence as species; this is the essence *qua* quiddity. The quiddity is always and only specific. Therefore, every strict and formal essence is a *quid*, a *somewhat*, but it is not necessarily a *quiddity*. This is not a mere conceptual distinction; on the contrary, we shall immediately see its real scope.

When the quiddity has been delimited in this way, we may ask what this specificity may be *in re*, what is the quidditive essence?

It might be thought that the species is that which Husserl called «ideal unity.» I have before me an individual red color. By a noetic mental act I apprehend (Husserl would say «I intuit,» but we may set aside this problem of the inward character of the act) the redness in itself independently of this individual red thing. This constitutive unity of «the» *(el)* red or of «the» *(lo)* red is for Husserl the species. Every individual reality would, therefore, be capable, in this view, of being brought within the species *(especiable)*. But this is impossible. In the first place, what Husserl calls the species presupposes a dissociation between «this» redness and «the» redness. In the second place, «the» (redness) is something «ideal,» the ideality of which, however, has a precise structure: unity of identity. There reappears here the old Platonic and Aristotelean theme of the ἕν καὶ ταυτόν. This structure, however, is not independent of that dissociation; there is idealization only to the degree to which there is dissociation; but it is not *a priori* evident that every reality whatsoever is susceptible of such dissociation. A real thing which, by its own inner character, would be unique, would not admit the dissociation between «this» and «the;» for that dissociation, there must be various individuals. The matter is even clearer if we look at the structure of the ideal, that is, the unity of identity. It is not a matter of a mere objective identity, the result of a noetic act, but of a unity whose term would be something «physical,» something real. Along this line of thought, the unity of identity rests upon the moment common to a multitude of individuals in relationship to which that unity of identity can be objectively conceived. By way of the structure of the ideal we arrive, then, at the same conclusion at which we arrive by way of the consideration of the dissociation between «this» and «the»: the primary and basic presupposition of specification, that is, the establishment of species, is the *multitude* of individuals. This multitude is not only a condition for arriving in fact at a knowledge of the species, but is rather the intrinsic condition for there being species *in re*; that is, for there being specification of an individual substantive reality. There is species only when there is a unifiable multitude. Where this is not the case, there is physical essence but not species. Species is not ideal unity.

On this basis, it might be thought that this unification is that which exists when, in this multitude of individual realities, similarities and differences exist *in re*. The unity of similarities would constitute the species. In this case, the species is not something merely ideal but something which, in its way, is real. This is what is customarily said. This position, however, appears to me to be equally untenable, for at least two reasons. In the first place, this would apply equally to all types of things indifferently, including artificial things (buildings, chairs, instruments, etc.) and, in general, to all «meaning,» a position which is unacceptable because these things have objective concepts but do not possess essence and, therefore, could hardly have species. Only the real, as such, can have essence and, therefore, only in the real is there species. Similarities and differences are not enough to constitute species. The domain of the specific is much more restricted, then, than the area of what indifferently are called «things.» The fact is — and this is the second reason — even when we consider «reality-things» the essentiable, the unification of the multitude of individuals by way of similarities would constitute a «class» of real things; but «class» is not necessarily «species.» Even though both concepts have been customarily employed indifferently, I believe that it is of fundamental importance to establish a strict distinction between them. Proof that they are not identifiable is the fact that, if we try to reach a real species, not just any classificatory concept whatsoever is adequate to this end. For example, this is a most serious problem among living things, namely, what is the criterion for establishing the species? As long as only the external macroscopic morphology is considered, the system of similarities can lead to crass errors; appeal must be made to functional criteria, which, unfortunately have not as yet been precisely established. This situation makes it clear that although every species may be a class, not every class is a species and that, consequently, the formal basis of specificity does not consist in being a class. In order to reach the quidditive essence by way of classification one has previously to know what the species might be; only that knowledge would permit us to ascertain the route which must be followed to establish the class. The lack of discrimination with which the concepts of class and species are used becomes clear when it is noted that the predominance of the classificatory concept generates the appearance of numerous «subalternate» species, in such fashion that what is species when viewed from certain levels proves to be genus when viewed from others. This is a relativization which is inherent in the concept of class. By contrast, the physical species is something *toto caelo* different; it will not tolerate this relativity. The classificatory concept then leads us to believe that 232 the «physical» species is the «last» species. But this conclusion is pure metaphysical logicism. *In re* species is not class nor is there any room, consequently, to speak of «last» or «lowest» species. And the fact is that a «conceptive» class does not include, in the most favorable of cases, any more than the conjunction of notes which univocally characterize a thing, that is, the essence in the wide sense of the term. It is a *quid* (what) which is not strict and formal essence.

Hence it may be necessary to establish, among objective concepts themselves, a difference of capital importance. All conceptive apprehension of the real is achieved by means of concepts, of which some are more or less general than others. It is along this line that we establish the difference between the «general» and the «special.» However, on this ground alone we do not get beyond the essence *qua* class. If we wish to apprehend a truly specific essence conceptively, i. e., by way of concepts, we have to take our point of departure in an already attained «vision» of the species; and the system of concepts through which we apprehend this specific essence expresses conceptively its real metaphysical moments. It is along this line that we establish the difference between «generic» and «specific.» Although the etymology of the words is the same, the «general-special» order is one thing, the «generic-specific» order another. The first is given in every «class;» the second, only in the physical «species.» Not everything general is generic, nor is everything special specific. The series from the general to the special, in a word, is, by its nature (*de suyo*), indefinite; given one concept, it is always possible, in principle, to find another which makes it more special. By contrast, the series from generic to specific is defined and in this sense finite; the species is something ultimate, it is ἄτομον εἶδος. The confusion of the generic with the general and the special with the specific has proved to be the source of serious confusion between class and species.

It is clear that it is possible to speak of a «natural» class or classes which are not mere «conceptive» groupings but truely natural groups. This is strictly true; even more, we shall see immediately that it is a fundamental truth. This does not mean, however, that a natural class is a species. It is necessary, consequently, to distinguish rigorously between natural class and species.

We said, a few pages back, that the strict formal essence is the minimum of notes which must be present, and cannot be absent, if a thing is to be wholly and solely what it is. In this sense, however, as we have seen, the strict and formal essence has two different aspects — the constitutive and the quidditive. The essence, *qua* constitutive, is the conjunction of the constitutive characteristics of a thing. When, consequently, this «constitutive» essence is found simply «repeated» or «replicated» in a multitude of similar or perfectly equal individuals, I will say that this multitude is constituted as a natural class. This unification of the many, by way of similarity or equality, in its *quid*, in its constitutive essence, is not «specification;» nor is it quiddification; rather it is «inclusion in a class.»

I may put it formally thus: the natural class is based on the mere multiplicity of individuals having the same constitutive essence, the same constitutive *quid*, within the *multiplicity*. By contrast, the species, the quiddity, is based on a very precise line, on the line of the physical and real *multiplication* of its constitutive essences. Multiplication is a physical process of «producing» a multitude. Without multiplication there would be only pure multiplicity of individuals. All multiplication leads to multiplicity, but not all multiplicity is the result of multiplication. Mere multiplicity rests on itself and constitutes only a natural class of constitutive essences. Only as the term of multiplication do the multiple individuals of a multitude form a species. That is: only those individual realities can be united in a species whose constitutive essence is susceptible, not only of repetition, but of multiplication as well; only in the latter case, is there quidditive essence.

It is not a mere conceptual distinction, because not only is it not *a priori* evident that all realities have a multipliable constitutive essence, but also, as a matter of fact, that there are, on the one hand, natural classes, that is, constitutive essences which are merely repeated, which are not, consequently, constituted as species and,

(margin notes: 233, 234)

on the other hand, there are constitutive essences which cannot be established in species, which cannot be organized as quiddities, precisely because they are unique. We shall see immediately which classes these are. Let us limit ourselves, at this point, to the example of some constitutive essences which tolerate neither multiplication nor multiplicity. In the historical course (to put it in this way) of the innumerable genetic mutations, very many living organisms arise which do not belong to the same species as their progenitors, the majority of which, nevertheless, have but a fugitive life, do not propagate themselves and this, not by any accident, but because they lack the biological stability necessary for propagation. These mutations were not indeed lethal, but were non-specificable; these organisms belong neither to the species of their progenitors nor do they establish a new species. For this reason they can be grouped in conceptive classes with other living things on the basis of one or another characteristic, but they can never be established in a natural class, a species, or a quiddity. Nevertheless, these essences evidently possess an individual physical essence, a constitutive essence in the strict sense, a constitutive *quid*. The essence, consequently, is one thing, the species and the quiddity another. And, therefore, the true problem does not lie in the way in which a specific quiddity realizes itself in individuals, that is, in the manner in which a quiddity is individualized, but, precisely the reverse, it consists in determining whether, and under what conditions, there exists a quidditive expansion, a quiddity, for a determined individual constitutive essence.

In order for a constitutive essence to be quiddifiable it is necessary and sufficient that it should tolerate or imply a physical unity of multiplication. Multiplication, I have said, is physical action. But of what kind?

1.   There must be a causal, productive action in order that, starting with an individual constitutive substantivity, others may be produced.

235   2.   This action must be produced, in some way or other (this is another question), by the substantive reality itself. If this action were not given in any way whatsoever, in the substantive reality itself, there would be no multiplication.

3.   This is not yet enough, however, to satisfy our problem. It is necessary, in addition, that this causal action, whatever its mechan-

ism (efficiency, etc.), to put the matter in this way, should be an action of an intrinsic type, such that the first individual on which the causal action rests may be a «model» of the individuals produced. It must be a «paradigmatic» causality, involving the constitutive characteristics, that is, the individual essence. Its result, in the range of the series of individuals, is the establishment of a homonymous line. Giving the term a metaphysical meaning, much wider than it possesses in paleontology and in biology, I should say that this causal action, in addition to producing individuals, constitutes a *phylum*. This is not a matter of a mere «relation» of similarity, more or less profound, among the individuals, but a strict physical reality. The *phylum* is a physical reality much more real, even, than the electromagnetic or gravitational etc. «field» can be. And those constitutive characteristics, by reason of which each individual belongs really and physically to a determined *phylum*, a r e p r e c i s e l y those which constitute the species: the individual essence has been specified (established in a species). In this sense, to ask ourselves what anything is, is to ask, not for the class of realities to which it belongs, but for the *phylum* from which and within which it emerges physically and really into reality and to which it belongs by reason of its constitutive essence. The essence is then quidditive. Such is the «physical» concept of species and quiddity. The necessary and 236 sufficient metaphysical condition for «quiddification» of the species is phyletic multiplication. Therefore, the physical essence is not, in the first place, specification but constitutive individuality; if, however, it is «*phylumable*» (able to be established in a *phylum*) it can be established in and as a species. It is clear that it is not required that there be multiplication *in fact*. In an individual which stands as the head of the species there is no multiplication in fact, but upon it a *phylum* can be established: it is intrinsically multipliable. And this intrinsic capacity, not its actual realization, is what constitutes the specificity of the essence. What happens is that actual multiplication is the only way in which we can come to know whether there is a species. The radical principle (*razón*) of specifiability is phyletic multipliability, and the formal principle (*razón*) of the species is the capacity of belonging actually or virtually to a *phylum*.

Where this cannot take place, there is constitutive essence but no species; there is no quiddity in the usual sense. This non-speci-

fiability can be of different types. There is, first of all, a non-specifiability by reason of «poverty» of constitutive notes; this is the case,
as we shall see, with all the singular individuals which exist in the
world. There are essences which, by reason of their very poor intrinsic endowment, are capable only of repetition or reduplication. There
are, in addition, non-specifiable essences of another type, exactly the
type to which I alluded earlier when I spoke of genetic mutations.
This example must be understood correctly, however. This example
may lead some to think that the non-specifiable is the anomolous,
the monstrous. This is not the case. It is true that mutations can
produce and in general do produce, probably even in a majority of
cases, monsters. In the example, however, we were not speaking of
monsters. For every monster is such only within a determined species; the monster, therefore, formally presupposes the species and
is of no use for our problem. What I was referring to was mutations
237 the result of which is not a monster but another living thing with
characteristics proper to itself, with its own «original» essence; if
I may be permitted the expression, a sketch, an «essay» of nature
to constitute a species, but an essay which was shipwreck in this
order. We should not confuse, then, an effort or trial which failed
and hence is non-specifiable, with an intra-specific monstrosity. The
effort is frustrated, not because of individual deformation of the
specific characteristics, but because of an innovation in the constitutive characteristics which I might call «defective.» The species,
as a matter of fact, involves not only the «constitutive,» but a constitutive such that it would be endowed with a certain stability in
the sense of dynamic continuity, of phyletic perduration. When there
is an innovation, there is a constitutive essence; however, if it lacks
that stability, if it is a labile constitutive, there is indeed a constitutive essence, but there is no quidditive essence, there is no species;
there is no specific innovation, but only an individual innovation.
Compared with other essences capable of specification and quiddification the labile essence, and therefore its non-specifiability, is «defective.» Finally, it is not possible to exclude, at least *a priori*, the
existence of another kind of non-specifiability, an incapacity of multiplication because the constitutive essence is of such richness and
perfection that it is and can only be constitutively unique. This
would not be a matter of a species which exhausts itself in the indi-

vidual, but of a non-specifiable, non-quiddifiable individual, and these are entirely different things. It is a «perfective» non-specifiability. We may content ourselves with leaving the door open to this type of essential non-specifiability. To sum up, there is non-specifiability by reason of poverty, «defective» non-specifiability, and «perfective» non-specifiability.

However, let us set aside *a priori* questions. We are attempting an intramundane metaphysics and, therefore, what we have to know is whether and in what form non-specifiable individuals may exist in the world; that is, what kind of essences realities in the world possess. The world, as we have seen when treating this point, has 238 three zones of reality, very different in character, but intrinsically articulated among themselves.

There is, before all else, material nature in the restricted sense of «inanimate.» We saw, when treating of the individual substantivity that, strictly speaking, that which has substantivity in this area is the material reality taken in its entirety, since each of the so-called elementary particles is are a mere fragmente of that reality. Hence it follows that only matter taken integrally possesses essence. Essence, that is, belongs only to the individual substantivity. This essence of «the» matter is not, to be sure, individual in a strict sense; but neither is it singular, but rather must be recognized as being a «unique,» constitutive essence. Nevertheless, we can consider the elementary particles as realities in and for themselves. Contemporary physics cannot say, at present, whether these particles are truly elements, since some produce other different ones, either by natural instability or by reaction, in such manner that it is not possible to say of all the particles whether or not they possess structure and hence, whether or not they are elements. For this reason, it is preferable to call them, as some have called them, «fundamental» particles. Be that as it may, when the particles are taken in and for themselves, we find that they possess some notes which not only determine them univocally but which are their «constitutives»: charge, mass, spin; we may add, if one wishes, the note of «abnormality» (*extrañeza*). These particles, consequently, have constitutive essence. However, each one of them «repeats» exactly all and only the constitutive notes of particles of its own type. Hence it is that these particles are not, strictly speaking, individuals, but rather mere singular individuals, *singuli*. The difference between two electrons or between two μ-ons of the same sign, for example, consists simply in the fact that one is not the other, since they are completely without internal 239 differences; they are merely numerical unities. It is true that these particles produce each other. This production, however, does not have a phyletic character, since the most diverse particles can give rise to a same type of particle and *vice versa*; even more, in reactions involving highest energy values, all kinds of particles are produced simultaneously by interaction. Their numerical multitude, consequently, is not the result of a true multiplication, but is rather a «mere» multiplicity. Hence it is that their constitutive notes, their constitutive essence, do not show membership in a *phylum* but only in a determined group; that is, they do not constitute *species*, but constitute only *class*, a *natural class*. Every *singulum*, because it has constitutive notes proper to itself, has a *quid*, a constitutive essence; but this *quid* is not *quiddity*, is not a quidditive essence. In order that it should be, it would be necessary that the particles possess a *phyletic* unity. Only then would the constitutive essence constitute membership in a *phylum*; only then would there be a quidditive essence, species, able to be articulated into *genera* and differences. This is not the case with the elementary or fundamental particles. For this reason, the *singuli* are not «speciables,» but only «classifiables» (*enclasables*). The same must be said of atoms, of molecules and, perhaps, of crystals as well. Many times, by an inevitable freedom of language, one speaks of «chemical species» to designate the «simple bodies,» the atoms. The atoms, however, in reality, are not chemical «species» but chemical «elements.» Atoms, molecules, crystals (?), are mere *singuli*.

Living things constitute the second zone of the world. As we saw, when speaking of individual substantivity, living beings do not possess strict substantivity nor, therefore, strict individuality, but possess, 240 rather, a *primordium*, a sketch of individuality superior to mere singularity; this is what I then called «quasi-individuality.» One perceives, in animals above all, a «quasi-individuality» which progresses as one ascends the zoological scale. Nevertheless, just as in the case of the elementary particles, we can take living things in and by themselves as though they were strictly substantive reali-

THE «ESSENCE» ITSELF OF THE REAL

ties. And then we discover something more than mere natural classes in them.

We discover, in the first place, a specificity, because true phyletic unities do exist among living things. In fact, the physical and causal act of the multiplication of living beings has a precise metaphysical structure: it is «generation.» Generation ,as we shall see immediately, is not simply identical with the multiplication of living things. In order that *multiplication* be *generation* at least two conditions are required. There must be, on the one hand, an action which «rests» in the generator or generators, but in a very special manner, namely, an action executed not only «by» them but «from» themselves. On the other hand, the paradigmatic causality must, in living things, take on a form which is also very special; it must be homonymy by «transmission» of characteristics of the constitutive essence of the progenitors to the constitutive essence of the beings generated. The manner of transmission does not affect the case: it may be a strict transference but it may also be a mere «exigitive» conformation. When these two conditions are present, and only when they are present, do we have «generation.» Hence, it follows that generation is the constitution of a *phylum* and at the same time the constitution of phyletic characteristics in the constitutive essence of the being engendered. The specific characteristics are nothing else but these: the moments of the constitutive essence which show that it belongs to the *phylum*. For this reason, with generation, then, we have the constitution of the species. It is true that biology has not yet succeeded in giving definitive criteria of specificity: distinction between species is many times undecisive and fluid. Nevertheless, the moment of fecundity enters into all criteria, even though only in a negative fashion: organisms which are in principle (*principialmente*) infertile in their crossbreeding do not belong to the same species. Therefore, phyletic or specific is always and only a «generational» unity. For this reason, specificity, the quidditive essence, is always «genotypical.»

However, this is not the only thing we encounter or find in living things. In fact, if, of the two conditions which are necessary for generation, namely, that there be an act executed *by* and *from* the progenitors and that, in that act, *all* of the quiddifiable characteristics should be transmitted, only the first is fulfilled, then there is

241

no generation in the strict sense; there is, in this case, only «origination;» the new living thing, rather than being «engendered» by the «progenitors,» «originates» in them, «proceeds» from them. Such is the case in «mutation.» For this reason, it can be said only with risk of grave equivocation that the first bird had a «reptile» for a «father;» we will say only that the birds proceed from the reptiles or «originate» in them. In such a case, the constitutive essence of the «originating» or «originators» are «more than specifiable» since they give rise to a new individual constitutive essence, not only with reference to what concerns its substantivity, but also with reference to what concerns the phyletic or quidditive characteristics. For this reason, this new essence is not of the «same species» as the essence of the originators. This phyletic or quidditive novelty can be of a different character or quality. It can be, in its turn, an individual constitutive essence speciable by generation. Then it is a question of an individual which becomes head of a new *phylum*, of an individual which inaugurates a species. In that case, the constitutive essence of the originating beings have a peculiar way of being «more than specifiables;» they are what I may call «meta-specifiable» or «meta-quiddifiable» essences. It may, however, be the case that the new individual is not «speciable.» Then the originating essences are «more than speciables,» but in another sense; they are simply «mutables» or, if one wishes, only «meta-essentiables,» but not «meta-speciables.»

To sum up, the multiplication of living things is either of the generating or of the originating type and, in the latter case, it is either of the meta-specifying type or of the mutant type. For this reason, there are, among living beings, three types of constitutive essences: there are «speciable» or «quiddifiable» constitutive essences; there are «meta-speciable» or «meta-quiddifiable» constitutive essences; and there are «non-specifiable» or «non-quiddifiable» constitutive essences, «unique» essences.

Men constitute the third zone of the reality of the world. From the point of view of his insertion into the field or zone of living things, the human animal proceeds or originates in another animal *phylum*. In this *phylum* he has had, then, at a given moment, not generation, but mere origination. The human animal, in a word, possesses, among other peculiarities, a non-transferable intelligence by reason of which he confronts both things and himself as realities.

Thanks to this character, the individual quasi-substantivity has terminated in a strict individual substantivity. However, the originating being of the human animal was not only «meta-essentiable» but «meta-speciable» as well. Men, in a word, multiply by generation, that is, possess a phyletic unity: the individual constitutive essence of every man is specifiable, quiddifiable. As a consequence, man is the head of a new *phylum*, has inaugurated a species. And since he is the only animal which possesses strict individual substantivity, it follows that he is the only animal whose phyletic unity is strictly and rigorously essential specifiability. Only the human species is, strictly speaking, *species*. However, the abstract unity of the species, of the quiddity, is what is expressed in a definition. Hence it is that 243 the human species is the only strictly definable species. It is not a matter of chance, consequently, that, as a matter of fact, only of man has a rigorous definition by proximate genus and ultimate difference been given. Naturally, this still leaves unresolved and undetermined the problem of the value of that definition.

Material reality, purely biological reality, the human reality, these three zones of the reality of the world, show us what that which we call species *is* and what it is *not*. It is the group of notes genetically transmissible and perdurant by interfecundity. These and these only are quiddifiable notes.

It is clear, of course, that not everything which is genetically transmissible is necessarily quidditive. Constitutive characteristics which do not belong to the quiddity can also be transmitted. Reciprocally, not all that is quidditive is necessarily transmissible; such is the case with the origin of new species. For this reason, the concept of species here expressed should be clarified in view of these two circumstances. These circumstances are not to be denied; they do not, however, invalidate this concept. In the first place, for the constitution of a *phylum* it is not enough to look only to one generator or one generated; it is necessary to have in view the totality of the engendering and the engendered. Then many constitutive characteristics are automatically eliminated, because they are transmitted only in isolated cases or groups; the group of characteristics transmitted in *all* cases is precisely what we mean by the «speciable» or «quiddifiable.» Despite appearances, this concept of species is not a merely residual concept; for this group of constitutive characteristics,

16

which are transmitted in every case, has, as we shall see immediately, a positive unity proper to itself. They are not characteristics which suffice to constitute a complete constitutive essence; neither, however, are they a mere «fragment of essence.» They are what I shall call a
244 «constitutive schema,» the «schema» according to which the constitutive essence of the engendered is erected. And this constitutive schema, genetically transmitted, is the very definition of *phylum*. In the second place, it is true that not all that is «quiddifiable» is always transmitted. However, attention must be paid not only to what is transmitted in all cases, but also to what is perdurable by interfecundity. The reptiles, despite the fact that they gave origin to the birds, continue to engender reptiles; but interfecundity between birds and reptiles does not exist. That is to say, the constitutive *schema* admits «grades» or «degrees» of schematism. Mammifers have in common with reptiles, fishes, amphibians, etc., the fact that they are all vertibrates. To be vertibrate is to have a certain proper constitutive schema, a zoological «plan» which is perfectly defined; but just as, nevertheless, not all the vertibrates are interfecund, this schema is not specific, but at most generic. Every new species and every non-specifiable individual always arises within a generic constitutive schema, already predetermined (*prefijado*). However, it is only specific when, in addition to being genetically transmitted, it is enduring, precisely and formally, through interfecundity. The convergence of different *phyla* in the constitution of certain species is not a matter of chance for our problem. The minimum of constitutive notes genetically transmissible and enduring through interfecundity: here we have, in one sum, the inner character of the *phylum* and the inner character of the species. The *phylum* is the constitutive schema and the species is that which establishes the membership of an engendered being in the *phylum*; the fact of being constituted according to one same constitutive schema. Later I will return to this concept of generation and species.

This is a strictly philosophical, and not merely biological, concept of species. No distinction whatsoever exists between a «biological» species and a «philosophical» species and the difficulties which can exist in determining the one are identical with the difficulties which
245 can exist in determining the other. The fact that no one can, as a matter of fact, learn *all* the generating processes, does not prove

the falseness of the concept but only indicates the approximative and partial character of many characteristics considered to be specific. What happens is that if, for one or another reason, the irreducibility of one specific note to any others is known *a priori*, then *eo ipso* all the generational processes which bear upon this note are known *a priori*; such is the case with man in what refers to his intelligence. Even in this case, however, the cognizability of the irreducibility of the note in question does not mean that an adequate knowledge of what constitutes the human species is also attained. Sometimes that which constitutes the irreducible peculiarity of a thing is called its nature. This, however, does not give us *all* that constitutes the human species: for that we have to know, not only that man possesses an intelligence which cannot be reduced to animal psychic processes, but, in addition, all the constitutive notes of what, with inevitable, but nevertheless irritating, vagueness is usually called «animal» or «animal organism,» as a generic character of the human species. For, we may ask, what concrete type of animal organism is that which enters into the structure of the human species? These things are necessary, not only for the «positive,» but for the philosophical, knowledge of man as well. The definition must contain a genus which is «proximate.» Which is the single note, or the notes collectively, which are truly proximate in this case? Only when we shall have knowledge of these will we be able to say that we know the specific inner character of man. Merely to know that he has intelligence is not enough. That is enough to insure the knowledge that man is of «another» species from the rest of animals; but it does not tell us of what kind, concretely, «this» other species may be. For this there is no other 246 path than the application of the criteria usual in biology and especially the genetic criterion. The histological and anatomical characteristics can many times — but not always — be decisive; but never are they any more than the «expression» of the specificity, never what constitutes it, because they are not constitutive, but only constitutional, characteristics. The knowledge of a species is, then, always and without exception, partial and approximate. However, as a rigorously philosophical concept, it is the group of constitutive notes by reason of which a constitutive essence belongs to a determined *phylum*.

Let us now cast a backward glance at the problem we have outlined. We have been asking how the essence could be formally and
entitatively individual without, as a consequence, entailing the condition that the individual substantivities be essentially distinct or
different. We approached this problem along two paths. The first,
starting from the idea of specific essence, of quiddity, consisted in
clarifying what is to be understood by «essential difference.» And we
saw that not every essential difference is a difference «of» essence,
of species, of quiddity, but that it may also be a difference «in»
essence, species, or quiddity, that is, a distinct manner of physically
realizing the same specific essence, a distinct manner in which the
quidditive essence physically structures the reality. These differences,
we saw, are not accidental but entitative moments of the essence
itself *qua* essence. This path, however, does not touch the basis of
the problem, because it begins with the supposition that the reality
is always, and only, the realization of a specific essence. But the
real problem lies precisely in knowing whether every *quid* is the
247 realization (*actualización*) of a *quidditas*. In other words, one must
begin with the individual substantivity and ascertain in what measure
its constitutive essence is essentiable, quiddifiable. Such was the
second path which we undertook to follow. And contrary to what
is always said and presupposed, I have tried to make it be seen that
not every constitutive essence is quiddifiable, that is, that essence
is not identical with quiddity. Therefore, not only are individual
essential differences not necessarily differences of species, but neither
do constitutive essences always form species. There are essences of
merely singular individuality; they do not form species, but natural
classes; they have *quid*, constitutive essence, but not *quidditas*, quidditive essence. Their singularity belongs, formally, to their constitutive essence, but does not introduce a difference of species, because
the species does not exist. In addition to these essences there are
other, quasi-individuals; they are the constitutive essences of living
beings. Among these, some are «specifiable,» quiddifiable; others are
«meta-specifiable;» others, «meta-essentiable.» In the first, the individual differences are differences «in» the species; in the second,
they are differences «of» the species or quiddity; in the third, the
individual set of characteristics is not a «difference» either «of» or
«in» species, but rather only a «proper constitutive» system; they

are «unique» essences. Finally, there are constitutive essences, the human, which are «specifiable» and in which, therefore, the individual differences are not differences «of» the species, but «in» the species.

To sum up, every constitutive essence is entitatively and formally individual. Specification is always a derived, and not always an existent, moment. Individual differences are always essential. I say, in other terms, even in the case in which the constitutive essence is also quidditive essence, the radical and formal element of the essence as moment of the substantivity is its constitutive character; that is, the essence *simpliciter* is the constitutive essence. And this essence is always individual.

As moments of substantivity, we have said, the constitutive notes 248 are absolutely metaphysical in condition, in the sense of *factual*. We may now add, this factual absolute, this constitutive self-sufficiency, has in its very essence, and as essence, an individual entitative character. The ultimate units (*piezas*) on which the entire world is based are not only something factual, are not only a pure *factum*, but are also a pure *factum* which is constitutively individual. Entitatively and formally, the essence is constitutive individual ultimacy.

III. *The Essence: Its Unalterable Constitutive Content*   249

Ungrounded and ultimate in the order of constitution, the notes of the constitutive essence possess a character of ultimacy not only absolute and individual but also, in content, such that they are constitutively unalterable. Inalterability does not mean that the notes cannot change; this would be absurd in principle and false in fact. In this sense there is no intramundane physical essence which is unalterable. The inalterability to which I am referring lies in another order; it is exactly and formally in the order of sameness. Every note, whether essential or not, is susceptible of physical alteration. What happens is that there are notes which, while themselves changing, do not change the sameness of the real thing; they only modulate or modify it. Then, this real thing, to be sure, ceases to be «the» (*lo*) same, but continues to be «the» (*el*) same. All the notes which belong to the order of concretion share this condition or character. Therefore, these notes whose alteration leaves the sameness of the thing intact do not, ultimately, touch the sameness of the thing; they

lack ultimacy in this constitutive order. By contrast, if the notes of
the constitutive essence are changed, one no longer has «the» (*el*)
same thing as before simply modified, but rather just the reverse;
what one has is an «other» reality, an «other» thing. In this sense,
and in this sense alone, do we say that the notes of the constitutive
essence are unalterable. The essence constitutes exactly and formally the moment of the sameness. To go against the essence is not a
countersense, but rather a «counter-reality;» it is the physical destruction of the substantive reality.

250 «the» (*el*) same and never «the» (*lo*) same is a primary characteristic
When speaking of the substantive reality, we saw that to be always
of every substantive reality, as substantive. Now, however, we may
advance a step further and say that this characteristic belongs to the
substantivity derivatively, because what it belongs to primarily and
formally is the content of the essential notes, as essential. For example, it is well known that white cats with blue eyes are deaf. These
three notes are inalterable. However, they are such only because
they are the consequence of a genetic structure. And this structure
is the true constitutive note. The inalterablility belongs to those
three constitutional notes, precisely in as far and in as much as
it belongs to the constitutive genetic structure. Every physical alteration of (that structure) is the total destruction of one thing or the
origination of another thing.

I have spoken of sameness. Let us avoid two reefs. In the first
place, traditional philosophy is accustomed to say that identity is a
transcendental character of every entity; every entity is identical
with itself. It might then be thought that sameness might be this
identity, this identicalness. But this is not the case. Even without, at
this point, positing the question of the equation between being and
reality, we must energetically insist upon the distinction between
identity (identicalness) and sameness. What real things have in their
character as physically real is a sameness; they are or are not «the»
(*el*) same in their possible alteration. Identity, by contrast, is, at
most, the objective concept of sameness. In the second place, it
might be thought that sameness might be the permanent character
of substance in contrast to the alterability of its accidents. The difference, however, between substantivity and substantiality is fundamental on this point. Sameness affects precisely and formally sub-

stantivity, and not substantiality. Permanence of substance does not suffice to insure that there be substantive sameness. There is, as we have seen, insubstantive substances, substances which began by being substantive but which, however, while persisting as substances, have lost their substantive sameness; such is the case with substances which compose an organism. Reciprocally, the organism preserves 251 its sameness so independently of the substances that, precisely in virtue of that independence, it can exchange them «singularly,» i. e., one by one. The sameness of substantivity, consequently, is one thing; the permanency of substantiality, another.

I may repeat then, the constitutive essence is that which possesses, by reason of its content, this ultimacy of sameness as a consequence of which it is inalterable. Every alteration in this essence gives place, *eo ipso*, to another constitutive essence. And this is not merely a formalistic and negative character. Quite the contrary. Precisely because it is inalterable, in the sense explained above, is its inexorable physical alteration the origination of an other essence as essence. And this is something completely or entirely positive and filled with real content. The alteration which constitutively affects the world in all its aspects and moments, when it touches what is inessential, «modifies» reality. When it touches the essential, however, since the essential is inalterable in its character as constitutive, it results *precisely for that reason* in the «origination» of a new essence. The constitutive inalterability of the content of the essential notes is thus, paradoxically, a genesis of essences. Physical essences can originate and do originate one from another in their proper and formal essential content precisely because they are inalterable in themselves. It is necessary to understand correctly this implication between inalterability of constitutive content and origination of essences, because traditional philosophy, in projecting the problem of the inalterability of essences has, in a certain manner, closed the path to an adequate understanding of the origination of essences.

In a word, in not distinguishing the «constitutive» essence from the «quidditive» essence, that is, in having identified quiddity and 252 essence, traditional philosophy found itself compelled to make a double affirmation. On the one hand, it affirmed that the physical essence (which, in this conception is no more than the singular reality of the quiddity, of the essence, of the species) is alterable in the sense of generable and corruptible, but «nothing more.» On the other hand, it affirmed that the quiddity, the specific essence, is inalterable in the sense of invariable in the course of time. As a matter of fact, neither of these affirmations is, strictly speaking, true or exact.

Let us start with the first affirmation, according to which the physical essence is generable and corruptible, but «nothing more.» This «nothing more» is not necessarily true when taken in all its rigor and universality. In the first place, traditional philosophy has always laid it down as a presupposition that the term of «generation» is a physical essence which is only numerically distinct from the generating principle; that is to say, that the generated is a mere singular. The «nothing more» means, in this line of thought, that generation is, so far as the essence is concerned, nothing but «repetition.» Now this may be true, but it is neither generally or necessarily so, because, in general, the reality has, in its very essence, a strict and formal individuality. In such a case, generation is not «repetition» of the essence and «nothing more» but a strict «genetic constitution» of the new individual essence *qua* constitutive essence (including in that essence its quidditive moment, only, however, insofar as it is constitutive). Constitution here means the act of constituting. The concept of «genesis» here embraces three metaphysical moments. In the first place, it is an act of the generating principle itself. In the second place, it is an act which, in the order of essence, does not merely transmit quidditive characteristics by «repetition» plus certain extra-essential individual characteristics, but which, further, is a unique and total act in which the constitutive essence of the engendered, its strict and formally individual essence, is con-
253 stituted. Since this essence involves richer and more numerous characteristics than the quidditive ones, the result is that the «generation» is not simple «repetition,» is not an act which merely «reproduces» but which, maintaining the particular «sameness» of the generating principle, causally determines the «otherness» of a strictly and formally individual essence. In this dimension, genetic constitution is «genetic determination» of a constitutive essence by the constitutive essence of the generating principle. The genetic determination affects, therefore, not only the quidditive moments but the total system of the constitutive characteristics as well. In the third place, the constitution itself, that is to say, the genetic determination, has an in-

trinsically «processive» character: it is a processual genesis. The constitutive essence is not just something which «is or is not,» but something which achieves *to be* genetically. This process is not univocally «determined» once and for all without qualification; rather, the genetic determination itself is processive, to the point where interference with the process can alter the definitive physiognomy of the constitutive system; that is, its formal essential individuality. The constitutive system of what is generated has an intrinsic power of reaching different ultimate constitutions; and it is precisely the genetic determination that processively produces the final constitution. The power of reaching different final systems is not then undifferentiated «potency,» but rather has a precise structure; more than a potency it is a «potentiality» of reaching different individual essences, a potentiality variable from an initial, as it were, «all potentiality» and a «nul-potentiality» at the end of the genetic process. It is not a merely biological concept: I believe that a strictly metaphysical character must be accorded to it. For this reason, rather than «potentiality of development» I prefer to speak of «potentiality of constitution,» a causality of processive conformation proper to 254 every generable essence. Strictly speaking, the name «generation» should be reserved exclusively for this processively determinating «genetic constitution.» Therefore, generation is not a mere «repetition» or numerical «reproduction» of a quidditive essence, but the «production» of a formally individual constitutive essence by processive determination.

In the second place, as we have already seen earlier, a constitutive essence not only can «engender» others with the same quidditative characteristics, but it can also «originate» others, whether specifiable or not. In such a case one is confronted by a genetic causality of meta-specification or of simple meta-essentiation.

Hence it follows that the physical essence is not necessarily a singular which is born, reproduces itself, and is corrupted and «nothing more;» rather, it is a constituted essence which, in addition to being born and being corrupted, either «repeats» or «engenders» or, finally, «originates» a new constitutive essence. Employing the Greek concept of «genesis» we will say that every constitutive essence is the genetic term of another and that this genesis includes the three possibilities of repeating, engendering, and originating.

Equally unsustainable is that other affirmation according to which
the specific or quidditive essence is inalterable in the sense of invariable in the course of time. Taking the essence as τὸ τί ἦν εἶναι,
as species (εἶδος), the Greeks thought that essences were physically
ingenerable and incorruptible, that is, immutable and eternal. It is
true that individually all substances save the stars and the θέος are
corruptible; but they engender, as we have said, others of the «same»
species, in such wise that this univocity of the specific generation
makes of the species, for the Greeks, something strictly ungenerable
and immortal: men are born and die, but humanity neither dies nor
255 is born; it «always» (ἀεί) is. And this eternity is rigorous and strict,
because the time of the substantial generation of individuals is cyclical; it is eternity, perpetual youth, as eternal return. Hence it is
that, for Aristotle, quiddity (τὸ τί ἦν εἶναι) as correlative of the definition, the species (εἶδος) and the substantial form (μορφή) are all
identical, and, for Aristotle, the validity of logic and of metaphysics
rests upon this identification. Christianity rejected this cyclical concept of time. Time has a lineal structure; it has a beginning and
an end. In that case, the strict eternity of the species and of physical
quiddities disappears, though it is preserved in an attenuated form
in mediaeval philosophy. Before all else, the essences would be eternal only considered as divine ideas; because they are co-eternal with
God they are immutable. Hence was born the thesis of the essence
as objective concept or as a meaning which rested upon itself, as
well as the Hegelian thesis of the essence as formal concept, as
moment of absolute spirit. These essences, realized *ad extra* in things,
do not have strict eternity but they do have an attenuated eternity;
they endure unchanged while time endures; within it specific essences
are neither generable nor corruptible: they are «perdurably» immutable.

But this conception is not necessarily acceptable, not even in its
attenuated form. Before all else, it is undeniable, because is a perfectly established fact, that the world has witnessed extinction of
specific essences. Even more, it is another fact that specific essences
have not co-existed with cosmic time; they have, at most, their hour
of epiphany. Whence it follows that the specific essences themselves
as species «are born and die» within cosmic time.

Even more, in addition to birth and extinction, we have seen that specific essences have an extremely precise coming to be, or birth: by meta-specification. The origination of specific essences by meta-specification is what we call evolution. For it is not a question of just any biological innovation whatsoever, which might be limited to simple variations within the same species, but rather of an innovation which affects the specific characteristics themselves; that is, the question of a process in which the new individual may be head of a *phylum* (in the widest sense of this concept and term). To learn whether this evolution exists as a matter of fact, is a scientific problem, a problem for science; nowadays, the invincible persuasion obtains that evolution is a matter of unquestionable fact. The explication of the mechanism of evolution is, at the same time, a scientific task in its own right. Presupposing this fact, however, and independently of how it is to be explained, evolution is a strictly metaphysical structural character: from the point of view of an intramundane metaphysics, evolution is that character according to which quidditive essences have a genetic constitution in the process of time and have it precisely because, in their constitutive content, they are unalterable. The ambit of the specific essences is not only τάξις, order, but is rather «essential genesis.» This genesis does not consist in the mere fact that some species are produced by others. This might be nothing else than an «equivocal generation» as the ancients would say. However, this is not the question here; rather its contrary is under consideration. Origination, in fact, has, before all else, a «systematic» character. Each specific essence springs, not just from any other essence, but from one or from various species which are perfectly determined and at a precise moment in time. Every specific essence has an intrinsic «evolutive potentiality,» highly variable according to the species and according to the moments of its natural history. To my way of thinking, it is a metaphysical and not merely a biological concept. For this reason, I prefer to call it «potentiality of meta-specification.» In virtue of it, the specific essence which has been originated, retains many of the phyletic characteristics of the species from which it has been originated; meta-specification has a character of relative progressive continuity. By reason of these moments of system and progressive continuity, the origination of a new specific essence is not equivocal generation but «evolution.» The

ambit of specific intramundane essences has, for this reason, a rami-
fied structure; it is not so much a building but a tree. The metaphysics of specific essences is a genetic metaphysics; that is to say,
in contrast to the classical idea of the permanency of essences it is
necessary to affirm the idea of an evolution of essence in the line,
or order, of the specific.

All of which makes it very clear to our eyes that the problem
of the unalterability of the specific essence has, in traditional philosophy, been displaced from its true position. Starting, as it were,
with something so obvious that it did not even need to be discussed,
namely, the identity of essence and quiddity, the traditional philosophy arrived at the problem of the inalterability of essence by a
double path: that of sameness as objective identity and that of inalterability as temporal permanency. And both ways of approach dislocate the problem of the inalterability of the specific essence.

(a) In the identification of essence and quiddity the formal character of the inalterability of the species proves to be the immutabl-
ity of its definition, that is to say, its identity with itself. As radical
and primary structure this is unacceptable. The physical essence is,
before all else, constitutive essence and, therefore, its inalterability
is not formal «identity» but physical «sameness» in the possible
alteration of the substantive reality. The first is at most the objective
concept of the second.

(b) When inalterability is taken as immutability by identity, there
can be no greater *physical* inalterability than temporal permanency.
258 Inalterability would then be indestructability. But this is to go outside the question. Permanency is always and only a consequence of
the constitutive character of the real. Therefore, one must approach
the problem of the inalterability of essence by way of the constitutive
content of essence and ask oneself, not whether essence perdures,
but whether it tolerates, or does not tolerate, or in what measure it
may tolerate an alteration which would not destroy its sameness.

In this order, the constitutive essence, as well as its possible
moment of quidditive essence, may not be perdurable and have,
nevertheless, an essential inalterable content. The inalterability is a
metaphysical character in the order of sameness.

This sameness is not only something of degree. That is to say, it
is not a question whether a reality might be the same so long as its

notes do not change much or many of its notes do not change at all and whether it ceases to be the same when there is a great change. It is not a question of more or less. It is a question of ultimacy, or of the level at which the change takes place. The least change at the ultimate level, that is, in a single constitutive note of a real thing, would inexorably make of it an «other» reality. Because notes are ungrounded, every variation in them gives rise to an equally ungrounded, that is, ultimate, system; therefore, to another essence. A change, however, introduced in the rest of the notes of the reality, might leave its sameness intact; the reality will be the (la) same even though it is not the (lo) same.

This idea of change in a constitutive note may appear to be a purely formalistic and merely conceptive (conceptual) operation; if a moment of the definition, of a thing, of its concept, is changed, evidently one has an «other.» This is true, but this is not the question because what I have obtained by this operation is not an other thing but the concept of an other thing, while our problem concerns a real and physical alteration. No essence produces or engenders an other specifically or individually different essence by a change of definition, but, on the contrary, a change of definition is the conse- 259 quence of a physical change in the reality of what is defined. Again, the issue concerns a physical process; and it is there, in the physical reality, and not in any mental operation, that the primary issue of the problem lies. Every physical constitutive essence is alterable in itself or into the other reality which it produces. Alteration into an «other» is genesis. What is constituted is «other» precisely because the constituting essence conserves its physical sameness. Otherwise, there would be an other one but not an «other;» there would be «two onés» but not «one and other.» There comes to mind the problem of the Platonic Parmenides. In this case or manner the inalterability of the essential content of the constitutive essence is what makes genesis possible. If the genesis affects only the individual constitutive characteristics qua individual, then the genesis concerns only the individual alterity, it is a process of «constituting genesis,» as we have said. However, if it affects the quiddifiable characteristics as such, there is then this «quiddifying genesis» which must be called «evolution.» These two concepts and the realities conceived in them are perfectly separable; in general, there is constituting genesis without quiddifying genesis, there is generation, but not evolution. The obverse, or reciprocal process, however, is not certain; there is no evolution without genesis.

This permits us to unify the two concepts in a single metaphysical concept and to trace out the abstract *schema* of the articulation, in this respect, of the essences in the world, that is, the structure of the cosmos.

In the world, as it is in reality, essences depend upon each other by an «essential genesis,» by an essential genetic process. This is the concept common to constituting genesis and to quiddifying genesis. 260 The «essential generation» is not a «substantial transformation» in the Aristotelian sense. This genesis is a process which primarily and formally concerns substantivity, and not substance. It would, however, have to affect the substance and, nevertheless, we would have to say that it is something *toto caelo* different from a substantial transformation. For Aristotle, substantial transformation is the fact that one same «subject,» prime matter (πρώτη ὕλη) takes on first one form (μορφή, εἶδος) and then another, through the action of the first. Aristotle calls this process «generation and corruption.» Generation and corruption are, in the form, the fact of acquiring or losing reality; they are not a becoming, but only absolute beginning and absolute annullment. In generation an other form emerges, which is either a replica or a substitution of the first by another specifically distinct; there is, however, no change within the form itself. As a consequence, in generation, as substantial transformation, what is transformed is the subject or, at most, the compound (τὸ σύνολον) but not the form itself. The forms are immutable (τὰ εἴδη ἀκίνητά ἐστιν, *Meta.* L 1067 b 9); they are generated and they are corrupted but they do not become. However, in opposition to Aristotle, it must be affirmed that the form itself becomes, that is to say, that in essential genesis there exists a «transformal» process, a true transformation of the form itself. It is not a process in which each form would do no more than «inform» one same subject exercising in it «formal» causality; rather, it is a process in which the form itself is transformed and, therefore, exercises in the subject a true «transformal» and «transforming» causality. For this, it is the same whether the transformation produces the new form entire or only certain of its moments. Essential genesis, then, is a process in which the forms

do not succeed each other in one same subject but a process in which
the first form, in and *from itself*, is transformed into an other in a
systematic and progressive way. And as this process is an «essential»   261
genesis and not a «substantial» transformation, it is of no interest
here to elaborate the contrast with the Aristotelian concepts any
further.

This makes it clear to us that in its each and every moment the
world is constituted of certain basic constitutive essences upon which
depend the appearance and the constitution of the rest, a dependence
which is, concretely and formally, an essential genesis. Correlatively,
in virtue of this generic-essential structure, what these basic essences
of the world may be is something which may vary in the course of
time. Naturally, the question is not whether the essences have within
themselves, intrinsically, a kind of undifferentiated impulse (*Drang,
élan*, etc.) to give rise to others. Quite the contrary: this presumptive
impulse is, in every case, something differentiated. First, because
no matter what may be the intra-essential factors which intervene
in the essential genesis, it is undeniable that no one of them would
give rise to a genetic process if the essence were not embedded in
a «configuration» of other essences, a configuration which is a factor
in the circumstance that the new essence, which is produced, is not
just any essence whatsoever, but a determined essence. And, as it
is physically «essential» for every essence to find itself in a configuration, precisely because it forms part of the world, that is, because
every intramundane essence is essentially respective (*respectiva*), it
follows that the presumptive impulse to produce other essences
already conceals or possesses a primary determination, is not an
undifferentiated impulse. In addition, however, it is not a question
of a strict impulse but of something different; of the fact that every
constitutive essence has, as its intrinsic metaphysical moment, the
condition of being something more than something constitutive of
a substantivity, a genetic-essential potentiality of producing an other
essence, individually and specifically different. It is not an «impulse»
but a «potentiality.» And this potentiality is not undifferentiated,
but has, in every case, its own different metaphysical structure, dif-   262
ferent according to whether it may be the essence which possesses
it and the processive moment in which it is considered. Every essence cannot produce just any other essence whatsoever, but, rather,

various precisely determined ones; at the beginning of the process, all of them are, perhaps, equally possible and only the process progressively determines only one among them. Configuration and potentiality are the two factors of essential determination. Such is the metaphysical structure of the world, insofar as its inalterable essences are concerned. Precisely because they are inalterable can they be the source of an essential genetic process.

There still remains unresolved the question of which may be the fundamental, in the sense of basic, essences, and whether the genetic process is a positive production transmitting all the individual notes of a substantial reality — something, under all aspects, totally inadmissible, for example, in the case of man. However, nothing in it opposes the intramundane universality of the genetic process as such. Fathers do not transfer the mind or soul to their sons, but this does not militate against the sons being really and truly engendered by the fathers. Analogically, even though the genetic process does not produce the human spirit by transmission from the animal psychic structure, nevertheless, it continues or remains true that the human species is the term of a zoological evolution; this, however, is enough for our present concern or inquiry.

To sum up, essential notes are ungrounded notes and, as such, constitutive. Considered in themselves, they are «ultimate» notes. 263 This ultimacy possesses three characteristics: that of being a factual condition, entitatively and formally individual in character and of inalterable constitutive content. Considered not in themselves but in relation to the other notes, the essential notes, since they are ungrounded, are «grounding» principles of the others. This is what we must now rapidly see.

264   SECTION TWO

ESSENCE: GROUNDING MOMENT OF SUBSTANTIVITY

Considered with respect to the rest of the notes, the essential notes, we have said, are the grounding notes of all the others, whether constitutional or not, in the order of substantivity. This last clarification is necessary in order to understand correctly in what the grounding character of the essential notes may consist. For «ground» (*fundamento*) is a concept which can have different meanings.

First of all, it might be thought that the constitutive notes are only the base on which the rest are supported. Ground (*fundamento*) would then be «foundation,» «base;» grounding would mean «basic.» Nevertheless, this is not the case. We have already said that the constitutive notes do not form a system which «stands underneath» (ὑποκείμενον) the other notes; they form rather a sub-system «within» the total system of notes of a substantivity. The substantivity is not constituted by a «stratification» but by a unitary «determination.» The constitutive notes as grounding subsystem are not points of rest, but «determining» moments. Here we come upon the second meaning of the concept of ground (*fundamento*). Ground (*fundamento*) is «determination.» This grounding character of essence as determining may itself in turn be understood in two ways. To determine can be understood in the sense of «cause to emerge,» cause to blossom or bloom (*brotar*, φύειν). This is a concept of ground reached by way of intrinsic origination and moves, therefore, along the line of substantiality. Thus there are innumerable notes which an organism, for example, may possess simply because each one of them emerges from one or from a number of the substances which compose the organism in question. For example, a man has 265 a certain weight because this weight emerges from the material substances which compose the human organism and only from them. In the last analysis, basicness and originating determination are the two unique concepts with which traditional philosophy has understood the internal grounding process of the real entity, because it has conceived this thing first and formally as substance. However, if we understand the reality of a thing primarily and formally as substantivity, then the determining ground takes on another character completely different from «emergence» and «origination.» Let us consider, for example, precisely the weight of a man. As emergent it is, as we have just said, an accident of each of the substances which compose his organism. Independently of this origination, however, that weight has a biological «significance» which is quite precise within the system of notes of the human substantivity. As we said in its place, this signification is nothing other than the expression of the «position» of the weight within that system. Now this determination, which is not «origination,» is what I would call merely «functional» determination; given a subsystem of constitutive notes, the substantivity cannot fail to possess such and such other notes. For this, it is a matter of indifference whether the function be «originating» or not, or whatever may be the possible mode of «origination.» The only decisive point is that the notes in question should be univocally determined in function of the rest. And what this function determines is what I have called «position.»

This functional determination is distinguished from originating determination in two points. First, in that which I have just indicated; even though the note might emerge from a substance, the formal *ratio* (*razón*) of origination is not the formal *ratio* (*razón*) of position; even less, in the case in which the note is not possessed by emergence. Second, because the originating determinant is only one, or
266 at most a series, of the substances which enter into the substantiality, while in the functional determination there enters into play for each note the totality of the notes of the substantiality. In a word, every «position» is «with respect to» something; *in casu* it is a matter involving the substantive system. And, therefore, it is the entire constitutive system, and not a part of its notes, which determines the position and therefore the significance of the note in question. Originating determination is a kind of «point-to-point» correspondence; each substance determines «its» corresponding note; at most, it may determine various notes. The functional determination, by contrast, brings into play, for each constitutional note, the totality of the constitutive system. Using a terminology accepted among mathematicians, we might say that the originating determination is a «function of points» of one or more variables, while what we have called merely functional determination is more in the character of a «function of sets.» The totality of the constitutive notes is a *prius* with respect to each one of the other notes of the substantivity. In this sense, the constitutive notes are something very like *(así como)* the properties of all the properties of the substantivity. In the example so frequently cited, the position and the significance of weight in the human substantivity is determined in function, not only of the animality, but also of the rationality; only with respect to both notes

is the function of weight univocally determined. Animality and rationality are, in this sense, the properties of all the human properties,
including the most elemental and material. It is needless to add that
I adduce this example only as an example; that is to say, without
that citation implying the acceptance of the definition of man as
rational animal. And above all, let us recall once again that I do not
take this proposition as a definition of the quidditive essence of man
but only as an essential proposition which enunciates the constitutive 267
essence. Animality and rationality do not determine the position and
the anthropological significance of weight as «genus and difference»
but only as physical notes. Only as physical notes are they the properties of all human properties.

We note, then, that the essential notes are grounding notes in an
exact and formal sense, as functional determinants of each one of
the notes which a reality or real being possesses in relation to its
substantivity. In a word, when the signification and position of each
note with relation to the constitutive notes has been fixed, as these
notes form a system, the primary system of the substantivity, it
follows that each note forms a system with the essence and, therefore, the notes grounded in this manner also form a system among
themselves; or better, we have constituted the total system of the
substantivity. Thus it is that the conjunction of the essential notes
go to construct and constitute the entire constitutional system. This
«construction» has two aspects. First, a «material» aspect: the essence determines the inner character and the position of each note of
the substantivity. Second, a formal aspect: the essence confers the
character of system on the entire constitution of the substantivity,
and is the fundamental subsystem, the foundational subsystem, of
the substantivity. The formal *ratio* (*razón*) of the essence is the sufficiency of the notes for the constitution «by themselves and of themselves» of a substantive system. Precisely by reason of this, the rest
of the notes of the substantivity receive systematic sufficiency, and
achieve it «by something else,» that is to say, by the essence. The
essence is system by and through itself; the rest of the substantivity
is system *ab alio, ab essentia*. Thus there is clarified the grounding
function of the essence in the order of substantivity, as distinguished
from the originating function of the substance.

268   And this is what succeeds in giving a more precise reply to the question of the essence as a physical moment of the real thing, the constitutive essence as distinct from the merely quidditive or specific essence. The essence, we said earlier, is not essence by reason of or through the notes as they are considered according to their *consideratio absoluta*, but rather by reason of the function which these notes fulfill in the real thing. And this is a double function. One is the «ultimate» function (absolute, individual, inalterable) of constituting the substantivity. The other is the function of determining the character and the position of the rest of the notes. Ultimacy and systematization are the two characteristics of the constitutive essence, as such.

All the notes which are not constitutive, that is to say, which do not belong formally to what is essential, are «inessential.» The difference between the essential and the inessential is, then, a difference between notes according as they may or may not be constitutive of the real thing. It is not, as Hegel thought, a difference which I might permit myself (for reason of greater clarity) to call a difference of «condition,» as though all the notes of a thing might be, in and by themselves, in their mere indifference to being, inessential, while all those would be essential insofar as they were the presuppositions of the *to be* of the thing in question. This latter view is unacceptable for two reasons. First, because it is not a matter of an indifference to being, but of a character of the reality itself, very precisely and formally determined, according to which there are, within one same substantive reality, essential and inessential notes. The inessential embraces, certainly, the compass of indifferent notes, that is to say, those notes which the thing may or may not have, while maintaining its substantive sameness. Indifference here does not mean «indifference to being» but «contextural indifference» in the order of sameness, contingency: the thing is «the» *(la)* same whether or not it has the note in question. But further — and this is the second reason — indifference is not the formal character of inessentiality. It would 269 be a serious error to think that only the indifferent, even though it be in the sense of the contingent, is inessential. This is not the truth; there are many notes which a substantive reality necessarily possesses, but which are nevertheless inessential; that is to say, all the constitutional notes which are not constitutive, but which are necessarily determined by these (the constitutive notes). They are not essential because they are not constitutive, and they are, nevertheless, necessary. The essential is, formally, all and only the «ungrounded» or constitutive. The inessential is formally, all and only, the «grounded.» Both the indifferent and the constitutional notes are grounded, that is, are functionally determined by the essence within the substantive reality. What happens is that the character of this ground is different in each case. As a consequence, the question of the inessential is the question of the structure itself of the fundamentality of essence.

This fundamentality is not, as Husserl thought, «meaning,» but is, rather, a moment of the reality as such. Therefore, the inessential is not that which remains «outside» of the meaning of anything, but rather that which is physically grounded in its essence. Furthermore, fundamentality is a moment of the constitutive essence and not of the quidditive essence. As a consequence, the inessential is not, as Aristotle thought, that which is formed by the individuating moments, since the notes of the constitutive essence are on their own account individuals and have, in general, not only singularity, but also strict individuality. The inessential, consequently, is what is grounded in a constitutive essence and in its strictly and formally individual moments.

On these suppositions, the fundamentality of essence as functional determinant of the notes of the substantive reality may take on, 270 as I have already been indicating, a different character according to what may be the character of the notes themselves.

There are, before all else, those notes which are not constitutive, but are, indeed, constitutional. These latter notes derive necessarily from the constitutive notes. For them, consequently, the essence is «necessitating.» Here we have the first type of fundamentality of essence: *necessity*. This «essential» fundamentality must, however, be understood correctly. Unqualified necessity may be understood, in the first place, from the point of view of substance; it is that necessity with which a substance possesses its properties because they «blossom» (*brotan*) from it with necessity. It is a necessity of origination or of production. This necessity determines the appearance of the note; without that necessity that note would not exist in the thing. There is, however, another type of necessity: «systema-

tic» necessity. Only this latter is a formally essential necessity. It is that necessity with which, given a system of constitutive notes, the thing must necessarily possess such and such other constitutive notes related to the first notes. This necessity does not determine the production of the notes; it does, however, determine the connection of the notes with the essence. On its own account (*de suyo*), a note may or may not be constitutional; only with relation to the subsystem of constitutive notes does it acquire one or the other character. This connection with the essence has two aspects. In the first place, it determines the inner character or quality of each note: in virtue of its constitutive notes the thing must have such and such precise notes. This necessity is not formally to be identified with necessity of origination or production from the substance. The essence is what determines the necessity with which a note of a certain character must belong to the substantivity. The confusion of the two necessities is the inevitable consequence of the confusion between substantivity and substantiality. It is certain that there are substantivities which coincide materially with the area of substantiality, and this fact leads to the confusion of the two orders of necess-
271 ity. There are also, however, realities whose substantivity exceeds the compass of the substance; for example, living beings insofar as they are functional combinations. In such a case, the necessity by which a living being possesses a certain note, is not identical with the fact of its substantial origin, for the simple reason that this origination might not exist when it might be a matter of a systematic property; its character itself is then determined by the essence, by the system, but not by the substance. Systematic necessity, however, determines not only the character of each note, but also its «position» in the substantive system in the form which has already been explained, and a point on which it would be useless and monotonous to return and insist. Necessity of origination or production, therefore, is one thing, systematic necessity, another. Only this second belongs intrinsically and formally to the constitutive essence, and it alone is a formally essential necessity. Such is the fundamentality or functional determination according to which the essence is necessitating with respect to the other constitutional notes.

There are, however, other notes which a real thing effectively possesses and which are not constitutional, but simply indifferent in its regard; these are the notes which belong, in any manner what-soever, to the order of concretion. Thus, its position in space is a matter of indifference to a body, relative to the properties which it possesses — to cite but the most trivial example. One does not see, at first glance, what determining function the essence might be able to exercise relative to these notes. Nevertheless, let us pause to reflect upon the character of the indifference they exhibit. It is true that, given a certain note, its possession may be a matter of indifference to the thing. However, instead of taking the note as our point of departure, let us take the thing itself, its constitutive nucleus. Then we will discover two circumstances which are decisive for our prob-lem. In the first place, we see that, not the note, but rather its «type» has already been determined without indifference by the substantivity. No man has, by his proper essence, necessarily to occupy «this» 272 place on the surface of the earth; he can occupy many very different such places without compromising his contextural identity. If, however, he were pure spirit, he would not have the capacity of occupying any place. The essence does not determine «this» place, but it does de-termine that the body must occupy «some» place or other. This shows us that the «indifference» in question is not «indefinition» (*indefini-ción*); the indifferent is not the undefined *simpliciter*, but is rather indifference within an ambit or definite type of notes, an ambit or type defined precisely by the essence. The essence determines the type of activities and passivities which the substantive reality «can» possess. To nothing can there accrue «just any» note among the infinite range of notes which can be conceived, but only notes of the determined type. In the second place, this fact also shows us in what sense a note may be indifferent. The note in itself is indifferent; its ambit, however, is not only determined, but is determined with necessity. It «is indifferent» to a body that it occupy «this» place; it «can» occupy various places; but it «necessarily has to occupy» some place. This unity between capacity and necessity is what we can call «possibility.» The word lends itself to equivocation because, employed in the plural, it almost always means human possibilities; in order, however, not to force the exposition with new words, I will continue, for the present, to employ the word «possibility,» granted that the context does not lead to confusion. The essence, then, necess-arily determines the range of the possible. And this «necessary possibility» is what constitutes the second mode of fundamentality: «possibilitation» (*posibilitación*). The essence is that which «possibilizes,» «establishes,» these notes «as possible.»

The essence, then, functionally determines, necessitates, and establishes as possible, the notes in the order of concretion. And the notes which are necessitated and made possible are, within the thing, the ambit of the non-essential. These two types of founding are irreducible. Precisely for this reason, because I was thinking of the «possibilitated» (*posibilitadas*) notes, I have so often said at the beginning of this work, that the essence is the principle from which flow, at least, the necessary notes of the thing. This phrase is doubly provisional. First, because I prescinded, for the moment, from the possibilitated notes. Second, because, with respect to the necessary notes, I spoke of a «flowing.» The word contained an ambiguity which, at that moment, was deliberate. I did not undertake to distinguish the «emanating» as a «blossoming» from the «emanating» as a functionally necessitating determinant. Of just how the essence may be a «principle» we shall speak in another article in which I will distinguish between the types of possibility.

The failure to have seen the fundamentality of essence in this way is the reason why the idea of what I called the suppositionality of essence in Hegel has always remained vague and vacillating. Hegel takes his point of departure in the being of the notes and bends them back in the interiority of the essence, and then he unfolds the essence, thus making of it the foundation of the notes of being. However, what Hegel does not perceive is that this fundamentality has a precise structure.

The essence determines, not only the notes which belong to the thing necessarily, but also the ambit within which the thing plays with relative indifference of its essence. For this reason, apart from other more profound reasons of which we have spoken at the appropriate time, the fundamentality of essence remains imprecise in Hegel. If we compare the two types of fundamentality, we will easily discern what they have in common. Each of the «possibilitating» notes, I have been saying, is indifferent, but its type is determined with necessity. As a result, one ought strictly to speak, not of necessity and indifference, but of necessitating necessity and possibilitating necessity. The formal structure, then, of fundamentality is precisely

«necessity» of the functional determination. Should we wish to re-as- 274
sume the employment of mathematical language, I would say that the
necessitating functional determination is a «uniform» function, while
the possibilitating is a «multiform» function. In both cases, however,
it is a necessary function. That which determines — I say anthropomorphically, that which selects — one of the values among the different possible values, is the configuration in which an essence is
constituted «relatively» to the other essences in the world. The essence, then, is that which grounds or establishes the inessential notes
as their necessary functional determinant.

Up to this moment, in expounding the constitutive character of
the essential notes, I have practically always limited myself to saying
that they are the ground whence the substantivity derives all its
other constitutional notes. I have done so, first, because it would have
complicated the exposition uselessly if allusion had been made on
every occasion to the adventitious notes, and, second, because the
most important thing about essence is to ground the constitution.

In this way is stated with complete rigor what the essential notes
are: they are the ungrounded or constitutive notes of the substantivity, the system of notes necessary and sufficient to insure that a
thing possess all its other constitutional notes or the ambit of the
adventitious notes. As such, they are «ultimate» notes in themselves
(absolute, individual, unalterable) and «grounding» (necessitating and
possibilitating) with respect to the rest. The essence is thus that to
which the characters which we have encountered in the substantivity belong formally and in the first instance. The substantivity, I
have said, is a closed and total, that is, sufficient, system of constitutive notes. The substantivity possesses this closure, totality, and
sufficiency, because its essence is a self-sufficient system of constitutive notes. The substantivity is constitutionally individual because 275
the essence is constitutively individual. And the substantive is always
the (el) same, exactly and formally because the essence has a constitutive and unalterable content.

This is a notion or idea of the «physical» essence from the point
of view of its notes. Even at the risk of tedious repetition, we repeat
that it is necessary to understand this character correctly. When traditional philosophy has spoken of physical essence it has always
understood the term in the order of substantiality: physical essence

is the «substantial principles» of the physical reality of the thing. What we have here called physical essence, however, is something understood in the order of substantivity: physical essence is the «system» of the constitutive notes of the substantivity as such. In the first case, it is a moment of the s u b s t a n c e ; in the second, a moment of the substantivity. Hence, the profound difference in the very concept of the constitutive. When it is said, in current usage, that the essential notes are constitutive of the thing, the term is employed without placing particular emphasis on it, in its merely usual meaning, according to which the constitutive is opposed to the consecutive, whatever might be the character of the object (real, mathematical, etc.), and the manner of consecutiveness. In the case of essence, it designates the substantial principles, the intelligible expression of which is the «metaphysical» essence, the quiddity. By contrast, here the decisive thing is the very concept of «constitution,» substantive individual, something which is not given save in the strict order of the real. Constitution, I have said, is the mode in which each real thing is «one» *qua* reality. The constitutive designates the conjunction of notes which, because they form a system «by themselves» are ultimate and grounding notes in the constitutional order, in contrast to the other constitutional notes which form a system *ab alio*, in virtue of the constitutive notes. The constitutive is, to express it in 276 this way, the primary constitution, the primary (element) of the constitution. And (it is) primary in a double sense: because they are the constituting notes of the other constitutional notes and because they are (those notes) which, by themselves, constitute the complete physical unity of every substantive reality *qua* reality. In this sense, that to which the constitutive is formally contrasted is precisely the quidditive, understanding by quidditive, not the abstract and intelligible unity of the specific notes, but their physical reality in each individual. The constitutive essence does not coincide with the quidditive, not only because the constitutive essence is not always quiddifiable, but because the quidditive, although considered physically in every individual, is not that which primarily constitues the unity of the real thing *qua* real, for this unity is not merely singular, but strictly and *essentially* individual. Only in this sense of «constitutive system» do we say that this system is the physical essence of the substantive reality. Whence it follows that the «physical» is not to be opposed to the «metaphysical» but is rather the metaphysical *par excellence.* Physical is not the synonym of «empirical» or «positive,» but rather, the physical itself is susceptible of a double consideration, positive and metaphysical. The physical, in a word, may be considered, on the one hand, as that which is «real,» in this sense, is the term of positive knowledge. But the physical may be considered as the formal and ultimate structure of the reality considered as such; and in this sense it is the term of metaphysical cognition. For this reason, that which is usually called «metaphysical» is, for me, much more «conceptive» than «metaphysical;» strictly speaking, the metaphysical essence is merely conceptive essence. I have developed these ideas extensively in my courses; a rapid allusion to them suffices here.

Since the essential notes form a system «by themselves» and constitute a «primary unity,» there ineluctably presents itself to us the problem of knowing, not indeed what the essential notes are, but 277 rather in what the proper function of the essential unity within the substantivity might be. It is the problem of the essential unity as unity, the second of the four great questions which arise regarding essence.

THE UNITY OF ESSENCE

The first step toward the determination of the concept of essence consisted in rigorously conceptualizing what the essential notes might be. We must now enter upon the second step, that is, we must ask ourselves what may be the very unity of the essential notes. Only then will we be able to understand, in a third stage, the inner character of essence as a moment of the substantive reality.

The problem of the unity of essence is, apparently, formalistic in character. This, however, is mere appearance. We have already encountered the same situation with respect to individuality. Apparently, it was a matter only of the internal indivision and the external division of all the other. Immediately, however, we saw that under those negative formalisms something positive, much richer in content, lay hidden: a «constitution.» This same situation, and in even greater measure, transpires with the unity of essence. It is a character filled with real content: it is that which confers on the thing its proper and intrinsic formal unity, its substantive unity; a unity which is not the mere bundle of essential notes but a unity which is actualized in them. The unity is that which *primo et per se* is actualized in the notes. In what does this unity of the essential notes consist? In order to ascertain this, let us begin by laying out the problem correctly.

SECTION ONE

THE PROBLEM OF THE ESSENTIAL UNITY:
THE UNITY OF ESSENCE

279   Let us return and take up our position at the point of view of the notes. The essence, I have said, is formally characterized by the self-sufficiency of the notes, that is, by the capacity which the notes have of forming a substantive system «by themselves.» This «by themselves» is a moment proper to every note. Consequently, each of the notes has the «capacity» of forming, in conjunction with the others, the essential unity. The problem of the essential unity is, then, before all else, the problem of the character or quality of this «by themselves.» Thence depends the character of the «capacity» and, therefore, of the unity itself.

What is understood by the «by themselves» is something apparently clear. Let us take any note at random, for example, human sensibility. By reason of its own proper concept, sensibility «in itself» does not imply being united to rationality nor being separated from it. As a consequence, the expression «by itself» would mean «in itself,» in its proper concept. On this supposition, each note in the essence would be nothing other than a moment which renders the essence «possible.» Only in taking all the essential notes «together» do we have no longer the possibility but the actuality of the essential unity; all together, in a word, these notes produce by themselves this unity. As capacitated to produce this unity by themselves, the notes are the «internal possibility» of the essence. The essential unity would be the act of these possibilities. For this reason, the problem of the essential unity would be the problem of the actuality of these internal possibilities.

Stated in this way, without qualification, this is true from a certain point of view. The problem is not, however, correctly formulated, 280 because, so long as we are not told the character of these internal possibilities and the character of their act, everything remains up in the air. The foregoing exposition takes its point of departure, simply, from the identity between «by themselves» and «in themselves,» that is, «in their proper objective reason (*razón*).» And this sets the problem on a false path, both with regard to the possibilities and with regard to their act.

(a) Above all (this formulation is incorrect) with respect to the «character of internal possibility.» Starting with the fact that «by themselves» means «in themselves,» possibility would have a precise character; it would mean that every character «in itself,» that is by its formal objective reason (*razón*), is indifferent to the unity and that, therefore, it is not impossible for them to constitute that unity. Every note is what it is with perfect «independence» of the others, and the possibility would be simply «non-contradiction.» In the example adduced, it was a matter of showing that the formal reason (*razón*) of sensibility neither includes nor excludes its unity with what has rationality as its formal reason (*razón*) and vice versa. We have already discussed this thesis in the second part of the work, when we examined the idea of essence as objective concept. What interests us now is to confront this conception with the results already achieved in the first step, namely, that the essence is, from the point of view of its notes, the physical system of the constitutive notes of a substantive reality. When the question is brought to a focus in this way, the insufficiency of the thesis we are examining and of this form of stating the problem of the unity of essence is obvious.

In the first place, we are told that the essential notes are formally «independent.» As a «physical» character, however, this independence can only mean what we have already stated, namely, that the essential notes are ungrounded, derive from no other constitutional note and, therefore, derive from no other constitutive note. If this

281 were not the case, the essential notes would be, not constitutive, but merely constitutional. This, however, does not, nor can it mean that, physically, the notes are independent, *simpliciter*. Because «derivation» is not the only kind of «dependence.» And, in effect, *in re*, physically, the notes not only are not independent, but quite the contrary; they are precisely «solidary.» The essential notes, as a matter of fact, form a «system,» the «constitutive system.» Because they are such, the notes are, as we have said, interdependent among themselves: each note, in its physical reality and in «this» individual substantive reality, cannot occur without the others. Objectively and in abstraction, sensibility has no relation to reason. Physically, however, and in the concrete, «this» sensibility, in «this» determined man, can not occur without «this» reason: they are two physically solidary notes. They are, to be sure, independent, in the sense that one does not derive from the other; they are, however, dependent, in the sense that the one cannot occur physically without the other.

In the second place, this solidarity is not simple non-contradiction. That is to say, it is not because, by its proper reason (*razón*) it is not impossible that sensibility should be united to reason, but rather that physically, this sensibility, in this individual man, has, as its intrinsic moment, being turned to this reason, being determined *from itself* (*desde sí misma*) to form a unity with this reason. It is not simply «sensibility» in an unqualified sense, but «sensibility-of» this rational essence.

That is to say, «by itself» does not mean here «in itself,» in its proper concept, but means, rather, a physical encatenation as an intrinsic moment of the physical reality of each note. No one (of these notes) can exist physically without relation to all the others. Hence, the internal possibility of the essential unity is not its objective possibility, but rather this physical possibility which we call solidar-
282 ity. This, and only this, is what we express when we say that the essential notes have the capacity to form, «by themselves,» a constitutively sufficient system. This was what I was alluding to when discussing the idea of essence as objective concept. I said that non-contradiction is a negative unity, while the essential unity is something positive. Now we see in what, minimally, the first moment of this possibility may reside: in physical solidarity.

(b) The thesis we are discussing is no less inadequate on the point of the *character of the actual unity of the essence.* Each of the notes, we are told, is possibility of unity with the others, and, taken «together,» they would not be mere possibility of unity, but rather, they would be the very actuality of this possibility, that is, they would be the actual unity itself. But, how are we to understand this unity as actuality? This is the decisive question for the articulation of our problem.

Aristotle understood the formal reason (*razón*) of the unity (ἔν) of the real through one character only: actual «indivision» (ἀδιαίρε-τον). It mattered little that a reality might be divisible; what mattered was that it was not divided. To the degree that this latter was the case, there is «one» reality and to the degree that this was not the case, there are «various» realities, various «ones» or units. This, however, despite the fact that it is, to all appearances true, is inadequate; indivision (not being divided actually) is a merely negative character which follows on unity, and is not what constitutes that unity formally. Hence the existence, which Aristotle examines, of different types of unity. I would say, however, that the substantive reality is undivided because it is one and not the reverse. Unity, then, is a positive character of the substantive reality. Of what kind?

Traditional philosophy has conceived the unity of the being from another point of view as well: the being is «one» when it has one sole essence and everything which that (single essence) implies; where there are many essences, there are many beings. The actuality of the unity would be the actuality of the essence. But this is of no use to us for our problem, because what we are looking for is not the unity of the being by reason of its essence, but the unity of the essence itself. Only in the measure in which the essence is one, is the substantive reality which possesses that essence one. 283

In this manner, the negative of indivision has sent us back to the positive internal unity of the essence which establishes what is real, in «one» substantive reality. In what, then, does the positive unity of the essence itself consist; that is, how are we to understand the actuality of this unity? On this point the correct articulation of the problem depends.

It would seem that the answer has already been given in what we have been repeating with such insistence, namely, that the essential

notes are the constitutive notes which, taken «as one,» are «by themselves» necessary and sufficient to insure that the substantive reality
possesses all its other notes. This means that, though indeed each
note in isolation from the rest is incapable of performing this function, nevertheless, all «together» do perform it. The essential unity
would formally be an act of what Kant calls «synthesis.» It is a matter
of indifference, for our problem, what character is assigned to this
synthesis: a real synthesis or a blind synthesis based on transcendental apperception (Kant). The sole thing which is important to us
here is the affirmation of the formally synthetic character of the
real (thing) and therefore of its essence. With respect to this synthesis, each note in isolation is only mere possibility.

   But when we examine this closely, it is impossible, for a reason
which is, ultimately, simple. This reason is that, as we have said,
each constitutive note is not physically independent of the others,
but rather solidary with them. This moment, of one note «turning
284 toward» the rest, is a moment intrinsic to each note, but of such
character that the note in question is physically turned to the others,
though «with anticipation», beforehand (de antemano). Hence it results that, in its physical reality, each constitutive note is united with
the others, precisely because it is something which, by itself, demands
them «by anticipation» and which, for this reason, cannot have reality without them. That is, the synthesis of constitutive notes is not
the act which constitutes the unity of the essence, but rather that,
on the contrary, it is the unity of the essence which, «in a certain
way,» constitutes the synthesis in act. The unity is not there because
there is a synthesis of notes, but there is a synthesis of notes because there is unity. It is what we express when we say that the
essential unity is primary and not consequent upon a synthesis. If it
were a matter only of notes according to their proper objective reason
(razón), the essential unity would be synthetic. It is, however, a
question of a physical and real unity, and hence the unity is primary.
«At once» does not mean synthetically, but realized in a primary
unity. This it is which primarily constitutes the systematic solidarity.
This primary character of the system, this «systematism» as such, is
the second moment of the positivity of the essential unity: the notes
are solidary among themselves, but in the primary unity of the
system.

Then, however, an inevitable conclusion emerges. On the one hand, the notes are the internal possibility of the unity, which is their act; on the other, however, as we have seen, the unity, as actuality, is a primary unity and is, therefore, that which establishes the notes as essential. From the first point of view, the unity is the synthesis of the constitutive notes; from the second, the constitutive notes are the analyzers (*analizadores*) in which the primary unity is actualized. These are not two points of view between which a choice can freely be made, because what makes the notes internal moments of the essence is their intrinsic moment of turning toward the others, and it is precisely this moment that constitutes the primary unity of the 285 essence. Whence it follows that, while the first point of view is not completely false, it is not the radical or basic point of view. The basic thing is not that the unity should be the act resulting from some notes, but that the unity should be primary with regard to those notes. This last consideration puts us on a different path, the only viable one for our problem.

Let us state this problem then briefly and rigorously:

1. The essence is a system of constitutive notes; therefore, as system it is a «one,» it is an essential *unity.*

2. This essential unity is a character orientated toward the formation of system by the (notes) themselves. It is what, from the point of view of the constituting function, I called ultimacy: a function of the notes which consists in forming, by themselves, a system endowed with sufficiency, that is, a function of auto-sufficiency. Hence it results that the problem of the essential unity is none other than the problem of the character of this «by themselves.»

3. This «by themselves» does not mean «in themselves.» To speak of notes «in themselves» is to speak of them in terms of what they are according to their proper objective concepts. By contrast, «by themselves» is a moment of the notes in the order of their proper and formal physical reality.

4. This physical moment of the «by themselves» has *two aspects* toward the discovery of which the whole earlier discussion was directed. One is the aspect according to which this moment belongs to each note as an *intrinsic* moment of it. Consequently, each note is «from itself» turned toward (directed toward) the others and establishes a unity with them, this unity which, provisionally, I called

solidarity. The second aspect is that according to which each note is turned, by itself, toward the others «with anticipation,» that is to say, that moment according to which the notes not only form a unity but that this unity is *primary*. The «by itself» has two aspects: it is intrinsic (from itself) and it is primary (by anticipation, before-hand). As a consequence, to be intrinsic and primary, these are the two aspects of essential unity.

286   Hence it follows that *the problem of essential unity*, as the problem of the «by itself,» turns upon two questions: on the formal reason (*razón*) of the intrinsic essential unity, and on the primariness of this unity. Let us take up these questions in turn.

287   SECTION TWO

ON THE FORMAL REASON OF THE UNITY OF THE ESSENCE

We have been saying that, «by itself,» each note is turned to the others «from itself,» that is, *ab intrinseco*. It is clear, we may repeat, that it is not a question of the proper objective reason (*razón*) of each note, but of its physical reality: it is «this» note in «this» given system which is intrinsically turned to the others. What is this intrinsic turning?

In its proper character (*de suyo*), «turning» is, in general, a species of «relation» between two or more terms, according to which one of them is referred to the other and, therefore, involves (or encloses) in its mode of reality a grounding moment, a ground, of its relation with this other. Therefore, the problem of turning always comes down, in the last analysis, to that of the character of this ground, which, as such, is a physical moment of the term in question. In our case, it has been the question of a «turning» which belongs intrinsically and formally to the physical reality of a note, as reality. Whence it follows that its ground is a constitutive moment of the physical reality of each note. Therefore, the «turning» is not yet, properly speaking, a «relation» because, strictly speaking, every relation presupposes the already constituted reality of its related things (*sus relatos*), while the fact is that this turning of which we are speaking does not presuppose the note but is, rather, one of the moments which constitute it (the note) in its physical reality. This constitutive character of the «turning» is what I have been in the habit of calling «respectivity;» I shall very soon concern myself with it anew with greater minuteness and attention to detail. Now we may say simply that respectivity is not, properly speaking, a relation, but rather, the pre-relational and constitutive moment of that which is «respective.» The thing «is» not in respectivity with others but is 288 constitutively «respective.» When this respectiveness is «external,» that is, when it is a question of the respectivity of two or of various substantive realities, we have, as I indicated earlier, what we call «world.» When, however, this respectivity is «internal,» that is, when it is a question of the notes internal to one same substantive reality, then we have what we have called intrinsic «turning» (facing) of one note toward the rest. Thus, for an adequate description of a note in its intrinsic and proper physical reality, it is not enough to rest content with what it is «absolutely» (to express it thus), but it is, rather, necessary to include this its «respective» moment as well. If, then, we consider, in this respectivity, that to which the note in question is respective, we will say that this note is respective to something «other.» If, however, we consider the respectivity as a constitutive moment of the reality itself of every note, that is to say, as a mode of reality of the latter, then we will say that the moment in question, in its physical reality, is intrinsically, formally, and constitutively «note-of» the other. The intrinsic turning to other notes is an internal respectivity and the physical character of each note, insofar as it is constitutively respective, is to be «note-of.» For example, human sensibility is not only «sensibility,» but is rather «sensibility-of» this rational physical essence. This «of» is not a moment «added» to the note, but, rather, belongs formally and constitutively to the physical reality of each note. That is to say, it is not the case that sensibility is that which it is by reason of its «absolute» entity, so to say, and that it is «human» by reason of the fact that it forms part of the man, but that, quite the contrary, sensibility is already, in its constitutive physical reality, a constitutively «human» sensibility and for this reason forms part of the man. The reality of human sensibility is completely and only unitarily 289

«sensibility-of» this human essence; the «of» belongs to it constitutively. The note is not «note» + «of» the others, but rather it is
«note-of» the rest. It follows that this «of» not only is not an added
somewhat, for example, to human sensibility, but rather that the
distinction between «note» (sensibility) and «of» (human) is a mere
distinction of abstractive reason *cum fundamento in re*, but not a
real distinction, as it would be if it were an «added somewhat.» The
turning intrinsic to each note is, concretely, this «of.» Stated in
other terms, no note has a proper substantivity, none is something
«substantive.» Only the constitutive system *as* system possesses substantivity. And, in it, each note has a physically and constitutively
«genitive» character, is «note-of.» Genitive does not mean generating;
it is not a question of a genesis; that would be absurd. «Genitive»
is a grammatical term. And in using it here what I want to say is
that there is, in the reality in question, a physical character according
to which each essential note is «of» the others. It is not a merely
conceptual, but a physical, respectivity.

What expresses this unitary character of the note and of the «of»
with greatest clarity is, perhaps, the grammatical form in which the
genitive is frequently expressed in some Semitic languages. In our
Indo-European languages, in order to express this «relation,» the
subject «of» which the thing is, is placed in the genitive by means
of a nominal inflection. For example, in order to say «the house of
Peter,» one will say *domus Petri*, which literally is «house of-Peter; »
the «of» morphologically affects Peter and not house. In some Semitic languages, however, sometimes what is put in the genitive case
(so to say) is the house, because what they seek to express formally
is only the house's belonging to Peter; and thus they would say
«house-of Peter.» This is what is called «constructed state» of the
noun (house) in contrast to «absolute state» in which Peter remains.
290 The house is not house and «nothing more,» unqualifiedly: it is rather
formally «house-of» Peter, while the latter is only the unaffected and
absolute term of this singular «relation.» Together, they form a unitary whole; for this reason in the constructed state, as is well known,
the two terms form an indissoluable semantic, morphological and
even prosadic unity. In this unity, the constructed state expresses,
then, with absolute rigor, the fact that the noun in that state involves a moment which *hic et nunc* belongs to it intrinsically, the

turning to the absolute substantive and, therefore, forms a systematic unity with it. It is needless to make clear that when I said that house is placed in the «genitive,» it is not a matter of a termination of the type of the inflection of the noun; rather it expresses the «idea» of the genitive by means of something which has nothing in common with the inflection of the noun, but rather by means of certain modifications of a different character. Solely for semantic reasons and in order to make myself understood by those who are not familiar with the Semitic languages, I have explained the constructed state as though it were an inflectional genitive. Since in Spanish there is no noun inflection, I have made use of the preposition «of» with a hyphen, either to Peter (inflection) or house (constructed state).

In the example cited, it is a question of a «relation» of belonging to Peter, a relation which is extrinsic to the house as such, but which is *hic et nunc* intrinsic to its juridical condition. If, however, we transpose these considerations to the physical reality of anything, then the constructed state «note-of» would not express a «relation» but something *toto coelo* different: internal respectivity. It expresses the fact that the very reality of the note is that which, by and from itself, that is, constitutively, is «reality-of» the other notes of the system. Each note is *ab intrinsico* a note of «constructed» physical character, as reality. «Genitive» does not, then, mean «generating» nor «modifying» (inflective) but «constructed.»

Here is where we touch the *primary* difference which exists among things. Taking up the instance of Peter's house, this relation 291 to Peter is intrinsic only to the juridical condition of the house *hic et nunc*. But «to be this house» is not «to be of Peter;» the house can change masters and yet would continue to be the same house. Nevertheless, what is absolutely intrinsic to the house is to be «someone's.» This someone may be unknown, may even be of «no one.» But the «no one» is, explicitly and formally, a turning to a living human being. And this turning to a living human being is absolutely intrinsic to the house as such. Without it, it would not formally be a house. This turning of things to the living human being is what makes them «meaning-things.» Meaning is, precisely and formally, the constructed character of things as moments of human life. In this constructed character the possibilities of life are constituted. Reciprocally, the «of» expresses, in this order, that things are, for-

mally, «things-of» life. If this constitutive «of» were struck out of
them, they would cease to have reality, as meaning. Nothing more,
however; because the physical reality of the house, for example,
would persist. By contrast, if we turn our attention to the reality,
not insofar as it is a thing which is a moment of life, but as a physical reality as such, then the «of» has a different character and
range. If, *per impossible*, we succeed in striking out, for example,
in this human sensibility the «of» according to which it is really and
physically «note-of» the human essence, both the sensibility and the
entire human essence would cease to exist. In the case of the house,
if we strike out the constitutive «of» of its materials, there would
cease to exist not only the house as house, but the physical reality
of that which a house is, as well. Here the «of» constitutes the
«reality-things.» For this reason, the «meaning-things» do not have
292 essence, but precisely only this: meaning. This is what we mean to
say when we affirm that each essential note has a formally and
intrinsically constructed character. Here, let us recall, physical reality
is reality *qua* reality; therefore, its physical character is *eo ipso* a
formally metaphysical character.

The «constructed» in this «constructed» state is such according
to the systematic unity of the essence. On the one hand, in effect,
the «of,» because it is an intrinsic moment of *a* note, brings it about
that this note has and only can have this, its physical reality, in
intrinsic and formal unity with those others «of» which it is a note.
By reason of being by itself a «note-of,» it is, *eo ipso*, a reality in
formal and intrinsic unity with the other realities of the system. On
the other hand, however, this same thing happens with *all* the notes
of the system in question. Sensibility is, certainly, only «sensibility-
of» the rational, but, in its turn, the rational also is «rationality-of»
the sensibility. That is, all the notes have a constructed physical
character. Whence it follows that the only thing which has an absolute
character is precisely the system itself. Later we shall justify this
affirmation. Each note belongs to the system not merely as a «part»
of it, but as a «moment» of its unity. The system, and only the
system itself, is that «of» which all and each one of the notes «are.»
Because it is constructed in character, this total unity is intrinsic
and formal: such is the essential unity. In its first aspect, as the
equivalent of a «from themselves,» the «by themselves» consists in

the intrinsically and formally constructed character of each note in the order of its physical reality. «To be turned» from itself to others is simply to have physical reality only in this unity with them. The solidarity to which we referred earlier was the provisional designation of this metaphysical character.

Even at the risk of proving insistent, I will tend to return repeatedly to this idea of the constructed state, examining it in its different aspects. We are striving, in effect, to give a metaphysical 293 conceptualization of essence and its notes, as a moment of substantivity, in contrast to the usual idea of the essence as a moment of the substantiality. To this end, we will have to find a conceptual *organon* different from the usual; and the constructed state provides us with this *organon*. It is not a matter, then, of a mere description or illustration, but of real and physical structure, independently of the vicissitudes of its grammatical expression.

With this statement we have characterized, in a global manner, so to say, the inner character of the essential unity (unity of essence): it is the intrinsic unity of a system in which the constitutive notes have by themselves the «constructed» physical character of being «notes-of.» This, however, is but the first step in our problem, since of this unity, which is intrinsically systematic, we have now to ask what may be its formal reason (*razón*), that is, what may be the proper character of this systematic unity as such?

In order to fix, with some exactness, what we have called essential or systematic unity, let us begin by recalling to mind the modes of entitative unity which distinguished classical philosophy. These modes are very various, but they can be reduced to three fundamental types. There is, in the first place, one which I would call *unity of conjunction*; it is that unity which is formed of different entities, each one of which has its own proper reality separate from that of the others, independently of their conjunction. Although it has not been customary to speak of more than two types of this unity, I think that three such types should be distinguished: simple conjunction, addition, and ordering. In the second place, there is a *unity of inherence*, proper to an accident with its substance; the formal reason (*razón*) of the accident consists, in a word, in being actually or aptitudinally inherent to the substance, and the different accidents are, 294 categorically, the different modes of inherence. In the third place, there is the *unity of substance*, whether it be composed of different principles, of which one is potency and the other is act (substantial unity of composition) or whether it is innocent of all composition of parts (the unity of simplicity). The first two types of unity are accidental (*unitas per accidens*): only the third would be true and strict unity (*unitas per se*), because the substance (οὐσία) would be by itself the rigorously and absolutely one being (ἕv).

This conception of this unity of the real is wholly based on the idea of substance and accident. In a word, in the unity which we have called conjunction, its elements are the unities (μονάς) conceived in the manner of substantial unities. In the unities of inherence, it is true, there are sometimes unities of various accidents and not only of accident with substance; however, it is always because each one of the said accidents is directly inherent in the same substance as the others, in such wise that then, indirectly, they form a unity among themselves, as the result of their inherence in the same substance. Finally, there is also *unity per se* which is not that of the composition of substantial principles, but is, rather, the unity of the potencies and of the substance; however, it is the reason why these potencies flow necessarily from the substance, in such wise that it is the unity of substance which constitutes these unities. This entire conception of the unity of the entity turns, then, about the idea of substance. This is no mere chance; it is that since Aristotle the entity *simpliciter* (ἁπλῶς) is substance (οὐσία); the substance is the one *per se* (ἕv καθ᾽ αὐτό) and all the rest is one only through reference to it.

On this basis, what we have called essential, or systematic, unity 295 does not fall under any of these types. It is, to be sure, a unity *per se* (ἕv καθ᾽ αὐτό), but it is not unity *per se* of the type of substantial unity. Nor is this a matter of chance. It is that here, the reality *simpliciter* is not the substance, but the substantivity. And the essence is a moment of the substantivity and not of the substance. This forces us to assign to the essential unity a proper formal *ratio* (*razón*) different from the preceding.

The essential unity, evidently, is not the unity of conjunction, because none of its notes has proper substantivity by itself independently of the system of which it is a moment. This we have already seen over and over again a number of times. The unity of conjunction is unity *per accidens*, while the essential unity is *unum per se*, a ἕν καθ᾽ αὐτὸ.

However, this unity is not substantial unity. We have seen, in effect, that substantivity is not formally substantiality. Even in those realities in which the compass of substantivity coincides exactly with that of substantiality, this coincidence is only «material,» and not «formal.» The substantivity does not have the character of subject, but of system, and its formal reason (*razón*) is constitutional sufficiency. Now the essence is formally a moment of the substantivity and, as such, its constitutive notes also have, as we have seen, the character of system; it is the subsystem or fundamental system. The essence is not a moment of the «*perseitas*» of a substance, but rather a moment of the constitutional sufficiency of a system. As a consequence, its unity is not the unity of a substance which would be the subject of its properties, but is rather a unity of the «properties» themselves among themselves. It has not been said anywhere that the supreme type of *per se* unity is the substantial unity. There are systematic unities which are superior to substantial unity. Such is the case of all living beings, and above all of man. In living beings the area of substantivity surpasses the ambit of substantiality *stricto* 296 *sensu*. The fact is that substantiality is only one type of substantivity among others. Therefore, it is an error to try to reduce the latter to the former. All intramundane substantive realities have, as we have seen, a moment of substantiality; in them, however, their substantivity has metaphysical priority over their substantiality. For this reason, in the metaphysical scale of entities, we witness a progressive substantivation of the substantiality and not the reverse, a substantification of the substantivity; the moment of substantiality is clouded over in favor of the moment of substantivity. Thus, the essential unity is a unity *per se*, but of a formally systematic, and not substantial, character. It is a unity «among» the constitutive notes themselves and not their unity as substantial moments or principles.

It might then be thought that the essential unity is a unity of inherence. We have indicated, as a matter of fact, that the accidents can have a unity among themselves by the fact of being inherent in one same substance. Would that not be the case of the unity of the essential notes «among themselves?» This is impossible, because the essential notes form a unity *per se*, while the unity of inherence is a unity *per accidens*.

To sum up, the essential unity is a unity neither of conjunction, nor of inherence, nor of substance. It is, to be sure, a unity *per se*, but not, however, of substance. Just as substantivity is something superior to the dualism substance-accident, so also is the essential unity a unity of a superior type: it is precisely a unity of system. And then it is not difficult to form a concept of what the formal reason *(razón)* of this unity consists in.

It is, in the first place, a unity *per se* which is systematic in character. In order to understand what this means, let us repeat what we have insisted on all along, namely, that the essential notes have in their physical reality a constitutively constructed character. They are formally «notes-of;» some are «notes-of» the others, of all the others. For this reason, the absolute substantive «of» which they are notes is not a subject of them but, rather, the unitary system itself which they form among themselves in virtue of the constructed character of each one. Their formally constructed character brings it about that the notes form a unity *directly* among themselves, not *indirectly* by way of the same substance in which all were inherent. The *per se* character of the essential unity means to be one «directly,» by reason of its intrinsic and formally constructed character. This is what, in its turn, permits us to form a more rigorous concept of what it is to be «note-of.» At first glance, every note is «of» someone and therefore it seems that every note of a substantive reality is «note-of.» This, however, is false, because this presupposes that «of» which an essential note is a note: that is to say, its absolute term is primarily and formally a subject; in that case, every note, whether essential or not, would always be «note-of.» The absolute term, then, of the essential notes is not a subject, but the unity itself of all the notes. Whence it follows that only those are «notes-of» which, by themselves and directly, form a system. It is exactly what we said before, namely, that the formal reason *(razón)* of the essential notes consists in the fact that they are capable of forming a system by themselves. Only the essential notes find themselves in the constructed state, only they are «notes-of.» To call essential the notes necessary and sufficient to form a system by themselves is the same as to say that all and only the «notes-of» are essential, all and only the notes in constructed state. Other notes form a system not directly, but as grounded in the essential notes. Therefore, these grounded notes are not formally «notes-of'»; they possess another type of reality of which we will try to form a concept in another place.

Hence follows, in the second place, the formal reason (*razón*) of 298 this essential unity. The formal reason (*razón*) of the accident is «to inhere» in a substance; for this reason, its unity is formally unity of «inherence.» An essential or constitutive note, then, is «note-of.» «This note» cannot have physical reality save «with» all the other notes of «this» determined physical essence. As a consequence, the formal reason (*razón*) of the essential note is to «cohere» with the others. The essential unity is formally a unity of «coherence» *per se.* This coherence is the formal unity of the system as such.

Coherence is a metaphysical character; that is, a physical character of reality but, it is to be noted, of the reality as such. It is not a matter of the real correlate of an objective concept. In the latter sense the essence would be that in which the thing «consists,» in contrast to that which the thing merely «is,» without consisting in it. Thus, for example, this paper «is» white, but it does not «consist» in being white. By contrast, man not merely «is» corporeal, but, at least partially, «consists» in corporeity. I myself, in order to simplify the exposition in other terms, have customarily spoken of consistency, in order to counterpose it, for example, to subsistency, and I have qualified the essence of consistency in this sense. This, however, is a merely indirect concept of essence, a concept delimited by mere counterposition. Taken, not in counterposition, but in itself, as a physical moment of the real, essence is not consistency, but coherence, because consistency derives from coherence; reality consists precisely in that in which and by which it is coherent. However, the physical (principle) of the coherence is not to be confused with other physical characteristics which some realities can have. On the one hand, one might think once again of consistency as that real character according to which some realities are consistent, in contrast to others, which are inconsistent. Neither, however, is essence, because not everything coherent is necessarily consistent; the inconsistent itself has its own peculiar coherence. Coherence, that is, the essence, in the real as such, lies beyond consistency and inconsistency. On the other hand, the word coherence may lead one to think of a material property of bodies considered macroscopically. Consistency, however, is not this, either. The coherence of bodies is, much rather, «cohesion.» It is a word which has the same etymological origin as coherence. It is normal, however, for etymologically equivalent words to be ascribed to differently specialized semantic lines. Making use of this liberty, we will say that bodies have cohesion because, as realities, they are coherent. Coherence is the condition, nothing more than the condition, for there being cohesion, and not, inversely, as though cohesion was the unique type of coherence. Cohesion is only the macromaterial form of coherence. In a word, coherence is a physical character of reality, but, however, as reality. And this coherence *per se* is the character and the formal reason (*razón*) of the essential unity.

Nevertheless, having said this, one has not said all that needs to be said concerning essential unity. Essential unity, in a word, is the unity of coherence *per se* of the constitutive essence. Its primary character is its status as physical: every essential constitutive unity is physical. The reciprocal situation, however, is not certain: it is not enough that the primary unity of a reality be physical in order that this unity should be, unqualifiedly, formally essential. It is necessary, then, to clarify somewhat more the physical quality and character of the unity of the constitutive essence, as essence. On the other hand, we also saw earlier that the essence is primarily and 300 formally the «constitutive» essence; however, let us add, this essence can be, in addition, quiddifiable, that is, can have as one of its moments what I have called quidditive essence. This quidditive essence seems to have, in its own turn, a certain unity precisely as quidditive. And then it is asked what is, speaking more precisely, this quidditive unity within the coherential physical unity of the constitutive essence? Here we encounter the two questions which we must rapidly elucidate.

Before all, (the question of) the physical status of the unity of the constitutive essence *qua* essence. We have already indicated this in describing the proper character of the essence at the opening of this part of our work: there are different ways of conceiving the physical character of essence *qua* essence. And, in the same place, we rapidly expounded and rejected a notion of the physical unity of the constitutive essence as insufficient, though underwritten not only by ordinary language but also, and above all, by a great philosophy, the philosophy of India: the *Upanishads* understand essence as the *rasa-*. Now, however, to enter upon a brief discussion with that philosophy, we may proceed to interpret this notion in function of the concepts which we have been developing in our idea of essence. Let us take any substantive reality whatsoever. Each one of the notes which we have called constitutive of it would be like the physical «manifestation» of a proper virtue or force of an active principal intrinsic to that reality: *each note*, in and by itself, would be, as a note, a mere manifestation of this active principle of it, a principle which would be the true note, or, better said, the truly constitutive (element) in it. Constitutive note, then, would be this virtue or active principle. Let us then, concentrate all these virtues or active principles in one same reality, in one same «element.» This element which concentrates in itself all the dynamic virtues or active principles whose «manifestation» are the «formal notes» would be, unitarily, 301 «the» active principle of the entire thing, its essence. Its unity would be a unity of «concentration.» This essence is not an abstraction, but a tangible and separable physical reality: the sap, the semen, etc. For this reason I have called it «element.» It is a kind of active extract of the reality in question. It is precisely the essence as *rasa-*.

Interpreted thus, by means of the concepts which we have been expounding here, this idea of essence contains, in some very important points, a secure vision of the problem. Let us not permit ourselves to be deceived by our western mentality of Hellenic provenance. In the first place, there must be emphasized in a rigorous manner and in the first place, the properly and formally physical character of essence. The sap is nothing at all comparable to the objective correlate of a definition or anything else of a similar kind. Even more, even though in this idea there does not appear as a concept that which we have here called «the constitutive,» nevertheless, *in re, rasa-* is always what physically constitutes the reality in question, by way of a kind of active operation, a «constituting operation.» It is not simply the operation «executed» by the active principle, but rather is the proper active character (*svabhāva-*) of what we have called principle. For an Indian, the essence is formally «constituting» in the active acceptance of the term, while for a Greek the essence is simply that which the thing formally «is.» This constituting essence is not

only a principle from which the notes of the thing «are born» (φύειν),
but an intrinsic moment of the note itself, included in its «formal»
reality, so to say, something like the life which the leaf of a tree
possesses; if it were not alive in itself it would not be a leaf. The
302 leaf is nothing other than the already constituted morphological manifestation of its proper and formal life. Essence is not «morphology,»
as for a Greek, but rather «constitutionality.» Even leaving aside for
a moment this manner of understanding the constitution as an active
operation and as manifestation, it cannot be denied that this conception of essence places the accent on the physical character of the
constitution itself, in contrast to the Greek concept for which the
constitution would be the simple formal configuration in which a
reality «is» (está). Nothing is truer than this physical character and
— if I may be permitted the redundancy — nothing is truer than this
constituting character of the constitutive element (lo constitutivo).
Not only this, but also that the essence, as that which constitutes
the reality, is not this unity of typical traits which the Greeks called
eidos, species. It is not that essence as rasa- lacks them (such traits);
it has them effectively and could not do otherwise than have them.
Its traits, however, do not present any aspects in common with those
of the eidos of the thing. The Greek eidos would be, for an Indian,
the already «constituted» essence (svarūpa-); the true essence, however, would be the «constituting» essence; and as such does not have
the least «formal» relation with the traits of the eidos. And this is a
truth which cannot be denied. I insisted on this point earlier, that
the constitutive note of an albino is certainly to be found in some
modality of some nuclear acid or similar substance (I do not know
which), in something, in any case, whose «traits» have nothing in
common with albinism as a trait, as a note of an eidos.

All this is true in general terms, and precisely on this truth rests
whatever is acceptable in the Indian notion of essence. Nervertheless,
it is not an adequate notion. As I had occasion to note some pages
earlier, there springs to mind the fact that in this conception of
essence, essence is something substantial; rasa- is a substance. So
true is this that it is perfectly separable. For this reason I have
called it «element.» The essence, however, is a moment of the substantivity and not of the substantiality; much less, is it an «element.»
Physical is not a synonym for either substantial or elemental. The

essence has a physical character; it is, however, in the order of substantivity. On this supposition, essence as *rasa-* is neither necessary 303
nor sufficient.

Before all else, it is not *necessary.* Not all the realities in the
world, in a word, have *rasa-* in the sense advanced; material realities
lack it. However, since in treating of an intramundane metaphysics
we encounter the fact that the most important realities in the world,
as realities (living things and man are not simply «other» realities
than the material, but rather have a higher level of reality than these)
have *rasa-,* we are able to prescind from this first consideration and
examine the idea of *rasa-* in itself.

This idea is not *sufficient,* because by it we are not told in what
the essentiality itself of *rasa-* consists. In the first place, the fact
that *rasa-* as essence has a «constituting» character does not mean
that the constitution has, necessarily, an «active» character. The proper characteristic of essence is, simply, «to constitute.» That the constitution is achieved or completed actively is a thing or matter which
concerns the mechanism, so to say, of the constitution, but is not
that in which the constitution formally consists. The essence, in a
word, is a physical moment of the substantivity and, therefore, the
constitutional notes are not grounded in the essence under the form
of origination, but under that of functional determination. The former is proper to substance; the latter, of substantivity. In the second
place, however, and above all, even prescinding from the constituting
character of essence, it does not tell us in what its formal essentiality
may consist. There is not the least doubt, in a word, but that of
rasa- itself it can and ought to be asked what its essence may be. It
does not help us at all in this matter to be told that in the *rasa-*
everything is essence and that in it resides the «whole» essence of the
thing; we must be told what this «whole» is, what its content may 304
be, that is to say, in what the fact that a note may be essential consists; even more, it is necessary to know in what its total unity
consists. So long as these points are not made clear, we will indeed
know that the *rasa-* is essence, but we will not know in what *rasa-'s*
being essence consists; we shall not have apprehended the *rasa-* in
its precise character as essence. In our present situation, we are
without precise ideas on both these points. This is clear with regard
to what concerns the «content» of the *rasa-,* its constitutive notes,

as constitutive. Nor is this any the less the case with regard to what concerns its unity as such. The essential unity of the *rasa-* cannot be simple «concentration.» It is true that, «materially,» the essence contains the notes necessary and sufficient to insure that the essentiated reality should have all its other notes, and in this sense it is possible to speak of «concentration» of constitutive notes. But this proves to be nothing more than a material unity. Nothing is said of the formal character of this unity, which might be that of conjunction, of substance, etc. We have, however, already seen that the formal reason *(razón)* of this unity is coherence. The idea of *rasa-*, therefore, has not cleared the field of the problem of the constitutive notes nor that of the formal reason of its unity. It does not indicate to us in what the essentiality of the *rasa-* consists; and this is no matter of chance or accident: the most ancient *Upanishads* (and it is to them alone that I am making reference in the present exposition and discussion of the *rasa-*) have all the characteristics of an archaic philosophy similar to that of our own pre-Socratics, and, just as in the case of the latter, it would be illusory to ask of them conceptual clarifications which could only have been made much later. Nevertheless, it was important not to pass over this notion of *rasa-*, not out of a motive of mere informative curiosity, but because it corresponds to a natural point of departure of the intelligence when it confronts reality, that is to say, the consideration that the essence is «something» essential which, in one form or
305 another, encloses in itself everything which the thing is (the essentiated reality). In this «something» India saw a kind of force or «concentrated» active principle; Greece, by contrast, saw in this «something» a shaping principle in the sense of eidetic moment (μορφή). Inchoatively, however, both mentalities take their point of departure from the same point. The terminus of the way of the *Upanishads* was reality as an «offspring» *(bhūtāni)*, not in the pejorative, but in the etymological sense of the term; the terminus of the way of the Greeks was reality as being (τὰ ὄντα). The essential unity of the constitutive essence, then, is, to be sure, a physical unity, but it is a unity neither of concentration nor of the eidos: it is a unity of coherence.

Here we have what I have been trying to make more precise with respect to the essential constitutive unity. I have been saying, however, that this essence can be quiddifiable, that is, may have as its intrinsic moment a quidditive essence. The quidditive essence contains an undeniable unity. We can recognize, in effect, whether two or a variety of substantive realities do or do not belong to the «same» species; this fact shows unequivocally that among the notes of the constitutive essence of a reality there is a certain unity which is properly quidditive. Of what unity, or kind of unity, are we speaking here? That is the question. That «both» essences are not simply identical is clear, granted that not every constitutive essence is quiddifiable, and, therefore, constitutive unity is not simply a quidditive unity. As a consequence, with respect to these substantive realities, whose constitutive essence is speciable, a serious problem arises: can it be that two essential unities exist in them? This is the second question which must be addressed if we are to succeed in clarifying and making precise the idea of essential unity.

In order to decide this question, it is necessary to circumscribe it in a rigorous manner. Before all else, it is not a question of the relation between the unity of the physical essence of each or every substantive reality and the unity of the species, because the unity of the species includes, as one of its moments — and not the only one — the to be «common» to all individuals. Under this aspect, the 306 unity of the species is a unity in the sense of «community.» However, in order that anything may be common to all the individual substantive realities in their physical essence, it is necessary that it begin by being possessed by each one of them. What is common, however, as common, has only a conceptive unity. By contrast, what is common, as possessed by each physical essence, has the physical character of the latter, which is a constitutive essence endowed with a unity which is not only a unity of community but is, rather, wholly the contrary: it is a unity which rests upon itself in its constitutive and incommunicable «individuality.» As is well known, Aristotle, in contrast to Plato, has already distinguished these two kinds of unity of ἕν. As a consequence, the radical question concerning essential unity resides in the very structure of the constitutive essence within it, within each individual substantive reality, and not in its possible community with others.

The question, then, is the following. In view of what we have called constitutive essence, each substantive reality has its entitative unity individually or numerically (as it is customarily said), which makes it, for example, «this» man and no other. «This» man, however, is, in addition, «man» and not «dog,» that is, has a specific essence which is proper to him. «To be man,» however, is a unity of notes different from «being-dog,» a proper essential unity. And as «to be man» is proper to «this» man, we are asking what type of unity his proper «being-a-man» might have in «this» man, that is, the specific essence, *qua* essence.

Obviously, this specific essence or quidditive essence *qua* essence does not have a physical and numerical unity in each individual. It has only what we have here called coherence of the entire constitutive essence of which the quidditive essence is its specific moment. If this were not the case, in each essentiated reality there would be two essences distinct in number, the constitutive essence and the quidditive essence — clearly an absurdity, because then there would be not one but two essentiated realities. In the essentiated reality, there is but one physical essence, the constitutive essence, and one sole physical essential unity, the coherential unity of its notes. However, I have already observed that although the quidditive essence possesses a certain proper unity *qua* essence, since on seeing a substantive reality I can sometimes recognize *in it itself* that it is of the same species as others — something which would be impossible if the specific characteristics did not possess a certain unity within each essentiated reality. Bringing together both statements, that is, the absence of physical unity and the possession of a certain specific unity, we will say that, between the two «unities» there is only a distinction of reason founded in reality. This, however, does not tell us in what the essential quidditive unity consists, but in what it does not consist, that, namely, in being physical unity. To ascertain the character of the unity in question, we had a path indicated to us when it was said that it is distinguished from physical unity with a *real* basis: if we make clearer what this basis may be, we will have *eo ipso* made precise in what the specific essential unity as such might positively consist in each individual.

Traditional philosophy, taking as its point of departure the view that the community of species is in itself «mere community,» finds the foundation of this community in the simple similitude of the individuals among themselves. Hence it follows that within the entitative and numerical unity of each individual there is something like a unity of specific physiognomy: the *unitas formalis,* the formal unity. It is not numeral unity; still it is a true unity, save that it is «less» than the numeral, *minor numerali.* The proof, we are told, lies in the fact that I can define this unity while prescinding from the physical unity of each individual. This formal unity would be the unity proper to the essence *qua* essence. And it is the unity which would be distinguished, with a distinction of reason founded in reality, from the entitative unity of each individual.

This conception of the essential unity *qua* essential is erected, as has been seen, on the identity of essence and quiddity. This, however, is not exact because not every physical essence is quidditative; it may be only constitutive. There is no need to insist on this point further. However, even when we pass over this important point and limit ourselves to the quiddity, it is not possible to conceptualize the quidditative unity as a formal unity. And this for various reasons. In the first place, the fact that the quiddity would be definable within each individual independently of its individual physical entity, proves only that there effectively exists a quidditative unity *qua* quidditative, but does not prove that this unity would be precisely a formal unity; that is, it leaves open the character of the unity which has been defined. We will see that definability is compatible with other conceptions of the quidditive unity. In the second place, it does not tell us what function this formal unity fulfills within the physical entity of the individual. And this silence does not befall by chance: the fact is that the formal unity as such is not able to fulfill any positive function in the physical reality of the individual. Let there be a reality A; the fact that another reality B should be simply similar to A, that is to say, the mere similitude of B to A does not and cannot fulfill a function within the constitution of B. Now, the idea of formal unity is based on the idea of similitude; for this reason, the formal unity does not fulfill any function in the essential constitution of a substantive reality. And this situation, when examined closely, is unsatisfactory: can it be said that the unity of the specific traits of an individual substantive reality performs no function in its constitution? In the third place, it is not that this formal unity does not exist; what happens is that the specific unity is not mere formal unity. And this is the decisive point. The formal

unity exists because constitutive similitude exists effectively between
the different individuals. However, this community, by way of similitude, is the community of a simple «class,» a «natural» class, in
the greater number of cases; this and nothing more. What similitude
constitutes is a class. Every species, to be sure, is a class, but not
every class is a species. Which means that both communities — that
of the class and that of the species — are distinguished from each
other by their very mode of being common. In the commonness of
the class, the individuals simply «are» (*están*) in community because
there exists a similitude of traits by their formal unity. Despite all
the appearances to the contrary, the idea of formal unity is founded
on the idea of similitude; and in this resides its radical insufficiency:
it leads to a class, but not to a species. By contrast, the community
of the species possesses, *in re,* a basis different from mere similitude
and, as a consequence, its community is something different from
merely «being» (*estar*) in community. Which means that, within each
individual, the quidditative unity *qua* quidditative is distinguished
from the physical unity by a *ground* different from mere similitude
to other individuals and that, consequently, it is an other *type of
unity* different from formal unity, a unity which fulfills or performs
eo ipso a *positive function* within the constitutive essence.

Before all else, the *ground* of the specific unity. This is something
which we have already expounded; let us recapitulate, from the
point of view of the problem which now occupies us, some of the
ideas which have been developed earlier. The specific, we said, is
certainly something «common;» however, something which is common by reason of being «communicated;» only in the measure in
which something is communicated or is communicable can there be
310 something specifically common. This communication is what we have
called multiplication by transmission. Specific community *qua* community is not «mere similitude» in which it «is» (*está*) but a similitude which one «achieves,» that is, a «genetic similitude.» Hence the
ground of specificity: it is that within each individual which brings
it to communication, that is, generation. What is generation? That
is to say, what is it that is transmitted in it? In generation the entire
constitutive essence is not transmitted, because every generable essence possesses a strict individuality. What is transmitted is not,
nevertheless, formally a «physical part» of the constitutive essence,

nor even of the substantive reality. Generation does, to be sure, involve a «transportation» of substances from the generators to the generated. What makes this transportation formally generation, however, is the fact that, by the action executed by the genitors, these «transported» substances constitute a «replication» (and not a mere replica) of the constitutive character of the generators, that is, a replication of the inner character of some of their constitutive notes (we have already seen which). It is what I have called the «constitutive schema.» What is transmitted then, is the constitutive schema itself. Therefore, the generated reality has, in its constitutive essence, a constitutive schema «equal» to the constitutive essences of its genitors. As a transmissive action, therefore, generation consists, formally, in the replication of the «constitution;» generation is, formally, «re-constitution.» And this re-constitution is what we earlier called paradigmatic causality; it is, rigorously speaking, «re-constitutive» causality. Generation is, formally, a phenomenon of substantivity and not of substantiality; it is the transportation of substances, but the re-constitution of the substantivity. That what is transmitted is, precisely and formally, only the constitutive schema: such is the rigorous concept of what we have been calling «moment» of the constitutive essence. And the quidditative essence consists in this equality of the constitutive schema insofar as it is genetically transmissible. The quidditative essence is, then, a mere moment of the constitutive essence. This quidditative essence is not «the» (la) complete essence qua essence of the substantive reality because, as we have already seen, that is, in itself, something merely «to be differentiated» (deferendo) and, therefore, cannot possess reality qua essence but rather «in» its «essential difference;» this intrinsic unity of the quidditative essence, in its essential difference, is the constitutive essence. Reciprocally, the constitutive essence is quiddifiable only when it can transmit genetically that which, in it, is only an essential «moment» of it, its constitutive schema; and this its moment is the quidditative essence. Stated in other terms: the necessary and sufficient condition to insure that a constitutive essence is specifiable or quiddifiable is that it should be schematizable. Not every constitutive essence is «constructed» on a physical schema. The reality of the species in each individual is not, then, in the first line the reality of a universal in a singular, but rather the reality of a constitutive schema in a constitutive essence. For this reason, the species as problem is not the problem of universals, but rather the problem of whether or not every essence is or is not physically erected on a constitutive schema.

To sum up, specific community *qua* community is not «mere similitude» but «genetic similitude.» Its ground within each one of the individuals is generation, the re-constitution of the constitutive schema. From the point of view of the generating principle, that is, as principle of generation, the replicating constitutive schema is what we have called *phylum*. From the point of view of what is generated, that is, as terminus of generation, the replicated constitutive schema in it makes of it a reality which emerges as such within a *phylum*.
312 They are but two aspects of one sole phenomenon: belonging (either as principle or as term) to a determined *phylum*. We are then able to describe the phenomenon of specificity, as we have already done earlier, from another point of view: the quidditative essence, or species, is the group of characters by which a substantive reality belongs to a determined *phylum*. Both physical concepts of specificity are perfectly identical: within each individual, its specific moment is its constitutive or phyletic schema, grounded on the generability of its constitutive essence. This notion of species is physical and not conceptive. It is the concept which, though in a manner clearly inadequate, resounds (echoes) in the ancient Indian texts, in which things are, as we have said, *bhūtāni*, «offspring,» and not simply «entities» (ὄντα) endowed with conceptive structure (genus, difference, species).

Having established this, and having clarified the ground of specificity and its content, the constitutive schema, we proceed to ask what may be the *character of the unity* of this constitutive schema within each individual of the species.

The quidditative essence is what is replicable, what is re-constitutable. What is replicable is always and only a moment of the constitutive essence. I can, however, understand the replicable *within it* (the constitutive essence) in two different ways. I can understand it in the first place *insofar as it is a moment of the constitutive essence*. And then, as a mere moment of this essence, what is replicable has no physical unity proper and peculiar to itself; it has only the coherential unity of the constitutive essence of which it is only a moment.

I can, however, consider what is replicable, what is re-constitutable of the constitutive essence, in a different way, namely, not simply as a moment of that essence, but insofar as replicable, insofar as re-con- 313 stitutable. And the question now becomes the following: does what is replicable *as replicable* have any proper unity even though it may not be the physical unity of coherence? That the constitutive schema, that is, the quidditative essence, possesses unity within the constitutive essence is something which cannot be denied; not, however, by reasons of «typicity» so to say, but for a different, very concrete reason: by generation. Generation is re-constitution of the constitutive schema. Hence, the phenomenon of genetic transmission has disengaged (*desgajado*) the constitutive schema as an autonomous moment of constitutive essences. It has disengaged it, first of all, in the line or order of transmission itself. Not, to be sure, in the sense of conferring «separate» or «separable» reality on the constitutive schema (that would be the Platonic χωρισμός), nor in the sense of the identity between the essence of what is to be the engendered (*generando*) and the substantial form (this was the Aristotelian conception), but in the sense of being the unique moment which is «equal» in the generation of the strict individual reality of the constitutive essence. Generation, in a word, is a phenomenon of substantivity and not of substantiality. Genetic equality is not, consequently, formally the unity of the trunk whence the individuals emerge, but rather the equal mode of being constituted as substantivity: namely, by replication of the constitutive schema. It is the equality of a recurrent moment of the substantivity, not the equality of a substantial principle. And this unity of the constitutive schema, disengaged genetically, is precisely the strict definition of *phylum:* such is the autonomy of the constitutive schema disengaged as something «transmissible;» and this autonomy of the constitutive schema, as something generable as generable, is the unity of that schema, the unity of the quiddity, within each constitutive essence. Generation 314 disengages, in this way, this unity of the constitutive schema within each individual. This unity, however, is not merely negative; that is to say, it is not a question of a «mere group» of notes, indifferent in itself (*de suyo*) to being a moment of a complete unity (the unity of the constitutive essence), but is, rather, a positive unity. For, if it is, to be sure, clear that the constitutive schema is not the complete essence of the essentiated reality, it is, nevertheless, the «to be differentiated» (*deferendo*) moment of it and, in addition, possesses true positive unity. This unity is the precise and formal term of the genetic disengagement as such.

Of what type is this unity? It is not, let us repeat it even to the point of satiety, a physical coherential unity. Neither, however, is it simple formal unity, in the scholastic sense. It is not, in a word, «physiognomic» unity of traits but, rather, a «generable» unity resting on the physical reality of the generating notes. The generating notes, then, form a physical subsystem within the constitutive essence; it is the subsystem generative of each individual. And this subsystem is, *eo ipso*, the physical «quiddifying» subsystem. Its term, even though it does not have a proper unity within the constitutive essence, nevertheless possesses a unity *sui generis*: the unity of the generable as such. This unity, in a word, is, before all else, the terminus of the generating physical subsystem. In what sense, however, is it its terminus? It is not such only in the way in which an act is the terminus of a potency which executes it; in this sense, the act of a potency is, insofar as it is merely the terminus of that potency, something only «possible.» The unity of the generable, however, is something already «actual;» for the generating subsystem, at the same time that it is «potency» of the substance in the order of the production of generation, is also a subsystem which «delimits» a moment of the substantivity in the order of replicability. The «replicable,» as such, before being effectively «replicated,» is already delimited 315 in act, as replicable, in the constitutive essence. That is, the generator has two aspects: one, that of being a potency of the substantiality, and another, that of being a subsystem of the substantivity. Under the first aspect, it is the capacity of «producing» the replication; in the second, it is the «delimitator» of what is replicable in the constitutive essence. Under the first aspect, it has not yet passed into act; generation is still merely possible. In the second, however, it is already in act, since the replicable as such is already actually delimited as a moment whether or not there is effective replication. The act is not only the act of a potency, but also an act with a different and distinct character: the act of a systematic delimitation of the substantivity. Generation, I have said earlier, disengages the autonomy of the constitutive schema, of what is replicable. Now we can give a strict and rigorous concept of it: disengagement is actual delimitation, the actuality of what is replicable, as replicable.

The constitutive schema, or quiddity, is, then, within the constitutive essence, a unity superior to the merely formal. It is not, to be sure, a physical coherential unity. However, insofar as it is the actual terminus of a physical subsystem, it is a more-than-formal unity. I would say that it is a «lesser» unity than the numeral, *minor numerali*; «greater,» however, than the formal, *major formali*. This *sui generis* unity is what I would call «phyletic unity.» And this is the unity which is proper to the quidditative essence within the constitutive (essence). Between the phyletic unity of the quidditative essence and the physical coherential unity of the constitutive essence there is a mere distinction of reason, because the constitutive schema does not form a complete system but is, rather, only the moment to be differentiated (*deferendo*), as such, within the sole complete system, that of the constitutive essence.

This moment which is already actually delimited is what gives 316 the replicable its unity of physiognomy, its formal unity. This formal unity exists, but it is grounded in the phyletic unity. And this is the reason why definability does not prove that the quidditative unity is merely formal. It does indeed prove that, in the quidditative unity, there is *assertivé* a formal unity; it does not, however, prove *exclusivé* that the quidditative unity consists only in it (the formal unity). The formal unity of the quidditative is no more than half of the quidditative unity: the unity of physiognomy. Another half is necessary: that the physiognomy be transmissible. The two aspects, taken together, are the phyletic unity of the quiddity. The phyletic unity is the moment of the coherential unity disengaged by the generating subsystem; it is also what confers a certain quasi-coherential unity on each individual with all the other individuals of its species, something which we might call «coherential respect or respectivity» of the individuals among themselves, and its phyletic unity resides in this respectivity. And this is what, once constituted, defines the definition. The definition defines what is already delimited, but the phyletic unity is that which, by delimitation, makes the reality definable.

In one word, the quidditative as such has, within each individual, a unity whose *ground* is generation, and whose proper *character* is to be phyletic unity, less than the numeral, but more than the formal and only by way of a distinction of reason distinct from the coherential unity of the constitutive essence. Thus the phyletic unity fulfills a *proper function* in the very structure of the constitutive essence. Only by bringing it into view have we shown the internal articulation of the quidditative essence with the constitutive essence.

The quiddity, or constitutive schema, is the specific moment of the constitutive essence. It might be thought, therefore, that its proper function is a primary function which it possesses of itself and which 317 would consist in conferring its specificity on the individual reality. This is not exact, however, because the quiddity is not a primary moment of the reality as such, but a derived moment, and that only of some realities. The existence of the quiddity depends, in effect, on the specificability of the constitutive essence; the individual is not an individual realization of the specific, but rather, on the contrary, the species is the expansion of the individual constitutive essence. As a consequence, this, and only this, is what, in the last analysis, possesses the properly specifying function.

This proper function is not, then, a function which, primarily and formally, fulfills the phyletic unity by itself, as though it were that function which imparts structure to the essence of the substantive reality, but rather, on the contrary, it is a function which it receives, in the first instance, from the constitutive essence.

The phyletic unity, I have said, is the moment of the coherential unity itself, disengaged within it by its generating subsystem. This subsystem is something physically real and belongs formally to the constitutive essence and to its coherential unity equally with the rest of the notes of the constitutive essence. Moreover, this subsystem is not a mere additive to the constitutive essence, as though *after* this last is what it is, it might have, *in addition*, superrogatively, a subsystem capable of replicating the coherential unity. This is not the true situation. Its proper capacity of replication belongs to the constitutive essence of these realities *essentially*, *qua* constitutive; replication is not essential to it, but the power of replication *is*, in such wise that without this generative or generating subsystem, the presumptive constitutive essence would not be such a constitutive essence. The constitutive essence of these essentiated realities is *essentially* quiddifiable, and has its proper constitutive schema *essentially* delimited in act, something which does not happen in the case of singular realities, each one of which would be what it is even 318 though it did not constitute a class with others. To be essentially quiddifiable does not mean to belong essentially to a species which would be κατὰ φύσιν anterior to the individual, but means rather to be essentially disengaging the moment of specificity from within itself. If, then, it is true that without coherential unity there is no phyletic unity, it is no less true that in these realities, without phyleticization, without actual delimitation of its constitutive schema, there would be no coherential unity. Hence the proper function which the quidditive has received from the constitutive. The «potentiality» of re-constitution in these realities is a constitutive or essential moment of the primary constitution of the individual. In these realities, the individual would not be able to have individual reality if it were not generable. And this generability is a turning of each individual to the rest, as others, not to such and such determinatively, but to the rest simply and merely as others. As a consequence, the turning to the rest, as others, is here co-essential to the individual essence itself. In these realities, then, the individual would not have individual coherence if it did not have a coherential respect to the rest. And reciprocally, it would not have coherential respect, if it did not have coherential unity. That is, the structure of its individual coherence is, *eo ipso*, the disengagement, the actuality of the rest, as others, within each individual. In a certain way or sense, then, each individual essentially carries others within itself.

This coherential respect is full of serious metaphysical consequences. Each individual, I say, carries, in a certain way, the rest within itself. This certain way consists precisely and formally in three metaphysical characters. Before all else, the constitutive essence, as such, is what it is, without the least reference to other realities. Not every constitutive essence is quiddifiable, and even when it is, the formal reason (*razón*) of essentiality is not specificity. When, 319 however, it is quiddifiable or capable of being established in a *phylum* it is constitutively referred to other individuals, and in its constitutive individuality, there is something counter-distinguished to these others, which, by reason of the turning toward them, it (the constitutive individuality) carries in itself. That is, every individual essence is, then, something «in itself» with regard to the others. To be in oneself, as counter-distinct to other, is the first characteristic of the way in which it carries them in itself. The individual reality is something «in itself» only in the measure in which it can be included in a *phylum*. In addition, however, in this phyletic unity and only in it, each individual essence has something «in common» with the rest, and it has this common element insofar as it has a received constitutive schema. The question here is not that each individual has, by reason of its own character, antecedents and descendents. That it has antecedents is necessary, and even though it may not have descendents it is necessary that it have the capacity to have them. This is not the question here, however; here the question is that of the essential reason of this double necessity; that is to say, the delimited actuality of the generable as such, of the constitutive schema, within the constitutive essence of each such being. By reason of having this constitutive schema, delimited in act within its proper constitutive essence, each individual essence possesses its «received» and «common» constitutive schema. Individual antecedents or descendents, that is, «antecendency» and «descendency» as such, are possible only as grounded in the received and common character of the constitutive schema delimited in act in each individual. «In itself,» «originated,» and «common,» these are the three moments of phyletic unity, of coherential respect as such, the three modes according to which the others are present in each individual essence. Therefore, 320 these are three metaphysical characters which, *per modum unius*, the constitutive essence of generable realities possesses in virtue of the coherential respect, of the turning toward others as others. And since this turning, this respect, is the actual terminus (in the sense explained earlier) of a physical subsystem of the constitutive essence, it follows that the coherential unity has, *from itself* and essentially, in delimited act, its turning toward others and is, therefore, essentially something in itself, something originated, and something common. This the proper and peculiar function which the coherential unity of the constitutive essence confers, by disengagement (*desgajamiento*), on its phyletic moment; it makes of it a unity with itself, a unity of origination, a unity of communication. Without this function, not only would there not be εἶδος, *species*, but also that which there is would not be εἶδος, *species*. Reciprocally, thanks to it (that function), εἶδος, *species*, is something more than the formal moment of the specified reality; it is the expression of the phyletic unity, that is, of the coherential unity insofar as it is communicable.

Just as, however, not every constitutive essence is quiddifiable, and just as, even in the case in which it is quiddifiable, the quidditative essence is grounded in the constitutive, it follows that the essence, as such, is nothing other than the constitutive essence, and that the essential unity is, formally, the coherential unity. Therefore, the formal reason of the essential unity is coherence. Here is the first element that we have been seeking.

This, however, is not enough for the complete characterization of the essential unity. This unity is not only intrinsic to the notes. It is not only that each note is turned to the rest «from itself,» but that in addition, it is turned to them «in anticipation» (*de antemano*). That is, the essential unity is a «first order» (*primaria*) unity. This is the second question which we propose to illuminate in order to grasp the character of essential unity. The essence is the primary coherential unity of the real as such.

SECTION THREE

ON THE PRIMACY OF THE ESSENTIAL UNITY   322

In saying that the essential unity is a primary unity, what we wished to make understood is that the unity itself is *in some way* «anterior» (πρότερον) to the notes which are one in such wise that the primacy is not that these are to be considered «components» of the unity, but, quite contrary, that they must be thought of as «analyzers» of the unity itself. That is: the notes do not ground the unity, but the unity grounds the notes. This is what I have been expressing at various times when I said that man is not man because he is animal and rational but is animal and rational because he is man. The first phrase expresses the human reality in function of its notes; the second, expresses this same reality by the primary unity of those notes. When this has been established, we ask, «Is the essential unity *qua* unity 'anterior' (πρότερον) to the notes themselves? And, if it is, in what does this character of primacy of the essential unity *qua* unity, *qua* ἕν, consist?»

That the unity, I may say without qualification, is anterior to the notes is something, to my way of viewing the matter, undeniable. It is, before all else, a plausible thesis, because there are irrefutable signs that this is the situation of fact. In effect, when I seek to understand any reality, I look for the group of properties which are constitutively its own. Every property discovered, however, is the note of this reality as intelligible unity. Only by directing my attention to something «one» can I understand what the real thing is. If this were not the case, we would not have known the properties of one thing but we would have known various things. The unity, the ἕν, is then, the primary supposition in the order of knowledge and, above all, of knowledge of essence; it is a *prius* κατὰ λόγον. Not only this, but if I intend to construct or produce some reality, my operation is ordered and orientated precisely by the idea of producing «one» thing. 323 For example, it is not enough for me to produce wheels and springs, but wheels and springs such that they constitute «one» watch. The unity, the ἕν, is the primary supposition of every «made» reality: it is something primary, τέχνη. Both the λόγος and τέχνη, have, then, as primary supposition of all notes, known or made, the ἕν. Obviously, this is merely a sign or index that the same thing transpires in the reality of nature, φύσει. It is only a sign, because, on the one hand, the structure of knowledge, of the λόγος, is not the structure of reality. And, on the other hand, though indeed it is the truth that τέχνη moves among realities and makes reality, nevertheless, it is not necessary to believe with the Greeks that τέχνη is an imitation μίμησις, of nature, but rather that it has a proper structure of its own precisely as «making;» and this means that there is no reason why the structure of the real should be the same as the structure of human making of realities. Therefore, λόγος and τέχνη are nothing more than two signs of the fact that unity is the primary moment of the real as real. As signs, however, they have an enormous consequence: they make our thesis plausible, something obvious. The obvious, in a word, is that which leaps to confront anyone who approaches it. When we seek to involve ourselves with the real and take the route either of λόγος or τέχνη, the first thing which arises to confront us, the first thing which offers itself to us — the obvious thing — is the priority of the unity with respect to its notes. The proper mode for the intellection of the obvious is plausibility. Hence it is that our thesis is, at the very least, plausible.

This thesis is, however, more than obvious and plausible: it is real and certain. And it is this for considerations formally foreign or alien to λόγος and τέχνη; for considerations which attain to and touch the φύσει ὄν, to the real as reality in and for itself. In order to see this it is enough to repeat, from another angle of vision, what 324 we have already said about the unity of essence. No note in the essence has substantivity in and by itself; rather, each is, intrinsically and formally, in a physical sense, «note-of» the rest of the notes. That is, the notes are what they are physically only in the unity of the system, a unity *per se*, whose formal character is to be coherential unity. This is the reason why the unity is «anterior» to the notes. In a word, as we have seen, the «of» expresses the physical, constructed character of each note. The terminus in the constructed state and the absolute term do not function *ex aequo*, but rather the first presupposes the second, of which it is precisely the «of.» That is, the absolute term is present to the constructed terminus as a «previous» real term which makes the construct possible. In «house-of Peter,» Peter is present to the house as an anterior moment in the global structure «house-of Peter.» Without the house, to be sure, there *would not be* that which is of Peter; without Peter, however, the house that is there *would not be* «of» Peter. Peter is, therefore, something prior to the house in the precise sense that without Peter the constructed state as such would not be given. The absolute terminus is, therefore, first present to the constructed condition and, second, it is present to it as something previous in it. When this connection is extrinsic, as is the case in the example we have cited, the whole does not have the character of being something *per se*. However, when it is a matter of something intrinsic and physical, the whole possesses this same structure, but as a physical and constitutive character. In the case of essence, the absolute term is, as we have said, the unity itself of the system. Hence it is that the unity is physically present in the notes, as something which is also physically «anterior» to them. The unity, therefore, is «in some manner»

anterior to the constituting character of the notes. Reciprocally, because it is primary, the unity is something more than a mere «relation;» as a moment of the essence it has a reality proper to itself.
325 Precisely for this reason, the essential unity is the absolute physical terminus of the constructed state of its notes. This it would not be if it were not something more than a mere relation; and it would be mere relation if it were not primary.

On this premise, what is this manner of anteriority? That is to say, in what does the primariness of the essential unity *qua* unity consist?

The fact that the unity is the absolute terminus might lead one to think that it might be a subjectual reality insofar as it is reality, a real subject with respect to which the essential notes would be its ulterior «entitative» determination, its «properties;» the notes would be the properties of the unity. The unity would be, then, not simply the moment of some «one» thing, that is «the one» (*lo*), but would be «the» (*el*) one itself (αὐτὸ τὸ ἕν), as reality in and by itself, as substance, οὐσία. Thus, the anteriority of the unity with respect to its notes would be an anteriority of substance with respect to its further determinations. This was Plato's thesis. Fundamentally, it derives from Parmenides, for whom the one not only is substance, but is the one unique subject. Following Aristotle, Simplicius tells us that, according to Eudemus, being (τὸ ὄν) for Parmenides is said, not in many ways (πολλαγῶς), but only in one (μοναγῶς). And from his own point of view, without, however, excessive historical deformation, Aristotle seems to suggest that, fundamentally, this Eleatic unicity (of being) is the unicity of substance. It is not the case that for Parmenides the one would be only the «sign» (σῆμα) of the unique reality of being, because for him, as for Aristotle himself, even though the concepts (λόγοι) of being (ὄν) and of one (ἕν) are distinct, nevertheless, *in re*, they are identified by mutual conversion (τῷ ἀκολουθεῖν ἀλλήλοις). But this conception of the one is impossible for two reasons. In the first place, it is impossible because essence is a mo-
326 ment of substantivity and not of substantiality and, therefore, the character of the essential unity cannot be substantial. Unity is not support, but system; it is coherence and neither inherence nor substance. In the second place, «the» (*el*) one does not exist in reality

whether as substance or as substantivity. It is impossible to substantialize the one — Aristotle already saw this — because what Parmenides and Plato called «the» (*el*) one does not exist, while only the beings (*los*) exist; and therefore, neither can «the» (*el*) one exist, but only «the» unities. However, neither does the one itself (αὐτό τό ἕν) exist as substantive reality; being and, therefore, the one, lack all substantivity. The (*el*) one cannot be substantialized, made substantive; the one is only a moment, primary, to be sure, but still only a moment, of substantivity.

One might think, then, that as a primary moment of substantive reality *as* substantive, unity is one more note of substantivity. Its anteriority would consist, in that case, in being the basic note of all the rest. This would not be possible unless this note were a genus, the supreme genus common to all substantive realities, in such wise that each one of the essences would be, by reason if its content, the specification of unity as supreme genus. Here the one, in and by itself, appears, not as a substance but rather as one of the supreme genera of reality (γένος τοῦ ὄντος). The anteriority of unity would then be generic in character. This is a conception formally distinct from the earlier, but which, historically, has always appeared in association with it: for Plato, the one is precisely a generic substance. Aristotle definitively showed the impossibility of the one being a genus. It is, to be sure, like being, something common to all realities; however, to all without exception, including the specific differences. Every difference is, in a word, «one» difference, and by reason of being such is already, therefore, «within» the one. The difference, however, is added to the genus and is, therefore, «outside» it. As a 327 consequence, unity is not generic but is, rather, a character which accrues to all realities, but which is above, so to say, all its particular determinations, transcending all of them. For this reason, later philosophy called this characteristic of unity, of the good, etc., just as of being itself, a transcendental character, that is, a character which concerns the being as such (I would say it concerns the reality as reality) in order to distinguish it from the character of the genus, the species, etc., which are characters which concern such and such an entity (reality), as such and such. We shall return to this point later. This Aristotelian conception is, as we have said, definitively true; the fact is that it is of no use to us in regard to our problem, save in a negative way. The transcendental character of the one does indeed effectively prevent us from falling into the error of conceiving the primacy of unity as the generic primacy of one note, as the primary physical basis of substantivity; unity is not one note more, not even the primary note, because it is not a note, but the unity of notes. It serves nothing more than this, however; this conception does not tell us in what, positively in our case, the priority of the unity in the constitutive essence of the reality consists. It is, to be sure, a physical primarity, but neither a substantial nor a generic one. In what, then, does it consist?

We said earlier that in its character as physically constructed, according to which the notes are «notes-of,» the absolute terminus is unity which, therefore, is present in those (notes) as something prior. This is to say, the character of the notes is to be «of» the rest; the character of the unity is to be «in» all. Presently we will see the

328 precise articulation of these two moments of (de) and in (en). What we need now is to justify the assertion that the absolute terminus is the unity itself of the system. Every note, in a word, is a «note-of» all the rest and, consequently, as we have repeated to the point of monotony, its turning to all belongs to it intrinsically. This same thing happens in the case of all the notes. Therefore, the physically constructed character of all of them is something rather like a «momentual autonomization» of the «of» as such. Hence it follows that that «of» which the notes are «notes-of» has a precise character. For each note, the rest are not merely all the rest, but are its totality; that is to say, the notes are not simply «all» but rather are the unitary «whole,» the unity itself. As a consequence, the absolute term of the «of» is this unity, which it was our obligation to justify.

On this supposition, the unity, because it is the absolute terminus, is present to all the notes as something previous or prior «in» them. It is present, however, not only to all of them pro indiviso, but also to each one of the notes; each one is, effectively, «note-of» the unity. Therefore, the unity is in each note as an absolute and prior moment of its own proper physical reality. It is a strictly physical being (estar). As a consequence, the unity is in each of the notes and not outside of them; however, it is present in them as dominating them in their physical reality. The unity, to be sure, does not dominate each note according to the proper concept of the latter, but rather

according to its physical reality *hic et nunc*, that is, as a note constitutive of the essence. The anteriority of the unity «in» each note
is, then, «dominance.»

How does it dominate? Precisely because each note, according to
its physical reality, evokes from itself the totality of the rest of the
notes. The way in which the unity dominates intrinsically in each
note is the «exigency» of the whole. The unity is only a moment of
each note and this moment is «exigential.» Hence it is that the es- 329
sential unity of the notes is not mere unity *per se*, but is a unity
the «perseity» of which has an extremely exact and positive character:
exigential perseity. Every note, then, not only is (*está*) in intrinsic
union with the others, but also this being (*estar*) is something more
than a mere being (*estar*); it is an exigitive being (*estar*). It is a unity
not only in the negative sense of indivision, but also in the positive
sense of exigentiality.

In themselves, to ask, to have need of, to evoke, etc., are terms
which have a clear meaning in the order of operation; we must,
however, translate them into the entitative order, the constitutive
order. Other metaphysical terms are in the same situation. For example, when Aristotle wanted to conceive matter metaphysically as
the entitative moment of the reality, that is, as prime matter, he took
the concept of potency (δύναμις) belonging to the operative order
and, by force of an abstraction, transposed it into the entitative order:
prime matter (πρώτη ὕλη) would be the potency of its substantial
form, while the latter would be the act of the former. However, first
he had to effect this same mental transposition in order to conceptualize entitatively the real as being in «act.» It was a difficult
effort. The concept of act is clear, in the operative order, as when,
for example, we concern ourselves with human actions. Let us take
the case of anyone who is executing a work (ἔργον). Let us consider
in this action first, the operation itself, and thereafter, what is done,
the work. The one who executes or carries out a work is in activity,
in ἐνέργεια; and in this operative sense, activity is opposed to passivity or affection, πάθος. Aristotle had, however, to transpose the
concept into the entitative order. For this purpose, if, in the activity
in which one stands while producing a work, I fix attention not on
that in which one is, that is to say, in *activity*, but rather in the very
fact of being (*estar*) in it, that is to say, in the fact of being (*estar*)

330 actuating, then ἐνέργεια is not opposed to passivity, πάθος, but to potency, δύναμις, and comes to mean not activity but actuality. As a consequence, ἐνέργεια comes, in the entitative order, to mean the actuality of the real. On the other hand, let us fix our attention on the work itself. In man's action the process of producing the work continues until the action finishes, is terminated. Thus, in the operative order, if I consider the work, not as something produced or executed by my action, but concentrate on the work in itself, then «completion» (achievement) does not mean that the *action* is completed, but that the work is something «realized,» and completed in itself (ἐντελεχές, *perfectum*). This moment of completion is an entitative moment of the work; the real is ἐντελέγεια, actuality in the sense of plenitude, in opposition to becoming (γίγνεσθαι). Whence ἐντελέγεια comes to coincide with ἐνέργεια to designate and conceptualize the real as actuality. They are two concepts which, as may be seen, are not identical, indeed far from it; yet, by converging in the idea of actuality, they explain why Aristotle employed them indifferently in order to designate the being as «act.» If I have lingered over these terms and concepts, it is not to expound their meaning, something long since understood, and which Aristotle himself undertook to emphasize (e. g., *Meta.* 1050 a 21-23), but rather in order to interpret their metaphysical origin as a difficult transposition of concepts taken from the operative order to the entitative order. To demand (*exigir*), then, is a clear term in the operative order. As is well known, *agere* is to move by an internal impulse, in distinction from *ducere*, to move from without, by putting oneself at the head of something. In this sense, *agere* is opposed to *quiescere*. Hence, in contrast to *educere*, to make something emerge from without, we have *exigere* (to demand), which, in one of its etymological meanings, signifies «to make arise out of, emerge from» within to the outside. This, however, is in the operative order. It must be transposed to the entitative order. If, in the *exigere* we concentrate, not on the

331 point that the action *leads* to a distinct terminus, but on the state, or better, on the way in which the one demanding (*exigente*) is formally *constituted*, then we will say that the to demand (*exigir*) is a moment of the *mode of the to be* of something. The operative *agere* becomes a physical necessity. It is an internal necessity, from itself (*ex*). A necessity, however, not in the causal order (necessity

of having a cause in order to exist or something similar to this), but rather a necessity in the order of the formal constitution. To demand (*exigir*) is *to be constituted* in the concrete plenitude of its proper formal reality, being necessitated only from itself, formally and positively, by the formality of an other, that is, to involve by physical necessity in its own formality the formal reality of an other, in such wise that, without the latter, the former would be physically impossible. This entitative exigency is the positive character of that *per se* unity which we called coherential unity: not only is it a unity indissoluble *by itself*, but a unity exigetive of the other from itself. The formal ground of essential unity is «coherence» and the positive structure of this co- (*con*) is exigency. Coherential unity is the entitative exigency of the whole on the part of every note. And to the degree that this exigency is intrinsic to each note, the unity is in each note as a dominant and prior moment in it. For this reason, the manner in which unity is present in each note is not bare presence (παρουσία) but presence in the mode of exigency; it is exigential dominance.

This mode of presence of unity in the notes makes patent the two characteristics of that unity. Because it is exigential, the unity is something intrinsic to each note, only, however, as a «moment» of it, not as a substance or as an additional note. Further, however, unity, despite being «in» each note and only in it, is, nevertheless, something prior to it (the note) in the exact sense that the exigency 332 of the other notes is what makes each one of those notes an essential note. In order to conceptualize this structure with greater exactness, we must make clear, then, in succession, in what the anteriority of the exigential unity consists, what is «that which it makes» in each note, and in what this «making» itself consists. Since the three questions overlap, some repetitions are inevitable.

(a) In the first place, let us consider the anteriority of exigential coherence. As anterior, unity is, in each note, a *prius* to its own reality. Of what priority, however, are we speaking? Something may have priority in many ways. It may have priority in the order of knowledge. Here, however, this kind of priority is not in question; we are concerned, rather, with the order of reality: that moment of the reality is *prius* by reason of which a thing is what it is. This real priority may, in its turn, be of different kinds. It can, for example, be the priority of a cause with respect to its effect. But this priority is not in question either; we are concerned, rather, with the intrinsic constitutive order. And even within this latter order, there occur different modes of priority. In the constitutive order, in a word, reality is actuality. In this sense, the moment of actuality has priority over its content; it is a question, in the final analysis, of the priority of act over potency. Such, for example, is the case of the Aristotelean form in the substantial composite: the form is «in» the composite as the determinant principle of its reality, simply because it is the bare act of prime matter. In this type, the priority is «mere» actuality. In the unity of essence, however, it is a question of something in some way different. Essential unity is not «mere» actuality, but is an actuality of an extremely special type. Because, in virtue of this unity, each note is essential, not only in the sense that it is effectively such, but also in the sense that it is such exigentially, demanding (*exigendo*) the rest in internal coherence. Hence it is that the unity is not anterior to the notes s i m p l y as *every act* is anterior to its potency, but rather as *this exigential* act is anterior, so to say, to its realization; that is to say, because it is an exigency which is actually orientating each note toward the rest. The priority is, then, a priority in the constitutive order, but of a dominant and exigential nature. Only if we take these characters of actuality and exigency together will we have understood adequately what the priority of the coherential unity in each note is. This is what I have called the «primarity» of the essential unity. Each note is the reality of its intrinsic exigency. That is to say, the exigential coherential unity is what brings it about that each note is what it is: an essential note. This affirmation, however, demands some ulterior clarification.

(b) What is then «that which makes» the essential unity? I have just said that exigential unity brings it about that each note is really and physically what it is. «Reality,» however, is, in this case, something ambiguous. It can mean, on the one hand, the absolute content of each note. It may, on the other hand, mean to be really «note-of;» for example, to be «sensibility of» a human essence. This last is what constitutes the essential reality as such, its «to be essential.» Because, in the first sense, the content of each note in the «absolute state» has nothing to do with the absolute content of the rest. This state, however, does not possess, by itself, complete physical reality, because no note is in an essence in this state; the essence, in a word, is not a mere conglomerate of notes. It is perfectly possible that some notes can be separated from the essence of which they form part and take on absolute entitative status; such is the case of substances which compose a substantivity. So long, however, as they form part of a substantive reality, even though conserving their substantiality, they nevertheless lack sub-stantivity and, therefore, if they are essential, their complete phys-ical reality consists in being «note-of.» That is, all the notes of an essence, as essential notes, exist physically only as «notes-of,» not in the absolute but in the constructed state. Therefore, every note has, physically, a relationship to all the others; that is, only its con-structed state constitutes, in each note, its essential reality as such. Hence it follows that what coherential unity brings about, that is to say, the terminus of coherential unity as primary moment of the essence, is precisely and formally the essential reality of each note, its «being-essential,» its essentiality. The essentiality of each note does not rest on itself nor on its union with the other notes, but on a moment intrinsic to it, namely, on the essential unity. Such is the primariness of the essential unity. Primariness is the priority accord-ing to which the unity exigentially determines the essential reality, as essential.

Stated in other terms: the proper function of unity is «essentia-tion» and the formal character of the notes, as essential realities, is to be «essentiated.» We employ the term «essentiated,» as we have done before, to express the character of the realities which, effec-tively, «have» essence; «essentiated» meant, then, simply «to have» essence. Here the word retains the same fundamental meaning, but with a more precise shading. It does not mean, simply, «to have» essence, but «to be» a formally essential reality, «to be essential,» to belong formally to an essence. To be essentiated is here to be «note-of.»

However, we must not let ourselves be thrown off balance by an easy mistake. We might fall back anew into the error of consid-ering the unity as the «source» of the notes. This is not the case: the unity, we have already said, is not something hidden beneath the notes, nor outside them, but something real only in them; it is the system of the notes itself, their internal respectivity. The primariness, then, of the unity is not the priority of some notes over others as their source, but the priority of the internal respectivity over each one of the notes which are respective to each other. We have already seen that τέχνη is a sign of this; but nothing more than a sign, because we do not know whether man makes things as nature makes them. If, however, we imagine that this is the case, then it is necessary to say that, if man were able to make a watch which would be real in the way in which natural things are real, that is, if we could make a watch at one blow (*golpe*), so to say, we would certainly have to make the pieces themselves at one blow (*golpe*), though these pieces would not, for that reason, cease to be constituted «in respectivity;» there would be, in what they themselves are, each one of itself, a kind of anteriority of their integrity as a watch over each one of these pieces which compose the watch. If nature were to produce watches, the «first thing» that, in its making, nature would have would be precisely the watch «before» the pieces, with an anteriority which is neither temporal nor causal, but merely «momental»: the *raison d'être* of the reality of each piece is the structural unity of the watch, its internal respectivity. This is also true when there is question of external respectivity, that is, of the world; on this point I said, in one of my courses, very many years ago: «God has created the world as such: the structural respectivity of things. Each one of them has been primarily constituted in respectivity to the others.»

Hence it is that of one same constitutive essence two equally true affirmations can be made: a determined constitutive essence is such because it possesses such and such notes and the constitutive essence possesses such and such notes because it is a determined constitutive essence. There is no contradiction nor vicious circle because the two affirmations are both true, each one from its point of view. From the point of view of the pieces, the truth is that the pieces compose the watch; however, from the point of view of the watch itself, that of «being a watch,» the truth is that its essential unity is what constitutes the *raison d'être* of the reality of each piece. The watch is nothing outside the pieces, but rather the exigential moment of each one of them, with respect to all the others. And the fact is that the notes and the unity mutually imply each other, but in a different way, in the coherential system which is the constitutive essence. In the constructed state, in a word, the absolute term is present, as I have said, in the constructed term as something which, while in it, is, nevertheless, prior to it. For the same reason, the constructed term is present in the absolute, but as posterior to it. The two terms constitute one unique global character, but one which in each of the terms is endowed with a precise meaning: it is a common term which rests on the absolute term and affects the constructed terminus as something which is founded on the absolute. For example, in the case of Peter's house, there is a unique character, possession. Peter is the absolute term; his presence in the house is established in a title of Peter and has a precise character: he is the possessor. The house is the constructed term; it is present to Peter, but he confers on it a mode of possessionality based on Peter himself: it is possessed by him. The common character is possession, and the mode of respective presence of Peter and the house, according to the structure of possession, is different: Peter, as possessor, is «in» the house; the house, as what is possessed, is «of» Peter. «In» and «of» are the two modes in which possession is constituted as a unity in «house of Peter.» This articulation occurs not only when it is a question of an extrinsic connection, but also, and above all, when it is a question of something intrinsic and physical. In our case, the common character is «essentiality,» and presence is concretely «actuality.» Essentiality belongs to both terms, to unity and to the notes, but to each in a different way. Unity is the absolute term. Based on itself, it is actual in the notes as something prior to them. Its essentiality consists in conferring essential reality on, in «essentiating,» the notes. These notes are, in their turn, actualized in unity, and for this reason their essentiality consists in being «notes-of,» in being «essentiated.» The way in which unity is actual in the essence is, then, different from the way in which its notes are actual: the unity is actual by being «in» each note, and each note is actual as being «note-of.» These two moments of «in» and «of» are the two moments of the actuality of the constitutive essence *qua* essence. They are not, however, two correlative moments; rather, the «in» is prior to the «of;» each note is, in a word, «note-of» only by reason of the unity which exigentially is actual «in» the note in question. This is the reason why, from the point of view of the «of,» the notes

337

compose the essence; however, from the point of view of the «in,» the essence itself, as unity, is the reason or *ratio* of the essential reality of each note, that which *constitutes* the essential character of the notes.

In a rigorous metaphysical sense, therefore, the essential unity is not unity «of» the notes, but rather unity «in» the notes. And as the «in» is a *prius*, it follows that the notes, as I have said again and again, are the analyzers of the actuality of the essence *qua* primary unity, that is, they are the actuality of the unity in them. To impart to this idea its ultimate precision, we may employ, as we have done all through this study, the word «to be» (*ser*), not in the ontological sense, but as an indispensible grammatical tool in our languages. Then we can say that the constitutive essence is the *to be* (*ser*) of the essentiated reality. Now, however, we understand that the word «to be» (*ser*) here has a double sense. It means, on the one hand, what the constitutive notes of the reality are; to be, then, means «constitutive» or essentiated. On the other hand, however, it means that which is the primary unity; «to be» then means «essentiating.» As the unity, that is, the essentiation, is primary with regard to the constitutive or essentiated, which for the same reason is posterior to that unity, it will necessarily have to be said that the essence, as a system of constitutive notes, *qua* constitutive, is, to be sure, the reality, but is, nevertheless, always and only reality «as been» (*sida*); «to be» here means «been» (*sido*). «Been» does not have, in this place, the sense of a temporal *past*, but the sense of a *passive* present, a kind of resultative present. By contrast, the essence, as a system of constitutive notes *qua* systematic unity, is reality as strict «to be» (*ser*). With this, the two concepts of anteriority and posteriority acquire a final exactness. Anteriority is, concretely, «to be» (*ser*) and posteriority, «been» (*sido*). To say that the unity is anterior to the notes is the same as saying that it is «to be» (*ser*); and to say that the notes are posterior to the unity is the same as saying that its being is «been» (*sido*). So far as the constitutive notes are concerned, then, the essence is the «been» of the unity which «is.» The essential reality is something «been» (*sido*) of its own «to be» (*ser*). This is «what» the exigential unity «achieves.»

It is necessary, however, to understand correctly this character of «been,» which the essential to be of the notes has with respect

to the unity which «is.» I said that the «been» is a kind of resultative
present. But nothing more than «a kind of.» Because neither is the
present temporal nor is the result here of a factitive character. Therefore, it must be asked in what this thing that we call «to do» or «to 339
make,» in virtue of which the notes «result» in to be «been» (sidas),
consists.

(c) In what does the «to make itself» as such consist? Strictly
speaking, the question has already been answered when we said
that it is the anteriority of the exigential unity. We said, in a word,
that the exigential unity has the anteriority of an act. What I insisted
on at that point, however, is the special character of this act: its
exigentiality. Now, by contrast, it is necessary to insist precisely on
the character of the act which the exigentiality has, and in which,
as a consequence, «to make» does not have a factitive meaning, but
rather the constitutive meaning of «to actualize,» of being a constituting act. We have indicated this already a short space before;
but I have already noted that, since the three questions overlap,
some repetitions are inevitable. We say, then, that the making itself
of the exigential unity is to «actualize.» «To be» and «been» (ser and
sido) have, in regard to each other, the status of act to actualized.
Hence it becomes necessary to reject (descarter) two possible interpretations of what we have called «to be» and «been» (ser and sido),
having their origins in two great philosophies.

It might be thought, before all else, that what we here understand
by «to make,» «to do» (hacer), was a primary activity, that is to say,
that the essential unity, insofar as it is primary, would be «unifying»
(uni-ficante) in the factitive sense of the word. In that case, «to be»
(ser) would be activity and «been» (sido) would be the precipitate
of that activity. It is clear that those who think this way do not
understand activity in the sense of the Aristotelean categories; because, for Aristotle, activity and action are accidents, and here we
are making reference to the reality which Aristotle calls substance
(let us leave aside, once more, in this instance, the distinction between
substance and substantivity). Both for some ancient neo-Platonists
as, many centuries later, for Leibnitz, substance would be, in itself,
a kind of underlying activity. Those ancient neo-Platonists understood
the ἐνέργεια of Aristotle in this way and Leibnitz himself spoke of 340
ἐντελέχεια as a substantial act, vis. This would not be an activity

which the substance «has» by reason of its active potencies, but rather an activity in which the substance itself *qua* substance, «consists;» substance would be active of itself. The essential unity itself, however, cannot be activity, nor do the notes prove to be the resulting «beens» (*sidos*) of it. Whether or not there might be substances which are activities in themselves and not by means of active potencies which need extrinsic activation, is a question which touches on the diversity of essential types which can exist; but it is not something which touches the essence itself as such. Whether or not the substantial act might be active in itself, the essence would reside, not in its formally dynamic moment, but in its actualizing moment. The unity is not «uni-fying» (*uni-ficante*); it is actual; but it is not active, and therefore, it is merely a «moment,» the moment of actuality; as a moment it is an act which is (*está*) resting upon itself and by reason of being this (*estarlo*), is the actualization of the «to be essential» of the notes. «Been» (*sido*) is not the result of an activity, but of to be actualized.

It would be equally false, however, to think that the unity «is» formally processual and that «been» (*sido*) would indicate the terminus — even though it be provisional — of this process; «been» (*sido*) would be «having become» (*devenido*). This would be an interpretation which would lead us to Hegel, or, more accurately, to an Hegelian interpretation of what we are saying. Essential unity cannot, however, be processual in character, nor is the «been» (*sido*) the «having become» (*devenido*). That is to say, essential unity not only is not activity, but also cannot be movement. For here there is no question of what brings it about (*hace*) that something comes to be real, but rather the question concerns the character of the internal structure of this reality once it is real. The origin of intramundane things is always processual, and from this point of view, not only the notes, but also their unity, are something which «been» (*sido*). 341 But this is not the question here; we are concerned rather with the actual internal articulation of the real insofar as it already is. So long as there is processualness, there is not yet any real thing, nor, therefore, constitutive essence. In the instant in which this essence exists, processuality — let Hegel think what he will — is already left behind; however, it is then and only then (when the essence exists) that the problem of the formal structure of the constitutive essence rightly emerges: its unity and its notes. The duality of unity and notes is a momentual duality not in the originating becoming of a thing, but rather, in the reality which has already come to be. Unity and notes are moments of the actuality, not momentual phases of a becoming. And this is true when we are considering not only a becoming in which that which has become is something other (e. g., a product) but also when we are treating as well of these realities which we say are intrinsically becoming realities in themselves. In reality, as becoming, the becoming is internally qualified, but it is qualified by reason of the character, the constitutive essence, of the reality as becoming *qua* reality, not *qua* becoming; the constitutive essence is what makes possible and qualifies the becoming, but not the reverse and, therefore, it is in the actuality of the essence that this articulation of unity and of notes has already been given. At no matter what point the question might be taken up, becoming is not the «formal» character of the essence, neither in that aspect which concerns the unity which «is,» nor in that which is concerned with the notes «been» (*sidas*). Between the unity and the notes no process mediates: it is simply a momentual duality between act and actualization. All that has come to be is actualized, but not all that is actualized has become. *To be* (*ser*) and *been* (*sido*) are two moments of actuality and not of becoming.

Now we may better understand that the «been» of which we are speaking here, stated negatively, does not have the character of a *passed*, whether in the temporal sense or in the sense of an «already was» in the Hegelian acceptance of the word (*gewesen*); rather it 342 has, in a positive way, the character of a *passive* present, in which the passive character is neither factitive nor processual and in which presentness has no temporal meaning but is, rather, the passive present in the order of actuality. «Been» expresses a primarily and formally «actual» moment of the essence, the actuality of the unity in its notes and, therefore, the notes as actualized by the unity itself.

«To be» and «been» *(ser* and *sido)*, unity and notes, are nothing but the moments of the actual reality of the constitutive essence *qua* actual. Exigentiality, as I said at the beginning, has not an operative but an entitative character. By reason of its notes, the essence is the reality of its intrinsic exigency; it is, I might add, the «been» (*sido*) of its proper «to be» (*ser*); we now say, finally, that it is the entitative actualization of its coherential unity. The three formulae are equivalent and, taken together, they express the primacy of the essential unity. Such is the character of the essential unity: by its formal reason (*razón*) it is coherential unity, and by its entitative rank it is a primary unity.

From the point of view of its notes, the constitutive essence is the system of notes necessary and sufficient in order that the substantive reality might have all its other notes. From the point of view of its unity, the constitutive essence is the primary coherential unity. These are nothing but two aspects of one single reality, the reality of the constitutive essence. In the light which illuminates the analysis of both aspects, let us return now to consider the constitutive essence in its integral physical reality, as a moment of the substantive reality: it is the problem «essence and reality,» the third of the four steps which we have set before ourselves in order to conceptualize essence.

343   ARTICLE III

ESSENCE AND REALITY

Strictly speaking, we have, in the course of the present study, already said, fundamentally, all that there is to be said on this point. We have, however, said it in a line of reflection which, step by step, has laid bare to us the different aspects of essence. For this reason it is now right to begin from the essence so conceived and, taking our stand on it, construct, in a unitary way, the concept of essence as the essential moment of the substantive reality. Since this undertaking involves a synthetic vision of essence, the concepts obtained earlier will necessarily re-appear, not in another order, but indeed in another perspective, within which alone they will achieve their final metaphysical precision.

The guiding thread of this entire investigation has been the idea that essence is a physical moment of the substantivity. Substantivity is not substantiality. Substantivity, in a word, has the formal character of a system of notes and not of a subject of notes. It is a character of the unity of the notes among themselves, but is not a hidden subject beneath or beyond them. It is not the «perseitas» of the substance, but, rather, sufficiency in the order of system. Therefore, essence, as a moment of the substantivity, is the moment of a system and not the determination of a subject. This is what we have been expressing when we said that the essence is, in the substantivity, the sub-system or fundamental system.

This character of essence leaves us engulfed in serious problems: before all, in the problem of how to apprehend and to express es- 344 sence conceptually; while essence is considered as the determination of a subject, the natural *organon* for apprehending essence would be the predicative *logos*. When that concept is abandoned, the problem confronts us anew: what is the *logos* of essence? However, in addition, we find ourselves obliged to ask ourselves about the essence itself from this other point of view. Now, every reality is, from antiquity, capable of being considered from a double point of view. In the essence of each real thing, there can be seen, on the one hand, that which the thing is in its content, so to say; thiat is, that according to which it is «such» a thing and not another «such.» On the other hand, however, the essence can be seen as that according to which the thing is «real.» The first constitutes the order of «suchness;» the second is the «transcendental» order. Therefore, the problem «essence and reality» leaves us planted amid three questions:

1. Essence and *logos*
2. Essence and «suchness»
3. Essence and transcendentality

It is hoped that the reader will indulge, not only the re-appearance of concepts which have already been explicated, but also the wearisome repetition of the explications themselves.

SECTION ONE   345

ESSENCE AND LOGOS

As reality, we have repeated many times, the essence is not the objective correlate of a definition, but rather the physical structuring moment of the real, a moment formally individual *qua* essence. On the other hand, the essence as physical reality is, as we have just recalled to mind, a fundamental system of notes, that is, a mode of unity which the notes, of which the essence is found to be formed, possess directly and among themselves. Since this is the case, in our effort to understand essence metaphysically, we find at our disposition the two classical resources: substance and definition. Therefore, we have found ourselves obliged to forge a conceptual *organon* adequate to the demands of the case.

In order to achieve this we appeal, naturally, to language. And this, not only, nor even principally (as did the Greeks) because language is «significative,» φωνή σημαντική, but because it signifies by «expressing.» And between every expression, whether it be linguistic or not, and the mind itself there is an intrinsic unity, both profound and radical: the *forma mentis*. This unity, that is to say, this mind «conformed» in this way, is what we call, precisely and formally, «mentality»: mentality is *forma mentis*. This is the reason why the *to say*, the λέγειν, is not only to say «something,» but is also to say it «in a certain way,» that is, with certain modulations proper to a determined mentality. Let us set aside, for the moment, the social character and the modifications of every mentality and of what is enunciated in it; that is not our present theme. We must be content with affirming that the structure of language always permits there to shine through, in one way or another, certain conceptual structures which are proper to the mentality. Let us explain ourselves further.

First of all, language permits certain conceptual structures to shine through or appear. This affirmation is not to be confused with four other affirmations which are completely different from it, namely: first, the affirmation that the function of language is primarily to express concepts; second, the affirmation that language is the *locus* where conceptual structures are expressed *primo et per se*; third, the affirmation that the primary function of intellection is to forge concepts of things; fourth, the affirmation that every structural moment of intellection has its formal expression in language. On the contrary, I have limited myself to affirming that in every linguistic structure a conceptual structure shows through in some way. The four affirmations cited above are, furthermore, in formal rigor, false,

346

while what we have here affirmed is an undeniable fact which is easily testable. Let us say, nevertheless, that in spite of being false, those four affirmations enunciate four serious problems, which, when joined to what we have affirmed here, constitute five fundamental aspects which must be clarified if one wishes to stay afloat in the problem of «*logos* and reality.» But this, too, is not our theme. Here we limit ourselves to taking language as the mere index of conceptual structures.

These structures then, I have said, are in great measure proper to a determined mentality. It is not the case that these concepts are «subjective,» but rather that, even while being true and fecund, they are always so only in an intrinsically limited way. And in this sense, every *logos* always leaves open the problem of its basic adequacy to conceive the real.

Classical philosophy rested on a perfectly determined *logos*: the 347 predicative *logos*. On it is mounted the whole of «logic» as the primary *organon* for the apprehension of the real. The predicative *logos* involves a subject and certain predicative determinations, predicated of that subject by way of the verb *to be*. That subject is looked upon, in the first instance, as a substantial subject, and the *logos par excellance* is that which expresses its intrinsic mode of being, the definition. Now this fundamental rank of the predicative *logos* has, for the results of our problem, at least three limitations: the identification of the essential *logos* with the definition, the identification of the *logos* with the predicative *logos*, and the identification of the subject of the *logos* with a subjectual reality.

Let us consider first the identification of the essential *logos* with the definition. For Aristotle, the definition (ὁρισμός) is always and only the *logos* of a quiddity (τὸ τί ἦν εἶναι) since, for Aristotle, every reality has a specific essence. Every essential proposition would then be a definition. The rest may be, as the manuals of Logic say, «descriptions,» but not definitions. (We may set aside what are usually called historical definitions, genetic definitions, etc., for these, strictly speaking, are not such at all, but mere characterizations, more or less univocal, of their objects.) This distinction between definition and description rests entirely on the existence of the *quiddity* and its identification with the essence. That difference will consist simply in the fact that when we cannot arrive, or we have not yet arrived, at the quiddity, this latter escapes us, remains hidden; therefore, we cannot define it and we must content ourselves with describing more or less «inessentially» the real thing. The description is formally «inessential,» while the definition is formally «essential.» (The so-called nominal definition is more properly called 348 a description.) In both cases, however, it is presupposed that the essence of the thing is identified with the quiddity.

This position is not accurate precisely because the essence of the real thing is not identified with its quiddity. This identification of the essence with the τὸ τί ἦν εἶναι is, fundamentally, the most serious correction which must be made in Aristotle's system on this point: the constitutive essence is not the same as the quidditive essence. Consequently, since essence and quiddity are not identical, neither are essential proposition and definition to be identified. A proposition which enunciates all and only the constitutive characteristics which a thing possesses καθ' αὐτό and without the subject entering into what is predicated, would be a strictly and formally essential proposition, since it would enunciate the *quid* of the thing in question, its constitutive essence. Such is the case of the proposition which will state that the electron is an elementary particle of electronic mass 1, of negative charge 1, and of spin ½. Nevertheless, this proposition is not formally a definition since the *quid*, the constitutive essence, forms a «class» but not a «species;» it is not a quiddity, a τὸ τί ἦν εἶναι; effectively, «elementary particle» is not a *genus in re*; it is only the designation of a natural class. Neither, however, is this proposition a mere external description, as though the quiddity lay hidden behind it, because in this case the quiddity does not exist, despite the fact that the notes expressed by the said proposition belong to the constitutive essence of the thing. This is the case of every non-quiddifiable constitutive essence. Hence it is that, in addition to non-essential descriptions and definitions, there are essential propositions which are not definitions. Every proposition is essential which enunciates all or some of the formally constitutive notes of the substantive reality; that is, the proposition which expresses the 349 notes of the constitutive essence, whether or not it is quiddifiable. The definition is only one of the possible types of essential proposition, the proposition which falls back on those constitutive notes which form the essential quidditive moment (when such exists) of

the constitutive essence of the reality. In order that an essential
proposition be a definition, two conditions must be met, conditions
which must be understood with complete formal rigor. First, it must
be a proposition which enunciates notes which, in themselves, belong
materially to the quiddity of the thing. Second, it must be a proposition such that the materially quidditative notes are exactly and
formally articulated in the form of proximate genus and ultimate
difference. The lack of either of these conditions would diminish,
in the essential proposition, its character as definition. This is evident
with regard to the first condition; if the proposition expresses constitutive characteristics which are neither quidditative nor quiddifiable, this proposition would express the constitutive essence and
not the quiddative, and there would be no definition, but rather a
simple essential proposition. However, it is necessary to insist especially on the fact that neither is there a definition if, the first condition having been fulfilled, the second is not fulfilled. In a word,
I can state the quiddifiable constitutive notes, that is, the quidditive
notes, taken, however, in their simple physical reality, one after the
other and in a certain order. This proposition would not be a definition, because the notes are not formally and expressly articulated
in that proposition as «metaphysical» moments (genus and difference
as such), but rather only successively enumerated as «physical» realities. Let us take, as an example, the classical formula according to
which man is a rational animal. This proposition can be understood
in two ways. One, merely enumerative: man is rational «and» animal.
In this sense, animality and rationality are two physical notes which
belong to the constitutive essence of each man, and which, because 350
they are quiddifiable, also belong to the quiddity. They belong to it,
however, only materially. For this reason, the proposition, understood
in this way, is an essential proposition, but it is not formally a definition. In order that it should be, it is necessary to understand it
in another way: taking the notes not as physical notes, but as metaphysical moments endowed with a precise articulation: animality as
genus, and rationality as difference. The formula then does not say
that man is rational «and» animal but that he is a «rational-animal,»
a unity metaphysically determined by two moments. Only then do we
formally express a quiddity and only then is the proposition formally
quidditive, a definition. Without genus and difference there is no

definition. For this reason, Aristotle called the genera «principles of definition» (ἀρχαὶ δὲ τὰ γένη τῶν ὁρισμῶν εἰσίν).

Based on the example which we have just cited, the manuals of Logic have been accustomed to distinguish two classes of definitions, the «physical» definition and the «metaphysical» definition. The first would be that which states the physical and separable principles or parts of the essence, as if I were to say «man is a composite of organic body and rational soul.» That definition would be metaphysical which states the metaphysical parts of the essence, its genus and difference, as when I were to say, «man is a rational animal.» It would seem, then, that what I have called the «essential proposition» is precisely the physical definition. This, however, is not the case. For the distinction of the two definitions presupposes the identity of essence and quiddity; whence it results that these «two» definitions are in reality nothing but modes or ways, one material and the other formal, of stating one same definition, the definition of the quiddity. The example of man shows us this clearly enough. It is 351 supposed that the physical essence is purely and simply the merely numerical and singular realization of the metaphysical essence, of the quiddity and, for this reason, that by means of which it is possible to define the essence from two points of view; what is defined, however, is always one and the same. By contrast, we have in this study distinguished the constitutive essence and the quidditive essence. The first not only is something more than the mere singularity of the second, but can be and is given sometimes without that other; there are, in a word, non-quiddifiable essences. Whence it follows that the proposition which states the constitutive essence is not another way of defining the quiddity but is, rather, something completely different. The difference leaps to view, because in these same manuals the metaphysical definition is called a «perfect» definition, a fact which clearly indicates that, in those words, the distinction of the two definitions is relative, is merely a difference of point of view. By contrast, by distinguishing the constitutive and the quidditive essence, the propositions which state them prove really distinct. As, traditionally that which states the quiddity is accustomed to be called definition, I reserve this name for that use and I call, by contrast, that which states the constitutive essence, essential proposition. Hence it is that what I have said on this point earlier must be completed in the following form: an essential proposition is a proposition which enunciates notes formally constitutive, whether or not they are quiddifiable, providing always that they be stated, if they are quiddifiable, in a non-quidditive form.

These essential propositions, which are not definitions, have one pecularity: they are not necessarily «completed» or perfect. The definition, with its proximate genus and ultimate difference, is, in principle, a proposition which expresses the essence of what is defined in an exhaustive manner. An essential proposition, however, which is not a definition, since it contains no more than a «series» of constitutive notes of the substantive reality, always leaves the door open to further predicates. It is not, and does not pretend to be, conclusive: it is an «open» proposition.

Hence it is that the effort to understand what is essential in the 352 reality need not be an effort to define it. As a matter of fact, only of man — we have already seen why — a strict definition has been given, one which is open to question, hardly free from opposition, perhaps, but a strict definition nevertheless; no other reality has been univocally apprehended in proximate genus and ultimate difference. By contrast, of all realities, including the human, constitutive notes have continuously been discovered, that is, essential notes of those realities. Differently from what happens in the case of the definition, this knowledge of the constitutive essence is progressive. First, because we are never certain that we have encountered all the constitutive notes of any thing; no one has ever defended such a chimera; second, only on the most rare occasion are we certain of having given a note which is truly constitutive, because almost always the note might prove to be only a constitutional note and the constitutive note might lie at a profounder level. For this reason, the apprehension of a constitutive essence is inexorably progressive and problematical. The goal of essential knowledge is neither to intuit nor to define, but rather to apprehend the necessary and sufficient constitutive notes which would insure that a substantive reality would possess all the rest of its notes. For this reason (we note this in passing, without entering into the question) we do have essential propositions about an individual reality: those which state its constitutive notes when these are not specifiable. It is not true that only the universal can be known. What happens is that only the universal is definable, something very different, because essential knowledge is not of necessity a definition. The problem of intellectual knowledge of the individual is not a problem of definition. This mere allusion to this question must suffice at this point.

353   To conclude: an essential proposition is not identical with a definition. The essential *logos* is not of necessity a defining *logos*. To have identified these two things is the first limitation of the traditional concept of the essential *logos*.

However, there is an even deeper limitation in this concept: that of thinking that the predication itself is the first and primary function of affirming the real *qua* real, in such wise that names (nouns) would be only «simple apprehensions,» that is, mere designations of concepts, wholly alien to affirmation. This, however, is not accurate. The primary form of affirmative apprehension of the real is the nominal form. And this is so not only because, as we shall see later, there are nominal phrases, but also because the simple noun fulfills at times the function of affirmatively designating the reality of some thing, without the intervention of the verb «to be». Before the division of the *logos* into simple apprehension (*simple aprehensión*) and predicative affirmation, there is a previous *logos* which is, withoat differentiation, what I have been accustomed tocall «aprehensión simple,» which is at the same time and simply, an affirmative denomination of the real. It is a pre-predicative *logos*, the «nominal *logos*.» Therefore, the *logos* cannot be identified with the predicative *logos*.

This nominal *logos* can take on different forms, according to which the nominal forms themselves may be. Classical logic has subscribed to one of them, namely, to that one according to which the reality is composed of simple substance — things. And this is the third limitation of classical logic: the identification of the real correlate of the noun (name) with a substantive thing. There is a nominal *logos* with a different formal structure.

In a word, «things» (in the widest sense of the term) taken in themselves are expressed in all languages by «nouns.» Taken in their mutual connections, however, things are expressed nominally in dif-
354 ferent ways. They are expressed in the first place, by way of a nominal «inflection.» This morphological structure allows there to become apparent the conceptualization of a very determined aspect of the reality. The inflection, in fact, affects each noun intrinsically;

that is, in the inflected noun there is expressed the connection of one thing with another, not as a mere «connection,» but as a «modification» of the absolute reality, and, therefore, the thing is expressed as a subjectual reality endowed with intrinsic modifications. However, it is always a matter of a thing and its name, although with a different shading in each (grammatical) «case.» For this reason, the connections, more than connections, are modes or states of being, precisely πτῶσεις, «inflections» of the real thing «in the absolute.» Hence it is that the declined (inflected) noun can occupy, in principle, any position in the phrase: it has, in itself, the expression of its proper inflective moment.

At other times the connections are expressed by way of «prepositions» which are added to the name. That is, the connections are conceived, not as intrinsic modifications, but precisely the reverse, as such and such connections of things. Things are, therefore, primarily independent from one another and one adds them to this reality according to a «net» of more or less extrinsic «relations» which link them. Here the connection is «relation.»

However, there are times when language expresses things connected by nouns morphologically constructed one upon another, in such a way that the connection is expressed by way of the prosodic, phonetic, and semantic unity of two or more different nouns. This is the «constructed state.» By reason of it the nouns in the constructed state occupy a perfectly defined place in the phrase, without being able to be separated from the name in the absolute state. In this third morphological resource, a new and original aspect of the reality shows through in conceptual form. Both in the nominal inflection and in the prepositional arrangement the accent is placed on each thing in and by itself, either modifying it intrinsically or relating it 355 extrinsically. In the constructed state the real is conceived as a unitary system of things, which are, therefore, constructed one after the other, forming a whole among themselves. Here the primary thing is not the things, but the unity of the system. The connection, then, is neither inflection nor relation, but intrinsic system.

These are three different conceptualizations of the reality, each one of which corresponds to a different aspect of that reality. For this reason, they are not mutually exclusive, but, rather, languages employ one or the other resource in different form or measure. The

Indo-European languages employ only the nominal inflection and the prepositional arrangement. Other languages, the romanic, for example, employ only prepositions. Of the Semitic languages, some employ both inflection and prepositions and the constructed state, while others have lost the nominal inflection and employ only the last two resources. What is important for us here, however, is not the nominal morphology, but the conception of reality which appears in or through it. The constructed state, as a morphological resource arising from a peculiar mentality, has discovered to us the conceptualization of a structure of the reality, according to which the reality itself is then *primo et per se* a unity of system (systematic unity). With this, the expression «constructed state» does not now designate here a mere morphological resource, but rather a real physical structure. In this real sense, and only in this sense, have I employed and will I employ the expression in what follows. We have here, then, the adequate conceptual *organon* which we were seeking for our problem: the nominal constructed *logos*. The essence cannot be conceptualized either in function of the substance or absolute subject nor in function of the definition, nor in any relational function, but only in function of the intrinsic «constructivity.» The constitutive
356 essence, in a word, is a system of notes and this system is not additive or inflectional concatenation of notes, but rather an intrinsically constructed system of notes.

This intrinsic constructivity of the essence as system is expressed in two moments: the essence has some notes in the constructed state, that is, as «notes-of» and these notes have a unity which is the absolute moment «in» them. The absolute terminus of the essence, then, is not each note according to its proper content, but precisely the reverse, the unity itself. This unity is formally a primary coherential unity, in such wise that the essence, as reality in system, is a reality intrinsically constructed according to two moments: the «of» of the notes and the «in» of the unity. They are not two merely correlative moments, but the coherential primacy of the «in» is what gives the notes their «of;» that is, their essential character. The «of» is constructed according to the «in»: here we have the intrinsic constructivity of the essential reality. For this reason and this reason alone essential reality has its peculiar character; the essence in itself is not simple actual reality, but rather, reality actualized from its own actual and intrinsic exigency. This character is the implication of the two moments of the constructed system, insofar as it is constructed in the order of actuality. The essence in itself is not, then, either substance or substantial determination. First, because the reality is not formally substance, but rather substantivity; and second, because this substantivity has the formal character of system. Its essence, then, is a system intrinsically constructed of notes. Such is the metaphysical character of the integral physical reality of the constitutive essence.

This constructed reality of the essence, however, can be considered from two points of view which corespond to two aspects of the essential reality: «*suchness*» and *transcendentality*.

SECTION TWO   357

ESSENCE AND SUCHNESS

The essence is the primary coherential unity of certain very exactly characterized notes, with a characterization which is not merely specific, but formally individual (whether singular or not) in itself *qua* essence. We must never lose sight of the fact that we are treating of the constitutive physical essence. The essence of the real thing «determines» (I shall presently explain the term) all the characters which a thing possesses; and, therefore, it is a reality in itself, as momental as one may wish, but a reality which is perfectly characterized: it is this one and no other. Here we have the first and most obvious aspect of the essence in its integral physical reality: the essence is what makes the real thing «such» as it is. To ascertain «what kind» this essence might be, that is to say, of what kind this «such» might be, is the task of positive knowledge or science. To metaphysics, however, formally belongs the conceptualization of this «suchness» itself. The essence, then, is essence, before all else, in the order of suchness. This «such» is not the same as that which appears in the expression «reality as such» and other similar expressions. For in these cases, «such» is an abbreviated way of saying «in as much as,» for example, reality in as much as it is reality, essence in as far as it is essence, etc. Here, instead, «such» means «such as it is.» I believe that it is superfluous to insist further on this point, because the context itself allows of no confusion.

It is, however, necessary to sharpen the outlines of the concept of «suchness» with greater precision. Scholastic philosophy has spoken of the entity in the «categorial order,» that is, in the order of 358 generic, differential, specific, and individual entitative determinations of the entity (these latter would be extra-essential for scholasticism) determinations which are distributed among the different «categories of entities.» The categorial order is, then, the order of determination and, reciprocally, all determination belongs necessarily to one category or other. This observation might lead one to think that what we have called «suchness» coincides exactly with catergorial determination. Nevertheless, this is not the case, neither with regard to what refers to the categorial nor with respect to what refers to the determination. A grave ambiguity is contained in the Aristotelean and scholastic idea of «category,» even when that idea is taken «ontologically.» We shall concern ourselves with that ambiguity later. Let us employ, consequently, only the idea of «determination.» It would be an error to believe that suchness and determination are synonyms. All suchness is certainly determination, but not all determination is suchness. The fact is that Aristotelean philosophy and scholastic philosophy have always conceptualized determination in function of substance and definition; as a result, what we have called suchness becomes *eo ipso* determination like all the others. Suchness, however, is not a determination in this sense, because it cannot be conceived in function of substance or definition, but only in function of the constructivity of a system. Naturally, this does not prevent the possibility that outside this precise problem, we might employ the terms «to determine» and «determination» in their wide usual acceptance, since all suchness is, in some sense, determination. What is it then to be «such?»

Let us begin with the essential notes. The essential notes are not formally essential by reason of their content, but by reason of their constructed state, that is, by reason of the «of.» Only by being «notes-of» do they have formally essential reality. This does not 359 mean, however, that their content is alien or indifferent to the essence. Quite the contrary. Precisely because the essential notes are physically, intrinsically, and formally «notes-of,» its very content is «of» the systematic unity. In saying that the essential notes are essential, not by reason of their content but by reason of their «of,» what we are affirming is, not that the content does not form part of the essence, but that the content belongs to the essence only in virtue of the «of» (de). To be a «note-of» is, then, also to be «content-of.» And the «content-of» is precisely the suchness of the notes. If the pure «of» constitutes the formal reason of the essential reality of the notes, the «content-of» is what makes the essence «such» essence. As a consequence, the essence is not «such» because it «has» these and no other determined notes, but rather because of the peculiar and precise way in which it has them. This mode is not the differential determination of a genus, but rather the constructivity of the physical notes, that is, to be «notes-of.» Hence, in the order of suchness, the notes have, constructively, a precise function: «to suchify,» «to make such and such.» In this order the constructed state of the notes means formally to be a «suchifying» reality. To «suchify» is not to determine a subject by a note, but rather it is to confer such content upon a system by being «notes-of.» And this does not belong to every note of a substantive reality. The merely constitutional notes and the adventitious notes are «determinants» of the substantive reality, but they do not make it «such» reality, they are not «notes-of» because they do not belong to the substantive system directly, by and of themselves, but rather in function of the essential system. «To be such,» to «suchify,» is formally a character or exclusive function of the «notes-of.» The remaining notes presuppose that the reality is already such, they presuppose reality already «as such» (talificada) and they confer ulterior determinations on its suchness. This supplies us with a first conception of essence from the point of view of the «suchness» of its notes. We have seen, in a word, that the essence is the group of notes necessary and sufficient to form a system by themselves. Now we can give this concept a final 360 precision. This group is the group of all and only the «notes-of.» And, since to be «note-of» is to be «suchifying,» it follows that, in the last analysis, the essence is, from this point of view, the group of notes necessary and sufficient to compose a reality which would be «such» in the exact sense of the concept which we have just explicated. It is, if I may be permitted the expression, suchifying auto-sufficiency.

But «suchifying» of what? Precisely of the other term of the constructed state of the absolute term, that is to say, of the unity itself. Not only the notes, but also the essential unity itself, is «such» in such wise that the essential suchness is a character of the physical essence in its integral reality. What is this suchness of the essential unity as unity?

It is a suchness conferred by the notes. In the order of suchness, then, it is the essential notes which «suchify» the unity. Nevertheless, this does not mean that in this order the essential unity ceases to be primary and coherential. Quite the contrary. And this is precisely what will make it possible to understand the suchness of the unity better.

The unity, in a word, is found «in» each note as an intrinsic exigency of the whole. This exigency is what confers on each note its character as «note-of.» It is this character which makes the notes «suchifying.» As a consequence, thanks to the primarity of the essential unity, and thanks only to it, do the notes enter the essence by «suchifying» the unity; so that, in the last analysis, it is the unity itself which is, in this respect, the primary reason of its proper suchness. The essential unity, I have said, consists in essentiating the notes. In this order, then, to essentiate means to actualize the suchness as an essential moment; to actualize the notes is to «make
361 them» suchifying. The actual content of this suchness depends on the notes; this fact, however, that this content should be «content-of,» that is, that by way of it the essence is «such,» depends on the unity itself. Presently I shall clarify this assertion by an example. As a consequence, the primacy of the essential unity appears in the fact that the essential unity is «auto-suchness.» The essential unity is not an empty and undifferentiated unity, which would do no more than make the notes something unitary, but rather, is a unity intrinsically and formally «such» *qua* unity. To be dog or to be man is, before all else, in this order, to be precisely «such» unity. Even more, this suchness of the unity, just like the suchness of the notes, is formally individual *qua* suchness. If the essence is only singular its suchness, too, is only singular. If, however, it is what we have called strictly and formally individual, then it is necessary to say

that not only to be dog or to be man, but also to be this dog or this man is to be «such» unity precisely and formally individual. Each such thing has its proper and irreducible essential individual suchness. Therefore, in speaking of «such» unity, I am referring always to this individual unity of the essence *qua* essence. The essence of a substantive reality is not only the system of constitutive notes, but also the fact that it is a moment by reason of which the individual physical suchness of each note is in a certain way exigentially «demanding» the rest.

By this I am not referring to what I said earlier, in a more general way, namely, that each note does not have nor can have physical reality save in unity with the rest of the notes. Here I am referring precisely and formally to the suchness of the notes itself, that is to say, to the fact that the character of each note in its full and concrete content is not what it is, except by implicating the particular character of the rest of the notes, also in their full and concrete peculiar content. For example, in any higher animal 362 whatsoever, its biological chemism, taken in its fullness, is a chemism which is such as it is *in its character as chemism*, implicating, for example, optic sensibility and, in the case of man, implicating rationality. To implicate, not in the sense that *in case* rationality were to prove to be a chemical phenomenon, or in the reverse situation, that rationality might intervene in the atomic mechanism of chemistry — an absurd supposition if there ever was one — but implicating in the constructed sense, that is, in the sense that the very structure of the chemism is intrinsically constituted solely by being exigentically «of» rationality. And in order to understand this well, I might add that I am referring to the notes in the «fullness» of their suchness; that is to say, I am not referring to the simple chemical mechanism, but to chemism understood as a series of processes in dynamic and reversible equilibrium, that is, to chemism in what it can and must give of itself chemically in the order of biological stability, in the line of the conservation of the substantivity. The chemism of an organism, in a word, can be considered from two points of view. First, (it can be viewed) as a chemism in and by itself; second, as a note of an organism. Only in this second sense is it rigorously «such» a chemism, that is, a chemism by reason of which the organism is «such» an organism, chemically constituted

in this fashion. It is true that in the first sense, it is also customary
to speak of the chemism «such» as it is. Then, however, we are
considering the chemism in question independently of the fact that
it is a note of this organism, and in doing so what we actually do is
confer on it mentally a substantivity of its own, and in that case,
the chemism is, in the strictest sense, «such» a chemism, because its
properties are «notes-of» this chemical edifice and, therefore, are,
rigorously speaking, «such.» In forming part of an organism, however,
this same chemism has lost its primitive substantivity and with it
363 has also lost its primitive «suchness;» it conserves only its substantiality and its determining content. In being converted into a moment
of the new substantivity, it also acquires a new «suchness.» Only by
recalling its prior «suchness» are we able to continue speaking then
of «such» a chemism as it is in itself independently of the organism.
Neither outside the organism nor as forming part of it, are the
«determining» character and its character as «such» identified in the
chemism. And insofar as it has this character of «such,» the chemism
is constituted in a form «such» that it demands exigentially the
«suchness» of the other notes. The same must be said of every other
note. That is to say, if we were able to see in this its ultimate and
full reality any note whatsoever of a living being, we would see that
this note is not «such» as it is, except in and by its exigential
unity with the others, that is to say, as demanding them, and that
this «demand» is a moment of the complete intrinsic constitution of
the note in question.

    This entitative structure shows itself clearly in a thousand ways
in the operative order; for example, in what, so many times in my
courses, even distant ones, I have called «exigetive displacement» of
certain functions by others in living beings. In the activity of living
beings, there comes a moment in which a function cannot be or
continue to be what it itself is unless there enter into action other
types of function. For example, there comes a moment in which the
chemism of a higher animal, such as a dog, cannot continue in its
«normal» chemical functioning unless the dog optically perceives
certain stimuli; in a word, only by these perceptions can it give an
adequate chemical response, that is to say, carry out the chemism
in the line of the stable biological equilibrium, in which normalcy
resides and in function of which the chemism of the dog is «such»

in the sense explained. It is not only that the chemism opens the 364
door to «another» function by itself, to optical perception by itself,
but rather that, on the contrary, it brings perception into play by
the effects of the chemism «itself.» The same thing happens with
rationality in man. There comes a moment at which man cannot
maintain his «normal» biochemical functioning except by involving
himself in the situation as *reality*. The biochemical activity has thus
disengaged the perceptive activity in the higher animal and the intellective activity in man. It is a «disengagement» because the intellective activity is not biochemical in itself; however, it is a strictly
«exigetive» disengagement and *intrinsic* in the order of suchness,
because the biochemical activity cannot, in certain cases, continue
being «such» as it is chemically, if it does not demand *from itself*
the perceptive activity or the intellective activity or both at the same
time. It is not a question of both activities being rooted in the same
subject, but rather that the one, so to say, prolongs itself exigetively
in the other. This disengagement has unitarily, in the unity of
suchness, two aspects. The new disengaged function stabilizes the
disengaging function; however, at the same time the latter has «lib-
erated» the superior function. For example, insofar as it is disengaged
by the biochemical activity, the first function of the intelligence is to
insure the biochemical stability; that is to say, it is a biological
function. In performing this function, however, it has not only
achieved the stabilization «of» the functions in question, but it has
also released the intelligent function «by the service of» trans-chemical
necessities, including trans-biological ones. The unity of both aspects
is found, in its turn, in the fact that this «superior» function not
only has been demanded by the «inferior,» but also that it is sustained
by it, precisely by that very thing which in this inferior function
(and in order to be what it is) demands the superior function; this
is what I have been accustomed to call «dynamic subtension» of some 365
functions by others. Exigetive disengagement, dynamic subtension,
and liberation, are three moments of the unity of suchness in the
living being: the plenary actuation of each function «demands», in
one form or another, appeal to the others.

These phenomena are all of the operative order. I have, however,
insisted at great length on them in order to make the idea of exigetive
unity in the order of activity more comprehensible, with the purpose

of carrying it over into the entitative order. This unity in activity is not, properly speaking, «constructed» because what is constructed concerns only the entitative order. It is, however, a strict exigential unity. The exigetive element, then, of the activity is a disengagement, precisely because the entitative structure is exigentially «constructed.» What we call being «such» is not to possess a *unitary cadre* of notes, but a *primary exigency:* constructivity in the order of suchness. In this sense, and only in this sense, to be «such» is anterior and superior to having such and such notes. For example, it is not only that man, in order to stabilize his chemism, does not make use of his intelligence simply because he possesses it or has it as a resource, but rather that *he has to* recur to it because what he «is» as vegetative and as sensitive he is in *entitative exigency* (I emphasize the word) of his intelligence. If this were not the case, what would give its impulse to the intelligence so that it would enter into action? By contrast, the matter is clearer if the chemism is already entitatively in exigential unity with the intelligence. The essence of man, in his individual essence *qua* essence, is not «such» because «it has» chemism, sensitivity, and intelligence, but rather because his chemism *qua* chemism «is» constructively sensitive and because his sensitivity *qua* sensitivity «is» constructively intellective. It is not a question of 366 a synthesis nor of a unity which would consist in the fact that the three notes are notes of one substance (this is a question alien to that of essence) but of the primary unity of suchness in the «constructed» reality of man. In this order, the «of» *(de)* is constructed according to the «in,» that is to say, the note is constructed as «such» note-of, because it demands such other notes.

Of what kind of others? We have already indicated this a number of times: of all. Up to this point we have explained what the primary unity in the order of suchness in general is. It is now necessary to say something of this character of «all» in this order. Only in that way will we have completely characterized the essence as suchness.

The exigential unity *qua* exigential leaves the notes in this formal unity which we have called «coherency.» Therefore, the problem of what the «whole» might be in the order of suchness is nothing other than the problem of what might be the form of coherence that the exigency of «suchness» imposes on the notes. This form has two moments.

In the first place, as we have just seen, each note is not «such» as it is, except by reason of that which impresses on it the exigency for all the others. Then, however, this whole cannot be unlimited, for, if it were, no note would be able to be «such» as it is, for its ultimate characterization would remain always incomplete, indefinitely. Some scholastics and Leibnitz thought, on the contrary, that every individual has infinite notes. This, however, is impossible. What happened is that they have confused the physical notes with the objective predicates. Of one individual reality there are always infinite possible predicates because, apart from other reasons, the points of view from which, in principle, the single individual reality can be considered are infinite. There is no reason, however, why these objective predicates should be physical notes. One same physical individual note can be considered from infinite points of view, to which 367 correspond infinite objective predicates; nevertheless, it is physically only one individual note. The essence is a unity of physical notes and not a unity, whether analytical or synthetical, of objective predicates. As a unity of physical notes, the essence is a totality limited in its notes. This limitation of notes impresses a concrete form on their suchness: each one is what it is by way of a mutual «co-limitation» of the notes in its suchness. And this «co-limitation» of the suchness is this form of coherence which we call *clausura*, closure. Closure does not mean that there are not more notes (a negative moment); rather, it means positively that each note is «such» a reality in a complete and full way only because the determination of the «suchness» is limited. *Clausura*, closure, is, then, the suchlike *(talitativa)* form of the primary coherential unity. We have already come across this concept when we were speaking of substantivity as system. There, however, the closure was not primary. For this reason, only the essence should be called closed, because it alone is enclosed by itself. The essence is «constructed» in its notes according to «such *(talitativa)* closure.»

In virtue of this moment, the essence is completely characterized. This characterization must, however, be understood correctly. Because it is a question of considering a limiting (ὁρίζειν) as the reason *(razón)* of a determination, it might be thought that the characterization is precisely a «definition» (ὁρισμός), that is, the determination of a genus by a difference. Even setting aside, however, the

general distinction, which we have expressed so many times during
the course of this treatment, between essence and the real correlate
of a definition, there are two grounds of distinction which refer very
closely to our present theme. First, because we are talking about
physical notes; the genus and the difference, however, are not physical
notes, but «conceptive» moments of the entire reality. And second,
368 because they are not correlatives; the genus does not determine the
difference, but only is that which is determinable by it; only the
latter determines the former. By contrast, in treating of physical
notes, their closure is that in virtue of which each note not only
determines the others, but also that each note is also determined by
them. Closure is rigorous «co-determination.» And this brings us to
the second constitutive moment of the «whole» of the notes in the
order of suchness *(talidad)*.

The first (moment) was *clausura*, closure. The second is the moment to which we have just alluded. It is that, what we call closure,
might constitute a reality in many different ways. One way would
be, for example, «enclosure.» If we take the physical notes of an
essence in series (so to say), their unity of closure might be conceived
like that character by reason of which this series has a first element
and a last element. This would be a «lineal» closure: A is such by B,
B by C, to N, which would be such by the penultimate note M. This,
however, is not the present case, because if it were so, N would
determine all the notes, but would not be determined by any other.
This, however, is impossible, as we have said. Therefore, if one
wishes to maintain the idea of a «series» of notes, it would have to
be a series in which the last note, N, would be determined by the
suchness of the first, of A. In that case, no note would be in an
absolute sense (en absoluta) either primary or ultimate: it is a
«cyclical» enclosure. Taken *stricto sensu*, this denomination is merely
symbolic, because the essential notes do not constitute a series of any
kind. What is meant is that in the constructivity of the essential notes
«such» as they are, all the notes «co-determine» each other mutually
and, therefore, if we could «see» (let us say it once more) the integral
physical suchness of any note whatsoever, it would show us constructively in its breast not only «other» notes, but all the others. We
369 said this earlier, but here we touch on the proper reason *(razón)* of
this structure. It is not only that the chemism of man is sentient

and that his sensitivity is intellective, but, in addition, that his intellect is sentient and his sensitivity is vegetative, etc. It is not a question of each note *resting on* the prior (this is the idea of the lineal series) but that each note in its mode of being «such» is intrinsically *of* all the others, in a positive way, exigentially. With this explanation, there is no difficulty in retaining the word «cyclical» because it continues to prove expressive. We will say, then, that the coherential whole of the notes in the order of suchness is *cyclical closure.*

Hence, it follow that the suchness of each note is, in a certain way, only a moment of a unique or single suchness; by reason of its cyclically enclosed unity, the notes are constituted in a single suchness. We have seen, in a word, that the content of «such» a note depends solely on the note; its «suchness,» however, in itself, as suchness, depends on the unity as a primary moment of the essence. Therefore, the suchness which the unity confers on each note it confers as a mere «point of application» (if I may be permitted this expression) of the primary suchness, enclosed and cyclical, in which the essential unity consists. Because it is enclosed and cyclical, the essential unity is «such» all at once, so to say. And only by reason of this fact can each one of the notes be «such.» The essential unity, as unity, is a primary unity of suchness. For this reason, to pass from one essence to another, is not a question of adding or of subtracting notes, but rather of remaking *ab initio* and *ab intrinseco*, that is, originatively, the very cycle itself of the primary unity; the content of one «same» note in its full suchness is «different» in two different essences. These coherent cyclical unities are the unities of suchness. Here we encounter the constructivity of the suchness of the essence.

No essence is an exception to this structure. To be sure, all intramundane essences have this character of cyclical closure in the unity of suchness. Since, however, this character is strictly metaphysical, it follows that the cyclical closure admits of grades of coherence which confer a different «such» *(talitativo)* character on the essence itself. There are conceivable, for example, realities in which the notes are cyclical to the point of being non-dissociable. The cyclical closure (in this case) would be strict simplicity. We can, however, descend still further, and conceive notes each one of which would concentrate, by elevation, what in lower metaphysical strata is found dispersed in notes which are actually and formally different. By this route we arrive, finally, at the point of conceiving an essence which would be but a single «note» *(sit venia verbo)*. This would not be uniqueness born of poverty (that of having but one note), but a unity of eminent richness, to be whole in a single note. The cycle would have come to be concentrated in a single point. It would be the greatest and the absolute simplicity. This, however, here goes no further than being something of which it is possible to conceive; its reality is not intramundane.

This idea of the unity of suchness provides us with a second concept of essence. From the point of view of the notes, we have seen that in the order of suchness *(talidad)* the essence is that group of notes necessary and sufficient to constitute a reality which would be *such*. We may add here that, from the point of view of the essential unity, the essence is the primary enclosed and cyclical unity which *brings it about* that the real is precisely «a such.» These two concepts correspond to the two moments of *that which* the essence is in its integral physical reality. The essence is that by reason of which the real is «such» as it is, and not in any other way. It is «such» because the notes which comprise it are such and because the unity which constitutes them as essential is «such.» This is the way in which the essence is «constructed» in the order of suchness. The essence is, therefore, a *quid tale*.

371   This suchness is formally individual *qua* essence, that is to say, insofar as it is an essential *quid*, something essential; it is constitutive essence, that which constitutes the real in its being «such.» This is clear; it might happen that the essence, in addition to being closed and cyclical, is closed and cyclically constructed according to a schema. The coherential unity has, in such a case, a third moment: the moment of *schema*. Then we have the quiddifiable essence: it is a closed, cyclical, and schematic unity. The consequence is that it is not that the essence, «in addition» to being specific, is individual, but just the contrary: the essence, «in addition» to being individual, is specific. The essence, in addition to being «such individual» of the reality is «such individual» of a species in contrast to others of the same species. And this manner of being «such» confers on its *quid tale* that triple character of unity with itself: communicated unity

and communicable unity, that we have expounded in the proper place. This triple character is formally and exclusively proper to certain essences alone, those we call schematizable. It concerns only the order of suchness, and within it, the individual only insofar as the individual is counter-distinguished from the rest of the members of the same species. The constitutive essence, by contrast, *qua* constitutive, lacks this triple unity of suchness.

Here we encounter the physical reality of the essence in the order of suchness: it is that according to which the thing is «this» and not the «other,» that is to say, it is the manner in which the real thing is «constructed» as «such.»

SECTION THREE   372

ESSENCE AND TRANSCENDENTALITY

This, however, is not the unique, nor the most radical, aspect of essence. For essence is not only that according to which the thing is «such» a reality, but also that according to which the thing is «real.» In this sense, the essence does not belong to the order of suchness, but rather to a superior order: the order of reality as reality. This character — let us call it this for the time; earlier I called it formality and I will return to it later — of reality stands above suchness, as much if we understand it in the exact sense which we have just explained as if we understand it in the usual sense of determination in general. And it is above suchness, not because this character was a supreme «such» note (we have already seen that Aristotle showed once and for all that this is impossible) but rather in the sense of being a character in which all the things and all the notes formally converge; even all the ultimate differences of all things, whatever their suchness may be, that is to say, independently of that suchness. This peculiar way of being above any suchness whatsoever in the sense of being related to all without being one further suchness, is what scholasticism called «to transcend.» It is the transcendentality of the real. The order of reality as reality is a *transcendental order,* in contrast to the order of reality as «such» reality, which is *the order of suchness.* As a consequence, the essence, insofar as it is that according to which the thing is real, belongs to the transcendental order.

Before entering on a transcendental consideration of essence, however, it is necessary to make this idea of the transcendental order a little more precise.

³⁷³
I. *The Idea of the Transcendental Order*

In order to make this idea more precise, we will turn our attention, in the first place, to modern philosophy and to classical philosophy. Thus, we will achieve a focus which will permit us thereafter to enter positively into the theme.

1. *Transcendentality in Modern Philosophy and in Classical Philosophy*

Modern philosophy, from Kant to Husserl, has been in good measure a «transcendental idealism.» The name itself seems to suggest that what, in this philosophy, is understood by transcendental is precisely the contrary of what mediaeval philosophy understood by transcendental. At the risk of admitting that we are treating here of a term which is strictly equivocal, it will be necessary then to make precise what is the transcendental order, beginning with modern philosophy.

This philosophy not only has a content which is more or less new, but also, with Descartes, inaugurates a new idea of what philosophy itself is: a meditation on reality, resting on the only unshakable reality: the reality of the I. This unity between the I and reality is precisely what is meant by truth: that is real which is as I think it is. Therefore, the order of reality, as transcendental order, would be the order of truth. And this order is constituted in the I as first reality. This primarity of the I would make of it the transcendental as such. In this line of thought, then, transcendentality is a character of the I. Its conceptual clarification is reached by way of two fundamental counterpositions.

(1) On the one hand, the «I» is the reality of «each one» (to 374
be each one is not the same as to be a person) with its peculiar
psychic and psychophysical vicissitudes and states in counter-
distinction to the «I's» of others. It is the empirical «I,» intrinsically
diverse. On the other hand, however, «I» am the I which mediates
over all things; it is not the I insofar as it is different or distinct
from all the other I's, but insofar as it is different from all that is
not I; it is a «pure I,» pure of all vicissitude and, therefore, intrinsically the (lo) same in all. Then, what we call «things,» whether
ideal, fantastic, or real, have, for the moment, a negative character:
not to be I; they are the «non-I.» However, since what the I does is
confront them, this negative character turns into a positive character:
the things are ob-jectum, objects. Thing is object. Reciprocally, this
pure I is not only what confronts objects, but it also consists formally
in going to them, in issuing out of itself, in «transcending»: it is a
«transcendental» I. It is a secondary matter, for our inquiry, how
the pure I may be conceived: a knowing I (Kant), a conscious I
(Husserl), etc. The decisive point is that the pure I stands above the
empirical I and that transcendence toward objects constitutes the
compass of its possible truth, that is, the transcendental order. The
concept of the transcendental is thus obtained by a first counterposition: the counterposition «pure-empirical.» This, however, is not
enough.

What then is this transcendence toward objects? It is not that
the I already has an object before it and goes toward it in order to
secure a representation of it, but rather, on the contrary, that it is
its very going which brings it about that that toward which it goes
becomes an object. To transcend is not a «seeing» but a «doing,» a
going toward the «non-I» by «making» of it the object. That is to
say, the object is not apprehended, but «posited;» only then can a
representation of it take place. For object does not mean here each 375
one of the objects, but only that in which all objects converge and
have to converge, namely, in being objects; what I will call «objectuality.» The posited is objectuality as such. To be is objectuality.
And this character is, for this reason, strictly transcendental. The I
is transcendental not only because it transcends of itself toward the
non-I, but also because, in transcending, it «posits» the transcendental
character of objects, that is to say, because its positing is transcen-

dental. And since this is an action of the I, it depends on the structure of the I; the structure of the I is the *a priori* condition for the possibility of every and all objects as such. The manner in which this structure is conceived matters little: whether as a system of conceptual forms (Kant) or as a constituting intentionality (Husserl) or any other different way. It will always be the case that the I determines *a priori* the objectuality as such. And with it truth as transcendental truth, that is, as capacity to know an object truthfully, does not consist in the capacity of the understanding to conform itself to objects, but precisely the reverse; it consists in the capacity of the understanding to conform to objects according to its own transcendental structure: it is transcendental idealism. This is what Kant called his «Copernican revolution.» Transcendental idealism means an idealism which affects only the transcendentality, that is, the objectual character of all that there is that can be known by the understanding truthfully.

And at this point there appears the second fundamental counterposition which defines the transcendental. The transcendental is objectuality; objectuality, however, as I have already indicated, is not a determined object. Hence, the distinction between objectual *meaning* of transcendentality and its *use* as the effective determination of an object. It appears that this use might be achieved in two 376 ways. One way would consist in the fact that transcendental position (or positing) rests upon something *given* (impressions of the senses, elemental data of consciousness, etc.). The *(lo)* given is not an object, but only a chaos of elements; and what the transcendental I then does is give these elements the form of an object, that is to say, objectuality. Then we have not only objectuality, but a determined object. The set of objects determined in this fashion is what transcendental idealism calls «experience.» If the other way is tried, however, namely, to determine an object with no given, with only the *a priori* conditions of objectuality, overflowing, therefore, the limits of the given and of that which can be given, then this use determines, not an object of experience, but a «transcendent» object, one that lies beyond all experience. For idealism this is chimerical because the I can never convert objectuality itself into an object, nor be, therefore, the source of the representation of it; at most, it succeeds in conceiving a possible object, or, to state it better, a not-impossible object, but nothing more. In order that there be a real object, something given is necessary. The transcendental, then, is «positing,» but only as the elevation of the given to a determined object; it is the objectual character of the objects of experience. The transcendental I is the I which objectualizes experience. The counterposition «transcendence-experience» succeeds in outlining thus the concept of the transcendental in idealism.

This philosophy has placed the accent on the moment of ideality and all of its effort seems to have consisted in reaching transcendentality within ideality. With this it seems that the terms have been inverted with regard to mediaeval philosophy, for which the transcendental order is the order of being as being. For this reason, «transcendentalism» is always a term which has for modern ears 377 clear and strong idealistic resonances.

Nevertheless, is it really this way? Here we are apparently assisting at an inversion of the concept of the transcendental. Only apparently, however. The concept of the transcendental I has, as a matter of fact, two moments: the I is transcendental because it is pure, that is, because it consists *formally* in transcending i t s e l f toward the non-I and because it consists *terminatively* in positing or constituting the transcendentality of the non-I. Now these two moments are, indeed, transcendental, but in the classical sense. Before all, with regard to what refers to the formal character of the I: to be pure I. Idealism reaches this concept from a point of departure in the empirical I. Idealism makes us see without effort that the pure I and the empirical I, although they are not two numerically distinct I's, are not identical. It has never, however, made clear in what its internal articulation consists. And this is, nevertheless, what is essential. In reflecting on it, we immediately become aware that «empirical» is precisely the suchness of the I, that is, that man as a reality is an I whose suchness is all its vicissitudes and psychic and psychophysical states. Only by taking its point of departure here and not abandoning it, does idealism reach its concept of the pure I: it takes the empirical I, the I as reality, and that of which it purifies it is not its reality, but its determined suchness. With that, what remains in the I as «pure reality.» This and nothing else is the pure I. And precisely this and nothing else is also the transcendental I. The pure I is not transcendental by opposition to every *other* object,

but by opposition to *every* object. And the totality of objects is the non-I. As a consequence, that to which the I goes immediately is a «non,» although the I itself does not «posit» it. The I would be the only thing which «is» *simpliciter* in and by itself; the I-ness is the «non» of the non-I, the non «not-I,» that is to say, the yes of reality
378 as reality. And this is precisely what constitutes transcendentality in traditional philosophy. Even though formally the I might consist in going toward the non-I, this aspect is not its primary aspect; the primary aspect is that the I is a *reality*, which can consist in going toward the non-I, but which begins by being a reality. The aspect of going toward the non-I is inscribed, so to say, within the character of reality, and not the reverse. Quite the contrary, that is to say, if the pure I were a reality only because it goes toward the non-I, the pure I would be reality because it is posited by my knowledge of myself, by my self-consciousness; that is to say, it would be something posited by a second pure I and so on *ad infinitum*. But this is impossible. The pure I is the I as pure reality and this is the reason why the reality of the I, as reality, is a transcendental aspect of the I: the transcendentality of the I in the sense of a going toward the non-I is based on its character as pure reality. The empirical I and the pure I are nothing but the reality of one same I considered either as «such» an I or as a «real» I, specifically as real. Empirical and pure are, then, the suchness and the transcendentality of the reality of the I. The I remains, consequently, withdrawn from the idealist inversion. As a consequence, the sole innovation of idealism, on this point, is to be found in the manner in which it conceives the transcendental reality of the I, that is, as a going toward the non-I; however, it is not determined in what this character of «going» might be, posited as antecedent to its character as reality. To say «I» is nothing but the idealist way of conceiving the reality of the subject as pure reality. The concept of the transcendental itself, however, issues unscathed from this operation.

The same must be said of the second moment, the terminative moment of the transcendental I, namely, that the transcendental dimension of things consists in being posited by the pure I. Here
379 the inversion of the concept of the transcendental appears more undeniable. Kant himself called transcendental idealism «a Copernican revolution» which is as much as to say «revolution in the

transcendental.» In what, however, does the revolution consist? Not, to be sure, in transcendentality. Idealism calls transcendental the I or consciousness insofar as these are *a priori* determinations of objects as such; that is to say, of their objectuality. But this is equivocal. This determination, in a word, is not transcendental by reason of being posited by the I, but rather by reason of the fact that what is posited is, independently of the fact that it is posited, the *a priori* determination of that in which all objects must converge not by reason of being such and such but rather by reason of being objects. This *a priori* might be subjective as idealism claims; it is not this subjectivity, however, which constitutes the transcendentality, but the being something common to every object insofar as it is an object. And, once more, this is the classical conception of transcendentality. What is peculiar to idealism and its revolution does not lie in the concept of the transcendental but rather in its root and in the character of its terminus. In its root: in being posited by the I. In the character of its terminus: in being objectuality. And these two innovations are essentially connected: nothing can be an object without being posited (in one way or another: this is a question which idealism solves too rapidly) by an I and, reciprocally, the pure I, when it confronts things, makes objects of them. This, however, is an idealist conception of reality, not a new conception of the transcendental as such. Hence it follows that «transcendental idealism,» in the question which concerns us, is a false expression. For transcendentality is not inscribed within idealism but, quite the reverse, idealism falls within the transcendentality of the real. Metaphysically, there is no «transcendental idealism,» but, if the expression is valid, an «idealistic transcendentalism.»

The transcendental has not changed. We cannot, however, be 380 satisfied with saying this, because, in addition, the very idealist conception of reality is inadmissible. And it is necessary at least to have indicated it in order to outline with greater exactness the idea of the transcendental order as the order of reality as such.

In the first place, idealism, like many other philosophies which are not idealist, conceives the reality of the subject as an «I» and an «I» which, in its transcendental purity, consists formally in «going toward» the non-I. This, however, is impossible. For «I» is not the reality of the subject but quite the reverse: it is the reality

of the subject which has being an I as a property, to phrase it this
way. To be «I» is a moment, and neither the unique nor the primary
moment — of the reality of the subject *in actu secundo*, operatively;
it is not an entitative moment. The reality of the subject lies beyond
the «I.» Further, even though we restrict ourselves to the operative
order, this pure «I,» despite the fact that «it goes toward» the object,
nevertheless, does not formally consist in this going toward it, but
consists rather in actualizing it, in giving it mere actuality in the
intelligence. These two things not only are not the same, but the
second can and is given, even though the first may not be given. And
this is the case whether we conceive the real subject as knowing,
as conscious, or in any other manner whatsoever. Consciousness, for
example, not only is not reality proper in the first act *(acto primero)*
but neither is it such in *acto segundo*, because consciousness is not
an act, but only a property of some acts, of conscious acts. «I» is
not the reality of the subject, whether in the order of suchness, or
in the transcendental order, no matter what concept of the subject
may be entertained (knowing, conscious, vital, etc.). In the operative
order of *actus secundus*, the «I» appears to me, then, as a character
381 of a reality properly anterior to it; it is impossible, therefore, to
take the «I,» whether empirical or pure, as the reality of the subject,
no matter how problematic this reality might be; nevertheless, the
character of the «I,» precisely because it is «I,» consists formally in
referring itself back to that reality. The «I» resides *within* the order
of the real.

In the second place, philosophy, with Descartes, has inscribed the
order of the real within the order of the true: that will be real which
is really such as I think it. This, however, is equivocal. If what this
means is that my true knowledge expresses the real, then it is not
to be denied. This does not permit us, however, to invert the terms
and to say that to be real consists formally in being the terminal
moment of truth. This is impossible; we have already seen as much
in making our analysis of truth. The moment of reality presents
itself in intellection not only as *independent* of the intellective act,
but also as *anterior* to it, as a *prius* relative to the presentation of
its independence: it is independent because it is real, and not the
reverse, in such wise that it is indifferent to reality to have truth
or not to have truth. If it were not so, the very truth would not be

able to be considered as real, but only as the terminus of another truth and so forth *ad infinitum*. The «radical» pole of reality does not consist in being an «I» nor does its «terminal» pole reside in being truth. The order of reality as transcendental order is not the order of truth; that is, the transcendental order is not the order of reality as truth, but rather it is the order of reality as reality.

In the third place, and finally, that toward which the pure «I» moves has, for idealism, the character of object. With this, metaphysics, which up to Kant had been w h a t C l a u b e r g was the first to call «ontology,» with Kant changed into that which we might call «objectology.» And this, too, is impossible. For that toward which 382 the pure «I» moves, and even more, that which is actualized in the intellection as a previous or anterior reality, does not have the formal character of object. It would have that character if the «I» were to consist formally in a «going-toward» the non-I; then and only then this non-I would spring up before us upon «encounter» and would be, therefore, *ob-jectum*, object. The I, however, consists only in actualizing the non-I, and then this non-I is not an object for two reasons. First, because not the whole of the intelligible is formally objectual. In saying this, I am not referring to the fact that my way of engaging myself with things is not always (neither as phenomenon nor as vital act) a confrontation with them as objects; rather, I am referring to something much more profound and radical, which affects intellection itself as such. However, since this is not our present theme I may content myself with leaving this fact firmly indicated. Second, because even in the case of intellecting *(estar intelligendo)* an object, *res objecta*, what I formerly intellect is not the *res* insofar as it is object, but insofar as it is *res*. Once again, even in the very case of objects, the moment of reality presents itself to me, in the intellection itself, as a *prius*, not only with respect to its truth, but also with respect to its objectuality. Contrary to what idealism affirms as something obvious, *thing* is not *object*. Just as substantivity is not subjectuality so, too, reality is not objectuality. The order of reality, as reality, is not the order of objectuality, but the order of reality simply as reality.

To sum up, this rapid discussion with transcendental idealism has made three points clear to us:

1. Transcendentality is beyond all possible ideality, that is, the transcendental in the order of the real.

2. That the order of the real is not grounded on the order of 383 the true, but is rather anterior to the latter whether we consider the subjective pole of the «I» or consider the terminal pole of intellection; that is, that the transcendental order is not the order of the real as true, but rather the order of the real as real.

3. That this reality as reality is not objectuality but simple reality.

Thus we approach the concept of the transcendental order as the order of reality as simple «reality.» Because the phrase does not lend itself to confusion, I will, in what follows, drop the adjective «simple» and limit myself to saying that the transcendental is reality as reality.

This is, formalistically at least, the classical concept. I say «formalistically,» that is, so long as real and reality do no more than oppose themselves to idealism in a sense which has been explained. However, insofar as we would wish to take these concepts in and by themselves, we see ourselves forced to open discussion with classical philosophy. How then does scholastic philosophy conceive the transcendental order?

We have already answered this question a number of times: that character is transcendental which belongs formally to all things, notes, and differences, whatever might be their «suchness,» by the mere fact of being (things, notes, or differences). And here begins what is peculiar to scholasticism. For scholasticism, what the intelligence conceives primarily and that to which, in the last analysis, all of its concepts are reduced, is «being;» every thing, we are told in effect, is intellected to the degree that I understand that it «is» this or the other; and the thing considered in this way, the thing insofar as it «is,» is precisely what is called «a being.» Hence it is that that in which all things coincide is *to be*. What, however, we may ask, is to be understood here by *to be*? This is the question.

Esse, to be, may before all else be considered as that which the 384 «is» of the copula expresses: it is copulative or logical being. In this sense, we say that everything about which we can form a proposition, «is.» Its *to be* is *concipi* a *to be* which, as such, is given in and by the conceptive act of intellection, an *esse in anima*. This latter *esse* is of two types. There is an *esse* which, in addition to being *in anima*, is also *extra animam;* it is the being which something has independent of all conceptions, real being, *esse reale*, substantive being. To it is opposed that which only has *esse in anima*, the *ens rationis*, but which *in re* neither has nor can have *esse*. The chimera, privation, certain relations, etc., do not have being in themselves, they are non-being; however, I conceive them «as though they were,» and for this reason they are indeed *ens* but *ens rationis*. By contrast, things which have being *extra animam* have existence, are *ens reale*. Here, *esse* means to exist and, therefore, to actuate by producing effects, something which is not given in the *ens rationis*, in the unreal being. The subject of this verb *to be*, in the sense of existing, is *ens*. This subject, however, like every subject of a verbal action, can be understood in its turn in two ways. It can mean the subject which effectively is enacting *(in actu exercito)* the verbal action; then, *ens* is a participial substantive, the being which actually exists, and for this reason involves, as does any participle, a temporal connection. However, *ens* can be taken as the merely possible subject of the action designated by the verb in its substantivated infinitive. Then *ens* is not a participle, but rather a simple name which signifies, not what is effectively existing but rather that which, by its own character, is a possible subject of the verbal action, that is to say, what is apt for *to be*, what has existence only aptitudinally; this is the being considered nominally. This, however, needs some clarification. In the first place, aptitude here does not mean lack of existence; because what we would then have would be being in potency, potential being. 385 This is not the question here. Here, aptitude does not mean lack but rather *precisivity*, that is, that being is that which is apt to have existence, prescinding from whether and not denying that it actually has it or does not have it. In both cases it has aptitude, even though, in the first case, it would be an actual being and in the second case a potential being. Therefore, in both cases it is being in the nominal sense, and in both cases for the same reason: because it is the possible subject of t h e substantivated infinitive «to exist.» In the second place, this subject of the infinitive is taken solely and formally in as far as it is the subject of that infinitive. For this reason that which is endowed with this *esse* is also *ens*, in a sense, however,

different from the participial being; the thing, in as far as it is apt
for having this infinitive *esse*, is called *essentia*, essence. The essence
is not the mere *quid* — this would be, according to the scholastics,
the abstract essence — but rather the *quid* insofar as it connotes
aptitudinally the act of existing. Hence being, considered nominally,
is mere *essentia;* it is, however, *realis* not because it exists as a matter
of fact, but rather because it is apt for existence *extra animam*, and
as such is something real and not something merely of reason. The
esse of nominal *ens*, that is to say, *esse* a c c o r d i n g to which
something is formally *essentia*, is called *esse essentiae;* as a consequence, it became necessary to call the act of actually existing,
the *esse* of the participle, *esse existentiae*. These are not two classes
of *esse*, but rather there is one same concept formed with greater
or lesser precision; that is, *esse* «immediately» has this double
meaning. A nominal *esse* is precisely what is expressed in the copula
because, although the copula can at times signify existence, the only
thing which the copula as copula expresses of itself *(de suyo)* is that
which is conceived as *esse nominale*, and it is in this that *esse logicum*
consists. The same thing happens, in the last analysis, in every being
of reason. And as these three moments of the *esse* (the *esse existen-*
386 *tiae*, the *esse essentiae*, and the *esse logicum)* enter in some manner
or other into every intellective act, it becomes comprehensible why
post-classical scholasticism ended up by affirming that the intelligence
is the faculty of *to be.*

Abstracting from the singular position of Duns Scotus, for the
whole of scholasticism, *esse reale*, considered nominally, and it alone,
is transcendental. Nevertheless, not all things, in a word, exist as a
matter of fact; therefore, participial being is not transcendental being.
All things, however, both those which exist and those which do not
yet exist, and even those which we consider «as though they were,»
coincide in their aptitude, real or conceived as real, to exist, independently of what their suchness might be. And this is true when
it is a question not only of complete or partial beings, but also when
it is a question of ultimate differences. «Independently» means
«whatever» might be the suchness, and not that the suchness remains
outside the being as such. To be sure, the suchness, considered in its
determination, does not enter formally into the concept of the being:
if that were the case, the concept of being would be formally con-

tradictory. The different suchnesses, however, do enter into the concept in question, either confusedly (Cajetan) or indeterminately (Suárez, etc.); that is, they are formally beings. And this does not mean that «being» must be only that in which they coincide, and in such manner that the differences *qua* differences excluded the suchnesses; that is to say, it is not that «being» is that in which they coincide and suchness that in which they differ. It means, on the contrary, that the suchnesses, precisely insofar as they are different, are also beings, that is, that the differences, *qua* differences, are also formally beings; on the contrary supposition, they would be «non-beings,» a nothing, and would therefore not even be differences. For this reason, speaking strictly, it is not true that the supreme *genera* differ among themselves (for to differ is to be compounded of a common moment 387 and a differential moment) but rather that, entitatively, they are primary diversity, they are *primo diversa.* Nevertheless, «they are,» they are beings, and their presumed differences are not differences, but rather immediate modes of being. This is the reason why the concept of being is not universal: it is transcendental. There remains unresolved, however, the problem of the more precise structure of the concept of being and of the manner in which it represents «the» beings, its *inferiors.* This, however, is not our theme. Here it is enough to have expounded in a summary manner what the being and the transcendental order are for scholasticism: the transcendental order is the order of real being nominally considered, the order of being apt for existing, the *ordo entis ut sic.*

Nevertheless, this does not mean that the «being» as such, is entirely empty. Quite the contrary. It is true that the suchness is not formally and determinatively included in the concept of being; the supreme *genera* of being are only *special modes* of being. It is also true, however, that being as such can be considered from two points of view; and what is offered to me from each of the different points of view is the same *ens qua ens*, though in different *general modes* of being; that is, in modes of being which follow on the sole fact of being *ens*. In a word, when being is considered in itself, it has, as we have said, a positive content proper to itself, the *quid*, in virtue of which scholasticism calls the being from this point of view *res*, «ratified» *(rato)* being, ratified in order to exist; and this same content, negatively considered, is undivided, that is, is *one*. The being

23

can, however, be viewed from another point of view, the being
with respect to other things. Negatively, each one is not the other, it
is a *quid;* a *quid aliud,* however, that is to say, an *aliquid,* a something.
From this point of view, the respect of a being, as being, to another
388 being is negative, and cannot have a positive character unless this
other being should be such that, by reason of its own proper character, it would be able to coincide with every being as such. This
being is, according to Aristotle, the ψυχή, the soul, which can coincide
with all or everything which has a reason of being, either by knowing
it or by appetizing it, by the mere fact of being a being. Therefore,
the being as such, considered in its coincidence with the intellective
soul, has, as being, this respect which is *verum;* and considered in its
coincidence with the a p p e t i t i v e soul, has, as being, another
respect: the *bonum.* These respects are positive, but extrinsic. Thus,
we have the six classical transcendentals: *ens, res, unum, aliquid,
verum, bonum.* This is the transcendental order according to scholastic
philosophy.

This conception, if it expresses that which is opposed to transcendental idealism, is unassailable; we have already seen this. If,
however, it expresses what is to be formally and exactly conceived
concerning the transcendental order, then it stands in need of further
discussion, both with regard to that which concerns the general idea
of the transcendental and with regard to that which touches on the
general modes of being, that is, the transcendental order, as order.
To abbreviate the exposition, the discussion will be, at the same
time, the positive exposition of what we might want to say about
these two points.

389   ## 2. *The Idea of the Transcendental*

To be sure, that is transcendental in which each and all agree
independently of their suchness. This idea is unalterable. One must,
however, carefully distinguish the transcendental itself from that
which *primo et per se* has transcendental character. For idealism,
the transcendental is the position (positing) of the pure I: it inscribes
ideality, therefore, within transcendentality and, by that fact, the
transcendental order is the order of reality insofar as it is object.
For scholasticism, what is transcendental is the *to be;* it therefore

inscribes the *to be* within transcendentality, and by that fact the transcendental order is the order of reality as being (ente). Nevertheless, if one examines the matter closely, in the expression of this idea three concepts always appear as intertwined: to be, reality, existence. These concepts are employed, despite all efforts to the contrary, somewhat promiscuously. This contributes considerably to the confounding of these ideas, despite the energy which scholasticism expends in affirming, in each case, that reality and existence are synonyms, or that *to be* means the same as existence. Hence the necessity of asking ourselves again, though in laconic fashion, what reality, existence, and *to be* really mean. We shall examine the question in two steps.

a) *Reality and Existence.* Without concentrating for the moment on the word *esse*, we may ask ourselves what scholasticism understood by reality, what *esse reale* is. The question is justified because what is understood by reality is not something as obvious as it might seem but, rather, a question which inevitably rests upon the primary and fundamental way in which things present themselves to us when we engage them intellectually. Consider, for example, the fact that the whole of transcendental idealism rests on the intellective confrontation of things as objects. For scholasticism, this confrontation, that is to say, the proper and formal act of the intelligence, is «to conceive;» it suffices to recall, in a word, that a beginning is made by saying that the first thing which the intelligence «conceives» and that into which all its «concepts» are resolved, is being. Since the primary way of apprehending things intellectually is fixed in this way, according to scholasticism, it is thence that it 390 derives its idea of reality. A rapid inspection makes clear to us three moments in that idea which it is useful to disengage and separate: (1) Reality is, in the first instance, everything which, on being conceived, presents itself to me as not receiving its being from the conception itself, but is rather, *extra animam*, where *anima* is taken only in the sense of the conceiving act of the intellect. If the expression be permitted me, reality is «extra-animity.» (2) This «extra-animity» is, to be sure, a moment extrinsic to the reality; however, it is its *ratio cognoscendi*, that procures for us a more exact concept of reality. Reality, in a word, is not something which can be defined, but is, however, something which can be explicated by counterposition. For scholasticism, however, that to which the real is counterposed *primo et per se*, in its status as «extra-animic,» is precisely the «intra-animic,» which is the unreal. The «intra-animic» is unreal because it is nowhere to be found, is fictitious, chimerical, merely thought, etc.; it is the non-existent. The real, by contrast, as opposed to the unreal, is the existent. «Extra-animity» is existence. (3) The existent, by reason of being such, produces real effects independently of whether it is conceived or not; a real chair, a real rock, etc., act on things and are counterposed to an unreal chair or rock, which exercise no action but which are mere «spectres» of reality. It is the moment of ἔργον, of *wirken*, etc. I can conceive the effects of what is only conceived; a conceived effect, however, is not an effectuated effect. By contrast, the existent has effectuated effects on things. And these three moments taken together inexorably yield the equation: reality = existence.

It is not the case that this is not true *simpliciter:* it would be absurd to pretend that it is not. None of these three moments, however, is primary or univocal, precisely because they rest on 391 the idea that the proper and formal act of the intelligence is to conceive. This, however, is not the truth; to conceive is not the primary and fundamental way in which we confront or engage things intellectively. We saw this when speaking of the essentiated reality. Here it will be enough to repeat that statement in summary fashion.

Man has different ways of apprehending things. One is by sensing them; in this man shares univocally the condition of any animal whatsoever. To sense is not a selecting of concrete things (material and formal), in the apprehension, but rather, is, before all else, a way of holding these things as apprehended. To this mode there corresponds in the things sensed a formality proper to them according to which they are sensed. What is sensed as such, then, is, if one wishes, «thing,» a stimulating thing, however, *qua* stimulating; the sensed as such has the formal character of a stimulus, or, as one is wont to say, stimulus is the proper and constitutive formality of pure sensing and of the purely sensed as such. Man, however, has another way of apprehending things: apprehending them as reality. This is intellective apprehension. The proper formality of what is intellected *qua* intellected is reality. Stimulus and reality, I repeat once more, are the two formalities of the apprehended as such. They are not merely juxtaposed. Something can, to be sure, be present as pure stimulus and not be present as reality. Nevertheless, what is present as reality may be a stimulus; the only reservation must be that it is not then «pure» stimulus, but «stimulating reality,» and its mode of apprehension is not «pure sensing,» but rather «intellective sensing,» or, what amounts to the same thing, «sentient intellection.» There is no need to enter into details on this last point; it is enough to leave it underscored. The important thing is that the first thing which man intellects is «stimulant reality,» stimulating, but reality. The proper and formal act of the intelligence is not «to conceive» but to apprehend the thing itself, not in its formality as «stimulating» but in its «real» formality. Conceiving is a further operation founded 392 on this first mode of confronting things. When this is established, if we wish to explicate what reality is, we shall have to center our reflection, not on the concepts, but rather on this duality of formalities, because the thing itself, as we have just indicated, has different characters according to these formalities.

(1) Reality is not «extra-animity.» Or better, the idea of «extra-animity» is not sufficiently clear and univocal, but is weighed down, rather, by a trying imprecision. What really is understood by *extra animam? Extra animam* is the opposite of *intra animam*. This opposition is established by considering the conceiving function of the intelligence. *Intra animam* would be that which has only an *esse objectivum* in the concept; by the same token, *extra animam* would be everything which has a being independent of this *esse objectivum:* «extra-animity» is extra-objectivity. And this extra-objective is what would be the real. Here, however, is where the inexactness lies. For things are present, not only in the concepts, but in sensation as well. If the thing present in pure sensation were sensed as real, there would be no question. But this is not the case. What is sensed in pure sensation is not reality, but stimulus; that is, the thing itself, in pure sensation, lacks the formality of reality. What is present in the stimulus, the stimulus-thing, is more than *esse objectivum;* it is something strictly extra-objective; therefore, according to the conception which we are discussing, it is *extra animam*. Nevertheless, as we have just said, the stimulus-thing does not have the formal character of reality. Therefore, if by *«extra animam»* is understood

all that is extra-objective, it is clear that extra-animity is not, without qualification, the synonym of reality. All that is real is *extra animam*, is extra-objective; but not all that is extra-objective or 393 *extra animam* has the character of reality. Between the *esse objectivum*, which is only *intra animam*, and the real *esse extra animam*, there is the *esse* of the stimulus-thing *qua* stimulus which is extra-objective and *extra animam* and which, nevertheless, does not have the formality of the real. Reality, then, is not the synonym of extra-animity. As a consequence, the decisive dualism on this point is not the «objective-extra-objective» dualism, but the dualism «stimulus-reality.» The first refers to the merely conceiving function of the intelligence, while the second refers to its primary function: it is the dualism «pure sensation-sentient intelligence.» Here, and not in conceptual extra-objectivity, in extra-animity, must the problem of reality be incardinated.

(2) To be sure, the mode of apprehension is always — whether we are dealing with pure sensation or with intellection — a moment extrinsic to what is apprehended *extra animam*. The proper character of the mode of apprehension, however, is a manifestation of the very character of things. Things, in a word (I never tire of repeating this), have different characters according to these two formalities. If we compare what we have called «reality» with the pure stimulus, the first thing to be seen is that the «stimulus-thing» is not something *unreal* (chimerical, fictitious, purely thought, etc.); neither, however, is it something formally real: it is simply *a-real*. That to which the real is to be counterposed, in the first instance, in order to explicate its character as reality, is not the unreal, but the a-real. Insofar as it is constituted as pure stimulus, the thing is present in an «affecting» form. The animal, to be sure, moves among «things» which are present to it, more things according as its status in the zoological scale is the more elevated. However, these things are present to it always and only in an affecting form; they are always and only complex unities of stimulation. Their perceptive unity and relative 394 stability are due to what I have been accustomed to call «formalization.» It is not necessary here to enter into this problem, because the sole thing which is of importance now is the formal character of stimulus. In what does the a-reality of the stimulus consist? To put it simply, in the fact that the «stimulus-thing» is exhausted in

the stimulation (actual, retarded, reproduced, or signifying); that is, it is present, but as mere suscitation of certain psycho-biological responses. By contrast, the same thing, intellectively apprehended, is present to me, but in a formally different fashion: not only is it present to me, but is so formally as a *prius* to its very presentation. Entirely the contrary (is the case of) of the «thing-stimulus» which is constituted and exhausted in its pure presence as stimulus. The priority is what permits and forces one to pass from the mere extrinsic moment of «being apprehended» to the inner character of the thing such as it is anteriorly to its apprehension. This priority does not mean mere «independence.» That what is present is something independent of the apprehender and of his apprehension is something common to the pure stimulus and to the reality. The animal behaves (and therefore responds), to a considerable degree, as orientated in his state of being stimulated to the independence of the stimulus with regard to his biological state. The moment of independence brings us, at most, to a «correlation» between sensation and what is sensed in their reciprocal independence of variations. The *prius*, however, is something absolutely different: it is the positive and formal «reference» *(remisión)* to what the thing is before the presentation. As I have been accustomed to say for so very many years, the thing is present to me as something «of its own» *(de suyo)*. A-reality consists formally in not involving this moment of the «of its own» *(de suyo)*, but rather, at most, the moment of independence. Independence is nothing more than mere extra-animity. The reality, by contrast, is the thing as something «of its own» *(de suyo)*. The thing is actualized in the intelligence, presents itself to us intellectively, as being «of its own» *(de suyo)* before being present to us. And this is illustrated even historically; more than twenty years ago I wrote that the primary 395 form according to which pre-Socratic philosophy conceived (here we are speaking of concepts) real things, as real, was by conceiving of them as something «of their own» *(de suyo)*. This it was which by difficult comparisons later and only later led to the conception of φύσις, of nature. I repeat, however, it is not, in the first place, a matter of conceiving things in this way, but rather of confronting them in apprehension according to the formality of reality. Reality is this «of their own» *(de suyo)* of things. This is not, clearly, a definition; it is, however, an explication. All explication places the thing explicated in a certain line or order. In the case of reality, it has been customary to place it in the order of concepts. Here, by contrast, we place reality in the order of immediate confrontation with things. And in this order, the reality is the «of its own» *(de suyo)*. Let us try to make this character more precise.

First of all, reality is not formally «nature;» that is, to be «of its own» *(de suyo)* does not consist in having internal operative principles. Nature is only a moment founded on the reality of the thing; formally, reality is always and only the «of its own» *(de suyo)*. A thing may be «of its own» *(de suyo)* in many different ways. All involve, as an intrinsic moment, nature. In the first place, however, not every way of being «of its own» *(de suyo)* consists in being only nature; there are things which are «of their own» *(de suyo)* not only by having nature, but further, by having other moments (personeity, etc.) articulated in union with the nature, in such a way that they are «of their own» *(de suyo)* only in this unity. Therefore, nature is only a moment of being «of its own» *(de suyo)* but nothing more. In the second place, even in those things which are «of their own» *(de suyo)* only by having nature, nature is not the synonym of reality, of the «of its own» *(de suyo)*. Nature is always and only the manner
396 in which something is «of its own» *(de suyo)*, but it is not, primarily and formally, the «of its own» *(de suyo)* itself. Nature, in a word, is not only an internal system of operative principles of the thing. On the contrary, only when these principles are intrinsic in the sense of belonging to the thing «of its own» *(de suyo)* are the principles in question nature. That is to say, the «of its own» *(de suyo)* is anterior to nature and is its ground.

Neither does the «of its own» *(de suyo)* coincide *formally* with existence; that is to say, to have reality is not formally to exist in contradistinction to being non-existent. The idea of reality remains centered for scholasticism in two theses: first, the real is the existent as existent; second, the real is *essentia* insofar as essence connotes existence aptitudinally. Taken as formal concepts, neither of these two theses is formally exact.

Let us start with the first. To be sure, everything non-existent is unreal and everything unreal is non-existent. This cannot be denied; it is not, however, sufficient, because what we are seeking here is the formal reason *(razón)* of reality. That the formal reason *(razón)* of reality is not simple existence is something which is already deduced from what scholasticism itself counterposed to *ens reale*, that is to say, *ens rationis*. The *ens rationis* is not formally the non-existent, but rather the non-existent conceived or imagined «as though it were» existent. Scholasticism saw this clearly. This, however, is equivalent to saying that the *ens rationis* has, «in its way,» a certain existence. This already indicates to us that the formal *ratio (razón)* of reality and of unreality is to be found in the *mode*, so to say, of existence rather than in mere existing. And this is, in fact, the case. To exist «only» *intra animam* is that mode of existence which consists in having only objective existence in and by intellection. Then to exist «really» is the mode of existing which consists in having existence «of itself» *(de suyo)*. And this is to be seen even more clearly if we 397 turn our attention to another type of «things» which are not formally *entia rationis* and which, nevertheless, are not real. For the Greeks, their gods appeared among men in different forms; for example, Jupiter as charioteer. What kind of reality does Jupiter-charioteer have? To be sure, Jupiter-charioteer does not exist really; Jupiter is not really a charioteer. For the Greeks, however, this figure of the charioteer is not a subjective illusion; this view is nothing more than a theory held by certain intellectuals. If men see Jupiter-charioteer it is because Jupiter has this figure and with it walks upon the earth, even though no one actually sees him. This figure, then, has, in its own way, a certain existence. Nevertheless, Jupiter-charioteer does not exist really. Why? Precisely because this figure or image does not belong to Jupiter «as his own» *(de suyo)*. In order for Jupiter really to be a charioteer it is not enough that he exist in a certain way in this figure, but it would be necessary that the existence of this figure (his existence in this figure) should belong to him as an existence «of his own» *(de suyo)*. Only then would Jupiter-charioteer really exist. But this is not the case. The real Jupiter has an existence «proper» to him; that which he has «of his own» *(de suyo)*, and which is not that of a charioteer. This proves that existence is not, without qualification, *formally* the *ratio (razón)* of reality. More than existence, what formally constitutes reality is the mode of existence: existence «of its own» *(de suyo)*. This type or mode of existence which is not «of his own» *(de suyo)* is what constitutes metaphysically the «to appear,» «appearance.» Jupiter is not really a charioteer; he does, however, appear as a charioteer, wears the form of a charioteer. This is the metaphysical dualism between appearance and reality. It is a metaphysical dualism and not a logical or psychical dualism. The appearance is more than *ens rationis* and more than something merely «logical,» as for example, the *Schein* of Hegel. The appearance is also something more than subjective illusion; at least it is not necessary to interpret it as subjective illusion, even if one adds that this illusion is grounded *in re*. And, still, it is not reality. Neither is the apparent figure, taken formally in and by itself, reality, because as appearance it has no existence «of its own» *(de suyo)*, but rather a reality «supported,» so to say, by the reality of which it is the appearance. Nothing can be «pure» appearance. Hence it is that, on the one hand, it seems to be reality, precisely because it rests on something which does have existence in its own right *(de suyo)*; on the other hand, however, it is, taken formally in and by itself, perfectly unreal. This ambivalency of the apparent figure is what we call «spectre» of reality. «Spectre» is a strictly metaphysical concept.

This metaphysical articulation between reality and appearance is what, to my way of thinking, provides us with the key necessary to understanding the «Hymn» of Parmenides correctly. The things that we see, «opinion» (δόξα), is not simple sensible illusion; neither, however, is it the «true being» (ὄν), but is rather the mere figure (μόρφη) as it «appears,» that which Parmenides and all the Greeks after him called being (ὄν), which alone truly «is», precisely, I would say, because «of its own» *(de suyo)*, the ὄν is *to be*, and nothing other than *to be*.

Thus, if things had, as we said earlier, principles which did not belong to them «of their own» *(de suyo)*, they would have neither nature nor real essence. This is the case with many «things» in the primitive mind; the things would be mere «places» *(loci)* of the presence and action of the gods or other realities. Correlatively, the existence of things as mere figure or appearance would make of them something unreal. This is also the case with many «things» in the primitive mentality which are nothing but «spectre» of the gods or of other realities. A world whose things would be nothing but «apparition» of the divinity would have in itself no real existence; it

would be a spectral world. Therefore, only when the two moments of 399
essence and existence belong to the thing «of its own» *(de suyo)* do
we formally have «reality.» The «of its own,» «in its own right» *(de
suyo)* is, then, anterior to essence and existence. We will say in
passing that this is, to my way of thinking, what makes it possible to
understand certain metaphysical speculations of India correctly.

Here the «of itself,» «in its own right» *(de suyo)* is confused
neither with the *a se* nor with the *per se*. *A se* is to have existence
from oneself; *per se* is the capacity of existence without the necessity
of a subject. «Of itself» *(de suyo)*, however, is to have existence in a
certain way *ex se*, when the existent thing is taken *hic et nunc*, that
is to say, whatever may be the ground of what exists, which is a
different question *(asunto)*. Thus, then, so far as existence is concerned, reality consists *formally* in the moment of the «of its own,»
«in its own right» *(de suyo)*; reality is, in some manner — we shall
see which — anterior to existence itself.

First, however, let us consider the second thesis: the real would
be, for scholasticism, *essentia*, insofar as it connotes aptitude for
existence. Of this connotation, however, we may ask: is it what
formally constitutes the essence, that is to say, does the essentiality
of essence reside in it? When I say of anything that it is dog or man,
here *primo et per se* I do not mean the aptitudinal character of dog
or of man for existence, but rather something «prior,» namely, that
the thing is «really» dog or man. And here «really» means that
«dogness» or humanity is what the thing is «of itself,» «in its own
right» *(de suyo)*. The thing is not really a dog or a man because
«dogness» or humanity are not something chimerical, nor because they
connote existence, but because they are something that the thing is
«of itself» *(de suyo)*; the conjunction of notes which constitute dog
or man belong «of right» *(de suyo)* to this thing. Here, then, «of
itself,» «in its own right» *(de suyo)*, is opposed to the merely stimulating; man, for example, is not what stimulates the animal in the
form of master or in any other stimulating form whatsoever, but 400
rather something which «of itself,» «in its own right» *(de suyo)*,
is man.

In a word, both existence and essence presuppose the reality.
What it this anteriority? Obviously, it is a matter neither of causal
nor of natural anteriority; it is not the case that «reality» is a cause

nor that the thing should first be real and only after that be existent and endowed with essence. It is anteriority only in the sense in which a formal *ratio (razón)* is anterior to that of which it is the formal *ratio (razón);* without existence and essence there would be no reality; what formally constitutes the reality, however, is this mode of «of itself,» «in its own right» *(de suyo)* according to which the thing is existent and is essentiated. Neither is it a question of «reality» being a term «superior» to existence and essence. This is not true, whatever may be the concepts one may have of these two moments. If one considers existence to be the act of the essence considered as physical potency of existence, that is to say, if one thinks that these two moments are really and physically distinct *in re,* it would be absurd to think of a term higher than both, because there is nothing superior to act and potency; the former is the very actuality of the latter, and this actuality is the thing itself in its unity. If it is thought, contrariwise, that existence and essence are only two different conceptualizations of one and the same thing, then the *ens reale* has both meanings «immediately,» and again no superior term is possible. All this is true. It is true, however, when one takes one's point of departure in the fact that the thing has already been conceived according to these two, essential and existential, moments; when this distinction is presupposed, there is no higher term, because reality is then always and only existence, whether actual, or potential, or aptitudinal. The fact is, however, that in the beginning of metaphysics there is no need to take one's point of departure in different conceptualizations of the moments of the real thing; quite the reverse, 401 we take our point of departure in the real thing *qua* real. Thereafter, I can consider the real thing *existentially* or I can consider it *essentially;* in both cases, however, and before this, I apprehend and consider the thing *really,* that is to say, under the aspect of what it is «in its own right,» «of itself» *(de suyo).* This prior consideration is not a *confused* apprehension; that is to say, it is not the case that «reality» is essence or existence in a confused state, in such wise that the explicit concept of the thing would involve these two moments; even less is it the case that «reality» is something which *prescinds* from these two moments, a case in which there would be neither essence nor existence; rather both moments *are included* in the «reality,» not confusedly, however, but *indistinctly;* the reality

is as much essence as existence. Every real thing, in a word, because
it is something «in its own right,» «of itself» *(de suyo)*, is, *qua* real,
formally limited with regard to all other things, including among
them the intelligent subject and its proper intellection. The reality
of any thing extends as far as its «in its own right,» «of itself» *(de
suyo)* extends, and it ends where this «in its own right» *(de suyo)*
terminates. And in this «in its own right» *(de suyo)* is included,
indistinctly, what, in a further distinction, will be existence and essence, the existential moment and the essential moment. Reality is
formally the «of itself,» the «in its own right» *(de suyo)*; formally
it is not «to exist» whether actually, potentially, or aptitudinally; it
is rather indistinctly at the same time essence and existence, because
this is the formality according to which the thing is «in its own right»
(de suyo). Only as grounded on this formality, that is, in the reality
qua reality, will we be able to discover its two moments of essence
and existence.

(3) Reality, to be sure, possesses this character of ἔργον, a
character which, if I may be permitted the expression, I would call
«ergic;» that is, it acts on other things, realizing determined operations. This «ergic» character is considered a character of what is real.
This is completely justified. Only it is nothing univocal. The ergic 402
character, in a word, is nothing but a *ratio cognoscendi*; it presupposes, therefore, that one already has a concept of the *ratio essendi*
of the real. When reality is conceived as mere existence, it is understood that a real effect is an existent effect. At this point the
difficulties begin. The effects of a real chair are real; of this there
is not the least doubt. The chair, however, *qua* chair, is not real,
because «chair» is not a character which belongs to it «of itself» *(de
suyo)*. It is a «meaning-thing,» not a «reality-thing.» This does not
proceed from the fact that the chair is artificial; a cave is not artificial;
nevertheless, the fact that it is «habitation» makes of it a «meaning-
thing.» For this reason, the effects which the chair produces are not
real if the chair is considered *qua* chair; the chair does not act
upon other things *qua* chair, but rather acts upon them, for example,
qua wood, or by reason of the form which it possesses. This is to
say, the «ergic» character presupposes the reality. And that only is
ἔργον which something produces by reason of what it is *really*; that
is, by reason of the notes which it possesses «of itself» *(de suyo)*.

All this brings us back to the point of departure of this discussion. The chair and its effects *qua* chair are *extra animam;* nevertheless, they are not, for this reason, real. Extra-animity is not reality, because something can be *extra animam* and be either stimulus-thing or meaning-thing. In neither of these two cases is it reality-thing. Reality is not «extra-animity» and nothing more, not even as extrinsic predicate, but is rather being «of itself,» «in its own right» *(de suyo).*

To sum up: no matter from which point the question is approached whether in the first way in which the real presents itself, or in its proper *ratio (razón)* (that is, reality *qua* reality) or, finally, in its ergic character, reality is not mere existence, but is, rather, something primary and irreducible which can be explained by saying that it is the «of itself,» «in its own right» *(de suyo).* It is clear that 403 one might then think that reality is taken as a synonym of what we call «to be.» This is not the case either. Reality is not formally existence; neither, however, is it formally «to be.»

b) *Reality and Being.* Scholasticism, I said at the beginning of this discussion, has intermingled the concepts of to be and of reality. On the one hand, it speaks of *esse reale* as of an existence (actual or aptitudinal). This equation, however, despite appearances, is not maintained in an inflexible manner, but rather the *esse,* as *esse,* takes on a meaning peculiar to itself. In a word, when it was sought to refine further the entitative character of essence and of existence, we have seen that scholasticism has felt itself obliged to speak of an *esse essentiae* and an *esse existentiae.* As a result, it has inevitably left an *esse* floating above essence and existence. It matters not at all that it is said that *esse* is not a common notion, but rather one which has these two meanings «immediately; » for it will always be the case that it is a question of an *esse reale,* but *esse,* and this is the decisive point, no matter how great the shadow in which the meaning of this *esse* may remain. Even more, scholasticism has spoken of the copulative or logical *esse.* Again in does not matter in what form the copula involves an *esse;* it involves it and is not identical with the *esse reale* and this is enough for us. With this there is underlined the inevitable tendency to consider the *esse,* the *to be,* as something which embraces existence, the essence, and the copula, without formally signifying any of these three moments. Nevertheless, scholasticism did not take this path. It has never admitted that *esse* is subdivided into *three esse's* which would be *esse ex aequo*, but rather, on the contrary, it energetically maintains the prerogative of the *esse reale* as existence in the order of *to be*, in such wise that the rest of the «*esse's* (the *esse* of the essence and the *esse* of the copula) would be *esse* as an analogical expansion of the *esse existentiae* as *esse*. We have already seen that both, *esse essentiae* and *existentiae*, constitute 404 *esse reale*. As a consequence, by making use of this concept of *esse reale* we will say that the scholastic conception of *esse* entails two affirmations, not explicitly formulated, but nevertheless undeniably implied: (1) that the *esse* of the copula is based on a primary and fundamental *esse*, on the *esse* of the real as *esse;* (2) that the *esse reale* itself is primary as *esse*, that is, that «reality» is a «determination» (again I employ a very inexact term in order to simplify the exposition) of «to be;» whence it follows that reality is *one* type — no matter how primary and excellent one would wish to conceive it, still *one* type — of *to be*. That is to say, not all *to be* is reality; reality, however, is reduced to *to be:* «reality» would be the primary form of «to be.» However, neither of these two theses is formally and rigorously exact. Let us examine them separately.

First of all, the thesis that copulative *to be* is grounded on a primary type of «to be.» That copulative *to be* does not rest on itself, but that it is founded either proximately or remotely on something that is real, is not only not to be denied, but is precisely what we are seeking to affirm. What happens is that we are told that the real here is an *esse reale*, substantive *to be*. And here the question lies, namely, in ascertaining whether that on which copulative *to be* is founded is formally and directly «reality» without qualification, or rather a «to be,» however substantive one might wish, but still a «to be.» So as not to linger too long on this question, we may abstract for the moment from all express allusion to scholasticism, and enter directly in *medias res*. Leaving to the second thesis the examination of the idea of substantive *to be* or *esse reale* in itself, what we ask, then, is the following: Is the copulative to be founded on a substantive *to be* qua *to be?* Naturally, we do not have to concern ourselves with the copulative in all its extension; that is, embracing those affirmations which fall back on mere beings of reason *(entia rationis);* the only thing important for us here is the copula of those affirmations

405 which refer to real objects, as when I say «this man, Peter, is white.» We restrict ourselves, then, to this last type of affirmation. In them — and in this they coincide with all the rest — the «is» is something which concerns the objective meaning of my affirmative intellection. It is not exhausted, however, in this objective meaning, but rather it reaches to that of which I affirm that it «is,» to the *res objecta*, to the objectual. Objectivity (truth) is not to be confused with objectuality.

In the affirmations in which we are interested, the *res qua objecta* is based on the previous presentation of the real thing as real. This reality of the thing is what, in the first instance, belongs in an intrinsic manner to the integrity of the intellection; it is, in a word, its immediate ground and its direct formal term. My affirmative intention, and with it the copulative *to be*, are grounded directly on the reality and not on a presumptive substantive «to be;» that is, they are not grounded on the «to be Peter» or «to be white,» but on «white Peter.» The interpretation, which we are now discussing, thinks quite the contrary. We have, on the one hand, «to be Peter,» and, on the other, «to be white.» Formally, these two beings have nothing to do with each other: to be Peter is not to be white, and *vice versa*. The copula, however, would be a species of «autonomization» of the moment «to be,» common to the two terms and would express (according to these interpretations) that the «to be» Peter is found to be affected by the «to be» white, or that «to be white» consists in «to be Peter.» The *to be* of each terminus would be modified by the *to be* of the other, by which «to be» takes on a certain autonomy. The result is that the substantive to be of Peter and that of white are converted into the complex of substantive *to be's* or, better, into the «to be» of the complex: the συμπλοκή or complex of «to be Peter» and «to be white.» Such would be the copula: a «to be» based on substantive «to be.» Such, however, is not the case. The copula

406 directly expresses a complex, but not a complex of *to be's*, but rather, of real moments of the real as real, and not the real as «to be.» This is to say, it expresses «white Peter» and not the «to be white» of «to be Peter». The reality, and not the substantive to be, is the previous ground, the *prius* of the objectivity of the affirmations and of the copulative to be. The real complex which the copula directly expresses is not a complex of *to be's*, but a real complex or structure

qua real. There is, to be sure, a complex in the affirmation, but the affirmation itself is not complex. The judgment consists formally only in the affirmative intention; the complex is that to which the judgment refers. This real complex is ordinarily intellected in a direct manner, and is expressed by the verbs in all their voices and aspects. Only when the real is excessively complex does it turn into *res objecta* and my intellection then unfolds itself into the presentation of the real complex and into the affirmative intention, into «it is.» To express this new «to be» recourse is had to some verbs of reality; then, however, these verbs have lost their meaning of reality and take on a merely copulative meaning. The copula arises, then, directly from a «de-realization» unfolding in the intellection of the reality, and not from a presumptive «to be» which would seem to be hidden in every verb, as though, for example, «to «walk» would be «to be walking; » this would be a pseudo-logical artifice. When I say «Peter walks,» to walk is a real element in Peter. The copula proceeds, then, from an unfolding of the reality and not from a complex of two «to be's,» the «to be» of Peter and the «to be» of to walk, nor from the analogical expansion of these beings. This is the reason why the copula terminates in the reality, even though, for this reason, I have had to make a *res objecta* of the real. The reality is the *prius* of the copulative *to be* and not the reverse, as though reality were a type of *to be*, namely, real *to be*.

Let us say as an illustration — and nothing more than an illustra- 407 tion — of this philosophical interpretation, that historical comparative linguistics shows us that this is the origin of the copula in our Indo-European languages. In Greek, for example, some verbs, such as μένειν, ὑπάρχειν, πέλειν, γίγνεσθαι, φύειν, etc., are verbs of reality; they come, however, to *acquire* a copulative sense which before they did not have. These verbs, in a word, employed by themselves with a subject, formally mean a moment of the real. When, however, it was necessary to designate the reality of the subject with some important additional note, that is, with a further noun, the moment of reality remained centered in the nominal complex, and the verb lowered its meaning of reality to express the simple affirmation of the unity of the signified complex. Such was the historical origin of the copula. The same thing happened with the proper verb *asmi, ahmi*, εἶναι, *esse*. Originally, it was only a verb of reality which signified, not *to be*, but existence. By the same process, it was converted by small stages (this should be underlined) into a copula, into «to be.» However, εἶναι, *esse*, has no more relation with *to be* than, for example, had πέλειν as a verb of reality with πέλειν as copula: the copulative value of *esse* is an acquisition and not something which lay hidden in the «to exist.» What happens is that by a super-position of both meanings, there was produced that «mirrorism» which consisted in thinking that «to exist» was a meaning of «to be,» as if «to exist» was «to be existent.» This was the origin of the expression *esse existentiae* and of other similar expressions.

That this is a «mirrorism,» that is to say, that the direct intellection of the real is not a «specialization» of the meaning of «to be,» becomes clear from another linguistic fact that still persists in our languages, namely, the nominal phrase. As is known, primitively (as 408 can be seen, for example, in the vedic and in the avestic) the nominal phrase is not the elipsis of a «to be» which is read between the lines, but is rather an original and an originative type of strictly «a-verbal» phrase; only in the more advanced stages of some languages, for example in sanskrit, will it be possible to speak of elipsis. The nominal phrase expresses the real complex directly and without copulative verb. It is true that it is found limited to decisions, identifications, etc.; these cases, however, are precisely those in which the purpose is to express the nude reality in all its force. And precisely then it is expressed without the verb «to be,» merely by the nominal complex.

The affirmative intellection, then, involves three moments together: the reality, the copulative «to be» or affirmative affirmation, and the truth. Of these, however, the reality is the primary and grounding moment, not only of the truth but of the copulative «to be» as well. The copulative «to be» is not grounded on a «to be» of the real, upon a substantive «to be,» but rather on the substantivity itself, on the reality as such. The copulative «to be,» then, is one thing, and the reality, another. Their possible unity, we have seen, does not reside in a «to be» masked in the «reality,» but rather in the unity of unfolding in the intellection. At least, naturally, if one were to say that «reality» is simply the *esse reale*. But this is inexact. It is the second of the two theses that we have to examine.

The expression *esse reale* comprises two terms: *esse* and *reale*. In what relation are they found in the unity of what they signify? On the one hand, *esse* seems to add nothing to *reale*. As Aristotle already says, ἄνθρωτος and ὤν ἄνθρωπος *(Meta.* 1003 b 28) are the same (ταυτόν). On the other hand, the two terms *esse* and *reale* seem undeniably necessary to designate what they signify; otherwise, it would have been enough to speak only of to be or only of reality. The *esse* belongs to ἄνθρωτος not only insofar as ὤν (participle) but also nominally, as simple εῖναι. This indicates that *esse* possesses a certain nuance proper to itself. As I said above, it is not 409 necessary, in this case, to say that it is a term which «immediately» has these two meanings. The *esse reale* as *esse* involves this apparent antinomy of adding nothing to *reale* and of possessing, nevertheless, something which, without going further, we may call, a nuance proper to itself. What then is the *esse reale*, the substantive «to be» as being?

One might think what is usually said, to wit, that reality is the eminent mode of «to be.» But let us examine this way of thinking a bit more attentively. For example, what is it to be iron? To be iron means, on the one hand, that the thing has such and such qualities. But these notes are not «to be» iron but are «iron» alone; therefore nothing which makes any allusion to «to be.» And the same happens if what one wants to say is that the iron exists. We have already seen it: essence and existence are simple distinct moments of something indistinctly or undifferentiatedly previous, the reality. The reality is previous to the duality: «essence-existence,» because both the one and the other are exactly moments of the real. Hence it is that the essence is not to be understood *in the first place* by way of its aptitudinal «relation» to existence, but rather, must be understood in a different perspective, namely, as something in and by itself as reality. And this reality of the iron, or better, the «real» iron, is not the «to be» of the iron. The real, *qua* real, is not included in the *esse*. And this is not to be changed. However, the expression «to be iron» can be understood in another sense, not in the sense that it is iron but in the sense that the iron *is*. We need insist only in passing on the fact that here «to be» does not mean that in which the reality consists, but rather that I take the word in its complete amplitude: the mere «to be» which embraces each and all of the moments of the

real. This «to be» is not the formal moment of the iron reality, but
410 rather something like an «affirmation» *(sit venia verbo)* of the iron
reality in its particular iron reality; therefore, something in one or
another form, grounded on this reality. Naturally, it is not an affirmation in the intellection. «To be» is something independent of the
intellection; the things themselves «are.» Therefore, «to be» is a
moment of the real; it is an actuality of the real, which belongs to it
by itself, even if there should be no intellection of it. As actuality
of the real, however, it is a «further» actuality of it; that is to say, it
is the actuality of something which is «anterior» as reality. The reality
is the «of its own» *(de suyo);* and only because the thing is «of itself»
(de suyo) can it re-actualize this its reality «of itself» *(de suyo)*. And
this re-actualization is the «to be.» Then the thing, already «of itself»
(de suyo), also «is.» And this is true, not only for what concerns the
iron, but also for what concerns the intellection of the iron; to
apprehend something as «to be» *in re*, presupposes the presentation
of the thing as reality. Before intellecting the thing as actually being,
and in order to be able to intellect it as being, the intelligence apprehends the thing as something real. No matter where you take up
the question (whether from the side of things themselves or from the
side of the intellecting of them) the reality is anterior to the «to be,»
and the «to be» is an actuality of the already real in and by itself.
Supposing then that the iron, already real, also «is; » then the iron
itself as naked reality, remains affected by this its ulterior actuality
which is «to be.» This naked reality which we call iron, insofar as it is
enveloped in this second actuality of it, which is «to be,» takes on the
character of something which «is iron; » the real iron is now «to be
iron.» Therefore, by the very fact that the iron «is,» the iron itself
turns out «to be iron.» Here we have the origin of the substantive
«to be.» Hence flow two fundamental consequences: (a) Reality is
411 not the «to be» *par excellance*, as though reality were inscribed in
the first place «within» «to be; » rather that the reality as already
real is the ground of the «to be; » it is the «to be» which is inscribed
«within» the reality without being identified formally with it. It will
be asked what is this that I call «further actuality.» We will see it in
summary manner immediately; for the moment, it is enough to have
indicated it by saying that it is like an affirmation or re-affirmation of
the reality in its reality. There is no *esse reale*, real being, but rather

what I would call *realitas in essendo*, the reality in its «to be», or better still, the reality «in to be.» *Ultimately*, there is no substantive «to be,» but rather naked substantivity. Things are, in the first instance, reality and not «to be». The real, however, insofar as it «is,» is precisely what is called «being» *(ente)*. Therefore, the real, as real, is not «being» *(ente)* but simply «reality.»

In having said that «to be» is a further act of the real, but that it belongs formally to the real itself, it also remains said that although «reality» is not «to be,» nevertheless, what we call «to be» is not to be diluted into a series of presumed connotations, but rather, possesses a «nuance» proper to itself which is strictly unitary. The antinomy which, at the beginning of this discussion, I stated about «to be», now is resolved by maintaining the two terms, but on distinct or different planes. On the primary plane, that is, on the plane of reality, «to be» adds nothing to the real; there is not «to be,» but rather unencumbered reality. On the plane of an ulterior act, however, not only is there «to be,» but this «to be» also has a proper unitary character. Scholasticism, in its effort to reduce the reality to «to be,» has diluted, as Aristotle did, what we call «to be» into different types of «to be.» By having distinguished here in a certain manner (we will see what manner) «to be» and reality, «to be» takes on a strict unity proper to itself. «To be» is not the same as reality, but «to be» is something proper and unitary.

This unity of the «to be» might lead us to think that the transcendental is then the «to be» itself. This is Heidegger's thesis. 412 We shall concern ourselves with it after we have spoken of being in a positive manner. For the moment, it is enough to repeat that the «to be» is a «further» act of the real, as already real; «to be» is grounded on the reality. And, therefore, the transcendental is not the «to be,» but rather the «reality.»

Let us sum up the path over which we have come. Copulative «to be» is not a primary, and primarily, an expression of the «to be» of the reality, but of the reality itself. In its turn, the substantive «to be» is not something primary, but something grounded on the reality. As a consequence, there does not exist a unity of «to be» which will embrace, analogically, copulative «to be,» the «to be» of the essence and the «to be» of existence, but rather, there is no more unity than the unity of the reality, the unity of the «of itself,» which actualizes itself further in two formally *independent* ways, which are alien to each other: substantive «to be» (a moment of the reality as a further act of it) and the copulative «to be,» the affirmative intention (moment of the complex intellection). In even more complex forms of intellection, the copulative «to be» may also express substantive «to be.» This, however, does not stand in opposition to what we are saying, first, because here I have referred only to the primary structure of intellection and, second, because, if the copula can express, and sometimes does express, the substantive «to be,» this is precisely because it expresses the reality in the first place; and since this reality involves the «to be» as its ulterior act, it follows that the affirmative intention at times can and must also express the «to be.» It is not necessary here to enter into further detail concerning the precise articulation between the copulative «to be,» the reality, and its «to be.» What has been said suffices.

This discussion with scholasticism about the idea of the transcendental leads to a decisive conclusion, namely that it is necessary to distinguish not only between being *(ente)* and «to be,» but also
413 between reality, being *(ente)* and «to be» *(ser)*. «Reality» is not a type of «to be» but rather is the thing as an «of itself» *(de suyo);* it is simply the real thing. «To be» is a «further» act of that which is already real *in re.* «Being» is that which is already real insofar as it «is.» As a consequence, the transcendental order is not the order of objectuality; neither is it the order of the entity *(ordo entis ut sic);* neither is it the order of «to be,» but rather it is the order of reality, *ordo realitatis ut sic.* This does not hinder us, when it is not a question of employing these terms in their most formal acceptation, from continuing to use the words being, entitative, etc.; this is what we have been doing all through this study. It should, however, be clearly understood that, speaking formally, they are only further moments of the real. Once this has been understood, nothing prevents us from looking at the structure of our languages, in which those terms or words are many times unavoidable.

To sum up, reality is the «character» (we have to express ourselves in some manner) of things as «of themselves» *(de suyo)*. This character is primary in things and, *consequently,* first in intellection.

(a) *It is primary in things.* It is, in a word, that according to which things are things; reality is what formally constitutes that which we call things. Things begin and end where the «of itself» (*el «de suyo»*) begins and ends.

(b) *It is primary in intellection.* Man is open to things by way of his sensibility; that is, he has access to things, in the first instance, by sensing them. Every theory of the intelligence necessarily comes equipped with a theory of sensibility. Pure sensation opens us to things, and presents them to us as mere stimuli independent of the act of sensing; they are stimuli-things. The formality of things, insofar as they are purely sensed, is «stimulativity.» This pure sensibility is what the animal has; but man also has it. Man is not only that which distinguishes him from the animal, but also that which he shares with the animal. Man, however, senses things not only as 414 stimuli, but also as realities; the stimulus itself is ordinarily sensed as a stimulating reality, that is, as a «real» stimulus. The opening to things, as realities, is what formally constitutes intelligence. The particular formality of intelligence is «reality.» Now this formality is not something primarily «conceived» but rather something «sensed»; man not only conceives that what he has sensed is real; he senses the very reality of the thing. Hence it is that this mode of sensing things is an intrinsically intellective mode. And just as sensibility is not then pure, but intellective, for the same reason, its intellection is not pure, but sentient. «To intellect» and «to sense» are essentially distinct and irreducible; they do, however, constitute a metaphysical structural unity, sentient intelligence, which we shall not try to elucidate here. This expression does not mean that the intelligence does not intellect anything except the things which the senses offer to it; neither does it mean that the things sensed are a sensible «knowledge,» an «information,» which even the animal possesses (in this sense even Aristotle himself sometimes attributed noetic characteristics to the αἴσθησις); it means that sensibility and intelligence constitute, in their irreducible difference, a structure of apprehension which is metaphysically one, in virtue of which the act of apprehension is one and unique: the sentient apprehension of the real.

In order to understand the inner character of this sentient apprehension of the real correctly, it is necessary to fix our ideas, even though only rapidly. In modern philosophy it is customary to call what is sensed (for example, colors, sounds, etc.) «sensible impressions.» This expression, however, suffers from a serious equivocation,

because it immediately suggests the idea that these «qualities» are no more than subjective impressions. But this idea is false. These
415 qualities in themselves are not impressions, but the thing sensed in the impression. Impression is not the designation of a sensed object, but rather is the designation of the mode in which something is sensed. Impression not only is not something subjective, that is, something which does not have any other character nor any other term than that of the subject, but rather that, on the contrary, impression is the way of being open to something which is not subjective, to what is sensed itself. In the impression there is present to me «impressively» something which in itself in not impression. Let this be presupposed; in pure sensation, that which is sensed, *qua* sensed, is sensed in the formality «stimulus;» and the mode according to which the stimulus-thing is present to the sentient (subject) is impression. In sentient intellection (or intellective sensing), because it is sentient, that which is apprehended is apprehended also, in the first instance, in the mode of impression. The only difference is that what makes the impression is not only stimulating qualities, but «real» stimulating qualities. Which means that in sentient intellection, the impression has two moments: one, the moment of sensed quality; the other, the moment of its real formality. Both moments belong to the thing which is sentiently present to me; and the mode in which they are present to me is, for both moments, impression. This is to say that in sentient intellection there is sensed, in the mode of impression, not only its qualitative content but also its proper formality, «reality.» This formality, insofar as it is sensed in impression, is what I have, for many years in my courses, called «impression of reality;» an impression which not only is not subjective, but which also presents us with the formality «reality» as something belonging to the thing sensed. It is not a second impression numerically added to the impression of the sensed qualities, but the impression of the proper formality of the qualities sensed. If I call it impression of reality I do so to distinguish this moment of impression of the sentient intellection from what is usually called sensible impressions, which are nothing but qualities; that is, that
416 the reality *qua* reality is originatively sensed, given in the form of impression. By reason of its quality, what is sensed is constitutively specific; this is the reason why pure sensation opens on stimuli-things

and remains situated in a limited order of things. By contrast, the impression of reality, as I have always said, is unspecified. This negative term now takes on a positive meaning: the impression of reality is constitutively transcendental. When a subject intellectively senses any stimulating quality whatsoever, the intelligence is open to the reality-things and, therefore, is situated not only among specifically determined things, but in reality, that is, beyond all specificity, in the dimension of the transcendental; open, therefore, not to limited things, but to any thing whatsoever. For this reason, the first intelligible, *primum cognitum*, in primarity of adequation *(primitate adequationis)* is the sensed real. And in it, the *primum cognitum* in primarity of origin *(primitate originis)* is the reality in impression (impression of reality). Only afterwards, the intelligence forms concepts, not only of the sensed qualities, but also of the sensed reality *qua* real, that is, the concept of reality. I repeat, however, that it is not the case that the senses sense only things, and that the intelligence afterwards conceives them to be real, but rather that in sentient intellection the thing is *already* sensed as real, and the conceiving intelligence conceives as real that which the sentient intelligence has already formally sensed as real. The transcendental is already given in the impression of reality. That which is first and formally intellected sentiently and that in which all of the concepts of the intelligence are resolved, is not being but reality. Contrary to what scholasticism, in its post-classical phase, has been saying for more than half a century, the intelligence is not the «faculty of being,» but the «faculty of reality.»

This does not mean, I must again insist, that the formality 417 «reality» consists in the way in which things are present to the intelligence. Quite the contrary: we have just said that «reality» is, before all else, the primary element of things in and by themselves. And this is not a mere a s s e r t i o n . Because in the sentient intellection, in the impression of reality we have the real present to us, not only as something independen† of the act (this happens also with the stimulus) but the real is present to us as something whose presence is c o n s e q u e n t on that which it already is «in and of itself» *(de suyo)*. It is what I have expressed by saying that the real is present to us, but as something which is *prius* to its presentation itself; it is the very mode of being presented, which means the primarity of the intellection of the real in its reality is based on the primariness of the reality as something «in and of itself» *(de suyo)*.

With these remarks I have made clear, rapidly and with large strokes, what I understand by «transcendental» *qua* transcendental. The transcendental, however, is an «order.» What, then, is the transcendental order, not *qua* transcendental, but *qua* order? It is this second aspect of the question which we must discuss with scholasticism.

3. *The Idea of a Transcendental Structure*

Let us clarify, before all else, what we understand by order. Order does not mean here the dominion, the line or direction according to which we consider reality, that is, transcendental consideration in contrast to mere consideration of suchness *(consideración talitativa)*. By order I understand, rather, the very structure of reality in its transcendentality, which it possesses by reason of its transcenden-
418 tality. Order means, therefore, internal structure. It is in this precise sense that we ask whether scholasticism describes a strict-order in the transcendental and in what this order may consist.

Scholasticism has called this order «general modes of to be;» that is to say, those modes which belong to every being by reason of its status as being alone. These modes are the six classical transcendentals: *ens, res, unum, aliquid, verum, bonum*. This is not a matter of mere enumeration; rather, among these entitative moments there exists an internal grounding. Scholasticism, then, undeniably admits a strict transcendental order. The problem resides in how it understands this order.

The transcendentals are customarily divided into two groups; for the purposes of the present discussion, however, it is better to divide them into three groups. First of all: *ens* and *res*. Strictly speaking, these are not two transcendental properties or attributes; rather, for scholasticism, they are only two «expressions» of a single thing, the being. *Ens* means that the thing «is,» and *res* means «that» which the thing is; that is to say, its ordination to *esse*. Without this aptitudinal ordination to *esse* the thing would be «nothing.» Therefore, *ens* and *res* are perfectly synonymous and express, with two words, not a transcendental property but the transcendental itself. After this, there comes a second group: the *unum* and the *aliquid*. For scholasticism these are, formally, nothing but negations. *Aliquid* is nothing but the *quid* insofar as it is not another *quid*. *Unum*, in itself, is nothing but the negation of division. To be sure, for many this is nothing but the formal *ratio (razón)* of the transcendentality of the one and they, therefore, add that the one connotes or positively includes the particular undivided entity of the *ens;* however that may be, the fact remains that the formal *ratio (razón)* of the unity is indivision. There remains, finally, the third group, *verum* and *bonum;* these are formally positive, but extrinsic, moments of the entity, that is, those moments according to which the entity as entity is capable of being intellected and appetitized by an intelligent and willing entity. Hence it results that, properly speaking, the transcendental «order» *qua* order cannot be positively anything save truth and goodness. The negative moments, precisely because they are negative, posit nothing *in re*. And since *ens* and *res* are synonyms, it follows, as we have just said, that *in re* there is only *ens* with two properties or attributes (we shall not enter upon this important discussion because it would lead us too far afield at this point), truth and goodness. At most, insofar as the *unum* connotes the particular undivided entity of the *ens*, it might seem a transcendental property. And then, granting this concession, the *ens* as *ens* would have the following three properties or attributes: *unum, verum, bonum*. These three notes are not merely juxtaposed, but are found intrinsically based each on the preceding: every *bonum* is based on a *verum* and every *verum* is based on an *unum*. To the degree that the entity has these three notes intrinsically established among themselves, in this manner, the transcendental is, in the scholastic view, a strict order or structure in the sense already given of these terms.

All this is, indeed, fundamental truth; truth, however, which demands further discussion. What we are asking, in a word, is not whether this order, as it has been described, is given effectively, but whether this order responds, without qualification, sufficiently to the idea of a transcendental structure, that is, a *structure* of the real *qua* real. This is the question. Let us examine it step by step, in order to enter directly upon the development of the theme.

First of all, *ens* and *res*. We are told that these are absolutely synonymous. Is this exact? The reply depends on the idea which one holds of «to be.» If «to be» is reality and reality is existence, then

420 the formal identity between *ens* and *res* is evident. We have, however, already seen, first, that reality is not existence whether actual or aptitudinal, but is, formally, the «in and of itself» *(de suyo);* and second, that reality and «to be» are not the same, for «to be» is an «ulterior» act of the real. With the reservation that I will later give an explanation in positive terms of this point, I have distinguished reality, «to be,» and being. As a consequence, though synonyms in the scholastic sense, I believe, nevertheless, that, effectively, they are not synonyms, but that «to be» is grounded on «reality.»

In the second place, the negative notes: *unum* and *aliquid.* We are told that they are mere negativity. Is this, however, exact? A negation is something which is given only in the mode in which the being is considered, in its objective concept, but not in itself. It will be said, however, that the transcendentals are, *in re*, nothing but the thing itself. Granting all this, their distinction has a ground *in re.* What is this ground? This is the question, and scholasticism itself has perceived the difficulty of the problem both with respect to the *unum* and with respect to the *aliquid.*

What is, effectively, the *unum* for scholasticism? Its formal *ratio (razón)*, we are told, is mere indivision; since, however, this proves insufficient from any point of view, it is added that this negation «connotes» or «includes» something positive, the positive undivided entity of the *ens.* Is it, then, a question of a mere connotation? That is to say, what is understood here by connotation and inclusion? This question is not a mere dialectical subtlety. For, in a word, if it is indeed true that, as a transcendental property of the being, the unity of «indivision» is something formally negative, it is no less true that this «in-division» is the metaphysical consequence of the *positive entity*, which is positively «one,» of the *ens*, and that, for this reason, this positive entity, although it may not be the «property,» the *unum* itself, nevertheless, fulfills a true transcendental «function,» since it

421 is what determines the unity as «property.» We reach the same conclusion, if it be admitted that the *unum* is not formally only a negation, but includes or signifies the undivided «entity» of the being. For, in the first place, there remains unshaken that which tells us what this «inclusion» itself is; and above all, because it always turns out that what is included is the entity of the being insofar as it is «undivided,» that is to say, a negation. The positive character of the

intrinsic indivision of the being is what fulfills a transcendental function ordered to the unity. What that inclusion may be will be clarified only on the basis of this function. What is this function? This question should have been posited by itself; it is not enough to say that the unity, as transcendental property, «connotes» or «includes» the positive entity of the being. The negativity of the *unum* is not, then, transcendentally sufficient.

The case with the *aliquid* is the same. The *aliud*, the otherness of the *quid*, is, consequently, something negative. On what, however, does this alterity fall back? Scholasticism itself lacked a precise conception on this point. It was customary to say, at times, that the *aliud* opposed the *quid*, set the *quid* over against, *nothingness;* that is to say, that *aliquid* is *non-nihil.* But this is a mere verbal conceptualization: the nothing, precisely because it is nothing, is not even a term to which reality can be opposed or which can be distinguished from reality. To do so would be to make nothing «something.» For this reason, others have thought that the *aliud* is another *quid;* and in that case the «aliquidity» would be the mere consequence of the *unum:* the division from all the rest. Then, however, it would not, in the strict sense, be a transcendental property in the scholastic sense, because the *aliquid* understood in this way rests on the multitude of beings, a multitude which, in some manner, belongs to the formal *ratio* of the being. The transcendentality of the *aliquid* is, then, extremely problematical. The decisive point, however, to my way of seeing the matter, is not this difficulty, but rather the 422 metaphysical necessity of this multitude which — equally with the positive entity in the case of the *unum* — if indeed it does not belong to the being as a transcendental «property,» nevertheless, fulfills a transcendental «function.» Within the multiple, in a word, the alterity of the *aliquid* is given only in a previously determined line, the line of being. In this line, there is the precise moment of the *alter* being referred to the *unum* precisely in order to be able to be *alter.* And this «reference» (let us call it this for the moment) is a strict «transcendental function,» since it is the possibility of a transcendental property.

As a consequence, the negativity of the *unum* and of the *aliquid* involve, transcendentally, what we have called «function.» It is the insufficiency of the negative in the transcendental order.

There remains the third group: *verum* and *bonum*. Save for some isolated scholastics, for whom these properties are merely negative, practically the whole of scholasticism understands that we have here positive moments of the being (el ente). Since, however, nothing can be added positively to the being (since it formally transcends all its modes and differences), it follows that these two moments are positive solely because they are two extrinsic relations of the being, as such to a determined being, the ψυχή, the intelligent and volitional soul. Here, however, two serious questions arise. Scholasticism itself stated the first of them. There is nothing in the being as being which includes in its formal *ratio (razón)* the existence of an intelligent and volitional entity. As a consequence, if the relation to this being is extrinsic, it is not possible to see how truth and goodness could be transcendental properties of the being; since that intelligent and volitional being does not exist, the being as such would have no reason *(razón)* either of truth or of goodness; nevertheless, it would
423 have a reason *(razón)* of *entity*. St. Thomas himself recognizes this to be the case, even when he is making reference to the intelligence and the will of the Creator: if, *per impossible*, he tells us, the Creator were not intelligent and volitive, the creature would have indeed a *ratio (razón)* of being, but no similar principle of truth or goodness. The transcendentality of truth and goodness, consequently, in scholasticism itself, is obscure and full of difficulties. Many are of the opinion, effectively, that only on the basis of the proof of the existence of creation, that is, only on the supposition of the «transcendental relation» of the finite being to an infinite intelligent and volitive being, would it be possible to speak of the *verum* and the *bonum* as transcendental «properties.» Others, and with good reason, think that even should the relationship to an intelligence and a will be extrinsic, nevertheless the *verum* and the *bonum* belong intrinsically to the being as such. Since the intelligence and the will of which one is speaking here are not an actual intelligence and will, but merely possible, what is being said is that *if* this intelligence and this will did exist, there would be truth and goodness because, whether or not there are intelligences and wills, the being, as such, is intrinsically intelligible and appetible; the intelligibility and the appetibility are the entity itself as such. All this is certain; however, both in the first and in the second conception, these transcendental

properties involve an extrinsic relation to an intelligence and a will (whether as transcendental relation or as possible relation). And in the measure in which this relation is extrinsic, the character of transcendental «property» of truth and goodness remain obscured. Nevertheless, not this, but a second question, is decisive.

This second question is the following: the intelligence and the will of the intelligent and volitive being are not formally attributes 424 or characteristics of its entity as such; that is, intelligence and will are not transcendental moments of the intelligent and volitional entity, but moments of its special mode of «to be,» moments of its «suchness.» Hence, they are not transcendental «properties.» Nevertheless, they have a strict transcendental «function» (both the transcendental relation and the possible relation are nothing else than this), since it is only with regard to the intelligence and the will that the being, as such, has the transcendental properties of truth and goodness. Once more, as with regard to the negative transcendental properties, there appears here, in the case of the positive properties, the same problem of the transcendental «function,» a function by which, and only by which, the being, as such, possesses transcendental «properties.» This problem of the transcendental function merits being stated in and by itself.

To sum up, a close inspection of the transcendentals of scholasticism has made us see that in the transcendental order *qua* order we encounter, on the one hand, the transcendental itself, the *res* (not the *ens*) and, on the other, a transcendental structure of reality, a structure which consists, not only in certain transcendental «properties,» but also in certain transcendental «functions.» Only by bringing the question to a focus in this way will we be able to know what that is which we call «to be,» and leave the problem of the transcendental character of essence, which is the objective toward which this entire discussion is directed, formulated in a precise manner.

What, then, is the transcendental order, *qua* order? Every real thing can be considered from two points of view. On the one hand, each thing is «such and such» a determined thing; on the other hand, however, it is a «real» thing; that is, it is something «in and of itself» *(de suyo)*. The first aspect of the thing is the order of «suchness;» the second is the «transcendental» order. These two orders are different, but they are not juxtaposed orders, since «reality» is 425 a character which transcends all moments, modes, and differences of the «suchness» of the real. They are not, however, absolutely independent. Precisely because «reality» is a merely transcendental character, not only is it implied in every moment of «suchness» but also, reciprocally, the suchness «determines» (let us put it this way) *in re* the properties of the real as real; that is, its transcendental properties. And since these properties are not identical, without qualification, with suchness, it follows that the suchness itself can be considered under two aspects: according to what it is in itself, and according to that which it determines transcendentally. And this latter is what I call, thematically, «transcendental function.» This function is not necessarily found limited to the reality of the thing which is «such;» there are, in a word, «suchnesses,» intelligence and will, for example, which fulfill a transcendental function, not only with regard to the intelligent and willing reality, as reality, but also with respect to all reality as reality. A transcendental function is, then, the function by which a suchness constitutes the transcendental properties of the reality. In virtue of this function, the reality, as reality, not only possesses certain transcendental properties «materially,» so to say, but is also «formally» a true transcendental *structure.*

Its description in not a question of simple speculation or of a dialectical combination of mere concepts. Quite the contrary: since the transcendental structure is determined by the transcendental function of the suchness, it is to the concrete analysis of the latter that one must turn one's gaze in order to discover this structure. It is not my undertaking or purpose to expound the transcendental 426 structure in a complete manner, but I am going to limit myself to those concepts which are necessary for the transcendental consideration of essence.

Things, such as they are in reality, are, before all else, things, reals, each one in itself and by itself; further, however, these things are found really linked among themselves in one form or another. Both these moments of «suchness» have a transcendental function; it does not matter, as I have already indicated in our earlier discussion and as we are going to see presently with greater exactness — that the multitude does not belong to the formal concept of reality. This double moment lays bare to us two aspects of the transcendental structure. One is the transcendental structure of each real thing, in and by itself; the other, the transcendental structure determined by the linking of each thing with the rest. We shall postpone until later the consideration of the first structural aspect because it is precisely the problem of «essence and reality.» We shall now say something, and only something, about the second.

Real things, I say, are linked with one another; stated in another way, they form a totality. This totality is not an extrinsic addition of real things, but an intrinsic totality, what the Greeks called σύστημα. This totality does not have the character of mere connection or order; that is, a vinculation of the things such that the active or passive operations of each thing are found in interdependence with the operations of the rest. This is true, but it is not the primary truth. The primary factor resides in the fact that this operative connection is found to be based in the very constitution of things, a constitution according to which each thing is formally what it is in reality in function of the constitution of the rest of things, other things. It is not a question, then, of an «operative» connection but of a «constitutive» characteristic. (Here I take constitution and constitutive in their usual sense and not in the exact acceptation in which I have been employing these terms in this study.) This character is not consequential to each thing; rather it belongs 427 intrinsically to its formal reality, in such wise that each piece of a watch is by its constitution something the reality of which is formally a function of the constitution of the other pieces, or the rest of the pieces. This intrinsic and formal moment of the constitution of a real thing, according to which this thing is a «function» of the rest, is what I have been in the habit of calling «respectivity.» Respectivity is not, properly speaking, a «relation.» And this for two reasons. First, because every relation is based on what the related things already are; respectivity, by contrast, determines the very constitution of the related things, not, to be sure, in their character of reality pure and simple, but in their mutual connection; respectivity is antecedent to relation. Second, because respectivity is not, *in re*, something different from each real thing, but rather is identified with it, without, however, the latter ceasing, for this reason, to be respective.

On this basis, the respectivity is a character which concerns «that which» things are in reality, their «suchness»: each thing is as it is, but «respectively.» This «respectivity» at the level of «suchness» is what I have formally called κόσμος, *cosmos*. This cosmic respectivity, however, possesses a precise «function»: it determines, in real things, a way of being real *qua* real. Respectivity, then, not in the order of «suchness,» but in the order of reality as such, is what I have called *world.* World is not the simple totality of real things (the cosmos is also this), but the totality of real things by reason of their character of reality, that is, as real: respectivity as mode or character of reality. World and cosmos are not identical either formally or materially. They are not formally identical because even if the cosmos were of a character different from that which it actually is, the world, nevertheless, would be the same as it is now. Neither are they materially identical, because in principle there might be «*cosmoi*» which were cosmically independent among themselves, but all would coincide in being real and therefore would constitute, in a certain way (we will not at this point enter on the problem how) one single world.

428

This concept of world is the primary and fundamental concept. The other concepts of world presuppose this one. Contemporary philosophy (Heidegger) customarily understands by world that in which and from which human existence understands itself and encounters (by understanding) the rest of things; that is, what we call «our world» or «my world.» The world, however, in this sense, is grounded on the world as respectivity of the real *qua* real. For this «our» and this «my» express, not the originative character of the world, but the world as the horizon of the system of possibilities of man; they express the appropriation of the world in «sketch» *(bosquejo, Entwarf),* but not the world itself. Only because man is a reality constituted *qua* reality in respectivity to the rest of things, that is, only because man is already «mundane» as reality, can he make the world «his own,» in the existential and vital sense, as «sketch» *(bosquejo).* Worldliness, mundanity, is nothing else than the respectivity of the real as real; it has nothing to do with man. Finally, we have to note that, if respectivity does not formally concern the character of reality, what we will have is either merely biological respectivity, the «medium» of living things, or the mere cosmic «environment» as a field of action and reaction. Neither medium nor environment are, however, formally world; world, I repeat, is the respectivity of the real in its formality of reality.

We have here the transcendental «function» of the cosmos (suchness) in the order of reality as such: to determine a world. What is the character of this function? Mundanity is a moment or note of the reality of every thing as real. It is not something strictly «added» to the reality of each thing, but is identical *in re* with its reality; and nevertheless, it is strictly a property or note of the real *qua* real: it is its pure respectivity in the order of reality as reality. Therefore, world is a transcendental character of reality as such and the «function» of the cosmos is, as a consequence, a strictly transcendental function. But this must be clarified.

First of all, the function of the cosmos is strictly transcendental. The fact that the cosmos is always and only of a determined «suchness» is no obstacle to this notion, because this same circumstance is found in the intelligent and volitional being, and, nevertheless, its function is strictly transcendental. The possible multitude of the «cosmoi» offers no obstacle to the transcendental unity of the world, just as the multitude — including the essential multitude — of intelligences and wills offers no obstacle to the transcendental unity of the *verum* and the *bonum*.

On this supposition, we say, the respectivity called world is transcendental; even more, it is the first transcendental «complex» of reality as reality. Let us begin with this last point. I call «complex» those transcendentals which formally belong to each real thing by the mere fact of its being real, but which, however, express what follows from the pure character of reality in order to the multiplicity of real things. By contrast, those are «simple» transcendentals which express, without addition, the reality in and by itself. And I say that world is the first complex transcendental, the grounding transcendental of all the other complex transcendentals: *aliquid, verum, bonum*. All three are complex; they express, in a word, what the character of reality of each thing, as referrable to the rest of things, really is. And this reference is nothing other than the respectivity of the real *qua* real, that is, the world. Only because a *res* as *res* is respective to the rest, can it be and is it an *aliud* with respect to them. The same thing happens with the *verum* and the *bonum;* they involve a respectivity of the intelligent and volitional reality to reality as intelligible and willed. Only because the intelligent and volitional real thing is in the world of other real things, only for this reason is it possible that there should be intellection and volition and, therefore, transcendental *verum* and *bonum*.

To be sure, the first point, the strictly transcendental character of the world, still remains. It is, apparently, the most difficult, since it will be said that not every real thing *qua* real, is respective. There can be real things, including the cosmos, which have no relation to each other, nothing in common; above all, there is a reality, God, which is formally extramundane. Under these conditions it does not seem possible to say that respectivity, the world, could be a transcendental character of reality. Nevertheless, let us reflect on it more closely. We appeal precisely to the reality of God. It is true that, so long as the existence of God has not been proven, it is not possible to find support in it and, in the beginning of metaphysics, the existence of the divine reality has not as yet been proven. But, even though this reality has not been proven at the beginning of metaphysics, neither is it excluded and, therefore, it is licit to treat it as a presumption in the theory of the transcendentals. To be sure, God could have created realities which would be wholly unrelated among themselves; I do not like these considerations of the *potentia Dei absoluta*, but in this case let us admit them. These realities would have no relationship among themselves «cosmically» but they would all coincide in being real; and this, which would seem to be no more than a simple coincidence, is something more than that, because in being the effect of a single creative reality, essentially existent, *eo ipso* those created realities, although by their suchness they have no relation among themselves, are, nevertheless, in respectivity with reference to their character of reality. If one wishes, God has created them in this form of respectivity, which is to have no relation among themselves cosmically. Still, these things which are without cosmic unity are respective insofar as their character of reality is concerned; that is to say, they have unity as a world. That difficulty would seem more serious which refers to the divine reality itself: the world is respective to God, but God is not respective to the world. God is «irrespective,» is extra-mundane, because He is a reality which exists essentially. Nevertheless, this has to be understood. «World» can have two meanings. One is the meaning which I would call «formal;» that is, the character of a zone of reality. In that sense, it is not, strictly speaking, a transcendental, because there is another reality, that of God, which does not lie within this zone of reality, but outside of it. «World,» however, may be the designation of a «disjoined» *(disyunto)* characteristic; it is not a division of real things, but rather that character according to which the reality as such is necessarily and, by reason of its reality, either respective (mundane) or irrespective (extra-mundane). And this disjunctive necessity *qua* necessity is what belongs to reality as such; if we call it «world» it is because, in this case, we qualify the disjunction by its clearest term, and, *quoad nos*, the only one which is immediately undeniable. Appropriating an expression which Scotus forged for other properties (Scotus never thought that «world» was a transcendental) I would say that «world» is a complex transcendental, but a «disjoined transcendental.» A complete disjunction which concerns the real as such is *eo ipso* a transcendental disjunction. The necessity to which I alluded before becomes convertible, disjunctively, with reality as such. I have already indicated, however, that since only the formally mundane term is primarily accessible to us at the beginning of metaphysics, 432 we can and must say that, for these cosmic realities, the world is a transcendental. This is exactly what, some pages earlier, I wanted to express by calling «intramundane» philosophy the consideration of reality *qua* reality but only in the mundane term of the transcendental disjunction.

To sum up, the transcendental order is the order of real things as real, that is, as t h i n g s «in and of themselves» *(de suyo)*. These things are «in and of themselves» in and by themselves *(de suyo);* they are the simple transcendentals *(res* and *unum).* And they are also respective «in and of themselves» *(de suyo);* they are the complex transcendentals, whether disjoined (world) or conjoined *(aliquid, verum, bonum),* the latter of which are founded on the disjoined. This is the transcendental structure of reality, a structure determined by the suchness in transcendental «function.» This transcendental structure rests, then, on two primary transcendentals: reality and world; the former, a simple transcendental, the latter, a complex transcendental.

I have already remarked that it was not my purpose to develop
this theme completely. However, while setting aside other points of
the question, it is, nevertheless, necessary to complete what has been
said with a decisive conclusion which follows from it concerning the
transcendental structure. This consequence is that, in virtue of what
has been stated, the reality of a thing must be considered according
to two moments which are transcendentally different from each other.
In the first place, the primary and radical moment is the thing in its
own proper reality, the thing as actually real in itself. In the second
place, however, and resting on this primary actuality, there is the
actuality of the real thing as a moment of the world: this is the
«mundane» actuality of the real thing, that is, the respectivity of real
433 things by reason of their reality. The actuality of the real thing as
a moment of the world is not formally identical with the actuality
of the real in itself, but does presuppose the latter and rests on it.
The actuality of the real thing in the world is what is formally «to
be» *(ser)*. Here «to be» does not mean to exist, nor is it the mere
quid of the existent, but rather «to be» falls back on the «reality»
without qualification, on the «in and of itself» *(de suyo)* which is,
indifferently, something essential and existential and antecedent to this
distinction. This «reality,» already actually in and by itself, has an
«ulterior» actuality, beyond its simple reality: it is its actuality in the
world. That a thing, iron, for example, «is» does not mean that the
iron exists or that the existent is iron. Because existing iron and existence as iron are not «to be iron» but «iron» simply. «To be» means a
kind of re-actualization of the reality as iron; and this «re-» is the
actuality of the real iron as a moment of the world. Only respectively
to the rest of real things can and must it be said that the iron «is.»

This distinction between «to be» and reality, with the anteriority
of the latter, is clear even in language. For example, if we want to
say that anything succeeds in attaining reality, we can express this
fact from two points of view: first of all, from the point of view
of the reality as such, that succeeds in becoming real which was
not real before. In this sense, we speak of generation (γίγνεσθαι)
blossoming or birth (φύειν), etc. I can, however, also express this
same point paying attention, not to the root of reality, but rather,
in a certain way, to its respective term *ad quem*, to its actuality
in the world. Then this becoming is not formally generation, but a

«coming into the world.» The first is to reach reality, the second is to reach «to be». This last is what is always expressed in the metaphor of φῶς, of light. The becoming of a living thing as coming into mundane respectivity is, for this reason, «enlightenment,» an εἰς φῶς παριέναι, as Plutarch says; to live is to see the ligth of day, 434 τὸ φῶς ὁρᾶν (Sophocles). The world is like the light. Therefore, to come to be *(ser)*, to come to be *(estar)* in respectivity with the rest of things, is a φαίνεσθαι, is an εἰς φῶς φαίνεσθαι (Sophocles), a πρὸς φῶς ἄγειν (Plato). To be *(estar)* in respectivity with the rest of real things *qua* real, this is what, to my way of viewing the matter, constitutes «to be» *(ser)*. «To be» is neither φαίνεσθαι, nor φαινόμενον; φαινόμενον is nothing but the condition in which reality remains *(queda)* by reason of the fact of «to be» *(ser)*; but «to be» itself *(ser)* is the actuality of the real thing as a moment of the world. Only because it «is» is the thing «phenomenon.»

«To be,» therefore, is not formally identical with reality, but presupposes reality. Reality is an absolute formality, while «to be» is a respective character. Only respectively does it make sense to speak of «issue into the light,» «come out into the light,» «bring to light,» «come into the world,» etc. By contrast, genesis and birth concern the real *qua* real in an absolute sense.

Hence it follows that a reality which is constitutively irrespective would have reality in an eminent sense, but would not, for this very reason, have «to be.» God is essentially existent reality; therefore, irrespective, extra-mundane. For this reason, it cannot properly be said of God that he «is,» he is not ὄν; rather it must be said that, just as his reality is extra-mundane, so he stands beyond «to be.» He is the «above-to be;» προ-όν, as with great exactness the first neoplatonizing theologians called him.

«To be,» then, is the mundane actuality of the real. This respectivity, however, as we have already said, is identical *in re* with the real thing itself. Hence it also follows that this actuality, which we call «to be,» is, in the thing itself, its intrinsic real re-actualization; and this is precisely what we call «substantive to be.» Substantive «to be» is not formally identical with reality, but is distinguished from the latter at least by a distinction of reason, a distinction of reason, however, founded in *re*. This foundation is transcendental respectivity. This is the reason why, to my way of seeing the matter, «substantive 435 to be» does not say that the substantivity is a type of «to be,» «the» type of «to be» *par excellance*, but signifies, on the contrary, the «to be» of the substantive; this is to say, that substantivity is anterior to «to be.» It is not *esse reale*, but *realitas in essendo;* it is substantivity «in to be.» Precisely for this reason, «to be» is an «ulterior» act of reality; its further respective actuality. In this sense, and only in this sense, is it necessary to say that «to be» is always the «to be» of the reality. And the reality, insofar as it «is» ulteriorly, is, for this reason, *ulteriorly* «being» *(ente).* Being *(ente)* is not formally the synonym of reality. So true is this that God, as we have said, is reality essentially existing but is not a being, ὄν, but πρo-όν. Being is only the real thing *qua* actual in respectivity, in the world. In sum, world is the first complex transcendental and the property which the real thing possesses according to this complex transcendental is «to be» *(ser).*

This distinction between reality and «to be» is the root of an important difference in the consideration of the real. According to these two actualities, the real thing has different proper modalities. In a word, the real thing *qua* real, in its first and primary actuality, can have a causal connection with other real things; the real thing, in its grounding respect to other realities has what, a few pages earlier, we called «condition»: it is potential, actual, necessary, probable, contingent, free, etc. This connection or causal respect, however, is not transcendental respectivity and, therefore, these modalities and conditions do not formally concern «to be,» but the reality in and by itself. By contrast, when the real thing is considered as actual in the world, that is, considered as actual in its transcendental respectivity, the real thing has «to be» *(ser).* This «to be», then, this actuality of the real as a moment of the world, has, among others, a modality 436 proper to itself: this is time. Time is purely and simply a «mode» of «to be.» It is clear that, just as world is the transcendental property determined by the cosmos in transcendental «function,» so also «time,» is the mundane actuality, «to be» *(ser)* as respective moment, determined by the change of the real thing in transcendental function. «To be» is constitutively «flexive.» Time is not a falling from «to be» *dejar de ser;* (that would be annihilation), but is always to be «other.» To say that time is a mode of «to be,» might seem to be a formula equal to that found in other philosophies; it might be such materially, but what I am saying formally is different, because the idea of «to be» is also profoundly different. «To be» is the respective actuality of the real. And the modes of this actuality are «was, is, will be» (past, present, future): these express the modes according to which the real thing «is» respectively to other real things. An extra-mundane reality is an extra-being, and, for this reason, essentially extra-temporal: it is «eternal.»

In its difference from reality, «to be» *(ser)* has, then, a unitary character proper to itself. It is, however, a unity which is merely respective. This is to say, «to be» is not a kind of supreme enveloping character, embracing the real completely and every being of reason; if this were the case the transcendental order would be the order of «to be.» This is a gigantic and fictive substantivization of «to be.» «To be,» and, correlatively, «non-to be,» have a merely respective character; real things «are» but «the» «to be» has no substantivity. The same thing happens with space. It is customary to say that things are «in» space. This is false: things are spatial, but they are not in space. Space is merely respective; it is the space which things leave *(dejan)* between one another; it is not a receptacle of things. The same must be said of time. And, in another order of problems, modern philosophy, since Descartes, has given substantive status to consciousness. Consciousness, however, has no substantivity whatsoever; and this, not because it is only an act, but because it is not even an act, but only a character of some acts, of conscious acts. 437 And there is nothing of chance about the fact that these three substantivizations came about all at once: that of consciousness (Descartes), that of time-space (Newton-Kant), that of «to be» (Hegel).

Reality, world, to be: here we have, insofar as it has reference to our problem, the structure of the transcendental.

Now it will not be too much to confront, in summary fashion, this conception of «to be» with other, more usual conceptions of it in philosophy. And, first of all, those philosophies which do not distinguish, but rather identify «to be» and reality. In the first place: the idea of *esse reale;* this is the scholastic thesis, in contrast to which we have defined our own position. Taking our point of departure in this identification as expressed in *esse reale,* an idealist criticism of reality has transformed *eo ipso* the idea of «to be» *(ser)* itself. Making of reality a mere sensible impression (giving the term

impression a subjective meaning) the result will be that *esse* is
percipi; this is the thesis of empirical idealism. Making of reality a
result of thought, it follows that *esse* is *concipi;* this is the thesis of
logical idealism. To be, however, is neither one nor the other; in the
first place, because thought moves in a formality already prior to it
(to be): the formality of the real; and, second, because this formality,
in the act of sentient intelligence, presents itself as a *prius* to its
own presentation. Idealism, in its two forms, empirical and logical,
is then, unsustainable, and, as a consequence, so too are its two
formulas concerning «to be» unsustainable. However, as can be seen,
the radical error resides in having identified «to be» and reality, and
of this identification both the two forms of idealism and the idea of
esse reale are guilty.

Reality and «to be,» then, can be distinguished. Hence: one of
two things: either reality is made one type of «to be» among others,
or, on the contrary, «to be» is considered as an ulterior act of the
438 real. Taking the first alternative, it might in its turn be conceived
that what we call «to be» is a position of thought; not that reality
itself should be a position of thought, but that its «to be» is such;
«to be» would then be objectuality. Then *esse* is *poni;* this is the
position of transcendental idealism *(Sein ist Setzung,* Kant affirmed).
However, in contrast to this thesis of idealism about «to be,» there
stands another, according to which reality would certainly be one
type of «to be» among others; but «to be» itself would not be a
position, but, quite the contrary; it would be the character under
which the whole of reality presents itself in a «permitting-that» (a
sein-lassen-von) the present *(lo presente)* would be showing itself to
us in and of itself; this would be «to be.» This is Heidegger's thesis.
To be sure, for Heidegger, this «permitting-that» *(dejar que)* is not an
act of thought; this, however, does not change his thesis about «to
be.» Before both theses, which make of reality a type of «to be,» we
have energetically maintained the thesis that «to be» is an ulterior
act of the real, the actuality of the real as a moment of the world,
independently of whether there are or are not men. We have already
seen our attitude with respect to transcendental idealism. Because
of the importance of the theme, we may reflect for a time about
Heidegger's thesis, despite the summary character of his positive
expressions about «to be».

For Heidegger, man is the being to whose «to be» belongs the «comprehension of the to be» of himself and of what is not himself. However, both in treating of himself and treating of any other thing whatsoever, «to be» cannot be confused with being.

1. Things, comprehended as such things, are beings, and something «ontic.» (Heidegger does not speak of things, but of beings; at times, however, to simplify the exposition, I will employ these two words; it is enough to know that, for Heidegger, thing is formally «being.»)

2. To be *(ser)*, however, is different; its domain is the «ontolog- ical.» It is the «ontological difference.» It is not a conceptual difference, but is a differentiating *(acontecer diferenciante)*, an ascentional happening, which carries us from the comprehension of the being to the comprehension of «to be» and maintains us in the latter. Because it refers to being, this ascension carries us beyond the totality of beings; it is, therefore, the happening *(acontecer)* of the Nought in a special state of mind *(animo):* anguish. The Nought naughts *(anonada)* the being in our comprehension of it; however, by the same token, it makes to appear *(patentiza)* in it the other extreme of the ascension: pure *to be.* The Nought of being, in a word, leaves us in «to be» *(ser)* but in a certain way: with nothing that is, without «being;» this is precisely pure «to be». To be «is» only in and by the happening of the ontological difference, that is, in the happening of the Nought: *ex nihilo omne ens qua ens* (that is, the «to be» of the being) *fit.*

3. What is this «to be» *(ser)?*

(a) «To be» is not a being, but rather always and only the «to be» of the being.

(b) The being is something which may be there or may be there without comprehension, while there is no «to be» save in the comprehension of «to be». As comprehension of «to be» belongs to the «to be» of man, it follows that his «to be» is the presence itself of «to be.» His «to be» consists in the fact that «to be» *(Sein)* «is here» *(Da);* that is to say, the «to be» of man is *Da-sein.* This expression does not mean that man is existence, in the current acceptation of this term, but that man is the *Da* itself, the presence of *Sein,* of «to be.» The *Da* is the comprehension itself as the presence of «to be.» Therefore, there is «to be» only to the degree that there is *Da-sein* and according to the manner in which there is *Da-sein.* It is not a

question of a presence as term or object of comprehension, but
rather that, as the comprehension of «to be» belongs to the very «to
be» of *Da-sein*, it follows that presence, that is to say, the *Da-sein*, is,
if one wishes, the very passage *(trascurso)* of pure «to be»; it is the
440 «to be» of the «to be». The *Da-sein* is the presence, in a certain
sense «ontico-ontologico» of «to be» itself in its purity, in contrast
to, and differently from, every being. Hence, for Heidegger, the fundamental prerogative of *Da-sein* in ontology.

(c) The mode of «to be,» the meaning of the «to be» of Da-sein,
is «temporeity» *(Zeitlichkeit)*. The comprehension of «to be,» the *Da*,
is temporeal *(temporea)* comprehension, that is, the *Da* itself is temporeal. *Da-sein* is temporeal, not because it is «in» time, but because
it is the originative time itself, that is to say, not time as something
which courses through a before (was, *fue)*, a now (is, *es)*, and an
after (will be, *sera)*, but as something which consists in not being
anything but an exstatic «opening,» in three articulated dimensions,
in the exact and special unity of the «instant.» By t e m p o r e i t y
we are «as we are» and we are, therefore, in being, but «beyond»
all being. Only in this exstatic beyond, do we comprehend the being
«in its to be,» because this exstasis consists positively in «leaving»
(dejar) the being as being, that is to say, in leaving the being «actually
being» *(siendo)*; therefore, in this «exstasis» we comprehend, in one
or another manner, the «to be.» T e m p o r e i t y is «at once» the
meaning of the «to be» of *Da-sein* and the «to be» itself as meaning.
In other words, as t e m p o r e i t y is originative historicity itself,
it follows that the *Da-sein* is the historicity of «to be» and reciprocally, « t o   b e » is the historicity of *Da-sein*. Hense it follows
that it cannot be asked what «to be» is (as I ask what beings are)
but I can only ask and must only ask myself what its «meaning»
may be. The meaning of «to be» is «to be» as meaning.

(d) This does not mean that «to be» is anything subjective. On
the contrary. This presence of «to be» in comprehension, in the *Da-
sein*, is the truth of «to be». The comprehension is the truth or
patentcy *(patencía)* of «to be.» The *Da* is that patency itself. This
truth is, then, the «to be» of *Da-sein*. Therefore, to say that there
441 is only «to be» in and by the *Da-sein* means that «to be» «is» not,
save in that patency itself, in the truth, and that, therefore, the «to
be» of truth is nothing other than the truth of «to be». Reverting to

the expression with which Aristotle expounds the action of νοῦς ποιητικός, namely, that it is illumination, οἷον τὸ φῶς, Heidegger will tell us that the presence of «to be» in the *Da-sein* is like light. In the truth which is the «to be» of *Da-sein*, «to be» is not present as a thing — this would be to make a being of «to be» — but that «to be is the luminosity *(luminosidad)* itself.» «To be» is the luminosity *(luminosidad)* of every being and what constitutes the very essence of man. Hence, not only is it not subjective, but «to be is the transcendent itself.» For this reason, the comprehension of «to be» is a transcendental comprehension.

To sum up, because he is the being to whose «to be» there belongs the comprehension of «to be,» it follows that he is the being which consists in «to be,» the «domicile» and the «shepherd» of «to be.»

I have said of the philosophy of Heidegger more than strictly concerns the point which we are treating; however, I wanted to handle the matter in this way in order to provide an adequate frame of reference for the meaning of his affirmations concerning «to be.» Heidegger has the unquestionable merit, not precisely of having distinguished «to be» and being (as we have seen, this distinction, in more or less turgid manner, is already to be found at the basis of scholasticism and even of Kant) but the merit of having posited the question of «to be» itself apart from that of being.

However, how does to be become a question? This is the decisive point.

Heidegger places the problem of «to be» in the line or order of comprehension. Stated in this way, without qualification, it is unobjectionable. In a word, only by showing itself to itself and from itself in comprehension is it possible to speak of «to be,» just as we can only speak of colors by seeing them in themselves. If Heidegger were content with saying that there is a comprehension of «to be» and with undertaking to explicate it in its irreducible originality, there would be not the least objection in principle to oppose to him. This, 442 however, prejudges nothing concerning «to be» itself. What would have been reached by this route would not have been an ontology, but a theory of ontological knowledge, so to call it. Nevertheless, Heidegger is in search of an ontology. To this end he conceives the comprehension of «to be» in a manner which is, in its own turn, ontological: he considers the comprehension of «to be,» not only as the act in which «to be» *shows* itself to itself and from itself, but as a *mode of to be*, that is to say, as a mode of the very same thing which is showing itself, of «to be.» Then the possibility of the comprehension of «to be» is not, at bottom, anything other than the possibility of «to be» itself. This is what Heidegger has before his eyes when he takes his point of departure in the assertion that «to be is given in the comprehension of to be.»

When the question is brought to focus in this way, the analysis of the thought of Heidegger is seen to embrace three successive steps:

(a) *The self-giving of to be* in comprehension is not the self-manifestation of anything which in itself would be alien to its self-manifestation (this is what happens in the case of beings) but is a strict «self-giving;» it is, to express it in this way, an *actually* being *(estar siendo)* that which it, «to be,» is. The self-giving of «to be» is the «to be there» *(ser-Da)*, is *Da-sein*, is the time-passage of the «to be» in its ontological purity, in contrast to being.

(b) *To be itself*, in this its purity is given and is *only in the Da-sein*, in the comprehension of «to be.» «To be» «is» only being *Da*, giving itself in comprehension.

(c) The comprehension of «to be,» in «which «to be» gives itself and actually is *(está siendo)*, belongs to the very «to be» of *Das-sein;* in such wise that then the *Da-sein* is the «to be» of «to be,» is a primary ontico-ontological unity; the *Da-sein* is, in a certain way, the being which consists solely in «to be,» a kind of substantivization of «to be».

We note, however, that Heidegger's theses are neither subjectivism nor idealism of any kind whatsoever. That anything «should be» o n l y i n comprehension does not mean that it is «by» comprehension, or that it is only a moment of comprehension. In Heidegger's conception, «to be» is not a product of man, is not something that man makes. «To be» is given, is not produced; «to be» has its own proper truth. The analysis of temporeity is precisely the «exposition» of this character of «to be.» Once this is said, however, it is necessary to add that none of these three theses, which we have analytically stated, can be sustained without qualification.

(a') The givenness of «to be» is, to be sure, something more than to be mere term of comprehension, if by term is meant only that upon which the act of comprehension falls. Under this aspect, the term would be a term which is, in a certain way, *extrinsic* to the act, as act. In every act of apprehension, however, what is apprehended fulfills a more profound function than that of being the term upon which the act falls: what is apprehended is not only the term of the act, but also what confers on this act its *intrinsic* concrete actuality. Actuality, in a word, does not mean only that the act is in the state of being actually (*estar siendo*) executed, but also that what is executed has intrinsic determined actuality, which would formally be the act of apprehending *this* thing and not *another*. The act is actual, then, in two senses: as an act which is executed and as an act of determined intrinsic quality. And this quality, that is to say, this actuality, is perfectly concrete: it is the quality of apprehending this sound and no other, this color and no other, this square and no other, nor any other different figure, etc. As a consequence, to apprehend is not merely to seize from without, but rather *to be* as what is apprehended. As Aristotle already said, τὸ δ' αὐτό ἐστιν ἡ κατ' ἐνέργειαν ἐπιστήμη τῷ πράγματι (knowledge in act is identical with the thing known; *De anima* 430 a, 20); ἡ τοῦ αἰσθητοῦ ἐνέργεια καὶ τῆς αἰσθήσεως ἡ αὐτὴ μεν ἐστι καὶ μία (the act of what is subject to sense and the act of sensing are one and the same; *Ibid.* 425 h, 25). When something is making a noise and I am hearing, the audition does not consist only in an act which 444 seizes the sound, just as the vision of a color is not only the act which seizes this color, because then difference between seeing and hearing would be merely terminal and extrinsic to the act. On the contrary, hearing consists in the fact that the act is intrinsically auditive and vision is intrinsically seeing; that is, «soundness» (so to call it) is, in one form or another, a moment, an intrinsic and formal quality of the act of hearing, *qua* act. When, then, I am hearing a sound, the sound of anything and the intrinsic auditive quality of my act of hearing are perfectly identical *qua* actuality. And the same happens with any act of νοῦς. Stated in other, more rigorous, terms: in apprehension, the actuality of what is apprehended, as apprehended, and that of the act of apprehending as apprehensor, are one and the same act; if one wishes, there is only one act, which is common to the mind and to the thing. As a consequence, the mind takes on the formal quality of the thing. For this

reason, some medievals thought that the unity between the intelligence and that which is intellected by the intelligence is superior
and more intimate than even the unity between matter and form.
Therefore, to be apprehended is not «to show oneself to» but a true
«self-giving» and a self-giving such that in it the senses and the
intelligence «are» in act the same as what is sensed and what is
intellected. It is clear, however, that this does not mean that this
sameness or identity of actuality is a sameness of «to be». Aristotle
himself adds: τὸ δ' εἶναι οὐ τὸ αὐτὸ αὐταῖς, the «to be» of what
is sensed and that of the act of sensing is not the same (De anima
425 b, 26). In a word, I am able not to be hearing a sound despite the
fact that the bell is ringing; and, on the other hand, the sameness is
able not to have a character properly «physical» as happens in sensing
(we may set this question aside), but can be a sameness of a different
character, as happens in the pure intellect; and this is one of the
445 differences between sensing and pure «to intellect». In conceiving a
square, I am not «physically» a square, but I am such in a non-physical
manner. This manner of «to be» is what scholasticism, with good
reason, calls «intentional.» Intentionality does not mean, then, what
it later comes to mean in phenomenology: the «intending» character
of the act and the character of mere «intended» correlate of the object.
Intentionality is not correlation «in intention» but is a mode of «to
be.» First of all, it is a mode of «to be» of that which is intellected
qua intellected; and it is this mode of «to be» which is the same as
the «to be» of the act of intellection as intellection of this particular
thing or of that other. And this non-physical mode of «to be» is the
intentional. In other words, the actuality of any thing is double:
actuality in the sense of the belonging to the thing, is one thing;
actuality in the sense of being in the state of giving itself (estar
dándose) to the intelligence and of being in the state of making the
intelligence intentionally what the thing is, is another. These are two
perfectly distinct and different actualities, of which the second is
grounded (in one form or another) on the first.

It was absolutely necessary to turn back to these old ideas. If
Heidegger tells us that «to be» not only shows itself, but that it gives
itself, he not only says something which is true, but also must
complete the idea by saying that it is a self-giving which brings it
about that the intelligence is the same as that which is intellected,

in casu, the same as the «to be.» And reciprocally, in the apprehension of anything, this anything not only *is showing itself,* b u t a l s o *a c t u a l l y is (está siendo).* As can be seen, however, this is not exclusive of «to be»; it happens with all things and all real notes. The pecularity of «to be» has nothing to do with the self-giving, but must be sought in the character of what is given. At least, naturally, that this character consists exactly in the fact that, while in the being its reality is distinct from its actuality, in the act of giving itself, when we treat of «to be,» we find that its character is nothing other 446 than its pure self-giving. And this is what Heidegger thinks. Can it be sustained? This is the second point of our question.

(b') For Heidegger, «to be» is the «element» in which every act of comprehension moves. To comprehend a chair is to comprehend it as «being» *(siendo)* a chair; to apprehend a pure number is to apprehend it as «being» *(siendo),* etc.; even what we call reality would be nothing other than a type of «to be.» «To be» would be the special light in which and according to which we have access to things. While we leave them in themselves, they inundate us correlatively, with the light of their «to be,» they give us their «to be.» Differently from the being, «to be» not only actually is *(está siendo)* in its self-giving, but, even more, «is» only in this, its self-giving. Still more, it is «to be» which «gives,» it is that giving itself; that is to say, there is no «to be» save in the *Da-sein.* This position cannot, however, be upheld.

In the first place, the «self-giving» of anything does not involve the moment of «to be» more than if that something were already given as reality. To something which is present as pure stimulus, we can never «leave» *(dejar)* that it «be» *(sea)* that or that other. Only that is «left» in this way which already presents itself as something «in and of itself» *(de suyo).* The stimulus, however, is not present as something «in and of itself» *(de suyo),* but only as something independent of the senser. The «independent» cannot be «left to be» but rather, the senser adapts himself to it, or, to speak anthropomorphically, only takes account of it. By contrast, the thing present as reality involves intrinsically in its presentation, not only the character of reality as a character «independent» of me, but also involves it in a very precise and distinct form, namely, as reality which certainly is present independently of me, but which, moreover, possesses this

26

character (of independence) as something «in and of itself» *(de suyo)* before its presentation and as the ground of that presentation. Reality is present not only as something which «is» *(está)* present here, but present as a *prius* to its presentation itself. And it in this moment of
447 priority that it is grounded as something inexorable, that we call «leaving» the thing in its reality. To leave is to take account of the thing as reality; and this taking account of is grounded, as something necessary, in the presentation of the reality as a *prius*. This taking account of is not an arbitrary possibility to which man puts his hand *ad libitum*, but is something necessary; it is a «having to» take account of, precisely because the thing is present as the reality that it is, *prius* to its presentation. Even more: if man has t e m p o r e i t y, it is precisely because, in apprehending a real determined thing, he not only «is» *(está)* in this thing, but also «co-exists» *(co-está)* in «the» reality, in the transcendental; and for this reason, because the character of reality is transcendental, man as reality which perdures and transpires in time, takes on, by transcendentality, time as his condition; and the time that is thus re-assumed is t e m p o r e i t y. The «leaving that» is grounded, not in temporeity, but, rather, on the presentation of something as a *prius* of reality. I do nothing here but state the idea; its development here would take us too far afield. If to be «actually is,» in its self-giving in «allowing-that» the thing «be,» it follows that the «to be» is grounded in the prior presentation of reality. Reality is not, therefore, a type of «to be,» but, quite the contrary, «to be» is something founded in reality: «to be» is given in the leaving of the real thing in its reality, but is not the reality itself.

On this basis, everything depends on our stating concretely why, in this leaving *(dejar)* understood in this way, what is actually exercising being is precisely the «to be.» At this point Heidegger appeals to light: οἷον τὸ φῶς. What is this φῶς? It is simply «clarity» or, as Heidegger tells us, «luminosity» *(luminosidad)* itself. This luminosity is what «to be» is; the «leaving» is a letting in of light, that is, the «leaving» would show us the «to be» of each thing because, basically, every thing «is» only in the light of «to be.» Let us not
448 abandon this metaphor, but continue it and it will show us that «to be» is not what Heidegger suggests. In a word, let us return to the question what this φῶς is. It is *lux*, that is to say, clarity. But what,

in turn, is clarity? It is something that is based on a luminary, a *lumen*, φέγγος. This luminary has an intrinsic quality, which the Latins called *splendor, fulgor*, etc.; or, if one wishes, brilliance, effulgence. The Greek language, as is will known, lacks a word to express this quality. This *splendor* is something which the luminary has «in and of itself» *(de suyo);* it is the moment of its own proper reality and nothing more. But what we call clarity, *lux*, extends to its environment *(alredador).* Considering this «environment,» and only considering it, does that brilliance take on the character of light, of clarity. That is to say: (1) Light, clarity, is possible only when grounded in the splendor or effulgence of a *lumen;* light is, originatively, a moment of the luminary. (2) Light or clarity is nothing other than effulgence itself in its illuminating function, in function of the luminous environment. (3) Thus, every thing has a double «lumenic» actuality (so to call it): one, actuality as effulgent «in and of itself» *(de suyo)* and, without losing this actuality, it has another, that of being visible «in the clarity of the light.» And since this clarity proceeds from the thing itself, it follows that this ultimate clarity is, as it were, a re-actualization of the first: it is the effulgence seen in the light which flows from it.

And this is precisely what furnishes us the key to our problem. For, what is this environment *(entorno)?* Environment, in its widest sense, is that which surrounds something; the reason why a thing exercises this function of environment (production of light) it does, is because something is respective. Surrounding is «respectivity» and light is the effulgence of respectivity. Every thing is real as an «in and of itself» *(de suyo).* This moment, however, of reality includes transcendentally all other realities. That means, then, that reality is 449 not only the «in and by itself» *(el de suyo)* of each thing, but reality in transcendental respectivity. And this respectivity is exactly the world in the transcendental sense of that term. The world is the effulgence in function of the luminous environment, of clarity, of light. And the actuality of the real thing in the world *qua* world is the actuality of a real thing in clarity of light: it is the «to be.» Reality as «of and by itself» *(de suyo)*, effulgence *(brillo)*, is the ground of the reality as illuminatory (light); and the actuality of a real thing in this light, in the world, is «to be.» World is reality in respective function, and the actuality of the reality in this world is «to be.»

Reality is clarifying «in and by itself» *(de suyo)*, it is respective «in and by itself» *(de suyo):* such is the unity of the two moments of reality and of «to be». It is otiose to add that this idea of light is simply metaphor; nevertheless, it is necessary to fix its meaning exactly with relationship to the use which Heidegger makes of it. But «to be» itself is not clarity, but is the supposition of all clarity: actuality in respectivity.

Hence, it follows that «to be» is not something which «is» only in the *Da* of comprehension, in the *Da* of the self-giving, but is also a moment of reality even if there were neither comprehension nor *Da*. To be sure, «to be» is not something ontic, that is to say, it is neither a thing nor the note of a thing. However, something may be neither thing nor note of a thing and nevertheless be a transcendental moment of the thing itself: such is «to be.» The light is a moment of the luminaries and nevertheless has, in a certain way, a unity apart from their effulgence *(brillo);* it is not for this reason, however, a kind of greater luminary, nor, therefore, is «to be,» as the actuality of the real in its respectivity, one more real note. Neither, for this reason, does it follow that «to be» is something which is only in giving itself in a *Da*. What happens is that in the case of the real there is a special respectivity, the respectivity to this intelligent «thing» which is the νοῦς; and for this reason the actuality in this respectivity is *also* «to be.» However, as the real thing apprehended
450 is already in itself respective to all the rest, it follows that, on apprehending its reality, *eo ipso* we apprehend its «to be.» «To be,» then, intervenes twice: one time as a moment of what is apprehended as reality; another, as a moment of what is apprehended *qua* apprehended. These, however, are not two «to be's», but the second is, as it were, only a ratification of the first: it is exactly to be, not *simpliciter*, but «insofar as it is to be.» What is constituted in the *Da*, and what would not be there without the *Da*, is not the «to be,» but the «insofar as» of «to be.» This «insofar as» is not conceptual in character. It is not a question of the apprehension and the *Da* being a «conceiving,» but rather that in the apprehension and in the *Da* the reality of the things and the «to be», which they have before being apprehended, is «re-actualized.» Conception is always a further function. The *Da* is nothing but a «respect» between *n* «respects» of the thing. The difference between reality and «to be» is a more than

conceptual difference; it is not, however, a happening in the *Da*. It is a difference between two moments of the actuality of every thing: the actuality as an «in and by itself» *(de suyo)*, and the actuality as a moment of respectivity. And as this second actuality, which is «to be,» is based on the first, it follows that it is not true that «to be» *ex nihilo fit*, but rather that, on the contrary, *ex realitate fit*.

To sum up:

1. «to be» is based on reality; reality is not a kind of «to be»;

2. «to be» is the moment of the actuality of the real in this respectivity which transcendentally constitutes the world; therefore, «to be» has nothing to do with the *Da-sein*. «To be» is given but not as thing or note; rather it has another way of being given: as respective actuality;

3. «to be» is always «to be» of the real thing, not because «to be» is actual *(esté siendo)* only in its self-giving, but because, as act of the real thing, it is a «further» act, beyond its primary reality «in and by itself» *(de suyo)*; it is a further act of the reality *qua* reality.

(c') The fact is that Heidegger takes his point of departure in 451 the supposition that man is the being to whose «to be» there belongs the comprehension of «to be,» in such wise that man is then the dwelling-place and the pastor of «to be». But this position cannot be maintained. To be sure, man moves ever in «to be»; the «element,» however, in which man moves primarily and constitutively is not «to be,» but reality. Man moves in «to be,» but because «to be» is a moment, an act, of that which is already real, and not because «to be» is that which primarily and formally characterizes human intellection. The actuality of «to be» in the *Da* of comprehension is grounded on the previous actuality of «to be» in reality. As a consequence, what formally characterizes man is not the comprehension of «to be,» but the manner of apprehending things. In saying this I am not making reference to apprehension as an act of a «faculty,» that is to say, I am not once more incardinating, as Heidegger would say, the problem of «to be» in «subjectivity,» because here I take «apprehension» not κατὰ δύναμιν but καθ' ἐνέργειαν. If man had no more than a stimulative *(estimulica)* apprehension, it would not be possible to speak of «to be.» As we have said, it is possible to speak of «to be» only in the degree or measure in which there is apprehension and presentation of things as real. Therefore, what formally belongs to the «to be» of man is not the «comprehension of to be,» but the «apprehension of reality.» What is the inner character of this apprehension? We have already indicated it. In pure sensation, things are apprehended and are found present only as stimuli; and this pure sensation is what formally constitutes animality. Pure intellection, however, consists in apprehending and in the fact that things are present as reality. Man does not originatively 452 apprehend things as pure reality, but as stimulating reality or real stimulus. Man does not intellect reality purely, but senses reality itself, senses its formal character of reality. Hence it follows that human sensation is not pure sensation, and that the primary and fundamental human intellection is not pure intellection, but that sensation (because it is sensation of reality) is intellective and intellection (because reality is something sensed) is sentient intellection; both expressions say the same thing. As a consequence, what formally belongs to the human reality is sentient intellection. Man moves in «to be» not because «to be» is *Da-sein*, but because *Da-sein* is sentiently open to real things, which, as real, «already» are on their own account *(de si).* The *primum cognitum*, the first intelligible, as we saw earlier, is not «to be,» but reality, and sensed reality in the impression of reality. Openness is not compression but impression. As sensation constitutes animality and intelligence is what presents real things as real, it follows that to say that man is sentient intelligence is the same as to say that he is the animal of realities. Man is not the «comprehender of to be,» he is not the dwelling-place and pastor of «to be,» but he is the «animal of realities.» And, I repeat once again, I take the expression καθ᾽ ἐνέργειαν.

Fundamentally, the entire philosophy of Heidegger is a commentary on this idea that man is the «comprehender of to be.» There is nothing strange about this. Heidegger took his point of departure in phenomenology and, despite the profound and radical transformations which he introduces into it, he remains, nevertheless, within the orbit of phenomenology. For phenomenology, what is primary and grounding is always and only consciousness as a being within which and only within which things are given for what they really and truly are. Heidegger overcomes the idea of consciousness by way of the idea of comprehension, and he overcomes the idea 453 of the «self-giving» of things by means of the idea of φαίνεσθαι, of appearing in the sense of showing oneself. This self-manifestation is self-manifestation as «actually being» *(siendo)*. «To be,» then, is the possibility that things show themselves and that man comprehends them. With this, the radical character of man becomes the comprehension of «to be.» This, however, cannot be upheld, first, because the primary function of man is not to comprehend «to be,» but to confront the reality of things sentiently and, second, because «to be» lacks the note of substantivity; «to be» is only «respectively;» and this respectivity is not respectivity to man, but to the reality of all, the whole. Therefore, it is reality and only reality that has substantivity.

Let us sum up. We proposed to ascertain in a summary fashion what the transcendental order is as a strict transcendental structure. We have seen that this structure includes, on the one hand, the reality as something «in and by itself» *(de suyo);* reality is the transcendental itself or simple transcendental. But this reality has a second transcendental moment, which is complex: respectivity or the world. And the actuality, that which is already real in itself, as moment of the world, is «to be.» Reality and «to be» are two different and distinct moments of the real, not, however, because reality is a type of «to be,» as Kant and Heidegger aver, but quite the reverse, because being is a «further» moment or actuality of the real, a moment which has nothing to do with intellection.

With this we have made the idea of the transcendental order precise, to the degree it was necessary for our problem. We have made it exact, in the first place, in as far as it is transcendental and, in the second, insofar as it is order. The transcendental order as transcendental is not the order of objectuality, nor the order of entity, nor the order of «to be,» but the order of reality as reality. In this order, reality possesses certain determined properties (let us call them so) by reason of the suchness of the real. This determina- 454 tion is a transcendental function, and the properties determined in this way constitute a strict transcendental structure. This is the transcendental order. And in this order, fixed in this way, must we now seek out essence.

II. *The Transcendental Consideration of Essence*

Let us repeat once more that essence must be considered in two orders. First it must be considered in the order of suchness: essence it that which constitutes the real thing as being «such» reality, the essence is a *quid tale*. The essence, however, is not only that which makes the real such *(talifica)*, but also that according to which, and solely according to which, the thing is something «real.» This second consideration of essence belongs, then, to the transcendental order. In order to enter into this consideration we have been obliged, first of all, to form a rigorous concept of this transcendental order: a task less simple than it might at first appear, because the theme bristles with difficulties and because the classical and modern traditions have woven about it concepts, long consecrated, which it was necessary to discuss carefully in order to bring before our eyes, in its purity and rigor, the idea of reality as reality. Hence, the extension of the earlier discussion; it was unavoidable.

Having done this, we have traced out the road toward the apprehension of essence in its transcendentality. The transcendental, we have said, is before all else a *character* of the real, but it is further a *structure* of the real as real. The order of suchness and the transcendental order, in a word, are not two independent orders; rather, the first determines the second: this is what we call the transcendental function. And this function determines, in the real, not only a character, but also a true transcendental structure. Hence it is that the transcendental apprehension of essence must be achieved in two successive steps. First, it is necessary to conceptualize the essence purely and simply in its mere transcendental character and then, in a second step, to conceptualize the transcendental structure of essence.

1. *Essence: Its Transcendental Character*

In our consideration of essence in section two we saw that, both from the point of view of its notes and from the point of view of its primary coherential unity, essence is that according to which the real thing is «a one such»: essence is «suchness.» Suchness is not mere specific determination, but fulfills a structuring function: it is that according to which the real thing has a constitutive structure. This essence is formally individual *as essence*, it is constitutive and not quidditative essence. The proper function of essence is not to specify, but to constitute «physically.» This «suchness» *(talitativa)* structuring function is a true function, because suchness is not synonymous with categorial determination, but is that constructed character according to which each note is «note-of.» With these remarks we have defined the notion of essence in contrast to mere specification, whether conceptive or physical (in the sense, for example, of substantial form). However, *eo ipso*, this essence is also that according to which the essentiated is real. The two dimensions are not formally identified, because the real *qua* «real» has characteristics which are not identical with the characteristics of the real *qua* «such.» Hence it follows that the essence, together with the «suchifying» structuring function, exercises a second transcendental function. It is a function of another order, but a true function, the transcendental function of the constitutive structure, that function according to which the essentiated is *eo ipso* a reality without qualification *(sin más)*. These are not two functions really different from each other, but they are distinct functions with a basis *in re.*

What we are now seeking, then, is, before all else, the transcen- 457 dental character of this function, that is to say, the determination of the transcendental «properties» grounded in that function.

In order to respond to this question, let us prescind for the moment from essence as «suchness,» in the strict sense in which we have defined this idea, and consider suchness provisionally as mere determination, that is, in the sense of mere content of something that is real. It might then appear that the idea of essence is discovered to be affected by an intrinsic ambiguity. On the one hand, essence would be mere determined content, and, on the other hand, essence would be suchness in the sense defined earlier. Under the first aspect, it would appear that any real quality or content whatsoever might possess essence, while, under the second aspect, the essence would appear to be only a part of the real thing, that is to say, what is essential to it in contrast to what is non-essential. We shall see immediately that this ambiguity is merely apparent: it is precisely the problem of the essentiated reality from the transcendental point of view. Now, however, in order to begin, let us abstract, for the moment, from this question and let us consider the essence as mere content or determination. F i n a l l y, i n t h e l a s t analysis there is the aspect of essence which has entered into the preceding exposition and discussion of the usual idea of the transcendental order.

I. *Essence as mere determination.* The transcendental order, we have said, is the order of reality *ut sic*, and reality is that character which we have called «in and by itself» *(de suyo)*. Now anything, in virtue of being a «proper» determined content is «in and from itself» *(de suyo)*, is reality. The «in and by itself» *(de suyo)* is, then, the transcendental character of all and every determined content. In the order of apprehension we have seen that a content might not have the formality «reality» but have instead the formality «stimulus.» 458 Therefore, what we have called formality of «reality» is precisely the transcendental moment of the presentation of things. The condition of being a stimulus is not transcendental in character, because it is always specific. On the basis of this supposition, essence is the determined content insofar as it establishes or implants the thing as something «in and from itself.» Such is the transcendental function of suchness as determination: to constitute the real in its reality *qua* reality. And to be «in and from itself» is what makes the content formally «essence.» Essence is, before all else, a transcendental concept and not merely a concept of «suchness.» The essence is the determination in transcendental function. This establishment of the thing as something «in and from itself» is precisely what, on so many occasions, we have called reality *simpliciter*. In employing this expression, we left it floating in a deliberate ambiguity. For this formula can mean either the conjunction according to which something is reality, for example, silver or iron, or it may mean that with it, we have a reality without qualification: it is the ambiguity between suchness and the transcendental. In the line of the transcendental, we now say, the essence, more than «reality» *simpliciter*, is «that» *simpliciter* of the real itself as such. Transcendentally considered, the essence is the «in and from itself» *(de suyo) simpliciter*. In other words: essence is absolutely identical with reality.

Hence it follows that the very concept and the term essence are equivocal. In the exposition and the discussion with scholasticism, we have spoken of essence and of existence as moments founded on a

prior «*de suyo;*» before considering the thing essentially and existentially, we said, it must be considered really. Then essence meant what
it meant classically: a moment of reality. Now, however, essence is
not a moment of reality, but is rather the reality itself. To the degree
to which we distinguish determination and suchness, essence will tend
to appear to us as a moment of reality, but in a different dimension,
namely, as moment of substantivity. For the time being we will 459
continue to consider suchness as mere determination. And in this
dimension, essence is not a moment of reality, but the reality itself.
In this context, essence is anterior not only to the fact that it exists,
but also anterior to its own aptitude for existence; that is, the concept of essence which we are proposing is beyond the essence and
existence of classical thought. Essence, then, (1) is identical with
reality and (2) is anterior to the dualism «essence-existence.» Both
concepts of identity and of anteriority were expounded when we
discussed the idea of the transcendental; however, in order to avoid
mistaken interpretations of them, it will not be superfluous to recapitulate what has been said.

In the first place, then, to speak of the *identity* of essence and
reality. Stated negatively, this identity is not the identity between
res and *ens* as known in classical philosophy. For, in this latter, the
res is the *quid* insofar as it connotes existence, whether actual or
aptitudinal, while *ens* is this same *res* insofar as it is «qualified» by
this existence. Here, in contrast, *res* is not identical with *ens*, neither
under that aspect which concerns the *res* nor that which concerns the
ens. It is not identical under that aspect which concerns the *res*,
because *res* is not the *quid* in order to existence, but rather the *quid*
in order to the *de suyo*, the «in and from itself.» Neither does that
identity exist under the aspect which concerns the *ens*, and this for
two reasons: because «to be» is not the same as to exist and because
«to be» is not the same as reality. The identity of essence and reality
has nothing in common, then, with the identity between *res* and *ens*.
Neither does it mean what a certain scholastic thinker (Soto) thought
it meant: for him, the essence is the *quid* considered «absolutely» and
not connoting existence whether aptitudinal or actual. For Soto, in
a word, between essence and existence there is, at least, a modal
distinction *ex natura rei*, in such wise that the essence is only a
moment of the reality, that moment which *ex natura rei* prescinds

from existence. What we have affirmed here is that the essence is
460 identical with the reality as something *de suyo*, «in and from itself.»
The essence does not prescind from existence, but includes it «indistinctly.» We shall, however, return to this last point in what
follows. Negatively, then, the identity of essence and existence is not
the identity of *res* and *ens* nor is it the *quid* considered *absolutely*.

Positively, the identity of essence and reality means that both
concepts express purely and simply the *de suyo*, the «in and from
itself» of anything. If one wishes to employ the word *res*, it will be
necessary to say that *res* is the real itself insofar as it is *de suyo*.
The determined content of anything is not essence (in the classical
sense), nor is existence itself real unless both moments belong to the
thing *de suyo*. And this thing *de suyo* is what constitutes the essence.
Here, as we have seen, the *de suyo* is to be understood as mere *ex se*.
The thing is real insofar as it is *de suyo* and insofar as it is *de suyo*,
its content is essence. This essence which is the real thing itself, what
is *ex se*, embraces, then, both essence and existence in the classical
sense. Such is the identity of essence and reality. This does not mean,
however, that as aspects, so to say, of the thing, essence and reality
are totally identical concepts, in such wise that the duality of terms
is useless. Reality, in a word, means the character of being *de suyo*;
it is, then, the transcendental property, or better, *character* of the
thing; it is transcendentality itself. Essence, by contrast, is the real
quid, the determined content of the thing in transcendental *function*,
that is, insofar as, by being «such» the thing is *eo ipso* «*de suyo*,» is
transcendentally real; it is the *quid* referred to the transcendentality
of the *de suyo*. The difference between reality and essence is formally
only a difference between transcendental property or character and
461 transcendental function. This is not a mere conceptual subtlety. We
have seen, in effect, with respect to the intelligent and volitional
«thing» that the transcendental function of this «suchness» is much
more vast than that of merely determining the transcendental
character, the mere being something «*de suyo*,» of the thing in question. The intelligent and volitional «thing» not only is something *de
suyo*, but also by being «such,» its function is much vaster than the
being *de suyo*, because «it brings it about that» by respect to «such»
a thing, the being itself, as such, is intrinsically true and good. We
saw the same thing with regard to the difference between cosmos

and world. Immediately we will see it again with regard to the essence itself as such.

Essence understood in this way not only is identical with the real, but even more is, in some way, anterior both to classical essence and to existence. We have already said that there is no question here of an anteriority whether causal or natural, as though the essence were the ground of the existence; that is to say, it is not a question of the anteriority of the essence, understood in the classical sense, with respect to existence. This was Hegel's thesis. It is impossible for two reasons. First, because it would be an untenable ontologism; if, of the two terms, one would have to be anterior to the other, it would have to be existence and not essence. Secondly, because Hegel still moved within the orbit of the classical concept of essence, that is to say, essence understood as a *quid* in the order to existence. Here, by contrast, we move within the orbit of a concept of essence which is beyond the classical concepts both of essence and existence; essence here is the *quid* in the order to the *de suyo*. And in this concept, *this* essence is anterior to the two classical terms in the sense in which a formal *ratio (razón)* is anterior to that of which it is the *ratio*. The formal *ratio* is «ground,» but only to the degree in which it is formal *ratio*. And in this formal *ratio*, the two classical terms are included, not confusedly, but *indistinctly:* the essence is both 462 existence and essence in the classical sense, because both have to begin by being *de suyo;* and this order to the *de suyo* is precisely the essentiality itself of the essence of which we are speaking. The anteriority of the essence is, negatively, absence of distinction between essence and existence in the classical sense in that other concept of essence. Positively, it means that being *de suyo* is the formal *ratio* and the ground of the fact that both existence (actual) and the aptitude for existence are moments of something which is *already* real. This is exactly what I expressed in the «Introduction» to this study, when I said that I was going to consider the essence in itself and not with respect to existence. It might have seemed that it was a truncation of the theme of essence; however, what I kept before my eyes was not essence simply insofar as it prescinds from existence, but rather this other concept of essence according to which essence is indistinctly anterior to both essence and existence in the classical sense. And the fact is that classical philosophy *begins* by distinguishing, in the form that it already had, the concepts of essence and existence; and then it explained the former by its aptitude for existence. This, however, was not a viable process. It is necessary to *begin* with the real as real, that is, as a *quid* or essence *de suyo*, and *afterward*, only afterward, would it be possible to distinguish *within* this essence what are usually called essence and existence. This, consequently, is a «further» distinction.

What is the ground and the meaning of this distinction? Real things are primarily sensed as real. And in this their sentient intellection, things show themselves as altering; that is to say, alteration itself is sensed as real; the alteration of the real is sensed in its very reality. I am not referring only to the change which all things suffer in one or another form, but above all to that alteration according to which things cease to be what they are; what was before *de suyo*
463 ceases to be such to give way to other things *de suyo*. To be sure, we do not know whether this happens with the whole of the real. For the time, however, it is enough that this should be the case with intramundane realities. And by limiting ourselves to these, as we so many times have done in the course of this study, we have to affirm that, as a matter of fact, all intramundane realities are, in one degree or another, labile, subject to change. It is what I call the «labileness» of the real. It is, then, a character which affects its suchness: such as they are, things are intrinsically labile. The labile character of intramundane things, however, has a strict transcendental function, that is, it determines a transcendental character in the real itself as real: its «limitation» as reality. This is a transcendental limitation. This limitation is not a second transcendental character; it is not the case that things are real and further limited, but that the limitation belongs intrinsically to the *de suyo* itself. The real is *de suyo*; it is, however, *de suyo* limited as reality; the real is «really limited.» This is exactly what I said so many times when I said that «*de suyo*» means reality as *ex se*, but not, however, *a se*. I will return to this idea immediately.

In order to understand what this limitation is, we must take a few steps backward. Essence, as we have seen, is qualitative autosufficiency in transcendental function, that is, insofar as it constitutes something *de suyo*. The real is, therefore, transcendentally sufficient. However, real or transcendental sufficiency is not the same

as plenary sufficiency (we shall see presently what the meaning of
this adjective might be). And this non-plenary sufficiency is what I
have called transcendental limitation. Essence is intrinsically and
transcendentally limited. Now the essence as already intellectively
«sensed» as limited, considered formally from the point of view of
its very limitation, that is to say, as something limited *de suyo*, forces 464
the intelligence to «conceive» the real, the *de suyo*, the essence according to two concepts, different *as* concepts, to which there
correspond two aspects of the essence. Each one of these concepts
conceives the same reality, the same *de suyo*; in each of them, however,
I have only «reduced» aspects of that reality, that *de suyo*, neither
of which gives me the essence, the *de suyo* in its entirety. This reduction necessarily works or operates along two lines.

In the first place, the essence considered from the point of view
of «suchness,» we have seen, has an unalterable constitutive content,
unalterable, however, in the order of formal sameness; physically
every essence is totally or partially alterable. This physical alterability
is the labileness in suchness *(talidad)* of the essence; and in transcendental function it shows us a reduced aspect of the essence:
sufficiency as something merely «ratified» in order to this *de suyo*,
in order to the reality. Here «ratified» is not what is usually understood by this term, namely, closed in the order to existence, but
rather expresses a formally transcendental character in the order to
the *de suyo*, that which is enclosed in the order to the *de suyo*.
However, since suchness is something positive, and, in transcendental
function, is essence, it follows that «ratified» is not the essence
itself, but a conceptive «reduction» of the essence: it is the suchness
conceived transcendentally insofar as it is limited. As a consequence,
«*rato*» is, first, a conceptive transcendental character. In the second
place it is a «reduced» character of the essence; it is that which the
adverb «merely» expresses; it is the essence in its «merely *rato*»
aspect. In the third place, it is a transcendental character, not in order
to existence (that was the classical conception) but in order to the
de suyo. The *de suyo* in the line of qualitative limitation remains conceptively reduced to the mere *rato* in the transcendental order.

This essence, however, reduced to something ratified, is not all 465
the *de suyo* of the essence, but precisely something reduced; it is
only an aspect of the essence. The essence, in effect, is not real only

insofar as it is ephemeral, but rather is real *simpliciter*, it is *simpliciter de suyo*. The *de suyo* is, then, something «more» than merely transitory, ephemeral. And insofar as it is more than merely transitory, even though limited in the line of this very «more,» the essence is something «merely existent.» However, we must not fall into any illusions; this also is a question of a merely reduced aspect of the essence. If, from the essence as reality, as *de suyo*, we separate (the expression will be forgiven us) its aspect as ratified, the real essence is not totally annulled; rather there remains to us another aspect of it, namely, the hollowness, so to say, which the subtraction of the ratified leaves in the essence as reality *de suyo*. And this second conceptive aspect is the essence as something «merely existent.» Merely to exist is not here a character «added» to the «ratified,» it is not a «predicate» of the *rato*, but a «reduction» of the essence as something *de suyo*. Only in order to the *de suyo* does the essence appear as something «merely existent.»

Seen from this point of view of its transcendental limitation, the essence, as limited reality, remains «reduced» in this way in two aspects. It remains reduced, in the first place, to something «merely ratified;» furthermore, it also remains reduced to something «merely existent.» Without reduction, however, the essence as something *de suyo* is positively reality *simpliciter*, is the *simpliciter real*. Hence it is that these two aspects of the reduced essence, namely, the «merely ratified» and the «merely existent» do not coincide *save in a certain way* with the classical notions of essence and existence. The difference lies precisely in the «merely.» To say of anything that it is «merely ratified» is not to say that it is *de suyo simpliciter*. Neither, however, is to say of anything, that it is «merely existent,» to say that it is *simpliciter de suyo*. Let us permit our reflection to linger on these ideas for a moment.

466   Before all else, we repeat at length, this duality presupposes the *de suyo*, but it is not that which constitutes the *de suyo* formally. It is a question, actually, of two aspects of the real essence; to pretend that this duality comprises the real essence would be tantamount to asserting that a thing is constituted by the totality of the aspects which it offers. Only the *de suyo* is the formal *ratio* of reality and stands beyond its aspects as their ground. It is certain that the limitation is a moment proper to essential sufficiency. It is not,

however, anything extrinsically added to the latter; rather, the essence is intrinsically and formally limited in itself, in its proper *ratio (razón)* as essence. This is what we expressed when we said that essence is, indistinctly, both essence and existence, in the classical sense; now we see that, properly speaking, the essence is also indistinctly as much merely ratified as merely existent. Every essence is *ex se;* however it is not, for this reason, *a se. A se,* however, does not mean what it usually was taken to mean in a large part of scholasticism, namely, identity of essence and existence, but rather to be real by i t s e l f . For greater exactness, it ought to be said, as a first approximation, that the essence, in the sense of reality *de suyo,* is *a se* when it is essentially existent. This, however, is only a first approximation, because, rigorously speaking, the «aseity» is a character which ought to be understood directly in relation to reality, to the *de suyo.* To be *a se* is to be reality in a plenary sense; and «to be» in the plenary sense consists in not tolerating reduction. This is the case with God. His plenitude does not consist in the identity of essence and existence, but in plenary sufficiency in the order of reality. When it is said that A and B are identical, this identity may have three meanings. It can mean that A is formally B, or that B is formally A, or that the thing is not what A and B are formally, but is rather something which absorbs, in a superior unity, what A and B are, 467 so that the latter are identical not by formal identity but by elevation. This is the case with reality *a se.* In the reality *a se,* essence and existence are identical; not, however, formally, but by elevation. It is in this that the plenitude of reality consists. All things are real, but none, save God, is «the» reality.

All essences are intrinsically limited; it is a transcendental limitation. To be sure, it is a question of an intramundane transcendental. If, however, we should wish to refer to a transcendental which embraces God himself as well, we would say that «sufficiency-limitation» is a detached transcendental. Let us limit ourselves, then, to intramundane essences. Their limitation does not affect only that which it has been customary to call existence; rather what it does affect is indistinctly the real itself as such, the *de suyo* itself. In the limited essence there is no priority whatsoever of any reduction over any other. It is true that no intramundane essence, insofar as it is merely ratified, is essentially existent; but it is no less true that no

intramundane existent, insofar as it is merely existent, has such or
such transcendentally ratified content. This is the reason why «merely
ratified» and «merely existent» do not coincide, *save in a certain
way*, with the essence and existence of classical thought. For classical philosophy, the essence is (according to different conceptions)
either a ratified *quid*, whether actually or only aptitudinally existent,
or mere capacity for existence, of receiving the act of existence. Here,
by contrast, what the ratified and the existent are «merely» shows
that it is a question only of «reductions» of the real essence, of what
is *de suyo*. The «merely ratified» essence is not classical essence,
because the latter is such in the order of reality as existence, while
468 the merely ratified essence is essence in the order of reality as a
de suyo. The same must be said of existence. Even more; here we
have not spoken of «existence» but of the «merely existent.» There
is no essence and existence, not only because there is not this «and»
(I shall return to this point) but above all because there is nothing
save either the «merely ratified» essence or the «merely existent»
essence. And both the one and the other are equally «poor» (we
should say insufficient) in the order to reality.

In the reality *a se* there is no possibility of conceptive «reductions.» For, even taking essence and existence in the classical
sense, the plenitude of reality of God does not consist in a priority
of essence over existence nor of the latter over the former. It is not
only the case that essence is such that it involves existence (existential
essence), that is to say, it is not only the case that the essence is
distinct from the essence of intramundane realities, but also that the
existence is pure essentiality (essential existence). In God, to exist is
something *toto caelo* different from what to exist means in intramundane realities. Not only essence, but existence is, in the being *a se*,
something transcendentally different from what these are in the
«merely ratified» being and in the «merely existent» being of intramundane realities. This is the reason why God, as reality, is beyond
this duality and this identity: He is the plenary *de suyo*.

Neither in God nor in any other real essence is there, then, a
priority between these two «reductions;» by being such, they are
mere conceptive «reductions.» It is one of the serious errors of all
the existentialists, to believe that, at least in the case of human
reality, there is a fundamental anteriority or priority of existence

over essence; no such priority exists, not even when the two terms
are understood as «merely ratified» and «merely existent.» It is a
question, not of a priority of existence, but of a different essential 469
structure. We shall concern ourselves with this in relationship to the
transcendental structure of the real essence as such.

The ground of this conceptive duality, I have said, is the limitation
of the real as such, transcendental limitation. It is the «talitative»
labileness in transcendental function. It might be thought that the
ground of this duality is causality, that is, the fact that the whole
of the real is grounded on something distinct from itself, on
something *by reason of which* it is real; this is what it was customary
to hold, above all in classical philosophy, with relation to essence
and existence. However, even prescinding from the difference between
these two «moments» of classical metaphysics and the two «reductions» of which we are speaking here, it still does not seem to me that
the *fundamental experience* which motivates the duality in question
is the fact of causation. Not that it is false *simpliciter* that causality
intervenes in the experience of real things and, therefore, in the apprehension of the intrinsic character of their reality. In the final
analysis, however, when all is said and done, things, whether caused
or not, are already here. And the truly surprising thing in experience
is that what is already real ceases to be real *by reason of an intrinsic condition*. And this is anterior to all causality, whether productive or destructive. That there is this double causality is evident. The
decisive consideration for our problem, however, is the intrinsic and
formal character of the reality of the real. It is one thing to see the
real in its collision (productive or destructive) with other realities,
and another very different thing to apprehend a reality in itself as
transcendentally labile. To see a house that is falling to pieces because
someone is destroying it is not the same as seeing a house which of
itself is gradually disintegrating. The first is an apprehension in
causal connection; the second is an apprehension of the real thing in
itself. Even when we see the house falling to pieces because someone 470
is destroying it, what is decisive is seeing that the house *is actually*
falling to pieces and not seeing that it is falling to pieces because
someone is destroying it. Reality is intrinsically labile; the transcendental function of this labile character is limitation. The mar-
velous thing is not that everything comes to be for a time but that

everything, in one measure or another, passes aways. The ground of our duality lies in the radical experience of the labileness of the real.

This labileness, and, therefore, this limitation, is not something primarily conceived, but rather something primarily sensed. It is a fundamental *experience* of sentient intellection. Only because we sense the real in its very limitation can we and must we conceive those two reduced aspects in the real. It is true that I have repeatedly called them «conceptive» reductions; but this was in order to set them in contrast to real moments. The limitation, however, which is intellected in the concepts in question takes its point of departure in the *de suyo* intellectively sensed. The impression of reality (in the sense proposed some pages earlier) is an impression not only of something which «is here» but rather of something which is labile in this its being. By this I do not mean to say that everything in its first presentation of itself in intellective sensation is formally and expressly sensed as something labile. For this last step, a conceptive reflection is necessary. The only thing that I am saying is that, when we apprehend something as labile, this labileness is sensed; and we sense it as a character which adheres in the very reality of what is sensed; that is to say, that the labileness is a moment of the impression itself of reality. The impression of reality is not an empty character, alien to the content of what is sensed, but is rather an intrinsic formality of every apprehension, of every perception of the real, and is found, therefore, intrinsically modalized according to the content perceived. One of these modal moments — one only among many others — is precisely this of being at times the impression of a labile reality in its proper character of reality. This is the reason why I say that we sense the real in its limitation as reality. This thing sentiently intellected is that to which the λόγος directly and primarily points. And only to the degree to which this λόγος achieves conceptive form in a reflection does the duality which we are studying appear explicitly and distinctly. Its primary ground, however, is a unitary experience of the real as real.

Let us return, in closing this discussion, to something which I pointed out two pages earlier. «Merely ratified» and «merely existent» are two «reductions» of the real essence as something *de suyo*. It is not a question of essence and existence, but of a single real essence, of one and one only *de suyo*. They are two aspects of a single «reduced» essence which, therefore, insofar as real, is formally beyond this duality. It is, however, one thing to say that these two aspects are different as aspects and another to say that they are two physically distinct moments, *tamquam res et res*, as Egidius Romanus said. Reciprocally, since they are merely aspects, these two reductions do not physically «compose» the real. In no order whatsoever, in which it is considered, is the real thing «composed» by the totality of the aspects which it presents for intellective consideration. There is no existence which would be the act of an essence, but one sole real essence, which is either merely ratified, or merely existent. With this it remains clear that, even prescinding from the difference between these reductions and the essence and existence of classical thought, there is no «real,» that is, physical, distinction or composition between essence and existence. And it is the ground of this duality which is solely the transcendental limitation of the real. The real is limited as real; its «limitation,» however, is a merely negative aspect. Every essence as something *de suyo* is *ex se*, intrinsically and formally, limited, but it is so by reason of its proper and intrinsic character. 472 That something is labile does not necessarily mean that it is such because it is compounded. On the contrary, the labileness itself in transcendental function is what makes it necessary to conceive the essence reductively, either as merely ratified or as merely existent; it is always a matter, however, of two conceptive «reductions.»

Hence it is that this conception partially co-incides with that of the classical thinkers who deny the real distinction. It coincides only in the negative dimension: there is no real distinction between the two terms of the duality, but only a «conceptive» difference (they would say «of reason») with a basis *in re*. There is, however, a difference in the positive dimension; because, as we have said, «merely ratified» and «merely existent» coincide only partially with the classical concepts of essence and existence. For the whole of scholasticism, the *quid* is essence only in the order to an aptitudinal existence; while here the essence is the *quid*, but in the order to the *de suyo*. And the same must be said of existence: it is not to be understood with regard to the *quid*, but directly with regard to the *de suyo;* only then do we have reality. The duality is only «reductive.» It is not a duality of reason between essence and existence, but between two reductions of the *de suyo:* as merely ratified or as merely existent.

Naturally, there is an entire series of «arguments» *pro* and *contra* the distinction of reason or the real distinction. They are repeated in a monotonous and uniform manner all along the course of the history of metaphysics; that is why I think that it is useless to reproduce them here. Those who maintain the real distinction would deny that the terms of the duality are mere aspects. In the last analysis, they appeal, whatever may be said, to a consideration of the finite being with respect to the infinity of its first cause. Personally, I do not see that there is anything which forces us to go beyond what 473 we have reached in the immediate analysis of transcendental limitation. Created reality is intrinsically and formally limited in and by itself; and there is no need to multiply entities beyond necessity. Intrinsic and formal limitation is the adequate explanation of the necessity of a first cause. «Merely ratified» and «merely existent» do not act or conduct themselves as physically distinct moments, but rather are but two mere aspects of one sole character: transcendental limitation of the essence as reality *de suyo,* as reality *simpliciter.*

Here we have the transcendental character of essence as mere determination, or, if one wishes, as mere «determinacy,» that is, as mere «suchness» *(talidad).* In this exposition we have treated the two terms as synonyms. I have, however, already noted that suchness in the strict sense is not mere determination. «Suchness» is that according to which the real is constituted physically and individually in «such» reality, in virtue of notes which primarily are «notes-of» in primary coherential unity. By contrast, determination is the mere content of certain notes which do not form part of the essence as suchness in the strict sense but which, however, determine it further, whether as constitutional derivatives from it, or as its own determinants in the line of concretion. These notes are, then, as we have seen, formally non-essential. The essence is not all that the thing is *hic et nunc,* but only that which is formally constitutive of it. This assertion might make it seem that the essence loses its radical metaphysical character to be reduced solely to «the essential» of something. This is, as I have indicated earlier, the problem of essentiated reality: what is it that has essence? In its proper place we have already treated this question, but only from the point of

view of the essential notes. Now it must be treated from the transcendental point of view. Transcendentally, that ambiguity of the
concept of essence will prove to be purely apparent. Let us take up
then this new aspect of the question.

II. *The essence as strict «suchness».* In order to examine this   474
problem, let us begin by studying, from the transcendental point of
view, the essence as the formally «such» *(talitativa)* element of the
substantive reality. Then we will confront the duality «essential-non-
essential.»

First of all, the essence as the formally «such» *(talitativo)* element
of the substantive reality. Let us recall, in summary fashion, the different aspects according to which the essence has shown itself to us
in the course of this study. We have seen, in the first place, that
the essence is a moment of the substantivity, that moment according
to which certain notes of it constitute, «by themselves,» sufficiency
in the order of substantivity. From this point of view, the constitutive
essence is the system of notes sufficient and necessary to form, by
themselves, a system; this is constitutive auto-sufficiency. This system,
however, is, in its turn, formally a primary coherential unity. As
coherential, this unity is a unity of self-closure, a unity which I have
called cyclical. As primary, it is a unity which «makes» the notes into
essential moments. The unity does not confer their content on the
notes, but it does confer on them their character as essential. The
notes are, then, «suchifying,» while the unity is essentiating. Both
moments, however, of the essence —its notes and its primary
coherential unity — are not merely two juxtaposed moments, but
rather every note is constitutively and formally «note-of;» and that
of which it is a note is the unity itself, which is «in» them. This
intrinsic «belonging» *(pertinencia)* of the two moments is what
constitutes the constructed state: the essence is intrinsic constructivity. (I have already noted that this concept is proper to intramundane essences, but one which leads, epagogically, to the possibility
of an essentially simple extra-mundane essence.) And in this line of
thought, every other note of the thing is formally non-essential. This
consideration of the essence is a «suchness» *(talitativa)* consideration;
essence is that according to which the thing is «a such» (or «such
a one»).

475   By its proper suchness, however, the essence has a transcendental function: it is that according to which the thing is a reality, that is, that according to which the thing is *de suyo*. This *de suyo*, now has a supremely precise character, determined by the constructivity in transcendental function. The belonging of the «*de*» of the notes and of the «in» of the unity, that is to say, the belonging of notification and essentiation to the constructive suchness of the essence is, in transcendental function, precisely the *de suyo;* and reciprocally, the *de suyo* itself has a transcendentally constructed character.

This is not a question of a mere conceptual subtlety which verges on tautology. Quite the contrary; here is where one can begin to see clearly what I said some pages earlier, namely, that the transcendental function of the «suchness» can be much vaster than the mere determination of a *de suyo*. Every note, in fact, is a «note-of» in and by a primary coherential unity, which, in its turn, determines, not the content of each note, but only its essentiality. In the transcendental order, this duality disappears, to remain absorbed in the *de suyo*. Because, if indeed it is certain that the notes have a content proper to themselves, nevertheless, it is no less certain that no note whatsoever is *de suyo*, that is to say, no note whatsoever, has, by itself, a proper reality; only the thing, the entire construct, is *de suyo*. If we sometimes speak of each note as a reality, it is by way of a mental operation by which we consider each note as though it were a thing. But this is a metaphysical fiction: no note whatsoever has reality save as «note-of» a unity. There is no other essentiated reality but the thing in its intrinsic constructivity. And it is this transcendental construct that confers reality on all and on each one
476 of the notes. Hence, the fundamental difference between the «suching» *(talitativa)* function and the transcendental function. In terms of «suchness,» the notes are what gives the character of notes to the thing *(notifican a la cosa)*. Transcendentally, however, the notes have reality only as moments of the *de suyo* in its entirety; from the transcendental point of view, the notes owe their entire reality to the *de suyo*. If this were not the case, we would have as many realities as notes; we would have, not one reality, but an aggregate of realities. The *de suyo*, determined as a construct, is a transcendental character of reality, one and the same for all the notes. And this is true not only with reference to the notes, but also

with reference to the unity itself. In the order of «suchness,» the unity is unity only by being «in» the notes, conferring essence on them. It is real, however, only in the *de suyo*. What then is this *de suyo*? It is, then, nothing other than the entire constructivity in its transcendental aspect. «Entire» constructivity means, as we have seen, the character «common» to the unity and the notes. In the order of «suchness»» this character is «essentiality» and the character of its community is «actuality»: the essence is, as a construct, essential actuality. This essentiality is actual in the unity as primary moment: the unity is actualizing, essentiating, actuality. It is actual in the notes as constructed moments: the notes are actualized actuality, essentiated actuality. This is constructivity in the order of «suchness.» This «entire» constructivity, then, in the order of «suchness,» that is, its common character of essential actuality, has a precise transcendental function: to establish the «suchness» as something *de suyo*. The actuality now is not only actuality of this «such» essence, but actuality of reality, this actuality which consists in being *de suyo*. The constructivity in transcendental function is that which concretely constitutes the *res*. There are many notes and there is one unity, but there is only one *res*. The *de suyo* is, if one wishes, a «construct of reality,» not only a construct of unity and notes. Transcendentally, essence is «construct of reality.» This is the reason why the essence is the *simpliciter* of the reality. The manner in which the things are concretely *de suyo* is by constructivity; and, reciprocally, all constructivity transcendentally determines a *de suyo*. 477

This becomes even clearer if we now consider the non-essential notes. We have already said, in the first part of this study, that the essence is an internal moment of the thing; within it the difference between the essential and the non-essential is to be found. With this it appears that the concept of essence remains restricted to one part of the real thing. Let us remember, in a word, the different meanings of this concept. In a first sense, essence is the conjunct of all the notes which a thing possesses *hic et nunc*. Among these notes there are some which univocally characterize the sameness of a thing in confrontation with other things or with its own variations; this is the second concept of essence. Among these latter notes, however, there are some which are the minimum necessary and sufficient w h i c h t h e t h i n g m u s t possess in order to be wholly

and solely what it is. This is the third concept of essence, essence
in the strict and formal sense. It is needless to repeat that essence
in this third concept is primarily and formally the constitutive, not
the quidditative, essence. On the other hand, however, through many
pages now, we have been saying that essence is the synonym of
reality. And then it would appear that, either we retrace the path
already traversed, by returning to the first concept of essence, or, if
we hold to the third, we leave outside the thing important characteristics of reality, all the non-essential characters. But this appearance
is false.

Before all else, what are these non-essential notes? We have
already seen this. They are not necessarily notes the possession of
478 which would be useless or indifferent to the thing. Quite the contrary, there is an entire series of non-essential notes, the constitutional notes, which derive, of necessity, from the essence, which then
is, more than constitutional, constitutive. There are also certainly
other notes which the thing may or may not have. The decisive point
for our present problem is not that these notes can not have reality,
but rather of what kind may be the reality which they have, when
de facto they are possessed by the thing. Both, then, in the first
group of notes as well as in the second, it is *always,* as we have
seen, a matter of grounded notes. In comparison with them, the
essential or constitutive notes are ungrounded. As a consequence,
what we must now ask is what may be the character of the grounded
notes when they are possessed by the thing. This is a question of
d e c i s i v e importance.

It is not a question of a juxtaposition of notes, as though the
thing «in addition to» essential notes, of ungrounded notes, might
have other notes grounded on them and which remain outside them.
This is absurd. No matter how many non-essential notes a real thing
may have, this thing is, nevertheless, in its ultimate concretion,
always and only one single thing and not various things. The grounded
notes form a unity of a special type with the constitutive notes. This
is not a unity of «inherence.» It would not matter if we employed the
term were it not that it already has a consecrated meaning in
metaphysics: the manner of the «to be» of the accident. The fact is
that the grounded notes are not inherent accidents, because the es-

sence itself is not substance but substantivity. I shall return to this point presently. The unity of the essential notes is, I have said, a unity of «coherence.» The unity of the non-essential notes with the essence is then a unity of «adherence.» There is no question here, naturally, of a material property. Even less does this mean «juxtaposed to;» rather the prefix «ad» has the exact sense of «in direction toward.» All the non-essential notes are notes which make of the thing, not reality *simpliciter*, but rather reality «in a certain respect» 479 (ad). Seen from the essence itself, they are, as I have said, positionally determined by it (the essence); seen from the point of view of the non-essential notes themselves, however, this positional determination is the character of *ad*. *Adherence* is a metaphysical character of the real. The real is, then, always «one;» its unity, however, is complex: it is a unity of coherence which is the ground of a unity of adherence. The metaphysical ground of adherence is coherence. In this sense, there is, in the real thing, a profound difference between the coherent notes and the adherent notes, between the essential and the non-essential.

The fact is, however, that this difference, and, in general, the triple meaning of the concept of essence, is a difference which refers to *that which* the thing is. It is a difference in the order of «suchness.» In it, the non-essential notes determine further the constitutive notes or the notes of «suchness» in the strict sense. This strict and formal essence has, however, a transcendental function. We are speaking, of course, of the constitutive and not of the quidditive essence. This it is, which, in its transcendental function, as we have seen, determines the *de suyo*, the reality of a thing insofar as it is real, the *res*. The non-essential notes, then, have no reality at all *de suyo*. Quite the contrary; it is the essence which *de suyo* possesses the non-essential notes. Only because the essence is reality, are the non-essential notes real. In the order of suchness, it is the non-essential notes which determine the essence. Transcendentally, by contrast, it is the essence which confers reality on them (the non-essential notes). The adherent is reality in and by the reality of the coherent. This transcendental character of the essence with respect to the non-essential is not «to sustain.» Substantialism reappears anew. The essence is a moment of the substantivity, that moment according to which the thing is *res*. The function of this *res* is not «to sustain» 480 but «to reify.» All that is non-essential is reified by the essence as *res;* and reciprocally, every *res* reifies all that derives from it or all that accrues to it. Transcendentally, there is neither retrogression to the first concept of essence nor restriction to the third. The strict constitutive essence in transcendental function does not limit itself to the establishment of something real; its function is much vaster: it reifies every non-essential determination in the order of «suchness.» It does so in such fashion that there is transcendentally but one concept of essence: the reality as something *de suyo.* The non-essential is not a second reality juxtaposed to the essential; rather, insofar as it is reality, it is transcendentally the same reality as the reality of the essential. What happens is that, mentally, we can consider a non-essential note in and by itself, and speak of that which it is *de suyo.* Then, however, we consider it not insofar as it is a non-essential note but simply as a real thing. This, however, comes from the mode of considering the note and not from its metaphysical reality.

Twice (with respect to adherence and with respect to reification) we have seen the concept of substance appear. However, despite the monotonous repetition of ideas, it is necessary to recall that the essence is not essence of substance, but essence of the substantivity. Essence is not substance, whether first or second. It is not second substance, because the essence is not necessarily quidditive nor quiddifiable, but formally and essentially is constitutive essence. Neither, however, is it first substance. Because reality, whether it is subjectual or not, is primarily substantivity, that is, a system of notes. And within it the essence is the subsystem or fundamental system, the determining system of the total system. Because it is cyclical, this fundamental subsystem is system in its own right in a constructivity. 481 And because it is positionally determinant of the other notes, it confers on these the character of system by adherence. The non-essential notes are not, then, an exception from the transcendental point of view. This is the reason why the function of the essence with respect to the non-essential in the order of «suchness» is not «to sustain» but «to reify.» In these two points (the reality as substantivity and the essence as constructivity) there resides, for all that concerns our problem, all our difference with Aristotle.

To sum up, essence is the strict and formal «suchness» in transcendental function, in the order to the *de suyo* and the transcendentality itself is the *de suyo*, the real *simpliciter*. This is the transcendental character of the essence. The essence does not, however, have only a transcendental character, but also possesses a strict *transcendental structure*. This is the other aspect of the transcendental consideration of essence.

2. *Essence: Its Transcendental Structure*

The transcendental order is determined by the order of the «suchness» in transcendental function. What, however, this function determines is not only certain transcendental «properties,» but a true, transcendental structure. We have seen, in a word, that the «suchness» *(talidad)* is something constructed, and what it determines transcendentally is the *de suyo* as a «construct of reality.» The real, the *de suyo*, is constructivity, and precisely in virtue of being such, this construct finds itself internally and transcendentally structured. In discussing the problem of «to be,» I appealed to this concept of transcendental structure: then, however, it was the structure of reality in that external-transcendental respectivity which is called *world*. Now, by contrast, what concerns us is the internal, transcendental respectivity of the real, of the essence in and by itself.

No dialectical disquisition is involved here. Quite the contrary. 482 Since what determines this structure is the transcendentally constructed character of reality, we must turn our attention to the analysis of constructivity in order to find a guideline for our investigation in this order.

First of all, because it is constructed, the *de suyo* involves not only the intrinsic belonging of the «notes-of» and of the «unity-in,» but also the fact that this belonging has its own transcendental character: «constitution.» This *de suyo*, however, not only has a transcendental character, but also, in virtue of those two moments of the constructivity (the «*de*» and the «*in*»), the thing is *de suyo*, according, however, to different internal respects of these two moments; these respects are what I have called dimensions. The second structural moment of the transcendental is «dimensionality.» Finally, the constructivity has a different transcendental function according to the «type» of «suchness» *(talidad)* in question. Constitution, dimensionality, and type: here we have the three transcendental structural moments of the *de suyo*, as such.

    I. *Essence and constitution.* Naturally, we may recall once more, we are speaking not of the quidditive, but of the constitutive essence. This essence has two moments: the essential notes and their unity. These two moments belong to the essence intrinsically. The notes endow the unity with its «suchness» and the unity is present «in» the notes making them «notes-of» (primary, coherential unity): it is the intrinsic constructivity of the essence. In transcendental function, this belonging constitutes the reality, the *de suyo:* it is the metaphysical construct. The question is not, however, exhausted by this analysis. For, in its character as construct, the *de suyo* constitutes a
483 constructed «unity,» that is to say, a unity of two moments. The *de suyo* is an *unum:* it is the transcendental unity. This unity is not the same as the essential unity, even though it is necessary to use the same word in order to designate it. The essential unity is the primary moment of the «suchness.» The transcendental unity is something different. We have seen that the «entire» construct of «suchness» *(constructo talitativo)* has a character common to unity and the notes: essential actuality. This actuality in transcendental function is formally the *res*, the *de suyo*. It is a metaphysical construct. In this construct, then, its character of «real» is common to the notes and to the unity *qua* real. And this common transcendental moment has as its proper character *to be unity:* it is the transcendental unity. The constructed character of the real *qua* real is, before all else, transcendental unity. Reciprocally, the transcendental unity is the actuality of the *de suyo* as metaphysical construct. Transcendental unity, then, is not to be confused with essential unity. Because it is a construct, the transcendental unity has a precise structure. This must be clarified in some detail.

    The primary coherential unity confers, in terms of «suchness» *(talitativamente)*, their cyclical closure on the essential notes; and this cyclical closure is that in which the indivision of the real positively consists. From this point of view, incoherence multiplies the real. Closure, we have said, has a character of suchness proper to itself: it is an individual constitution. And individual constitution is the way in which the essence determines the transcendental unity, the metaphysically constructed unity of the real as such. It is a transcendentally individual unity. What is the character of its structure?

When we were discussing this problem in terms of «suchness» we said that the idea of individual embraces four moments: the moment of numeral unity, of constitution, of concretion, and of incommunicable reality. For the time being we may set aside the moment of concretion. Of the other three moments, the first two referred to what we called singularity and constitution. As we shall see, transcendentally the difference proves to be absorbed into a higher character: the transcendental constitution. The fourth is the moment according to which each real thing is incommunicably separated from all the others. Constitution and incommunicability are, then, the two aspects of the individual transcendental unity. These mutually implicate each other, and the transcendental unity, in its proper structure, consists in this implication. Let us examine both aspects successively beginning with the second.

The cyclical closure in terms of «suchness» is, in transcendental function, that in virtue of which to be *de suyo* is to be «separated» from all the rest. This, however, is the most superficial aspect, because it is merely negative. In the transcendental order, the cyclical closure has an exact positive function, the real *qua* real belongs to itself. The real, as a *de suyo*, is thus a *suyo*. This is not a concept in the order of «suchness.» In the order of suchness, everything has «its» properties. Here, however, we are talking about the transcendental order, and transcendentally, the thing does not have «its» properties but is *suyo* its *own*, itself. This belonging to itself, this *suyo*, is the positive element which underlies the formal indivision, or undividedness. Because it is *suyo qua* reality, all of the real is incommunicable. Incommunicability is the negative aspect of this positive belonging to itself. Understood in this way, incommunicability is not a character which refers formally to existence — incommunicable existence as it is customarily called — but refers rather to the *de suyo* itself, which embraces, indistinctly, both essence and existence in the classical sense. Existence is incommunicable only insofar as it belongs to the thing as something which is *suyo*. The *de suyo* is beyond essence and existence in the classical sense. And it is this *de suyo* which, because it is *suyo*, is incommunicable in virtue of its formal *ratio (razón);* and only in virtue of the *de suyo* being incommunicable are both essence and existence, in the classical sense, incommunicable. In this respect, then, the transcendental function of essence is to establish the real as something which is *suyo de suyo.* Transcendental unity is, before all else, this unity which consists in being *suyo.*

This is not just a wearisome play of words. *De suyo* is the character of the reality of the real *qua* real; and *suyo* is the moment of the real's belonging to itself. This difference between the *de suyo* and the *suyo:*

1. is only a difference of reason; this is the reason why *suyo* is a transcendental moment;

2. is a difference of reason, but founded *in re;* there is one aspect under which something is *de suyo,* another under which it is *suyo;*

3. this *fundamentum in re,* however, is, in the real thing itself, a precise structure of grounding. The *suyo* is not merely something «added» to the *de suyo,* nor is it a matter of two aspects discernible *ad libitum* among a thousand others which might be excogitated. The *suyo* is, quite the contrary, a moment which belongs intrinsically to the *de suyo* in accordance with a structure of grounding: the real is *suyo because* it is *de suyo.* The *suyo,* incommunicability, is only a «resultant,» so to say, of the *de suyo.* This is the reason why incommunicability is not only a transcendental *property* but has, further, the character of a transcendental *structural* moment.

The *suyo,* understood in this way, is a character of the *de suyo;* therefore, it permeates *(transfunde)* the real in its entirety in all its moments, including the moments of «suchness.» A thing, for example, is *suyo* as living, as being endowed with such and such physical notes, etc. This is the reason why it is incommunicable. The *suyo* touches the notes and the essential unity, the real, in what is most proper and radical in it, its reality itself.

As a construct of «suchness» *(constructo talitativo),* the essence is, then, enclosed cyclical unity, a system of notes capable of forming by itself a system endowed with constitutional sufficiency. This character of «suchness» in transcendental function consists in determining a constructed metaphysical unity whose first structural aspect is to belong to itself, to be *suyo.*

With this it might appear that we have now reached the transcendental *unum* of the real. But this is true only in an incomplete manner. In terms of «suchness» the notes impart a suchness to the essential unity, that is to say, confer certain determined and particular characteristics. Its transcendental function, however, is higher than this: in its transcendental unity, the real not only belongs to itself (is *suyo*, is incommunicable) but also belongs to itself in a manner particular to each essence. In terms of «suchness» the notes impart «suchness» to the primary coherential unity; transcendentally, they modulate the belonging to itself. Every reality *de suyo* is *suyo*, but «in its own way.» This belonging to itself in a particular way is what we call transcendental «constitution.» The unity of incommunicability, to the degree to which it is grounded only in the *de suyo*, has the structural character of constitution. Here we have the complete transcendental *unum*. It is not merely a property but the transcendental *structure* of two moments: one, the moment of belonging to itself, the other, the moment of belonging to itself in a special, particular way. Clearly, this concept of a «special way» of being *suyo* has nothing in common with the substantial modes of which some scholastics spoke in relation to subsistence.

The concept of constitution emerged for us in passing in speaking of the essential notes, but in a somewhat unclear way. Then, constitution meant the intrinsic determination in terms of «suchness» of 487 the unity by its notes; every real thing has, in this sense, its proper individual characteristics, *its constitution.* Transcendentally, however, it is not a question of this kind of quality of the unity, but of an intrinsic way of belonging to itself. And it is in this transcendental sense that we speak here of constitution. These are not two independent senses: the second is the first in transcendental function. And the difference between these two senses leaps to view. In terms of suchness, there is, as we have said, a difference between the moment of numerical unity and the moment of qualified constitution. There are things which are only *singuli*, different examples only numerically, while in other things, there are constitutive differences in the order of «suchness.» It was necessary to distinguish, therefore, mere singularity from strict and formal individuality. Nevertheless, at that time, we already suggested that, «strictly speaking,» the singular, too, has its constitution, indeed, its singular constitution.

This suqqestion was made in the order of «suchness.» When, however, these «suchnesses» are taken in transcendental function, the difference between singularity and strict individuality remains absorbed in the *(lo)* transcendental individual. But the *singulum* and the *individuum*, taken in transcendental function, determine the *de suyo* as something that is *suyo*, as something that belongs to itself, in a particular way. That is to say, the *singuli* and the *individui* have equally their own transcendental constitution. And as both in the first and in the second t h e essence is constitutive and not quidditive, it follows that the transcendental constitution determined by the said essence is transcendentally individual; to be individual, in a word, is to belong to one's self, to be *suyo*, in a particular way. Essence is transcendental constitution.

489 This idea of transcendental unity as individual constitution was necessary. When Aristotle delineated the problem of the «one» (ἕν), he differentiated diverse senses of unity, and, in a special way, these four: the one as «continuum» (continuous, συνεχές), and as the «whole» (ὅλον), the one as «universal» (καθόλου), and the one in the sense of «each one» *(cada cual,* καθ᾽ἕκαστον). This last meaning alone concerns our present problem. And a double inadequacy is to be discovered in it. In the first place, in terms of suchness, «each one» *(cada cual),* as mere singular, is not distinguished from «each one» *(cada cual)* as strict and formal individual, what «each one» *(cada cual)* is according to a proper determination in suchness *(determinación talitativa propia).* In the second place, however, when the «each one» *(cada cual)* is taken in the transcendental sense, it remains reduced to something vague and imprecise, precisely because of the lack of the transcendental determination of constitution. «Each one» is transcendentally «each one» according to its proper constitution, according to the particular way of belonging to itself, of being *suyo* and, therefore, one.

As I see it, this is the positive concept of what scholasticism, without further clarification, called «inclusion» or, at least, «connotation» of the positive entity in transcendental indivision. When discussing this concept, I said that indivision, both as including and connoting the entity of the being, is an inadequate concept, because it leaves unanswered the question of precisely determining the positive character of indivision and the precise way in which this positive element is included in the structure of the *unum*. The intrinsic indivision is the coherential cyclical unity, whose transcendental function is belonging to itself, the being *suyo* of what is *de suyo*. And in its turn, the inclusion of this cyclical coherence in the transcendental indivision is precisely and formally the modulation of the belonging to itself, that is, the constitution. It is not only that, as a matter of fact, real things have constitution, but also that they must have it by reason of their proper kind of unity. This is the 489 reason why the constitution is transcendental. The real then has, not this vague and formalistic «property» of being «one,» but an exact «structural» character: transcendental constitution. And the function in the order of «suchness» which determines this character is the constructivity in the order of «suchness» as constitutive of the *suyo*. The essence as reality, as *de suyo*, has an exact transcendental structure, the first aspect of which is to be *suyo, constitutionally*, that is constitutionality. As I have said, essence is, above all, transcendental constitution.

Essence, then, as reality, as *de suyo*, is *suyo*, is transcendentally individual. The individual, however, has many further determinations, almost infinite in principle, which do not constitute the individual but which determine it in the order of concretion. This is the third moment of individuality, of which we must now speak. The difference of which we are speaking is rigorous and beyond appeal: «individual» is not a «concrete.» It always remains to say, however, in what, on this point, the transcendental character of this further determination may consist. In its formal and particular *ratio (razón)*, the real is the essence as a *de suyo*, and this essence is already individual in its character as essence; it is individual *de suyo*. The transcendental function of the individual character of «suchness» is much wider than that of determining the particular manner of belonging to itself. Just as the reality, as *de suyo*, transcendentally «reifies» all of its notes, which are non-essential in the order of «suchness,» so also the individual essence, as a *de suyo*, «individualizes» all the further notes in the line of concretion. The thing, we have said, is *res* and reifies. We may now add, then, that the *res* is transcendentally individual, and individualizes all that flows from it or that accrues to it, exactly and formally because it is already transcendentally individual. Transcendentally, concretional determi- 490 nation is individualization. Individualization means that these further notes are not only concrete, but also, by reason of their belonging to the essence, take on individual character; it is the essence which confers on them their character of individuals. For this reason it is necessary to introduce, at this point too, adequate words which would prevent confusions. Essence, insofar as it is already transcendentally individual, has individuity *(individuidad)*. The notes of the further concretion do not make the thing individual, but rather give it individuality *(individualidad)*. Already, in the order of «suchness,» the difference is profound: the individual is not made, but «is» once and for all, while individuality is acquired or is impoverished, and, in any case, always is modified. This is the difference between to be *«el» mismo* and *«lo» mismo*. The real thing, so long as it endures, is always the *(la,* feminine of *el)* same, but it is never absolutely the *(lo)* same. In transcendental function, the difference takes on another character: it means that individuity, precisely because it is such, individualizes; so that there is then only one sole individual in its two moments of individuity and individuality. These two moments must, however, be understood correctly. In the order of suchness, the ulterior notes have two different characters. Some notes flow from the constitutive dimension (by positional determination); they are constitutional notes. Others are strictly adventitious. The first «express» the constitutive dimension (the phenotype, for example, is the expression of the genotype); the second «concretize» the individual. In both cases, it is the notes which determine the individual in the order of «suchness.» (For this reason I have called them, in this context, without further distinction, «notes in the order of concretion.») In the transcendental order, however, the situation, so to say, is inverted; the essence proves to be an individual *de suyo;* and, thanks to this individuity, confers on the concretive notes their character as individuals. The essence «individualizes» *de suyo.* For 491 this reason, the difference in the order of «suchness» remains absorbed in the transcendental individual. This individual is unique.

To sum up, the essence, the real, the *de suyo,* has a structural moment proper to itself; it is transcendentally constitution with the character of individual. But it is not only this.

II. *Essence and dimensionality*. The essence is a transcendental construct. In it are found, naturally, the two moments of constructivity (the «of» of the notes and the «in» of the unity) in transcendental function, that is, as structural determinants of the *de suyo* as such. And we have just seen that this constructivity determines that transcendental unity which is the constitution. The constitution, we have said, is the mode in which the real (thing) itself is one. There is, however, another aspect: the unity of the essence in the order of «suchness» as primary coherential unity not only includes the notes but is «in» them exactly in its character as primary. And this character in the order of «suchness» determines, in transcendental function, another structural character, also transcendental. It is not simply that the constitution is an inclusion of the notes in the unity and that we now take this «relation» inversely. This would be true in the order of «suchness.» Here, instead, we are referring to the entire metaphysical construct as the structure of the *de suyo* itself. And in this line, we have said, the transcendentally real, that is, as *de suyo*, belongs to itself in each real thing *as* real, in its particular way. The constructivity, then, of the essence in the order of «suchness» determines another structural character different from that of this belonging.

We saw in the course of the analysis of the «real» truth that, in the order of suchness, the real is found projected from within, in its own notes. This projection is the formal «respect» of the real in its notes, a respect which is nothing other than the actualization of the real in them. The thing not only has hardness, for example, but is 492 actualized in its entirety in this note of hardness; the note is not «had» but «is» in it. It is nothing other than the constructivity in the order of suchness of the essence, the presence of the unity «in» the notes. This projective respect is what I have called dimension. And we see that that of which it is dimension is the substantivity, the constitutional sufficiency of something. In treating the theme of real truth, I introduced these concepts somewhat indiscriminately, that is, passing over the sphere of mere suchness and emphasizing the transcendental, at that point not yet distinguished as such. The same happened with the concept of constitution. There we were essaying a first introduction to these concepts of constitution and dimension. However, equally with constitution, dimension is a transcendental concept in the strict sense; and the difference between these two ways of viewing, that of «suchness» and the transcendental, will be seen immediately.

Considered in the order of «suchness,» it was a matter of a «respectivity» of the «in» of the unity with respect «of» the notes. By this primary exigential presence, the unity is in the notes actualizing them as essential notes. We said that, from the point of view of the notes, the essence is something «been» *(sido)* with respect to the primary unity. In transcendental function, then, this unity, this «in,» in its respect to the notes, is what determines a structural character of the *de suyo* itself. The essence transcendentally, that is, the real, the *de suyo*, is something that not only belongs to itself in its own way (constitution), but also is something which *de suyo* is «from itself» what it is. And in this respect, the *de suyo* is an *intus* of its own reality, is «interiority.» Interiority does not mean here anything occult; it is not a matter of something which lies beyond the essential notes or beneath them, because the essence is a
493 construct, a metaphysical construct, a construct of reality. The essence, I said, has the character of system, is the fundamental system of the substantivity. And the «in» of its unity, the interiority, is nothing else, transcendentally, but «systematicity» itself. Neither does it mean that it is an intimacy. Not everything real possesses intimacy; this is given (intramundanely) in human realities. Material things lack intimacy: they do, however, have this interiority which is nothing else than the transcendental character of the «in» in the order of suchness of the essence, systematicity in transcendental function. The *de suyo* is, in this aspect, a «from itself.» Correlatively, in transcendental constructivity, the notes are nothing other than the been *(sida)* unity, that is, been *(sida)* interiority. And this is precisely an *extra*, an «exteriority.» Exteriority does not mean exteriorization before other entities. Quite the contrary, nothing can exteriorize itself in this sense, because, anteriorly, that is to say, independently of this possible exteriorization, it has or «is» exteriority. Exteriority is a transcendental moment of the *de suyo;* it is nothing other than interiority formed *(plasmada)* to be the real itself. The essence, the real, is something, if I may be permitted the expression, «self formed» *(auto-plasmada)*. Transcendental constructivity is this intrinsic structure of interiority and exteriority. The interior is found actualized in

the exteriority; and, reciprocally, the exterior would not be exterior were it not the *ex* of the interiority itself. In the order of «suchness» the essence is the «in» of the unity and the «of» of the notes. Transcendentally, by contrast, the essence, as reality *simpliciter*, is interiority and exteriority as moments of this metaphysical construct which is the *de suyo*. The formal respect, then, according to which the interiority is shaped *(plasmada)* in its proper exteriority, that is to say, the very respect of the *ex*, is what constitutes what I call «dimension.» Dimension is a strictly transcendental character; it is the *in* in the *ex* as a moment of the *de suyo* itself. 494

Hence the profound difference between this view of the real and that of which Aristotle spoke. Aristotle sees the notes of the real as something which supervenes upon a subject, a substance. No note has «separate» reality, but only reality as «united» to a substantial subject. He calls these different ways of «to be» «categories» or supreme «genera» of being, of the ὄv. In the first place, however, even within Aristotle himself, this concept of category suffers from a serious ambiguity, because he does not distinguish sufficiently between two aspects of the categories. Only when they are viewed in their proper content are they supreme «genera» of being. By contrast, when they are viewed as different modes of «to be,» the categories have nothing to do with their generic character. The Latins translated category as predicament. Strictly, however, the categories are predicaments only by reason of their content, that is, as genera. Taken as modes of «to be» they are not predicaments. There is always this ambivalence, or better, this ambiguity, between category and predicament in Aristotle. This situation does not come about by chance. The fact is that Aristotle, by reason of the convergence which he sees between the reality and the predicamental *logos*, conceived the reality in subjectual form. Consequently, the categories, other than substance, appeared to Aristotle as accidents, that is, as something which is not real save upon a substantial subject. As a consequence, this is, as I have said, fundamentally a view of reality «from outside inward.» Hence it was enough that with Hegel, twenty-three centuries later, the real should be seen «dialectically,» in order that the reality might be conceived as an «interiorization» of the notes in which its «to be» consists. The real, however, is not, *primo* and *per se*, substance, but substantivity. And the substantive element *simpliciter* of the substan-

tivity is the essence. The essence does not have notes which are notes
495 of a subject, nor is it an *interiorization* as Hegel thought; it is a
primary *interiority* which, of itself, is already formed *(plasmada, ex)*
in its proper essential exteriority. It is a vision «from within outward,»
a vision from the primary «in» of the unity and from the «of» constructed of the notes, but both in transcendental function. The
metaphysical constructivity of the real is this structure of «interiority-exteriority» whose formal transcendental character is «dimension.»
Dimension is nothing other than the *ex* of the *in* in the construct of
reality.

   In the order of «suchness,» the real is, as we have seen, pluri-
dimensional: the thing actualizes itself in its notes in three respects,
namely: richness, solidity, actuality of being *(estar siendo).* These
three dimensions of «suchness» have a precise transcendental function
as moments of the *de suyo.*

   In the first place, *richness.* I have already indicated that, even in
the order of «suchness,» the richness of the essence cannot be confused with abundance of notes. The distinction, however, remained
obscure. It becomes clear now when richness is considered in transcendental function. What transcendentally determines the richness
is the «perfection» of the real as such. The essence, the real, is of
itself *(de suyo)* more or less perfect. An essence which would be
whole in a single note, would have the highest perfection. The constructed *ex* (according to which the interiority of the real is transcendentally exterior) is, before all else, its own «perfection.» Perfection is, then, here a transcendental moment. It is the first — first
only in enumeration — transcendental dimension of the essence in
as far as it is *de suyo,* insofar as it is reality.

   In the order of «suchness,» however, the real actualizes itself in
a second dimension, solidity. Solidity, in transcendental function, is
«stability.» The essence is a more or less stable *de suyo;* if this were
not the case, it would not be something *de suyo,* but would be
496 dissipated into a pure nothing. Stability is not the synonym of
static nor of quiescent in Hegel's sense, but is a transcendental
character which lies beyond these properties in the order of «suchness.» In this order, there are many different stabilities: there are
static stabilities; there are, also, dynamic stabilities. For example,
one speaks of the stability of the solar system (something which to

this day has resisted mathematical proof) and stable and unstable equilibria. In this last case, stability always involves a dynamic aspect, whatever may be the concept that is formed of it (stability in the sense of difficulty in issuing from the state of equilibrium or stability in the sense of facility in recovering equilibrium by internal forces). It will be said that these dynamic systems are not «things.» Undeniably, however, there are «things» to the stability of which, in the order of «suchness,» there belongs (in one form or other, this is not important here) a moment of «movement;» for example, the stability of a fluid mass in rotation (many stars and, above all, living beings.) Here we are not referring to anything of this kind, but rather to the fact that stability means that the real, whatever it may be in the order of «suchness» (static or dynamic) is stable in its reality itself. Nor does stability mean that the real is a thing like a permanent subject beneath its possible movements (in the metaphysical concept of movement). It is not that there are not stable realities in this sense. This type of stability, however, is neither the only nor the typical example of stability. Even more, the very necessity that there should be a permanent subject — the mobile — is a consequence of the transcendental stability of the real, and not the reverse. This consequence, in turn, is not necessary. Movement might be only a moment of the primary act itself (as scholasticism would say) of the real, a case in which it would not be possible to speak strictly of an «underlying subject,» but of a «moving substrate.» A moving substrate is one thing; a mobile subject quite another. We will not enter any more deeply into this problem which does not concern us here. The only thing that concerns us is that whatever may be the concrete character of the stability, this stability, as transcendental character, is a structural moment of the real, a transcendental moment of the *de suyo*. A thing which is essentially unstable is essentially unreal, if the expression be permitted me.

Finally, the real has, in the order of «suchness,» another dimension: its actual exercise of the act of being *(estar siendo)*. When we reached this point, this new dimensional character also necessarily remained obscure. The effectivity of actually exercising the act of being *(estar siendo)* is clear only in transcendental functions. The actual exercise of the act of being *(estar siendo)* in transcendental function is «duration.» This is a strictly transcendental character. Duration here does not mean how long a thing endures (this would be only the measure of duration) nor does it mean either the *distensio* of St. Augustine or the *durée* of Bergson. In all these cases, duration has a temporal character. There are, however, other cases in which duration is a-temporal *(aevum)* or extra-temporal (eternal). Here we are treating of none of these. Duration, in itself, is a transcendental character of all these «durations;» all of these are but modes of enduring. Nor is duration, as a transcendental character, formally identical with what some scholastics had in mind when they said that to endure is to retain «to be.» First, because it is not a question of «to be,» but of reality. In the second place, and chiefly, because in this definition duration is conceived by way of its effects. Duration is neither to retain «to be» nor to retain reality, but to be «enduringly;» that is, that by reason of its own transcendental structure every reality is *de suyo* enduring. Under any contrary condition, it would be evanescent, it would not have reality. And in this sense it (duration) is a transcendental moment of the *de suyo*.

498   Perfection, stability, duration, are three dimensions according to which the real is shaped *(plasmado)* from within in the intrinsic exteriority of its notes. They are three formal respects of the *in* in its *ex*. In them is expressed the transcendental dimensionality of the real. All the real is *de suyo* more or less perfect, more or less stable, more or less enduring. They are not three independent dimensions; for this reason, as I remarked in the proper place, these dimensions cannot be understood in mathematical form. Transcendentally, however, they are true dimensions. They belong to each other mutually; in each of them, however, the real is «more or less» (perfect, stable, enduring), that is to say, in their very unity they are something according to which the real is «measured.» And what is measured in this measuring, in the form of «more or less,» is what transcendentally constitutes the «grade of reality.» The concept of «grade» has its origin, obviously, in the order of «suchness»: there are things which are more or less hot, more or less developed, etc. Transcendentally, however, there are no grades of «to be» in this sense of gradation, that is, as though the grades of reality were only differences, so to say, of intensity. Essences have reality in different measure, but with a metaphysical, and not a gradual, distinction. With this clarification the word can be employed in metaphysics. What consti-

tutes this measure or degree is precisely the dimensional structure of
the real as such. Real things are real *de suyo* in different measure.
It is, in a certain sense, a transcendental capacity of reality. For this
reason, in their difference of transcendental measure, essences are not
distinct in degree, or grade, but rather have no common measure
physically: physically, they are incommensurable.

The real is *de suyo*, belonging to itself in its own way and,
further, is real in different measure. Constitution and dimension are
two transcendental structural moments of essence as something *de
suyo*.

III. *Essence and typicalness (tipicidad)*. The real, the essence, 499
belongs to itself, in its own way, and from itself. This constitution
and dimension have, in their turn, a different character according
to the «suchness» of the essences in question. This diversity in the
order of «suchness» can, in effect, be understood in two ways. First:
diversity which is formally of the order of suchness; second, diversity
in the order of «suchness» according to its transcendental function.
The first point of view would lead to a catalogue or classification
of essences. This is not what we are looking for here; we have
already made some allusion to it in speaking, for example, of the
dimension of stability in the essence. The only thing we are looking
for here is the diversity of essences according to a difference in their
transcendental function. All material essences are diverse in the order
of «suchness» in their formal «suchness» (material bodies of different
character, organisms of different types, etc.); nevertheless, they all
have the same transcendental function. What we are looking for,
then, is not a diversity in the order of «suchness» *qua* order of
«suchness,» but a diversity in the order to a difference of transcendental function. We call this difference transcendental «typicalness.» Stated in stricter terms, this is a matter of a difference in the
metaphysical construct *qua* metaphysical.

Every reality, every essence, is *de suyo* in the double structural
moment of constitution and dimension. This ordination to the *de
suyo* is the transcendental function of every essence without exception; it is precisely what makes it something formally real. Among
essences, however, there are some whose transcendental function
consists simply in establishing them as realities and «nothing more.»

This «nothing more,» negative in appearance, is a positive moment of transcendental typicalness. It is the type of essence that I would call transcendentally «closed.» By this statement, I am not referring to the closure of the essence in the order of «suchness;» every essence, without exception, possesses its notes of «suchness» according to a closed, cyclical unity; and this closure, in transcendental function,
500 is, as we have seen, the *de suyo*. I am referring to something else; namely, the moment according to which, by reason of being something *de suyo*, the closed essence is something «in itself.» Its entire transcendental reality is exhausted in being «*de suyo en sí*.» This is what the closed essence consists in. The expression «*en sí*» has already made its appearance when we were treating of the *ratio (razón)* of the essential unity. Then, however, «*en sí*» meant: (1) a moment of «suchness» and (2) a moment of «suchness» exclusive to quiddifiable essence, that is, of each individual reality with respect to others of the same species. Here, however, «*en sí*» is a transcendental moment of every closed essence as such.

It is clear that no essence constitutes an exception to this rule, in the sense that no essence falls short of being something «*en sí*.» What happens is that there are essences which, in transcendental function, not only are «*en sí*» but are «*en sí*» in such wise that it belongs to their particular *de suyo, in actu secundo*, to behave, not only according to the notes which they possess, but also in view of their particular character of reality. *In actu primo* (the only decisive factor in this point) this structure is what constitutes the «open» essence. Openness is here a transcendental structural character. These essences are not «*en sí*» and «nothing more,» but in their very way of being «*en sí*» they are open to their character of reality *qua* reality and, therefore, are open, in principle, to the whole of reality as such. These are, without any shadow of doubt, the intelligent and volitional essences. Since that which possesses will is grounded (whatever may be the manner of understanding this grounding) in the note of intelligence, we may limit ourselves to this last and speak only of the intelligent or intellective essence. Every intellective essence is transcendentally open and, reciprocally, every transcendentally open essence is, *eo ipso*, intellective, because intelligence is, formally, apprehension of the real as real, and, reciprocally. The intellective essence is open *de suyo* to everything real as real. The closed essences are, then, those which are not intellective. Intelligence, which is an essential note, has a transcendental function exclusive to itself. For this reason, the difference between the intellective and the non-intellective is a transcendental difference and not only a difference in the order of «suchness.» Open and closed are two transcendental «typicalnesses.»

Let us clarify these concepts. In the first place, openness does not point, formally and in the first place, to the term to which it is open. Here, then, we are not treating of the fact that, by reason of being open, the intelligence coincides in principle with all reality *qua* real. Openness does not mean the condition of the term to which it is open but the very structure of the intellective essence insofar as it is something *de suyo*. In the second place, the *«en sí»* of essence is not the Kantian *«en sí.»* Here *«en sí»* means only the establishment of something as a *de suyo*. This *«en sí»* neither includes nor excludes, without qualification, a transcendental openness. When it excludes such openness, the essence is «only» *de suyo*, «only» *«en sí.»* When it includes such openness, then the real is something *de suyo* «open in itself,» is intelligence. Hence it follows that the intellective essence has a peculiar transcendental function. The essence which is intellective in the order of «suchness» in transcendental function establishes this essence before all else as something real, as something which *de suyo* is something *«en sí.»* At the same time, however, it establishes that essence as something transcendentally open to that which it — the intellective essence — is not in itself, or to its own proper «to be» in itself. These two moments are not structurally independent, and in their mutual transcendental belonging formally consists the type of metaphysical construct to which we have been alluding. In this is grounded the «coincidence» with the whole of the real *qua* real and, as a consequence, the *verum* and the *bonum*. By reason of this «coincidence» the transcendental function of the intelligence exceeds the mere establishment of the intelligence as a reality proper to itself. This «exceeding» however, that is, the «coincidence» is not something primary, but is, rather, the consequence of the transcendental structure of the intellective essence: the transcendental openness.

It is necessary to understand correctly the relation of the *«en sí»* and of the «openness.» It might be thought that the intellective essence is properly and formally (as something *de suyo)* only something «*en sí*,» and that its presumed reference to other realities or to its own reality is an addition, so to say, to this character of the «*en sí*;» in this case the openness would be only a presumed and problematic «addition» to the «in itself.» The intelligence, like any other reality, would be formally «only in itself,» and its presumed openness would not be a formal moment of the reality of the intelligence as such. This was the error of all forms of subjectivism: the intellective essence, by reason of being something «only in itself,» would be a closed essence. But the intellective essence is not *de suyo* only something in itself *(en sí)*, placed only later in relation with other realities, but its openness belongs constitutively and formally to its proper reality in itself. The intellective essence is *de suyo* «open in its very self.»

But it would be no less an error to understand this structure from the opening alone, as though the intellective essence were something like the openness itself, in such wise that its character of «*en sí*» would be the precipitate of that which the intellective essence is «openly.» In the case of the human essence, this would mean that man is pure happening or event. But this is impossible. Openness is, to be sure, an essential moment of the intellective essence as reality; it is, however, a moment which «modifies» — we may say more exactly — that «makes a type of» *(tipifica)* that which the intelligence is as reality *de suyo* «*en sí*.» That is to say, the openness is a tran-
503 scendental character of the «*en sí*.» It is not an addition; even less is it something which floats above itself. Only because the intellective essence is real in its very self can it be open to reality as such. In the case of man, man «is,» not by happening, but rather he happens precisely because he is as he is, as «*de suyo en sí*.» Openness is a transcendentally typical modification of the «*en sí*.» Because it is transcendental, it is not a mere addition to the «*en sí*;» however, because it is only a transcendental *typification*, it is inscribed intrinsically and formally, *a limine*, in the «*en sí*.» This precise articulation of the «*en sí*» and of the «openness» in the intellective essence is, then, a transcendental structure.

This transcendental typicalness of the intellective essence, insofar as it is *de suyo*, has a very clearly defined character considered in the *suyo* itself as resulting from the *de suyo*. We have seen that the essence, by reason of being *de suyo*, belongs to itself in its own way, and that this transcendental structure, the constitution, has, as its character, the individuity which individualizes everything that derives from the «suchness» or that accrues to it, in such wise that, transcendentally, there is but one single individual. The *suyo* of the closed essence is simple individuity. In the case of the open essence, however, the openness transcendentally modifies this metaphysical construct of the *suyo*. Every essence, in a word, belongs to itself. In being open, however, it behaves, in the operative order, not only according to its properties in the order of «suchness,» that is to say, it does not behave only in the manner deriving from its being such only in itself and nothing more, but behaves, rather, in a manner deriving from its particular character as reality; it behaves not only according to what it is in the order of «suchness,» but also according to its transcendentality as such. This means that, in the transcendental constitutive order, an open essence not only belongs to itself, but belongs to itself in a particular manner.

The closed essence is, so to say, only «materially» *suya*. This is 504 not the occasion to examine in detail the differences between the way in which an inanimate reality and a living thing, above all, the animal, belong to themselves. These differences are not properly transcendental but much rather of the order of «suchness.» Transcendentally, the living being belongs to itself only «materially;» transcendentally, it is a «closed» essence. Its openness, in a word, is only «stimulative» *(estimúlica)*; it is open to stimuli, but is not so, formally, to the character of the stimulus as reality. At most, we might say that the animal, above all the superior animal, is a *primordium* of open essence; it is, if one wishes, a «quasi-open» essence, in which phrase the «quasi» expresses the character of mere *primordium*. For this reason, the animal has only individuity; it is *suyo*, but only «materially,» that is, only as transcendental individual. By contrast, the strictly open essence is *suya* «formally and reduplicatively» as I have been in the habit of saying; it not only *belongs* to itself, but also does so in that particular manner of belonging to itself which is *self-possession*, possession of self, in its proper and formal character as reality, in its proper «*ser-suyo*.» It is its reality, as such, that is *suya*. *In actu secundo*, this possession of self is precisely *life*. To live is to be in possession of oneself *(poseerse)*, and to possess oneself is to belong to one's self in the formal and explicit aspect of reality. Life as transient *(transcurso)* is the mere «argument» of life, but is not life itself. In life man possesses himself «transcurrently,» but this transcurrency is life only because it is possession of self. When the possession of self is taken as a character of the first act, this manner of being *suyo* is precisely what constitutes the person.

Just as, then, in the constitutive order, every essence, without exception, is «individuity,» so, too, the open essence is, in the constitutive order, transcendental «personeity.» Personeity is the type of the individuity of the open essence. Just as the individual, transcendentally considered, individualizes everything which derives from its «suchness» or accrues to it, so also the open essence, because it is personeity, «personalizes» (in principle) everything that derives from its «suchness» or accrues to it: it has «personality.» Life in its biographic discursiveness is personal only by personalization. In and by itself, it is not «personal,» but strictly «a-personal.» It is personal only by reason of being the life of a living thing which is already person, that is, which has the character of personeity. Personeity is not personality, but, without personeity, personality would be impossible. It is not enough to say that my acts are mine, those of each person, because by doing only this, one has not shaved down to the person. Personeity does not reside in the fact that my acts are mine, those of each one, but rather that my acts are mine because I am my «own» me, so to say, that is, because antecedently I am personeity. Person is the *suyo* of the open essence. It is a transcendental character. For this reason, it is impossible for an intellective essence not to be person in some form or other (by its own condition or by assumption, etc.); what is impossible is that there might exist an intellective essence which would not be a person, which would *simpliciter* be without personeity.

Man belongs to this type of essence. Intramundanely, he is the only essence which is person. For this reason it is necessary to clarify somewhat this transcendental condition of the human person, both in what refers to its *de suyo* as well as in what refers to its «openness.» It might be thought that our earlier exposition means that (inversely to what happens with every other intramundane reality), in human reality there is a priority of existence over essence. This is the case with all existentialisms. But this is not true. Mere existence is, as we have seen, only a «metaphysical reduction» of the *de suyo*. Without a priority of the *de suyo*, man would not be reality. 506 Furthermore, to exist as a character of the *de suyo* and to conduct oneself with a view to existence would be impossible if man did not have to conduct himself with metaphysical necessity and *a priori* with respect to his existence. And this necessity, precisely because it is such, is something which follows from the transcendental structure of man, that is, from his essence, from his *de suyo*. There is no priority of existence over essence; rather, it is a matter of an essence which *de suyo* conducts itself operatively with regard for its proper reality, because, and only because, it is a transcendentally open essence. It is one thing to be open to one's proper reality; quite another thing that the essence should determine itself processually from the mere act of existing. The latter is metaphysically impossible. Man, by reason of his intellective «suchness,» is *de suyo*, that is, transcendentally, an open essence. And the *suyo* of the open essence is where the person transcendentally resides.

Furthermore, in the case of man, it is necessary to make clear just what this openness itself may be. All intelligence is openness to the real *qua* real. But this tells us nothing about the particular character of this openness. From the latter depends the very character of intelligence itself; because, in principle, intelligences can be conceived which differ essentially in the order of «suchness.» Therefore, it is not enough to say that comprehension is openness. What constitutes the openness of this intellective essence which is man, is not primarily *comprehension*, but the discovery of oneself as turned from oneself, insofar as intelligence is turned toward sensation; that is, openness is *impression*. And, as I have already said, I do not, in saying this, refer to the fact that man exercises his intelligence on something already sensed prior to the intellection itself, but that in the order of «suchness,» human intelligence, not only in exercising its act of intellection, but in the very structure of intelligence as such, is turned toward sensation; in such wise that intelligence and sen- 507 sation form one sole structure, the sentient intelligence, thanks to which all reality is sensed in the impression of reality. The human opening is concretely, formally, and primarily sentient, an intellective openness having the character of impression. It is, therefore, a matter neither of intellection being an act ulterior to that of sensing, nor of intellection itself consisting in endowing what is sensed with an objective form (form of an object), different from the subjective form which it had in the act of sensing (Kant), but rather that, in its exercise, the intellection is in itself sentient, and sensation intellective, and that, in their essential constitutive structure, intelligence and sensation constitute a single structure. It is possible, and is a matter of fact, that there may be sensation without intellection, but the opposite is not certain; all intellection is ultimately sentient. This is the reason why man is «animal of realities;» and hence it follows that man is «personal animal.» Man proceeds to elaborate his personality in distention and protension, precisely because structurally he is already personeity, and is such as an animal *(animalmente).*

This reflection upon the human reality as an open essence is only a special case of the problem of the transcendental structure of essence as a *de suyo.* It was, however, suitable not to omit it, first, because it is the sole intramundane essence which is open; and secondly, in order to avoid confusion of concepts; and, above all, in order to eliminate conceptions which are only too current in contemporary thought. Open essence and closed essence are the two transcendentally distinct types of all essences in so far as «de suyo».

508 To sum up. Our purpose has been to form a conception of essence in its transcendentality. And we have seen, first of all, that the essence has a transcendental *character.* Transcendentality is the character of reality as such, that is, the *de suyo.* And the essence is what is constitutive of the real in transcendental function, that is, in the order to the. *de suyo.* This essence, as reality *de suyo,* not only has transcendental properties, but also is a strict transcendental *structure.* What is constitutive of the real is, in effect, of a constructed character. This constructivity in the order of suchness in transcendental function determines a metaphysical construct. This construct has its proper structure, a transcendental structure. This structure has three structural moments: as metaphysical construct, the essence is individual constitution, is a dimensional system, and has a determined type. The essence is *de suyo suya* in a manner proper to itself; it is, *de suyo,* an interiority in exteriority, according to different dimensions; it is *de suyo* closed or open to its very character of reality. The intrinsic consistence, belonging to each other, of these three moments constitutes the transcendental structure of the essence.

THE PRINCIPIAL CHARACTER OF ESSENCE

We said, at the beginning of this chapter, that it was our purpose to address the problem of essence in four successive stages: the determination of what essential notes are, the determination of the proper character of the unity of the essence and, in the light of this analysis, to clarify, in a third stage, the problem of essence and reality; finally, the fourth stage was to be the question of the principial character of essence. This is the last question which we have to treat.

When we were studying the problem of essence and reality, we employed many concepts which had already been reached in the first two questions, but we placed them in a different line, the line of reality as such. We may now recall that the concept of principle has already risen at various times during the course of the earlier exposition. Essence appeared to us as principle of the non-essential notes, but a principle of different character according as one treated of constitutional notes or of adventitious notes. Now our concern will be only to enquadrate these concepts in a unitary manner in the line of metaphysical principiality as such.

Aristotle saw clearly what it meant for anything to be a principle (ἀρχή): principle is always and only that from which anything comes in the ultimate instance (πρῶτον). Principle is the «whence» itself (ὅθεν). I immediately introduced the tripartite division of principles, which had already become classical: principle whence something «is» (ἔστιν), whence something «becomes» (γίγνεται), whence anything 510 is known (γιγνώσκεται). In the three cases, the principal character of the principle resides formally in its character of «whence.» Evidently, only the first of these three meanings interests us here, because we are referring to this principle which is the essence. Since here «to be» and reality are not synonyms, we will call this principle «principle of reality.»

In speaking of real principles, it would seem that reality is *eo ipso* already conceived in the meaning which this concept has had since the beginning of our European science. Nothing could be more illusory. The reality of the real has been understood historically in the most diverse ways. It has been understood, in the first place (and this order is purely enumerative) as «power» *(poder):* reality would be a system of powers or capacities *(poderosidad)*. This is the concept which appears, for example, in the wisdom and the religions, not only of primitive mentalities, but in a certain sense even in mentalities which are already «developed» (I will try to explicate this assertion immediately in a more precise manner). Here «power» is a proper character independently of the interpretations which, even within these mentalities, it might receive. For example, powerfulness does not mean «spirit» or «soul» or anything like these. The idea of power is not synonymous with that of «animation.» Quite the contrary. Animism itself presupposes the idea of power, and is only an interpretation of it, the animistic interpretation of power. Another way of understanding reality is to understand it as «force.» Not force in the physical sense of Newton and Leibnitz, to be sure, but a force *sui generis*, the force of the reality; this idea which is already expressed in our languages when we say that something happens, has to happen «by the force of things.» It may also be understood that the reality of the real consists in the fact that each real thing is something *de suyo*, something which, in relation to the earlier conceptions, might be called «naked reality.» With this idea our wisdom slowly was born in Greece. These three characteristics, power, force, naked reality — belong to *every* conception of the real at whatever historical level it may be considered. It is intrication into the character of which we have no need to enter here. We may be satisfied with saying that, in every apprehension of the real, these three characters are present. Inchoatively, however, they are capable of different developments as some characters dominate over others. Primitivism does not consist in considering reality as power, but rather, in including force and naked reality within the character of power, in which case power becomes the one decisive factor. By contrast, our wisdom, limited to naked reality, has, with dire results, forgotten the other two characters. We have no desire to assign them a preponderance which they neither have nor ought to have, but rather of inscribing them in the character of «nude reality,» in the *de suyo*. Things not only act *de suyo* on others, but also have, *de suyo*, a certain dominant power over them. Was it not precisely the unity of these characters which Anaximander expressed in his celebrated ἀρχή? This is not the time to go into this fundamental problem; it is enough, by this summary allusion, to set the problem of the character of the essence as principle in its proper frame of reference: the principle as the character of the *de suyo* itself. Principle means, then, the «whence» of anything in the sense of *de suyo*.

The entire question resides, therefore, in saying how the essence is principle insofar as it is something *de suyo*. The essence is the principle of the constitutional and the adventitious notes. Let us set these latter aside for the moment. The constitutional notes are those which constitute the complete substantivity of the real. That of which the essence is the principle, then, is the substantivity. The substantivity is a system of notes endowed with sufficiency in the order of constitution; within this system the essence is the grounding system, 512 the system of constitutive notes. And the way in which the essence is principle, its character as principle *(principialidad)* insofar as it is essence, is to be «positional determinant» or «functional determinant» of the notes of the substantivity. This is the ὅθεν, the «whence» of the essence. Taking the constructivity in the order of suchness and the transcendental constructivity of essence *per modum unius*, we will say that in a «con-struct» its formal character is «structure» *(e-structura)*. Here, then, structure has a meaning which is not restricted exclusively to transcendental structure. It means that a «con-structed» system is formally «structure.» The essential moments of the essence co-determine each other mutually in their unity. To be structure consists in this. And this «structure» is the determining positional principle of the constitutional notes. Formally, the «effect» of a structure is position. The essential as principle is a structural principle.

By these considerations, the position of this thesis relative to Leibnitz and Aristotle is established. Relative to Leibnitz, because the essence is not a *vis*, but pure structure; only because there is an essential structure is it possible to have a *vis* in certain cases and aspects of substantivity. Relative to Aristotle, because essence is not a moment of substance but of substantivity. For Aristotle the reality, in the eminent sense, is the substance and its essence is hylomorphic: a substantial form which actualizes a prime matter. We prescind, for the moment, from the fact that, for Aristotle, this essence is always specific. This conception, in my opinion, is not sufficiently viable for two reasons. First, because, among the essential moments, there is not, necessarily, any hylomorphic relation. The substantial principles of Aristotle have an extremely precise character, the form is the determinant, the matter the determinable. In a structure, however, 513 all its moments «co-determine» each other mutually; there is no actualization of a matter by a form. In a living being, its essential moments (in the case of man, soul and body) (co-determine each other mutually. For this reason, there is no composition of matter and form in the exact Aristotelean sense. In the second place, however, substance is not the ὄν *par excellance*. The real is *primo et per se*, non-subjectual but substantive. And, as we have seen, these two moments, of subjectuality and substantivity, do not coincide formally. They can sometimes coincide materially in an inanimate body, the substances which constitute it give rise to another substance; formally, however, it is the substantivity of this substance that confers the character of reality *par excellance* on it. The matter is even clearer in living beings. Their substantivity coincides neither materially nor formally with substantiality. An organism is not a substance; it has many substances and renewable substances, while it has but one sole substantivity, always the same. The essence of a living being is a structure. This is the reason why the structure is not an informing substantial form, because its notes co-determine each other mutually and because the structure is not a substance but substantivity. The articulation among the notes of a reality is structure when, by reason of it, it possesses systematic properties, something irreducible to the mere external coupling of elements. Structure is an intrinsic unity expressed in systematic properties. Habituated (as we are) to the idea of substantial unity, this idea of the unity of substantivity might seem to us looser, a unity of inferior rank. This is not the case; the true and radical unity of the real is the unity of substantivity. So much so, as we have seen, that there are substances which are non-substantive. This unity is not substantial; neither, however, is it accidental: it belongs to an order superior to substance. The division of the real into substance and accident is not metaphysically primary. 514 The primary and fundamental division of the real is «substantive-insubstantive.» The greatest metaphysical unity is the structural unity of the substantivity. In the substantial unity itself, what is primary as essence is the system of its constitutive notes *qua* system. This does not mean that substance does not exercise any function in metaphysics. The substance which does so, however, is the substance articulated with the substantivity. We have already seen that, in the order of suchness, this articulation can be of many very different types. I repeat, however, that substantiality is not the formal *ratio (razón)* of substantivity; it is not necessarily even a proper character of the substantivity. On the contrary, the ground of substantiality is substantivity; that is, the principle as such is structure. The essence is what is *simpliciter* real in the real, it is the *de suyo*, as such; and this *de suyo* is a construct the formal character of which, both in the order of «suchness» and transcendentally, is «structure.» It is clear (I insist to the point of monotony on the point) that I am referring to intramundane essences. When one treats of a *de suyo* reality which is essentially extra-mundane, the concept of essence is no longer univocal. Even in this case, however, in the order of concepts, we cannot conceive an essence save by taking our point of departure from the idea of structure and concentrating its moments, by elevation, to the point of reducing them, in the end, to something like a simple point. This would be the plenitude of substantivity. In the intramundane context, however, the essence is *de suyo* principle of the substantivity as structure.

This structure is the principle, not only of the constitutional notes of the substantivity; it is also the principle of its adventitious notes. Here, adventitious does not mean fortuitous, but due to the connection of one substantive reality with others; adventitious is «acquired.» The essence, as structure, is principle of these notes insofar as it constitutively predetermines the ambit of these active or passive connections of one reality with others. But, how does it predetermine them? This is a decisive question. To the degree that 515 they are pre-established, these notes, to which we are referring, are «possible» precisely because the only thing which the essence pre-establishes is their ambit; each one is, therefore, merely possible. What is the nature of this possibility?

The Greeks conceived what we here call pre-establishment *(pre-fijación)* of the possible as a δύναμις, a «potency.» This is true, but a radically insufficient truth. Speaking of those essences which we

have called «closed,» this δύναμις is strictly «potency;» and the
notes which are pre-established by it are, consequently, possibles in
the sense of potentials (with active or passive potentiality). Their
actuality depends on the connection with other realities according to
their potencies. Hence it follows that this actualization of the potency
in a determined note is a «movement» and the actualized note is
metaphysically what we have called «fact.» This is not, however, the
only kind of pre-establishment of the possible, nor, therefore, the only
type of possibility. There is, in a word, an intramundane essence,
man, who is an «open» essence and open in an extremely precise
sense: sentiently. By reason of this structure, then, man *partially*
pre-establishes his possible notes in virtue of potencies which belong
to him by reason of his status as a reality *«en sí.»* However, the
openness modifies the *«en sí»* to a significant degree and, therefore,
the character of its potencies. Between the bare possibility and its
act, man, in many, though not in all, zones of his operations, inexorably
interposes the sketch *(esbozo)* of his «possibilities.» Here, possibility
has a different character than the merely potential. With the same
potencies, man may have different possibilities. The potency passes
into act by mere «actuation;» the possibilities pass over into act,
however, by «acceptation» or «approbation.» Hence it is that the
actualization is indeed no mere movement, nor actuality a mere fact.
The actualization is a «to happen» *(sucede)*, and the note which is
actualized is an «event» *(suceso, o evento)*. This is a strictly meta-
516 physical difference. The fact is the actuality of a mere potency; the
event is the actuality of a possibility. It is clear, however, that these
are not two absolutely independent actualities; there are actualities
which are merely facts, but there are no events which are not also,
in some form, fact. The opening, in a word, is but a modification of
the *«en sí;»* it is not something which floats above itself. For this
reason, the possibility is a modification of the potentiality. Hence it
is that the same act, the same note, may be at once fact and event.
The formal *ratio (razón)*, however, by which it is fact, is not the same
as the formal *ratio (razón)* by which it is event. Therefore, the essence
predetermines *(prefija)* its possible notes, either in the form of bare
«potentializing» potency or in the form of possibility, more exactly,
in the form of «possibilizing» potency.

If we now trace back this operative difference to the structure itself, the difference between closed and open essence takes on a principial character *(principial)* radically different in each case. The structure of the closed essence is the principle «whence» something is a fact; the open human essence is the principle «whence» something is event. And, in this sense, this latter essence has the character of an «eventual» principle. Here, I repeat, eventual does not mean by hazard. The essential structure itself has to receive exact qualifications precisely in its character as principle. A closed essence as structural principle is *res mere naturalis;* and an open essence as structural principle is not only *res naturalis,* but also *res eventualis.* I do not call it *res historica,* because not every event has an historical character in a strict sense; for this, it is necessary that the event be social in some form or other. Evidently, this denomination as *eventualis* is, in a certain sense, *a potiori,* because not all the adventitious notes of man are eventual and because even those which are eventual never are purely eventual. The openness, I have said, is only a mode of the *«en sí»* and, therefore, the event is only a mode of the fact. 517 Without this positive structure of the *«en sí»* there would be neither biographical events nor history; and above all, history would not be formally *human* history. Taking at once the constructivity in the order of «suchness» and transcendental constructivity, we will say that «pure naturalness-eventness» is a metaphysical difference determined by the structural difference of the essence.

To sum up, as principle, the essence is structural principle of the substantivity.

GLOSSARY OF TERMS AND PHRASES PROPER TO THE ZUBIRIAN PHILOSOPHICAL IDIOM

NOTA BENE

Numbers in parentheses refer to page
reference in the Spanish
text edition of 1963

Numbers in square brackets refer to
page references in the
English trans-
lation

TERM

<table>
<tr><td>SPANISH</td><td>ENGLISH</td></tr>
<tr><td>absoluto</td><td>absolute</td></tr>
</table>

Zubiri's use of this important term must be carefully distinguished from its use in Romantic idealism. The context of Zubiri's employment of the term and concept is strictly realistic. It relates directly to the status of the «notes» (q.v.), of the essence. These are absolute if metaphysically ungrounded (v. ground). In a wider sense, «absolute» characterizes in general the position of being without ground, either as a lack or privation (weak use) or as needing no ground (strong sense) either in a limited fashion as in substantivity (q.v.) or unconditionally as in the case of God (q.v.). The concept is also closely related to the concept of factual (q.v.).

<table>
<tr><td>actualización</td><td>act, actual</td></tr>
<tr><td>actualidad</td><td>actuality</td></tr>
<tr><td>(acto) actual</td><td>actualization</td></tr>
</table>

All of these terms are fundamental in Zubiri's thought. The basic concept is *act*, which is taken, in the first instance, in the Aristotelean and scholastic sense, in which it signifies the exercise of being in some dimension and, by extrapolation, in the whole of the real. In this sense, the meaning of the term is best grasped in relation to that of potency, over which act enjoys a general priority, in the sense that, while every act is the realization or actualization of a potency, all potency eventually is grounded in act and actuality. In turn, the notion of *act* leads to those of actual, actuality and actualization. The difference between act and actual is «momentual» (314-315 [296]); actual is the act of the act; the exercise of the act as real. Zubiri, interpreting Aristotle, seeks to order these concepts with a certain seriality: potency, act, actual (400 [364]). Actualization, in turn, is the actuality of the process of the realization of something in the strict order of the real: the fulfilment of it as act; under another aspect actualization is the projection of something as a whole according to all its dimensions. Actuality, finally, is the condition of having been actualized and being in the condition of being actual, i.e., concretely exercising the act, which is the act of a potency, considered abstractly as a state or condition.

	adherencia	adherence
cf. coherence		
inherence		

The notion of adherence must be taken in analectical relation to those of coherence and inherence. Adherence is the state of the presence of the inessential in the structure of the thing; it is the widest and most constitutive note of the inessential, as such, but as present in the totality of the thing (478-479 [426-427]). Coherence, by contrast, is the formal *ratio* of the essential note and hence the metaphysical character of the real as such (298-299 [283-284]). Inherence, finally, refers, in one set of theories, to the manner in which all the subjects of adherence, whether accidents of properties, might be conceived as present in the thing. Zubiri, developing a notion of essence as structure, gives a particular accent to these classical and traditional notions.

	alteración	alteration
	inalterabilidad	inalterability
v. genesis		

Concerns the condition of the essential notes of the essence, their immunity, as constituting the essence, to change. The constitutive inalterability of the notes generates the character of sameness (mismidad q.v.) and, correlatively, it is the constitutive essence which is the moment of the sameness of one thing. Sameness and inalterability belong, in the first instance, to the essential notes and only derivatively to the substantivity (q.v.) (249-251 [245-246]). A certain implication obtains between the inalterability of the constitutive content and the origination of essences. The alteration of the inessential affects the reality; when alteration touches the essence, since the notes are constitutively inalterable, a new or different essence arises. Hence, a constitutive essence can originate (254 stet [249]) and every constitutive essence is the genetic term of another essence according to three possibilities: repetition, engendering, origination (254 [249]). Zubiri goes on to note certain things which inalterability does not imply: i.e., inalterability is not formal identity, but only physical sameness; it is not perduration but a metaphysical character in the order of sameness (257-259 [252-253]).

	aseitas	aseitas
	(Latin)	(Latin)

Zubiri's employment of this term and concept, already made classical by the «second scholasticism» (cf. Giacon, Carlo: *La Seconda Scolastica* 3 vols. Milano

1944-50) follows that usage, with some modification to meet the exigencies of his own thought. It is closely related, in dialectical fashion, to the correlative term «perseitas» (q.v.). A being — any existent — is said to be *a se* and to possess the property of *aseitas* if it is ungrounded in some one of the senses in which this latter notion may be invoked. Substance, *qua* substance, is *a se* and possesses *aseitas* because it resides basically in the sufficiency (q.v.) of its notes. An actual entity is *a se* and possesses this property if it is not caused by another and has actual being *(estar siendo)* (q.v.) *por sí mismo* (q.v.). In this sense only God is *a se* but is not *existent;* (v. existence). «Perseitas» resides in the possession of the capacity for existence (not actual existence) *por sí mismo.* Thus, the world is *per se* (v. world), but is not *a se* and hence does not possess *aseitas.* This is the reason why Zubiri believes that he can speak of and deal with an *intramundane metaphysics* (q.v.). In this matter he takes issue with Spinoza who (in Zubiri's view) confuses these terms and concepts (155 [170]) and is in accord with the thinkers of the second scholasticism (Suarez et alii). (Cf. Giacon, Carlo, *op. cit.* passim.)

caducidad   caducity
decrepitude

The fundamental apprehension of the real as subject to decrepitude; the radical experience of this caracter. It is something which is primarily sensed; however, it becomes most directly and completely apprehended in the sentient intelligence. It is a transcendental function of the transcendental limitation of the real as limited *de suyo* (q.v.). It is intimately involved in the experience and real process of change at whaterver level. Alterability is the condition of a thing as liable to change in its character of suchness.

clasura   closure

Closure is a character of the constitutional system (q.v.) (146 [163]). It is not, however, an incommunication with other realities, but resides within the order of the notes which constitute the system. Consequently, what closure confers on the constitutional system is its *totality*, i.e., precisely its character as a *whole.* It is directly related to the suchness (talidad q.v.) of the thing. As a unity of physical notes, the essence is a totality limited in and by its notes. This limitation of the notes impresses a concrete form on their «suchness»: each one is what it is by way of a mutual «co-limitation» of the notes in their suchness. This «co-limitation» of the suchness is the form of coherence which Zubiri calls «clausura» (closure) (367 [336]). Zubiri compares closure to cyclicalness, but insists that this is only a figure since «not all systems are circular, though all possess what circular systems have in their circularity: conclusion, closedness» (146 [163]). The relation of the notes in the constitutional system as establishing closure is «co-determination» (265; 367 [257; 337]). Closure also has a function in the transcendental order (q.v.).

esenciable   essentiable

v. *reality*

This term relates to the problem of the ambit or range of essence. According to Aristotle, this is the realm of the «natural» (383-385 [351-352]). Zubiri posits a question which is latent in, but not sufficently appreciated by, earlier thinkers. Since for him reality (realidad q.v.) is a more basic notion than either being (ser) or essence (esencia) while other thinkers have traditionally limited the question to what essences there are, Zubiri is led to go a step further and ask what, within reality, may be the *range* of essence, not merely in its actuality (q.v.), but in its intrinsic character as a possible dimension of reality. Only thus, in Zubiri's view, can the question of essence be addressed metaphysically. The question, however, cannot rest at the level of possibility; it turns about necessity of some kind. Reality takes the form of essence under some necessity. The question then arises, what kind of necessity (103 [128]) It is the necessity which brings it about that the thing be such (para que la cosa sea tal) (103 [ibi.]). To understand the range of essence it is necessary to understand what is meant by «such a thing». Since the «such a thing» is in the order of reality, it is necessary to determine the sense of «reality». Zubiri's position will be that the range of the «essentiable» is that range of reality which is susceptible to becoming «such» (tal). What then is the formal and intrinsic character of the «essentiable»? Zubiri replies that the essentiable and the essentiated can be determined in this intrinsic and not merely actual character only by the prior determination of the meaning of «reality» (175 [187]).

esenciado   essentiated

As the ambit of the «essentiable» must be determined in terms of necessity within reality, so the essentiated must be determined within the province of the essentiable. The range of the essentiated is, for Aristotle, substance (146, 147 [162, 164]). For Zubiri, it must be identified by way of the necessity which must be present in order that the real be real as essence. Things have essence, i.e., are essentiated only by that by reason of which they are real (111 [134]), in the sense of *realidad simpliciter* (q.v.) and not merely as reality as such (123-124 [145-146]). The essentiated is not such, however, simply as actual (q.v.) but transcendentally (q.v.) as well (474-481 [423-428]).

especie   species

Zubiri imparts particular weight and meaning to this classical concept especially by the way in which he relates it to the different dimensions of his concept of essence. The physical essence is that in a thing which makes it «one,» clearly circumscribed and determined, thing. One way of understanding this «circumscription» or determination is as a «species» — «that conjunction of features which permits us to locate a thing in the line ... of the *genera,* and which, within the *genus,* represents a determined figure ...» (176 [187]). Species is also discussed in relation to the «constitutive essence.» The function of essence is not exhausted in its specifying function; indeed, this is a lesser function of essence. More basic is its «structuring» function. «The essence as a physical moment of substance exercises a structuring and not (merely) a specifying, function» (92 [116]). Care must be exercised to distinguish properly the philosophical from the biological concept of species (244-246 [242-244]). A condition is indicated between *having* and *being* species (318 [299]). The reason (razón q.v.) of species is identified as «Those constitutive characteristics, by reason of which each individual thing belongs really and physically to a phylum (q.v.), are precisely those which constitute the species ...» (235 [235]). Specificity does not exist «in re» (229 [230]) and must carefully be distinguished from the concept of «class» (231 [231]). The unification of the multitude of individuals by way of similarities is what constitutes a «class» of real things; but «class» is not necessarily «species» ... «for if we try to reach a real species, not just any classificatory concept is adequate» (231 [231]). The problem of species is not to be confused with that of «universals.» «The reality of the species in the individual is not ... the reality of the universal in the singular ... for this reason the species as problem is not the problem of universals, but ... the problem of whether or not every essence is or is not physically erected on a constitutive schema ...» (311 [293]).

| esse logicum | logical existence (being) |

v. esse reale

The proper context for the study of «esse logicum» is the realm of real affirmation (404-405 [367-368]); it involves, consequently, the notion of the origin and force of the copula. «The copulative value of *esse* is an acquisition and not something which lay hidden in the «to exist» (407 [369]). The relation of the «esse logicum» to reality is explained thus: «the only thing important for us ... is the copula of those affirmations which refer to real objects ... In them ... the «is» is something which concerns the objective meaning of any affirmative intellection. It is not exhausted, however, in this objective meaning, but rather ... reaches to that of which I affirm that it «is,» to the *res objecta,* to the objectual. Objectivity ... is not to be confused with objectuality» (405 [367]).

| esse reale | real existence (actual) |

«Esse reale» Zubiri warns, exhibits a persistent ambiguity: «the tendency of the *esse,* the *to be* as something which embraces existence, the essence and the copula without formally signifying any of these three moments» (403 [366]). Scholasticism in particular exhibited this ambiguity. «Esse reale» must be considered under the specific aspect of reality. «Reality is ... everything which, on being conceived, presents itself to me not as receiving its being from the conception itself but is ... *extra animam* ... where *anima* is taken only in the sense of the conceiving act of the intellect. Extra animity is existence. The existent produces real effects independently of whether it is conceived or not» (390 [355]). The basic problem of the proper ordering of these three, existence, essence, copula, is the real issue in the determination of «esse reale.»

estructura   structure

This concept emerges so centrally that Zubiri may correctly be said to be advancing a «structuralistic» theory of essence, provided this term be protected from confusion with other uses of the term «structuralist» and «structuralism»; for the thrust of his theory is «essence» as «structure» and as «structuring.» For this reason he speaks of structure as the «essence of essence» (512 [453]). Structure in intimately related to the notion of essence as principle. Principle means for Zubiri, at least in its reference to essence, the «whence» or source of anything insofar as it is «de suyo» (q.v.). Essence is this principle in all entities which are «de suyo.» The particular manner in which it is principle, its efficasiousness as principle is the *construction* of the entity, the generation or imparting of its characteristics in the particular configuration proper to it (v. constructed state). Structure is the character of this construct of the entity *de suyo* viewed under its formal (as distinct from its genetic, etc.,) aspects (511-512 [453]). Zubiri also speaks of structure as the essence of the living entity (514 [454]). Of particular interest and importance is the notion of transcendental structure. Structure is transcendental by virtue of its relation to transcendental function (q.v.). Reality possesses a transcendental structure which consists both in certain transcendental properties and in certain transcendental functions (424 [383]). The transcendental function is that by which and only by which the reality *(res* not *ens)* possesses transcendental properties. The transcendental function is the function of essence. It functions by way of establishing the suchness (talidad q.v.) of the entity (425 [384]). The transcendental function is then the function by which a «suchness» constitutes the transcendental properties of the reality. In virtue of this function the reality, as reality, not only possesses «materially» but also «formally» transcendental *structure* (425 [384]). Transcendental structure is of two types: i.e., the transcendental structure of each thing in and by itself and the transcendental structure determined by the linking of each thing with others or all others (426 [385]).

evento   event

v. suceso

A technical use of this common term (a not unusual trait of the Zubirian idiom). Among human realities a radical difference is established between metaphysical conditions:

a) reality as the realization of possibility as potency = *fact* (hecho q.v.)

b) reality as the realization of possibility as capacities (possibilidades = active possibilities) = suceso = event

c) fact and event are not distinguished necessarily by the *content* but by *formal principles*

existencia   existence

It is a central point in Zubiri that essence, as he conceives it, is anterior to existence, just as his conception of essence itself points to something which is anterior to essence in the classical sense (7-10, 11, 461-462 [45-47; 48; 412-414]). This anteriority is neither causal nor of nature, as though essence were the ground of existence. Essence is anterior to both essence in the classical sense and to existence in the sense in which a *ratio* (razón q.v.) is anterior to that of which it is the *ratio*. This anteriority consists precisely, in Zubiri's view, in that essence is ordered, not to existence, but to the character of «de suyo» (q.v.) of the reality. It means that being «de suyo» is the formal *ratio* and the ground of the fact that both (actual q.v.) existence and the aptitude for existence are moments of something *already real* (462 [413]). By this line of thought the classical notion that it is existence which is the formal *ratio* of reality is modified, i.e., reality as denominated not by reference to existence but by reference to transcendental sufficiency (v. sufficiency). Transcendental sufficiency does not mean plenary sufficiency. Existence for that which is transcendentally sufficient but not plenarily so (i.e., as in essence) is an event and not a constitutive dimension of the reality «de suyo» as it is in the case of the transcendentally and plenarily sufficient. This latter situation is realized only in one case: God (465 [416]). Existence as such is pure essentially (468 [418]). In intramundane realities it is an event

estado constructo   constructed state

The «estado constructo» (constructed state) expresses the intrinsic system of the dimensions of the essence as dynamic; the real is conceived as a unitary system of things constructed in intrinsic relations to each other and thus forming a whole within itself. The concept «estado constructo» is the most inclusive expression of this total situation with respect of essence; thus it forms the most adequate *organon* for conceptualizing essence (355-356 [328]).

estar siendo   actual being
                                exercising the
                                act of existence

This phrase expresses most fully the actually of the essence, i.e., the *de facto* realization of its total intrinsic system of potencies, possibilities and capacities in the order of existence where it exercises real effects. This condition *ratifies* (v. rato) the totality of the dimensions of essence. Since the condition of «estar siendo» of the essence can be ratified only in a total process of conceptualization, this «estar siendo» is conceived adequately as the constatation of essence. Constatation, in its intrinsic sense, is precisely this ratification of the essence as realized (129-130 [150]). «Estar siendo» determines the important concept of «duration» with respect to essence. The «estar siendo» in its transcendental function (q.v.) is duration, not in the temporal sense nor in that of distention of S. Augustine nor in the *durée* of Bergson, but in the sense of the internal self-identity of the essence which makes it one, the same, identifiable, irreducible; short of «estar siendo» the essence possesses these notes only problematically (497 [441]). It is to be noted that «estar siendo» does not refer to the retention of being (ser) but to its actuality in the essence, with no relation to others.

exterioridad	exteriority

One term in the complex interiority (q.v.) — exteriority which Zubiri develops in relation and in opposition to both Aristotle and Hegel. Ultimately, his purpose is to dissolve the opposition interior-exterior to replace it with a view in which, instead of being thus opposed, they become constitutive dimensions of the real as such. Aristotle's, Zubiri says, is a view «from the outside inward» because his «categories», other than substance, are «accidents» without reality except as inhering in a substantial subject. Hegel sought to «interiorize» this relationship by the dialectic, i.e., by the dialectic the so-called accidents are seen to be *generated* equally with the substance by the inner dynamic of the real, the Idea (496 [440]). By contrast, Zubiri holds that the essence does not have notes which are notes of a subject (Aristotle) nor is it interiorization of the notes (Hegel) but is a primary interiority which of itself is already formed (plasmada) in its proper essential exteriority. The metaphysical constructivity of the real is this structure of «interiority-exteriority» the formal character of which is «dimension» (495 [440]).

fáctico	factive

v. factual

These terms are closely related to each other, but are both radicated in the more complex term *fact* (hecho) (q.v.).

físico	physical

A basic concept in Zubiri because his is, radically, a physical theory of essence; or, more precisely, a theory of the physical essence. In his employment and development of this term and concept, Zubiri adheres closely to his classical antecedents but presses his analysis beyond certain stereotypical interpretations of them which have become dominant in philosophical usage. The term «physical,» he notes, has long designated the character proper to inanimate bodies; this, however, is only a restriction or specialization of a much wider and more profound concept, rooted in ancient thought, which must be recovered for the purposes of metaphysics and specifically for the problem of essence. In this latter sense «physical» designates not a class of things but a mode of «to be» (ser). As a mode of «to be» (ser) it means to proceed from a principle intrinsic to the thing which is born or grows. «Physis» (φύσις), as substantive, came to designate this intrinsic principle. All the characters of the thing, as thus proceeding, are, consequently, physical. The physical is contrasted to the «artificial» and the «intentional» and comes to be the synonym of «real» in the strict sense of the latter term (11-13 [49-50]).

función   transcendental
transcendental   function

The function by which the suchness (talidad q.v.) «determines» the properties of the real as real, i.e., its transcendental properties (424-425 [383-384]). The importance of this function to the notion of essence is expressed by saying that the difference between reality and essence is formally only a difference between transcendental properties and transcendental function (460 [412]). The relation between transcendental property and transcendental function is clarified by saying: the transcendental properties of the thing are those determined by the transcendental function of suchness (420-422 [380-381]). This immediately raises the question of the relationships between transcendental function and suchness (talitativa) function, which Zubiri answers in the following manner: the talitative function determines the notes which make the thing «such» but the transcendental function alone determines that in their constructivity, as constituting a constructed unity, these notes have reality as belonging to that reality. Transcendentally, the notes have reality only as moments of the «de suyo» (q.v.) in its entirety (476 [424]). Transcendental function constitutes an important element in the concept of transcendental structure (q.v.).

fundamento   ground

Zubiri notes the importance of the Hegelian employment of this term: it is the «to be» which the essence has as a consequence of the negation of the negation (41-42 [74-75]). He elaborates on its possible meanings (264-267 [357-359]): as «basic», as «originating determination» as «fundamental determination». He identifies it as necessity (273-274 [264-265]): The formal structure of fundamentality is precisely necessity of the functional determination. In this sense, essence is that which grounds or establishes the inessential notes as their necessary functional determinant (273 [264]). The concept of foundation or ground is especially important and difficult in the case of relation; it is to be found precisely in what Zubiri calls «constitutive respectivity» (q.v.) of the essence and the notes (287-289 [274-276]).

genesis   generación
                        generation

Zubiri's first step is to free this concept from domination by its Aristotelean and Platonic associations (195; 213-214 [202; 214-217]). It is the ratio (razón q.v.) of the unity of the quidditative essence insofar as this unity is replicable. It is not necessarily repetition but rather genetic constitution (107; 252-254 [130; 248-250]). It is to be considered the ground of the specific community (community of the species) (308-311 [291-293]). A distinction is to be made between constituting genesis and quiddifiable genesis; these find their unification in essential genesis; but such unification is not to be confused with substantial change or transformation (191; 259-260 [200; 259-260]). It may be said to have two moments: 1) an act of the generating principle (252-254 [247-249]); 2) a unique and total act in which the constitutive essence of the engendered is engendered (ibid.).

generación   genesis-
                           generation

Related to notion of multiplication. Adds two conditions to multiplication: action executed by and from a generating principle and the paradigmatic causality which must be made homonymous by transmission of all the quiddifiable characteristics. It is the constitution of a *phylum* and the constitution of the phyletic characters of the constitutive essence of what is generated. The moment of fecundity always enters into the distinction of the species; phylectic or specific unity is always and only a generational unity. Specificity, specific character, the quidditive essence is always «genotypical.» It is the foundation of the community of the species. It may be conceived as the replication of the constitutive «schema» of the essence, its re-constitution; it is the *ratio* (q.v.) of the quidditive essence insofar as it is replicable.

hecho   fact

This complex term plays an important part and role in Zubiri's thought. Its most inclusive meaning involves «precision» (in the Scholastic sense of this term, especially in the Second Scholasticism; cf. Giacon, *op. cit.)* from a ground; something is taken «in and by itself» prescinding from whether it has a ground (196 [203]). In all, however, Zubiri seems to advance three concepts of fact: 1) that is «fact» which exists simply by existing; 2) that is fact which exists (whether contingently or necessarily) as an act of a natural potency (in the Aristotelean and scholastic sense (204-205 [209-210]); 3) The term also enters into dialectical relation to the notions of «closed» and «open» essences. The structure of the «closed essences» is the source of anything's being *fact* and, as such, «res mere naturalis.» The contrast is with the «open» essence which is «eventual» and hence «not mere fact.» Hence a basic dualism seems to emerge; fact-event, with the notion «historical» emerging over the horizon (515-517 [455-457]). Cognate terms are factive, factual.

inalterabilidad   inalterability

v. alteración

May first be considered as a character of the notes of the essence (249 [245]); may also be applied to the content of the essence both in the genetic order (that which can be transmitted to maintain the species through its individuation) and of the principle of its identity (q.v.) and sameness (q.v.).

identidad   identity

The traditional meaning of this term marks the point of departure of Zubiri's analysis of this important notion. He finds this traditional meaning not fundamentally in error, but inadequate to the demands of the problem of essence as he defines this problem. Traditional philosophy holds that identity is a transcendental character of every entity, i.e., every entity is identical with itself. This led to the impression that sameness *(mismidad* q.v.) is this identity, this identicalness. Identity and sameness must, however, be distinguished, to the profit of both concepts. What real things, as physically real, have is sameness *(mismidad)*. Identity is at most the objective concept of this sameness (250-251 [246-247]). There are, Zubiri affirms, three possible modes of identity: when it is said that A and B are identical and this identity may mean 1) A is formally B' or 2) B is formally A; or, 3) the thing is not what A and B are formally but is something which absorbs what A and B are into a superior unity whence A and B are identically but by «elevation» (466-467 [416-417]).

inesencial   non-essential

Differs from the «indifferent» of Hegel (268-269 [260-261]) as well as from the «individuating» of Aristotle and the «exterior» of Husserl; inessential notes (q.v.) are grounded (477-478 [425-426]) and have aspects both of adherence and of the status of the thing as thing *(res)*.

inteligencia   intelligence

The theory of «intelligence» constitutes a basic element in Zubiri's intramundane metaphysics as well as in his concept of God. In the first case, in his anthropology, he is concerned to establish its unity with sensibility (115-116 [138-139]). His most important contribution is the concept of «sentient intelligence» which expresses this functional unity most completely (414-416 [375-376]). Sentient intelligence is closely related to the «impression of reality» which is the core moment in which the traditional dualism between concept and percept is resolved. Its primary function is to apprehend the real thing under the specific formality delete, of its reality (64-65 [93-94]); by means of this act or capacity man is positioned among things as realities (realidades); for sentient intelligence, being (ser) presupposes reality (408-409 [370-371]); its function is transcendental, i.e., establishing the real as real through its specific properties of whatever order (423-424, 427 [382-383]).

interioridad   interiority

Equals «de suyo» (q.v.); not as «hidden» (Heidegger) but as systematization (492-493 [437-438]); not to be confused with «intimacy» (self-communion of a subject) which is exclusive to animate beings and perhaps to man; has as transcendental function the co-establishment as unity of the notes of whatever order; essence is the purest form of interiority in the order of realities (realidades) as such.

logos   logos

«Logos» concerns primarily reality (realidad) and the mode of its expression in discourse»; «logos» is the appearance of reality in discourse. The *organon* of the logos, consequently, is language, discourse, of whatever mode. Since, however, the structure of language, discourse, is not the same as that of reality, language, discourse, logos has many modalities (el λέγειν tiene modulaciones). The essential logos is that which enunciates or expresses the essence; it is not, however, identical with the predicative logos of classical philosophy which identifies the essential logos with the definition. The essential proposition (logos) is not closed, but open (351 [325]). More adequate to the expression of the essence is the nominal constructed definition (la esencia necesita del logos nominal constructo) (355-356 [328-329]).

materia   matter

Basis of individuation, but forms only natural classes, not true species (238-239 [237-238]). Defined as variable, but not progressive concretion (169 [181]). A moment in an evolutative process in the order of individuality (171-172 [183-184]). Provides the *schema* for the substantivization (q.v.) of reality (173 [184]). Substantivity (q.v.) belongs only to the material whole (172-172 [183-184]).

metaespeciación   transpecification

Capacity of transformation (evolution) within the quidditative (q.v.) order, reflected in the natural classes based on matter as principle in the order of individuation. There is not merely essential «taxis» but essential genesis as well (256-257 [251-252]). The genetic constitution of the quidditative essence is the basis of transpecification (257 [252]). «Essential genesis» is defined as «proceso en que la primera forma en y desde sí misma se transforma en otra de un modo sistemático y progresivo» (259-260 [253-254]).

metafísica   metaphysical

Conceptualization of reality itself, not identifiable with logic (against Hegel). Intramundane, the direct concern of philosophy; intramundane basis of transmundane investigation (47, 201, 357 [78; 207; 329]).

mismidad   sameness

Related to essence because essence is what constitutes the characteristic sameness of the thing. Not reducible to identity (249-250 [245-246]). Distinction necessary between «el mismo» and «lo mismo»; the former is that which is the same, the latter that which constitutes the sameness of that which is the same. Sameness is the basis of multiplicity and individuality as mediated by matter. The individual is the same (el mismo) but is not that by which the same is the same. Involved alike in processes of specification and transpecification. Differs from reduplicability and reduplication. Related to but not identical with permanence; «same» referred to permanence more closely allied to identity which is in turn more closely allied to what makes the same the same rather than to that which is the same by reason of sameness = constitutive essence.

mundo   world
v. cosmos

Cosmos and world were classically equated as the totality of real things (199 [205]). Zubiri distinguishes world and cosmos (l.c.) world = unity of all real things «in and by» its mere character of reality as counter-distinguished to its quality (talidad) (q.v.) (199 [ibid.]). Cosmos (l.c.) = the unity of real things by reason of content. There is but one world; there may be many «cosmoi».

naturaleza   nature

The ordinary concept of nature: the physical world as distinguished from the intentional or artificial (11 [48]). In the Greek concept nature refers to the mode of being (ser) and not to the originative principle (106 [130]). In the modern sense = the system of natural «laws» while recognizing the priority of things and the inadequacy of «laws» to express all that things possess (107 [131]). It is essence only in a material sense (180-181 [191-192]). Derives from «de suyo» (q.v.) (395-396 [359-360]), a counterprinciple to techné which = «mimnesis» of nature (323 [302]); modern techné, however, can produce natural things artificially (84-85 [109-110]) hence differs profoundly from earlier.

necessidad   necessity

As negative determination, not adequate (103-104 [127-128]); positive notion = determination (deletion of alternatives) in any order. Only essential necessity is real necessity (107 [130]); distinction between «necessity of origination» and «systematic» necessity (270-271 [262-263]).

nota(s)   note(s)

General meaning of the term: all parts and properties of the thing (res) (104 [128]); are to be distinguished into formal and causal (135-136 [153-154]); constitutional and adventitious (136-137 [154-155]); additive and systematic (147-148 [163-164]); actualize the substantivity (147-148 [ibid.]); not all constitutional notes essential, but all essential notes constitutional. Only essential notes establish the «suchness» (talidad q.v.) of the thing (358-360 [330-332]).

objetividad   objectivity
objetualidad   objectuality

Objectivity indicates, the terminal moment of the concept in its purely intentional dimension (71 [99]). Objectuality = status as content of moment of objectivity, but independent of the possibility associated with objectivity, e.g.: poetic image = objectual, but not objective.

patentización   manifestation

To be distinguished, e.g., from Heidegger's unveiling of being; nevertheless, moves in the same order of speculation with respect to essence. In Heidegger, unveiling involves the presence of the essence to the other; in Zubiri, it involves the manifestation of the essence in its «verdad real» (q.v.) (127-128 [148-149]). «Verdad real» is not logical truth (the realization of the real in *logos)* nor is it ontological truth; it is «truth» and «real,» i.e., the condition of the real in its total manifestation to itself and not to the presence of the other (117-119 [140-141]).

persona   person

Person is self-possession in the order of essence as primary actuality of the essence (504 [447]). Realized in certain states of human presence it is the «suyo» = constitutive self-coherence of the open essence (as distinguished from closed essence); hence, human from natural, for even though natural essence is open, it is not open as self-present possibility of capacity. Person is the basis of «personeity» = condition of «estar siendo» (q.v.) as person and of personality which is the deployment of personeity in an existential process (504-505 [447-448]).

«Person» is a metaphysical condition because it defines the intrinsic character of the thing in its manner of being real with respect to its fundament in reality (197-198 [196-197]). This particular metaphysical condition is present in certain states (not all) of human consciousness especially that called «existing.»

phylum phylum

To be understood in a philosophical and not simply zoological sense though these are not totally and mutually counterposed. Defined philosophically, it is related in a double way to the notion of «species» or, more strictly, «specificality,» i.e., the intrinsic reason why species arise or can arise. The radical reason of specifiability, i.e., the possibility of species as phyletic multiplication, while the formal *ratio* (razón q.v.) of the species, is the character of belonging to the phylum. The phylum is a strict physical reality. To ask what a thing «is» involves reference to the phylum, i.e., is to ask for the phylum from which it emerges physically and to which it belongs, therefore, by reason of its constitutive essence. This yields the physical concept of species as distinct from the logical concept. In this process, not actual, but simply intrinsic multipliability is necessary. Phylum and species involve the minimal system of constitutive notes genetically transmissable and constant by way of interfecundity.

por sí mismo by, of, itself
mismas

This phrase is used by Zubiri in a variety of contexts, with varying accents. The basic meaning is clear. It indicates a condition of a) independence and b) (self) sufficiency and (self) determination in the subject to which it refers. It is used with maximal force in the context of the essential unity, i.e., the unity which characterizes the essence. Zubiri focuses the sense of the phrase in this strong usage in the following points: 1) The essence is a system of constitutive notes; hence as a system it is one, has an essential unity, i.e., a unity proper to it as essence; 2) this essential unity, which establishes the essence as a system which is one, is a function of the notes; these possess *por sí mismas* the capacity of forming this unitary system, endowed with auto-sufficiency. Hence the problem of the unity of essence and the meaning of *por sí mismo*, as used in this strong sense, involves this character of the notes of having this capacity *por sí mismas* of forming the system as a unity; in this context, *por sí mismas* must be distinguished from the notes taken «en sí mismas.» To speak of the notes «en sí mismas,» is to speak of them as they are according to the objective concept of each. This character «en sí misma» of the note does not tell us immediately or of itself whether or not, or in what way, it possesses the capacity to enter into an essence as a system. Nevertheless, the capacity is rooted in the notes «en sí mismas,» in the notes in their proper physical reality. That capacity is a «moment» (q.v.) of the note «en sí misma» but is not identical with it. 3) This «physical moment» is a moment of the notes according to their physical reality. 4) This «physical moment» which is the *por sí mismo* has two aspects: one is the aspect according to which this moment belongs to each note as an intrinsic moment of it; hence, under this aspect, each note is «from itself» intrinsically turned toward the others in conjunction with which it constitutes a unity with them (the unity of the essence); the other aspect is that according to which each note is turned toward the others «by anticipation» «beforehand.» The «por sí mismo» resides in these two aspects: it is intrinsic «desde sí mismo» and primary «de ante mano» in the tendency of the notes to form a unity with the other notes of the essence. 5) Hence the unity of essence is intrinsic and primary, «por sí mismo.»

possibilidad   possibility

The «possible» does not constitute a world apart determinable solely by logical processes. Neither does it reside in mere contradiction. The essence in the «real» sense constitutes the internal possibility of one thing. It is the antecedent metaphysical condition of the created reality but is not antecedently determinable logically from the notion of the creator but is manifested by the actuality of his action. It is the bond between capacity and necessity. It is not to be identified with mere potency.

quidditas   quiddity

Not to be identified *simpliciter* with essence; error on this point of many earlier philosophers (e.g., Plato 216-217 [218-219]), Husserl (229-230 [229-230]) refers to physical reality, not to logical entity. It is a moment of the physical essence (220 [222]). Within the essence must be distinguished from the constitutive essence (223-225; 228-229 [224-225; 228-229]). It has a structuring function within the totality of the thing and the essence (222-223 [224-225]).

rato   ———

A legal term, especially in ecclesiastical law, which Zubiri turns to philosophical use; illustrated by his example from matrimony, «rato» but not «consummato» = all the condition for the actuality of an essence short of its actualization but which actuality adds nothing to the essence *qua* essence. It is the sufficiency of anything in the transcendental order of the «de suyo» (q.v.) whereby, if it were to be (actual) it would be established in the order of actuality according to the conditions of transcendentality. The «rato» is not the equivalent of essence in the classical sense (465-466 [415-416]). It is neither prior nor posterior to the existent from which it is distinguishable and distinguished transcendentally.

razón   reason
                                ground; order

Reality always prior to razón, even in God; not = to cause but has affinity to the «rato» (q.v.) when the «rato» is determined transcendentally. Nor does the intelligence have primacy over the reality; hence it follows that metaphysics cannot be a logic (against Hegel). Razón imparts intelligibility and intelligiable structure to discourse different from, but manifesting, the real.

realidad   reality
simpliciter   (unconditioned)

Variously represented by different philosophers (e.g., Aristotle, the rationalists, Husserl, etc. 2, 3, 4, 33-35 [41, 42, 43, 66-67]). Identified with the physical (q.v.). The *idea* of reality depends upon the concept of existence (389 [354]); three moments of the idea of reality — as the «extra-animam» which = existence and the effects of the existent which are its reality. The essence as structuring of the actual = reality; but only transcendentally distinct from this reality (not two «things»). It is the formal character of the intellect as such. It is the reason why truth abides in the intellect. It is a syntactical rather than a substantive or factive concept. It is prior to being (ser) because to be (ser) is conditioned by reality and not *vice versa*. Taken as the total simultaneous co-presence of all its conditions, it is the thing *(res)* = *realidad simpliciter.*

respectividad   respectivity
respecto

An entitative, not an operative, concept (181-182 [192-193]). In its extrinsic character related to the concept *world* (i.e., the extrinsic respectivities of things are constitutive of their *locus* in the world q.v.). The intrinsic respectivity concerns the interior coherence of their notes (essential, constitutive, etc.) (cf. constructed state). Most importantly of all is the respectivity of the thing to its ground (197-199 [203-204]) because this respectivity provides the metaphysical condition of the thing. Different in the thing known «cosa sentida» and in the thing as real (290-292 [277-278]). To be distinguished from relation which may or may not correspond to the respectivity (427 [385]). Has three metaphysical characteristics when conceived with respect to the internal coherence of the thing: being in itself (ser en sí), something common with others, origination (318-320 [299-300]).

ser   to be

The linguistic origin of the term, in contrast to the verb «estar,» lies for Zubiri in the fact that *ser* is a verb of reality, not of mere existence (407 [369]); this is fortified by its grammatical use (337-338 [313-314]); the essence as a system of constitutive notes as constitutive of the reality which is («sido»). «Ser» means «sido,» to be, in this sense over the distribution of its form (cf. «estar siendo»), not prior to «reality» but rather the priority belongs here, as always to reality (realidad). «Ser» = ultimate act of the real insofar as the real «is.» Therefore, «ser» is not transcendental in the order of the real «as real» and not as «is» (412 [473]). A «thing» («cosa») in its actuality = «ente» which embraces reality *ser-estar.* Aristotle is mistaken in taking substantive «ser» as ultimate in the order of being; rather it is posterior to «realidad.» The world, «mundo,» is the realm of «ser» in a more basic sense than it is the realm of «estar.»

sistema   system

A basic concept in all dimensions of Zubiri's thought; the constitutional (as distinct from but not opposed to constitutive) notes of the primary unity of a thing constitute a system through intrinsic respectivities (q.v.) (144 [161]). Formally, the system as such resides in the positional interdependence of the notes establishing the system (144-146 [161-163]). This positional character does not exclude, but rather extends to dynamic interdependence, which invariably involves positional interdependence as well. The system is characteristically marked by «clausura» (q.v.) and hence is «clausuarado» (146 [162]). This property does not, however, exclude movement and change, even evolutionary, but imparts to such movement direction, unity, etc. System has affinities, but is not to be confounded with, mixture and functional combination. The latter may be characteristic of system but are neither constitutive of nor inseparable from system (149-150 [165-166]).

sustancia   substance
sustantividad   substantivity

Mistaken by Aristotle as first form of reality (3, 156 [41, 170]) it is not the «ὄν» = that which *is par excellence* (512-514]453-454[); it is a «moment» of what is, not what is = thing (158 [112]); not to be identified with substantivity (151 [166]); has affinities with permanency, but is not identical with it (250 [246]); the same complex affinity relates to «sameness»; substance and sameness have affinity but not identity (251 [247]); historically, the evolution of the concept has proceeded in close relation to that of essence, but they must be carefully distinguished (1-5 [41-46]).

Substance is refined by Zubiri by his development of the notion of «substantivity.» Substantivity is realized in substance, but consists in the formal structure of the constitutional unity which is formally individual (and not specific or generic); it is directly related to the essentiable and the essentiated (q.v.) which are dimensions of reality but not its exclusive dimensions, for not every grouping of notes achieves substantivity (153 [169]); may be distinguished into simple and composite; this distinction involves not the *number*, but the *status* of the notes, i.e., whether these be merely additive or rather belong to the system as such or in such wise that, were they withdrawn, the system would be destroyed as system (147 [163]).

suyo   ——
de suyo

Embraces all the reality of the thing, hence all that makes it to be, to be this, to be this kind, actual, etc. (485-486 [431-432]). It is the positive principle of the indivision and the principle (razón q.v.) of the incommunicability of the thing (483 [430]). It results from the transcendental function of the essence which is to establish the real as something deriving from its own inner principle (de suyo) so that it is in fact (suyo) indivisible and incommunicable in its strict individuation. The principle, consequently, of the transcendental constitution of reality (488-489 [434-435]). In the human subject generates the status of *person* (q.v.).

talidad   suchness

Essence is essence in the order of suchness (357 [329]); suchness is not, consequently, an accidental concept, but a metaphysical concept. Suchness does not coincide with categorial determination. Every suchness is determination, but not every determination is suchness. Only essential notes constitute suchness (358 [330]). The suchness gives the specific content to essence (358-360 [330-331]); it relates to the constructivity of the essence, not to its accidents, properties or characteristics. The transcendental function of suchness is precisely to establish the thing in its essential, not accidental, character (457-458; 475-477 [409-410; 424-426]).

transcendentalidad   transcendentality

Essence belongs to the transcendental order (372 [341]); the notion of the transcendental differs in classical and in modern thought. The idealist notion is inadequate (380 [341]). The transcendental is the order of the real, not insofar as it is true, but in its strict character as real. The reality as reality is not objectuality (status as object of a mind or possibility of being such without reference to reality) but simply reality as such (and not as *such* reality). Transcendental and transcendentality must be distinguished. Transcendentality is that character in which all things converge independently in their suchness. Transcendental indicates the antecedency of the real to all modes of its apprehension, or apprehension of it; it is, therefore, the antecedency toward which all thought tends but which essentially transcends all such approaches (399-400 [363-364]). The transcendental is the real «completely 'de suyo',» the «prius» of all modes of presentation or representation. Transcendental structure is the specific structure given the real by its suchness; but it is not identical with that suchness, though not independent of it. Transcendental structure involves in each real thing the real in and for itself: essence, suchness, respectivity and incatenation with other things.

unidad   unity
(modos de)   (modes of)

Numerical unity and unity of content are to be distinguished, though they are not unrelated (140 [159]). Both occur in reality (141 [160]). Primary unity in the philosophical sense is the constitutional unity characteristic of a system (143-144 [161-162]). Systematic unity has three characteristics: the elements of the system guarantee certain of the properties; constitute, with the other elements, the basis of certain new systematic properties and all are integrated in a radical unity of the closure (q.v.) of the system. Unity may be distinguished in many ways: i.e., quidditive, phyletic, coherential, essential, transcendental (q.v.).

verdad   true (truth)

Most important is the relation of truth to reality. Since reality is «de suyo» and hence in no way dependent on any mode of presentation or representation to a mind (not even that of God) it has an intrinsic principle and property which establishes it in its reality «de suyo,» which is ontological truth. In this sense truth is reality *simpliciter* (q.v.). As such, it is the measure of all other forms of truth which in any way involve presentation of this «real truth» to any mode of presence. This leads in turn to the distinction of logical truth — which in its broadest sense involves all ways in which ontological truth is presented, or may be presented, to any kind of presentational order. *Real truth* is neither logical nor ontological; there is no element of conformity because in no sense are two terms involved; real truth involves *two conditions of a single term:* its own reality as actualized reality. It is real truth which imparts truth to all its presentational forms to any form of consciousness whatever.

SELECTED BIBLIOGRAPHY

I. WRITINGS OF XAVIER ZUBIRI

1. *Ensayo de una teoría fenomenológica del juicio*. (Doctoral Thesis) Revista de Archivos, Bibliotecas y Museos, Madrid, 1923, p. 188.
2. «Hegel y el problema metafísico», in Cruz y Raya, 1933, n. 1, pp. 11-40; reprinted in *Naturaleza, Historia, Dios* (cited below) 6th edition (1963), pp. 223-242.
3. «El Maestro Eckehart», in Cruz y Raya, 1933, n. 4, pp. 83-86.
4. «Sobre el problema de la filosofía», in Revista de Occidente, 1933, n. 115, pp. 51-80; n. 118, pp. 83-117.
5. «La nueva física. Un problema de filosofía», in Cruz y Raya, 1934, n. 10, pp. 7-94; reprinted in *Naturaleza, Historia, Dios*, 6th edition (1963), pp. 243-304, under the title: «La idea de naturaleza: nueva física».
6. «Filosofía y metafísica», in Cruz y Raya, 1935, n. 30, pp. 7-60; reprinted in part in *Naturaleza, Historia, Dios*, 6th edition (1963), pp. 33-60, under the title: «¿Qué es saber?».
7. «En torno al problema de Dios», in Revista de Occidente, 1935, n. 146, pp. 129-159; reprinted in A. Robert Caponigri: *Pensadores católicos contemporáneos*, 2 vols., Barcelona, 1964, I, pp. 349-379.
8. «Note sur la philosophie de la religion», in Bulletin de l'Institut catholique de Paris, 1937, 2a Series, n. 10, pp. 334-341.
9. «Sócrates y la sabiduría griega», in Escorial, 1940, n. 2, pp. 187-226; 1941, n. 3, pp. 51-78; reprinted in *Naturaleza, Historia, Dios*, 6th edition (1963), pp. 149-222.
10. «Ciencia y realidad», in Escorial, 1941, n. 10, pp. 177-210; reprinted in *Naturaleza, Historia, Dios*, 5th edition (1963), pp. 61-95.
11. «El acontecer humano. Grecia y la pervivencia del pasado filosófico», in Escorial, 1942, n. 23, pp. 401-432; reprinted in *Naturaleza, Historia, Dios*, 6th edition (1963), pp. 305-340; partial version in French in G. Lann *Le temps et la mort dans la philosophie espagnole contemporaine*, Toulouse, 1968, pp. 32-48.

12. *Naturaleza, Historia, Dios.* Editora Nacional, Madrid, 1944, p. 565; (editions 1951, p. 437; 1955, p. 407; 1963, pp. xi-483. Buenos Aires, 1948).

13. «El problema del hombre», in Indice, 1959, n. 120, pp. 3-4.

14. *Sobre la esencia.* Sociedad de Estudios y Publicaciones, Madrid, 1962, p. 521 (editions: 1972, p. 525; German translation: *Vom Wesen,* H. G. von Rotzer, Max Huber, Munchen, 1968, p. 390.

15. *Cinco Lecciones de Filosofía,* Sociedad de Estudios y Publicaciones, Madrid, 1963, p. 284; 1972, p. 284.

16. «El hombre, realidad personal», in Revista de Occidente, 2nd series, 1963, n. 1, pp. 5-29.

17. «El origen del hombre», in Revista de Occidente, 2nd series, 1964, n. 17, pp. 146-173, English translation in: A. Robert Caponigri: *Contemporary Spanish Philosophy.* Notre Dame and London, 1968, pp. 42-75.

18. «Trascendencia y física», in *Gran Enciclopedia del Mundo,* 1964, Vol. 18, pp. 419-424.

19. «Notas sobre la inteligencia humana», in Asclepio, Archivo Ibero-americano de Historia de la Medicina y Antropología Médica, XVIII-XIX (1967-1968), pp. 341-353.

20. «La dimensión histórica del ser humano», in *Realitas, Seminario Xavier Zubiri I:* Trabajos 1972-1973, Sociedad de Estudios y Publicaciones, Madrid, 1974, pp. 11-69.

21. «El espacio», in *Realitas, Seminario Xavier Zubiri I:* Trabajos 1972-1973, Sociedad de Estudios y Publicaciones, Madrid, 1974, pp. 49-54.

22. «El hombre y su cuerpo», in Salesianum, XXXVI (1974), pp. 479-486; Asclepio XXV (1973), pp. 3-15.

23. «El problema teologal del hombre», in *Teología y Mundo Contemporáneo: Homenaje a Karl Rahner,* Madrid, 1975, pp. 55-64; cf. Curso 1971-1972.

24. «El concepto descriptivo del tiempo», in *Realitas, Seminario Xavier Zubiri II:* Trabajos 1974-1975, Sociedad de Estudios y Publicaciones, Editorial Labor, 1976, pp. 7-47.

25. *Scritti religiosi* a cura di Albino Babolin, Gregoriana Editrice Padova, 1976, p. 227 (Italian translation with extensive introduction, noted below).

26. *Inteligencia Sentiente,* Alianza Editorial, Sociedad de Estudios y Publicaciones, Madrid, 1980, pp. 288.

II. CURSOS

1945-1946   Ciencia y Realidad. Introducción al problema de la realidad.
1946-1947   Tres definiciones clásicas del hombre.
1947-1948   ¿Qué son las ideas?
1948-1949   El problema de Dios.
1950-1951   Cuerpo y Alma.

1951-1952   La libertad.
1952-1953   Filosofía primera.
1953-1954   El problema del hombre.
      1959   Sobre la persona.
      1960   Acerca del mundo.
      1961   Sobre la voluntad.
      1962   (No course offered.)
      1963   Cinco lecciones de filosofía.
      1964   El problema del mal.
      1965   El problema filosófico de la historia de las religiones.
             El problema de Dios en la historia de las religiones.
      1966   El hombre y la verdad.
             Sobre la realidad.
      1967   El hombre: lo real y lo irreal: Reflexiones filosóficas sobre algunos problemas de Teología.
      1968   El hombre y el problema de Dios. Estructura dinámica de la realidad.
      1969   Estructura de la metafísica. Problemas fundamentales de la metafísica occidental.
      1970   Sobre el tiempo. Sistema de lo real en la filosofía moderna.
1971-1972   El problema teologal del hombre: Dios, religión, cristianismo.
      1973   El espacio. El hombre y Dios. (Given at the Gregorian University in Rome.)
      1974   Tres dimensiones del ser humano: individual, social e histórica.
      1975   Reflexiones filosóficas sobre lo estético.
      1976   La inteligencia humana.

III. WRITINGS ON XAVIER ZUBIRI

A. Books

1. Sanguinetti, Francesco: *Xavier Zubiri: pensiero filosofico e scienza moderna.* Editrice «La Garangola», Padova, 1975, p. 167.

2. Savignano, Armando: *Psicologismo e giudizio filosòfico in M. Heidegger-X. Zubiri-J. Maréchal.* Editrice «La Garangola», Padova, 1976, p. 253; on Zubiri: pp. 131-186.

3. Ellacuria, I.: *Sobre la esencia: Índices* Sociedad de Estudios y Publicaciones, Madrid, 1965, p. 195.

4. Marquínez Argote, G.: *En torno a Zubiri*, Madrid, 1965, p. 155.

5. Laín Entralgo, Pedro: *La empresa de ser hombre*, Madrid, 1958; on Zubiri: pp. 183-195.

6. Caturelli, A.: *La metafísica intramundana de Xavier Zubiri*, Córdoba (Argentina), 1965, p. 55 (cf. Humanitas (Monterrey, México), n. 7 [1966], pp. 77-97).

7. Gargorri, P.: *Unamuno, Ortega, Zubiri en la filosofía española*, Madrid, 1968; on Zubiri: pp. 123-168, 195-205.

8. López Quintás, A.: *Filosofía española contemporánea*, Madrid, 1970, p. 719; on Zubiri: pp. 196-272.
9. Varii: *Homenaje a Xavier Zubiri*, Madrid, 1953, p. 275.
10. Varii: *Homenaje a Zubiri*, 2 vols., Madrid, 1970; I, p. 787; II, p. 786.
11. *Realitas: Seminario Xavier Zubiri I: Trabajos 1972-1973*, Madrid, 1974, p. 514.
12. *Realitas: Seminario Xavier Zubiri II: Trabajos 1974-1975*, Madrid, 1976, p. 576.

B.1 Notices on the *Cursos* of Zubiri.

1. Gómez Arboleya, A.: «Los cursos de Zubiri», in Homenaje, 1953, pp. 119-137.
2. Fernández, J.: «Los cursos de Zubiri», in Alcalá, 1954, n. 55, p. 4.
3. Del Campo, A.: «El último curso de Xavier Zubiri sobre Cuerpo y Alma», in Cuadernos Hispano-americanos, 1951, n. 22, pp. 122-124.
4. Del Campo, A.: «Un nuevo curso de Xavier Zubiri acerca del mundo», in Indice, 1960, n. 141, pp. 276-293.
5. Riaza, M.: «Curso de X. Zubiri sobre la realidad», in Aporia, 1966, n. 2, pp. 268-269.
6. López Quintás, A.: «Un nuevo curso de Xavier Zubiri: El hombre: lo real y lo irreal», in Revista Tercer Programa, 1967, n. 5, pp. 57-80.

B.2 Notices on *Sobre la esencia*.

1. Artola, J. M.: «En torno a *Sobre la esencia* de Xavier Zubiri», in Estudios Filosóficos, 1963, n. 30, pp. 297-332.
2. Fernández de la Mora, G.: «La teoría de la esencia en Zubiri», in Atlántida, 1966, n. 22, pp. 363-380 (The same article appeared earlier in Pensamiento español, 1963, pp. 59-76).
3. Zaragüeta, J.: «Una obra de Zubiri», in Revista de Filosofía, 1962, nn. 81-82, pp. 255-279.
4. Aranguren, J. L. L.: «La aparición del libro de Zubiri» (in re *Sobre la esencia)*, in Revista de Occidente, 1963, n. 2, pp. 243-246.
5. Legido, M.: «La meditación sobre la esencia de Zubiri», in Salmanticensis, 1963, n. 10, pp. 363-381.
6. Rubert Candau, J. M.: «*Sobre la esencia* de Xavier Zubiri», in Verdad y Vida, 1963, nn. 81-84, pp. 395-408.
7. Cerezo Galán, P.: «Contribuciones al estudio de *Sobre la esencia* de Xavier Zubiri: De la sustancialidad a la substantividad», in Documentación crítica Iberoamericana de Filosofía y Ciencias afines, 1964-1965, n. 1, pp. 15-27.
8. Arellano, J.: «Contribuciones al estudio de *Sobre la esencia* de Xavier Zubiri». «La idea del orden transcendental», in Documen-

tación crítica Iberoamericana de Filosofía y Ciencias afines, 1964-
1965, n. 1, pp. 29-83.

9. Ramos Gangoso, A.: *Exposición sumaria y crítica de Sobre la
esencia del Dr. Xavier Zubiri*, Santiago de Compostela, 1964, p. 72.

10. Ciguela, J. M.: «La metafísica de la esencia de Xavier Zubiri», in Nordeste Resistencia, 1965, n. 7, pp. 185-219 (Chaco, Argentina).

11. Antonio Méndez, R.: «La esencia en Zubiri», Franciscanum, XIV
(1972), pp. 3-56, 147-176.

B.3 Major Articles on Zubirian Themes.

1. Babolin, A.: «Il pensiero religioso di Zubiri», in Xavier Zubiri:
Scritti religiosi, a cura di Albino Babolin, Gregoriana Editrice,
Padova, 1976, pp. 9-65.

2. Babolin, A.: «Il pensiero religioso di Xavier Zubiri nella critica
d'oggi», in Aquinas, XV (1972), pp. 7-24.

3. Babolin, A.: «La teoria filosofica della relegazione di X. Zubiri
come momento negativo dell'alienazione», in *Temporalitá e alienazione*, a cura di E. Castelli, Roma, 1975, pp. 434-453.

4. Babolin, A.: «La teoria filosofica dell' essenza di Xavier Zubiri»,
in *Studi di filosofia in onore di Gustavo Bontadini*, 2 vols., Milano,
1975, Vol. II, pp. 429-454.

5. Ellacuria, I.: «Antropología de Xavier Zubiri», in Revista de
Psiquiatría y Psicología Médica de Europa y América Latina, 1964,
n. 6, pp. 405-430; n. 7, pp. 483-508.

6. Ellacuria, I.: «La religación, actitud radical del hombre», in
Asclepio, XVI (1964), pp. 97-155.

7. Ellacuria, I.: «La idea de filosofía en Xavier Zubiri», in *Homenaje
a Xavier Zubiri*, 1970, vol. I, pp. 459-524.

8. Ellacuria, I.: «La idea de estructura en la filosofía de Zubiri», in
Realitas, 1974, pp. 71-139.

9. Ellacuria, I.: «La historicidad del hombre en Xavier Zubiri», in
Estudios de Deusto, 1966, n. 28, pp. 246-286; n. 29, pp. 523-547.

10. Ellacuria, I.: «Introducción crítica a la antropología filosófica de
Zubiri», in *Realitas*, 1976, pp. 49-138.

11. Del Campo, A.: «La voluntad y la libertad según Xavier Zubiri»,
in Papeles de Son Armadans, 1959, n. 66, pp. 276-293.

12. Del Campo, A.: «La función transcendental en la filosofía de
Zubiri», in *Realitas*, 1974, pp. 141-158.

13. Ferrer Arellano, J.: «Unidad y respectividad en Zubiri», in Documentación crítica Iberoamericana de Filosofía y Ciencias afines,
1964, n. 1, pp. 85-109.

14. Solaguren, C.: «Estructura temático-metódica de la metafísica de
Zubiri», in Verdad y Vida, 1965, n. 90, pp. 255-369.

15. Andrés Fernández, F.: «Los presupuestos antropológico-metafísicos de la afirmación de Dios en Xavier Zubiri», in Revista de filosofía, XXV (1966), pp. 125-153.

16. Caba, P.: «Física y metafísica de la luz», in Augustinus, 1966, nn. 42-43, pp. 191-237.

17. Casado, Carlos Fernández: «Naturaleza y artificio en la obra del ingeniero» (in re Zubiri's distinction between ancient and modern technology), in Realitas, 1976, pp. 351-404.

18. Cruz Hernández, M.: «El hombre religado a Dios», in El problema del ateísmo, Salamanca, 1967, pp. 231-248.

19. Laín Entralgo, Pedro: El Estado de Enfermedad, Madrid, 1968; on Zubiri: pp. 174-192.

20. Laín Entralgo, Pedro: «Die menschliche Krankheit in die Metaphysik von Xavier Zubiri», in Studhoffs Archiv, Vierteljahrsschrift fur Geschichte der Medezin und Naturwissenschaften, der Pharmazie und der Mathematik, LI (1967), pp. 303-317 (Wiesbaden).

21. Monserrat, Javier: «El realismo zubiriano en el conjunto de una teoría crítico-fundamental de la ciencia», in Realitas, 1976, pp. 139-202.

22. Marquínez, Germán: «Zubiri visto desde Latino-américa», in Franciscanum (Bogotá), XIX, n. 55, enero-abril, 1977, pp. 129-145.

23. Rivera, J.: «El origen de la filosofía en Xavier Zubiri», in Cuadernos hispano-americanos, 1968, n. 222, pp. 552-583.

24. López Quintás, A.: «Realidad evolutiva e inteligencia sentiente en la obra de Xavier Zubiri», in Homenaje a Xavier Zubiri, 1970, Vol. II, pp. 215-248.

25. Riaza, María: «El enfrentamiento de Zubiri con la fenomenología de Husserl», in Homenaje a Xavier Zubiri, 1970, Vol. II, pp. 559-584.

26. Riaza, María: «Sobre la experiencia en Zubiri», in Realitas, 1976, pp. 246-313.

27. Inciarte, F.: «Observaciones histórico-críticas en torno a Xavier Zubiri», in Anuario Filosófico (Pamplona), IV (1971), pp. 185-244.

28. Baciero, C.: «Metafísica de la individualidad», in Realitas, 1974, pp. 159-220.

29. Baciero, C.: «Conceptuación metafísica del 'de suyo'», in Realitas, 1976, pp. 313-351.

30. Widmer, H.: «Das Strukturprinzip der Wirklickkeit, Aspekte des Wesenmodelles nach dem spanischen Philosophen Xaiver Zubiri», in Freiburger Zeitschrift für Philosophie und Theologie, XXI (1974), pp. 67-138.

31. Gregorio, Eva: «Il problema di Dio in Xavier Zubiri», in Rivista di filosofia neoscolastica (Milano), LXVIII (1976), pp. 269-305 (cf. this author's thesis listed below).

32. Sanguinetti, F.: «L'origine dell'uomo secondo Xavier Zubiri», in *Filosofia e crisi della cultura*. Editrice «La Garangola», Padova, 1974, pp. 151-190.

33. Montero Moliner, F.: «Esencia y respectividad según Xavier Zubiri», in *Realitas*, 1974, pp. 437-455.

34. Savignano, A.: «Il pensiero fenomenologico di Edmund Husserl secondo Xavier Zubiri», in Aquinas, 1977, n. 1, pp. 4-42.

(Note: dates refer to scholastic year during which thesis was presented and defended.)

C. Doctoral Theses on the Philosophy of Xavier Zubiri.

1. Battilani, V.: *L'antropologia di Xavier Zubiri*, Universitá degli Studi di Padova, 1974.

2. Cau, P.: *La filosofia di Xavier Zubiri*, Universitá di Genova, 1968-1969.

3. Dotti, M. G.: *Ricerca e significato del filosofare di Xavier Zubiri*, Universitá degli Studi di Parma, 1969-1970.

4. Ellacuria, I.: *Principalidad de la esencia en Xavier Zubiri*, Universidad Complutense de Madrid, 1965-1966.

5. Garosi, L.: *Il discorso metafisico di Xavier Zubiri*, Universitá degli Studi di Parma, 1969-1970.

6. Gregorio, Eva: *Il problema di Dio in Xavier Zubiri*, Universitá degli Studi di Parma, 1974.

7. Martínez Santamaría, C.: *El acceso del hombre a Dios*, Universidad Pontificia, Salamanca, 1976.

8. Ramírez, C.: *The Personalist Metaphysics of Xavier Zubiri*, Georgetown University, Washington, D. C., 1969.

9. Trio Badillo, I. E.: *El tema de la libertad en el pensamiento español contemporáneo*, Cap. II, «Zubiri», Universidad de Navarra (Pamplona), 1970.

INDEX

INDEX

A

Term	Spanish text	English text
Absolute		
— as metaphysical condition of the ungrounded notes	206-209	211-213
Accidents		
— in Aristotle and other classical	164	177
— writers	293	279
— as different modes of inherence, reflected in the judgment	125	147
— two modes of distinction from substance	164	177
Actuality		
— and *act* in Aristotle	329-330	307
— *act* and potency	400	364
— difference from *act*	314-315	296-297
Actualization		
— defined	117-118	140
— and *dimension* (q.v.)	161	175
— as pluridimensional	120	142
— simple and complex	120-122	142-143
	124-125	146-147
— and knowledge	443-445	398-399
— not a potency	515-516	455-456
Agathon (Good)		
— correction of Platonic idea of	111	135
— role in essence	110	134
Alteration		
— as destruction and as becoming cf. *genesis*	258-259	252-253
— real —, as basis of classical distinctions between essence and existence	462-463	413-414

Term	Spanish text	English text
Anaximander		
— his idea of «arché»	511	453
Appearance		
— essence as, in Hegel	40-41	73-74
— as existence, which is not self sustaining, but sustained	396-398	360-362
Apprehension		
— distinction between «aprehensión simple» and «simple aprehensión»	353	326
— the metaphysics of the act of	443-447	398-401
— defined	457-458	409-410
— two fundamental modes of, in man	391-392	356-357
Aristotle		
— on essence	75-95	101-120
— metaphysics of knowledge in	443-445	398-400
— on substance	3, 77-82	41, 103-107
	85-88	110-112
	154	169
— on accident	164	177
— on nature and techné	83-85	108-110
— on natural vs. artificial entities	77	103
— on nature as the essentiable	83-85	108-110
— on properties	104	128
	127	148
— on the inessential	269	261
— on «species»	80-82	106-108
	88-89	112-113
— no essential difference between members of the same	216-218	219-221
— inalterability of	251-257	241-252
— unity of	99	122
	186	195
	229-230	229-230
	282	271
	293-294	279-280
	306	290
	487-488	434-436
— on act and potency	329-340	307-315
— on the idea of «principle»	509-510	451-452
— on God, as thought of self	44	76
— as subject	86	110
— on the soul	387-388	433-434

	Spanish text	English text
Term		
Artificial		
— as opposed to physical: see *Physical*		
— as opposed to natural: see *Technical*		
'aseitas'		
— «plenum» of reality	466-467	416-417
— and «perseitas» confused in Spinoza	155	170
Augustine St.		
— on time as distensio	497	442
automorphism		
— and becoming, in Hegel	58	87
Averröes		
— as elaborator of Aristotle's ideas	94	117
Avicenna		
— as elaborator of Aristotle's ideas	94	117

B

	Spanish text	English text
Bergson, H.		
— duration in, and in Zubiri	497	442
being (ser)		
— in Hegel	37-39	69-71
— in Heidegger (q.v.)		
— linguistic origin of	407	369
— grammatical utility of	337-338	313-314
— not primary	196-197	203-204
— and reality	403-417	366-380
	437-438	393-394
	449-450	403-405
— in Scholasticism	403-417	366-380
— substantive	410-411	372-373
— relation to copulative being and reality	412	473
— posteriority of substantive- to reality	434-435	391-392
— as «reactualization» of the real	408-409	370-371
	442-453	397-408
— and world	432-434	389-392
— problem of unity of	403-404	366-367
— respective unity of	436-437	392-393

Term	Spanish text	English text
Bonum (good)		
— as transcedental, in Scholasticism	387-388	353-354
— problematic character of conception of, as transcendental	422-423	381-382
— defined	432	390
— and «openness» of essence	501-502	445-446
— v. Agathon		
Brentano, F.		
— as predecessor of Husserl	5	42

C

Cajetan (Tommaso de Vio, Cardinal)		
— confused notion of the existent and its qualifying determinations in	386	352
Category		
— ambiguity of term in scholastic usage	357-358	329-330
— and in Aristotle	494-495	439-440
— as structural moment of substantivity	157-158	172-173
Cause		
— and experience of the existent and the merely «rato» (q.v.)	469-470	419-420
— the divine idea as exemplary —	63	92
— paradigmatic causality		
— — as condition of multiplication	234-236	234-236
— — special, in generation	240-241	239-240
— — as reconstitutive	310	293
Change (Cambio)		
— as unity of «to be» (ser) and «not to be» Not-to-be (no ser) as conditioning the applicability of the principle of contradiction	70	98
Christianity		
— philosophically related to Greek thought	200	206
— transcends Greek thought by idea of world as the created	200	206
— time in Christian thought	254-255	249-250

Term	Spanish text	English text
Class		
— and species (q.v.)	230-232	230-232
— natural	232-233	232-233
— — and species	233	233
— — the, not constituted in the species	234	234
Closure (Clausura)		
— as character of the constitutional system	146	163
— confers character of *totality* (q.v.)	152	168
— and «suchness»	366-367	337-338
— cyclical and co-determination	367-370	337-340
— function of, in the transcendental order	484-485	431-432
Coherence		
— as metaphysical character of reality as such	298-299	283-284
— positive structure of	ibi	ibi
— correlatives: coherence-adherence/essential —	329-331	307-307
inessential	478-479	426-427
Conceive (to) (Concebir)		
— as final function of the intelligence	391-392	356-357
	450	404
— formality of real not —, but sensed	413-414	374-375
Concept		
— formal	36	69
— — and essence; cf. *Hegel*	36-58	69-87
— objective	36	69
— — and essence	59-73	88-100
v. *objectivity, objectuality*		
Consciousness		
— acts of, but no — as such	28-39	61-63
— actualization as formal character of	29	62
Concretion		
— and problem of individuation in the perspective		
of the species	167-168	180-181
— variable and progressive	168-170	181-183
— and individuality	491	437
— and transcendentality	489-491	435-437

Term	Spanish text	English text
Condition		
— real or metaphysical	197-199	204-206
	202-205	208-211
	435-436	392-393
v. absolute, factual		
Configuration		
— and essences	261-262	255-256
Consistency		
— as more than the pure «is»	298	283
— as grounded in coherence (q.v.)	298-299	283-284
Constatation		
— specific ratification (q.v.) of reality	129-130	150-151
cf. Estar siendo, dimension		
Constitution		
— primary structure of the thing	137	156
— something physical	137	156
— something individual	137-141	156-160
— as mark of «to be a unity»	140	159
— unity of, as unity of system	146	163
— — as primary unity of system	143-144	163-164
— affected by dimensionality	142	160
— genetic cf. *generation*		
— and transcendentality	483-489	430-431
Constructivity		
— essence as	356	329
— transcendental aspect of	475-482	424-430
— metaphysical, of the real	494-495	439-440
Contingency		
— as metaphysical condition of the created	201-204	207-210
— not structural moment of reality	203	209
Contraction		
— no — of species, but expansion of individual	168	181
— every reality is individual but not — of the species	184	195
Contradiction (Principle of)		
— evident in concepts, problematic in application to reality	67-68	95-96
— noncontradictoriness of system of concepts not demonstrable positively	66-67	94-95

Term	Spanish text	English text

Copula
— cf. *esse logicum*

Cosmos
— as transcendental function ... 428-429 ... 386-387
— as distinct from world (q.v.) ... 427-428 ... 385-387

D

definition
— essence as objective correlative of ... 75 ... 101
— expresses essence, condition under which ... 75-76 ... 101-102
— no-, of ideal or artificial entities ... 76-77 ... 102-103
— only substances have ... 77-78 ... 103-104
— problematic character of all ... 89-90 ... 113-114

deictic (function)
— as nominal indication ... 16 ... 52
— as primary apprehension ... 16 ... 52

Descartes
— initiates a new idea of philosophy ... 373 ... 342
— substantivization of consciousness in thought of ... 436-437 ... 393-394
— dissociation of ideas of substance and essence, in ... Int. 3-4 ... 41-42
— concept of essence in ... 33-35 ... 66-68
... 59-73 ... 88-100
... 99 ... 123

«de suyo»
— reality as ... 393-395 ... 358-360
— relation to nature ... 395-396 ... 360-361
— does not coincide with existence ... 396-398 ... 361-364
— nor with classical concept of essence ... 399-400 ... 363-364
— ergic character of ... 400-401 ... 364-365
— and determination ... 457-458 ... 409-410
— and interiority ... 492-494 ... 438-440
— transcendental character of ... 475-477 ... 424-425
— three structural moments of ... 482 ... 430
— and «suyo» ... 484-485 ... 431-432
— transcendental types of: essence, open and closed ... 499-508 ... 443-450

Term	Spanish text	English text
determination		
— meaning of	264-265	257-258
— functional	264	257
— originating	264-267	257-259
— essence as mere —	457-473	409-422
— categorial	357-358	329-330
— internal	140	159
difference (essential)		
— in classical philosophy	215-218	218-220
— and individual —	224-225	226-227
— «in» and «of» the quiddity	225-226	227-228
dimension(al) (ality)		
— all reality as	120	142
— and essence	491-498	437-443
— a transcendental concept	491-492	437-438
— a transcendental mark	492-494	438-439
— and interiority	494-495	439-440
— and exteriority	ibi	
— as moments of constructivity	ibi	
— three- of «suchness»	495	440
— expressed by three formal respects	141-142	159-160
	497-498	442-443
— and constitution	498	443
distinction		
— physical and conceptive	12	50
dominance		
— as anteriority of essential unity in each note	328	306
— exigent	331	309
duration		
— as transcendental mark	497	442
— as measure of other dimensions	497-498	442-443
— cf. time		
cf. Bergson vs. Zubiri		

E

essence		
— morphology of	Intro 3	41
— dissociation from substance	3-5	41-43

	Spanish text	English text
Term		
— classical sense of	399-400	363-364
— in Hegel	36-58	69-87
— in Husserl	23-32	56-64
— in St. Thomas	182-183	193-194
— term misused	110	134
— notion of	7-10	45-48
— something physical	176-178	187-188
— and existent	72	100
— physical, as object of present treatise	275-276	266-267
— function of	181	192
	93	116
	100	124
— not that of specification	183-185	194-195
— as substantive individual	185-186	195-196
— as generating system	268	260
— transcendental	484-485	431-432
— individual character of	246-247	244-245
— intrinsic constructivity of	356	329
	474	424
— and suchness — q.v.		
— and inalterability q.v.		
— and existence, ground of distinction between	462-463	413-414
— «reduced» essence	463-466	414-417
— transcendentality of	372-508	341-450
— transcendental function of	484-485	431-432
— identification with reality	457-461	409-413
— open and closed	499-507	443-450
— formal *ratio* of	207-208	212-213
essence, constitutive		
— and specific essence	219-225	221-226
	276	266
	305	288
	311	293
— condition of its specification	311	293
— three types of	242	241
	254	249
— and «being» (ser)	337-338	313-314
— and processuality	340-341	316-317
essence, metaphysical		
— should be called «conceptive»	178	189
— as distinct from physical	176-178	187-189

Term	Spanish text	English text
essence, as principle		
— in Hegel	54	84
— anteriority of	59-62	88-90
— substance anterior to, in Aristotle (cf. Aristotle)	512-514	453-455
— as grounding principle of substantivity	176	187
	264-277	257-267
— as ground of constitutional, but not constitutive, notes	270-271	262-263
— as ground of essential and inessential	54-55	84-85
— essences as «archai»	209	214
	248	245
— — priority over reality q.v.		
— — priority over being (ser) (q.v.)		
— — — over essence and existence in the classical sense	400-401	364-365
	461-462	413-414
— — «principiality» of	509-517	451-457
essence, quidditive		
— from the aspect of its unity	305-316	289-298
— its unity as replicable moment	312-316	294-298
— as more than specifiable	241-242	240-241
essentiable, the		
— ambit of	100-101	124-125
— general exposition of	103-108	127-132
— as the «natural», in Aristotle	83-85	108-109
— presupposes «necessity» and «reality»	101	125
— intrinsic and formal character of	175	186
essentiated, the		
— general account of	109-174	133-185
— place within the essentiable	101	125
— identified with substance, in Aristotle	83-85	108-110
— essentiated reality and substantive reality	146-148	163-165
— — — and dimensionality (q.v.)	134	153
— — — an «reality simpliciter»	143	161
— as formal character of essence itself	175	186
— as transcendental	474-481	423-429
esse, logical		
— in scholasticism	385-386	385-386
— origin of the copula	407	369
— relationship to substantive being (ser) and reality	412	473

Term	Spanish text	English text
esse, real		
— in Scholasticism, ambiguous	403-404	366-367
	408-409	369-370
— as transcendental	386-387	352-353
— as reality	389-390	355-356
estar siendo		
— as ratification of the constatation	130-131	151-152
— transcendental function of is duration	ibi	
evolution		
— systematic philosophical treatment of	249-262	245-255
	309-320	292-300
— in the order of individuality, in the world	171-173	183-185
— scientific and metaphysical aspects of	256-257	251-252
— intramundane universality of the genetic process	262	256
existence		
— opposition to essence, in classical theory	7-10	45-48
— in Hegel	41-42	73-74
— not formal *ratio* of reality	389-403	355-366
— and the merely existent	462-466	413-417
— anteriority of essence over —	461-462	412-413
— no anteriority of, over essence	468-469	418-420
exteriority		
—as character of the notes	494-495	439-440
extra-animity		
— concept of: inexact in scholasticism, corrected by Zubiri	389-390	355-356
event		
— conterposition to *fact* (q.v.)		
— metaphysical condition of human reality	204	210
— and «res eventualis»	516-517	456-457

F

Term	Spanish text	English text
fact		
— three concepts of	204-205	210-211
— and «natural thing»	516-517	456-457
— as actualized note of closed essence	515-516	455-456
— and event, as the two great differences in the metaphysical condition of the real	204	210

	Spanish text	English text
Term		
factic, the		
— as different from the factual v. fact	208-209	213-214
factual		
— as the absolute in the essence, different from the factic (q.v.)	208-209	213-214
filetization		
— and coherential unity	318	299
— cf. *phylum*		
finitude		
— in what the finiteness of things consists	46	77
flexión, nominal		
— defined	353-354	326-327
form		
— as physical essence (q.v.) in Aristotle	92	116
	193	201
force		
— in terms of substantivity	162	176
— as interpretation of the «real» in «reality»	510-511	452-453
forcefulness		
— logical and natural	188-189	197-198
function, transcendental		
— definition of	424-425	383-384
— and transcendental property	420-422	380-381
— and transcendental structure	425-426	384-385

G

Galileo		
— his idea of nature rejected	106-107	130-131
generation		
—what is added in	240-241	239-240
— not necessarily repetition, but genetic constitution	252-254	248-250
— as ground of the specific community	308-311	291-293
— as *ratio* of the unity of the quidditative essence insofar as replicable	312-314	294-296
— cf. *genesis*		

Term	Spanish text	English text
genesis		
— three metaphysical moments of	252-254	248-250
— constituent and quiddifiable	258-259	253-254
— essential — unification of above; not substantial		
transformation	259-260	253-254
God		
— «aseitas» and plenary reality of	466-467	417-418
— as transcendent being (sobre ser)	434-435	319-320
— as transcendentality also in His existence	468	418
— essence of in terms of structure	514	455
	370	340
— and the possibility of a «perfective aspeciability»	237	236
— intelligence of, distinct from human, *qua* intelligence	46	77
— ideas of, and things	52-53	82-83
	63-64	92-93
— reason subordinated to reality in knowledge of		
vision	48-49	79-80
— necessity of creative «fiat» for finite reality	ibi	ibi
— ultimacy of the created	201	207
— creates the world as such	355	328
— the created homogeneously possible and contingent		
relative to —	200-201	206-207
— problem of God and world as transcendental	430-432	388-390
Goedel		
— his theorem and the principle of contradiction	66	94
ground		
— possible meanings of	264-265	257-258
— in Hegel	41-45	73-76
— as necessity	273-274	264-265
— of relation	287-289	274-276

H

Term	Spanish text	English text
Hegel, G. W.		
— essence as formal concept in	36-58	69-87
— truth of the thing in	100	123
— intellection as positing in	113	137
— essence as generating principle in	100	123
— fundamentality of essence in	196-197	203-204
— indifferent being (ser) in, not primary	196-197	203-204

Term	Spanish text	English text
— substantialization of being (ser) in	436-437	393-394
— unity as process in	340-341	316-317
* — the «real» as interiorization	494-495	439-440
Heidegger, Martin		
— his concept of the world not radical	428	386
	432	390
— his idea of being (ser)	438-453	394-407
— being (ser) as transcendental in	411-412	372-373
— «temporeity» in	440	396
hylomorphism		
— the relation between essential moments not necessarily hylomorphic	512-514	453-454
Husserl		
— dissociation of ideas of essence and substance in	Intro 5	42-43
— consciousness as pure essence	ibi	ibi
— essence as eidetic unity of meaning (sentido) in	23-32	56-64
— meaning of transcendental idealism in	373-379	342-347

I

I	Spanish text	English text
— concept of, in idealism	373-379	343-346
— in Zubiri	380-381	347-348
idea, (the)		
— in Hegel	44-45	76-77
— divine, exemplary cause, but not essence of things	63-64	92-93
ideation		
— not the formal intrinsic character of intellection (q.v.)	113	137
idealism		
— dissociates ideas of essence and substance	Intro 4	41
— essence of	49-50	80-81
— idea of transcendental in	373-383	342-350
— rejection of, in its empirical and logical forms	380-382	347-349
	437	394
identity		
— three possible modes of	466-467	401-402
— and sameness (mismidad)	250	246

	Spanish text	English text
Term		
impression (the)		
— in modern philosophy	414-415	375-376
— of reality	414-416	375-377
	470-471	420-421
— and «openness» (q.v.)	451-452	405-406
	506-507	449-450
inalterability		
— as character of notes of the essence	249	245
— of constitutive content of essence	251-258	247-253
incommuniciability		
— and transcendental unity	483-484	430-431
— and *Suyo* (q.v.)	484-485	431-432
— as transcendental structural property and moment	485	432
indiscernible(s)		
— and singularity	167	179
individu(al) (ity) (ation)		
— and individuation as *moment,* not principle, of the thing	137-138	156-157
	166	179
— purely numerical	138-139	157-158
— as constitutional function and internal determination	166	179
— and substantivity	165-166	178-179
— what it means to be «this» (esta)	166	179
— not by concretion, but by constitution	168-171	181-183
— the constitutive, as	212-213	216-217
— formal *ratio* (razón) of	168	181
— concretion as third moment of	491	437
— and «individuity»	491	437
— strict, as system of notes	144	161
— transcendental and concretion	489-491	435-437
indivision		
— positive aspect of	484-485	431-432
	488-489	434-435
in-essential (the)		
— not the «indifferent» (undifferentiated) of Hegel	39	72
	54-55	84-85
	268-269	260-261

Term	Spanish text	English text
— not the «individuating» of Aristotle	261	255
— not the «beyond meaning» of Husserl	261	255
— as grounded	477-478	425-426
— as adherence	478-479	426-427
— as reified	479-480	427-428
— the essential, seen from the point of view of the	477	425

infinitude
| — and cf. finitude | 46 | 77 |

insusbstantive
| — formal *ratio* of and difference from the accidental | 164 | 177 |
| — and cf. *substantive* | | |

intelligence (theory of)
— unity with sensibility (q.v.)	115-116	138-139
	413-414	374-375
— sentient, and impression of reality (q.v.)	414-416	375-376
	451-455	405-408
	506-507	449-450
— primary function of: apprehension of real things insofar as real	64-65	93-94
— formal character of	113-116	137-140
	173	185
	392-393	357-358
— and reality:		
— being (ser) presupposes — even in intellection	408-409	370-371
— and distance between thought (pensar) and to be (ser); reason as «to go forward»	47-48	78-79
— as being (ser) and reality as «there is» (hay) in the problem of truth	112	136
— and «openness»	500-501	444-445
— dual function of	501-502	445-446
— transcendental function of	423-424	382-383

intellected (first)
| — not *Ens*, but the impression of reality | 414-416 | 374-377 |

Intentional (ity)
— opposed to physical (q.v.)	11-12	49-50
— (ity) not formal character of consciousness	29	62
— nor of intelligence cf. Husserl, Phenomenology		

Term	Spanish text	English text
interiority		
— and *de suyo* (q.v.)	492-494	438-440
— different from interiorization	494-495	439-440
— three formal respects (q.v.) of	497-498	442-443
interiorization		
— in Hegel	494-495	439-440
intimacy (intimidad)		
— as note of the human reality	492-494	438-440

J

judgment		
— brief theory of	405-406	368-369
— implications of, in affirmative intellection	407-408	369-370
— cf. *esse logicum*		

K

Kant		
— and Aristotle	86	111
— his idea of intellection	507	450
— critique of his idea of nature	106-107	130-131
— critique of his idea of unity as synthesis	283-284	272-273
— substantivization of space-time in	436-437	393-394
— distinction between being (ser) and subject of being (ente)	441	397
— essence as objective concept in	59-73	88-100
— concept of transcendental in	374-382	343-349

L

Leibnitz		
— antecedents in Aristotle	86	111
— conceptive truth in	100	124
— on radical origination of things	63	92
— essence as objective content of idea in	59-73	88-100
— «unum in se» in	99	123
— infinite predicates, but not infinite physical notes	366-367	336-337

Term	Spanish text	English text
— essence as «vis»	512-514	453
— substance as activity	339-340	315-316
Language		
— five basic points for a theory of	346	320
— as «novum organon»	345-346	319-320
— as index of conceptual structures	346	320
— essence of, compared to classic Greek view of	345	319
— and substantivity	163	177
— expression of essence as something physical	178-190	189-199
liberty		
— as metaphysical condition	203-204	209-210
life		
— living beings as inchoatively strict individualities	166	179
— as specifiables	240-242	239-241
— variable and progressive concretion of individuality	169	181
— as unique	172-173	184-185
— human	504	447
limitation		
— as transcendental property	462-463	413-414
— and «suchness»	464	415
logos		
— and essence	345-356	320-329
— nominal, the	353	326
— predicative		
— limitation and insufficiency of	218-219	221-222
— configures reality as subjectuality	161-163	175-177
— priority of the antepredicative	353	326
light		
— metaphysics of	433-434	490
	447-449	402-404
— in Heidegger's thought	440-441	396-397

M

man		
— between substantivity and subjectuality	159-161	173-175
— strict individuality in	166	179

	Spanish text	English text
Term		
— variable and progressive concretion in his individuality	169-170	181-182
	249	245
— as meta-specifiable	242-243	241-242
— the proximate genus «animal» in the the composition of man	153-154	169-170
	245-246	245-246
— as «animal of realities», in opposition to Heidegger	451-452	405-406
— three fundamental actualizations of his intellection	131-132	151-152
— as confronting things as realities	173	185
— his two fundamental modes of apprehension	391-392	356-357
— as person	504-508	447-450
— basis of moral subjectuality in	161	175
— the reality of the subject does not reside in being «I»	380-381	347-348
— intimacy of	492-494	438-439
— not totally «event» (suceso)	209	214
— no priority of existence over essence in	505-506	448-449
— and time	447	402
— and freedom	203-204	209-210
mathematics		
— and reality	163	177
matter		
— forms only natural classes	238-239	237-238
— variable, but not progressive, concretion in	169	181
— as moment of evolving process of, in order of individuality	171-172	183-184
— as *schema* for substantivization of reality	173	185
— substantivity belongs only to the material whole	171-172	183-184
metaphysics		
— as conceptuation of reality itself	357	329
— cannot be a logos	47	78
— intramundane- condition of	201	207
	463	414
metaphysics (mediaeval)		
— unity of known and knower in	444	399
— confuses *objectivity* and *objectuality*	70	98
— ontological truth as radical truth in	64	93
	100	124

Term	Spanish text	English text
— states problem of essence in line with Aristotle	94	117
— structure of essence and essential difference in	216-217	219-220
— unlike Aristotle, views the possible in its respect to God	154-156	169-171
— inadequate account of the unalterability of species in	251-258	247-248
— attenuates the eternity of the species	254-255	249-250
— species as unity of similarity in	230-232	231-233
— inadequate solution of problem of individuation in	167-169	180-182
— gives primacy to individual, but only as realization of the common	215	218
— types of unity in, and in classical philosophy	293-294	279-280
— unity of the essence as actuality in	282-283	271-272
— identity as transcendental character of every being (ente) in	250	246

mentality
| — «forma mentis», unity of thought and expression | 345-346 | 320-321 |

metaspecification
| — potentiality of | 256-257 | 251-252 |

movement
| — as actualization of the potency | 515-516 | 455-456 |

moral, the
| — in function of the substantivity | 159-161 | 173-175 |

multiplicity (multiplication)
— mere, and natural class	233	233
— and elementary particles	238-239	237-238
— postcedent to moment of individuality	165-166	178-179
— as condition of the species	233	233
— characteristics of	234-236	234-236
— difference between — ity and -ation	233-234	233-234
— difference from generation	240-241	239

mutation
— see *origination*

meaning
— essence as, cf. Husserl

	Spanish text	English text
Term		

N

nature		
— ordinary concept of	11	49
— in the Greeks	106-107	130-137
— in the moderns	ibi	ibi
— in Hegel	44	76
— not only materially essence	180-181	191-192
— and «de suyo»	395-396	360-361
— and techné	83-84	108-109

necessity		
— negative determination of, not sufficient	103-104	127-128
— only real necessity is essential necessity	107	130
— of origination and systematic	270-271	262-263

Newton		
— Newton's Law considered as predicative *logos* and its transformation into substantive expression	162	176
— substantivization of space-time in	436-437	393-394

note(s) — in general sense		
— types of		
— — formal and causal	135-136	153-154
— — constitutional and adventitous	136-137	154-155
— — additive and systematic	147-148	164-165
— — systematic as a) mixed type and b) functional combination	149-150	165-166
— priority, as «real-things» to «meaning-things»	105	129
— as actualization of the substantivity	157-158	172-173
— metaphysical condition of grounded	206	211
— essence and «indifferent» notes	271-272	282-283
	514-515	455-456

notes(s) constitutional		
— defined	136-137	155-156
— grounded	188-189	197-198
— constitutive	189	198
— essence and grounding of	270-271	262-263

note(s), essential		
— problem of	187-188	196-197
— grounding character of	123-138	145-157
— «respective» character of	287-289	274-276
— and actuality of essence	337-338	313-314

Term	Spanish text	English text
— alone confer «suchness»	358-360	330-332
— capacity to form system	297-298	282-283.
— the pure «of» as formal *ratio* (razón) of reality of	358-360	330-332

O

object
| — and essence | 31 | 64 |

objectivity
| — as terminal moment in purely intentional dimension | 71 | 99 |

objectuality
— the fact that something is an object	70-71	98-99
— distinction from *objectivity* (q.v.)	ibi	ibi
— false notion of in idealism	375-382	343-344

one
— as transcendental in scholasticism	387-388	353-354
	418-419	378-379
— transcendental function of, slighted in scholasticism	420-421	380-381
— as simple transcendental	432	390

order
| — sense of in transcendental | 417-418 | 377-378 |
| — cf. transcendental | | |

organism
| — as functional combination | 149-150 | 165-166 |

origin
| — as distinct from *position* | 151-158 | 167-168 |

origination
| — as distinct from *generation*, (q.v.) | | |
| — does not transmit all the quiddifiable characteristics | 241-242 | 240-241 |

P

Parmenides
| — three «ways» of, and Aristotle | 69 | 97 |
| — reality-appearance duality in *Hymn* of | 398 | 362 |

Term	Spanish text	English text
— Platonic, and alteration	259	253
— subtantification of «the» (el) one and «the» (el) being, (ser) in	325-326	304-305
particles, fundamental		
— characteristics of	238-239	237-238
— cf. matter		
patentization		
— as discovery of the thing in *real truth*	127-128	148-149
— distinction from «unveiling»	ibi	ibi
— cf. dimensions		
perfection		
— transcendental concept of	496	441
permanency		
— distinct from sameness (mismidad)	250-251	246
— as character of substance	ibi	ibi
perseitas (in Scholasticism)		
— and substantive sufficiency	154-156	169-170
— cf. Spinoza		
person		
— character and structure of real	198	205
— elaborated concept of	504-506	441-448
phrase, nominal		
— metaphysical significance of	407-408	369-370
philosophy (Greek)		
— its idea of the world	199-200	205-206
— eternity of species in	254-255	249-250
— cyclical conception of time in	ibi	ibi
— conception of essence in	301-305	285-286
— conception of the *technical* in (q.v.)		
— and language	345	320
— system as intrinsic totality in	426	385
— idea of potency, but not of possibility in	515-516	456-457
phenomenology		
— idea of the intentional in cf. *intentionality*		

Term	Spanish text	English text
phylum		
— as strict physical reality	235-236	235-236
— and species	243-244	241-242
— and generating and generated	304-305	288-289
— and unity of *constitutive scheme*	ibi	ibi
physical		
— general meaning of	N-11-13	49-50
— as the truly metaphysical	276-292	266-278
Plato		
— fails to distinguish essential and in-essential	54	84
— structure of essence and essential difference in	216-217	219-220
— problem of difference and essence in	229	230
— one as supreme genus, refuted by Aristotle	326-327	305-306
— substantification of «the» (el) one and «the» (el) being (ser) in	325-326	304-305
— his idea of individual unity corrected by Aristotle	306	289
plausibility		
— result of signs, words, techné	322-323	301-302
power		
— as the «real» of «reality»	510-511	452-453
«por sí mismas»		
— and the «en sí mismas»	279	268
— a false way	279-283	268-272
— and *solidarity* (q.v.)		
— recapitulation concerning	285-286	273-274
— as «constructed character» of each essential note	292	278
possibility		
— not a world apart	71-72	99-100
	200	206
— in rationalism	61	90
— not mere non-contradiction	65-66	93-94
— essence as internal p. of anything	67	95
— as metaphysical condition of the created	200-202	206-208
— diverse manners of	202-203	208-209
— as unity between power and necessity	271-272	263-264
— distinct from mere potency	515-516	456-457
— and appropriation in man	159-160	173-174

Term	Spanish text	English text
position (positing)		
— in transcendental idealism	437-438	393-394
— concept of, in Zubiri	144-146	144-145
	157-158	172-173
— as functional determination	264-267	257-259
— not intrinsic characteristic of intellection	113	137
potentiality		
— as factor of essential determination in the evolutive structure of the world	261-262	255-256
— of constitution and processual	253-254	249-250
— as distinct from possibility	515-516	456-457
precision		
— logical and living	196	204
predicament		
— cf. *category*	494-495	439-440
prepositions		
— philosophical meaning of	354	327
Presocratics (the)		
— concept of nature in	395	360
principle		
— concept of, in Aristotle	509-510	451-452
— character of essence as	509-517	451-457
priority		
— types of	332-333	310-311
prius		
— characteristic of reality before	393-395	358-360
— anterior to presentation of reality	414-416	375-376
— and independence	446-447	401-402
probability		
— quantitative measure of possibility	203	209
— and constitutive essence	340-341	316-317
processuality		
— and constitutive essence	340-341	ibi-ibi
proposition (essential)		
— anterior to definition	348-350	322-324
— not same as physical definition	350-351	324-325
— as open	351-352	325-326

33*

	Spanish	English
Term	text	text
property(ies)		
— in the Aristotlean sense	104	128
— as note(s)	100	124
— differentiated by the manner of being proper	159-161	173-175
projection (projectivity)		
— structure of	127	148
— cf. actualization		

Q

quiddity		
— as essence, eidos and species in Plato	216-217	219-220
— not ideal unity, rè Husserl	229-230	230-231
— not unity of similarity	230-232	231-232
— refers to physical reality	218-219	221-222
— essence is not	219	222
— moment of physical essence: only derivatively conceptive unity	220-222	222-224
— quidditive and constitutive essence distinguished	223-225	225-227
	228-229	229-230
— defined	227-228	228-229
	243-246	241-244
— structuring function of	222-223	234-235

R

rationalism		
— essence as objective concept in	59-73	88-100
— confuses *objectivity* and *objectuality*	70-71	98-99
rasa-		
— conception of essence in Indian philosophy	300-305	285-289
rato (Spanish)		
— meaning and nature	464	415
— «merely rato» not equivalent of classical essence	465-472	416-421
— neither prior nor subsequent to «merely existent»	469-470	419-420
— basis of distinction between these	ibi	ibi-ibi
— not a *real* distinction	471-472	421-422
reason		
— in Hegel	36-37	69-70
— priority of reality over	45-50	77-81

Term	Spanish text	English text
reality		
— substance as, in Aristotle	In-3	41
— idea of, in rationalism	33-35	66
— as the merely «factic» in Husserl	24	57
— as physical (q.v.)		
— on what this idea depends	389-390	355-356
— what must be understood by	100	124
— as formal character of the intellected as such	114-116	137-139
	392-393	357-358
— truly real and true reality	119	141
	11	49
	116-117	139-140
	123	145
— what brings it about that there is truth in intellection	112-134	136-153
— and negativity	50-51	81-82
— ambit of, cf. *essentiable*		
— and essence	30-32	63-65
	343-508	318-450
— priority of over essence	400-401	364-365
— identity of with essence	459-461	411-413
— as syntactic, cf. *respectivity*		
— and bring (ser)	403-417	366-377
	433-434	390-391
	437-438	394-395
	449-450	404-405
— «in essendo»	410-411	372-373
— and «de suyo»	413-417	374-377
— and existence	389-403	355-366
— and nature	395-396	360-361
— and appearance	396-398	361-363
Reality, *simpliciter*		
— ambiguity of term	457-458	409-410
— and dimensiones (q.v.)	133-135	153-154
— the notes of	135-137	154-156
— structural unity of cf. *constitution, unity*	135-142	154-160
— and substantive reality	146-147	163-164
— and substantivity (q.v.)	295	281
— as system of constitutive notes	193	201
realization		
— as necessary co-positing of new properties	67-68	95-96

	Spanish text	English text
Term		
reference		
— as transcendental function	422	381
relation		
— and respectivity (q.v.)	287-289	274-276
	427	385
res		
— transcendental in Scholasticism	387-388	353-354
— as synonym of «ens» in Scholasticism	418-419	378-379
— — not so in Zubiri	419-420	379-380
— comparison of meaning of, in Scholasticism	458-460	410
— as the transcendental itself	424	383
— as reality	460	412
— constructivity of	475-477	424
— natural, eventual, historical	516-517	456-457
respectivity		
— entitative and not operative	180-181	191-192
— extrinsic cf. world		
— intrinsic	287-289	274-275
cf. *state, constructed*		
— of thing (cosa) and its ground	197-199	204-206
— not relation	427	385
— and function, transcendental structure and ground	426-427	384-385
cf. *totality*		
— distinct in *meaning-things* and *reality things*	290-292	277-279
Respect, coherential		
— and co-herential unity	202	208
— three metaphysical characteristics of	318-320	299-301

S

sameness		
— as second meaning of essence	16-17	52-53
— «el mismo» and «lo mismo»	249	245
— not identity	250-251	246-247
— nor permanence	ibi	ibi-ibi
— of essence, not gradual, because ultimate	258	253
sensibility		
— proper and constitutive formality of	115-116	138-139
	392-393	357-358

Term	Spanish text	English text
— unreality of	392-395	357-360
— unity with intelligence	413-414	374-375
— intellective	414-416	375-376
	506-507	449-450
— and human essence	291	278
singular (singulum)		
— and individuality (q.v.)		
— as having «constitution»	141	159
— function of essence with «respect» to	211	215
— forms only natural classes	238-239	237-238
system		
— defined	144-146	161-163
— as «closed»	146	163
— tridimensional, constituted of		
— constitutional notes as moments of		
— primary unity	144	161
— and mixture	149-150	165-166
— and functional combination	ibi	ibi-ibi
— as alone absolute	292	278
— as totality	152-153	168-169
solidarity		
— defined	280-282	269-271
soul		
— in Aristotle	387-388	353-354
— and «true» and «good»	422-423	381-382
space		
— as merely «respective»	436-437	393-394
— substantivized by Kant and Newton	ibi	ibi-ibi
species		
— and physical essence	176-178	187-189
— and constitutive essence	91-93	115-116
— notion of, defined	243-244	241-242
	311-312	293-294
	320	300
— philosophical and biological concepts of	244-246	242-244
— as condition of having and being (ser)	318	299
— *ratio* (razón) of speciability	234-236	234-236
— and inalterability	251-258	251-253

	Spanish text	English text
Term		
— the problem of the unity of not that of the universals	311	293
— priority of individual over	165-171	178-183
	229-230	230-231
	234	234
— and class	230-233	231-232
— inadequacy of Aristotle's concept of	88-89	112-113
Spinoza		
— confuses «aseitas» and «perseitas»	155	170
spirit		
— in Hegel	44-45	76-77
— cf. *intelligence*		
schema, constitutive		
— defined	244	242
— ground of species	309-311	292
— and quidditative essence	313	295
— unity of	312-314	294-296
— cf. *phylum*		
state, constructed		
— as organon to conceive essence	355-356	328-329
— defined	289-290	276-277
— as expression of internal respectivity	290	277
stimulus		
— proper and constitutive formality of	115-116	138-139
	391-392	356-357
— problem of, reality of	115	138
	393-395	358-360
structure		
— defined	511-512	453-454
— as essence of living being	512-514	454-456
— as essence of essence	ibi	ibi-ibi
— of open and closed essence	516-517	456-457
structure (transcendental)		
— and transcendental structure	424-425	383-384
— and «suchness»	425-426	384-385
— two types of	426	385
— and «respectivity»	429-467	387-418
	481-507	429-450

Term	Spanish text	English text
Suarez		
— admits non-specific essential notes	185	195
— does not indicate their function	ibi	ibi
subjectivism		
— fundamental error of	502	445
subjectivity		
— cf. substance		
— confused by Aristotle with substantivity	87-88	111-112
— subject *of* and subject *to*	159-161	173-174
subsystem		
— the constitutive, as fundamental	191-193	199-201
subtension, dynamic		
— concept and meaning of	363-365	334-335
sufficency		
— and substantivity	151	167
— not identical with subjectuality	154-156	169-171
— nor with capacity to exist	ibi	ibi
— as totality	151-153	167-169
— and the intra-mundane	463	414
— in «suchness» and transcendental	464	415
— «ex se» and «a se»	466-467	417-418
suppositionalness		
— in Hegel, criticized by Zubiri	55-58	85-87
substance		
— as subjectuality	156	171
— not the «ὄν» par excellance	512-514	453-455
— as moment, not thing	158	173
— not formally identified with substantivity	151	167
— and permanence	250-251	246
— historical evolution of the concept in relation to that of essence	In-3-5	41
	1-5	43
substantivity		
— defined	164-171	177-183
— as closed and total system of constitutional notes	187	196
— constitutional character of	146-147	163-164
— and species	176-178	187

Term	Spanish text	English text
— involves sufficiency (q.v.)		
— not every grouping of notes capable of	153	169
— simple and compound	147	164
	150-151	166-167
	156-157;	171-172;
	185	195
— priority over substance	250-251	246-247
— beyond the substance — accident duality	296	281
— and substatiality, distinguishable even in material realities	161-163	175-177
suyo (Spanish)		
— transcendental function of essence and transcendental unity	484-485	351-352

T

	Spanish text	English text
technic (techné, technology)		
— Greek concept of	77	103
— and nature, in Aristotle and in Zubiri	83-85	108-109
— and meaning thing (q.v.)		
— necessity of changing concept of	107	130
— as mimesis of nature	323	302
— structural unity of, anterior to reality of parts in	334-335	311-312
think (to)		
— necessity of conceiving «in» but not «for» thinking	57	87
this		
— ambiguity of	167	180
— four proper moments of	170	182
Thomas, St.		
— view of essence	182-183	193-194
— failure to explain the individual function of essence	183-185	194-195
— transcendentality of «verum» and «bônum» in	423	382
time		
— as mode of being (ser)	435-436	392-393
— as respectivity	436-437	393-394
— in Heidegger	5	42
— temporeity	447	402
— cf. *duration*		

Term	Spanish text	English text
tipicity		
— of essence	449-507	404-450
— in so far as transcendental	499	443
totality(ies)		
— unity of, in the operative and constitutional orders	152	168
— things as totalities	426-427	385-386
transcendentality		
— essence and	372-508	341-450
— superior to «suchness»	372	341
— in classical and modern philosophy	373-388	342-343
— idea of the transcendental	388-417	354-377
— «ordo transcendentalis» as «ordo realitatis ut sic»	412-413	373-374
— not independent of order of suchness	424-425	383-384
— the transcendentals in Scholasticism	387-388	353-354
— simple and complex transcendentals	429-430	387-388
— disjunctive and conjunctive transcendentals	430-432	388-390
truth		
— reality and	112-134	136-153
— essence as radical —, in Hegel	42-43	74-75
	45	77
	51-53	81-83
— and intelligence	112	136
	116	139
— as actualization of the thing (cosa) in the intel-		
ligence	112-114	136-137
— subordination to reality	381	348
— transcendental, in idealism	374-375	343-344
truth, conceptive		
— and ontological	65	93
truth, logical		
—grounded in real	119	142
truth, ontological		
— what is usually understood as	34	67
— not radical	64-65	93-94
— not to be confused with real (q.v.)		
— and essence	51-53	81-83
truth, real		
— and ontological	34	67
	117-119	140-142

	Spanish text	English text
Term		
— ground of logical	119	141
— guide to structure of reality	120	142
	123	145
— defined	120	142
— complex character of	122-123	144-145
— pluraldimensionality, consequences of its	123-124	145-146
	127	149
true (the) (verum)		
— as transcendental, in Scholasticism	387-388	353-354
— problem aroused by	422-424	381-383
— complex conjoint transcendental	432	390

U

ultimacy		
— in «specific» conception	216-219	219-221
— Zubiri's view of	219-220	221-222
— factual, and individuality	211	215
unity		
— numeral and of content	140	159
— constitutional, primacy of	143-144	161-162
— systematic	148-149	165-166
— formal and quiddity	307-309	290-292
	314-315	296-297
— exigetive	365-371	336-340
— as community	305-306	289-290
unity, coherential		
— and phyletic	317-320	298-300
unity, essential		
— problem of,	278-342	268-317
— and constructed state	292-293	278-279
— what it is not	294-296	280-281
— what it is	296-300	281-284
— formal *ratio* of	287-291	274-278
— primary character of	322-342	301-317
— as unity «in» the notes	337-338	313-314
— as distinct from transcendental	482-483	430-431

| | Spanish | English |
Term	text	text
unity, phyletic (specific)		
— as generational	240-241	239-240
— «maior formali, minor numerali,» only «ratione» distinct from transcendental	315	297
— grounds formal —, and definability	315-316	297-298
— its function	316-317	298-299
unity, transcendental		
— distinct from essential	482-483	430-431
— defined	484-485	431-432
— in Aristotle	487-488	434-435
— as transcendentally individual	483	430
— as structure	486	433
universal(s)		
— advance in Scholasticism over Aristotle's theory of	94	117
— problem of, not problem of the species	305-311	289-293
unspecifiability		
— three types of	236-237	236-238

V

version		
— of the essential notes among themselves	287-289	274-276
— defined	ibi	ibi
— cf. respect, coherential		
vision		
— mental, priority to predication	218-219	221-222

W

will		
— transcendental function of	423-424	382-383
world		
— as the whole of real things	199	205
— redefined by Zubiri	199-200	205-206
	427-428	385-386
— three zones of reality in	171-173	183-185
	237-238	236-237

Term	Spanish text	English text
— metaphysical structure of	261-262	255-256
— as pure *factum*	209	213
— as created by God	334-335	311-312
— as extrinsic respectivity (v. Heidegger)	274; 288; 428	265; 275; 386
— as transcendental	428-432	386-390
— and being (ser)	432-434	390-391

TABLE OF CONTENTS

                                                                           Págs.

Translator's Introduction   11

PART ONE: The Problem of Essence   39

   Introduction   41
   Chapter One: The Problem of Essence   45
   General Note   48
   Chapter Two: A Provisional Determination of the Concept
      of Essence   51

PART TWO: Some Classical Ideas Concerning Essence   55

   Chapter Three: Essence as Meaning   57
   Chapter Four: Essence as Concept   67
     Section One: The Essence as Formal Concept   69
     Section Two: The Essence as Objective Concept   88
   Chapter Five: The Essence as Real Correlate of the Defi-
     nition 101

PART THREE: Essence, Structural Moment of the Real 119

   Chapter Six: Introductory Recapitulation 121
   Chapter Seven: The Compass of the «Essentiable» 127
   Chapter Eight: «Essentiated» Reality 133
     Section One: Reality and Truth 135
     Section Two: Structural Unity of Reality *Simpliciter* ... 154
     Section Three: Formal Character of the Unity of the Real. 160

Págs.

Chapter Nine: The «Essence» Itself of the Real   187

  Section One: The Specific Character of the Essence   187

  Section Two: Internal Analysis of Essence   196

Article I: The Essential Notes   197

  Section One: Essence, Ultimate Moment of Substantivity ...   202

    Subsection I: The Essence: Its Factual Metaphysical Con-
    dition   202

    Subsection II: The Essence: Its Individual Entitative
    Character   214

    Subsection III: The Essence: Its Unalterable Constitutive
    Content   245

  Section Two: Essence: Grounding Movement of Substan-
  tivity   256

Article II: The Unity of Essence   267

  Section One: The Problem of the Essential Unity: The Unity
  of Essence   268

  Section Two: On the Formal Reason of the Unity of the Essence   274

  Section Three: On the Primacy of the Essential Unity   301

Article III: Essence and Reality   318

  Section One: Essence and *Logos*   319

  Section Two: Essence and Suchness   329

  Section Three: Essence and Transcendentality   341

    Subsection I: The Idea of the Transcendental Order   342

      Para. 1: Transcendentality in Modern Philosophy and
      in Classical Philosophy   342

      Para. 2: The Idea of the Transcendental   354

      Para. 3: The Idea of Transcendental Structure   378

    Subsection II: The Transcendental Consideration of Es-
    sence   408

      Para. 1: Essence: Its Transcendental Character   408

      Para. 2: Essence: Its Transcendental Structure   429

Págs.

Article IV: The Principial Character of Essence   451

Glossary of Terms and Phrases Proper to the Zubirian Philosophical Idiom   459

Selected Bibliography   481

Index   489

Page

Article IV. The Principal Character of Essence 471

Glossary of Terms and Phrases Proper to the Aubrian Philosophical Idiom 479

Selected Bibliography 481

Index 485